D0594286

Individual Behavior

Individual
Behavior

A PERCEPTUAL APPROACH
TO BEHAVIOR

REVISED EDITION

ARTHUR W. COMBS
University of Florida
Gainesville, Florida

DONALD SNYGG
State University of New York
Teachers College
Oswego, New York

HARPER & BROTHERS

PUBLISHERS, NEW YORK

INDIVIDUAL BEHAVIOR:

A Perceptual Approach to Behavior, Revised Edition

Copyright, 1949, by Harper & Brothers

Copyright © 1959 by Arthur W. Combs and Donald Snygg

Printed in the United States of America

The Library of Congress catalog entry for
this book appears at the end of the text.

CONTENTS

FOREWORD

THE perceptual approach to behavior described in this book was first stated by Donald Snygg and the present author in an earlier edition published in 1949. The point of view expressed in that volume seemed so novel at the time that it was felt appropriate to title the book, *Individual Behavior: A New Frame of Reference for Psychology*. Time, however, does not stand still and what was new but a few years ago has become widely accepted and practiced today. Now, ten years later, there still seems little reason to change the basic outline of the perceptual point of view stated earlier, but it can hardly be called "new" any longer. The point of view just emerging at the time of the first edition has come of age as one of the most virile and exciting movements in current psychology.

The foreword to the first edition stated the purpose of the book as one of giving expression to what looked like the beginning of an inevitable trend in understanding human behavior. Subsequent events seem to have amply corroborated that observation. In the last few years new developments in perceptual psychology have occurred with such rapidity that, like Alice in Wonderland, one must run as fast as he can just to keep up. Almost every psychological journal reports new and intriguing studies bearing upon some aspect of the personal frame of reference. Much of this research has supported the perceptual approach and that, of course, has been gratifying. Some errors and inconsistencies have been uncovered, and that has been challenging and helpful. Old concepts have been refined and expanded and some new concepts have been developed. All this activity has proved so fruitful as to make necessary the extension and development of the perceptual approach to behavior presented in this new edition.

The close collaboration Dr. Snygg and I enjoyed in writing the first edition when we lived but a few miles from each other was an intensely exciting and rewarding experience for each of us. We had hoped to repeat this team arrangement when a new edition was called for, but, unhappily, this was not to be. The great distance between us occasioned by my move to Florida and the pressure of other duties upon Dr. Snygg made it necessary for him to withdraw from this project. As a consequence I have written this volume alone. Dr. Snygg's influence, however, will still be discerned in this volume in much of the material carried over from the previous book. His influence may be observed too, in many of my own contributions, I am sure, for the stimulation and growth afforded by the intensive collaboration with such a man, I find, is a continuous, developing thing. I count that period of our former partnership as one of the most truly creative experiences of my life. I am also indebted to him for his critical reading of several of the early chapters of this edition. Although I have worked alone this time, therefore, I believe it is fitting that this edition of *Individual Behavior* should carry the names of both its original authors since the basic development of the perceptual frame of reference was, and still is, our joint contribution. As the author of this edition, however, the responsibility for whatever errors it contains must be laid at my door.

I have often been asked by students, "Where did these ideas come from?" This is always a difficult question, for who can ever be sure of the origins of thought? It is even probable that there can be no "new" ideas in human behavior; only new ways of looking at what has always been. While the first edition was still in press, I remember discovering other authors whom I had never read before and finding they had written many of the same ideas, sometimes even in identical words! There seem to be great trends in human thought and when the time is ripe "new" ideas occur to numbers of people in widely separated places by a kind of psychological osmosis from the very times in which they live. I believe many of the ideas in this book are of this character. Others can be more specifically traced to particular authors or experiments in clear figure in my perceptual field. No matter how carefully he tries, however, the developer of a frame of reference, will seldom be aware of all the influences acting upon him to determine his ways of thinking and no bibliography can ever include more than a small fraction of those who have contributed to the formation of the ideas contained within it.

Since a frame of reference is a way of looking at events it can be applied to the interpretation of all research within its scope including that which may have been originally designed from a different point of view. Many of the studies I have included in the documentation of this volume were first designed in the more traditional frame of reference of objective psychology. I am especially grateful, however, to those writers and researchers who have honored this point of view by studies designed to test its basic premises. It is largely because of their productivity that this book has been made necessary. Indeed, the number of authors who should be recognized as contributing to these views is so great that in order to avoid filling these pages with too many distracting footnotes and hundreds of names, I have included a separate Reference Index for documentation. In this index the reader will find listed, page by page, reference to those authors whose work is relevant to the topics under discussion.

For their special contributions to the preparation of this manuscript my particular thanks and appreciation are extended to the following:

To Mrs. Marion Maines and Mrs. Virginia Brannan, my successive secretaries, for cheerful and efficient secretarial service far beyond the call of duty,

To my very good friends, Ted Landsman and Daniel Soper, for critical reading of the entire manuscript and innumerable helpful suggestions,

To my wife, Mildred, and my daughter, Carol, for hours of labor on the difficult task of checking the manuscript, the bibliography, and the production of the figures.

To the hundreds of students who have explored these concepts with me in the past ten years I owe a deeper debt than I can say. Their enthusiastic response to this frame of reference has been a continual inspiration, while their doubts, frustrations and criticisms have been challenging and stimulating beyond measure. In a very real sense, this book is as much their contribution as mine.

A book, no matter how disciplined and objective its author, can never escape being an intensely human and personal document. So it is with this one. This edition of *Individual Behavior* represents the most inclusive, consistent, and useful way of understanding behavior of which I am currently capable. As psychologist, teacher, counselor, researcher, and human being, both professionally and personally, I have been engaged for as long as I can remember in a search for more adequate understandings of the nature of man and his behavior. This book is the product of that quest. It is offered here in the hope that it may prove equally helpful to others engaged in a similar search.

ARTHUR W. COMBS

June 14, 1958

PART I

The Perceptual Frame of Reference

CHAPTER 1

The Challenge to Psychology

WITH the explosion of the first atomic bomb at Alamogordo in 1945 man embarked upon a new era—the era of the social sciences. The magnificent achievement of our physical scientists in setting free the sources of energy in the atom has given man, for the first time in his long struggle to wrest a living from his environment, the promise of almost unlimited control over his physical world. At long last he has at his command sufficient power and know-how to feed, clothe, and house the entire world. Despite this knowledge, however, millions of people are starving and millions more are ill clothed and ill housed. The greatest problems of our time are no longer the problems of production and control of "things" but of communication and coöperation among people. Having won control over our physical world, we find ourselves confronted with a new problem, the problem of how to control ourselves!

It is not, after all, atomic bombs we fear, but the people who might use them. We have achieved control of "things" only to find ourselves faced with the equally vital problem of learning to live with one another. The explosion of the atomic bomb gave dramatic emphasis to problems that have existed for centuries but became critical in our time because of two great trends: (1) the ever-increasing interdependence of people in modern society, and (2) the tremendous increase of power in the hands of individuals.

We are often impressed with the competitive features of our society and like to think of ourselves as essentially a competitive people. Yet the fact of the matter is that we live in the most coöperative, interdependent society the world has ever known! We are thoroughly and completely dependent upon the good will and coöperation of millions of our fellow men, from the engineer who keeps the electric turbines running through the night to the modern missile expert on whom we

3

depend to defend us in time of war. We are equally dependent upon
the less romantic occupations. We need garbage men to keep our cities
livable, laborers to dig our pipelines, and stevedores to load and unload
our ships. There is perhaps no better example of this interdependence
than the modern supermarket. Behind the gleaming displays stand veritable armies of people who have coöperated in one form or another
to bring the displayed products together for our use.

Our society is so complex and interrelated that few of us could live
more than a very short time apart from his fellows. Whether we like
it or not, we are thoroughly dependent upon the good will of others.
Even our great industries, often referred to as examples of free competition, on closer analysis turn out to be monuments of human cooperation. We are likely to forget that the great contribution of Henry
Ford to modern industry was the development of the assembly line,
a highly organized method of getting people to work together in the
manufacture of a product. Our great "competitive" industries are, themselves, remarkable examples of coöperative endeavor.

Accompanying this growth of interdependence has been a vast increase in the power available to each of us. The great industrial and
scientific advances of the last century have contributed to make individuals more important than ever. The power of the "common" man
for good or evil has been immensely increased. Any citizen in our
society has hundreds of horsepower at his disposal at the nearest light
switch. He can purchase firearms at his hardware store. When he sits
behind the wheel of his car he has a fearful projectile at his command—more than a ton of metal capable of propulsion at speeds ex-
ceeding a mile a minute. Properly handled, his car is a "pleasure car"
for himself and his friends. Improperly handled, it becomes a jugger-
naut wreaking terrible death and destruction. We would not dare to
drive a car, if we could not count on others to stay on their own side
of the road and obey the rules of the highway. The welfare and safety
of each of us rest upon the coöperation and understanding of our fellow
citizens. In an interdependent society there can be no unimportant
people!

Our society has become so complex and its people so interdependent
that the failure of one individual among thousands can disrupt the delicate balance of organization to such an extent that millions may suffer.
The behavior of an individual is no longer the concern only of his own
little group. It concerns all of us. To deal adequately with the prob-

lems of human relationships we need to understand, as never before, the whys and wherefores of human behavior. Time presses upon us and we need to seek ever more adequate ways of viewing behavior if we are to meet the challenge of human destiny. To live effectively in our modern world we need to gain the very best understandings we can achieve concerning the nature of man and of his behavior.

People can behave only in terms of what seems to them to be so. How we attempt to solve the great human problems of our time depends upon the ideas we hold about what people are like and why they behave as they do. If I believe a man is honest, I will trust him. If I believe he is dishonest, I will take steps to protect myself against him. How I behave toward him and how he behaves toward me will be a direct result of what each of us believes the other is like. In a broader sense, how we deal with our great human problems in industrial relations, in our homes, in our schools, in our communities, even in our diplomatic negotiations with other countries, will depend upon the ideas we hold about the nature of man and why he behaves as he does. Our success or failure in dealing with the problems before us will depend upon the adequacy of our understanding. It is the knowledge to make our understanding adequate which the modern science of psychology attempts to provide.

Psychology—The Science of Behavior

People have always been interested in the problems of human behavior. In a sense, all of us deal with human behavior every day of our lives. The salesman, the teacher, and the business administrator are constantly observing the activities of other people and adjusting their own behavior accordingly. A science, however, cannot be built upon this kind of casual observation. What makes a science is the careful, disciplined approach taken to the solving of problems—whether it be the behavior of airplane wings under stress, of chemicals in solution, of atoms in an atomic pile, of winds in a hurricane, or of people behaving, and misbehaving, with each other. Careful, controlled observation is the essence of all science—whether it concerns the physical sciences like physics, chemistry, and mathematics, or the social sciences like sociology, anthropology, and psychology.

Science is not static and unchanging, however. Like everything else we know, science is continually growing and progressing. Things are seen one way today, and tomorrow someone discovers a new and better way to look at the same problem. In the eternal search for knowledge science must continually explore and test its concepts. It does this in two major ways: (1) the accumulation of data through observation, and (2) the organization of data into frames of reference, theories, or systems which make understanding useful and meaningful.

It is through the development of theories and frames of reference that psychology seeks to provide adequate understanding of people and their behavior as the basis for the solution of the great human problems of our time. This book is but one attempt to organize the data of psychology into a useful and effective frame of reference. Before this point of view is more closely investigated, however, it will pay us to examine more closely some facets of the relationship between observation and theory.

THE ACCUMULATION OF DATA FROM OBSERVATIONS

Every science is based upon the careful accumulation of data from observations about the behavior of its subject matter. In the 70-odd years of its existence as a scientific discipline psychology has amassed thousands upon thousands of observations about people and their behavior. People have been observed in all kinds of situations and with varying degrees of exactness. We have compiled a vast literature including observations of children and adults, of males and females; of people at work and at play, in the home, at school, in industry, or in the community. Nothing has been too private or too sacred to be left out in this search. Psychologists have invaded every aspect of life to observe human behavior and thus further our understanding of people. Some observers have even penetrated the delivery room to observe the behavior of babies at the moment of birth. Others have made observations of persons under torture in the concentration camps of the last war. We have recorded observations of the sick and the well, the successful and the failures, the rich and the poor. Psychological journals are bulging with observations of human behavior.

Psychologists' observations of people and the ways in which they behave, have been made with every degree of control, ranging from informal observations of a group of children in a playground to precise measurements of the conditioned eye blink. The majority of data about behavior are of a normative or objective character. That is, they are observations made from the point of view of an outsider, someone other than the behaver himself. These observations permit us to state that, given a particular situation, "the chances are" that people will act thus or so. Such observations are helpful to us when we are dealing with masses of people. They make it possible for us to predict the probable number of persons who will do some particular thing we have in mind. By means of certain kinds of tests (which are simply devices for making controlled observations), for example, we can predict the probable number of college freshmen who will make it through to graduation, or the probability that a particular soldier may become a good pilot.

Other psychologists have attempted to make more personal observations of people. They are not content with knowing what a group of people *may* do. They hope to understand what a particular individual *will* do. As a consequence they have directed their observations to the behavior of individuals in an attempt to discover the nature of personality and the sources and forms of human uniqueness. Whatever the purpose behind the observations, however, psychology is forever seeking to accumulate new observations about human behavior, wherever it occurs. Indeed, we have almost more data than we know what to do with. Our problem now is to discover what it all means. For this we need the second great function of science: the organization of data into meaningful frames of reference.

THEORIES AND FRAMES OF REFERENCE

A frame of reference, or a theory, is nothing more than an organization of data, or a way of looking at data, to make them meaningful. Facts, by themselves, have little meaning or value. It is only when facts are combined into some sort of framework, that they become useful to understand or deal with problems. The temperatures, wind directions, and barometric pressures reported by observers all over the country to a weather bureau have little meaning as isolated facts. They do not have much more meaning even when we see them all together plotted on a large map of the United States. It is only when we bring all these data into a meaningful relationship to one another by a theory of weather changes, that they come alive for us, i.e., that they serve as a basis to predict the weather conditions for the next 24 hours. All science is continually engaged in the search for new and more adequate frames of reference, or theories, by which accumulated data make the most effective and efficient sense.

A fact is not an independent thing that we can memorize, depend upon, and know will always be true. When we feel our railroad coach moving it may be because we are leaving the station, but it may be because we are watching a moving train on the next track. What one believes to be true will depend upon the way in which observations are organized and upon the point from which the observer makes them. In the same way ". . . a bomb dropped from an airplane over a European city is seen by the aviator to fall in a straight line, by an anti-aircraft gunner to describe a parabola, by a North Polar observer to rush counterclockwise, by a Martian to perform a spiral movement about the sun, while to an observer on Sirius it would seem to follow a curved path through the heavens . . ." (Diehl). What seems to us to be true or a fact depends upon the frame of reference from which we make our observations. Theories are attempts to bring order and meaning to observation by providing a frame of reference for making observations; they give to facts the meanings which make them useful.

Theories vary with the purpose of the observer. There are almost unlimited numbers of ways in which facts can be organized or looked at. What is more, each of these ways may be quite useful and acceptable, depending upon the needs for understanding we have at a given time. The same data looked at in different ways lend themselves to quite different kinds of orientations. One might look at the data concerning the number and age of automobiles in the state of Montana, for example, from a number of different points of view. One could interpret these data in terms of the problem of safety on the highway, the probable replacements the auto companies need to turn out next year, the kind and numbers of roads needed in a particular area, the number of quarts of oil required for the following year, or the probable number of seat covers to be sold in the state within the next six months.

As Angyal suggests: "The utility of a theory consists essentially in that it serves as a guide, as a point of reference, for empirical studies, which otherwise are likely to result in an utterly chaotic and incoherent mass of data. The utility of a good theory is twofold: it allows us to question nature intelligently and offers a background for the interpretation of empirical data." Theories provide an interpretation of what is. This makes it possible for us to ask new questions leading to further extension of our knowledge. No theory is, of course, ever "right." Good theory is only the best approximation of meaning we can make in our time. Every theorist must recognize the tenuousness of his conceptions and look forward to the certainty that his theory will one day be superseded by some new and more inclusive, or more satisfying explanation of events.

Theories vary also as to the amount of data they attempt to include. Some theories refer to fairly minute aspects of a major problem, others attempt to include great masses of data covering a broad field of understanding. Generally speaking, the more inclusive the frame of reference, the more useful the theory becomes. Whatever problem we face, the most useful frame of reference will be one that most adequately helps us understand and use all of the facts before us.

Let us investigate this principle by examining Fig. 1. As man reached a point in his development where it became necessary for him to deal with numbers of things, represented in Fig. 1 by the marks between A and B, he developed a number system, represented by the triangle ABC. The development of this number system made it possible for him to deal with his environment more effectively than he could before and to understand many new concepts. In time, however, this number system became inadequate as new facts were discovered and new needs arose, represented in Fig. 1 by the marks between

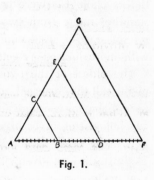

Fig. 1.

B and D. New facts could not be dealt with in the old number system and out of this need a new frame of reference called algebra was developed, represented by the triangle ADE. The new frame of reference did not deny what had gone before but made it possible to deal with matters never before approachable. But even this frame of reference could not suffice forever and soon man's insatiable striving made it necessary to deal with still more new facts and problems, represented in Fig. 1 by the marks between D and F. This, in turn, led to the development of still another frame of reference, known to mathematicians as calculus, represented by the triangle AFG. This relationship of facts and frames of reference is characteristic of the progress of science. Through the continual search for facts and for frames of reference in which these facts can be comprehended the frontiers of knowledge are pushed forward.

All sciences are constantly engaged in this never ending search for better explanations of the largest possible number of facts. Often the best explanations are the simplest as well. This is often called the principle of parsimony. Indeed, one might well say that the goal of science is the reduction of the largest possible amounts of data to the simplest possible explanations. Perhaps the best example of this search for ultimate simplicity in our time is to be found in Einstein's comprehensive theory of matter expressed in the simple formula $E = mc^2$. Here a vast subject is reduced to an ultimate of simplicity.

Frames of Reference of Psychology

Psychology, too, has its frames of reference and its theories of behavior. Observations about human behavior made over the years have been organized in a multitude of ways, depending upon the problems the psychologists were trying to understand. These attempts at understanding range from two broad general approaches, called frames of reference, to a great number of smaller theories developed for dealing with more limited aspects of behavior.

The oldest of the two great frames of reference in psychology we might call the "external," or "objective," approach. In this frame of reference, behavior is examined from an outside observer's point of view. The psychologist observes his subjects through tests, laboratory experiments, and many other means in order to determine just what they will be likely to do in a given situation. As he places his subjects in one situation or another and observes their behavior change, he seeks to explain their behavior in terms of the situations to which they react. In this way the causes of behavior are assigned, with one modification or another, primarily to the environments in which the subjects are reacting. It has been observed, for example, that delinquents very frequently come from broken homes, from association with bad companions, from poverty-stricken homes, or from homes with immoral parents. These factors are, therefore, regarded as environmental influences producing delinquent behavior. Making their observations in this frame of reference, psychologists describe behavior in terms of the environmental stimuli which seem, to an outside observer, to be acting upon and producing the behavior of the individual. This has sometimes been called S-R psychology because it attempts to explain behavior, or the response (R) of the subject, in terms of the stimulus (S) to which he appears to be reacting.

This frame of reference has aided psychology tremendously, and during the three-quarters of a century of psychology as an experimental science, psychologists have amassed a huge amount of data about the circumstances under which different types of behavior occur. As a result of these studies progress has been made in the prediction of normative behavior, i.e., of what the "average," "normal," or "typical" individual, or even the "typical 10-year-old," may do under a given set of circumstances.

Such predictions are useful in fields like advertising, politics, or business administration, all of which are concerned with behavior of masses, and in which the prediction of what particular individuals will do is seldom necessary. However, in the great majority of situations this understanding of normative behavior is not enough. Most of us must deal with individuals; thus, it is usually necessary to understand the behavior of individuals with greater accuracy than normative methods allow.

To deal with the problems of individual behavior another frame of reference has emerged more recently, called the "personal," or the "perceptual," or the "phenomenological" approach to psychology. This approach seeks to understand the behavior of the individual from *his own* point of view. It attempts to observe people, not as they seem to outsiders, but as they seem to themselves. People do not behave solely because of the external forces to which they are exposed. People behave as they do in consequence of how things seem to them. We run very hard from the danger we *think* is there and ignore the danger we do not know exists. Behavior in this frame of reference is seen as a problem of human perception. *This perceptual view of behavior is the frame of reference of this book.*

Within these two great frames of reference for psychology, the external and the perceptual, are many more specific theories. Some of these are devised in the external frame of reference and some have been developed in the perceptual view. Some of them are restricted to a very small segment of the whole problem of behavior. Others are general attempts to organize large accumulations of data into meaningful explanations of problems of human relationships. Like any other science, psychology can be explored in many ways and on many different levels.

Theory Level and Application

There is nothing sacred about theory. Theory in any field of endeavor is nothing more than a systematic explanation of events useful to the purposes one has in view. Theory which holds for one frame of reference or one problem may be totally inadequate, even misleading, in another. Theory can be constructed on many levels and for many different purposes, but its maximum efficiency is reached only on the levels and purposes for which it is designed. To examine this question of theory level let us draw an analogy with physical science as illustrated in the left side of Fig. 2.

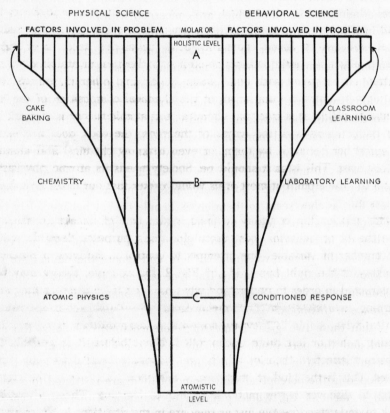

Fig. 2. Levels of Theory Construction.

We might think of all data about any subject as spread along a continuum from the molar or holistic level, where we are concerned with the totality of a problem, to the atomic level, where we are primarily concerned with minute aspects of events (the vertical axis of Fig. 2). On any level along this continuum we may construct theory which will be helpful in explaining the matters we need to deal with at that level. Beginning at the bottom of Fig. 2, atomic theory, for example, is useful in dealing with problems of the atom. At that level (C) and for those purposes, it is relevant and essential. On another level (*B*) theories of organic and inorganic chemistry are useful and pertinent for the pharmacist when he makes up a doctor's prescription. He may know little or nothing about atomic theory, however, and he is able to carry on his job quite effectively without this knowledge. This is not to imply that atomic theory does not hold for the chemicals with which he deals. Indeed, it does, but the pharmacist does not need to know atomic theory to carry on his profession adequately. On still another level, the molar level, colleges of home economics have developed theories of cake baking sometimes quite without reference to chemical or atomic physics. Cakes can be baked with flour, water, sugar, and other ingredients by people who know nothing at all of the chemical composition of the ingredients. While it is true that chemical and atomic theory is at work in the batter along with the hands of the cook, the cook does not need to guide her behavior by them, or even to know chemical and atomic theory exist. This is as it should be. Society needs its atomic physicists to control the atom, but most of us would prefer that our cakes be baked by cooks!

This relationship of utility to level is also true of behavioral theory. The theory of behavior most useful for one's purposes depends upon the number of variables one attempts to control in studying a process. Looking at the right hand side of Fig. 2, for example, theory may be constructed in order to understand what happens to children as they are learning in a classroom (the molar level). To do this it is necessary to deal with people as they are and with a large number of factors affecting behavior left quite uncontrolled. Nevertheless, it is possible to construct effective theories which are extremely helpful for our purposes. This is the kind of study many educators carry on in the classroom to discover better methods to induce learning. These educators seek to understand people just as they are in the situations in which they must deal with them.

Such studies, however, make some people very uncomfortable. Too many variables remain uncontrolled! Accordingly, one may seek to study learning on a level wherein more of the variables are controlled. One can, for instance, study learning in the laboratory instead of in the classroom, where theories of learning can be developed from experiments using tachistoscopic exposures (level *B*). In the laboratory one can go further and control the material being learned by removing meaning from it, as in the use of nonsense syllables. Other factors, too, can be controlled, e.g., the circumstances and the time the subject is exposed to the material, or the surroundings in which the experiments take place. In this way one can find new theories of learning applicable to the more "pure" situations constructed under such laboratory conditions. It is possible to go even further in the elimination of variables and to study a single stimulus-response unit, as Pavlov did in his experiments with dogs (level C). Here, too, it will be feasible to construct learning theories applicable to the kind of situations studied. Unfortunately, when learning is examined under these restricted conditions the subject of study is no longer people but an isolated process. Molar approaches cannot answer atomic questions and atomic approaches are far too narrow to provide practical solutions to molar problems.

Theory on any level is true and helpful for its purposes, but it hardly suffices at other levels. Any theory of behavior may be devastatingly criticized by the simple expedient of examining it at a level different from the level at which it was devised. Failure to realize this relationship of theory to level sometimes causes serious breakdowns of communication among scientists. To the laboratory psychologist, for example, the failure of the applied psychologist to control all the variables in his study of problems may seem like a shocking disregard for the rigorous discipline of science. In turn, the applied psychologist may regard his laboratory colleague's narrower interests with impatience and irritation over what seems a callous disregard for "the really important matters." Theories are not "right" or "wrong"; they are merely more or less adequate for the problems they were designed to deal with.

The great human problems of our time press upon us and we need the best possible understanding we can acquire about the nature of man and his behavior. In adopting any frame of reference or any theory of human behavior, however, we need to be keenly aware that all such theories are always only an approximation of the true nature of events. Sooner or later, the best of theories is likely to be superseded by something a little better, a little more accurate, a little more comprehensive, or simpler, or more useful for accomplishing our major purposes. This should not dismay us. Rather, it should give us courage to make the very best attempt we can to achieve the best approximations to the truth of which we are capable in our generation.

The remainder of this book represents an attempt to set forth a broad and inclusive personal frame of reference for the understanding of human behavior. This frame of reference may be applied to any level of psychological exploration, but in this book it has been applied with special reference to the aspects of individual behavior which are most essential for the solution of the immediate problems of our time. It includes the thinking and work of thousands of psychologists and social scientists interpreted in the frame of reference I have found most adequate to bring order and organization to the great quantity of data psychology has collected about human nature. It is presented here in the hope it may prove as useful and helpful to others as it has to me.

CHAPTER **2**

The Perceptual View of Behavior

HUMAN behavior, may be observed from at least two very broad frames of reference: from the point of view of an outsider, or from the point of view of the behaver himself. Looking at behavior in the first way we can observe the behavior of others and the situations in which such behavior occurs. It is then possible to attempt the explanation of behavior in terms of the interaction of the individual and the situations in which we have seen him operating. This is the "objective," or "external," frame of reference. The second approach seeks to understand behavior by making its observations from the point of view of the behaver himself. It attempts to understand the behavior of the individual in terms of how things "seem" to him. This frame of reference has been called the "perceptual," "personal," or "phenomenological" frame of reference and is the point of view of this book.

The Perceptual View of Behavior

In the personal, or perceptual, frame of reference we attempt to observe behavior from the point of view of the individual himself. As a matter of fact, that is what almost all people, professional psychologists or laymen, do as soon as they are confronted with the task of dealing with the behavior of an individual. "What does he want?"—"What is he thinking?"—"How does he feel about this?" are some of the questions they ask as they try to put themselves in his place to understand and anticipate his behavior. The clinical psychologist may have carried out research concerning the relation between juvenile delinquency and objective factors such as family income, the parents' age, the number of brothers and sisters, and the percentage of home ownership in the district; but when he is actually dealing with a delinquent boy, he is almost certain to ask "What does he think of himself?" and

"What does he think of his parents?" and otherwise attempt to see the situation from the point of view of the boy. Even the psychologist in the animal laboratory finds himself thinking "That rat is hungry" or "This rat is afraid." We take it as a matter of course that people's ideas, emotions, and opinions have an effect upon their behavior, and we are consequently alert and sensitive to them.

People do not behave according to the facts as *others* see them. They behave according to the facts as *they* see them. What governs behavior from the point of view of the individual himself are his unique perceptions of himself and the world in which he lives, the meanings things have for him. Recently, I heard a kindergarten child try to tell his teacher how pretty a little girl looked in her brand-new party dress. "She was pretty as . . . , pretty as . . . , pretty as a mother!" said the little fellow searching his mind for the prettiest thing he could think of. Now the fact of the matter is, from the outside observer's point of view, this child's mother could only be described as a very homely woman! To this little boy, however, his mother is the epitome of beauty and the criterion by which loveliness is to be judged. How this mother looks to other people is largely irrelevant information in trying to understand this child and his relationship to his mother.

Disregarding, for the moment, the objective facts about behavior some of us have learned, let each one of us look at his own behavior as we actually see it at the moment we are behaving. At once, we find lawfulness and determinism. From the point of view of the behaver himself behavior is caused. It is purposeful. It always has a reason. Sometimes the reasons are vague and confused, in which case his behavior is equally vague and uncertain; sometimes the meanings are extremely clear and definite. But everything we do seems reasonable and necessary at the time we are doing it. When we look at other people from an external, objective point of view, their behavior may seem irrational because we do not experience things as they do. Even our own behavior may, in retrospect, seem to have been silly or ineffective. But at the instant of behaving, each person's actions seem to him to be the best and most effective acts he can perform under the circumstances. If, at that instant, he knew how to behave more effectively, he would do so.

From the point of view of an observer who knows the location of an exit, the behavior of a fire victim rushing back again and again to a jammed door is completely unreasonable. From the point of view of the victim in those circumstances, it is the most reasonable thing he can do because the door is the closest approximation to an exit he can find. However capricious, irrelevant, and irrational his behavior may appear to an outsider, from his point of view *at that instant*, his behavior is purposeful, relevant, and pertinent to the situation *as he understands it*. How it appears to others has no bearing upon the causes of his behavior. The important thing is how it seems to the person himself. These personal meanings which govern behavior the psychologist calls perceptions. It is the fundamental thesis of this book that all behavior is a function of the individual's perceptions. In the remainder of this chapter, let us examine the fundamental premises upon which this point of view depends.

All Behavior Is Lawful

It is a necessary assumption of any science that its subject matter is regular and lawful. If this assumption could not be made, there could, of course, be no science. It is the purpose of science to discover the laws of events, but if the events with which the science deals are totally capricious and without meaning, there can obviously be no science at all. Like all science, then, we begin our study of behavior with the assumption that it is lawful and meaningful. Beginning with this assumption psychology may hope to discover the laws of behavior through careful observation and interpretation.

The Perceptual Field Determines Behavior

Behavior, we have assumed above, is lawful. To the behaver himself behavior always seems relevant, purposeful, and caused. But, if the behavior is caused, where are the causes? To the individual the causes of his behavior appear to be in the world around him and in his relation to it. As he experiences it, he eats, not because of stomach contractions, or a lowering of the sugar content of his blood, or because of habit, but because he is hungry, or because he does not wish to disappoint his wife, or just because he *feels* like eating. In any case, it seems to him that his behavior is a reasonable and necessary result of his present situation.

This situation is, of course, not the physical situation or the objective situation but the *perceived* situation, the situation as it appears to the behaver. An "hereditary" Democrat (or Republican) may believe that Republicans (or Democrats) are customarily wrong-headed, misguided, and—to some degree—enemies of society. If he believes so, he will act and vote accordingly. He will not doubt the validity of his own views and he will think that he is basing his behavior upon objective facts. It should be clear, however, to other people that his behavior is determined, not by the objective field, but by a personal, individual way of perceiving which is not identical to that of any other individual.

THE "FIELD" CONCEPT

Modern science has long since discovered that many matters cannot be understood solely in terms of the "things" with which it deals. Many of the complex events we hope to understand and predict can only be dealt with through an understanding of *interrelationships*. Even when the precise nature of these interrelationships is not known, it may still be possible to use them effectively. To deal with such interrelationships modern science has invented the very useful concept of a "field." When something occurs at one point in space apparently because something else happened at another point with no visible means by which the "cause" can be related to the "effect," the scientist often says the two events are connected in a field. This field serves as a kind of bridge between cause and effect by which the scientist can deal with a problem even though he may not be clearly aware of all intervening aspects. No one has ever seen electricity, for example, nor are we entirely certain just what it is or exactly how it works. In spite of this lack of exact knowledge, however, we are able to deal with the phenomenon by assuming the existence of an electric field. Using this field, scientists and engineers have been able to predict and control electric currents and to build devices using its properties.

A field, it should be recognized, is an inference. Whether or not it really exists in any tangible fashion, we do not know. Although no one knows exactly how this field is composed, or what it is that makes it operate, nevertheless, the concept is useful as it makes it possible to deal with events that behave predictably even though we may be ignorant of the reasons why or how. That an event can be utilized in a predictable way is sufficient to make it useful for the scientist's purposes. Thus, the field concept has proved tremendously useful to modern science; it has made it possible to by-pass some unsolved problems and to deal effectively with matters about which we do not know all we should like to know. The astronomer uses the concept to predict the orbits of the stars. The atomic physicist finds it helpful in understanding the structure of matter. The embryologist explains the determination of function by referring to the location of cells in a growth field. Psychologists, too, have found the field concept useful for the understanding and predicting of human behavior.

THE PERCEPTUAL FIELD

In this book we shall use the field concept to refer to that more or less fluid organization of meanings existing for every individual at any instant. We call it the perceptual or phenomenal field. *By the perceptual field, we mean the entire universe, including himself, as it is experienced by the individual at the instant of action.* It is each individual's personal and unique field of awareness, the field of perception responsible for his every behavior.

Several years ago a friend of mine was driving a car at dusk along a Western road. A globular mass, about two feet in diameter, suddenly appeared directly in the path of the car. A passenger screamed and grasped the wheel attempting to steer the car around the object. The driver, however, tightened his grip on the wheel and drove directly into the object. The behavior of both the driver and the passenger was determined by his own phenomenal field. The passenger, an Easterner, saw the object in the highway as a boulder and fought desperately to steer the car around it. The driver, a native Westerner, saw it as a tumbleweed and devoted his efforts to keeping his passenger from overturning the car.

In understanding this behavior it is not necessary to know what the object "really" was. Each individual in the car behaved toward it according to its nature in his own perceptual field. What a botanist or a geologist might have known about the object had no effect on the behavior of these travelers as they struggled to get the wheel. The behavior of each was determined, not by the objective facts, but by his own perceptual field. In other words, the factors effective in determining the behavior of an individual are those, and only those, which are experienced by the individual at the time of his behavior. These experiences we call perceptions and the entire field of these perceptions we call the perceptual field.

The concept of complete determination of behavior by the perceptual field is our basic postulate. It may be stated as follows: *All behavior, without exception, is completely determined by, and pertinent to, the perceptual field of the behaving organism.* The perceptual field has also been called the personal field, the private world, the behavioral field, the psychological field, the individual's life space, and the phenomenal field. The last term is derived from a school of philosophy known as phenomenology which holds that reality lies not in the event but in the phenomenon, that is to say, in the individual's experience of the event. It will be recognized that this is essentially the position we have taken—that behavior is a function, not of the external event but of the individual's perception of it. Because it is similar to the early view of the phenomenologists, perceptual psychology is sometimes called phenomenological psychology, and the perceptual field is sometimes referred to as the phenomenal field. In this book we will not use the term "phenomenological" but we shall occasionally use the term "phenomenal field" synonymously with the term "perceptual field," only because this synonym will serve to avoid repetition.

The Perceptual Field as "Reality"

The perceptual field is the universe of naive experience in which each individual lives, the everyday situation of the self and its surroundings which each person takes to be reality. To each of us the perceptual field of another person contains much error and illusion; it seems an interpretation of reality rather than reality itself; but to each individual, his phenomenal field *is* reality; it is the only reality he can know. This perceptual field is far richer and more meaningful than that of the objective, physical world. We do not live in a world of objects without meaning. On the contrary, we invest the things about us with all sorts of meanings; these meanings are for each of us the reality to which we respond.

The restriction of "reality" to the attenuated field of physics means a complete abandonment of everything that we ordinarily recognize as real. A friend of mine owns a desk at which he writes and on which his friends sit and spill cigarette ashes. An inquiry about the real nature of the desk had the following results:

"It is really cellulose."
"What is that?"
"A molecular combination of carbon, hydrogen, and oxygen."
"What are they?"
"They are made up of protons and electrons."
"What are they?"
"They are really charges of electricity."
"What are they?"

"They are not matter, just waves."
"What are they?"
"Not waves in anything, just waves."
"What are they?"
"All right, waves of nothing!"

In other words, what the desk *really* is depends upon the professional perceptual field of the person who answers the question. From the point of view of chemistry, my friend owns some rather refractory and unusable cellulose; from the standpoint of subatomic physics he owns no matter at all. Neither science says that he has a desk because neither science deals with desks.

No matter what we are told, our own perceptual field will always seem real, substantial, and solid to us. It is the only field and the only reality we can directly experience. It includes all the universe of which we are aware—including not only the physical entities which exist for us but such other entities as justice, injustice, and public opinion. It also includes experiences of love and hate, of fear, anger, and human compassion which do not exist outside the experience of people. So strong is our feeling of reality with respect to our perceptual field that we seldom question it. We accept that how it seems to us must truly be so. When others do not see things as we do, we are quite likely to jump to the conclusion that they must be either stupid or perverse; for what is right and proper seems to us so clear with respect to our own observation that no other conclusion seems warranted.

Our perceptions always have the feeling of reality at the instant of behaving. This may not be true in prospect, or in retrospect. Looking back at what we thought was so last week, we may feel now that our observations at that time were in error. But these are observations after the fact. At the time we acted, it seemed to us that the things we did, the thoughts we had, and the feelings we felt were reasonable, correct, and real. Even the murderer, at the moment he commits his crime, may feel that he is solving his problems in the only way he can under the circumstances. Later, reviewing his action, he may regret his decision and doubt the "reality" of his past thinking. On the other hand, looking forward today to the situation we will be in next week, we may plan very carefully what will be right and proper to do. When the time comes, however, we may behave quite differently because it may "seem" different at that moment. We behave in terms of the immediate meanings existing in our perceptual fields on both occasions.

Characteristics of the Phenomenal Field

A field, as it is understood in modern science, always has at least four properties: stability, fluidity, intensity, and direction. The reader may recall his experiments in his physics or science classes with iron filings and a magnet. When iron filings are scattered upon a piece of paper over a magnet they can be observed to line up in patterns of force about the magnet. That is, the iron filings placed in the electromagnetic field around the magnet respond to the force of the field and fall into patterns that reveal something of the character of the field. From the behavior of these filings it can be observed that the electromagnetic field is stable, that is, it tends to retain its character until some event causes it to change. At the same time, the field is also fluid. It can be changed, for instance, by the introduction of other magnets to the field. The intensity and direction characteristic of the field are revealed by the patterns taken by the iron filings. These same four properties are also characteristic of the phenomenal field although they are expressed in somewhat different fashion.

THE PERCEPTUAL FIELD IS FLUID. The phenomenal field is continually changing, and thus it is sometimes difficult to study. Like the Irishman's pig which ran around so fast that he could not count it, the phenomenal field is sometimes difficult to observe because, even as we attempt to look at it, it changes. It is this fluidity of the field, however, which makes change in behavior possible. Without a degree of fluidity, the individual would be unable to adjust to the changing circumstances in which he must live his life and find need-satisfaction. The capacity for change in the perceptual field also makes learning, reasoning, remembering, forgetting, and creativity possible.

THE PERCEPTUAL FIELD HAS STABILITY. Although the perceptual field is highly fluid it is by no means unorganized; the organization of the field necessarily gives it a degree of stability. To live successfully each of us needs an organized, stable, predictable field. Without some stability of the field we could not live at all. The nature of the organization producing this stability is the major concern of this book.

THE PERCEPTUAL FIELD HAS DIRECTION. In the same physical situation, or in objectively identical situations, the perceptual fields of different individuals will differ. Furthermore, during successive presentations of the same physical situation the perceptual field of even the same person changes. However, although the content and form of organization vary from individual to individual and from time to time, the perceptual field always has direction, i.e., it is always organized and meaningful. Our perceptions are never masses of meaningless and unrelated stimuli.

This organized characteristic of the perceptual field was first studied by the Gestalt psychologists who objected to the orthodox, stimulus-response psychology of their day and pointed out that, surely, human understanding is much more than an addition of unrelated stimuli. When we look at a picture we see much more than spots of paint; our response to a musical composition is much more than hearing a series of notes. The Gestalt psychologists pointed out that perception is always organized into what they termed a "Gestalt," or configuration. What is perceived, they said, is always a "total" and never an isolated event.

The perceptual field of any individual is both much more and much less than the field which is potentially available in the immediate physical environment. It is much more in that it includes many things not physically present. The most detailed perceptual field, however, includes only a very few of the vast (practically infinite) number of objects, details, and meanings which are present, or which might be present, in the fields of other individuals in the same physical situation. For instance, if any of us began to make a close study of the room in which we are at this moment, it is probable that we could spend months, years, or even a lifetime making a series of discoveries about it, even though

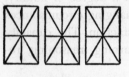

we may think we are already very familiar with the room. Fig. 3 actually contains all the three-letter words in the English language, but it is extremely unlikely that anyone not actively seeking new details and aspects in Fig. 3 would ever discover even one of them. Having studied Fig. 3 the reader may discover for himself how the

Fig. 3.

entire alphabet is contained in the figure by turning to Fig. 5 on p. 26.

At any given time, the field of a given individual is organized with reference to his need and the activity by which he is trying to satisfy his need at the time. The field of a professor playing golf, for instance, is very different from the field of the same professor engaged in teaching a class or in conversation with his wife. In each case, the field is organized around the activity of the moment and the perceptions occur which have bearing upon the professor's immediate problem. If thoughts of the lecture intrude into his golf game or if thoughts of his wife intrude into his lecture, it is only because: (1) the intruding activity has not been brought to a conclusion and, from his point of view, is still in progress; or (2) the intruding activity is more important to the satisfaction of the individual's need than the activity in which he is formally engaged. What is perceived is always a function of the individual's need operating in an organized field.

THE FIGURE-GROUND CHARACTER OF ORGANIZATION. The Gestalt psychologists observed that the meaning of any event was always a result of the relationship of any item to the totality observed. This relationship of the part to the whole they called the figure-ground relationship. The figure-ground relationship is familiar to all psychologists but the accompanying illustration, Fig. 4, will show some of its salient points. If the whole illustration is seen as a candlestick there is relatively little detail. As soon, however, as the observer looks for details in the base of the candlestick, the details in the top fade into ground. To illustrate the above point, the observer will note that the figure always is something. As long as any part of it is figure, it is meaningful. It is either a vase, a candlestick, two faces, or, at least, an undifferentiated object. When the illustration is seen as two faces there is a striking change in the character of the area between the faces as it fades down into ground. When the illustration is seen as a vase or a candlestick the same area emerges into figure, and a previously nonexistent solidity emerges that is striking. Objectively there has been no change, but the perceptual change can have a marked effect on the behavior of the observer. This process of emergence of figure from ground is known as *differentiation*, and makes possible change in our perception of events.

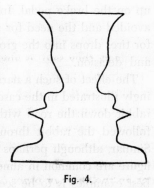

Fig. 4.

An example of the figure-ground relationship and its effect upon behavior may be seen in the difference between the field and the behavior of a motorist who is testing his brakes, and between the field and the behavior of another motorist who is stopping his car to avoid an imminent accident. In the first case the figure is rather diffuse and includes some awareness of his tires; consequently, he brings his car to a stop in a way that will not damage the tires. It is almost impossible for a responsible driver to bring his car to the required, abrupt stop under those conditions since, as soon as he feels the wheels slide, he eases

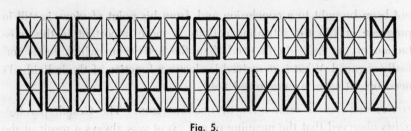

Fig. 5.

up on the brake pedal. In a real emergency, however, the object to be avoided and the need for stopping stand out so sharply that his concern for tires drops into the ground, and the brakes are applied with violence and decision.

The effect of such a narrowing of the figure upon behavior was amusingly illustrated in the case of a young man so intent upon chasing a jack rabbit down the road with his car that he suddenly discovered he had followed the rabbit through a barbed-wire fence and into a pasture. Similar, although perhaps less dangerous, samples of intent response to figure are common in almost everyone's experiences. Perhaps one of the best examples is to be seen in our experience at a movie. Entering the theater we perceive the screen and its content as ground, the aisle and seats as figure. Having found a seat we perceive the screen somewhat more precisely as we make ourselves comfortable. At this stage, we are still aware of our surroundings, of the edge of the screen, even of the screen as a screen. Shortly, however (if the picture is a good one), the images on the screen move into exclusive figure so that we lose practically all awareness of the ground surrounding us, to the extent that we feel so "alone" with the images on the screen that we may cry unabashedly in a manner which we certainly would not had all the strangers around us been clearly in figure.

The use of these illustrations should not mislead the reader into thinking that figure exists only in the visual aspects of the field. It may occur in any sense field or in any combinations of sense fields. In taste perception, for example, the figure-ground relationship can be observed when we attempt to bring into clearer awareness some particular component of a tasty dish whose recipe we are seeking to guess. In connection with the sense of hearing, the relationship may be observed when, lying in bed, we suddenly become aware of a dripping faucet or a rattling window which only a moment ago caused no annoyance to us at all when it existed as part of the ground of our perceptual field.

Anything in the field can become figure, including bodily fatigue, pain, and abstract ideas. As the Gestaltists have pointed out, however, two events may not appear in figure simultaneously. We may perceive Fig. 4 as a candlestick or as faces but not as both at once. How an individual behaves at any moment, however, is always a function of the total perceptual field in existence at that time. The meaning of any event perceived is always a product of the relationship of that figure to the total ground of which it is a part.

The intensity with which events are experienced in the phenomenal field will be a function of differentiation and levels of awareness. Although the perceptual field includes all the universe of which we are aware, we are not aware of all parts with the same degree of clarity at any moment. For instance, we walk through the living room without paying specific attention to the exact location of the lamps and the chairs, but our behavior indicates that we are aware of them. We do not bump into them. We know they are there even though we may be intent upon other matters. Awareness of these objects is at a low level of clarity adequate for the purposes of the moment. If our needs change, however, the same chairs we were only vaguely aware of a moment ago may emerge into very clear figure; for example, if our wives suggest redecorating. Until this moment the reader, if he is sitting down, has probably been aware at only a very low level of his point of contact with whatever it is he is sitting on. Were he not aware that he is firmly in contact with something he would not behave as he does; he would be busily trying to keep himself from falling. The reader may also discover that now that we have drawn his attention to his point of contact, the perception may be in very clear figure. Other low-level-awareness phenomena like breathing, the feel of the tongue in the mouth, or of the toes inside our shoes can also be brought into clearer figure when necessary. This process by which aspects of the perceptual field are brought into clear figure is called differentiation. At any moment perceptions in the field may exist at any and all levels of differentiation from the vaguest to the sharpest.

We have said that behavior is always determined by the nature of the perceptual field at the instant of behaving. It follows that at whatever level of awareness perceptions exist in the field, they will have their effects upon the individual's behavior. When we perceive clearly and sharply, behavior is correspondingly direct and efficient. When we perceive only vaguely, then behavior, too, is likely to be fuzzy and inaccurate. Perceptions at low levels of awareness, it is true, will affect behavior with less precision than perceptions more clearly in figure, but as long as they exist at all in the perceptual field, they must have their expression in behavior. The mass activity elicited by a fly buzzing around the face of an uneasy sleeper is an example. In the sleeper's field the fly functions as a vague, relatively undifferentiated annoyance and his response is made accordingly. When the level of awareness is sharpened and the fly, as source of annoyance, has been clearly perceived, behavior similarly becomes more precise and direct.

It should not be supposed that all meanings existing in the phenomenal field at low levels of awareness can always be called readily into clear figure, or reported to other people. Not at all! Many aspects of experience are destined to remain in ground all our lives. Consequently it may never be possible to bring them into sufficiently clear figure to relate them to others. However, reportable or not, since behavior is always the product of the total field, even vague awarenesses play their part in our behavior. Early in this century Freud noted this effect upon behavior and based a great deal of his theory of psychoanalysis upon what he called the "unconscious." Much of people's behavior, he observed, was motivated by events discernible by him but denied by his patients. He concluded, therefore, that behavior was often controlled by unconscious impulses. This is a point of view similar to the one we have been expressing.

Freud's description of behavior produced from low-level awareness as "unconscious," however, has turned out to be most unfortunate. The terms "conscious" and "unconscious" leave the impression of a clear-cut dichotomy instead of a continuous gradation of awareness from sharp and precise perceptions to vague and indistinct perceptions. The term "unconscious" has also been used by some people as though there were perceptions of which the individual is unaware. They have described the "unconscious" as a kind of "place" (even sometimes, as a kind of dark closet) where one could hide away things one does not want to look at. These are unfortunate aberrations of the perfectly useful idea that behavior may be significantly affected even by perceptions at low levels of awareness. In this book, we shall avoid the use of the terms "conscious" and "unconscious" because of the unfortunate connotations these terms have gathered about them.

DIFFERENTIATION, THE PROCESS OF FIELD CHANGE. Each of us is constantly searching his field for details and meanings which will better enable him to satisfy need. This process involves a continual change in the perceptual field by the constant rise of new characters into figure and the consequent lapse of other characters into ground, in the manner described above. This process, from the point of view of the behaver, is one of increased awareness of details and is, therefore, called differentiation. It is through differentiation that change in the perceptual field and, hence, change in behavior occurs.

An example of differentiation, or change in the field, may be seen in the process of becoming aware of an object. When persons are shown a figure or group of figures for varying lengths of time and asked to reproduce what they see, the first awareness is ordinarily of a vague, relatively undifferentiated whole, which then differentiates in more or less orderly fashion into more detailed parts. Since the properties of a newly emerging object are determined by its relationship to the rest of the field, at this stage it can easily be, and frequently is, distorted and misinterpreted. Illusions, hallucinations, and many cases of mistaken identity, as well as the common errors of proof reading, result. Who has not made errors like the traveler expecting a bridge, who mistakes a billboard for the anticipated span? Who has not been surprised to discover that a sign he thought said one thing on closer examination actually said something quite different?

The factors which appear to determine the nature and extent to which an event is differentiated are the need of the behaver and the opportunities for differentiation that are available. Since the figure is the only aspect of the field of which we are clearly aware, change in the field means change in the figure. The figure may become more precise, more detailed, and more intense, or it may become larger, more vague, and more diffused. On the other hand, the figure may become so large, so vague, and so diffused that it practically merges into ground. This probably does not happen except in deep sleep or unconsciousness, as under ordinary circumstances of daily life the individual is engaged in a continual search for the means of satisfying his needs; this requires a continual emergence of new characters into figure.

In the same way the figure is constantly shifting in size it is also changing in character as new characteristics and entities arise and differentiate from the ground. Since precision of behavior can only result from precision of figure, it is this emergence into figure which is the basic cause of more effective behavior. Change in behavior occurs with differentiation in the perceptual field. Thus, learning, problem solving, remembering, forgetting, and the like are all aspects of the process of differentiation occurring in the individual's phenomenal field.

SYNTHESIS, GENERALIZATION, AND PERCEPTION OF ABSTRACT EVENTS. It is the differentiations an individual is able to make in his perceptual field that determine the nature of his perceptions—both the direct perceptions of concrete events apprehended through our sense organs and the perceptions of complex events understood only through the medium of abstract thought. This broad use of the word "perception" is somewhat of a departure from traditional practice in laboratory psychology and a word of explanation seems in order. Historically, psychologists have used the word perception to refer only to, "a single, unified meaning obtained from sensory processes while a stimulus is present." To describe acts of knowing, understanding, or forming ideas, they have used the words "cognition" or "conception." In this book, however, the word "perception" is used to refer to *any* differentiations the individual is capable of making in his perceptual field whether an objectively observable stimulus is present or not. There seems little need for more than one process to explain these events. Differentiations in the phenomenal field resulting in perceptions of seeing, hearing, smelling, or feeling are precisely the same as those made in conceiving, knowing, or understanding. Although the subject matter varies, the process is the same. The differentiation of an idea or a concept is not basically different from the differentiation of a scent, a sound, or the printed words on a page.

Differentiation, as we have been describing it, seems to correspond to a process of analysis. But, it may be asked, do we not synthesize as well? Do we not also see examples of generalization? Are not synthesis and generalization the opposites of differentiation? To answer these questions, it is necessary to remind ourselves that the perceptual approach to understanding behavior is concerned solely with the problem of how events are experienced by the behaver. What seems like integration, synthesis, or generalization observed from an objective point of view, becomes—observed from the behaver's own frame of reference, simply another form of differentiation. When an individual, for example, perceives that "all these things have this aspect in common," what is occurring is not an "adding up" of separate and discrete perceptions. Rather, the observer has differentiated from his field of perceptions the unifying principle that "all these things have this aspect in common." Thus, what appears on the surface to be integration or synthesis, is—from the behaver's own point of reference—a differentiation of the relationship of events to each other.

Common Perceptions Make Communication Possible

Since the perceptual field cannot be observed directly by any other individual it may appear to the reader that in this frame of reference the causes of behavior are so secret that actual prediction of behavior must be beyond any outsider's power. Indeed, if the perceptual fields of different individuals were completely private, there would be no way of knowing another person's field and the prediction and control of behavior would, of course, be impossible. When I whistle to a dog, call to a friend, or lecture to a class, however, the dog, my friend, and the students, in a large percentage of cases, behave as if the sounds I make in my perceptual field are also present in theirs. In other words, changes in my own field are often accompanied by behavior on the part of others which indicates that a change has also taken place in their phenomenal fields.

It is probable that this relationship arises in the following way: each of us is born into a situation in which certain common characters and objects exist. For example, both the Eskimo and the South African tribesman are born into a world where things will fall if they are dropped, where there is ground under their feet, where there are people around them, where there are forms of precipitation, where there are colors and sounds to be experienced. Even among people as remote from one another as these, there is considerable agreement about the things they experience. There is even more among people in the same culture, who have many more common aspects as potential characters of their perceptual fields and of their individual "realities." Thus communication is possible through that part of the phenomenal field that is common to two persons. For instance, among most members of western society there are common gestures which make some communication possible although the spoken languages are different. However, they can do so only when the physical gesture has the same phenomenal significance. An American, to whom the nod means assent, will be unable to communicate by this means with a Greek, to whom it means negation, until he discovers the meaning of the gesture in the other's field. It is not the physical nature but the perceived character of the action that is important in determining behavior.

Communication is essentially the process of acquiring greater understanding of another's perceptual field and it can take place only when some common characters already exist. In speech, for instance, communication is possible only to the extent that the objective physical sounds or characters have the same meanings in the two fields. An American cattle fancier found his ability to communicate with a Scottish dealer much enhanced as soon as he discovered that "coo" meant not cow, as he had inferred, but calf. The same words often have very different meanings in the perceptual fields of different individuals. Even strangers of the same general culture often have difficulty communicating, but old friends who have shared many experiences can understand one another's fields so well that they can communicate and anticipate one another's behavior without using words at all.

The well-known phenomenon by which twins communicate with each other in a private language is possible because of the mutual nature of so much of their experience, so that there is an unusual correspondence between their perceptual fields. People who have common experiences tend to have common characteristics in their phenomenal fields and, as a result, show common tendencies in their behavior. Consequently, one finds at a social gathering the skiers, the bridge players, the teachers, the businessmen, or those who have been to Europe forming into groups despite the best efforts of a hostess to "mix them up." We feel more comfortable with persons whose phenomenal fields have much in common with our own. Because we see alike we also behave similarly and we can thus predict more easily what the other will do and how he will be likely to react to our own behavior. It is through the area of overlap in our respective fields that communication becomes feasible.

COMMON MEANING AS A FUNCTION OF DIFFERENTIATION.   Whatever meanings the individual possesses are the direct outgrowth of the kinds of differentiations he has been able to make. Since no two people ever have identical perceptual fields, no two people can ever have identical meanings. All human beings, however, have their humanity in common. In addition, large numbers of us live in common cultures. Consequently, many of us will, in the course of our experience, acquire many differentiations held by other people. The fact of our similar kinds of experience makes it likely that what one person has differentiated from a given situation is some assurance that others may do likewise.

Some differentiations are so common to the experience of all people that they are made almost automatically. In their early studies of perception the Gestalt psychologists were intrigued by a number of these common ways in which people order their perceptions. As a result oi their studies they isolated a number of principles of figure-ground relationships which seemed to them so universal that they were first ascribed to structural differences. There seems good reason now to believe that these common ways of differentiating are not so much matters of structure as learned ways of responding. Some of the common differentiations explored by the early Gestaltists are as follows:

1. Other things being equal, perceptions are differentiated in terms of the *nearness* of the events experienced. For example, in the line below it will be noted that those letters appearing together seem to stand out from the rest of the printed line.

a bc d e fg h i jk

2. Other things being equal, perceptions are likely to be ordered by the differentiation of *similarity* in the events experienced. In Fig. 6, for example, the circles and dots are not seen as a helter-skelter, unordered series of events. Rather, one's perceptions are ordered in terms of the similar aspects of the field and circles and dots are seen as alternate rows.

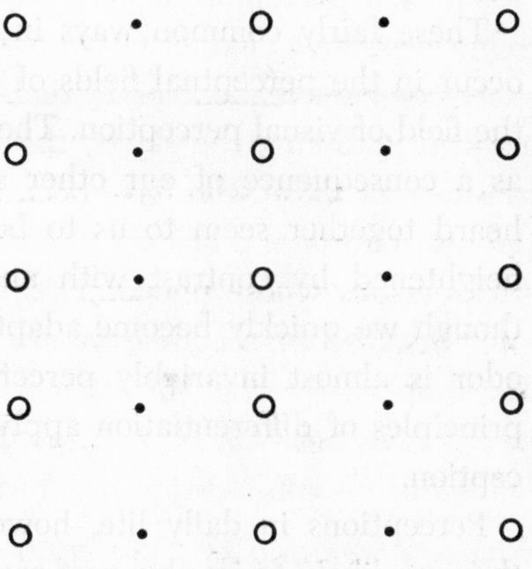

3. Other things being equal, perceptions are likely to be differentiated in terms of the **intensity** of the event experienced. In the sentence you are **now** reading, the **words** printed in **bold face type** seem to stand **out** from the rest of the **words** in the **sentence** as a consequence of their greater **intensity** (in this case, blackness) compared to the other words of the sentence.

Fig. 6.

4. Other things being equal, perceptions are likely to be differentiated in terms of their *common fate*. That is, events which seem to share a common direction, continuity, or characteristic are likely to be seen in figure. In Fig. 7, for example, the dots are perceived as two lines perpendicular to each other with the line with the dots from A to B seeming to belong together, and the dots

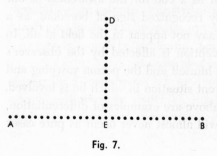

Fig. 7.

from D to E also seeming to belong together—but in a different category than the dots from A to B.

5. Other things being equal, perceptions are likely to be differentiated in terms of their *novelty* or *contrast*. That is to say, in a series of similar events what is new or contrasting is more likely to appear in figure in the perceptual field. In any classroom the appearance of a Hindu student in a sari will invariably capture everyone's attention. Newness or difference is a well known attention gainer.

6. Other things being equal, events sharing a *common movement* or *direction* are more likely to be differentiated. Events which appear to be moving in an otherwise still setting are more likely to appear in figure than the surroundings. When the rabbit "freezes" it is much more difficult to see him; the hunter who moves is much more likely to be shot for a deer than the hunter who stands still.

These fairly common ways in which figure-ground relationships may occur in the perceptual fields of different people take place not only in the field of visual perception. They may also be found in our perceptions as a consequence of our other sense modalities. The notes which are heard together seem to us to belong together. The taste of a food is heightened by contrast with another food of different character. Although we quickly become adapted to given odors, a newly introduced odor is almost invariably perceived quickly. The above figure-ground principles of differentiation apply to comparatively simple cases of perception.

Perceptions in daily life, however, are almost never simple. Rather, they are likely to involve vast areas of the perceptual field. Items within the field are interacting and interdependent, and any new thing in the field derives its properties from its relationship to the field as a whole. For instance, yawning by one person in a group will have a varying effect on the others since it will have varying functions in their individual perceptual fields. It may appear as a cue for the awareness of our own throat sensations, as a vaguely recognized sign of boredom, as a deliberate act of discourtesy, or it may not appear in the field at all. In any case, the character of the perception is affected by the observer's concept of the relationship between himself and the person yawning and his general concept of the total current situation in which he is involved. While the simple principles stated above are examples of differentiation, such common kinds of experiences will almost never occur as pure cases in ordinary life. What is perceived will always be a function of the individual's need and the antecedent field which he possesses at the moment.

The Understanding and Prediction of Behavior

The presence of common meanings in the perceptual fields of different persons makes communication possible. It also makes possible the understanding and prediction of the behavior of other people. The relation between one's own perceptual field and one's own behavior is relatively simple and well known to each of us because of our lifelong experiences in which we have been able to observe the relationship between our own perceptions and behavior. Because of this experience, the process of reconstructing another individual's perceptual field by observing his behavior is a relatively simple and easy task, which can often be done with little training. Since behavior is always determined by the individual's perceptual field, we need only to learn to read behavior backwards in order to understand the perceptions of another person. That is, we can infer from another's behavior the nature of the perceptions which probably produced it.

As a usual thing, when we see a man scratch, we can infer that he itched. When we see him yawn, we often share his field so vividly that we are impelled to duplicate his behavior. By this kind of inference from what we are able to observe, we can understand the perceptions lying behind a great deal of human behavior. We can accomplish this by asking ourselves "Now why did he do that?" or "Under what circumstances would I have done that?" To ask such questions effectively, moreover, we do not need to learn to do something entirely new. Everyone has been making observations of this sort all his life, so that the problem is one of learning to do more accurately, effectively, and explicitly what one already has learned to do albeit implicitly and unsystematically. When important people with whom we are conversing begin to fiddle with their watches or stand and walk to the door, all but the most eager and obtuse people can infer that they are impatient for us to leave. As a consequence, we are likely to take our departure without waiting to obtain an electroencephalogram reading or measures of our subject's heartbeat, blood sugar, or breathing rate.

The social scientist, attempting to understand and predict human behavior approaches the problem of prediction in exactly the same manner, that is, by inference from observed behavior. What the rest of us do, often haphazardly and implicitly, however, the professional worker seeks to accomplish more explicitly, more precisely, and with greater discipline and care. In Chapter 20 we will look much more closely at some methods of observation and inference commonly used by psychologists.

The Variables of Perception

In this chapter we have postulated that all behavior, without exception, is determined by the perceptual field at the moment of action. To produce change in behavior, then, it will be necessary to produce some change in the individual's perceptual field. To understand other people and to use ourselves effectively as instruments for human welfare, our own welfare as well as the welfare of others, we will need to understand, as clearly as possible, the factors controlling and limiting the processes of perceiving and the function of the perceptual field. Some of the factors controlling perception have been known and studied for generations by several disciplines. The importance of other factors bearing upon perceptual processes have been, only more recently, appreciated and subjected to experimental scrutiny. In the next seven chapters, we shall examine seven of these known variables of perception.

It should not be supposed that these seven factors are in any sense definitive. Indeed, it could be argued that several of these factors could be consolidated thus reducing the list of variables. On the other hand, it is conceivable that in the years to come still other variables may be differentiated as having important effects upon the perceptual process. The factors discussed in the remaining chapters have been classified in this way solely because it is convenient to discuss and present them so. The reader, of course, is free to interpret and order them in any way that seems most helpful for his own purposes.

Because the effect of human need upon perception is so fundamental and all-pervasive a factor we shall begin our exploration of the variables of perception with the problem of human need in the following chapter.

CHAPTER **3**

What Do People Need?

ANY understanding of human behavior must be based upon some knowledge of what people are trying to accomplish when they behave or misbehave. The teachers in a certain school who conceived the notion of cutting down misbehavior by granting a banner to the classroom showing the best deportment each week were completely unprepared for the results. Deportment improved in the lower grades but the upper grades went on a rampage. The lower grades worked for the banner while the upper grades felt disgraced if they won it! To deal effectively with others it is necessary to have the most accurate possible conception of what it is people are trying to do, for whatever we believe about their motives will inevitably affect our behavior toward them.

What, then, is it that people are characteristically trying to do? A glance at the behavior of people about us would seem to indicate that people are motivated by a vast number of needs, people have need for love, clothing, prestige, food, drink, automobiles, hate, revenge, exercise, lipstick, cigarettes, crossing streets, or even, sometimes, death. Behavior seems characterized by an almost unlimited number of motives, some of which may be quite antagonistic to one another. The opposing desires for living and for dying, for having money and for spending it, for being slim and for eating heartily, for example, are motives difficult, if not impossible, for most people to carry out at the same time. A conception of human motives based upon so large and conflicting a picture of what it is that people are striving for leaves us hopelessly confused when we try to understand human behavior. We need a simpler, more accurate understanding of motives in order to understand ourselves and to serve as an effective guide in our dealings with others.

Is there a simpler, more fundamental view of what it is the man is seeking that avoids this confusion? I believe there is. Indeed, I believe it is possible to reduce all these seemingly diverse and confusing goals toward

37

which people seem to strive to a single, all inclusive human need which motivates all human behavior at all times and in all places. In this chapter we shall examine this concept from three points of view: (1) the origins of need in the nature of man himself, (2) the fundamental need defined, and (3) the effects of need upon perception.

The Origins of Need in the Nature of Man and the Universe

MAN IS CONTINUOUS WITH HIS UNIVERSE

To the best of our knowledge about the evolution of life on earth, man, like all living creatures, has developed from a long and continuous line of animal life. Man is composed of chemical elements found in the soil, the rivers, and the mountains of his world. He is part of the universe, part of a vast and magnificent organization. Like rocks, rivers, plants, animals, planets, and suns, as a part of this great organization, man participates in its processes. Like everything else in the universe, man is affected by the organization of which he is part.

Man is himself an organization within the larger organization of the universe in which he exists. Indeed, he is an organization within a whole series of organizations leading outward from himself to the larger structure of the universe. This is familiar to school children who sometimes make a game of addressing themselves as "John Smith, 105 Main St., Santa Barbara, California, U.S.A., North America, the World, the Solar System, the Universe." These are some of the larger organizations in which man participates. Every one of these organizations of which man is a part has, in turn, its effect upon man and his behavior.

The man illustrated in Fig. 8, facing in one direction, for example, can look out from himself to a series of ever larger organizations of which

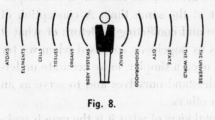

Fig. 8.

he is part, ending in the universe itself. But this is not the only way man participates in organization. Like the universe itself, he, too, is an organization of smaller organizations. His physical being, for example, is composed of a large number of other smaller organizations such as the skeletal, respiratory, digestive, excretory, and reproductive systems, among others. These organizations are diagramed on the opposite side of Fig. 8; they are composed, in turn, of organizations of cells, which are organizations of chemical elements, which are organizations of atoms and so on, ad infinitum. Man thus appears to be an organization in a long chain of organizations extending within and without himself as far as we have learned to see.

THE DYNAMICS OF ORGANIZATION

In this continuity of organization, the more intimately related the organizations, the more direct and specific is the effect of a larger organization upon a smaller. Let us take, as an example, the case of John Smith whom we mentioned before. John's family organization, the Smiths, will more intimately and directly affect young John's life and behavior than his neighborhood group which is represented by his street address. John's neighborhood, in turn, will probably affect his behavior more intimately than his city, state, or nation. Each one of these larger organizations, however, will have its effect upon John and will govern, less specifically but no less surely, his behavior. In the same manner, John's own organization will affect the organizations of which he is composed. What John eats will affect directly the organization of his digestive system and, less directly but no less surely, the cellular organizations of which that system is composed. As an organization within a larger organization, thus it seems clear that man is affected by the larger organizations of which he is a part.

The reverse effect seems also true. An organization made up of many parts is affected by the parts of which it is composed. The introduction of a new element, or a change in an old element necessarily affects the total organization of which it is a part. The birth of a child into a family certainly changes the organization of the family in many ways. Less directly but no less certainly, change in the family organization affects the community, city, state, and nation of which the family is a part. In this sense, man as an organization is both affected by and affects the organizations in which he participates. By his participation, indeed by his very existence, man produces change in the universe of which he is a member.

The action and interaction of man and his world which we have been discussing, is by no means limited to physical events alone. Similar effects may be observed in the realm of ideas, values, attitudes, and human thought. Here too, the world in which man lives both affects and is affected by the organization of human thought. People from the North think differently about Negroes than do people from the South. Russians think like Russians, and Americans think like Americans. The organization of man's ideas and understanding even produces changes in the environment in which he lives. One need only point out the way our entire world has been changed because of our new knowledge about atomic energy. Our ideas and values affect the culture in which we live and, in turn, are affected by it.

As a participating member of the universe, man must necessarily be affected by the organization of which he is a part. The characteristics of that larger organization will be characteristic of man as well, although with different expression and magnitude. Is there any universal characteristic of organization which we can select for examination which seems to have this relationship? There seems to be.

THE MAINTENANCE OF ORGANIZATION

Perhaps the most outstanding characteristic of our universe is the very fact of its organization. Our universe, above all things, seems characterized by the maintenance of its organization. Whatever else may occur, the universe maintains an order. This maintenance of its organization has been the subject of awe and thanksgiving for generations of philosophers, scientists, poets, and theologians. Various explanations of the existence of this organization have found favor with different groups of students. Everyone may choose the explanation that satisfies him. We shall not be concerned here with the explanation for this maintenance of organization. For our purposes it is sufficient that the phenomenon seems to exist.

The maintenance of organization by our universe seems also characteristic of the organizations of which that universe is composed. According to all our observations, it seems inherent in the nature of an organization itself. Wherever we turn for illustration organizations show this same enduring quality. To maintain their organizations is the dominant characteristic of all things. It appears true of living and non-living things, and of the universe itself. The simplest atoms tenaciously resist disruption, and heavenly bodies maintain their established orbits.

The universe maintains its organization, our world maintains its spheroid character, rocks remain rocks and water remains water until some influence forces a change in its organization. Even then, although one organization may be destroyed, its component organizations continue. Water may be broken into hydrogen and oxygen; these elements, in turn, maintain their organizations. Thus, the outstanding attribute of an organization seems to be its perpetual tendency to self-maintenance.

BIOLOGIC OPERATION OF MAINTENANCE OF ORGANIZATION

This characteristic maintenance of organization is not confined to in-animate objects alone. It is more true of the living than of the dead. Schrodinger, for example, has pointed out that living organisms actively create organization by concentrating energy and organizing matter. In spite of its fluid condition, the lowly amoeba hangs together and resists destruction. It actively seeks and stores food. When its environment dries up completely the amoeba may still encyst and protect itself from such disturbing forces. Plants, too, display this characteristic, for grasses bent by the lawn roller regain their upright state, and the notched tree soon adjusts itself to the damage and maintains its organization. Among higher animals, wounds cover with scar tissue, and the entire body be-comes a battleground as the organism adjusts to infection. In fact, as Dashiell expressed it, "Through all animal life an outstanding charac-teristic runs—the tendency of the organism to maintain its normality against internal or external disrupting agencies."

It is this tendency of the organism to maintain its organization, or equilibrium, that Cannon described in his concept of "homeostasis," mean-ing the tendency of the organism to maintain its stability. This general law of constancy of the internal environment has become a basic tenet of biology. Richter, for example, has reported a series of experiments with rats to investigate this tendency of the organism to maintain internal balance or consistency. In these experiments, when the "need" for water, constant temperature, sodium, calcium, phosphorus, and carbohydrates was surgically created, the organism responded vigorously to maintain its internal organization by actively seeking such materials in its en-vironment. When extraordinary requirements for salt were produced in rats by the removal of the adrenal glands, they became able to distinguish between water and a salt solution in concentrations of one part of salt in 33,000 parts of water. Normal rats made this distinction only when concentrations were as strong as one part of salt per 2000 parts of water. Richter concludes from his experiments that: "These forces have their origin in the deep biological urge of mammals to maintain a constant internal environment. The activities may be diverse, and there may be different goals, but the underlying biological drives remain the same." Experiments with other animals have demonstrated similar effects. There could be no life without the maintenance of organization, for life is dependent upon the relationship of parts to other parts. Without the stability of these relationships life could not continue.

As a result of his intensive studies of brain damage Kurt Goldstein was led to base his theory of the organism upon the homeostatic tendency of living beings. Even in cases of severe damage to the brain, he found his subjects maintaining organization by avoiding any situation which would place a strain upon impaired capacities. There seems little doubt that a major characteristic of life is a tendency to maintain organization or wholeness.

MAINTENANCE OF ORGANIZATION IN MAN

Turning to human beings, the art and science of medicine has been predicated upon this fundamental characteristic. The task of the physician is to remove, destroy, or immobilize the causative agent of disease and to help build up the organism to the point where the body can readjust itself. The physician or surgeon helps this process along, but it is the organism itself which brings about the cure through its own return to effective organization. This action has often been referred to as the "healing power of nature." Psychology has long overlooked this important principle, and it is only recently that we have come to recognize its operation in psychological as well as physical functions. Mental patients, for example, often get well despite lack of treatment and even, sometimes, in spite of treatment.

It has been commonly observed that even under the most severe psychological shocks most people manage to make adjustments. Certainly, it is true that most people do so without the help of psychoanalysis, psychiatry, psychotherapy, or other formalized treatment. As Fletcher said discussing this principle: "Rationalization of one's behavior is no less an act of organic defense against ego disturbance than is a change of blood count against infectious disease. The rise of temper against an insult is not essentially different from the rise of temperature against infection."

If this struggle to maintain the organization of the organism is seen in a purely physiological sense, the only possible conclusion is that the fundamental motive of human behavior is the preservation of the physical organism. But, this conclusion is inadequate because many things men do are not directed toward their physical survival. One needs only look around to observe that man does not seek to maintain only his physical self. If that were his only concern, we would have no suicides, nor would anyone ever join the army, fly a plane, or climb a mountain. If maintenance of the physical self alone were the goal of human beings, we would not eat too much, drink too much, or stay up late. We would even avoid such dangers to our bodily health as shaking hands, appearing in public places, or kissing beautiful girls. We would, indeed, live a sterile existence in more ways than one.

Man does not live in a physical world alone. The universe in which he lives and maintains his organization is a universe of ideas, values, societies, and people. Man, furthermore, is as much a part of these aspects of his universe as he is of its physical aspects. Like the larger organization of which he is part and the smaller organization of which he is product, he maintains the organization he is. The self man seeks to maintain is not just his physical body but the self of which he is aware, the self he has come to consider his personality, that unique being known as John Jones or Sally Smith. This self is called the perceived, or phenomenal, self.

The Basic Human Need

By the phenomenal self we mean those aspects of the perceptual field to which we refer when we say "I" or "me." In common with the rest of the perceptual field it has the feeling of complete reality. Its physical boundaries are roughly the skin or clothing surfaces. Man can extend these boundaries; for example, when he uses a cane, or when he drives a familiar vehicle. It is a common observation that many a man reacts to a crumpled fender as though it were violence to his own person.

Sometimes the perceived self may be experienced as if a portion of the body were excluded. When circulation in one's foot or one's fingers is cut off we have the feeling that these limbs are not there; we have no feeling of them and, thus, they are not part of us. This definition of the self in such a way as to exclude a portion of the body is illustrated by the case of a young woman who applied to the author for graduate work in psychology. Noting that she was very badly crippled, he asked if she had considered the degree to which her handicap might make things difficult for her. "I don't have a handicap!" she snapped. Clearly, she so defined her "self" as to ignore her crippled legs.

THE PHENOMENAL SELF DEFINED

The perceived, or phenomenal, self includes far more than the physical aspects of self. Perceptions of the self as strong, honest, good-humored, sophisticated, just, guilty, and a thousand other qualities may be a part of the phenomenal self of a particular individual. We shall even discover later that the phenomenal self may include, by identification, persons and objects entirely outside our physical selves. For instance, we are quite likely to react to attacks upon our sons, daughters, wives, husbands, or parents, as though these were attacks upon ourselves. Indeed, for all practical purposes they are. In short, the phenomenal self includes not only a person's physical self but everything he experiences as "me" at that instant.

It will be recalled that we have defined the perceptual field as the universe, including himself, as it appears to the individual at the moment. Although behavior is always determined by the total field, that portion which the individual regards as part or characteristic of himself influences almost all of his behavior. Since it is always the self which is perceived as behaving, behavior must always be appropriate to the phenomenal self. Aspects of the perceptual field having a specific reference to the self will, therefore, be of paramount importance in understanding the individual's field and, hence, his behavior.

Each of us has literally thousands of more or less discrete perceptions of himself in all kinds of situations. Among them are such perceptions of his physical self as being blue-eyed or brown-eyed, tall or short, fat or thin, blond or brunette. One will also have concepts of himself in social or judgmental terms when he sees himself as being afraid or unafraid, acceptable or unacceptable, liked or unliked, able or unable. The number of self perceptions a person may possess will be almost unlimited, but for each person they are unique to himself. They are his experiences of himself. All perceptions of the self a person has at a particular instant we call the phenomenal self, or the perceived self. It is the phenomenal self which each human being is forever seeking to maintain.

The phenomenal self, it should be understood, is not a physical entity, that is, it does not exist someplace in our bodies. To the individual himself the phenomenal self is real. It *is* himself. To the outsider observing the individual, the phenomenal self is pure abstraction inferred from the observed behavior and representing only an approximation of the self experienced by the behaver. Such a concept is useful in helping us to understand and deal with problems of human behavior. It helps us to focus attention upon those aspects of the perceptual field of particular importance in understanding behavior, and at the same time makes it possible to exclude many aspects of minor importance.

THE STRIVING FOR ADEQUACY: THE BASIC NEED OF HUMAN BEINGS

From birth to death the maintenance of the phenomenal self is the most pressing, the most crucial, if not the only task of existence. To maintain this personal organization of the self in the universe in which he lives, however, requires of a human being much more than mere survival. Man lives in a changing world, a world in which the organizations of which he is composed and of which he is part are continuously changing. A changing world requires changes in the organization of the self if it is to be maintained. Each of us needs to do more than merely change with the flow of events. Because we are aware of the future and must maintain ourselves, in the future as well as in the present, it is necessary to enhance the self against the exigencies of tomorrow. The self, therefore, "has to be maintained in the future, built up and enhanced so that the individual feels secure for tomorrow. And since the future is uncertain and unknown, no enhancement of the individual's experience of personal value, no degree of self-actualization, is ever enough. Human beings are, by nature, insatiable.

Thus, man seeks not merely the maintenance of *a* self but the development of an *adequate* self—a self capable of dealing effectively and efficiently with the exigencies of life, both now and in the future. To achieve this self-adequacy requires of man that he seek, not only to maintain his existing organization, but also that he build up and make more adequate the self of which he is aware. Man seeks both to maintain and enhance his perceived self.

Though the maintenance and enhancement of the self are two different words, this does not mean that man has two different needs. We express maintenance and enhancement as two different words, but both relate to exactly the same function—the production of a more adequate self. Both refer to man's striving to accomplish, like the rest of his universe, an adequate organization. I may shore up the timbers of my house to keep it from collapsing or I may plant trees to improve its looks. One activity maintains the structure, the other enhances the property. Both activities have a common result—a more adequate, better functioning dwelling for me and those important to me. In the same manner, I seek to become the most adequate person I can become in every situation in which I may find myself. I may do this by seeing my dentist to have my cavities filled, by reading a new book in my professional field, or, I may seek to enhance myself by buying a new suit of clothes or by making a speech at a national convention. Whether I seek to maintain myself as I am or enhance myself against the exigencies of the future, I am always seeking to be the most adequate personality I can be.

In the previous pages we have seen: (1) that man, like the universe of which he is a part, characteristically seeks the maintenance of organization; (2) that the organization man seeks to maintain is the organization of which he is aware, namely, his phenomenal self; and (3) that, because man lives in a changing world and is aware of the future as well as of the present, maintenance of the self requires, not simply maintenance of the status quo, but an active seeking for personal adequacy.

We can define man's basic need, then, as a need for adequacy. It represents in man the expression of a universal tendency of all things. It is expressed in man's every behavior at every instant of his existence. Asleep or awake, each of us is engaged in an insatiable quest for personal adequacy. This quest may find its expression in a wide variety of behavior aimed, in one form or another, at the maintenance or enhancement of our perceptions of personal worth and value. Other authors have spoken of this need as a need for self-actualization, or self-realization. In the field of psychotherapy this need has been described as a need for growth. In this book, whenever we refer to man's basic need, we mean that *great driving, striving force in each of us by which we are continually seeking to make ourselves ever more adequate to cope with life.*

NEED AND THE PREDICTION OF BEHAVIOR

Seen in this light it is possible to understand much of human behavior which would otherwise seem unreasonable. Even odd behavior such as wearing gaudy clothing, speeding, arguing with the police, or going over Niagara Falls in a barrel can not only be understood, but, if enough information is available, it can become completely and accurately predictable. If each act is seen as an attempt to preserve or to fortify the individual's perception of personal adequacy, behavior becomes meaningful. Rather than appearing inconsistent, behavior then becomes more predictable. Note how this point of view helps to clarify behavior in the following summary of a "typical" clinic case.

Eight-year-old Jimmy Allen, an only child, is brought to the psychological clinic by his parents at the insistence of his teachers. The parents are much incensed and regard all of this as a direct insult to the family and a threat to their feelings of adequacy. They raise a thousand complaints against the school and are completely at a loss to understand why the teachers should have suggested this consultation. Jimmy, they tell the psychologists, is a delightful child at home. He has his "moments" now and then, but on the whole, he is his Mother's and Daddy's darling, the center of a comfortable suburban home. Jimmy plays with a group of younger children whom he completely dominates much to the delight of his father. Jimmy's slightest wish is his parents' command. His manners are delightful with adults and he speaks like a polished young gentleman. With the adults at the clinic, he is calm, poised, and helpful. To the psychologist he seems too helpful for a child of eight. The parents feel that the school must be a terrible place because, as they point out, Jimmy just hates to go, and he cries and begs to be allowed to stay home. He has even made himself sick over it and had to stay home because he got so upset.

The school's report about Jimmy presents a vastly different picture. His teachers complain that he is "not bright," stubborn, and a "very nasty child." He does not get along well with the other children; he beats up those younger and smaller than he, and he attempts to "buy" those older and stronger with lollipops and licorice shoe-strings. In class he is constantly talking and showing off. He must always be the center of attention. He likes art work and this is the only thing he does well. Whenever his work is displayed, he brags insufferably. He has been known to cheat on exams. When he lost the leading part in the school play recently, he skipped school for three days in a row. With forty children in her class the teacher is at her wits' end and does not know what to do with Jimmy.

Jimmy joined the local Y, went four times, and never returned again. The boys' work director of the Y reports that Jimmy never got along with any of the boys, stuck to the director "like molasses" and wanted to do nothing but swim. Jimmy refused to participate in the gym classes and stayed out of the various Y clubs entirely. He was an excellent swimmer and enjoyed this sport immensely until one day he was sent home for holding two younger boys under water. Jimmy hasn't been back to the Y since that incident.

When we can see this child as he sees himself, his behavior becomes much more understandable. While we might analyze his behavior in terms of many specific needs, all these needs become a function of the one dominant aspect and that is the boy's need to protect and to enhance his own phenomenal self and to become the most adequate person he can.

Thus Jimmy has developed at home a concept of himself as being very important, as indeed he is, to his parents. At home he is able to achieve a feeling of adequacy by controlling his indulgent parents and adopting the accepted modes of behavior in an adult world. When he moves from this sheltered atmosphere, however, to the wider world of school and community, his associates do not react to him in the same way. They are unwilling to accept him at his own evaluation of himself. They are not even aware of the values he places on himself, but react to Jimmy only in terms of his behavior. All this must be very puzzling to Jimmy. Since his concept of himself is not accepted by his associates he is forced to defend himself, and he does so by means interpreted by others as "stubbornness," being "nasty," and cheating on exams. In his attempts to gain what he feels is his rightful due, he buys off the older boys and beats up the younger ones, he sticks close to the director of the Y and, of course, brags of his accomplishments and enjoys doing what he can do well.

A delight at home to his parents, a nuisance away in the community; his need for self-esteem surfeited at home and opposed in the community—seen in this way, Jimmy's behavior becomes consistent. Indeed, given enough information about a new situation, his behavior can be accurately predicted.

ONLY ONE NEED

Even such apparently conflicting tendencies in the individual as the desire for self preservation and the desire for death, seem conflicting only because they have been observed from a frame of reference inadequate to encompass such behavior under a single heading. From the point of view of the outsider, behavior often seems motivated by conflicting or antithetic goals. From the individual's own point of view, however, the goals are quite harmonious. This is well illustrated in the following excerpt from a counseling record concerning a young man in the depth of despair:

YOUNG MAN: I don't know what I would do. I've thought about hanging myself, sometimes. It's an awful thing. It's entered my mind several times.

COUNSELOR: That scared you pretty much.

YOUNG MAN: I often wonder what people would think if I did.

COUNSELOR: You find this not satisfactory either.

YOUNG MAN: It doesn't accomplish anything. I suppose if a fellow got low enough, he'd have the guts.

COUNSELOR: It scares you a bit that you've thought of that kind of out.

YOUNG MAN: To the point, sometimes, where I couldn't read a book on sociology. Sometimes I've thought, too, of going away—*but that's a kind of quitting, too. I don't like to be a quitter.*

In this example from counseling, it is clear that the thought of suicide is not the result of a death wish. If it were, this man would have committed suicide, because certainly, at that moment, the rest of his picture looked deeply depressing. Note, however, that the client rejected this possible solution, not because of a desire for self preservation, but because of his concern with "what people would think" if he committed suicide. Even suicide does not remove the individual from the necessity of maintaining and enhancing the self.

The soldier in wartime is not torn between a desire for self destruction and a desire for self preservation as he faces the coming battle. On the contrary, he is concerned solely with the adequacy of his phenomenal self. Although the situation will vary from individual to individual, it might roughly be described as follows: He may risk death on the one hand to *preserve* himself from becoming the kind of person who "lets his buddies down," and on the other hand, to *enhance* his self concept by being the kind of person who is "one of the gang," or as brave as the others. Many of us place our physical selves in jeopardy to achieve a more adequate concept of ourselves.

Students of human behavior have in the past postulated a number of basic human needs. Murray, for example, has described 28 needs which seem to him basic to human personality. In an article, published several years ago, I suggested a list of 40 such basic needs. Freud, the first of the psychologists to look at behavior from the point of view of the behaver, felt there were two basic needs: the desire for life and the desire for death. One might well ask, "What does it matter, after all, whether one conceives of human beings as having one need or many?"

THE EFFECT OF THEORIES OF NEED ON BEHAVIOR

We have already seen that each of us behaves according to his own conception of things. How we behave in dealing with the people and the things around us will be the direct outgrowth of our perceptions about them. Hence, the concepts we hold about what people are trying to do, must inevitably affect the way in which we attempt to deal with them. Inaccurate or conflicting concepts of human need will, of necessity, result in inaccurate and inconsistent behavior on our part toward others. It is important for anyone required to cope with the behavior of others to have the simplest, most accurate understanding of human need of which we are capable. Numerous and overlapping concepts of human needs are confusing and difficult to work with. We must have a broad and accurate concept of human need for the simple reason that we will behave according to what we believe to be true.

Perhaps an even more important reason for finding the simplest possible definition of human need, is in the very nature of the concept of need. When the psychologist speaks of need, he usually means some very basic, fundamental, even incontrovertible goal of human behavior. Needs for many psychologists arise from the basic physiology of the organism itself; there are, for example, "needs" for water, food, warmth, or sexual gratification. Thus the concept of need denotes an absolute necessity to human welfare, so that satisfaction of a need cannot be denied without the most dire results. This seems to me an unfortunate and even highly dangerous concept in many practical situations. For example, if one conceives a very homely girl as suffering from a "need" to be attractive, what shall one do to help her adjust? If this need is truly basic, therapy must be directed toward the attempt to improve her appearance; but this may be a task defying all the skill of a Hollywood make-up artist. Similarly, if homosexuality is regarded as a "need," what hope is there for treatment? What we believe to be true about people's need will directly control our own effectiveness in dealing with human problems. Too narrow or inaccurate a view of what people are striving for may even make it impossible for us to deal effectively with human problems.

Years ago, Adam Smith, an economist, postulated that people were motivated by a need for food, clothing, and shelter. Accordingly, a whole generation based its economic planning upon his assumption. The idea was partly true but completely failed to enable us to deal with many of our pressing economic problems just because it was only partly true. Adam Smith, in this assumption, overlooked entirely the psychological aspects of man's striving. His theory could not offer an explanation, for example, why Germany should twice go to war despite the fact that it had the highest standard of living of any country in Europe, or why General Motors workers should remain on strike for nineteen weeks ostensibly because of a difference with management over a salary increase of half a cent an hour.

Since 1914 the Children's Bureau of the U. S. Department of Labor has been publishing a pamphlet entitled "Infant Care" which is intended to guide parents in the care of young children. As these pamphlets have been revised in the course of the years, they represent an interesting mirror of the beliefs held by experts about the needs of children. They illustrate, too, how conceptions of need are translated directly into patterns of behavior. In 1914, for example, needs were conceived almost exclusively in terms of physical well being. Mothers were advised to pay attention to their infants only when the child really *needed* attention. They were warned not to succumb to the baby's demands to be picked up, carried, or played with. Babies were regarded as delicate beings who needed rest and quiet; but babies also needed to be guarded against lest they control the adults around them. The mother of 1914 was told, for example: "The rule that parents should not play with the baby may seem hard, but it is without doubt a safe one. A young, delicate, and nervous baby needs rest and quiet, and however robust the child, much of the play that is indulged in is more or less harmful. It is a great pleasure to hear the baby laugh and crow in apparent delight, but often the means used to produce the laughter, such as tickling, punching, or tossing, makes him irritable and restless. It is a regrettable fact that the few minutes' play that the father has when he gets home at night . . . may result in nervous disturbance of the baby and upset his regular habits."

In 1945, however, concepts of a baby's need had changed and mothers were then told: "A baby sometimes cries because he wants a little more attention. He probably needs a little extra attention under some circumstances just as he sometimes needs a little extra food and water. Babies want attention; they probably need plenty of it." Whatever beliefs we hold about what people need have an inevitable effect upon the way we consider appropriate to deal with them.

In the field of education, ideas about children's needs have produced similar wide swings in our methods of dealing with youngsters in the public schools. Our early school philosophies were based upon the idea that children's needs were largely perverse and animalistic and that the task of the school was essentially the task of civilizing them. Children were seen as having natural needs for self gratification, play, and amusement which had to be curbed or trained in more acceptable adult patterns. At a later period, the so-called Progressive Movement saw children's basic needs as essentially good, and it was considered the task of the school to encourage the expression of these basic needs. With such a view of children's needs, some schools swung as far toward giving children freedom of expression as previous schools had in repressing them.

THE CONCEPT OF NEED IN INDUSTRIAL PRACTICE

Perhaps one of the most interesting demonstrations of the importance of our concepts of human need may be observed in the famous Hawthorne Studies. These studies were carried out in the Hawthorne plant of the Western Electric Company. In setting up the experiments, the researchers were interested in finding out what would happen if the "needs" of workers were systematically varied. To accomplish this purpose, a small group of workers assembling telephone relays was isolated in a room where working conditions could be varied and where the workers' behavior could be studied carefully and systematically. The researchers believed that to achieve high productivity workers need improved work conditions. Accordingly, they gave employees rest periods of varying lengths and at one or more times during the day. In other experiments production changes were measured when the work day and the work week were shortened or lengthened, when lunches were prepared at company expense or provided by the worker. The experimenters found that employee productivity steadily increased with each variation in working conditions, even when workers had no rest periods at all, when they had to supply their own lunches, and when they had to work a longer week and longer hours per day! In reporting their results, the experimenters stated: "In many respects these results were puzzling to the investigators for they were not what they had expected. The general upward trend in output independent of any particular change in rest pauses or shorter working hours was astonishing. The improvement in mental attitude throughout the first two years of the experiment was also perplexing. Neither one of these developments could be related to the kind of working day in any simple one-one correlation."

Like thousands of industrial supervisors and foremen before them, the investigators in these experiments believed that employee productivity was a direct result of the working conditions and they designed their experiments accordingly. They were misled by their own beliefs about the nature of human behavior. What seems to have happened in these experiments was that the workers, feeling themselves to be set apart as a special group, became highly identified with the company and experienced a great lift in their morale. They felt like important people doing an important job and their production records mirrored their feelings. As a result of these experiments, management was impressed with "the stores of latent energy and productive coöperation which clearly could be obtained from its working force under the right conditions. And among the factors making for these conditions the attitudes of the employees stood out as being of predominant importance." Looking at the problem of productivity in this new way, the management of Western Electric Company started a research program in employee morale which, in turn, led to important changes in personnel policies and procedures which have become models for many other industries. With a more accurate conception of human behavior, they were able to deal with the human-relations aspects of industrial management with greater effectiveness than ever before.

In the modern world, and particularly as members of our society, we have to deal with people of all ages and all cultures. A theory of human motivation adequate for that purpose must be broad enough to include all human behavior in all cultures, at all times, and at any age. It must make all behavior from the founding of empires to the winking of an eye accountable in the simplest possible terms.

IS PERSONAL ADEQUACY A "SELFISH" NEED?

At first glance it may seem a very depressing and sordid picture of man as being perpetually concerned with the search for a more adequate self. It seems to make him a very selfish creature indeed. This picture will be true, however, only if we conceive of man as an isolated organization. We have seen that organizations are affected by the organizations of which they are part and that they are affected by the organizations of which they are the product. Man does not live as an isolated self but as the product of organizations present and past, and as part of organizations present and future. As part of larger organizations of which he is a unit, the achievement of personal adequacy requires the adequacy of the larger organization as well. The change or destruction of the larger organization changes or destroys the smaller as well. Thus, to maintain adequately and enhance his own organization requires of man that he seek ever greater adequacy of the organizations of which he is part. The juvenile delinquent seeks the maintenance and enhancement of his gang of which he feels he is a part but the destruction of any segment of society in which he feels he has no place or which threatens his existence. The well-adjusted man has a broadly encompassing self which is by no means restricted to his personal being but which is also concerned with the welfare of others. What he does to achieve personal adequacy contributes also to the adequacy of society. In later chapters of this book we shall want to examine this proposition much further.

The Effects of Need on Perception

Man, we have seen, is an insatiably striving organism forever seeking the maintenance and enhancement of the self. From birth to death he is continually engaged in the search for greater feelings of adequacy. Whether or not he is successful in this quest will be determined by the perceptions he is able to make in the course of his lifetime. If he could not see or know about himself and his world, he could not behave effectively toward his environment, and he would be unable to exist at all. His perceptions enable him to be aware and to behave in ways which lead to the satisfaction of his fundamental need. We would expect, then, that an individual's need would have profound effects on his perceptions, and this is exactly what proves to be so.

Out of all the things we *might* perceive, we perceive what is meaningful to us and what helps us to maintain the organization of our phenomenal field and, thus, to satisfy our fundamental need. Each of us can observe the effect of need on his perception when he gives just a little thought to his own behavior. Though we look at the newspaper every day, it is not until we feel a need for a new suit that we spend much time reading advertisements for clothes. We do not even see the bicycle shop we pass every day until our youngster's bike needs fixing. It doesn't seem important to us to study until the week before an exam. The passenger in an automobile does not know the unfamiliar road home because he was not watching the road on the way out; it was not a part of his need. We see what we need to see.

Many psychologists have been intrigued with this problem of the effects of need on perceiving and have amassed a veritable mountain of research demonstrating the effect in a wide variety of settings from food selections to politics. One of the earliest of these experiments was the "cafeteria feeding" study of Davis in 1930. She permitted newly weaned children to select their own foods from an assortment of items in any quantity they pleased and she found the children could and did select what, for them, was an adequate and well balanced diet. Children with special dietary needs, moreover, seemed to choose the "right" foods to satisfy their particular deficiencies! Experiments on food deprivation in which subjects were systematically starved have repeatedly demonstrated that, as starvation levels are reached, subjects find it difficult to keep their minds off the topic of food. They find themselves thinking about food continually. Osgood describes such an experience as follows: "An office that I pass each day is numbered 400D; inevitably, when the hour is near mealtime, I perceive this as FOOD. The car I used to drive had the euphemistic label SILVER STREAK on its dashboard; inevitably, when the hour was near mealtime, I would read this as SILVER STEAK."

Other research studies have shown that college students, asked to judge their college aptitude test scores, respond in ways that protect their feelings of adequacy. Children from wealthy homes, it has been demonstrated, perceive half a dollar to be smaller than children from poorer homes. When words are presented for very short periods of time in a tachistoscope, people tend to see the words they value most more quickly than those words having less value. Even the learning of pro-Communist and anti-Communist material seems affected by the political leanings of the learner, for Communist material is learned more readily and retained more tenaciously by persons with Communist leanings, while anti-Communists behave similarly regarding anti-Communist materials. I have found in my own classes that some of my most rabidly anti-Communist students sometimes describe passages from the U.S. Constitution as Communist-inspired!

It has been demonstrated that persons tend to associate favorable characteristics with members of Congress from their own party. It seems apparent that the effect of need on perception it to be found in every aspect of human endeavor. It is the custom on the campus of the University of Florida for all roads to be closed while students change classes; the campus police place signs in the road reading CLASS CHANGE. One hot day, as I approached my classroom I thought, "I'd better get a drink before I go to class as I probably won't have another opportunity to get one for two hours." As I entered the building I sought the drinking fountain and bent over to slake my thirst. As I did so, I glanced outside at the sign in the middle of the road which said just as clear as could be, LAST CHANCE. Even psychologists who should know about these things are not immune to the effect of need on perceiving. In a study of the evaluations of other people by clinical psychologists, Weingarten found that clinicians saw more problems in their clients in those areas in which the clinicians themselves had problems. Even when it was brought to their attention what the experiment was designed to show, they, nevertheless, continued to see in the cases they examined the problems they wrestled with themselves!

We have been able to mention here only a few of the research studies demonstrating the effects of need on perception. There are many more studies in the psychological literature exploring every facet of this fascinating problem. We shall want to look at further studies in later chapters when we examine the satisfaction of need more specifically through the individual's goals and values, the development of the self and its protection from threat. Whatever the behavior of the individual, it is always directed at the satisfaction of need. The search for adequacy is the central factor controlling the organization of the phenomenal field and the perceptions of which we are capable.

Need and the Problem of Motivation

A great deal of the time and energy of teachers, advertisers, administrators, social workers, and others concerned with human relations has been devoted to the problem of motivation; how to get others' to do the things they "should" do. It should be clear from our discussion in this chapter, however, that from the point of view of the behaver himself, he is never *unmotivated*. We have stated the fundamental human need as a continuous search for personal adequacy. In this sense each of us is always motivated. We are forever seeking the maintenance and enhancement of our perceived selves. People are never unmotivated from their own points of view, even though it may seem so from an outsider's point of view.

When people seem to us to be unmotivated, it is not because they are really so, but because we don't understand their goals. Thus, a child's resistance to learning arithmetic or spelling may cause the teacher to think the child is unmotivated and has no desire for self improvement. To the child, however, learning arithmetic or spelling may seem to have nothing whatever to do with his quest for self enhancement, at the moment, and, thus, he remains uninterested in the subject matter until the teacher threatens him with failure. When that happens, he may perceive the matter differently and seek to maintain his concept of self by getting by—but only just! People are never unmotivated although they may sometimes seem to the outside observer to be unaffected by the values the observer holds dear.

From the outsider's point of view it may seem highly doubtful that other people are always motivated to seek their most adequate selves. Yet this is exactly what proves true the moment we look at the situations with which people are confronted through their own eyes. The delinquent taunting the police, sassing his teachers, and walking about with a chip on his shoulder seems to the outsider hardly pursuing personal adequacy. Rather, he seems to be perversely seeking his own destruction. When one gets to know delinquents better, however, it becomes clear that such swaggering behavior is an outgrowth of deep feelings of inadequacy. Seen from his own frame of reference, the delinquent's behavior may be compared to whistling in the dark while passing a graveyard. It is a pathetic attempt to convince himself and the world about him of an adequacy he does not feel.

If it is true that each human being is always doing the best he can to be adequate according to his perception of events at the moment of his behavior, or misbehavior, it becomes obvious that a great deal of "blaming" people for their behavior, is misdirected and futile. People are always trying as best they can to be adequate. Thus, the problem of changing behavior is not one of motivating people but of helping them to perceive differently. In our experience working with parents over the years, we have rarely seen a parent who viciously set out to destroy his child. Time after time we have discovered that even parents who did terrible things to their children often did so "because I want Jimmy to be a good boy!" The problem was not motivation. The problem was how to help parents to develop better and more effective ways of perceiving themselves and their relationship with others. When this was accomplished the individual's own need for adequacy could be counted on to supply the necessary power for change.

The task of teachers, parents, writers, and anyone else whose task is affecting the behavior of others is a problem of perception. To change behavior it is necessary to help people change the way they see themselves and the world they live in. When people see differently they will behave differently. The need of the individual for adequacy, for the maintenance and enhancement of the self, will permit nothing less. The need for adequacy provides the direction, the drive, and the organization for every behavior. How it is expressed in a particular personality will be dependent upon the scope, the richness, and the availability of an individual's personal meanings. We need now to know more specifically and precisely what affects perceiving and the nature and organization of the individual's perceptual field. In the next six chapters I have attempted to set forth what I believe to be the most important factors, other than need itself, which determines each person's perceptual field.

CHAPTER 4

The Physical Organism: Vehicle of Perception

THE most self-evident factor affecting perception is the organism in which the process of perceiving occurs. The physical body in which each of us is more or less tenuously housed makes perceiving possible. We must have eyes to see, ears to hear, taste buds to taste, and olfactory end organs to enable us to distinguish odors. Even these organs, however, would not be sufficient without the marvels of our brain and nervous system. What limits the functioning of these organs must inevitably limit our perceptions as well.

We can, after all, perceive only those things which we have the equipment to perceive. Dogs and birds can hear high-frequency sounds which most human beings cannot. We are limited by our human auditory equipment to the sounds we, as human beings, can hear. We cannot perceive like honey bees, navigate in the dark like bats, or find our way home like pigeons. Our physical equipment sets broad limits to the kinds of things we can perceive directly. Within these broad limitations, however, we find that human perceptions can be extremely varied and extensive.

Physical Limitations on Perceiving

Human perceptions extend far beyond our experiences of sight, hearing, smell, taste, and touch. We have ideas, values, concepts, perceptions of relationships, and meanings that far transcend the limitations of our sense organs. It is possible for Helen Keller to live an extraordinarily rich and meaningful life though she is totally blind and deaf. Though it is, of course, necessary for us to have sense organs to perceive, our physical bodies impose fewer restrictions upon our perceptions than we are, at first glance, likely to assume.

An automobile is roughly limited by its structure. It will not run successfully under water, nor will it normally fly through the air. Within the broad limits of its structure as a vehicle for operation on land, however, it has tremendous potentialities. From a study of its mechanics and condition we can tell whether it will operate or not. But no matter how detailed our study of its carburetor, pistons, or tires, we cannot tell from such data where the automobile has gone, where it will go next, or even where it is now! In the same way the behavior of a human being cannot be understood through a study of the structure of the organism alone. We must, of course, have eyes to see and ears to hear. But given the necessary equipment for seeing and hearing, *what* we see and *what* we hear is affected little by the structure of our eyes and ears. The structure of the eye tells us *whether* one can see. It tells us nothing about what is seen. Our bodies provide the vehicle of behavior; they do not explain it. We are broadly limited by our fundamental physiology, but the variety, the richness, and the almost limitless patterns of human behavior can never be fully understood exclusively in terms of the physical organism.

Our physical bodies are only one of a number of factors affecting human behavior. Man's whole history has been one of escaping from the bonds of his physical limitations to understand, predict, and control the forces of the world about him. He has learned to move loads far beyond his personal strength, to hear and to talk with people at the opposite ends of the earth, to fly through the air and travel under the sea. If human behavior could be understood by a study of the physical organism alone, we should not need psychologists, sociologists, political scientists, or theologians. We could get all the advice and help we need from the physiologists alone. The vast development of the physical sciences has been perhaps the most outstanding achievement in man's development in the past hundred years. We are impressed by these achievements and inclined to carry over the principles applying to the physical sciences in all other aspects of living. Our physical selves, of course, have important effects upon our abilities to perceive; and to understand human behavior we need to have as keen an awareness of these limitations as modern science can give us. We need, however, to see such limitations in their proper perspective, without overvaluing or underestimating them. What effects does the physical organism have on perceiving? In the remainder of this chapter, we will explore something of the relationship of the physical organism to the perceptual field.

The Biological Origins of Awareness

Perhaps the most outstanding characteristic of all living things is their ability to react. The biologist calls this characteristic "irritability" by which he means the ability of the organism to respond to its environment. If one places a drop of acid in a solution containing one-celled amoebae, the amoebae move away from the acid. Conversely, amoebae move toward food particles. This ability of living things to react to physical events is true of all living things from the simplest to the most complex organisms. If animals did not have this characteristic they could not exist. Amoebae unable to move away from danger or toward food would very quickly disappear from the earth.

The peculiar organization of matter which makes this responsiveness to stimuli possible in animal life is unknown. Though we can isolate the chemical elements in a living organism, the peculiar organization of these elements which produce life still eludes us. Scientists seem to agree that irritability is a function of the particular *organization* of elements that make up a living organism. It is a property of protoplasm but not of the elements of which protoplasm is made. Whatever its nature, however, we can observe that every animal possesses some kind of awareness whether it be a primitive sort of irritability as in one-celled life or the highly developed ability to perceive in higher forms of life. All animals, regardless of complexity, seem able to perceive, that is, to give meaning to experience.

The Development of Spatial Awareness

The survival of any organism depends upon its ability to deal with those parts of the physical environment with which it comes in contact. From the environment it touches, it secures the energy and materials for maintenance. From the environment, too, it may receive injury and destruction. However, before either happens the source and the organism must come into physical contact. Food which remains an inch away is not food. As for danger, "a miss is as good as a mile."

As we trace the development of animal life from its most primitive beginnings in the single cell through more complicated organizations of cells in the sponges, worms, fishes, amphibians, to the mammalian forms of life, we find life characterized by an ever-increasing organization of structure for special functions. In the course of this evolution some cells become modified for special processes of digestion while others become organized into special functions for breathing, excretion, reproduction, and for awareness. As we trace the phylogenetic scale of animal life from its simplest beginnings to the complex being, called man, we find an ever-increasing development of specialized structures for increased irritability, or awareness. In human beings these structures seem to have reached their highest levels of development in our tremendously complex brain and nervous system. One of the outstanding characteristics of this development is the continual improvement of these organs, particularly the organs of vision and hearing, which make it possible for the animal to be aware of events at a distance from him.

Organisms without distance receptors can use, to maintain their organization, only materials which happen to bump into or with which they blindly come into contact. They are unable to seek out and secure such materials with precision or efficiency. At the same time they are unable to anticipate and avoid the disruptive forces in their neighborhood and they are at the mercy of any they happen to encounter. By developing distance receptors and motility any organism may considerably expand its field of action and increase its ability to maintain its organization. By enlarging the area of the physical field of which it is aware at any given moment, the organism gains access to a greatly augmented supply of the energy and materials it requires; it has thus acquired the means of detecting danger at a distance. It has also gained a wider field into which it can escape from danger. Any increase in awareness of its surroundings is valuable in aiding the organism to achieve effective maintenance.

A significant factor in the rise of man to his present degree of control over his environment has been the development of erect posture which has given him a wider range of vision than that of his four-footed competitors and, because he can keep his hands free for precise manipulation of the environment, he has been enabled to achieve and profit from a visual and tactual precision far greater than that of other animals. The value of any physical function to the organism is determined and limited by the other qualities of that organism. Vision is of no value to a tree. Because their short stature limits their field of vision, a high level of visual acuity would be equally useless to most breeds of dogs. The long-legged sight hounds, who can make use of visual acuity, are the only dogs who have good eyesight. The primates, living in trees, are high enough above the ground and also have the manual equipment to be able to utilize a higher degree of visual acuity. Because of their upright posture, this superior eyesight was still useful when our ancestors came down to the ground. Having a highly differentiated visual field gives man a tremendous advantage over the rest of the animal world.

The Awareness of Time

The extension of the organism's phenomenal field by the development of distance receptors involves much more than an expansion of space. The possession of distance receptors gives the organism a perceptual field of which time, as well as distance, is an aspect. Distance receptors cannot be effective unless some sort of time awareness develops along with them. In turn, the possession of distance receptors makes a sense of time possible. Objects at a distance are not immediately available or immediately disruptive. In relation to the organism itself such objects are in the future or in the past but not in the present. As a result, the awareness of objects at a distance brings with it an awareness of temporal distance and relations, i.e., of past and future. The animal whose total experience is a matter of events immediately impinging upon him has no need of a sense of time. It is only when events are perceived at a distance that such awareness becomes possible. The bridge I see in the road ahead is not here now, but I know that if I keep going I shall reach it. The ability to perceive remote events, thus, makes awareness of time possible.

An organism having achieved such a perceptual field lives in and commands the resources of a behavioral field vastly greater, in size and potentialities, for the satisfaction of need than an organism, mobile or immobile, whose behavioral fields are limited to the aspects of environment which touch their body surface. And this is not all. Through a complementary process of physical evolution and social invention it is now possible for a human being, by the use of symbols, to enlarge his phenomenal field to include events and objects which are far distant in time and space, to include ideas, principles, and concepts far beyond the range of his senses. Language, for example, makes it possible for us to experience events long past. When we read of dinosaurs we can grasp something of an era before man existed, and when we read science fiction we can plunge light years ahead of our time. Through the medium of words we can deal with honor, justice, and other abstract concepts unavailable to us through our sense organs alone.

From this point of view the perceptual field is an essential aspect of the organism's equipment for dealing with its environment. Until now, the development of the perceptual field has been primarily a product of evolution. Recently, however, we have taken an important part in expanding and enriching the phenomenal field. Evolution is too slow; we can now expand our individual potentialities with radar, Geiger counters, electronics, new systems of mathematics and other types of symbols, which can still further enlarge and enrich perceptions.

From the simple irritability of the single cell to the specialized functions of the sense organs, the brain, and the nervous system in man, there has been throughout the evolution of animal life an increasing refinement of the organism's capacity for awareness. The ability of man to perceive broadly and richly seems fundamental to man's superiority over the rest of the animal world. Though man is endowed with the physical machinery which makes such perceiving possible, we still need to know much more than we do now the richness and breadth of the perceptual field of the adequate personality come about. What limits does our physical structure place upon our perceptual fields?

The Growth of Awareness

We cannot observe the growth of awareness in human beings in the same manner in which we can observe physical growth. We can be sure that sensitivity to its environment exists in the embryo, for we can observe the reactions of the developing fetus from the fertilization of the egg to the birth of a new human being. It is impossible for us to know, however, exactly what the embryo's experience of his environment is like. The precise nature of the development of awareness we can only infer. [It seems reasonable, however, to assume that awareness progresses by a process of differentiation and organization concomitant with the development of the nervous system as other functions of our anatomy become differentiated with their developing organs.] The simple interchange of oxygen and carbon dioxide of the single cell becomes organized during prenatal development into the highly specialized organs of the respiratory and circulatory systems of the new-born child. The primitive elimination of waste products by a process of diffusion in the single cell becomes the special function of specialized kidneys in the mature human being. Similarly, the organization of the organism for more effective awareness is brought about by the development of the sense organs, the nervous system, and the brain. How this process is experienced by the fetus we cannot know, of course, but by the time of birth the physical organism has developed a highly complex and efficient system of structures which makes awareness possible, and has already had some months of experience in perceiving.

Our experience of awareness is not something which occurs all at once. It does not arise full blown, nonexistent at one moment, and complete and functioning in the next. It begins as a characteristic of animal life, and with the development of our highly specialized sense organs, our nervous systems, and our brains, we become increasingly able to perceive more and more sharply and clearly.[The human organism's perceptions probably begin as vague awareness which becomes clearly and sharply differentiated only with the development of the sense organs and the passage of time.]

AWARENESS OF THE PHYSICAL SELF. The perceptual field contains many perceptions of our physical selves which make it possible to be aware of what is going on within us and to move our physical bodies from place to place. Some of these perceptions, like the feeling of pain experienced as a result of a pin prick, are sharp and clear. Many other perceptions will be so vague that we cannot describe them to others. We may, indeed, not even be able to feel them very clearly ourselves. An example of such vague perception is an awareness that we are off balance and falling when walking. We perceive almost at once when we are off balance and we adjust our body posture automatically, although we could not put into words precisely what we felt that led us to make the necessary movements returning us to an upright position.

It should not be supposed that because perceptions exist they are necessarily reportable. Most of the perceptions we have about physical beings we can report only vaguely, if at all. There are at least three reasons why this should be.

1. The first reason has to do with the relationships of larger and smaller organizations discussed in Chapter 3. We spoke of the nature of our physical selves as a series of organizations ranging from single cells, to tissues, to organs, to systems, to the body proper. Any change in a suborganization affects its immediate parent organization most directly with an intensity diminishing as it becomes more remote in the chain of organizations. The same seems true of our awareness of the physical self.

We are most keenly aware of the larger or more immediate organizations, and we are less keenly aware of the minute or remote ones.

Our awareness of body functioning is somewhat like the perceptions of the general manager of a large industry about his organization. He is most keenly aware of the departments directly within his purview, or of problems reported to him by his department heads. He may be almost totally unaware of things going on in a far corner of one of his factory buildings. Of other matters on a higher level or organization he may have a vague awareness as, for example, he may have a feeling that something is wrong in the receiving department, but be unable to state exactly what bothers him. This problem may not come clearly into focus, however, until the day when the strained relationships in the receiving department cause it to fail in providing necessary production materials. At this point the manager becomes clearly and sharply aware of the problem. Other things being equal, we are aware of those aspects of our physical selves which are most immediately in our purview or which have an immediate and precise effect upon our overall functioning. A freezing hunter does not know his fingers are numb until he has to reload his gun. Athletes keyed up to the excitement of the game have often been known to finish the game before becoming aware of injuries. Farther down the scale of organization it is increasingly difficult to be able to call perceptions of body states into clear figure. It is notoriously impossible, for example, to perceive the precise location of abdominal pains. The best we can do is to ascribe them to general areas.

2. A second factor making for the vague character of many of bodily perceptions has to do with need. A great many of our perceptions about our bodily processes are vague because there is no real need to bring them into clear figure. Many of these perceptions could be so clearly perceived as to be reportable if we wished to turn our attention to them. Many of us have had the experience, perhaps in church, of having our stomach rumble in an embarrassing way. Following such obstreperous behavior of our digestive system we may become keenly aware of a great many more vague rumblings and movements going on within us as we turn our attention from the sermon to our bodily selves. We can perceive our heart beat quite clearly if we listen for it. Though we are always aware of our muscle tensions (otherwise we could not move), we do not ordinarily maintain these perceptions sufficiently clearly to be able to report them to others. Nevertheless, we can bring many of these into clear focus simply by concentrating upon them. If it

were sufficiently important to us to spend our time on it, we could undoubtedly bring many more aspects of our physical selves into clear
perception. This seems to be what the hypochondriac does when he fears
he is sick. He becomes sharply aware of body functions that most of us
ignore. We do not perceive them because there does not seem to be
any need to do so in our peculiar economies.

Finally, many perceptions about our physical beings are not reportable because we lack the necessary symbols by which we can communicate what we feel to others. We do not have words adequate to convey
some perceptions. We cannot report any definite place "where it hurts"
for our doctor when he asks us. Indeed, we may not be sure what it is
that hurts or even whether it hurts at all! Sometimes our awarenesses are
extremely vague as when we complain of being "kind of sick," "nauseated," or "blue."

3. Many other perceptions we react to so quickly that we are unable
to describe them, for their experience is so fleeting that it is impossible
for us to grasp them. Who can describe, for example, what he feels when
he corrects his stride to regain his balance while he is walking. We
just do not have the language to enable us to report such perceptions to
others. Indeed, the experience may be so vague to us that we cannot
grasp its meaning even for ourselves, much less to be able to report it to
others.

In the previous chapter we have seen that human beings are continuously engaged in a never-ending attempt to achieve a more adequate
self. This self, moreover, is not the physical self, but the phenomenal
self of which the physical organism is but a part. Though the phenomenal self includes the physical self, it extends far beyond to include
the vast area of our perceptions of interactions with other people and
the world about us. In Chapter 3, we have also seen that organizations
both affect and are affected by the organizations of which they are part.
If this is so, we would expect that our physical selves should both affect
our perceptual fields and be affected by them. This is exactly what
seems to be true.

Some Effects of the Physical Organism on the
Perceptual Field

There can be no doubt that the physical endowment of the individual has important effects upon his perceptual field. We have already

mentioned that to perceive one must have the equipment with which to do so. Other factors having to do with the physical organism will play an important part although these may vary considerably from individual to individual. Some of the factors in the physical organism affecting the perceptual field will be open to manipulation. Others will lie outside our control, or, at least, they will be beyond our control by any means of which we are now aware.

THE POSSESSION OF ADEQUATE SENSORY EQUIPMENT

Most obvious of the factors affecting perception will be the effective operation of the sensory equipment which makes perception possible. The adequate functioning of eyes and ears is an essential for visual and auditory experience, for example. One does not expect a blind man to see nor a deaf one to hear. Possession of the necessary equipment for taste, smell, and touch will also be important for perceptions to occur in these areas of experience. People lacking such essential physical equipment for perceiving live in a world different from the rest of us. Let us not make the mistake of supposing they have fewer perceptions than we. Though their perceptual fields may be limited in respect to visual or auditory perceptions, their perceptual fields may be far richer than ours in other respects. Interesting experiments with the blind and the deaf, for example, have demonstrated how such persons may develop certain common perceptual abilities to a degree of proficiency much higher than that of the sighted and those who can hear.

The functioning or nonfunctioning of essential sensory equipment for perception is usually dramatic and easily recognized. Perhaps more common, and certainly less simple to recognize, are instances in which there is impairment of function rather than outright loss. What each of us perceives seems to him to be so. The near-sighted child who cannot see as far as the blackboard but only as far as his book is missing important perceptions available to other children, but his difficulty may be overlooked by his teachers and his parents. Indeed, he may not even be aware of his problem himself since he has always seen this way. If he thinks about it at all, he may assume that this is the way other people see things. Persons with impaired vision and hearing are often quite unaware of their own disabilities.

The sense organs we possess provide us with the means by which we may perceive the world about us. They make possible our contact with the world of reality. We assume that what we see and hear is what is there to be seen and heard. Our perceptions are our own personal "realities." We are rarely led to question them. The child who has never seen or heard well assumes his experience is all there is until he sees or hears differently or is made aware that the experience of others is different.

The writer is "red-green blind." This is a form of color blindness in which a person is unable to see red and green quite as vividly as other people. I did not know of this defect until my senior year in college when one of my teachers gave a test of color vision to the class. I can recall painful instances during my childhood on family expeditions to pick wild strawberries. It always seemed that others could fill their pails much more quickly than I could fill mine and I became the object of much annoyance to the other members of my family who shoved me aside with such comments as, "For heavens sake, move over, you big lummox. You're standing right on 'em!" I remember, too, how irritated adults were if they sent me to the store to match a spool of thread. I could never do it right! Neither I nor my parents knew that I was color blind and, thus, we all behaved as though I could see normally.

Even today, it is somewhat difficult for my friends to understand that my perceptions are different from theirs. When people hear that I am red-green blind, they may pick up a red object and ask, "What color is this?" When I answer, "Red," they are crestfallen and say, "But I thought you said you are color blind!" When I assure them I am color blind, they want to know, "Well, how do you know it is red if you are color blind?" To this I always reply, "Just as you do. I have always heard this color you are pointing at called 'red' so that is the name I call it too. However, the fact that I call it red does not mean that I see the same as you." Suppose I ask you, "How do *you* know this is red?" For each of us, our own experience is real. We cannot know our senses are impaired without some standard of comparison. The healthy functioning of our sense organs has vital effects upon our perceptual fields.

LIMITATIONS OF THE CENTRAL NERVOUS SYSTEM

The existence of a normally functioning sensory apparatus is an obvious requirement for effective perception. Our sense organs make it possible for us to perceive our environment. Less obvious, but no less essential to the process of perceiving, is the existence of an adequate nervous system behind these receptors which makes possible the communication and interpretation of stimuli. Just how this happens in the nervous system is still a mystery. We know a good deal about the physiology and growth of the nervous system and we know something of the transmission of nerve impulses. However, the process of converting these simple impulses into the complex meanings of our perceptions is a mystery that still eludes us.

Just as a person may be born with certain weaknesses or impairments of his sensory equipment, so too, he may be born with deficiencies in his nerve structure. We know something about a few of these anomalies but much still remains to be discovered. There may be impairments of which we are still completely unaware. We know, for example, that children are sometimes born with serious handicaps directly related to malfunctioning of the nervous system. These include such disorders as Mongolism, and microcephaly or macrocephaly which seem to be the result of maldevelopment during the uterine period. Persons afflicted with such disorders seem unable to perceive as effectively and efficiently as other people. Even when given many opportunities, they are apparently less able to profit by their experience or to modify their perceptions in the light of what has happened about them.

Other disturbances affecting the central nervous system are certain types of glandular dysfunction. Best known among these is cretinism. Children suffering from severe thyroid deficiencies in early childhood may develop a malfunctioning body which seriously impedes their efficiency in perceiving. Such children are often classed as mentally deficient because of their failure to learn as well as normal children. We know very little about how or why this reduction of perceptual efficiency occurs, but apparently a lack of normal secretions from the thyroid glands impairs the functioning of the nervous system and this, in turn, has restricting effects upon the child's ability to perceive.

Impairment may also be caused by a mechanical injury to the brain or the spinal cord. Injuries of this sort may occur in the process of entering the world at birth or may be the result of accident or illness later in life. Whatever their origin, however, they may markedly affect the individual's ability to perceive efficiently. Children with severe brain damage, for example, are apt to be extremely distractible. They often seem unable to control their perceptions and attention jumps rapidly from point to point so that they never seem to alight long enough to catch up with themselves. The exact nature of the mechanics producing this unfortunate impairment of perceptive functioning is still unknown.

Other types of damage which we know produce serious limits upon perceiving may result if the organism has been deprived of oxygen for any reason (anoxia). This sometimes happens to deep sea divers who dive too deep or remain down too long. It occurs, too, to persons overcome by gas. Lack of oxygen apparently causes destruction of brain cells, giving typical symptoms of brain damage.

A further limitation of the nervous system upon perceiving may be observed in cases of cerebral palsy. In this and similar disorders, damage to the nervous system may more or less seriously impair normal body functioning. Thus, in cerebral palsy, a malfunctioning nervous system may cause muscles to work in opposition to each other causing a spastic kind of movement, instead of the smooth operation of muscle groups characteristic of most of us. The ability of such persons to perceive effectively and clearly may be quite unaffected. Any impairment of bodily functioning, however, has effects upon perceiving as a result of the restrictions it places upon mobility. People who do not get about as well as others do not perceive the same things in the same ways. As the vehicle of our perceiving, our bodies provide the platform from which we make our observations, and important changes in this platform inevitably affect our perception. The victim of cerebral palsy sees the world differently from the unafflicted, although he does not necessarily see it less richly or less completely. Similarly, the epileptic may be quite able to perceive effectively and efficiently, but he inevitably perceives himself and the world around him differently because of his handicap.

In recent years we have come to understand that certain diseases like *encephalitis lethargica* can have effects upon perceiving such that marked behavior changes may occur following an attack of this disease. Personalities have been known to change with dramatic suddenness following encephalitis so that patients appear to be quite different people. Such behavior changes must be the result of different ways of perceiving themselves and the world around them, but the details of how and why these changes occur we do not know. Similarly, we now know that any disease accompanied by high fever, especially in early childhood, may be followed by a more or less serious impairment of intellectual functioning.

Anyone who has had the misfortune to be seriously ill at some time in his life may have experienced the distortion of perception characteristic of delirium. This, too, is a physical effect upon perception; it occasionally happens when a person has a high fever. He may have wild delusions or hallucinations of weird happenings to himself or to the world around him. These seem to be concomitant effects of temporary impairment of the normal functioning of the nervous systems.

Fortunately, most of us have relatively intact and functioning nervous systems which make it possible for us to perceive with ease and accuracy. Indeed, it is remarkable that despite its complexity the human nervous system manages to function as perfectly as it does.

LIMITATIONS OF GENERAL HEALTH

Most of the above effects of our physical structure upon perceiving are obvious and dramatic. They are effects we are not likely to miss. Perhaps even more important, because they are so much more likely to be missed, are the less readily deservable effects upon perception resulting from debilitating, but not disabling, physical impairments. Any physical disturbance which seriously reduces energy reserves of the organism has its effects upon the scope of perception. When an individual is sick enough to be confined to his bed, it is easy for us to understand how his abilities to perceive may be restricted by his inability to get around. Listlessness or lack of interest may have similar effects. Whatever decreases alertness has inevitable effects upon perceptive efficiency.

Lesser degrees of illness, in which the individual is handicapped, but not incapacitated, may also have their effects upon perceiving, for whatever depletes our abilities to get around and become involved with life must necessarily affect our perception. We know, for example, that the physical and mental development of children is closely related. Even intelligence, which is, in a sense, the ability to perceive effectively and efficiently seems closely related to the general physical well being of the individual. "Studies of Genius" has shown us that children with high I.Q.'s are also generally taller, heavier, healthier, and in every way superior to average children. Intelligence has even been known to improve with improved nutrition. Whatever affects the general level of efficient bodily functioning may also affect the individual's perceptual field. Limitations of general health such as malnutrition, chronic focal infections, or long-continued fatigue may affect perception in at least three general ways:

1. *By reducing mobility.* When energy levels are depleted, we do not move around as much as when we are well. We prefer to hoard our limited supplies and to avoid activity. It is quite possible for people to perceive richly and broadly although confined for a lifetime to a small space but, other things being equal, most of us perceive more richly and

more effectively when our freedom of movement is unhampered. A person confined to his bed by illness may find his perceptions confined to tracing the patterns of the wallpaper. When we are fatigued, malnourished, or suffering from disease or chronic focal infections, we do not feel like exerting ourselves. It is an effort to move about, and we prefer to take it easy. Such inactivity saves energy, but also has restricting effects upon our perceptual fields.

2. *By reducing interest.* Interests are a vital factor in controlling the richness and variety of the perceptions we make. Any physiological condition which affects the degree or intensity of interest, whether directly or indirectly, must have its concomitant effects upon the ability to perceive. Thus, when energy levels are depleted by disease, malnutrition, focal infections, fatigue, or any other debilitating factor, interest levels will be sharply lowered and perception restricted. The man who is ill and tired finds it difficult to work up much enthusiasm for active participation in events. He is not interested in going to a meeting, attending a lecture, or getting involved in an activity, and so loses an opportunity for perceiving. Indeed, if he is very ill or in great pain, he may find it almost impossible to perceive more than his own unhappy state.

3. *By focusing attention under deprivation.* In the preceding chapter the nature of the organism's fundamental need for the maintenance and enhancement of the self was discussed. One of the prime requirements for the satisfaction of this need is the healthy condition of the physical organism which does the perceiving. This need has an organizing or limiting effect upon our perceptions. We would expect, then, that when the operations of our bodies are seriously impaired, there should be an organization of our perceptions with respect to such threats. This is exactly what seems to occur. We may go for long periods unaware of some portion of our bodies as long as it is operating smoothly or effectively. However, the moment some part of our physical self is injured or begins to function badly, we immediately become aware of that part, and our attentions are directed to it. All of us have had experiences of this sort in which our perceptions become focused more or less intensely on some portion of our physical bodies momentarily out of order, such as when we have injured a finger. Before the injury, we took our fingers for granted and accepted their functioning without question. But when we have smashed a finger in the car door, or hit it with the hammer, our perceptions become suddenly concentrated on the injured member of our organization. Indeed, we may momentarily be incapable of perceiv-

ing anything else. Even long after the first shock of injury has passed, we are keenly aware of our hurt finger during the period of convalescence.

Similarly our perceptions become organized whenever our physical selves suffer deprivation. When we are hungry our perceptions become focused on food, and when we are thirsty, our perceptions are concerned with drinking fountains, the kitchen sink, or mountain streams. Several psychologists have carried out interesting experiments by systematically depriving subjects of food or drink for long periods and examining the effects of such deprivation on perception. Subjects report an increasing concern for food or drink as the degree of deprivation increases until consciousness itself begins to be affected. They report spending many hours daydreaming about delicious food, memorizing recipes, or imagining sumptuous banquets. They became disinterested in other people and protested their places in the food line. On shopping trips they bought cooking utensils for which they had no real need.

THE EFFECT OF DRUGS UPON PERCEPTION. Alcohol and drugs, which are often used as a means of escape from the crueler facts of life, have interesting effects upon the perceptions of the individual. Such narcotics seem to create a feeling of well-being by reducing the clarity and sharpness of perception, or by temporarily providing a feeling of strength and freedom of action. These effects can be clearly observed in the use of alcohol. It is a common observation that light "social drinking" at a party helps to loosen the tongues of the guests and make them more at ease, especially when they are strangers to one another. As people become less able to perceive the reactions of others and experience a lessening of awareness of their own tensions or inadequacies, their inhibitions are relaxed and feeling tone is enhanced. With a deadening of awareness of self, individuals do not have to face so sharply the distasteful fact of not being what they would like to be. They are relieved of normal burdens of self consciousness and can behave in a less inhibited fashion. When an individual is in complete stupor, unpleasantness can be escaped entirely.

One of the effects of fear and anxiety is to restrict the individual's perceptual field. Anything, therefore, which tends to eliminate anxiety thus seems to leave the individual free to perceive both himself and the world about him. Drugs which tend to eliminate anxious feelings have even been known to result in changes in intelligence test scores.

Some narcotics seem to produce this effect of well-being not by the dampening of perception alone, but by temporarily giving the individual additional reserves of energy which, in turn, add to the person's feeling of well-being and adequacy. Alcohol, for example, is quickly converted to energy in the body, and this is experienced as an increase in strength or power so that the individual may feel more capable. The feeling of strength may also be augmented as the drug counteracts the effects of fatigue. Narcotics which are accompanied by dreaming may produce an added sense of well-being through fantasy which permits the individual to be, for a while, almost anything he pleases.

Such effects are not limited to narcotics. Actually, the same effects, to a lesser degree, may be produced by food or fatigue. Anyone who has ever worked with young children must surely have observed how quickly active youngsters react to food. A child who has been whining and irritable may, in a few moments, be transformed into a fairly pleasant human being by giving him a meal or a between-meal snack of milk and cookies. Apparently the sense of well-being induced by the restoration of energy gives the child an entirely different perception of himself and his world. Beyond a certain point the chemical products of fatigue seem to produce a deadening of awareness similar to the narcotic effects mentioned above so that the behavior has a spurious feeling of capacity which can sometimes prove highly dangerous. Automobile drivers, for example, after long hours at the wheel seem to become less aware of the need to stop. They feel, instead, quite capable of going on when they had much better not.

EFFECTS OF BODY STRUCTURE.   The general body structure with which we are endowed may not affect our perceptions directly, but it has important indirect effects upon the nature of our perceptions. Our bodies provide the vehicle or platform from which perceptions are made and we have already seen that what is observed is in large measure a function of the point from which the observations are made. The tall man sees things quite differently from the short man for the simple reason that his eyes are higher above the ground. Some years ago on a trip to New York, I got so engrossed in a mystery thriller that I did not notice the people who got on the train and took seats around me during the last hundred miles of the trip. When the train pulled into Grand Central Station, of course, everyone stood up. When I stood up with the rest of the passengers I was struck with a moment of panic, for everywhere I looked I was looking at belt buckles! When I boarded the train I had been a man of average height. Now, suddenly, I was a pigmy among giants. For a moment I had a very strange feeling that my whole world had lost its stability until I noticed that all the men standing around me carried bags marked "New York Knickerbockers," the name of a famous professional basketball team!

Almost any aspect of our general body structure or condition can have its indirect effects upon our perceptions. Children see differently from adults by the mere fact of being of different height. But perceptions may also be affected by our weight, skin color, strength, sex, and appearance. These effects will be particularly marked if our society has developed expectancies about them. Thus, the perceptions of the self held by stout women in Russia, where stoutness is acceptable, are quite different from that of the stout young American woman who must live in a world which values the slim, svelte figure.

Everyone's perceptions are deeply affected by his sex. Men and women do not perceive alike. From the moment of his birth our society begins to impress upon the child the fact of his maleness or femaleness, what is expected of boys and girls, of men or women in our culture. Similarly the values we place upon appearance have their inevitable effects upon the individual's perceptions. We call some people ugly and some beautiful. Some kinds of skin blemishes we regard with horror or disgust. The structure and appearance of our physical beings is the platform of perception and has its vital effects upon ways of perceiving.

HANDICAPS AFFECT PERCEPTION. Any kind of physical handicap may have its effect upon the perceptive field. Speech defects or various forms of physical abnormalities may deeply modify the perceptions of the individual afflicted with them. The perceptions of self and of the world about him are inexorably affected by the mere presence of such handicaps. For some the handicap may even become one of the most central aspects of living. Our folklore is replete with tales of persons who have spent their lives compensating for the existence of a personal inadequacy.

EFFECT OF BODY CONDITION ON THE PHENOMENAL SELF

We have previously pointed out that the phenomenal self is more or less roughly defined by the body surfaces of the individual. Thus, the body and its condition as a part of the field of the organism must affect behavior. It is probable that for most of us every field state includes more or less of this body condition as an integral part of the total field. Furthermore, in the course of our development we learn to differentiate more or less strongly the particular aspects of body condition which are more or less important in the definition of the phenomenal field. Which aspect we differentiate most strongly is likely to be a function of the phenomenal self. Thus, in our culture, men are more likely to be concerned with physical vigor, while for women the particular figure in vogue or facial beauty is likely to be most strongly differentiated. Frequently children are far more concerned with physical size and strength than with other aspects of the body, while adolescents are mainly interested in those aspects which make for successful competition for the attention of the opposite sex.

Since the physical body is the most constant aspect of our experience, it is not surprising that it should play a very large part in defining the phenomenal self. For most people the smooth-running body in good condition is likely to give a feeling of enhancement of the self, as it makes its owner feel adequate, competent, and in control of situations. Poor physical condition, on the other hand, may result in the definition of the phenomenal self as in some fashion humiliated. This is a frequent symptom of people with a physical handicap. I once worked with a young girl who was frightfully conscious of the size of her nose. In my estimation her nose was not in the least unusual, but she regarded it as a constant badge of shame and humiliation. She finally had plastic surgery which, in her opinion, helped her a great deal by reducing her nose, although no change was apparent to me. It is clear that she was attending to an aspect of her body dictated by her concept of herself. Furthermore, a slight change in this bodily characteristic apparently resulted in considerable change in her phenomenal self.

EFFECT OF THE PHENOMENAL SELF ON BODY CONDITION

It seems evident that the effect of the body on the phenomenal self is not the only direction in which this body-self relationship can operate. The reverse situation is also very frequent with the phenomenal self profoundly affecting the bodily condition of the individual. This is particularly evident in the new field of psychosomatics where bodily disturbances appear as the result of psychological problems. Physicians have discovered an increasingly long list of human diseases and ailments which seem to have their origin in the affective, emotional, or psychological life of the individual. The study of the interrelationship between behavior and the physical organism in which behavior occurs is called psychosomatics, and it is destined to play an increasing part in the practice of medicine. Fascinating as the topic of psychosomatics is, we shall not stop to deal with the problem here. That is subject matter for several books.

One of the most interesting examples in my experience of the effect of the self on the physical condition was the case of a young woman who had been overprotected all her life by a very domineering mother. At college she had stuck closely to another girl very much like herself. Immediately after graduation her friend left to be married but this young woman remained at home. Within a few days of graduation she developed eczema on one hand which rapidly spread to cover her entire body and particularly her face. Obviously, in such a condition it was impossible for her to seek a position. She traveled about from doctor to doctor and from clinic to clinic without success. When she went to a camp her eczema disappeared completely, but as soon as she returned to the city it returned in full force. During psychotherapy I observed that this skin condition became less and less pronounced while we talked. However, the slightest reference to her condition or any attack upon her organization would bring it back. Eventually this client came to achieve some insight into her condition but found it difficult to admit its nature even to herself. To admit any such shenanigans would be a threat to her concept of herself as a brilliant student of psychology. The fact, that others in whom she had faith thought her condition to be psychological was, however, disturbing. It was necessary for her to rid herself of the condition without accepting the cause as psychological. This she did by adopting a diet she heard about from someone she met on the street. Within a week her skin cleared up. Since then she has found a job and moved on to a better adjustment in other ways as well. It is significant that, in spite of discontinuing her absurd diet, her condition has not returned. From many examples of this type, it would seem possible that in certain types of physical disturbances, real changes in the bodily condition of an individual may be brought about by changes in the phenomenal self.

It is the thesis of this book that behavior is the product of the perceptual field. Perception makes possible such behavior as feeding, drinking, or sheltering one's self against the elements. Without perception reproduction would be impossible. Where the body goes, what it eats, drinks, enjoys, or avoids is the product of its perceptions. The perceptions available to the organism even determine whether it lives or dies. This entire book is, in a sense, devoted to the question of the effect of perception upon the physical organism since we attempt to understand behavior from a perceptual point of view.

CHAPTER 5

Time and Opportunity Affect Perception

THE physical body provides the vehicle which makes perceiving possible. The fundamental need for adequacy provides us with motive and direction. These factors impose important limits upon individual perception and behavior. But these alone are insufficient to explain the richness and diversity of human perception, or the variety of behavior produced by the perceptual field. It is a commonplace observation that people behave differently depending upon the time and place in which they are involved.

These determinants of behavior, observed from an external point of view, are also important in order to understand behavior from a perceptual frame of reference. Both time and environment are important variables in controlling the nature and extent of the perceptual field.

Perceiving Takes Time

Other things being equal, what an individual is able to perceive in any situation will depend upon the length of time he has been exposed to the event. This principle is familiar to anyone who has ever studied a painting. The longer one looks, the more he is able to perceive. The reader may test this now for himself by looking intently at the floor, the ceiling, or the walls of his room. He first sees the grosser aspects of the object. Very quickly, however, he will find he is noting more detail. Looking at a wall, for example, one may first perceive its general shape and color. Looking longer one may become conscious of the texture, of parts of the wall, of relationships, cracks, inequalities in the paint, and so forth. The same effects may be noted in our other senses. The more often one hears a piece of music, for example, the more he perceives. With each hearing, different nuances, not heard before, may come into figure. This process of discerning increasing detail out of the total field of awareness is called differentiation. We shall want to examine this phenomenon much more closely in a later section of this book.

Considering the effect of time upon perceiving, we must keep in mind that we are speaking of the duration of the individual's experience with an event rather than the observer's. Thus, while it may appear to an outside observer that a person is confronted by an experience, from that person's own point of view he may have no contact with the experience whatever. A child may sit in school all day, apparently exposed to the curriculum, but may actually experience and perceive quite different aspects of the situation. While the teacher labors under the delusion that a child is being exposed to arithmetic, he may actually be admiring the pretty girl across the aisle, examining the names of former students carved on his desk, or he may even, in fantasy, be hunting bears in Alaska. Perception is an internal, individual phenomenon and the perceptual field of one individual may be quite different from that of another, even in what seems to be the same situation. In considering the time of exposure to an event, therefore, we must see the problem from the point of view of the behaver.

The time required for perception to occur varies tremendously from a minute fraction of a second to generations. Tachistoscopic studies, for example, have shown that it is possible for a person to differentiate single words exposed in such machines at speeds of as little as one hundredth of a second. Subjects shown an object for very short periods of exposure report only seeing "something there." As the time of exposure is increased they may be able to perceive the object vaguely, and when exposure has been increased to a full second or more, quite complicated perceptions can be made. The perceptions we make of many events in the external world around us can be made with great speed. On the other hand, human beings lived with gravity for thousands of years before it was perceived and stated as a principle of physics. People had been looking at the sun for a long time before Copernicus helped us to perceive that the earth went around the sun instead of vice versa.

The purely mechanical aspects of perceiving are extremely rapid. Given something the individual "knows" and is "set" to perceive, he can perceive at incredible speed. Events new to the individual or buried in a larger, more complicated field take considerably longer to be perceived.

A second factor affecting the time required for perception has to do with the fact that most perceptions the individual makes are functions of previous perceptions. Before one can perceive the mechanics of multiplication, for example, he must have perceived addition. The child cannot perceive the need for the sand dome on the locomotive until he has first perceived that sometimes locomotive wheels slip. Many of our perceptions are based upon long series of previous discriminations extending back to our earliest beginnings. It seems axiomatic that to make differentiations a person must have lived long enough to do so, a fact we recognize in the construction of intelligence tests calibrated for various age levels and which teachers recognize in the concept of readiness or maturation.

A great many of our difficulties in communication seem to stem from our failure to recognize the importance of time in perceiving. The speaker who moves too fast loses his audience and makes himself ineffective. Communication may fail because the audience has not had sufficient previous experience to perceive the new aspects conveyed by the speaker. Since new perceptions derive their meaning in large part from already existing perceptions in the field, the time required to perceive a given event will be affected by the existing field. Listening to a lecture in advanced mathematics, would leave most of us hopelessly unable to comprehend for lack of the proper differentiations at earlier periods in our lives.

Opportunity Affects Perceiving

For perception to occur, there must be an opportunity for perception. We are accustomed to believing that what we perceive is so. Our perceptions seem to us to be an accurate picture of what exists. When we perceive a chair, we believe the chair exists; so much so, that we are willing to sit down on it. We can see for ourselves that the chair holds us up. What is more, other people in whom we have confidence also believe the chair exists. We can confirm our experience of the chair by testing our perception with our other senses; we can feel the chair with our hands, we can hear it when we move it, we can even smell it and taste it, if necessary. Best of all, we can corroborate our impressions from the reports of other people whom we trust and who agree that what we perceive is true.

Now, whether there is anything *really* there when we perceive is a problem philosophers have been arguing about for generations. To understand behavior, however, it is not necessary for us to settle that argument. Since behavior is a function of perception, it is the perceptions of people with which we must be concerned, and these perceptions can be studied whether or not they have any counterpart in reality.

To understand an individual's behavior the only reality we need to be concerned with is what *seems real to him*. If people believe an event is so, then for them it is so. As students of human behavior this is the reality with which we must deal. In the following pages, when it is necessary for us to discuss external events, objects, or opportunities we shall refer to the generally accepted beliefs people have about the world in which they live, leaving the question of whether these beliefs or perceptions have any counterpart in an objective world to the philosophers and logicians.

There is a vast world of people, things, and abstract ideas which we can see, hear, feel, measure, or perhaps only think about, which seems to us real and objective. This is the environment in which we live; it provides much of the raw material of our experience. This environment, furthermore, provides many opportunities for perception, which may be more or less concrete, or physical, contacts of the individual with his world, or which may be vicarious experiences.

CONCRETE OPPORTUNITIES FOR PERCEPTION. In the first place, the perceptions possible to any individual will be limited, in part, by the individual's own direct experience of the environmental factors to which he has been exposed. Eskimos ordinarily do not comprehend bananas, nor African bushmen snow, since neither has had the opportunity to experience them in his environment. In a similar way, each of us has come to perceive many aspects of the physical environments in which we have lived. The major sources of concrete experiences are:

1. The natural scene—the geographic and geologic features about us such as rocks, rivers, seas, mountains, and plains, as well as the recurring tides and our experience of night and day.

2. The constructions of man—the highways, harbors, buildings, machinery, furniture, signboards, papers, autos, and a million other items.

3. The world of living things—animals, insects, plants, microörganisms.

4. The experience of the self—one's own physical, emotional, and thinking being.

5. The interaction with others—the social existence of man and the impact of other people upon him.

VICARIOUS OPPORTUNITIES FOR PERCEPTION. Perceptions may also occur in the individual's field as a consequence of exposure to the experience of others, through reading, conversation, movies, and other means of communication. The development of language makes possible vast opportunities for perceiving on a symbolic level what we could not ordinarily hope to experience. Although I cannot directly perceive that it is dangerous to expose myself to rays from an atomic pile, for example, I can differentiate this notion through what others whom I respect have told me. Many of our perceptions are acquired through this kind of symbolic exposure. Certainly most of our formal schooling falls in this category, which may explain, in part, why so little of it is effective in changing behavior. Ideas which we have not differentiated ourselves from the broad background of our perceptual field are apt to remain isolated from the rest of the field and to have little effect on behavior.

What people perceive is necessarily limited by the opportunities to which they have been exposed in the course of their growth and development. This fact is nowhere better demonstrated than in the now famous Ames demonstrations in perception. These startling phenomena demonstrate with great clarity several important basic principles concerning perception:

1. *What is perceived is not what exists, but what one believes exists.* This principle is illustrated in the chair demonstration. This demonstration consists of a large wooden box into which one can look from several holes in the front. Looking into the box through one of these peep holes, one sees a chair as shown in Fig. 9. When, however, one goes around behind the box to look down inside it, there is no chair at all, only a series of white strings suspended in the otherwise empty space of the box, as shown in Fig. 10. What we have seen looking through the peep holes is not what is actually there, but only what the observer believes to be there. As Ames said,

Everybody believes that when we use our eyes, we look at "something out there" in our environment from which light rays come to our eyes and bring about images on our retinas. Everybody believes that "what is out there" contributes to what is in our visual awareness. But not everybody believes that we ourselves also contribute to what is in our visual awareness, although this is the case.

While modern physics has disclosed a great deal about certain aspects of the something "out there," and while modern physiology has disclosed a great deal about our stimulus patterns and bodily processes, relatively little has been learned about the nature of what we ourselves "subjectively" contribute to our perceptions of the "something out there."

You have, it would seem, sufficient evidence that what is in your visual

Fig. 9. Chair Demonstration (Seen from the Front). (From W. H. Ittelson, *The Ames Demonstrations in Perception*, Princeton University Press, Princeton, N.J. Reprinted by permission of the publisher.)

Fig. 10. Chair Demonstration (Seen from the Rear). (From W. H. Ittelson, *The Ames Demonstrations in Perception*, Princeton University Press, Princeton, N.J. Reprinted by permission of the publisher.)

awareness was neither in your stimulus patterns nor in the environment, but was your own contribution to the perceptual event.

Stated in terms of field dynamics, objects and events impinging upon our perceptual fields are perceived in the way which best "fits" the field of that instant. In Ames' demonstration it is significant that a "chair" requires less differentiation. It takes less time to perceive a chair than to carry the process of differentiating further and to break the experience down into a number of strings. We could equally well draw illustrations of this principle from many experiences of daily life wherein we hear or see what we consider reasonable to perceive. Because we are hungry and it is near lunch time, the call from the kitchen is heard as a call to come to lunch. Vague impressions of another person may be put together so that we believe we see a friend only to discover, after we have hailed him, that he is a total stranger. We often jump to apparently reasonable conclusions even though these conclusions may later prove to be wrong. This characteristic of people to perceive what fits into their mental picture rather than what exists, constantly creates problems for our courts in determining the credibility of witnesses. It is often difficult to recognize whether a witness is reporting what actually happened or what he believes "must have happened."

Since the perceptual field is always organized, what is perceived must be the product of this organization. If perception occurs at all, it must occur with meaning. Meaning is given to events by the relationships in the perceptual field in which they occur. The words read by each reader of this page have different meanings. Even the same reader rereading the page will perceive differently. Reading is not so much a matter of taking meaning *from* a book as bringing meaning *to* the printed page. This is not to suggest that the ideas set down by an author are unnecessary or without value. Not at all. Experience is, of course, essential to perceiving, but what is perceived is determined by the unique perceptual field of each person which includes much more than the direct experience of our senses.

2. *What is perceived is what we have learned to perceive as a result of our past opportunities or experiences.* To illustrate this principle, Ames has developed several distorted rooms, one of which is diagramed in Fig. 11. This room is obviously distorted with a tilting floor and ceiling when one looks at it from a distance. Coming close, however, and looking into the room without extraneous cues to guide him, the observer

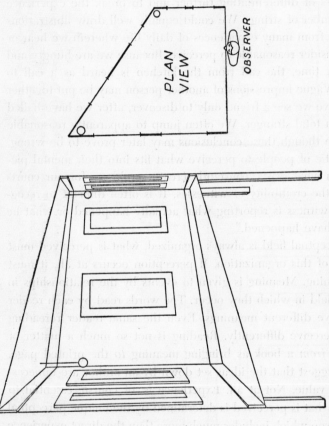

Fig. 11. This Is a Drawing of the Distorted Room. It does not show the distortion fully, because the back left corner does not appear to be far enough away from us. The reason for this is that there are so many things built into the room which violate the usual rules of perspective. For example, consider the two back windows. If they were the same size, the left one should look smaller than the right one, because it is farther away. It is actually larger, and when drawn larger, the left corner refuses to go back where it belongs. In order to realize how far away the back left corner is, we have to have the plan view, which is a horizontal cross section of the room. For the experiment, the observer is placed nearer the right wall than the left one. (From Earl C. Kelley, *Education for What Is Real.* New York, Harper, 1947.)

PLAN VIEW

OBSERVER

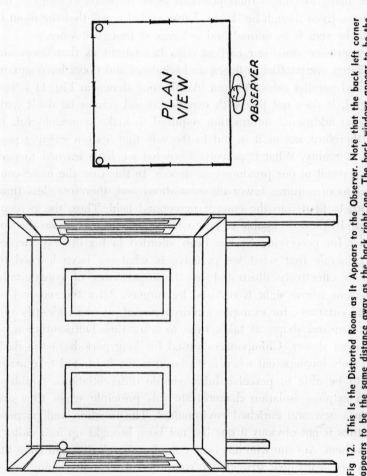

Fig 12. This Is the Distorted Room as It Appears to the Observer. Note that the back left corner appears to be the same distance away as the back right one. The back windows appear to be the same size. In the plan view, note that while the observer is actually to the right of the center (see Fig. 11), he seems to be in the center. (From Earl C. Kelley, *Education for What Is Real*, New York, Harper, 1947.)

discovers that the room looks perfectly normal with level floor and ceiling, windows of equal size and properly squared corners, as shown in Fig. 12. Even though the observer has seen the distortion of the room a few moments before, he now sees it like a normal room. Moreover, when he is given a pointer and asked to touch various points in the room, he badly misjudges their positions as he responds in terms of his perceptions. Even though he "knows," in a verbal sense, that the room is distorted, he sees it as normal and behaves as though it were.

Our experience since our earliest days has taught us that floors are level, ceilings are parallel to floors, and windows and doors have square corners and parallel sides. A room like the one shown in Fig. 11 is not meaningful. It does not jibe with experience and cannot be dealt with without the additional information required to make it meaningful. It is seen, therefore, not as it is, but in the way that fits our existing perceptions of reality. What is perceived is what we have learned to perceive as a result of our previous experiences. In this case the more conventional room requires fewer differentiations and, therefore, less time and effort, to fit it into the current perceptual field. Thus, the perceptions an individual is capable of now will depend, in part, upon the opportunities for perceiving he has been afforded in his life experience.

This principle that what we perceive is what we have learned to perceive is effectively illustrated by the experiences of congenitally blind persons whose sight is restored by surgery. After the removal of congenital cataracts, for example, children cannot, at once, identify objects by size and shape. It takes time to learn this. Differentiation of color is even slower. Chimpanzees raised for long periods in the dark are extremely incompetent when first placed in the light, and take many months to be able to perceive fairly simple differentiations. Children raised in extreme isolation demonstrate this principle when they are placed in a new and enriched environment. The function and purpose of bath tubs is not obvious if one has not been brought up in a culture that uses them. Anyone who has ever visited a church different from his own may recall his own struggles to comprehend what was going on in the service and the way in which it became clear when he learned to interpret the symbolism correctly.

When we are faced with incongruous events, we tend to perceive them in the way that is most familiar or meaningful to us at that moment. This is the basic principle upon which projective tests are constructed; namely, that, when an individual is asked to respond to an ambiguous situation, he will invest it with the meanings important to him. Even simple forms or diagrams may be interpreted and named in this fashion. Ink blots, for example, may be seen as all sorts of things by subjects taking the Rorschach test. The meanings we have learned, moreover, are often highly stable and difficult to change. Experiments of changing child attitudes toward people of other nationalities by showing the child movies, for example, demonstrate that, though new information may temporarily change child values, when the pressure to change has passed, perceptions gradually revert to earlier forms.

Apparently the proverb "seeing is believing" is not as sure-fire an indication of what is so as we are led to believe. Indeed, the existence of the principle that perceptions are largely learned calls for a reexamination of some of our most cherished and time-honored beliefs and practices in human relationships.

The Concept of Constancies

The physical world in which we live, of course, provides us with important opportunities for perception. In fact, just to exist in any situation makes demands on an individual's perceptual field. If I am immersed in water in the middle of a lake, this predicament imposes upon me perceptions that enable me to keep afloat. When the temperature gets low in my living room, it affects my perceptions and I become aware that I must keep warm. When my car is going too fast, I soon perceive that I must slow down before I have an accident. All situations in which people are involved have some effect upon their perceptions. Some of our experiences are so frequent, stable, or important, moreover, that they serve us as frames of reference for judgment.

Because of this interaction with the physical world around him, the individual learns to perceive when he is right side up or upside down, in warm places or cold. He also learns to orient himself in space by perceiving himself in relationship to objects in the environment. These perceptions become the individual's "anchors to reality" and provide a stable base for his behavior. Psychologists have called these perceptions "anchorages." They provide the individual with standards for judgment and meaning. Most of us, for example, have come to rely upon the horizon as a fixed point of reference for many of our perceptions. Similarly, we judge distance, weight, time, and appropriateness of behavior with refer-

ence to important or stable aspects of our own experience which can
serve as bases of comparison.

We do not, however, rely only upon our experience of the external
world to provide us with standards of judgment. We actively invest
some objects, events, or concepts with stability. We build up "constancies"
and, thereafter, depend upon them as platforms or frames of reference
to comprehend the world about us. Cantril says of these constancies, "We
create these constancies by attributing certain *consistent* and *repeatable*
characteristics to what they refer to, so that we can guess with a fair
degree of accuracy what the significances and meanings are of the various sensory cues that impinge upon us. We do this so that we will not
have to make fresh guesses at every turn. These significances we build
up about objects, people, symbols, and events, or about ideas all orches-
trate together to give us what we might call our own unique "reality
world."

The use of personal experience as frames of reference is done so
smoothly and naturally that we often do not even perceive that we are
doing it. When, however, we must behave without the use of such guides,
we become keenly aware of their importance. This is well illustrated in
the autokinetic phenomenon which concerns the apparent behavior of a
fixed spot of light in a completely dark room. Without a reference point
to which the spot of light can be referred, it is seen by most subjects as
drifting about in space. It is difficult to localize or pin down an experience when we do not have access to our usual points of reference. When
such anchorages are lost or when they become too variable to be de-
pended upon, sane people become quite ill. This seems to occur in sea
sickness, when many of one's normal anchors to reality become unpredictable and even the horizon seems to leave its moorings. An amusing illustration of this relationship is to be found in the experiences of
the test pilot who wanted to determine if there was any truth to the idea
that pilots fly "by the seat of their pants." Before take off the pilot had
several shots of novocaine injected into his posterior to deaden his perception of contact with his seat. As a result he became nauseated and ill
after turning and diving maneuvers which were no more than routine in
the ordinary course of his duties!

Our perceptions of the physical world generally are adequate because
inadequate perceptions of the physical world tend to be self correcting.
I may be unhappy because I arrived at my friend's party just as the party
was breaking up because I missed the proper turn and lost my way. But

when I go there again I shall still have to make the same turn and I shall be able to differentiate clearly and rely upon my differentiation. Physical factors have a high degree of predictability. The same stability often cannot be found in people and, consequently, adequate frames of reference are harder to discover. Thus, a child finds it easier to adjust his perceptions about the streets he must cross on his way to school than to discover what his teachers or relatives expect of him. Streets stay where they belong but people, sometimes, refuse to sit still long enough to know what they are about.

There is evidence to suggest that some forms of maladjustment have their roots in the individual's inability to cope with events because he does not clearly understand the "expectancies." Experimental neurosis can be produced, for example, by forcing animals to deal with capricious events. Rats or goats, for instance, which have been trained to escape severe punishment by making a particular choice of behavior, may become quite desperate when such choices are no longer possible because they are continuously shifting and changing. Need satisfaction is impossible in an unpredictable world. The development of dependable constancies and anchorages is essential to the individual's very existence.

Despite its difficulties establishing anchorages with respect to people is essential to successful living in an interdependent and social world like ours. Because we are so dependent on other people for need satisfaction, we must work out effective relationships with them. To do this, it is necessary to invest other people with elements of consistency and predictability. As a consequence, we attempt to classify people, to give them roles, status, prestige, authority, and the like, to provide handy reference tags to help us deal with them. The particular social anchorages or constancies differentiated by a particular person are the product of his experience with the important people in his world while he grew up. From those around him he learns about authority figures and what to expect of men and women. He develops expectancies about Negro people and white people, about labor and management, and so on; in time these expectancies may become so firm as to serve him as predictable guides. Some of these frames of reference about people will be quite unique, sometimes even bizarre. When this happens individuals have difficulty dealing with each other. Effective interaction must be based upon stable, accurate concepts of what other people are like. Fortunately, many of our expectancies about people are shared with others, because we have grown up in a common culture.

The Individual's Culture and Opportunities for Perceiving

It is not physical situations alone that force perceptions upon us. For most of us social demands are far more frequent and pressing in daily life. Demands are imposed upon the individual by his family, his friends, his community, and his nation; in short, by every life situation with which he is faced. Much of any person's behavior is the observable expression of his unceasing attempt to achieve need satisfaction when he is confronted with the necessities imposed upon him by the cultures in which he moves. Consequently, a very large portion of the perceptions we are able to make are a direct result of the particular cultures in which we have been brought up. Indeed, the social setting in which we live is so all-pervasive that even the inanimate aspects of our worlds are given meaning by the culture.

The experience of the individual in meeting the demands of life in his particular culture plays a large part in determining the richness and variety of perceptions in his phenomenal field. Many of these perceptions will be similar to the perceptions of his fellows in the same society. This is important, because it is only on the basis of common meanings that it is possible for one person to communicate with another. If similar meanings did not exist for members of a common culture, communication with his fellows would be extremely difficult and need satisfaction would be impossible. When one's house is on fire, to confuse the letter box with the fire alarm box does not contribute to the maintenance of self. Knowledge of the meanings of objects existing in the culture are essential to need satisfaction of the individual. Such meanings in the culture will therefore come to have counterparts in his perceptual field. It will be equally true of the concepts, values, ideas, and other abstractions existing in the particular culture in which he is brought up.

As W. Kohler expressed it, "The world *looks* today what our forefathers learned to say about it; we act and speak accordingly." What were once new ideas and concepts are matter-of-fact perceptions of people today. The matters the students of one generation learned to perceive with difficulty and painstaking effort are calmly accepted by the next. The germ theory of disease, the concept of evolution, or the controversy over nature-nurture, all difficult concepts for workers in former times, are used as the accepted basis for new explorations in our time. The culture we live in has vital effects upon the discrimination, conceptualization, and evaluations we learn to make of things we see about us.

THE FAMILY AS CULTURE TRANSMITTER

The human infant is born into an existing society—a structured, more or less organized society in which all individuals are bent upon maintaining their own integrations. The search of these individuals for need satisfaction produces a society which is not only responsive to the demands of its members, but also enforces upon its new members its own peculiar framework. From the moment of birth, if not before, this social pressure begins its work. From the very start socially acceptable differentiations are imposed upon the infant—for example, we present blue booties to a newborn boy, pink booties to a girl. Even the physical behavior of the child is subject, almost at once, to social control. Babies may be fed on schedule, subjected to hospital routine, and very shortly are taught "proper" habits of elimination, eating, and sleeping by their parents who, as products of their society, are guardians of its values.

From them we learn to define the world about us in terms of the culture into which we are born. We come to accept as our own "reality" the differentiations we acquire as a result of our experience with those who most closely affect us. We apply the labels of our culture to things and people around us. We accept also the values, taboos, and moral concepts of our culture and subcultures. The meanings of these things become part of our own "reality." A child can only see himself in terms of his experience and the treatment he receives from those responsible for his development. He is likely, therefore, to be strongly affected by the labels which are applied to events by other people. As his experience with them contributes to need satisfaction or frustrates such satisfaction he is likely to perceive things as good or bad, desirable or undesirable, friendly or hostile, etc. Once such perceptions have become part of his perceptual field they may persist as important determinants of behavior for the rest of his life. Such values, in turn, affect his perceptions so that even the things he sees and hears may become functions of his cultural experience. Autistic children, for example, who have learned to perceive adults as deeply threatening, dangerous, or untrustworthy, behave as though people did not exist. They have nothing to do with people and prefer to spend their time with things; they even treat people as "things" when it becomes necessary to use them for need satisfaction.

Persons with whom we are strongly identified provide us with anchorages or constancies in terms of which we make judgments about the world about us. In some instances this identification may be so strong that even the ordinarily stable world of things may be perceived awry by contrast. The following, for example, is a description of such an occurrence reported by Cantril in connection with the distorted room we discussed on page 85:

Since the room is seen as square, persons or objects within the room or people looking through the windows become distorted. I had shown this room to hundreds of individuals and among other phenomena had demonstrated that when two people look through the back windows, the head of one individual appeared to be very large, the head of the other to be very small. When the individuals reversed the windows they were looking through, the size of their heads appeared to the observer to change. But on this Sunday morning when my friend's wife was observing him and me, she said, "Well, Louis, your head is the same size as ever, but Hadley, your head is very small." Then we changed the windows we were looking through and she said, "Louis, you're still the same, but Hadley, you've become awfully large." Needless to say this remark made a shiver go up my spine and I asked her how she saw the room. It turned out that for her—unlike any other observer until then—the room had become somewhat distorted. In other words, she was using her husband—to whom she was particularly devoted—as her standard. She would not let him go. His nickname for her was "Honi" and we have dubbed this the "Honi phenomenon."

This observation was followed systematically in a series of experiments on married couples by Dr. Warren Wittreich. He found that if couples had been married less than a year there was a very definite tendency not to let the new marital partner distort as quickly or as much as was allowed by people who had been married for a considerable time. But, again, I hasten to add that it is not a simple matter of how long one has been married that determines how willing one is to distort the size or shape of one's marital partner! The original observation was made on a couple who were already grandparents. Preliminary investigation also seems to show that parents of young children will not allow their children to distort as readily as will parents of older children.

Examples of this use of our experience as yard stick for judgments are also common in daily life. We are familiar with the child who believes his father is right and the world is wrong or the mother who believes "they were all out of step but Jim!" Many of us have experienced, too, how our concept of a decent standard of living increases with our income.

The ways the individual learns to differentiate people will differ widely from culture to culture. What we call *man*, is *hombre* to the Spanish, *homme* to the French, or *inuk* to the Eskimo. The same is true of other objects. What they are called, what they are described as, and even their meanings may differ in different cultures. Certainly the American ideal of a "man" is far different from that of the Frenchman, the

Spaniard, or the Eskimo. Even what is included in the definition of self may vary from culture to culture. The Wintu Indians, for example, have a much more holistic concept of the self than we. They do not make the kinds of distinctions we do between the self and the body. The Wintu Indian is so much more anchored to his environment than we are that when he is bitten on the arm by a mosquito he does not speak of his right or his left arm; he scratches his "East" arm going downstream and, later in the day, coming upstream he scratches his "West" arm!

Even the same objective events may be perceived with varying degrees of differentiation in different cultures. Though we have only one word to describe snow the Eskimo has several words to designate varying conditions and properties. The precise character of snow is of far more import to the Eskimo than it is to us. Similarly, the Masai, an African tribe whose economy is based on cattle, have 17 words referring to different conditions of a cow. In such a society a cow carrying a calf is not to be lightly confused with a cow which is not.

A student from India at an American school had never seen snow except at a great distance on mountain peaks. During the fall months she asked many questions about it and looked forward with increasing excitement to the first snowfall. At last, one December day a snow flurry filled the air but the student from India did not recognize what she had been looking for for several months. Much to everyone's surprise she asked "What kind of insects are these?" In our own country, experience with the testing of children in various parts of the nation has shown that perceptions are highly limited by the environmental conditions surrounding the individual. Mountain children, for example, often give bizarre responses on intelligence tests.

There are differences between the perceptions of rural and urban children, children from the North and children from the South, from mountain and valley, from seaboard and the plains. Nor are such differences confined only to children. Adults, too, are limited in their perceptions by environmental factors. During the war, I worked in an induction station receiving men from the mountains of Kentucky, West Virginia, and southern Ohio. An intelligence test in use at this station was composed of a series of five pictures with instructions to cross out the picture in each series that did not belong with the others. One set of five pictures showed a trumpet and four stringed instruments, a guitar, a harp, a violin, and a bass fiddle. Many of the men crossed out the harp because they had never seen one or because, as they explained, "all the others are things in our band." On the basis of these tests we cannot assume that these men were less able to make differentiations or had perceptive fields less rich than their examiner. We can only suggest that their perceptions were formulated in a culture different from those who made up the test. Presumably, had the mountain men made a test and administered it to the psychologist, the psychologist would have appeared rather dull!

No one is ever free from the effect of culture upon perceiving. We are continuously sensitive to those around us and to the meanings of events for them. These meanings become a vital part of our own reality. The individual's perceptions tend to become more and more like the perceptions of the important people in his world. Acting on other premises, basing his behavior on perceptions unacceptable to them would make him and his behavior unacceptable to these important people and thus frustrate his search for adequacy. Perceptions unacceptable to people we value are essentially disorganizing and are, therefore, unacceptable to us. We can observe this in the ways in which people defend their points of view and the groups they belong to. Americans defend the perceptions of Americans even when subsequently they may discover them to be wrong. For some people, it is inconceivable that Americans could *ever* be wrong.

These effects have also been demonstrated in a number of researches on group influences on perceiving. Schein, for example, had a number of subjects judge the weights of a series of objects, first alone and later in the presence of other people making similar judgments. He found his test subjects were influenced to a marked degree by the judgments of the other people they heard responding. Hearing other people make judgments different from their own even influenced Schein's subjects to change their judgments when they were more correct than those of their fellows. In other experiments Negro children were found to have become aware of their social status very early in life. Their perception of the lower esteem granted the Negro in our culture even led a majority of young children to describe brown as a "bad" and white as a "nice" color.

CULTURAL DIFFERENCES AND INTERNATIONAL UNDERSTANDING. The effects of culture upon the beliefs, values, and self concepts of people create serious problems for human relationships and international understanding. The experience of people always seems real to them so that whatever has been differentiated as a result of a particular culture always seems right, proper, and natural. It is easy, therefore, for people raised in one culture to fail miserably to understand those raised in another.

When Queen Elizabeth and Prince Philip of Great Britain visited America in October, 1957, the royal party attended a football game between Maryland and North Carolina. The following is a United Press report of the British difficulties in understanding our game:

BRITISH PRESS PUZZLED BY ANTICS ON GRIDIRON

London, Oct. 20 (UP)— American football threw the British press for a loss today.

Every newspaper played up the visit of Queen Elizabeth and Prince Philip to the Maryland-North Carolina game at College Park, Md., yesterday. But they found it frightfully hard to follow.

The newspapers generally followed the lead of Arthur Helliwell in The People, who wrote: "Don't ask me to describe the match. It baffled me as completely as it baffled the Duke. Every few seconds play was held up while the players went into head-down huddles and bands and prancing cheer-leaders went into action."

The Sunday Express in apparent desperation fell back on cricket terms.

"The Queen and Prince Philip sat swaddled in yellow and blue two yards from the pitch (field)," it said.

The Sunday Observer tried hard.

The players were "padded and armored like stag-beetles," it said. "They worked up and down the field, tunneling through the uproar of music and shouting, jerking from one scrimmage to another, obeying some intricate and secret pattern of play."

But not one of the newspapers reported the score (Maryland 21, North Carolina 7), or even which team won.

(Jacksonville, Florida, *Times Union*, Oct. 21, 1957)

Minor misunderstandings like this one can sometimes prove amusing, but more serious misunderstandings have been known to result in the tragedy of war.

The problem of intercultural communication is perhaps nowhere better illustrated than in the difficulties encountered when new techniques are introduced into old, established cultures. With the best of intentions, attempts to "help" people of foreign cultures have failed miserably primarily because the helping agencies failed to appreciate and adjust to the unique values and beliefs of the people they wanted to help. To further understanding of these matters and to help innovators behave more effectively, UNESCO published a book entitled *Cultural Patterns and Technical Change.* The book describes a number of instances in which good intentions fell awry because of failure to understand that things are perceived differently in different cultures. The following are some of the more amusing of these incidents:

The British, who regarded the hill tribes of Burma filthy for taking almost no baths were, in turn, considered dirty by the Indonesians because they bathe only once a day!

The Western handkerchief for pocketing mucous is considered revolting by a number of other societies!

Among the Zuni it is customary to go to bed only when one is ready to die. Imagine, then, the consternation of the Zuni tribesman with a cold who is ordered to bed by the white man's physician!

In one community the proposal to install a village pump as a labor saving device for the women was met with unexpected opposition until it was understood that in *that* village water carrying was a time-honored mark of womanhood.

In an attempt to increase the food supply the British Government once supplied veterinary service to certain cattle-raising tribes. Unhappily, this only contributed to soil erosion and made the people poorer because the cattle increased and ate up all the ground cover, for the people loved their cattle and only killed them on ceremonial occasion!

The Permanence of Perceptions

Behavior, we have said, is the product of the total field of perceptions open to the individual at the moment of his behaving. How he behaves will be a function of the state of his awareness at the moment he is called upon to act. The perceptual field is continuously being organized and reorganized in the light of the new perceptions or differentiations as long as the individual lives. Once made, differentiations in the field probably remain forever. Awareness is an irreversible process.

This statement may prove a bit startling to the reader who knows that he has "forgotten" things. Nevertheless, there is evidence that this statement is true. Once an event has been experienced, this experience cannot be reversed. Perceptions once experienced form the groundwork for all later perceptions. A number of experiments on forgetting have demonstrated this point. One of the most interesting was that of Burtt, who read his infant son long passages of Greek poetry. In later years, Dr. Burtt, had his son learn a number of passages of Greek poetry by heart. Among the passages the child learned at ages 8, 12, and 16, were some passages which he had heard as a baby. He learned the passages he had heard as a baby more quickly than the passages he had never heard before! Forgetting, it would seem, is not so much a fading out of what we have learned as it is a matter of organization of the perceptual field in which some perceptions became less capable than others of being called into clear figure on demand.

Although it seems true that the effect of perceptions is permanent, it should not be supposed that we mean they are solid and unchangeable or lie fallow in the perceptual field until called upon. The perceptual field is an organization continuously changed and modified by the perceptions occurring within it. As the total field changes, moreover, changes are produced in the perceptions within the field as well. Thus, an individual's experiences exert an irreversible effect on the field. It should not be assumed, however, that the original event can always be recalled just as it happened. Isolated perceptions like the Greek passages of Burtt's experiment may remain unchanged for long periods. Had these been brought frequently into figure over the years, they would undoubtedly have changed considerably. I recently visited my childhood neighborhood which I had not seen since I was ten years old. I found it extremely difficult to recognize and was particularly shocked to discover that what I remembered as a bright, sunny, spacious neighborhood with considerable distances between houses was now a neighborhood of narrow streets, dark and overgrown with trees, and houses practically on top of each other. My perceptions, originally made when the neighborhood was new, when trees had just been planted, and when distances seemed greater because my legs were shorter, had changed but little in the years that passed. Had I returned more often to the old neighborhood in the years between, the likelihood is that my perceptions would probably have changed and I might have been less shocked.

The Effect of Past Opportunities on Future Perceptions

The perceptual field as it exists at any moment has a controlling and determining effect upon other perceptions which the individual can experience. We have already seen that many perceptions are dependent upon previous perceptions. This means that the opportunities for perceiving which the individual has had in the past must have a vital bearing upon possible further perceptions. This is nicely demonstrated in another of Ames' demonstrations in perception which illustrate that new events are perceived in ways consistent with what we have previously learned to perceive.

The need for adequacy cannot be fulfilled without a degree of stability in the world in which the individual lives. When, therefore, events are perceived at odds with long established experience, these events must somehow be brought into consistency with other more basic perceptions. This phenomenon is illustrated in the trapezoidal window demonstration. The demonstration consists of a trapezoidal piece of sheet metal with holes cut out to resemble window panes and with shadows painted on to resemble thickness, mounted on a shaft which is slowly turned by a small electric motor as shown in Fig. 13. All our past experience has taught us that, as an object moves away from us, it appears to grow smaller and, as it approaches, it appears to grow larger. Looking at this window as it rotates, the long edge always appears to us to be closest, and we see the window slowly oscillate back and forth instead of turning round and round. Even though we "know" the window is going round in a circle, we still "see" it waving back and forth, the long edge always near us and the short edge always away. Apparently, our past experience has taught us so thoroughly the nature of perspective, that we cannot controvert this evidence. So strong is this learned way of perceiving that even when a small box is hung on the corner of the window, it appears to break loose from the oscillating window and take off into space on an orbit all its own, as shown in Fig. 14.

Aniseikonic lenses are specially designed to distort the visual image delivered to the retina of the eye. Nevertheless, persons wearing such lenses often experience no distortion of vision whatever when they wear them in familiar surroundings. The image delivered to the eye is "seen" as quite normal despite the physical damage to the stimulus. Away from familiar cues, persons wearing aniseikonic lenses usually see other people somewhat distorted. Even this distortion, however, seems to be related to the strength of the constancies developed by the individual. In one experiment, for example, navy recruits saw petty officers less distorted than recruits like themselves!

The effect of past experience can also be demonstrated in the use of the old time stereoscope. When different pictures are exposed to the left and right eye in the stereoscope under controlled conditions, individuals tend to see what their past experience "sets" them to see. Thus, when a group of teachers from North and South of the border looked at a picture of a bull fighter with one eye and a baseball player with the other, the Mexican school teachers "saw" the bull fighter, while the American teachers "saw" the ball player!

Fig. 13. Monocular Distorted Room. (From W. H. Ittelson, *The Ames Demonstrations in Perception*, Princeton University Press, Princeton, N.J. Reprinted by permission of the publisher.)

Fig. 14. The Rotating Trapezoid Demonstration. (From W. H. Ittelson, *The Ames Demonstrations in Perception*, Princeton University Press, Princeton, N.J. Reprinted by permission of the publisher.)

The state of the perceptual field at any moment sets limits upon what new events may be perceived. New perceptions are dependent upon antecedent experiences. If this seems somewhat depressing that we are able to perceive only what our previous experience has made it possible for us to perceive, we need to remind ourselves that our previous experience has also made it possible to perceive events we might not have been able to perceive without that experience. Our previous perceptions both limit the new events we can perceive and open vast new possibilities for further perceiving. The fact that I have been a psychologist for twenty years probably means that I shall never become famous as a dress designer. My perceptions of the past do not permit me to grasp the fine points of that profession. I must be content with admiring the product of others. On the other hand, the experiences I have had which have made me a psychologist have opened a vast horizon of possible new perceptions not open to people without that experience. Because of my previous experience I perceive events differently than my colleagues in engineering, business, or homemaking. For them and for me perceptions narrow possibilities in some directions and open new vistas in others.

In this chapter we have seen that what an individual perceives will to a great extent be dependent upon the kinds of opportunities to perceive he has been afforded in the past. It will be recognized at once, however, that exposure to events in no sense completely determines the perceptions an individual will make. The opportunity to perceive does not guarantee that a particular perception will occur. Even with equivalent exposure the perceptions of different people are not alike. Exposure to events is only one of the factors involved in determining whether or not an event will be differentiated.

We have now explored four of these factors, namely, the physical organism, need, time, and opportunity. In the following chapter we shall examine still another factor affecting perceiving, the effect of goals, techniques, and values.

CHAPTER **6**

Goals, Values, and Techniques

ALTHOUGH each of us is motivated at all times and in all places by the same basic need for adequacy, the expression of this need in different people is as varied as human beings themselves. Some people seek the maintenance and enhancement of the self in possessions and, thus, spend much of their lives collecting things like money, houses, shells, old automobiles, or human heads. Others find adequacy in the ideas and concepts of religion, law, science, literature, art, or music. Still others find adequacy in various sorts of activities like running, driving, eating, farming, swimming, building houses, taking dope, or sleeping. These ways in which individuals seek to achieve the maintenance and enhancement of self we call goals, techniques, and values. They are the differentiations people make to achieve need satisfaction. The character of these differentiations in an individual determines in very large measure his personality structure and behavior.

THE DIFFERENTIATION OF GOALS

In the course of an individual's growth and development and as a product of his experience with the world around him, certain aspects of the perceptual field become more or less clearly differentiated from the remainder of the field because they satisfy need. These differentiations are called goals. Thus, certain objects, feelings, or events become differentiated as more or less related to the satisfaction of the basic need for a more adequate self. The newborn infant has few if any goals beyond the extremely undifferentiated one of maintaining organization. In time, however, with the differentiation of certain objects, persons, and sounds, which accompany the satisfaction of his basic need, his goals become more clearly defined. In time, the goals differentiated by a particular individual may become permanent and characteristic parts of his personality and are evident in so much of his behavior that other

102

people are able to predict with great accuracy what he is likely to do in a given situation.

This goal differentiation is interestingly illustrated in the use of the word "Daddy" by a friend's young son. The child's first use of this word was greeted in his family with much pride in his accomplishment until it was discovered that thunder arriving at mealtime was also "Daddy" to him! Apparently he had differentiated the word from the speech matrix as meaning a loud noise of which his father was but one producer. Similarly, a child's other goals become differentiated in the course of time with developing satisfaction from food, water, persons, toys, and the like. Even the concept of "mother" is not exempt from this process of gradual differentiation from the remainder of the field. Many a heartbroken mother has had the distressing experience of leaving her infant for a week or two and returning to find the child "does not even recognize his own mother!" Specific persons such as father, mother, sister, aunt, or grandmother, with the special meanings which our society attaches to them, take considerable time to differentiate.

In the course of differentiation of the child's goals from the remainder of the perceptual field, it is apparent that not all children will develop the same patterns. In fact, the opportunities and circumstances of growth present so vast a number of possibilities for differentiation that it is unlikely that any two individuals ever have identical goals. Thus, a very young child may differentiate a goal of "bed" as a source of security; while another may come to differentiate the same object as a place to play, to have a bowel movement, to be fed, or as a place of punishment.

Even where two children appear to have the same goals, it will probably be discovered on further examination that wide differences exist. In similar situations there cannot be like goals for different children because each one sees his situation from his own unique point of vantage. Even for identical twins in apparently identical situations this is true, for a moment's reflection will make it clear that each twin is a part of the other's environment so that twin A's environment contains twin B, but twin B's environment instead contains twin A.

Living in the midst of a particular family group the child will adopt the goals of those who are important in satisfying his need and, thus, he may become a Republican, a Methodist, an outdoorsman, or a gypsy, depending upon what is important to the people who surround him. This process of differentiating goals similar to (but not completely like) those of the group in which the individual moves gives a certain degree of continuity and similarity of goals among the various representatives of the same culture.

THE DIFFERENTIATION OF TECHNIQUES

It is probable that very little human behavior is the result of direct movement toward goals; rather it moves through a series of subgoals to reach its major goal of need satisfaction. If crossing the street to a friend's house is our goal, we cannot reach it without achieving certain subgoals in the process. For example, it may be necessary for us to descend the stairs, open the door, reach the curb, avoid a car, and so forth. Such chains of goals which provide the means of achieving adequacy we call techniques. During his growth, the child develops many techniques which make it possible for him to reach the goals he has previously differentiated. Techniques are methods of reaching goals and thus satisfying need. Like goals they are fundamentally designed to maintain or enhance the self. Everyone develops highly characteristic techniques. One person may characteristically placate people and win their good will by flattery; another may seek to attain self assurance by dominating and criticizing others. Our friends can usually recognize and identify the particular techniques that we are most apt to use—this is signified by the slang phrase, "He would!" Since behavior is usually best described in terms of its path, techniques are usually described in terms of the goals or the subgoals which they involve. For instance, reading, drinking, or movie going are typical techniques of escape from feelings of inadequacy, and the people who use them have as goals the acquisition of certain types of books, of liquor, or attendance at movies.

Techniques become differentiated in the perceptual field of the individual in the same manner as that described for the differentiation of goals. At first such techniques may be extremely generalized but with the passage of time they tend to become more and more refined. In any case, techniques are always the result of the individual's striving for need satisfaction. Thus, the young child who feels frustrated by someone and desires revenge or mastery over the object of his frustration, may at first be openly aggressive—fighting, kicking, and laying about him generally. In time, as he discovers that this technique does not bring real satisfaction of his need because of the violent reaction of others, he may come to differentiate a modified technique of attack upon a verbal level expressed, perhaps, in tattling, or verbally abusing the object of his aggression. Since even this behavior is likely to bring censure upon him as he grows older and, therefore, result in less satisfaction of his need, he may learn to modify his technique still further, as he discovers that he can reach the same end through gossip or undercover slander of his tormentor. Eventually he may even be able subtly to get others to do what he wishes while he remains in the background.

THE DIFFERENTIATION OF VALUES

We have seen that the process of differentiation of goals and techniques within the perceptual field is always related to need satisfaction. Some goals and techniques are differentiated as positive or satisfying and, hence, to be sought. Others may be differentiated as negative, destructive, or humiliating to the self and, therefore, to be avoided. In the experience of the young child these differentiations are made with a high degree of specificity, but before very long he begins to differentiate that some goals and techniques are more or less alike in their abilities to yield or inhibit need satisfaction. He perceives that some objects, goals, or techniques have similar properties; this differentiation of common value serves as a kind of frame of reference for making further differentiations. We call these frames of reference, which are more or less clearly differentiated in the perceptual field and serve as guides for seeking or avoiding values.

Whereas goals and techniques apply to specific aspects of behavior, values are differentiations of a generic rather than a specific character and, thus, affect a much wider field of behavior. For psychologists, social workers, teachers, and other students of behavior a person's values are, therefore, of great importance in understanding the behavior of others. When a person's values are known it often becomes possible to predict with great accuracy how he may behave in given situations. This use of people's values as important clues to their behavior, however, is not confined to psychologists or professional people. All of us become highly sensitive to the values of those around us in the course of our development. Very early we recognize the crucial character of values affecting a person's behavior. This provides us with guide lines to the behavior of others and makes possible a degree of prediction of what they will do. Even young children discover that "Uncle Joe does like kids" or that "mother doesn't want me to grow up" and are, thereafter, able to adjust their behavior in terms of these inferences.

It should not be supposed that all of an individual's values can be clearly and precisely stated by the individual. Values differ greatly in the degree of clarity with which they are perceived. Some values will be quite definite and precise in the individual's perceptual organization so that he may be able to express them aptly and succinctly in the symbolism of words. Others will be so vaguely differentiated that the individual may be quite unable to report the nature of the value determining his selection of perceptions. This latter state of affairs is illustrated in instances where outsiders may be able to perceive a value affecting our perceptions which we, ourselves, may be quite unable to identify clearly. It may also happen that an individual will lay claim to the symbol of a value acceptable to his social group but be so vague in his differentiation of its meaning that the value has little affect upon his behavior. It is a common thing, for example, to hear people claim to value democracy while behaving in most undemocratic ways.

Values will affect the perceptions of particular individuals depending upon the extent of applicability they seem to have to the behaver. Some values, for example, may be differentiated as applying only to a limited number of situations or goals. Such values might be a dislike of pickles, a disapproval of people who "scratch off" at traffic lights, or an appreciation of double camellias. Values may also be so extensive as to affect almost every area of one's life, such as a value which calls for respecting the dignity and integrity of people, or a concern for justice and fair play. There may also be any degree of applicability between these two extremes; for example, when a general value espousing the dignity and integrity of man is carefully circumscribed to apply only to one's own religious or national group, or when a specific value is extended to generalities and we assume "they must be nice people because they support the boy scouts."

THE PERMANENCE OF GOALS AND VALUES

When goals have been differentiated and have served to aid the individual to the satisfaction of need they tend to persist as a part of the field organization of that individual. The degree of this persistence is likely to be a function of the degree of differentiation from the remainder of the field. Generally the more the achievement of the goal serves to bring the organism to the satisfaction of basic need, the greater will be its differentiation from the remainder of the field, and the more likely it is to appear as a goal on future occasions. Almost any parent is familiar with the changes in an infant's behavior when he has been left with his grandmother for a week. On the child's return to his family he may have acquired new goals or techniques which he has learned brought satisfaction when used with "grandma." When he returns to his own home, these persist or disappear, depending upon whether or not they get results at home.

The more strongly goals lead to satisfaction of the fundamental need, the greater is the differentiation from the remainder of the field, and the greater is the likelihood of persistence. This is particularly well illustrated in connection with negative goals. Negative goals, which become differentiated in the field as objects to avoid, threaten the organization of the individual. His need, however, is to maintain his phenomenal self. Hence, such threats are likely to be very strongly differentiated— so strongly, in fact, that often a frightening object may be experienced only once to be avoided ever after. This may frequently be observed in childhood fears which persist far into adult life and may continue for the entire life span. Goals which seem to the individual less strongly related to need satisfaction are less clearly differentiated and easily displaced. I will give up the idea of going to the movies tonight when friends drop in to see me, since going to the movies was only mildly related to making me feel adequate anyhow. Ask me to give up my job, my wife, or other goals of vital importance to me and my reaction will be very different.

A second major factor contributing to the permanence of goals and values has to do with the selective effect such differentiations have upon perception. The emergence in the perceptual field of any goal or value determines to a great extent what related matters are likely to be differentiated thereafter. The possession of any goal or value has both a narrowing and expanding effect upon capacities for differentiation. The person who has differentiated "country music" as desirable and valuable, and "long-hair" music as boring and unpleasant has made a differentiation which cannot help but affect his behavior and further experience. Having these values he will avoid concert music and listen to hillbilly songs. This effectively closes him off from some kinds of experience while at the same time it opens up new possibilities in the area he has learned to value. The decision to become a school teacher probably shuts the door to the possibility of becoming a great physician but it opens up vast new areas of exploration unknown to the physician. By controlling the opportunities we have for further perceiving, the differentiation of goals and values tends to perpetuate itself in our perceptual fields.

The Effects of Goals and Values on Perceiving

Once established, goals and values have intimate effects upon perceiving. Indeed, the peculiar patterns imposed upon perception by goals and values produces much of the uniqueness of behavior we have come to describe as the individual's personality. The goals, values, and techniques we have differentiated as leading to need satisfaction serve us thereafter as reference points to the achievement of adequacy. Once clearly differentiated, they consequently exert a selective effect on later perception, and thus, they markedly affect behavior. As a consequence of this crucial relationship, many psychologists have been led to experiment with the effects of goals and values upon perception, and a vast literature has accumulated on this topic.

Perhaps the most striking and commonplace examples of the effects of values upon perception are to be found in the differing perceptions of men and women. The two sexes in our culture often have widely differing values which, in turn, have selective effects upon the perception of the two groups. Men brought up to value machinery are often appalled at the lack of care and respect given mechanical equipment by women. Similarly, women raised to be deeply sensitive to social and interpersonal matters are sometimes shocked at what seems like unthinking, unfeeling attitudes of men. Many a hostess has been distressed by the tendency of her guests to drift into male and female groups where similar values make communication easier. Several interesting researches have demonstrated that women seem to depend more on visual frames of reference in orienting themselves to the world around them, while men rely more heavily upon kinesthetic and tactual experience.

The effect of values on perceiving may also be observed in hypnosis wherein subjects may, for the sake of controlled experimentation, be given values they have not previously held. Subjects fond of fruit juices, for example, may be told they detest such things and, thereafter, under hypnosis may be observed to react with disgust at the sight of fruit juices. It is even possible to reverse the subject's normal aversions; for example, a subject who dislikes dogs can be instructed that he is quite fond of them. We have already observed in an earlier chapter how food deprivation affects the kinds of perceptions people have under semi-starvation conditions.

Much of modern psychological diagnosis relies heavily on the use of various types of projective tests. All of these tests provide more or less structured materials or situations to which the subject responds. The assumption is that whatever meaning he puts into such materials must be related to his own perceptual field. In the Thematic Apperception Test, for example, he is asked to tell a story about a picture, the details of which are purposely quite vague and ambiguous. Therefore, whatever story the subject tells, he is projecting into the picture from his own personality or experience; the skilled interpreter is thus provided a sample of some of the subject's meanings. In perceptual terms such tests make it possible to explore the individual's perceptual field with particular reference to the goals, values, and techniques important in his unique economy. These tests have been subjected to a great deal of experimentation, so there seems little doubt that they can provide us with important data about perception. What concerns us at the moment, however, is only the fact that the tests demonstrate so effectively the selective effect of the individual's goals and values on perception.

In an experiment in which subjects thought they were about to see words related to animals, they read sael as seal, and wharl as whale. The same subjects expecting to see words related to boats saw sael as sail and wharl as wharf. Several experiments have demonstrated that people perceive words of greater personal value more quickly than those of less importance to them. In our society certain four- and five-letter Anglo-Saxon words are strictly taboo, and experimenters have demonstrated that the reaction time to such words is considerably greater than the reaction time to less value-laden words. Even skin color may be seen as darker or lighter depending upon individual values. In one experiment, for example, Negro students saw the skin color of popular school principals most nearly like that they personally preferred, while the skin color of unpopular principals was seen as close to what the students disliked. There seem to be no aspects of perceiving unaffected by values. Study after study has demonstrated this intimate relationship.

The effect of values upon perception has important implications in all types of social problems. It has been shown, for example, that persons whose values favor a certain event or outcome tend to expect such desired outcomes. Thus the same poorly clad man may be seen by pro-labor observers as a "forgotten man" and an object of sympathy, while anti-labor observers see in him a "wastrel getting just what he deserved." Prejudice, group conflict, and break-downs of moral judgment and communication are frequently the unhappy societal products of unfortunate, personal values. Persons with strong values tend to perceive events in terms of their values, and therefore, they are more likely to see things as black or white than neutral observers.

We have already seen in the previous chapter how goals and values are affected by the culture in which the individual is raised. Once established such values continue to affect the perception of people throughout their lives. The great social problem we face in the desegregation of our public schools is vastly complicated because people raised in different cultures have differentiated different goals and values. These goals and values, in turn, affect the ways people are able to perceive the very same data. The dynamics of value development and change lie at the very heart of our great social problems and are the primary data of sociologists, social psychologists, political scientists and others interested in social change. More adequate understanding of human values is essential to the solution of our great human problems.

GOALS AND VALUES AFFECT REASONING AND LEARNING

Goals and values have important effects upon reasoning and learning. I remember the Kentucky moonshiner to whom I once administered the Wechsler-Bellevue intelligence test, who could not tell me how many pints there are in a quart although he had certainly been taught this fact in his early schooling. Knowing that my client did a considerable business in bootleg liquor, I framed the question differently asking, "Well, how do you sell your liquor?" He smiled tolerantly and replied, "Oh, boss, I just sell it by the jugful!" In his community to have done otherwise would have been to risk bankruptcy. In a culture where a jug is the standard container for spirits, there is no need to know about quarts.

In a fascinating series of studies on human reasoning, Maier demonstrated how the values people hold may interfere with their ability to solve problems. Given two sticks and a clamp and instructed to make a hat rack some subjects were unable to solve the problem, apparently because they could not differentiate the clamp as a hook. Others, used to seeing pliers as a tool, were unable to solve problems which required the use of the pliers as a pendulum weight. Deep-seated cultural values have a considerable effect on learning. College students from Southern states. for instance, show more distortion in reasoning where ethnocentricism, or racial attitudes, are involved than students from Northern states who do not have such strong values. Another experimenter has demonstrated that positive and negative values affect students' learning of psychology.

Students who have values similar to the values of their instructors seem to get higher class marks than students whose values differ from the values of their instructors although their marks are based on objective tests derived solely from textbooks.

GOALS AND THE LEVEL OF ASPIRATION AND INTERESTS

There seems almost no limit to the variety of ways in which goals and values affect behavior. (Even the hopes, aspirations, interests, and objectives toward which persons strive will be determined by the goals they have differentiated in the perceptual field and the strength of the values which individuals attach to them.)For example, I have for several weeks been working hard on this manuscript and resented almost every intrusion to the extent, on occasion, of resenting the very work which is the source of my livelihood. Other goals have arisen at times, but almost all of them have had to give way before the impelling force of finishing this book. And this would be expected since I am aware that one's prestige in psychological work is very largely dependent upon one's publications. To suggest the possibility of spending the afternoon at an exhibition of Ming china vases would be unlikely of any response, because it would not be consistent with the way in which I regard myself at this time, nor would it seem related to my most pressing current goals. The things toward which people aspire will, in the final analysis, depend upon the degree to which they perceive goals as contributing to the maintenance and the enhancement of the self.

The kinds of interests people hold are also a function of the goals and values that seem important to them. We are interested in what serves to satisfy need. (As long as goals and values lead to need satisfaction they remain important to us and we are interested in the objects or events they represent. When, however, such goals and values no longer provide us with feelings of adequacy, new interests arise as expressions of shifting patterns of goals and values.)A good example of this may be seen in the child learning to roller skate. Other children like him skate, and to maintain and enhance his phenomenal self he, too, wants to roller skate. When he puts on his new skates, however, he finds skating much harder than he had expected and, probably, Mother Earth less comforting than he had been led to believe. But the reactions of those about him are encouraging, and he is told that he is doing well. This evaluation is at variance with what he feels, but it results in further efforts and more commendation while he is developing his skill. He is interested in learning to skate. Eventually the time comes when he has developed some degree of skill and regards himself as able to skate or, even, as a good skater. Now, however, the commendation and plaudits of others are likely to be far less strong or frequent and his ability to skate is taken for granted. Much of the satisfactions involved are lost. Unless others have taken their place, it is likely that his interest and desire to skate will disappear.

Observations of this sort of behavior have caused people to think that we are interested in the things that are problems to us, and that we are likely to lose interest when they are no longer problems. This seems partly true and there is good reason for it. The feeling of personal adequacy derived from any accomplishment is always enhanced if there is a possibility of failure. The things we know we can do are less challenging than those we have yet to try. The adolescent who can't dance when this is expected in his group feels learning to dance is a problem; the adult who desires to keep up with his neighbors finds figuring out how to get a new car an interesting problem.

It sometimes happens that people set goals for themselves which are far above their capacities. This is characteristic of some college students. College students must have been fairly successful at school—otherwise they would not have reached college. Having been successful and having differentiated goals and values in these terms by comparison with less brilliant contemporaries in the grade- and high-school years, many come to college expecting to operate on the same level. College students, however, are usually more highly selected, and the competition for grades is much keener than the student has ever experienced before. His level of aspiration being higher than the conditions of his new environment warrant, he sets goals in terms of what was previously normal for him. This may bring him lower grades than he is accustomed to receiving. Not to reach his goals is a threat to his organization. He may insist on them all the more strongly because they are under attack. He may even raise them. Until he can readjust his level of aspiration according to his new environment or call upon new reserves of energy and application, he is likely to suffer severe feelings of failure and inadequacy. Fortunately, most college students are able to make this adjustment in a reasonable period of time. Occasionally, however, people with unrealistic goals are unable to accept their own limitations and continue to strive for impossible objectives for most of their lives.

The Effects of Techniques on Behavior

Like goals and values, when techniques are differentiated they become an integral part of the organization of the individual's perceptual field and are subject to the primary forces in its operation. We have already seen how this organization tends to persist and how techniques, as a part of the field, also persist depending on the degree to which they contribute to the satisfaction of the basic need of the individual. Furthermore, once differentiated, techniques tend to remain as a part of the fundamental organization. Thus, certain techniques of reaching goals may become characteristic ways of behaving for the individual depending upon his unique concept of himself. For instance, the child who regards himself as a "tough guy" is likely to act in accord with this concept and is likely to meet many situations in an aggressive manner even though this may lead to less ultimate satisfaction for him. It becomes what he considers the appropriate method of arrival at his goals for the sort of person he considers himself. Often the "radical" adopts certain kinds of behavior as appropriate for himself and shuns conformity in any form. The amusements of more conventional people are inconsistent with his conception of himself and are rejected for behavior he considers more sophisticated. In time, the techniques we differentiate as appropriate for reaching our goals may become so characteristic of us as to be integral parts of our personalities. Other people expect us to behave in a certain way. Indeed, others may be able to predict with great accuracy how we will behave in a given situation.

NEGATIVE TECHNIQUES

In the course of his development, everyone comes to differentiate both positive and negative techniques and to utilize or avoid such techniques, depending upon whether or not they lead to the satisfaction of his basic need. Thus, the child who has been subjected to extremely severe punishment administered consistently over a period of time may differentiate techniques for reaching his goals by meekness or fawning as attention-getting devices while, at the same time, he differentiates aggressive tactics as techniques to be avoided at all cost because they result in behavior on the part of others which threatens the self. Such techniques may, furthermore, become an integral part of the individual's field organization with, or without, repetition. While the majority of techniques probably become differentiated with repeated behavior, they are not a direct result of repetition. Indeed, they may become effectively differentiated with no repetition whatever. In traumatic or highly emotional situations, for example, a single incident may result in a relatively fixed differentiation.

CONSISTENCY OF TECHNIQUES

In everyday life many people utilize the same techniques to arrive at many different goals. The go-getter may find aggressive techniques so useful in satisfying his needs that he applies them almost indiscriminately to every activity. He runs down his business rivals, dashes from place to place, hangs a DO IT NOW sign in his office, bids wildly in his bridge game, and may even apply such techniques to courtship as he attempts to sweep a girl off her feet. Still another person may find a technique of suppression best leads to the satisfaction of need; he may literally swallow his pride, even when he is seething within. The opposite aspect of the relationship of goals and techniques may also be possible wherein an individual may utilize differing techniques to arrive at the same goals. A woman seeking to build up her self-esteem may try to accomplish this by gossiping about her neighbor, buying herself a new dress, powdering her nose, striving for a career, or raising ten children. For both goals and techniques the determining factor of persistence lies in the degree to which it is differentiated, either positively or negatively, with respect to need satisfaction in the total field. Techniques or goals most clearly differentiated in the individual's field organization will tend to persist.

The same is true of techniques

CLASSIFICATION OF TECHNIQUES

Attempting to maintain and enhance the self, a person differentiates many techniques in the course of his experience which lead more or less adequately to achieving this end. For the most part these techniques are concerned with what the layman calls boosting self-esteem which is another way of saying the enhancement of the self. For practical purposes it is convenient to classify such behavior in a number of categories. It should be recalled in any such classification, however, that there are probably no pure cases of the use of any of these techniques. Techniques can be roughly divided into three major categories: (1) mastery over people or things, (2) identification with a powerful individual or membership in a potent group, and (3) physical change in the body organization.

Need Satisfaction by Mastery over People

THE USE OF FORCE

Techniques for achieving mastery may be found in many devices, ranging from the completely obvious to some so subtle as to pass unnoticed by the ordinary observer. Among the most primitive of such techniques is, of course, the use of physical force. Beating people with a club to gain mastery is by no means obsolete in our society and, although our methods are often more refined, the essential principle still exists. Direct aggression or the wielding of superior force is still a major means of achieving mastery for many individuals. Although physical size is no longer as important for mastery as it once was in adult society, the clenched fist is still a favorite technique even of many adults for achieving their fundamental goals. The technique may be disguised as legal action, social position, employer-employee relationship, or presumed superiority of knowledge as in a teacher-pupil relationship, but the principle is the same. The force compels although the club has given place to more genteel devices. Coercion is used to achieve the end even though this coercion may appear in verbal or other symbolic dress. Almost anyone, after failing to achieve his ends by more subtle means, may explode in anger. This is true of nations as well as of individuals, so that force of arms is necessary to achieve the goals which diplomatic pressure has failed to gain.

From the social point of view the use of direct aggression is a particularly bad technique because it sets up a whole chain of aggressive reactions in which each victim attempts to forget his own humiliation by using his power to humiliate others. A man who has been humiliated at work may come home to bully his family; his wife, to regain her lost self esteem may nag at him and the children, who, in turn, seek self enhancement by aggressive behavior in the neighborhood.

SYMBOLIC TECHNIQUES OF FORCE

In order to maintain its own organization, our society frowns upon the use of direct physical aggression by its members. Therefore, in the course of his growth, the child may acquire symbolic techniques which are quite as effective as the more primitive techniques. Symbolic aggression is frequent in clinical practice. For example, a little girl brought up by her mother to be a "little lady," was referred to a clinic because she persisted in wetting her bed. The child had talked the matter over with her mother and agreed that one of the things she might do would be to refrain from drinking water after four in the afternoon. The following highly revealing conversation with the family cook took place that same evening:

CHILD: (*coming into the kitchen*)   Elsie, what do you suppose would happen if I were to drink four glasses of water after supper?
ELSIE: Oh My! Why, I suppose you'd wet your bed.
CHILD: (*vainly trying to suppress her delight*)   Oh dear! That's just what I did!

Apparently the child had learned to utilize bed wetting as an aggressive technique against her mother. It is a common observation that such aggressions are often expressed in play. A large part of a child's time in play therapy may be spent in such symbolic activities as breaking balloons, playing "accident," knocking down block houses, or making clay figures of mother and father to be smashed to bits.

While adult symbolic aggressions are less obvious than those of the child, they are, nevertheless, often effective. Veiled techniques, such as gossiping, whispering campaigns, excessive blame, or even "constructive" criticism may fool the average observer but should not deceive the psychologist. If people cannot satisfy their needs by one technique they must turn to more successful techniques. There are a great many ways to enjoy mastery over others that may be more or less disguised, and they are often not only accepted in society, but encouraged. Games of all kinds are primarily played to give the participants and their supporters an opportunity to enhance the phenomenal self by defeating worthy opponents. Ordinary polite conversation may be used by the speaker to build up his self concept by dominating the listener, while the listener is waiting for his opportunity to act as an authority. The humorist, Strickland Gilliland, once said "If you see one man talking to another on the street, it is not a conversation. The other fellow is just waiting to tell about his operation." As a rule, large informal gatherings break up into small conversational groups where people do not have to wait so long for an opportunity to talk.

DEMONSTRATIONS OF SUPERIORITY

Kidding, ribbing, hazing, and practical joking are further methods by which the individual may take advantage of a social situation to feel superior to a victim. Since it is essential that either the victim or the audience be important, ribbing, like gossip, is often a kind of flattery, and many young girls are well aware that the insults of preadolescent boys are really compliments of a rare character.

Ostentatious spending and making of gifts are other ways in which people find a sense of superiority or worth. Among the Indians of British Columbia, the most important way of acquiring such superiority was the public presentation of gifts which the humiliated recipients were unable to repay. Families lived in destitution for years and individuals sold themselves into slavery to secure the means of recovering their prestige by outdoing their enemies. This potlatch custom eventually became such a menace to the community that it had to be forbidden by the Canadian government, probably to the relief of all concerned.

Another interesting variation of the use of subtle aggression is often seen in clinical experience with the negative or dawdling child. This is a form of aggression put to effective use on a larger scale by Ghandi and his followers in India and has been used in our own country by labor in strikes and slowdowns in industrial disputes. In all of these cases the technique is useful to gain a feeling of power over those who would force one action or another on the individual or the group. The adoption of a negative "you can't make me do it" attitude is a potent means of regaining feelings of competence and independence.

Perhaps the most subtle and least recognized function of mastery in operation is to be observed in a certain type of leadership dependent upon the skillful manipulation of people. This kind of leader is able by means of subtle techniques to gain mastery over the group, and to sway individuals to his way of thinking without their being aware of the techniques in use upon them. He may thus be able to obtain mastery by planting ideas in fertile ground, by selectively praising his fellows' ideas and, if he is a good leader, he may even succeed in doing so while he remains completely in the background.

Need Satisfaction Through Mastery of Things

Fortunately for the human race, domination of others is not the only way in which people may build up and reinforce their phenomenal selves. Another way of achieving adequacy lies in the mastery of things. To achieve this end it is necessary that the individual have a feeling that he is able to do something that gives him power over his surroundings. At all ages, but especially in childhood, the control may be destructive, as when young children enjoy themselves by banging on the kitchen pans or tearing up the family magazines. Much of the pleasure in building with blocks comes from the pleasure in knocking them down. Among adults, too, such destructive attempts at mastery are not uncommon. Building contractors report that their men enjoy wrecking a building more than building one, probably because the destruction is faster and more spectacular thus providing greater awareness of personal power. Many an adult remains a fire-engine chaser long after childhood, and crockery-breaking booths are always popular at carnivals.

For most adults, however, it is probable that the greatest amount of mastery over things is gained from constructive behavior. The engineer takes pride in his bridge, the architect in his building, the small home owner takes pride in garden walls built with his own hands. It is probable that the inexorable breakdown of jobs to more and more minute details in assembly-line production has destroyed for many workers their opportunity for mastery over things as it was possible in the production of a complete article. As a consequence some industries have attempted to reverse this trend by giving workers opportunities to work with larger units of the product involving a number of processes, or some industries have turned to assigning a group to produce a unit leaving workers free to rotate the tasks within the group as they please. It is probably true that handling of giant machines in modern industry contributes to the feeling of power for some people. Many a man has probably not yet lost his secret desires to command the monstrous huffing-and-puffing railroad engine, which so impressed him in his youth.

Need Satisfaction by Identification with Others

The second group of techniques to maintain and enhance the phenomenal self is so universally used and is so different from the dominating techniques we have been discussing that some writers contend that it must be due to a completely independent motive, which they have called the need for social approval. For a number of years, during infancy and childhood, we are almost completely dependent upon adults for the satisfaction of our physical and psychological welfare. Children who win the good will and attention of adults are fed, clothed, and comforted. Children who incur ill will are punished, ignored, or humiliated. As a consequence, the sympathy and good will of other people are vitally necessary to every child, and much of this feeling of need for others survives into adult life. From a practical point of view, the adults in our present highly specialized economy are almost as dependent upon other people as children. Even if this were not true, it is not likely that any adult having had the normal experiences of childhood could fail to gain a feeling of security and self assurance from the approval of people he respects.

If the technique of seeking the approval of others were motivated, as many suppose, by an independent drive for social approval, then the approval of one person or group should be as satisfying as the approval of another. If, on the other hand, it is simply an alternative method to secure a consciousness of self worth, then we should prefer the approval of the individual or membership in the group which seems important to us. There is evidence that this is the case. People often travel long distances to see famous personages and, thus, identify themselves with success. The politician who said "If you can't lick 'em, join 'em" was simply expressing a common type of behavior. Even in times of peace, the less powerful members of a group tend to seek security by identifying themselves with a powerful group or a dominant leader. Large numbers of Canadian mental patients identify themselves in one way or another with the United States and claimed to be American secret agents, relatives of the President, or to be receiving messages from the "hearts of the American people." No similar preoccupation with Canada is apparent among patients in American hospitals. In the United States such attempts at identification with a strong group or leader are by no means uncommon; advertisers find that it pays to have their products endorsed by public figures. Many people like to use the soap their movie idol uses or smoke the cigarette approved by an All-American fullback.

Individuals tend to seek self esteem through winning the approval of groups or individuals they believe to be important but they tend also to withdraw from groups which no longer contribute to their feelings of importance. It is a common observation that, when an individual has achieved the highest office in an organization, his ardor for the work of that group often disintegrates rapidly and he may soon have broken his relations completely.

Need Satisfaction Through Body Change

A third major group of techniques seems to be that in which the individual seeks some form of bodily change which contributes to redefining his phenomenal self in a more favorable, or less humiliating, light. Often the excitement attendant upon thrills results in increased body tonus which is exhilarating to the individual and is likely to give a feeling of increased power and effectiveness. Such boosts to the self esteem are often consciously sought and paid for in amusement parks. Indeed, in some people this feeling becomes almost a permanent goal in life and much of their time is spent in a search for thrills. Gambling is a familiar example of this device. In the excitement and anticipation of winning or losing the gambler is able, for the moment, to forget his feelings of inadequacy and incompetence and gets a feeling of heightened tonus which is exhilarating and gives him a feeling of power. Lotteries and policy games are most popular in the poorest sections of cities, apparently because to many people they furnish the only hope of achieving property or power. Economically these people cannot afford to gamble, but psychologically they cannot afford not to gamble.

TECHNIQUES, ROLES, AND TRAITS

The techniques people differentiate in the search for need satisfaction, we have seen, often have a high degree of stability and provide a measure of predictability for behavior. The roles people play in life are to a great extent the product of the particular techniques an individual has differentiated as appropriate for a person like himself. Thus, seeing myself as a teacher, I have differentiated certain kinds of behaviors as proper expressions of that self. In a similar manner, I have differentiated certain kinds of behavior as appropriate to my conception of myself as an automobile driver, a father, a husband, an American, a friend, a Floridian, etc. The techniques which each of us differentiate are always an expression of our fundamental need to maintain and enhance the self. As a consequence of this close connection, techniques are often valuable clues to the self structure of the individual. When we know enough about his techniques it is often possible to make remarkably good inferences of the nature of the self to which an individual's techniques are related.

From the point of view of the outside observer the characteristic behavior produced by the individual's pattern of techniques, goals, and values provide the basic clues to understanding his personality. When we wish to describe another person we usually do so by describing his traits. We describe people, for example, as a devoted father, a fine swimmer, a hard drinker, or a person of great sensitivity and feeling, depending upon what we have observed about him. These traits are the manifestations of the individual's techniques of achieving need satisfaction as they can be observed by the outsider in overt activity of one sort and another. They are the means most of us use in daily life to describe other people.

Psychologists often find it useful to describe human personality in terms of traits. For many purposes it is enough to know that individuals are likely to behave in a particular fashion under given circumstances. Industrial psychologists, for example, may use observations of the ways in which people typically behave to develop more efficient production techniques or decrease fatigue and tension on the job. For more precise understanding of human beings, however, the trait approach to personality has more often than not proven disappointing. Traits describe what is characteristic of an individual's behavior but they are by no means an accurate indication of what a particular individual will do in a particular situation. The same techniques may have quite different expressions in behavior on different occasions. The teacher who knows she can help children by communicating her affection for them soon discovers that this communication must be quite different for little boys and for little girls, and even for individual little boys and girls.

Behavior is always related to the purposes of the behaver. Thus, a trait appearing at one time may not appear on another occasion even in what seems an identical situation. The teacher who today conveys her appreciation and interest in a child by praise and commendation may the next day keep him after school for punishment, not because she loves him less, but because her immediate goals have changed. Traits though they are often useful in describing behavior are likely to break down as criteria for prediction. Of much more value for the understanding and predicting of behavior are the individual's purposes expressed in his goals, values, and techniques of behavior.

Behavior we observe in others, like the symptoms of disease or the rumble of thunder in a storm, are but the external manifestations of dynamic processes within the system we are observing. Sometimes, it will be enough to deal with such surface indications. For deeper and more precise understanding, however, it will be necessary for us to penetrate behind the behavior trait to more dynamic factors in the unique character of the individual's personal self and the goals, techniques, and values through which this self is expressed.

CHAPTER 7

The Development of the Phenomenal Self

THE most important complex of differentiations in the individual's perceptual field is his phenomenal self. What a person thinks and how he behaves are largely determined by the concepts he holds about himself and his abilities. If a man believes he is Napoleon, he will act like Napoleon or, at least, like his concept of Napoleon. How we act in any given situation will be dependent upon (1) how we perceive ourselves, and (2) how we perceive the situations in which we are involved. The self is the most stable portion of the individual's phenomenal field and is the point of reference for everything he does.

As discussed in Chapter 3, human beings are continually and insatiably engaged in a never-ending attempt to achieve an adequate self. In view of this fundamental need, the self perceptions we possess have a tremendous role in determining every behavior. Indeed, the phenomenal self is so important in the economy of each human being that it gives continuity and consistency to his personality. It provides the central core around which all other perceptions are organized. When the individual's phenomenal self is understood, the various and diverse behaviors of people become consistent and predictable. The very perceptions we are able to make at a particular time are dependent upon the concepts we hold about ourselves and our abilities. Self is a basic variable affecting and controlling perception.

Human beings have, of course, always behaved in terms of some kind of understanding of the self. The use of the concept of self in the behavioral sciences is, however, comparatively recent. William James devoted a chapter to the self in his *Psychology*, published in 1890, and Freud developed his concept of the ego at about the time of World War I. Although these men pointed the way to fascinating possibilities for the understanding of human beings, a considerable period elapsed before the concept came into its own. It is only within the last twenty years that the self has been given serious attention as a basic tool of the behavioral sciences. Today, many psychologists have adopted the concept and it is currently the subject of a vast body of theory and experimentation.

What Is the Self?

The word self, in its dictionary sense, is a word we use to describe, or refer to, a particular individual, i.e., some unique personality we wish to single out from the rest of mankind. It is a term referring to a specific person and has been indispensable in the historical development of man as a conscious and thinking entity. When we wish to go further and describe the characteristics and attributes of a particular, given self, however, the job becomes a more complex and difficult one, for a self can be observed from innumerable frames of reference. A self may be described from the point of view of any number of people, including the individual himself.

What the particular qualities of a "real self" are, of course, we can never know, for the self can only be understood through somebody's perceptions. These perceptions may be more or less close approximations to the real self but surely they will never be entirely accurate. Unless it is more precisely defined the self is not very useful as a scientific construct. In fact, the question of whether a real self exists or does not exist is primarily an academic or philosophical question. It is probable that no one can observe a self—his own or anyone else's—directly. To understand human behavior, however, it does not seem necessary to do so. The ways in which the self is perceived can be studied, and that is all that is necessary for us to deal effectively with it.

Concepts of Self

The ways in which the self may be described are practically limitless. Individuals may see themselves as men or women, children or adults, Republicans or Democrats. More specifically, a particular individual may see himself as George Jackson, owner of a 20-foot sailboat, who lives at 627 Blackmoor Street, Alleghany, Missouri. These are descriptions which serve to differentiate the self from all other selves. They make it possible to distinguish a unique individual out of the mass of humanity. Each of us is possessed of a large number of such ways of describing and distinguishing ourselves as unique among other people.

These are descriptions of the self which the individual shares with others. People also have many other ways of seeing themselves, which are of little importance to outsiders but are the particular property of the individual himself. There may even be concepts of the self in a particular person which would be highly surprising to others. It is possible for a person to have concepts of himself completely at variance from the ways in which he is regarded by other people. George Jackson, whom we have mentioned above, may see himself also as a ukulele player, a great wit, a neat dresser, or a young man. Outsiders might be quite surprised to know of these concepts George has of himself, if indeed, they were interested at all. They might even find it funny that George considers himself a great wit, recalling the times they have been bored with his long-winded stories. Concepts of the self may be held in common by the individual and by outsiders or they may be the peculiar perceptions of the individual's own private world of experience.

The perceptions people have of themselves do not stop with description alone. Much more important, people perceive themselves in terms of values. We do not see ourselves simply as fathers or mothers, students or cab drivers. We see ourselves as good fathers or mothers or as bad fathers or mothers. We see ourselves as A, B, or C students, and as successful or unsuccessful cab drivers. People regard themselves as attractive or ugly, as pleasant or unpleasant, as fat or thin, as adequate or inadequate, or in terms of a thousand other descriptions of greater or lesser degree of value or importance.

Whatever his way of describing himself, each individual has developed a large number of such perceptions. These more or less separate perceptions are called concepts of self. By concepts of self we mean those more or less discrete perceptions of self which the individual regards as part, or characteristic, of his being. They include all perceptions the individual has differentiated as descriptive of the self he calls *I* or *me*.

The varied ways in which an individual perceives himself are by no means of equal importance in the peculiar economy of a particular human being. The particular concepts of the self held by a person seem to vary in at least the two following important respects:

1. Some self perceptions appear to be much more central, or basically part, of us than others. If only because our society expects very different conduct from men and women we are reminded of our sex dozens of times a day. As a result, our concepts of ourselves as man or woman are usually related to the very core of being. They seem to the individual as

basic and fundamental truths. What is more, because they do seem so basic he resists with great vigor and determination any attempt to change them. Other concepts of the self may not be so strongly defended because they do not seem quite so important in our particular organizations. A man may regard himself, for example, as a man, as a Presbyterian, as a teacher, smoker, and as a driver of a 1956 Dodge. He may also regard himself as an American citizen, as younger-looking than his age, as a good tennis player, and as the life of the party. Each of these perceptions will seem to the individual to be more or less true of his personality and he will energetically resist attempts by an outsider to change such concepts, depending upon how basic the concept seems to him. Thus, it may be quite easy to change the above person's concept of himself as the driver of a 1956 Dodge. We could, for instance, buy him a 1957 Cadillac. If he does not particularly value his concept of himself as a good tennis player we might change it fairly easily if we could manage to get him thoroughly trounced a few times. Changing his concepts of himself as an American, as a teacher, or as younger-looking than his age, would be more difficult depending upon the value these concepts hold for him. Trying to change his concept of himself as a man would probably be next to impossible. Concepts of the self vary in the degree of importance or centrality they have in the person's peculiar economy.

2. Concepts of the self vary in sharpness or clarity. Perceptions about the self may range all the way from concepts which are vague and barely discernible to concepts which are clear and sharply in focus. This is a figure-ground relationship. The mother in the psychological clinic, for example, may be quite certain that she is Jimmy's mother. This is a perception of herself in clear figure. However, whether she is a "good mother" may be far less clear to her. Indeed, it may be this very lack of a clear concept of self that causes her difficulty. The adolescent moving through his teens is at first highly doubtful of his status as an adult and only slowly he comes to see himself in that role clearly and sharply. In his early adolescence he is not quite sure whether he is a man or a boy, and thus he behaves in terms of his confusion. Little by little as he grows closer to his twenties his concept of himself as an adult comes more and more sharply into figure and his behavior as an adult becomes more precise and predictable too.

The self is differentiated with greater and greater clarity throughout life. We are continually discovering who and what we are. Consequently, at any moment, we will find the concepts of the self held by a particular person to vary widely from concepts in clear, sharp figure to concepts so vague and fuzzy as to be inexpressible by the person himself.

The Phenomenal Self and Self Concept

Each individual has had literally hundreds of thousands of more or less discrete perceptions of self. This myriad of self perceptions does not exist in the perceptual field as a mere enumeration of ways of seeing one's self. Rather, the concepts of self which each individual possesses is an organization which is the individual's own private conception of himself in all his complexity. This organization of all the ways an individual has of seeing himself we call the phenomenal self. We might also call it the perceived self.

By the phenomenal self is meant the individual's own unique organization of ways of regarding self; it is the Gestalt of his concepts of self. Whereas the concepts of self about which we have been speaking describe isolated aspects of the person, the phenomenal self is the organization or pattern of all those which the individual refers to as "I" or "me." It is himself from his own point of view. The phenomenal self is not a mere conglomeration or addition of isolated concepts of self, but a patterned interrelationship or Gestalt of all these. It is the individual as he seems from his own vantage point.

In Fig. 15 we have diagrammed the perceptual field representing all of an individual's perceptions by the circle A. The perceptual field, as

Fig. 15.

we have seen before, includes all of a person's perceptions, including those about himself and those about things quite outside himself, the not self. Within the total perceptual field we may think of a second and smaller circle B, including all those perceptions which an individual has about himself irrespective of their importance to him. This circle encompasses all those perceptions of self in a particular situation which we have called the phenomenal self. It will be recalled that the perceptions of self vary widely in their importance or centrality in the personality. Many of our concepts of self have little or no immediate value to us at a particular moment. Thus, if one turns his attention to his little toe, he can become quite keenly aware of that member of his body and regard it as a distinct part of himself. This perception may have little real value, however, in understanding any very large or characteristic aspects of a person's behavior. The phenomenal self is the self in a given situation.

To describe the organization of those very important or central perceptions of self involved in a great deal of the individual's behavior, it is sometimes helpful further to differentiate the perceptual field to include only those perceptions about self which seem most vital or important to the individual himself (diagramed in our figure as Circle C). We call this organization the self concept. In this way he may extract from the phenomenal field those particular concepts of self which are such fundamental aspects of his phenomenal self that they seem to the individual to be "he" in all times and at all places. This is the very essence of "me" whose loss is regarded as personal destruction. The Indian brave who conceived of himself so completely as a man that he maintained those perceptions even when dying at the stake is an example. Whatever these concepts are for any individual they are the very core of personality. The self concept is the self "no matter what."

Raimy, who first defined the self concept in 1943, said of it: "The Self concept is the more or less organized perceptual object resulting from present and past self observation . . . [it is] what a person believes about himself. The self concept is the map which each person consults in order to understand himself, especially during moments of crisis or choice." The self concept serves as a kind of shorthand approach by which the individual may symbolize and reduce his own vast complexity to workable and usable terms. The self concept represents for the individual his generalized self, just as the fifth grade teacher may describe "fifth grade children" in terms of her experience of them. In using such terms she recognizes that the children she refers to are quite different individuals, but to talk about the group as a whole it is necessary to symbolize them in some fashion. Just so the individual uses the self concept as the symbol or generalization of self which aids in perceiving and dealing with self. It is his attempt to reduce his self organization to its essence so that he may be able to perceive and manipulate it effectively.

THE PHENOMENAL SELF AS INFERENCE

This shorthand description of a complex self is helpful to outsiders, too. Psychologists, for example, frequently find the self concept a useful construct for studying individuals, because it represents the most stable, important, and characteristic self perceptions of the individual. The self concept can be used as a convenient approximation of the personality of his subject. In this way the psychologist is able to achieve an amazingly accurate prediction of an individual's behavior in a wide variety of settings. Though we may sometimes use the self concept as a convenient device for understanding the individual, it should never be forgotten that people always behave in terms of the *total* phenomenal field, never in terms of an isolated part. The self concept is a useful approximation of a larger organization; it is not synonymous with it. The self concept is never a sufficient explanation of behavior by itself. The phenomenal self as a discrete *physical* entity does not exist. Like the concept of the atom or the concept of electricity in the physical sciences, the phenomenal self is an inference which makes it possible for us to deal with a complex function not directly observable. The physicist infers from the behavior of the atomic pile the existence and relationships of the atoms within, or infers from the behavior of his voltmeters or ammeters introduced in the electrical circuit the nature and functions of electricity. In the same fashion the individual himself infers from his experiences who he is and what he is. He perceives of himself as tall or short, man or woman, liked or unliked, acceptable or unacceptable, able or unable, depending upon his experiences with the world about him, but most particularly from how people who inhabit that world treat him. All these perceptions contribute to his perception of himself, to his phenomenal self. To the individual himself the phenomenal self is always real; in origin it is an inference from his experience. The outside observer using the perceptual approach may also infer the nature of the phenomenal self or of the self concept from the nature of the individual's behavior.

From an objective point of view, the widely diverse behavior of any individual is likely to cause the external observer to feel that there is little or no consistency in the behavior he observes. It is the thesis of this book that this is only true when we observe behavior as an outsider. When we understand behavior from the point of view of the behaver it becomes clear that he is not acting inconsistently. Far from it. Although the phenomenal self is complex, it is by no means disorganized. Rather, it is a highly organized function which operates in consistent and predictable fashion. The activities which result from a given phenomenal self may represent varied and puzzling behaviors, but do so only when we fail to see the person in terms of his own perceptions of himself.

Characteristics of the Phenomenal Self

CLARITY AND CENTRALITY OF SELF PERCEPTIONS

Like all other perceptions the phenomenal self has the feeling of reality to the individual. His perceived self seems to him to be truly himself. However, it is probably not possible for the individual ever to perceive the total organization of his self perceptions clearly at any one moment. Rather, he perceives those aspects or concepts of self which emerge into figure from time to time as he goes about the daily business of satisfying his fundamental need.

CONSISTENCY OF THE PHENOMENAL SELF

Although the perceived self may include numerous concepts of self, it should not be supposed that the phenomenal self is a mere collection of self perceptions existing without relationship to each other. Quite the contrary is true. An organization, we have seen, is a relationship of things or events to one another. This is true of the phenomenal self as well. The concepts which make up the perceived self have a definite relationship to each other. The fact that the phenomenal field is organized requires a high degree of consistency in the perceived aspects of self.

This characteristic consistency of the self seemed so important to Prescott Lecky that he postulated a need for self consistency as the one basic need of the organism. He describes this characteristic as follows: "Immersed in an environment which he does not and cannot understand, the individual is forced to create a substitute world which he can understand and in which he puts his faith. He acts in consistency with the conception, derives his standards of value from it, and undertakes to alter it only when convinced by further experience that it fails to serve the goal of unity. Since this self-made scheme of life is his only guarantee of security, its preservation soon becomes a goal in itself. He seeks the type of experience which confirms and supports the unified attitude." For Lecky, "The goal for which the individual strives is the maintenance of a unified organization." This, he calls "self consistency."

It will be recognized that Lecky's position is similar to the one we have taken in this book. We have described the fundamental need of the organism as the search for adequacy. To achieve the adequate self, however, will require of the individual that he develop a high degree of consistency within his phenomenal self. An organized self must necessarily be a self-consistent one. It would be hard to conceive of a stable, effective, integrated personality characterized by inconsistency. Other things being equal, the degree of internal consistency in the phenomenal self will control in large part the degree of adequacy a particular personality may be able to achieve. The search for adequacy, then, must necessarily involve the individual in a search for self consistency as well.

One of the characteristics of organizations is that they resist change. The phenomenal self, as an organization, is also characterized by this effect. Casual observation of the behavior of the same individual in various situations would lead one to believe that the self undergoes wild and fluctuating changes in differing situations. What seem like wild and fluctuating changes in the phenomenal self, however, are in reality artifacts of the frame of reference from which they are observed. For example, the overbearing foreman who browbeats, threatens, and curses his men may become a fawning, obsequious lackey the moment the plant supervisor appears on the scene. At first glance it would certainly appear that his self has undergone a very decided shift in character. This appears true, however, only if we regard the matter externally. From the point of view of the foreman, his phenomenal self may have undergone no change whatever. Regarding himself as being of a level of competence, authority, ability, etc., greater than that of his workers but less than the plant supervisor, his behavior in the two situations can be observed to be a natural and expected outgrowth of such a concept in either case. There remains no necessity to infer any change in his phenomenal self in the two situations. If the self were newly structured by every momentary situation, any degree of consistency of behavior would become an impossibility.

STABILITY OF THE PHENOMENAL SELF

Once established in a given personality, the perceived self has a high degree of stability. The phenomenal self with the self concept as its core represents our fundamental frame of reference, our anchor to reality; and even an unsatisfactory self organization is likely to prove highly stable and resistant to change. This stability has been repeatedly demonstrated in modern research.

A rapidly changing self would not provide the kind of stable frame of reference the individual needs in order to deal with life effectively and efficiently. To be able to deal with life at all, he needs a firm basis from which to operate and the maintenance of his phenomenal self is essential. The very operation of his fundamental need leads to a high degree of stability in the perceived self. Anyone who has ever attempted to rebuild a child's feeling of competence once he has developed a concept of himself as incompetent and inadequate, can testify to the difficulty of bringing about such changes. Ordinarily it is only upon repetition of many experiences of adequacy and with much praise and encouragement that such a shift in the self concept becomes possible. Even in the traumatic situation of the man who has lost a leg in an accident or in battle, the redefinition of the self to exclude that lost member often requires an extended period and in some cases may never occur at all.

It is interesting that even a phenomenal self in which the individual regards himself as very inadequate, stupid, or inept will often be defended to the last ditch. Almost anyone knows how difficult it is to convince the person with severe inferiority feelings of his true level of worth. He is likely to be pleased by praise, even highly embarrassed, but continues to act in the same old ways. Any college counselor is familiar with such people who when told of a high score on a test, for example, profess that "there must be some mistake. That couldn't be me. Are you sure?" To accept such statements about themselves would require that they do things they do not feel able to do.

The very existence of the individual's need to maintain self imposes a selective effect upon his perceptions. Once the phenomenal self has become established, experience thereafter can only be interpreted in terms of that self. Thus all perceptions which are meaningful to the individual derive their meaning from their relation to the phenomenal self already in existence. Obviously this selective effect contributes to making the phenomenal self less likely to change. The woman who sees herself as misused and interprets all her experience in the light of that fact is not likely to change her position with any degree of readiness. So far as she is concerned, everything that happens to her is further proof of how right she was in the first place. In the same way, the child who feels rejected may interpret his parents' mildest rebuke as further evidence to prove what he already thinks—his parents don't love him. His resulting behavior may even cause his belief to come true.

The phenomenal self is an extremely stable organization which provides the core of human personality. Its existence gives stability and consistency to the individual and his behavior. To say that it is a stable function, however, does not mean that it is incapable of change. In a later chapter we shall want to examine more closely how such changes are brought about.

The Origins of the Phenomenal Self

In a previous chapter we have suggested that some kind of perceptual field exists for every individual even before birth. The precise character of this prenatal field must of necessity be closed to our understanding. We can do little more than speculate about what it must be like as the organism's awareness develops from the primitive "irritability" of the single cell to the awareness made possible by the highly specialized sensory equipment of the human fetus. Even with a highly developed nervous system, during the months the developing child spends in its mother's uterus its perceptions of the world outside its own skin must be extremely limited. Whatever the exact nature of this field, it seems probable that it is vague and undifferentiated, restricted for the most part to perceptions of pressure.

The major development of the phenomenal self begins with the birth of the child into the world of which he is going to become a part. It seems likely that James's description of the child at birth as existing in a "blooming, buzzing confusion" is a highly realistic description of the field of the newborn infant. As the infant is plunged suddenly into a world of sight, sound, taste, smell, and feeling, perception must be, at first, a hazy matter. We have some indication of what this may be like from the reports of persons who have been surgically cured of blindness. Suddenly plunged from a world of darkness into sight, such people tell us that at first they perceive only a blur, a kind of light-colored fog. Following this, they become increasingly able to differentiate items in their surroundings with greater and greater sharpness and detail. The experience of the newborn child is probably similar, although he begins, of course, with far less than adults recovering from surgery, for he does not have their highly developed senses of touch, taste, smell, and hearing or their vast stores of previous experience.

For the newborn only the most intense stimuli elicit responses. As time passes, more precise differentiations become possible and in the first few hours after birth the amount of stimulation necessary to bring forth a response may be observed to decrease rapidly. With sharper differentiation within the field behavior also becomes increasingly well defined.

It is a fascinating experience to watch a young child throughout the months after birth as bit by bit he organizes and orders his movements with greater and greater accuracy and precision. Research in child development, whether investigating sucking, locomotion, the Babinski reflex, or the ultimate development of language, illustrates this trend from generalized behavior to precise operation. Once his equipment for sensing taste, smell, sight, and hearing begin to function at birth, vast new potentialities for differentiation become available and the child launches upon a voyage of exploration destined never to cease throughout his entire life span.

This process of exploration and differentiation of himself and the world about him is the most outstanding characteristic of child behavior. Young children are notoriously "into everything." Everything must be examined, felt, and tasted with little or no regard for adult standards of safety or hygiene. Harassed adults attempting to keep up with a young child as he goes about this business develop a keen respect for the unceasing energy with which this process of exploration is carried on. Even when the child seems most quiet he may be deeply engrossed in some new and intriguing discovery not always approved of by adults, but fascinating and compelling to the young explorer. Nothing is exempt from the continuous process of differentiating, testing, and perceiving.

Among the earliest of differentiations made by the infant are those concerned with the discovery of self. This is not an easy or simple process, but rather a long and involved matter of exploration and discovery probably beginning with the differentiation of the distinctions between "me" and "not me." The earliest differentiations of self from the rest of the world are of a tactual, kinesthetic sort made as the child explores his physical being and its contact with his surroundings. As a result of such explorations he discovers such things as: These fingers are "me," but those blocks are not; all this within the confines of my skin is "me," but what lies outside my skin is "not me." Bit by bit as experience increases, the self becomes more and more clearly differentiated from the remainder of the phenomenal field.

While these differentiations are at first made slowly and with much difficulty, with the development of language the process of self differentiation is vastly accelerated. The development of language and the ability to communicate by means of words open new frontiers of experience. Language makes it possible to experience vicariously what would otherwise have to be experienced slowly and painfully. It even makes possible experiences one could never otherwise have. Few of us have the problems of queens or presidents, but we can differentiate and understand them through the spoken or written word. Language provides a "shorthand" by which experience can be symbolized, manipulated, and understood with tremendous efficiency. Above all, the possession of language vastly facilitates the differentiation of self and the world about.

The Development of the Phenomenal Self

We have already seen in a previous chapter how the physical body affects perception. As the child grows and explores himself, he discovers that he is male or female, tall or short, fat or thin, blond or brunette. Some of these perceptions he arrives at through his own explorations of self. Other concepts, particularly those which have to do with values, he acquires from his interactions with people about him. He discovers not only what he is, but also what he is not and attaches values to these discriminations. He perceives himself as "good" or "bad," adequate or inadequate, handsome or ugly, acceptable or unacceptable, depending upon the ways he is treated by those who surround him in the growing-up years. He learns about himself not just from his own explorations, but through the mirror of himself represented by the actions of those about him.

The self is essentially a social product arising out of experience with people. Although some of the individual's experience of self may be achieved in isolation from other people, by far the greater portion of his self arises out of his relationships with others. Human personality is primarily a product of social interaction. We learn the most significant and fundamental facts about ourselves from what Sullivan called "reflected appraisals," inferences about ourselves made as a consequence of the ways we perceive others behaving toward us. We learn who we are and what we are from the way we are treated by those who surround us; in our earliest years by our families, and in later years by all those people with whom we come in contact. People are continually discovering and rediscovering themselves from birth to death.

THE EFFECT OF THE FAMILY ON THE DEVELOPMENT OF SELF

No experience in the development of the child's concepts of self is quite so important or far-reaching as his earliest experiences in his family. It is the family which introduces a child to life, which provides him with his earliest and most permanent self definitions. Here it is that he first discovers those basic concepts of self which will guide his behavior for the rest of his life. In examining these effects of the family on the individual's self definitions we are likely to be particularly struck by the traumatic events in his family life: births, deaths, family upheavals or great periods of happiness or unhappiness. These are, of course, vital experiences in the life of the individual and have important bearings upon his perception of self. Of even greater significance, however, are the everyday interactions among the members of a family which often seem too prosaic and commonplace to notice. Yet it is these very commonplace experiences which probably have the deepest and most profound effects upon the development of the self.

Traumatic events in the lives of people are, of course, important, but we have often overvalued them. Far more important for most of us have been those events so commonplace that we do not even think to report them in describing ourselves. They may have been so trivial that we cannot even remember them when asked to recall them at a later date. Indeed, it may even be true that the traumatic events in our lives were only traumatic because of their relationship to the more fundamental and basic feelings about self acquired in the prosaic humdrum of daily life in a family setting. Thus, the death of a grandfather might be accepted with little or no trauma by the child who felt adequate and accepted in his family, but would seem an irreparable loss to the child for whom such a grandfather represented the only love and acceptance in a family setting where such treatment was lacking from mother and father.

The reverse may also be true. Events which sometimes seem to an outside observer as deeply traumatic and shocking may actually appear to the child who experiences them as only momentarily distressing if he has had much experience of adequacy in the everyday interactions of his family life. Fundamentally well-adjusted youngsters show a surprising ability to take even the most shocking experiences in stride with an aplomb that seems almost callous to adults. Some years ago the author worked with a 12-year-old girl brought to our psychological clinic for examination following a sordid attack by an elderly man in her home community. The parents of the child were fearful that she had suffered some irreparable psychological damage as a result of this experience and brought her to the clinic for study. To the amazement of everyone, after complete psychological study and a number of play-therapy sessions we could only conclude that the child had suffered no major permanent damage. She was a thoroughly normal 12-year-old, poised and charming as she could be. When asked, she discussed her unhappy encounter simply and matter-of-factly with the staff. She expressed a wish that it had never happened, described her assailant as "that nasty old man," then turned her attention to the more interesting business of present projects and events. Her experiences in her family had apparently provided her with so basic a feeling of adequacy and worth that she was able to accept even this shocking experience without being crippled by it.

THE FAMILY PROVIDES EARLY EXPERIENCE OF ADEQUACY OR INADEQUACY. The child's family provides the earliest experience of the individual's adequacy. As the child is successful or unsuccessful in making his way in his family, as he is loved and cherished or rebuffed and rejected, the infant experiences his first perceptions of adequacy or inadequacy. This is strikingly illustrated in some research with very young children. Even in the first few weeks after birth, deeply rejected children become listless, refuse to eat, and seem to "pine away." They behave as though they felt completely inadequate to deal with life, as though the struggle to live were just too much. Spitz, who studied hospitalized children, found similar striking examples of deep feelings of inadequacy and despair even in very young infants neglected by parents for long periods of time.

In his interaction with father, mother, and siblings, the young child begins his differentiations of self as liked or unliked, wanted or unwanted, acceptable or unacceptable, able or unable, worthy or unworthy, adequate or inadequate. These are the kind of perceptions through which the individual is able to symbolize his own degree of self actualization. The more positive self definitions he acquires, the greater is the feeling of adequacy and need satisfaction; and, conversely, the more negative self definitions he acquires, the more frustrated and unhappy he becomes. Experience later in life may change the concepts developed as a product of family living but never easily or quickly. The most basic of such self concepts may be so deeply rooted in the individual's organization that they cannot easily be changed even by the most drastic of later experiences.

It is seldom that families consciously and purposefully set about the business of creating feelings of adequacy or inadequacy in a child. Rather, these feelings arise as a product of the interactions of the various members of the family often motivated by quite opposite ends than those produced in the child. Ordinarily the self concepts differentiated by the child are acquired quite without regard to parental motives. It sometimes happens, for example, that parents with the best of intentions set such high goals for children as to give the child a feeling of incapacity and unacceptability because, try as he may, he can never seem to achieve the goals his parents set for him. If too long continued, the child may eventually reject his family and their values completely. Such feelings may persist to adult life where they produce behavior which causes other people to describe him as "lacking confidence," "having an inferiority complex," "lacking ambition," or "afraid to take a chance." The concepts of self differentiated by the child are the product of his personal experience of events and may have little relationship to the motives and intentions of those who surround him.

THE FAMILY PROVIDES EXPERIENCE OF ACCEPTANCE. The feeling of adequacy provided the child as a result of his early experience in his family contributes as well to his capacities for acceptance of self and of others. One can, after all, only deal with those aspects of self of which he is aware. Facts about self which the individual is unable to accept into awareness cannot be assimilated in the perceptual field; and if not part of the field, they do not affect behavior. It is only the self which the individual can accept which provides the basis for his behavior. The person unable to accept the fact that he does not know cannot listen to advice. The entertainer beginning to slip from public acclaim may be unable to accept this fact and so behave in ways quite inappropriate to the facts of the matter as perceived by other people. The accurate and realistic acceptance of self is essential to effective living. People unable to accept themselves are under serious handicaps, because they must necessarily deal with life from false or inadequate premises.

The capacity for acceptance is closely related to the individual's experience of adequacy. Generally speaking, the greater the feeling of adequacy, the greater the capacity for acceptance of self and of others. The origins of this capacity, like the child's earliest experiences of adequacy and inadequacy, lie first in the kinds of treatment he has been accorded in his early family life. Here it is that children first experience whether or not they are acceptable or unacceptable human beings. The very young child is so completely dependent upon his family and so exclusively confined to their company that the kind of acceptance or lack of acceptance he experiences from them is likely to have long-lasting effects. Children can accept what is acceptable to those they feel are important and must reject what seems unacceptable to those with whom they are highly identified.

This early learning of acceptance is illustrated in the case of "Edith Moore," a young woman with whom the author worked some years ago. Miss Moore had a shriveled hand, but so carefully had she kept it hidden that until she came for counseling help I was quite unaware of her handicap, despite the fact that she had been in one of my classes for a year. She was almost totally unable to accept her hand as part of herself. For years she had never been able to order food in a restaurant which would have required bringing her hand into view above the table. She had never owned an evening dress or gone to a formal party because evening dresses do not have pockets. Though she was confronted many times a day with the fact that her hand existed, she attempted to live her life as though it did not. This lack of acceptance was no accident. She learned not to accept her hand from the way in which she was treated by her family in the years of her growing up. Here are some of her own statements in the process of counseling, illustrating how this lack of acceptance was learned:

COUNSELOR: (Summing up what has gone before) So this has been kind of a secret that everybody knew, but nobody talked about.

CLIENT: Sometimes they tried to keep it even from me. I remember one day I overheard a telephone conversation from my aunt and they were talking about my hand. It made me feel terrible. I know my mother never told me, but I always thought that each child in the family, when he reached a certain age, was told not to speak of Edith's hand. They have never even spoken of it. It seems queer to me.

COUNSELOR: This makes you feel like a special case.

CLIENT: That's why I like to come up here to school. At home, we never speak of it. Sometimes I wish they would.

COUNSELOR: You think that if this thing had been brought out in the open as a young child that you wouldn't feel so badly about it.

CLIENT: Keeping it secret just makes me feel more uncomfortable about it. Another problem: I know that my family knows about it, but when I meet old family friends I always wonder—do they know or don't they? Will it be a shock to them, or do they already know? I don't know how to act.

COUNSELOR: Keeping this thing a secret has really seemed to make it more obvious to you.

CLIENT: I think so. I think that keeping it a secret in the family just brought more attention to it. I have gotten to feeling, from my family and the way I have been treated, that this thing has to be kept a secret. If my family thinks so, for heaven's sake, what will strangers think? It has to be hushed up and hidden. The way they acted, I don't know what to think.

COUNSELOR: Sometimes your family's attitude made you feel somewhat guilty.

CLIENT: Yes, it made me feel so much so that I have never even spoken of the matter. I guess that maybe I thought that because of my family's attitude of their never even speaking of it that maybe nobody is supposed to see it—like as if it was something bad in the family. I felt I was to blame.

THE FAMILY PROVIDES EARLY EXPERIENCE OF IDENTIFICATION. It is from his family, too, that the child first experiences feelings of self expansion and identification with others. In addition to his most personal self he differentiates also what is *my* mother, *my* father, *my* brothers and sisters, aunts or uncles, family or friends. These are more than mere differentiations of others; they are experienced more or less fully as real parts of the self, so that when they are lost by separation or death the individual often has the feeling that part of himself has been lost as well.

While at first such identifications occur through the individual's intimate experiences with his family, as he grows older his capacities for identification normally become much broader. As he becomes emancipated from his family and moves into the wider and wider world of adult life he may develop many other identifications. In this way he comes to feel that other people or institutions are also part of self and he accordingly behaves toward wife, country, church, fraternity, plant, or neighborhood as though these too must be maintained and enhanced. Such feelings of identification are extremely important for the existence of a coöperative and interdependent society. A society made up of persons who felt no identification with others would be an impossibility.

Though feelings of identification usually begin to develop in the family circle, this does not always occur. It is fortunate that most children grow up in families wherein they learn to identify with friendly adults, but some children are not so lucky and may be forced to make their way in their early years with little opportunity to form positive identifications. In later years they may in turn find great difficulty in developing strong feelings or identification with other people. Whether or not the capacity for identification develops depends upon the individual's success in finding need satisfaction in his interactions with those most closely associated with him. Families, friends, institutions, even nations are likely to become strongly identified with self when they contribute to feelings of adequacy, or may be rejected when they result in humiliation and failure.

THE FAMILY ESTABLISHES EARLY EXPECTANCIES. The family provides the individual with his earliest contacts with the society of which he is going to become a part. Families, as part of the culture, are the unconscious conveyors of culture to the new generations. It is from his family that the child first differentiates those goals, values, techniques, and ways of behaving acceptable to his society. From the way in which he is treated by his parents and early guardians he develops expectancies, concepts of what is appropriate behavior. He learns what is expected of boys, or girls, of children and adults, of *our* family, *our* church, *our* country, as distinguished from others. From those about him he learns, too, what is worth working for and what not, what one *should, ought, must* do to be acceptable to the world about him.

In addition to these fairly general kinds of expectancies, the individual also acquires expectancies of a much more precise character having to do with what is expected uniquely and more or less exclusively of him. He thus learns that "Sister is expected to do well in school but I am not." Or, "Joe can go around with anybody, but I have to go with the *right* people." Many of these kinds of expectancies are established very early in life and have vital effects upon behavior for years afterward. The closer they become associated with the individual's concepts of self, the more stable they become and the more difficult to change with the passage of time.

In later life these expectancies form the individual's level of aspiration. Depending upon the concept of self possessed by the individual, he will choose this goal or that as appropriate for such a person as he regards himself to be. The man who regards himself as a pretty good bookkeeper probably does not set a goal for himself to be President of the United States, nor does the successful physician adopt as a goal for himself retirement to a comfortable job as garbage collector. Whatever goals are considered worthy of the individual's consideration are dependent upon the way in which he regards himself and the kinds of self expectancies he has acquired in the course of his experience.

SOME EFFECTS OF THE CULTURE ON THE DEVELOPMENT OF THE PHENOMENAL SELF

To this point we have spoken of the development of the self for the most part as a product of the individual's experience with his family. The family itself, however, is a product and conveyor of the culture which produced it. Even the world of physical objects into which a child is born are subject to the particular interpretations of the culture, so that the phenomenal self becomes overwhelmingly the product of the culture.

Human beings are born into a culture and live in some sort of one the greater part, if not all, of their lives. Of course, it would be theoretically possible for one to develop a phenomenal self even if he existed entirely alone on a desert island. For practical purposes, however, the culture in which we move is so completely and inextricably a part of our experience as to overshadow almost all else in determining the nature of the concepts of self developed by each of its members. Even our definitions and values with respect to the purely physical aspects of our environment are left not entirely to our own experience but are colored, interpreted, and valued one way or another by the culture into which we are born, as they are interpreted to us by the acts of the people who surround us. Even the so-called "objective facts" which surround us are likely to be no more than the interpretations of the culture in which we are raised. Rain is seen quite differently in the farm community, where it tips the balance between success and failure of crops, and by the city dweller who regards it only as an interference with a planned picnic. Automobiles are seen quite differently by adolescent boys and their middle-aged fathers.

The inclusion by the individual of the meanings of his culture applies not only to things and events but to himself as well. The self concept of most people will be found to have many elements of similarity with what other people think of them. The child who is surrounded by parents, teachers, and friends who regard him as adequate and capable comes in time to adopt as his own much of their definitions of him. To regard himself as anything else would lead him into behavior unacceptable to his circle and would be unlikely to reach his maximum need satisfaction. The conceptual self is the product of the individual's experience, and since his experience almost always occurs in some cultural setting, it should not surprise us if the self has many elements in common with the individual's culture.

At first glance this would lead one to believe that the individual must always conform to his culture, but the concepts of self people possess are not always what one might expect from the culture they live in. Sometimes they may be quite different from what we would expect. We need but look about us to observe that many persons have developed meanings about themselves quite different from those we might expect from the cultures in which they move. Such differences in meanings may be the result of (1) a change in the culture or (2) a change in the self concept, or both of these.

CHANGE IN THE CULTURE

It must be remembered that the individual lives not in a single culture but in a whole series of cultures, at any moment. We might describe these as subcultures within a larger culture. At any moment a person may be living in a family, a school, a community, a church, a state, a nation, or a world subculture. What is more, the demands made on the individual by these various subcultures may differ very widely. Since the individual may be raised in a subculture, his self concept develops as a function of that subculture. When he moves from it into the larger group at some later date, his self concept may no longer be consistent with the demands of the new group. His actions may continue to be appropriate to the self concept he derived from the previous group and may appear to him to be completely adequate. To the new society his actions may appear to be "queer," "unusual," or even "quite daft," depending on how far they deviate from the expectations of the new social group.

The author remembers how impressed he was as a child by the old gentleman who was invited to the family Thanksgiving dinner. For years he had lived almost as a hermit. To the children he was an object of curiosity in his fancy dress suit, but the old gentleman was quite unconscious of his odd appearance. When the gravy boat was passed he disregarded the ladle and poured the gravy out, much to the astonishment of this young child. Obviously he was doing what he considered in his day to have been both "right" and "proper." He was completely consistent with himself and the culture he had known, but out of place in the one he had entered. Other examples of this sort may be observed in the adjustments of immigrants to a new country.

This inconsistency between the phenomenal self and the expectations of others offers an explanation for the increasing conservatism and rigidity to change observable in the later years of life. Having formed his self concepts in earlier life, the individual tends to maintain them. As life continues, the culture in the midst of which he lives undergoes changes. Thus its demands become different, while the self concept may remain more or less static. This has the effect of separating behavior from the cultural demand, and the individual is likely to feel threatened by the new factors in his culture. Under threat the need of the organism is to protect its organization, and its concepts become more strongly defended than ever. The likelihood of any momentous changes in the perceived self while under such attack must be extremely remote. It is not surprising therefore that age brings greater rigidity, since the very passage of time is likely to place the self under threat.

CHANGE IN THE SELF CONCEPT

The self concept may also change without any change in the culture. For instance, the teacher who has come to expect a particular behavior of a child may sometimes be quite bewildered by a sudden change in his behavior. Although the classroom situation may not have changed, the child's behavior becomes quite different because his concept of himself has changed. In a certain school Peter had always been a very shy and retiring child who never raised problems for the teacher. He was quiet, orderly, and gentlemanly at all times. In fact, the child seemed to be repressed and almost fearful of those around him. From Peter's own point of view, he regarded himself as being unimportant and pretty much incapable of dealing with his fellows in class. As a result he took a back seat and showed very little "push." Peter had been subjected to a great deal of bullying by a group of neighborhood boys of whom he was in mortal terror. He was unused to combat and did not know how to defend himself. Whenever he could he scurried off home through back streets to avoid his tormenters. One day, however, the gang caught him. They pushed him around. They called him names till Peter was wailing in tears. Finally, the leader of the gang knocked him down and sat on his chest while the rest of the boys stood around and jeered. Peter was terrified. When the leader threatened to kill him, however, it was too much and Peter lashed out in desperation. In a frenzy of fear he threw the leader from his chest and sailed into him. Much to his surprise he discovered himself beating up his tormenter, while the gang that had been jeering at him a moment before was now yelling encouragement. Having knocked the leader down in the first rush of his terror, he now pounced upon him, grabbed him by the hair, and beat his head on the ground. In a few moments the leader of the gang was sobbing with pain and begging to be let off. Peter let him go and was led from the field of battle as a hero. For months afterward the gang, impressed with his ferocity, treated him with respect. Peter's impression of himself changed too. He gained confidence in himself; he was looked up to and was no longer afraid. He became more active, got into more mischief, and even went so far as to defy his teacher in front of his new-found friends. All of this was puzzling to the teacher, who was unaware of Peter's new status. Peter's concept of himself had changed, while the school situations had not.

CHAPTER 8

The Effect of Self on Perceiving

The Individual's Frame of Reference

The phenomenal self is the individual's basic frame of reference. It is the only self he knows. Whether other persons would agree with his self definitions or not, the phenomenal self has the feeling of complete reality to the individual. It is himself from his own point of view. Wherever he is, whatever he does, the maintenance and enhancement of this self is the prime objective of his existence.

Gardner Murphy has described this feeling as follows: "To most men in most societies, the self may be full of blemishes, of sin, of incompetence, but it is the one beloved self, the lawgiver. In a fundamental sense, the self is right. My nation is right, my class is right, my family is right, and I am right. The altercation that follows an automobile collision and the account the driver gives later to his friends are hardly the primitive 'rage' that Watson traces to obstructed movements. They are portraits of the artist as the right kind of person; he has been insulted by the carelessness or incompetence of another driver who did not see what the traffic situation really was. The first postulate is that I saw the situation as it was; the accident was due to the fact that the other driver did not see it as I did." As the central point of the perceptual field, the phenomenal self is the point of orientation for the individual's every behavior. It is the frame of reference in terms of which all other perceptions gain their meaning. It is involved in greater or lesser degree in all perceptions. It provides meaning to what would otherwise be meaningless.

The self provides the frame of reference from which all else is observed. People are not really fat unless they are fatter than we. Negroes asked to judge skin color of other Negroes use their own color as reference. Even in regression under deep hypnosis the self "core" persists and individuals behave, not as a child, but rather as "self pretending to be a child." It has even been demonstrated that we discriminate our own forms of expression from those of others even when there is no "conscious" awareness that they are ours. Experiments which manipulate environmental cues in such a fashion that the relationship between the self and the external world is difficult to maintain are often so distressing to the subject that he may experience nausea. It is this separation of self from normal anchors in the environment which seems responsible for some of the nausea people experience in "sea sickness."

PERCEPTIONS ARE ORGANIZED AROUND THE SELF CONCEPT

Since the purpose of an individual's behavior is the satisfaction of his own need, the perceptual field is usually organized with reference to the behaver's own phenomenal self. The meaning of an object or event is thus his definition of the relationship between the object and himself. We have already seen in an earlier chapter that perceptions have a bearing upon the individual's behavior in the degree to which they seem to him to be related to the self. We are much more concerned about our own children than about others, about our school, our country, or our front lawn than we are about those relating to other people. The self is the individual's basic frame of reference, the central core, around which the remainder of the perceptual field is organized. In this sense, the phenomenal self is both product of the individual's experience and producer of whatever new experience he is capable of. Even when we are concerned with matters that have to do with other people, the degree of this concern will be roughly proportional to the degree to which we are able to identify with others. This is another way of saying the degree to which we feel they are also ourselves. When we feel identified with other people, it becomes possible for us to empathize with them and we can also experience the situation from their point of view. A situation then which is not dangerous to us may seem so because we recognize that it is dangerous to another. It seems fairly certain that this seeing the situation from another's point of view is not possible, however, unless some degree of identification exists. The different attitudes toward new weapons of people on opposing sides in a war is a case in point. Effective weapons introduced by the enemy are cruel and inhuman because they threaten us or our friends, similar ones introduced by ourselves are clever and humanitarian because they protect us and our friends.

All perceptions existing in the perceptual field acquire their meaning through their relationship to the existing self. It is only when events are perceived as having some important relationship to self that they are likely to produce much change in the individual's behavior. Thus most of us know all of the good reasons why we ought not to be prejudiced, yet most of us continue to be prejudiced in more or less degree. Most of us, similarly, have pretty fair notions of the kinds of things we should eat and the kind of care we should take of our physical beings to maintain the best of health. Yet this knowledge is likely to have little effect upon our behavior until such time as we discover the personal meaning of those ideas for ourselves.

THE PHENOMENAL SELF AND THE INTENSITY OF BEHAVIOR

Only when some relationship to self is perceived in any new event is it likely to have any marked effect upon behavior. The very meaning and importance of events is determined by the relationship perceived between them and the phenomenal self. Imagine for a moment all possible experiences as being arranged along a line, as in Fig. 16, from those which have a very close relationship to self at one end to those having little or no relationship to self (as perceived by the behaver, not an outsider, of course) at the other end. Now, keeping this diagram in

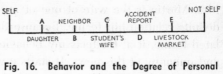

Fig. 16. Behavior and the Degree of Personal Meaning.

mind, let us suppose that I am driving my car to work on any morning. It is a pleasant morning and I am in no hurry. I am driving at a moderate speed along the highway, listening with half an ear to my radio. What is coming to my ears from the radio has very little relationship to me and has little or no effect on my behavior. I hear, for instance, the morning livestock quotations from the local stockyard. Since I am not a farmer, meatpacker, or buyer of meats, this information has little or no relation to me. It is information at point E on our diagram. Having no perceived relationship to me this information passes through my awareness with little or no effect upon my behavior. "It goes in one ear and out the other," as we sometimes say, and it does this precisely because I do not see that it has anything to do with me.

Now let us suppose that the next item of information which comes over the radio has a relationship to me approximately that of point D

on our diagram. As I drive along, the news report comes on and I hear the announcer tell of a very bad automobile accident which has just been reported at the corner of Fifth and Oak Streets. He goes on to say that a Mrs. Ethel Martin, who was driving one of the cars, has been taken to the hospital in very serious condition. I hear this information, and because I am a driver myself at the moment, it has somewhat more bearing upon me than the previous information about livestock prices. I perceive in this event a mild sort of relationship to self and I react mildly to it. I may say to myself, "Another serious accident. How awful!" I may even look about me uneasily for a moment or slow down the speed of my car temporarily. Because I do not perceive any very important relationship to myself, however, this item of information has comparatively little effect on my behavior.

Let us suppose, however, that this same item of information is perceived as having the relationship to me roughly indicated by point C on our diagram. Let us suppose, for example, that I know Mrs. Martin. I met her once at a tea last year. She is the wife of one of the graduate students in our department. Now the information which previously had little or no relationship to me is seen to have some definite relationship. Mrs. Martin is the wife of one of *my* students. She has a more or less definite relationship to me. Because this information is perceived as related to me, it also affects my behavior more markedly. I am distressed and unhappy at this news. It starts a whole chain of thoughts about Bill Martin, his family, his relations with the staff, his ambitions, background, and a thousand other details. The news occupies my thoughts for most of the rest of the way to the office and continues to affect my behavior even after I arrive there, for I talk to others about the matter. I may call the hospital. I ask questions about whether Bill knows about the accident or not and what we might do to be helpful. I inquire a bit among the rest of the staff as to Bill's financial condition with an idea that he may need special help in this emergency.

If Mrs. Martin were even closer to me, let us say, at point B on our diagram, it is possible that my behavior would be even more markedly affected. If, for example, Mrs. Martin were my next-door neighbor with whom our whole family had been on good terms for many years, the information about her accident would be perceived as much closer to self and the resulting behavior it set in motion would be much more extensive and personal. My very good friends are in a sense a part of me, and what happens to them is of vital concern to me. So, on hearing what has happened to Mrs. Martin I may be deeply shocked. I call my wife to discuss what we can do to help. I find it difficult to stop thinking about Ethel Martin all day long. I make plans with my wife and neighbors to take care of the Martin children, or to lend Ed Martin a car. When I get home I take in the wash Mrs. Martin left on the line, pick up the tools Ed left in his driveway, and congregate with my neighbors to discuss the details all over again.

Finally, let us suppose the information I hear over the radio has a relationship to me indicated by point A on our diagram. Let us suppose, for example, that Mrs. Ethel Martin is the married name of my daughter! Now the relationship of this simple piece of information has a vital and direct relationship to myself, and the behavior I exhibit as a result may verge on the violent as I forget about everything else and drive directly to the hospital!

Events acquire their meaning from the relations we perceive between them and our phenomenal selves. The perceptions we hold about self determine the meaning of our experiences. Generally speaking, *the more closely related an experience is perceived to the phenomenal self, the greater will be its effect upon behavior.*

This is an extremely important principle with wide implications for every aspect of human behavior. It is the fundamental problem of learning and explains why it is that so much of our schooling has had so little effect upon us. In a very real sense we might even define learning as the discovery of one's personal relationship to events or ideas. Most of us learned at one time the principal exports of Venezuela, but most of us have long since forgotten what these are, along with thousands of other similar bits of information whose relationship to ourselves was never made quite clear to us. Indeed, it is in this principle that we find the greatest single problem of education. Education has been highly successful in gathering information and making information available to people, but has been far less successful in helping people to make information so much a part of themselves that they would behave differently as a result. To be effective, education must find ways of helping people discover the personal meaning of events for them. Events which do not seem to have any relationship to self are likely to be ignored if, indeed, they are perceived at all. It is only when events are perceived as having some relationship to self that behavior is changed as a result of perceiving.

The Selection of Perceptions

Anyone comparing the ways in which he perceives with the perceptions of someone of the opposite sex can very quickly discover that men do not perceive in all things as women do. Nor do children perceive like adults, Americans like Russians, or schoolteachers like engineers. The self concepts we hold have a vital effect upon the ways we perceive. They determine the ways it is necessary and appropriate for us to behave and, as a result, the things we see, the ideas we note, and the objects we accept or reject.

At any instant, the things possible for us to perceive in any situation are almost limitless. Yet we do not perceive in any such chaotic fashion. What we perceive is always organized and has meaning, and that meaning derives from the phenomenal self. Men see what seems appropriate for men to see while women see what seems appropriate for them. In our society the use of taboo words is regarded a more serious offense for women than for men and this difference shows up when men and women are asked to report such words after they have seen them. Under these conditions men report more taboo words than women. People with low opinions of themselves underestimate their performance more than people with higher self concepts.

We need but to look about us to see thousands of examples of this selective effect of the phenomenal self upon perception. The same political candidate is seen quite differently by the Republican and the Democrat, and segregation is not the same seen by the Northerner or the Southerner. Professors do not see college-student behavior in the same way in which parents do, students do, or the city police do. Mr. and Mrs. Brown on the way home from the party discuss the people who were there. When Mrs. Brown asks her husband if he noticed "the dress that Helen was wearing," she may be quite annoyed to discover that her spouse did not notice Helen's dress at all. Being a man, there may have been other things about Helen more appropriate for men to perceive, however, which Mr. Brown did notice, but about which his wife does not think to ask him.

Little boys in our society are raised quite differently from little girls and come to see themselves quite differently as a result. When boys fall down and bump their noses, we are inclined to say, "Here, now! Little boys don't cry!" So little boys learn that it is not proper for boys to display their emotions. When little girls fall down and bump their noses, however, it is a very different matter! We rush to their assistance, pick them up, and comfort them as best we can. So little girls discover that crying is acceptable female behavior. In later life the results of these self concepts may make it difficult for the young wife to understand why her husband is "such an unfeeling brute" or may make it hard for a husband to understand why his wife "gets so upset over little things." The ways we see ourselves, once established, continue to select our perceptions throughout our lives.

The self even affects the relationships between the individual and other people through this selective effect upon perceptions. Harry Stack Sullivan, for example, pointed out: "If there is a valid and real attitude toward the self, that attitude will be manifest as valid and real toward others. It is not as ye judge that ye shall be judged, but as you judge yourself so shall you judge others." The principle that self acceptance is related to capacity to accept others has also been demonstrated in studies of counseling improvement. Even the individual's levels of aspiration are a function of the kinds of self concepts he holds.

We are only beginning to discover the tremendous importance of this fact in dealing with human problems. Every day brings to light some new and intriguing consequence of individual self perceptions. People behave in terms of the self concepts they possess, and this fact is tremendously important to anyone who must work with people in any capacity whatever. We are even beginning to discover that many, if not most, problems which persons bring to the psychological clinic are primarily problems brought about by unfortunate concepts of self.

In working with children who were poor spellers, for example, Lecky noted that otherwise normal children who were unable to spell seemed to make about the same number of errors per page in their written work *irrespective of the difficulty of the material!* When spelling tests were cut in half there were about the same number of mistakes on each half, again irrespective of the difficulty of the material. Lecky observed, furthermore, that such children did not make such mistakes in spelling when they were dealing with a foreign language. He concluded that these children must be spelling in terms of the concepts they held about their capacities as spellers. They were spelling in a manner consistent with the beliefs they held about their spelling abilities!

What is more, when methods were employed to help these children change their concepts of themselves, they learned to spell with little or no difficulty. Here is Lecky's own report of what can be done in this vein:

If we are able to change the self-conception which underlies this viewpoint, however, his attitude toward the material will change accordingly. With the resistance eliminated, he learns so rapidly that tutoring is often unnecessary.

Such a change in the pupil's attitude often results in improvement which is quite astonishing. A high school student who misspelled 55 words out of a hundred, and who failed so many subjects that he lost credit for a full year, became one of the best spellers in the school during the next year, and made a general average of 91. A student who was dropped from another college and was later admitted to Columbia was graduated with more than 70 points of "A" credits. A boy failing in English, who had been diagnosed by a testing bureau as lacking aptitude for this subject, won honorable mention a year later for the literary prize at a large preparatory school. A girl who had failed four times in Latin, with marks between 20 and 50, after three talks with the school counselor made a mark of 92 on the next test and finished with a grade of 84. She is now taking advanced Latin with grades above 80.

Two of the poorest spellers in the High School of Clifton, New Jersey, were used to demonstrate this method before a university class in psychology. Given twenty words to spell, one missed all twenty and the other nineteen. The school counselor, continuing the use of the method, reports that both are now excellent spellers and have taken up spelling as a sort of hobby. The results reported are taken from the work of three different counselors, showing that the method lends itself to general use in the school system.

Similar examples of the profound effects of the phenomenal self upon the individual's abilities to perceive accurately and effectively may be seen in any reading clinic. It is becoming increasingly rare in these days of periodic eye examinations and continuous checkups on child health to find youngsters unable to read because of faulty vision. Most of the cases coming to the reading clinic are poor readers who have nothing whatever wrong with their eyes. They are not unable to read in a physical sense, but are children who for one reason or another have come to *believe* they cannot read. What is more, because they see themselves as nonreaders, they approach reading expecting to do badly, and a fine vicious circle gets established which goes something like this:

Jimmy has been poorly taught to read and develops the feeling that he is not very good at reading. Because he *feels* he is a poor reader, he avoids reading as much as possible and thus avoids the very experience and practice which might make it possible for him to learn to read better. When asked to read, he does so, hesitatingly, without confidence, expecting to make mistakes, and he does. These mistakes are noted both by those around him and by himself and corroborate his impressions. His teacher, seeing him read so badly, may make the mistake of saying, "My goodness, Jimmy, you really don't read very well!" and send him home with a low grade on his report card—which proves what Jimmy has been thinking all along: "I don't read very well!" A very large part of remedial reading instruction is directed at helping children or adults to perceive more accurately and effectively not only the words on the printed page, but even more important, new and more adequate concepts of themselves!

THE CIRCULAR EFFECT OF THE PHENOMENAL SELF

This effect of the perceived self upon human behavior, it should be understood, is not limited to children who are unable to read and spell. A great many of us are the unwitting victims of our concepts of self in just the same way as the poor readers and spellers we have mentioned above. It is even possible that some of the readers of this book may be laboring under unfortunate concepts of themselves as unable to make a speech, do mathematics, drive a car, swim, or remember people's names. Indeed, this limiting effect of our phenomenal self upon perception sometimes produces great tragedies.

As Lecky has pointed out, we perceive in ways that are consistent with our concepts of self. A given phenomenal self perpetuates itself by permitting only such perceptions as are consistent with its already existing structure. People limited by their self perceptions behave in ways that seem to corroborate the self concepts they already hold. They seem almost to be "asking for" proof of what they feel about themselves, and indeed, they often get just what they ask for. The individual who, for example, feels that he is incapable of successfully making a speech perceives so many flaws in everything he does and turns his attention so intensely upon himself, expecting himself to fail, that he may stumble and falter or become tongue-tied with stage fright, which of course simply serves to demonstrate how right he was in the first place!

Perceptions are selected which are consistent with the perceived self of the behaver. Such selection occurs, furthermore, without regard to whether such perceptions seem to be complimentary or self-damaging in the eyes of an outside observer. It will be recalled that we have stated the fundamental need of all human beings is the maintenance and enhancement of the phenomenal self. Since the first need of the individual is to maintain his perceived self, perceptions inconsistent with what he believes are unlikely to occur because they would not fit his self structure. The girl who has a deep feeling of her own unattractiveness may feel we are cruelly baiting her when we tell her how pretty she looks. It seems inconceivable to her that we mean what we say. She may believe quite genuinely that we are "just trying to make her feel good."

There are literally millions of people in this world who are the prisoners of their own perceptions of self. Vast numbers of people believe they are able to do far less than they really can. As a result, they remain chained to unhappy, unproductive, and unsatisfying ways of life. Studies with various self concept scales at Vanderbilt University show that (1) patients are differentiated from nonpatients; (2) failures in paratroop training, from passers; (3) alcoholics, from nonalcoholics; (4) delinquents, from nondelinquents; (5) drop-outs, from stay-ins in school—all on the basis of self-concept. Can one conceive the kind of world we might achieve could we but find the means to release ourselves from the slavery of inadequate concepts of self? Here is a waste of human resources compared with which our losses in warfare or automobile accidents seem small indeed.

DISTORTION OF PERCEPTION

When individuals are confronted with events inconsistent with their self structure they may seek consistency of perception by doing violence to the facts. They may perceive a particular event in so distorted a fashion as to be almost unrecognizable to a disinterested outside observer. Thus, the senator who sees himself as a professional Communist hunter and savior of the nation may begin seeing Communists behind every bush or discover conspiracies where none actually exist. Labor and management in the midst of a strike often see events in a manner distorted beyond recognition by the onlooking public. Rationalizations, in which people may be found giving *good* reasons instead of *real* reasons for their behavior, are a form of seeking for better organization by which inconsistent events can be brought into closer harmony with existing self concepts. This is a form of self deception to which all of us succumb on occasion.

When it is unflattering to admit the truth, it is sometimes much easier to distort the perception enough to make it appear in a more flattering light. In our society the term "laboring" class carries distasteful connotations, so most people prefer to class themselves as "workers" rather than as "laborers." We can avoid the consequences of our mistakes by seeing them as none of our doing. We failed to make the meeting, not because we failed to start on time, but because the train was late, the streets were too crowded, or the clock did not go off. What is more, we may even believe this story! We would certainly object with vigor if anyone suggested it were not true!

Inconsistent or threatening events may also be dealt with by denying their existence entirely. A person confronted with a situation highly derogatory or destructive to his concepts of self may find it possible to maintain or enhance his integrity by the simple expedient of relegating the perception to someone else or denying its existence entirely. Thus, he may really not see what he would rather not see. The scientist who has spent his life proving the truth of a particular notion may be unable to accept the possibility of another solution and protects his phenomenal self by simply denying the new fact exists. Threatening derogatory comments about self can often be effectively dealt with by assuming they really refer to others. The teacher who asked the class to keep quiet was really directing her remarks "at Jane, not me!" In the next chapter we shall want to give more detailed attention to these kinds of distortions.

THE PHENOMENAL SELF AND ROLE

The concepts of self held by the individual determine the perceptions he will have of any particular event. Out of all the perceptions possible at any moment only those which are appropriate and consistent with the phenomenal self are available to him. This selective process determines the roles people play in any life situation.

The particular roles we feel called upon to play in life are the result of the goals and techniques we have differentiated as appropriate for us in those circumstances. Such roles will be appropriate to the phenomenal self existing for the individual at the moment. The professor and student act quite differently in the classroom. The behavior of each depends upon the concepts he has of himself and of the situation. The same person in the same situation at different times might feel called upon to make a speech, keep scrupulously clean, faint, tell a story, start a fight, or powder his nose (in preparation for a TV appearance, of course).

Though we speak here of "playing a role," we are not using the term in the theatrical sense of putting on a mask or playing a part not natural or appropriate to one's self. We use the term to mean simply the selection by the individual from his perceptual field of those goals, techniques, or ways of behaving that seem to him appropriate for the kind of person he feels himself to be in the situation he sees himself in. These roles will be the kinds of behavior that seem to him appropriate to or consistent with his phenomenal self in the situation.

Whatever roles we feel called upon to play will always be a function of need satisfaction. Whenever it becomes clear to us that our roles are inconsistent with our way of regarding ourselves, we will change them to others more likely to produce results and more consistent with our perceived selves. Changes of this sort may occur as follows:

The culture in which one moves can tolerate some differences in behavior from the expected. How much latitude it can tolerate will vary widely from situation to situation. When the individual's behavior passes this point of tolerance, it can no longer be accepted. The people about him begin to behave in unfriendly ways. At this point he may perceive that people do not act as he expects them to. His need satisfaction is frustrated. This results in feelings within him that "something is wrong." He feels unhappy and dissatisfied. In his subsequent search for need satisfaction he may differentiate new goals and techniques which bring him better results. This may or may not involve major changes in the phenomenal self.

Let us take as an illustration the case of the man who considers himself to be a skillful driver. With such a concept of himself the situation demands that he have no accidents. However, our driver may have differentiated his role as one of demonstrating that he is a skillful driver by an air of nonchalance, by taking chances, by coming close but not too close, and the like. One day he has an accident. This is terrible! An accident is not at all consistent with his concept of himself, and he does everything he can to place the blame elsewhere. What is more, his role as a "chance taker" has let him down and no longer leads to need satisfaction. His perception of this situation will lead him to the role consistent with his new perceptual field. He may develop a "drive with care" technique in place of the former "come close but not too close." This illustration assumes that only the required role is brought under doubt by our driver's accident. Of course, it will be recognized that if his concept of himself as a skillful driver is too greatly threatened, he may become not a safer driver, but a more dangerous one, to satisfy his need to defend his concept of self.

We have only begun to understand the importance of the phenomenal self in selecting and controlling human perceptions. In this chapter we have examined something of the role of the phenomenal self as a factor in perception. We have seen, too, that the phenomenal self is, itself, an organization of perceptions. In a later chapter we shall want to give much more attention to how the phenomenal self develops and its relationship to human feelings and emotion.

How the Self Concept Changes

As Raimy has pointed out, "the self concept not only influences behavior but is itself altered and restructured by behavior and unsatisfied needs." We have seen that the self concept is a stable organization. To say that it resists change, however, does not imply by any means that once it is established no further changes are possible. It is probable that throughout the lifetime of the individual change is constantly occurring in the self concept as he perceives the reactions of others to himself. In a sense, this is like learning about self through a mirror. He differentiates new aspects of self in terms of the reactions of those about him as they respond to his behavior.

The individual's own fundamental need requires change in his concepts of self. One cannot be truly adequate in a changing world without adapting to the changes going on about him. A static self concept existing in a moving world would soon be out of touch with the world about it. An adequate self must be stable but not rigid; it must be changing but not fluctuating.

THE NECESSITY FOR CHANGE

We have already suggested that the self is the product of the individual's experience. Each of us discovers who he is and what he is from events that have occurred in his lifetime, but most particularly from the ways he has been treated by those close to him in the course of his growing up. The process of self differentiation never ceases. We are continuously engaged in a process of self discovery, sometimes more rapid than others, but never completely absent from our experience.

The first step in the acquisition of new concepts must, of course, be some sort of experience inconsistent with existing self perceptions. The mere fact of living in a dynamic changing society imposes upon the individual a necessity for change. The varying roles the individual is called upon to play in the course of his interaction with his culture make it inevitable that sooner or later he will be subjected to experiences at odds with his existing self organization. This inconsistent experience may be perceived by the individual at any level of awareness. Thus, a person may be quite clearly aware that his new experience does not jibe with his existing phenomenal self. Perceptions inconsistent with existing concepts of self may also be experienced by the individual dimly and indistinctly as "doubt," as a vague feeling of tension, as a feeling that "something is wrong," "this is not me," or, more specifically, as a feeling of inadequacy or failure. This inconsistency may also be experienced in a positive sense as when one feels a sense of elation at a new skill mastered or new status achieved.

The ability to perceive difference between the self that the situation requires and the phenomenal self is dependent upon one's ability to see himself as others see him. As a member of a particular group or culture and responding to the world of things and events about him, the individual interprets these events in terms of his concept of the culture. Furthermore, he participates in this observation of himself, and he becomes more or less able to "see himself as others see him," or at least to see himself as he thinks others see him. When the author does not attend church on Sunday morning, he is aware of the fact that other people in his neighborhood look askance at such behavior. Similarly, the child as he grows older learns not only to behave in one way or another, but to evaluate his behavior in the terms of the culture in which he is reared. When he takes a piece of forbidden candy, he knows that his behavior is not acceptable. He not only behaves in a certain way but becomes able to interpret his behavior objectively, that is to say, in terms of the values of the culture in which he operates. This objective evaluation of his behavior in terms of the society in which he moves may or may not affect his concept of himself. For example, though he may evaluate his act of taking the candy as "stealing," he may continue to regard himself as a "good" boy. It is interesting that this is often exactly what seems to occur in many delinquents. Even though they may accept the label of "liar" or "thief" this acceptance is subject to the selective effect of the need for maintenance of the phenomenal self upon perception, which leads the child to defend himself by believing that his lying and stealing are "smart" or "good."

Unless awareness of discrepancy between the perceived self and cultural demand occurs, it is certain that the chances of change in the self are very slight. Almost anyone is familiar with examples of such lack of insight in everyday life. We see illustrations of this in such common expressions as, "Ye Gods! Can't he *see* what he's doing?"; "You'd think he'd know better"; and "Yeah! Just *try* and tell him." In such situations the individual's perceptions of self seem truly to have blinded him to the external evaluation of the facts.

Even the ability to see himself as others do is limited by the need for maintenance of the self concept. For example, in the illustration used above, the child who conceives of himself as good, but who has taken the forbidden candy, may deny in the most vociferous terms any suggestion that he is a "naughty" boy. Even though he "knows better" he must defend his concept of himself to protect his organization.

RESISTANCE TO CHANGE

The differentiation of new perceptions of self is comparatively easy when the economy of an individual does not already contain self perceptions in that area. Children who have not yet formed clear concepts of self in respect to a particular function are much more responsive to new experience than adults who have clearly differentiated phenomenal selves. When no preëxisting concepts of self interfere, the differentiation of new concepts is a simple concomitant of the kinds of experiences to which the individual may be subjected. Thus, repeated instances of success or failure in a particular area may quickly result in a self con-concept as adequate or inadequate with respect to that matter in a child who has no preëxisting concepts. The same experiences of success or failure experienced by a child who already has strong perceptions of self in this area may result in no appreciable change in the self concept whatever. Early experiences are likely to be highly important in determining the self concept because they limit the possibilities of later ones.

We have already seen in an earlier chapter that the fundamental need of each of us is to maintain and enhance the phenomenal self. The self concepts we seek to maintain, furthermore, are those currently in existence. The stability of the phenomenal self makes change difficult by causing us (1) to ignore aspects of our experience which are inconsistent with it or (2) to select perceptions in such a way as to confirm the concepts of self we already possess. As a result, changes produced by events inconsistent with well-differentiated self concepts are likely to be slow and laborious, if indeed they occur at all. What is more, the greater the importance of a particular concept of self in the economy of the individual, the more unlikely is any given experience to produce a major change.

A self concept resulting from many experiences over a long time may take an equally long time to change. The delinquent who has learned over a 14- or 15-year period that people cannot be trusted, or that he is unliked, unacceptable, an outcast, is not likely to respond at once to the first new or kindly experience the well-meaning teacher or social worker directs toward him. This is sometimes difficult for teachers and social workers to understand. A child with a long history of unhappy experiences develops a concept of self which is not easily open to change, and the harm that took so long to build up may take a long time to be reversed. A concept resulting from much experience requires a large amount of contrary experience to produce any basic change. Like a well to be filled up, even after a lot of dirt has been shoveled into the pit, the hole is still there and seems as deep as ever. One must shovel a long time before one begins to see any tangible results.

Persons who must work with deeply disturbed children often become discouraged and disillusioned because their well-meant acts of kindness or sympathy are rebuffed by the very children they seek to help. Their discouragement is the product of their own misunderstandings, however, and not a function of the perversity of those they seek to help. The child who has become a truly tough delinquent as a result of a lifetime of frustration, neglect, and failure develops a feeling about himself that he is unliked, unwanted, unacceptable, and unable. He has learned, too, that other people are not trustworthy. Expecting such a child to respond immediately to a single statement, "I like you, Jimmy," is like expecting to reverse Niagara Falls with a teaspoon! All his previous experience has taught him that he is unlikable and unacceptable and that people are untrustworthy—particularly when they say the very things he would like so desperately to believe but knows are not true. The worker who approaches such a child in this way had better be prepared to back up his spoken words by behavior, for he is certain to be tested if he is attended to at all.

Unfortunately, what often happens is something like this: The naïve or untrained worker approaches the child with a statement like that above, meaning in all sincerity what he says. The child finds such a statement completely inconsistent with his concepts of self and is impelled to reject the idea. At the same time, his experience has shown him that people are not to be trusted. As a consequence of these perceptions he rejects the proffered help or affection and may even attack or insult his benefactor. The astounded worker, in turn, seeing himself rebuffed so violently may conclude the child is incorrigible or hauls off and slaps him for his impertinence—thereby proving to the child what he has believed all along! Self concepts differentiated as the result of long and adverse experience do not change in a moment. Nor do they change as the result of words alone.

GRADUAL CHANGE IN THE PHENOMENAL SELF

While changes in peripheral aspects of the self concept may sometimes occur fairly quickly, changes in the important or fundamental concepts of self usually change only slowly and gradually. Such shifts may even occur so imperceptibly that the individual, himself, lacking the evidence of some striking event, may never be aware that any major change has occurred and assume that he always had the same attitudes he has now. Sometimes, too, the change in the way others treat the individual is so gradual that he is hardly aware of it and cannot put it into words. It is rare, for example, that the adolescent is suddenly conscious of being grown-up. In fact, it is more likely to be true that he still regards himself as a child far longer than is justified by his general development. This often results in behavior extremely annoying to adults who wonder why he doesn't grow up or "act his age." In time, with repeated evidence of his new status, however, most adolescents achieve a differentiation of the self more adequate to their new social status. It seems likely that gradual changes of this sort, as a result of repeated experiences, represent the most frequent type of change in the concept of self. Primitive societies, as a rule, handle this problem better by holding public ceremonies to dramatize the person's new adult status to the community and to himself.

Even changes in the self which at first glance seem to be quite rapid often turn out to be really very gradual. "Sudden" insights are more often than not likely to be based upon a whole series of prerequisite differentiations so prosaic as to be unnoticed but establishing the foundation which made the "insight" possible. A young woman who came for therapy with the author of this volume was the daughter of a minister. All her life she had led an exemplary life for the benefit of her family and the congregation. Going away to school and being forced at last to live her own life, she was deeply confused and upset. In the following series of statements from the eighth interview with this young woman, note how she struggles with her concept of herself and her relationship to the world about her as she attempts to differentiate just what she is.

Note, too, how a whole series of minor differentiations result finally in a "sudden insight" (shown in the last sentence in italics).

A couple of years ago I heard one of Dad's sermons in which he said, "A person has to like himself." From then on I took it for granted that I did. I decided I wouldn't change for anything—until this week, when I began wondering if I really did. I decided I liked myself but I also despised myself. Remember I told you I was afraid of failure because I had never really experienced it. Hooey! I've never really had anything but failure.

I've decided I'm a two-sided, two-faced person. I've always had to act one way although I felt another. I've always had to be something I'm not. I feel like a different person at home and away.

I'm not sure now what I'm like—I don't know what I am. I'm a man without a country. I don't think I ever knew really what I was. I give appearances, but down under I'm not that at all.

What is myself? It's funny how sure I was and now I'm not sure at all. I feel so miserable, afraid, and worried. I'm afraid of everything at the moment, but I can't find what I'm afraid of. I'm afraid to live like this for the rest of my life, but I'm even more scared as to what to do about it. I'm afraid even to think about it. The more I think, the more worried and scared I get—It gets worse and worse.

My problem is myself. Everything's wrong but I don't know what it is. What am I? I'm human, female, five feet seven, period. . . . I want to be sure but I'm not even sure of myself. . . . Maybe I know what I am but I'm afraid of it. I'm in a panic about myself.

I never felt I could be myself. I couldn't be because of my father's job. Now I know I must change myself, but what am I? I must know that.

This stared me in the face. I'm face to face with it, but I just can't do it. I keep getting this far and that's all. I'm stopped. One side of me says, "What can you do?" and the other side of me says, "You've got to, you've got to, you've got to." *It's a battle between what I think I am and what I really am.*

TRAUMATIC CHANGE

Changes in the self concept also may occur, but much more infrequently, with traumatic shocks in which the entire organization of the individual is threatened. This is well illustrated in the following case of a young woman from the files of a psychological clinic. As a child, she had been happy and carefree. She felt quite secure in her position and conceived of herself as a "good girl." One evening her parents had a rather wild party and she was put to bed with instructions that she was not to get out of it under any circumstances. Curiosity, however, was too much for her and she got up, lay on the floor and watched the evening's proceedings in the room below through a grating in the floor. Here she

fell asleep and in the night was overcome by coal-gas fumes in the
house. Later, she was discovered by her mother, who was furious at her
misbehavior. The child hung between life and death for several days,
during which time her mother did not let her forget that she would
never have been in that condition had she been a "good girl" and done
as she was told. This single incident was of such a traumatic nature that
the child completely revised her self concept and accepted her mother's
definition of herself. Even by the time she came to college, she was
thoroughly convinced that she was indeed a very "bad" person. She had
apparently developed a concept of herself as "guilty," and bowed to
her mother's slightest whim because she felt she "owed" it to her. She
gave up the career as a dancer she had wanted previous to her narrow
escape, to enter religious education in the hope of someday "saving" herself. Thus, under the traumatic shock of possible complete destruction,
a fairly violent change in the phenomenal self was brought about.

SOME CONDITIONS FOR CHANGE IN THE SELF

Whether or not a change is likely to occur in the perceived self seems
to be dependent upon at least three factors. These are:

1. The place of the new concept in the individual's present self organization.

2. The relation of the new concept to the person's basic need.

3. The clarity of the experience of the new perception.

The relation of the new concept to the total economy. We have already seen in the preceding pages that not all concepts of self have equal
value in the peculiar economy of a particular individual. Less important
concepts of self (from the behaver's own view, of course) will be more
easily changed by new experience than more central or personal concepts of self.

The relationship of the new concept to the subject's need. The phenomenal selves possessed by each of us are our nearest and dearest possessions. We have seen that the maintenance and enhancement of the
phenomenal self is the fundamental need motivating our every behavior.
It follows that new concepts of self which seem to the individual to
satisfy this need are more likely to be accepted into his personality
structure. Experiences which seem to the behaver to be threatening to
his existing concepts of self (even if such experiences seem enhancing
to the outsider) are likely to be rejected with great vigor. This means
that other things being equal, change in the self is most likely to occur

in situations which do not force the individual to self defense. Change can and sometimes does occur under threat, but generally speaking, the absence of threat increases the mobility of the self concept.

The clarity of the experience of the new perception. Change in the self concept can only occur as a consequence of some new experience of self. The more vivid such experience, the more likely is it to result in changes in self perception. In general, first-hand experiences are likely to be much more effective in producing self-concept change than are symbolic experiences. What happens to us directly is much more vivid and clear than the words that people speak to us. The experience of failing an examination, for example, is far more real than a parent's warning of the possibility of failure.

CHAPTER 9

The Availability of Perceptions in the Field

T O live effectively and efficiently in our modern society requires that we be able to cope successfully with the situations in which we find ourselves. It requires also that we be able to adapt and change our behavior to fit the varied requirements of the moment. In a world changing as rapidly as ours, anything less leaves us in danger of behaving inappropriately. The kind of adaptability and efficiency of behavior required for modern living can only occur if we have a field of perceptions maximally open to our use. Perceptions must be available to us when they are needed. Since behavior is a function of our perceptual fields, effective, efficient behavior can only occur from the widest possible field of perceptions. Whatever restricts and inhibits the perceptual field will have serious effects upon the individual's ability to deal with life.

Differentiation and Need Satisfaction

Whether or not satisfaction of need is possible for the individual will depend upon the differentiations he is able to make in his perceptual field. If it is necessary for me to be 20 miles from this spot in two hours, I shall certainly not be able to satisfy my need if the only means of travel I can differentiate is walking. Recently a new drinking fountain was installed in one of our college buildings. The need of the writer was momentarily frustrated until he had differentiated that *this* fountain worked by a foot pedal instead of the usual handle. How adequately we are able to satisfy our own and others' needs will depend upon the differentiations we can make in our perceptual fields. It is not enough, either, that perceptions should be *possible* in the field. They must also be available for use at the instant they are needed.

Whether or not it is possible for the individual to achieve need satisfaction will depend upon the level and character of the differentiations he is able to make at a particular instant. If these perceptions result in behavior adequate to meet life situations, need satisfaction is achieved and the individual feels happy, satisfied, and operates with a minimum of disturbance. If they are not adequate, he is likely to feel unhappy, frustrated, and ineffective and may even make his situation worse by the behavior to which such feelings lead him.

A great deal of the work of the clinical psychologist is directed at assisting clients to make more adequate differentiations than have previously been possible for them. The handling of parents who bring a bedwetting child to the clinic is a case in point. If they have perceived his bed wetting as "Jimmy is just being nasty," their behavior toward him is bound to be a function of that differentiation. Seeing his behavior as "being nasty," differentiations involving punishment, restraint, shaming, or "teaching Jimmy to behave" are likely to follow. On the other hand, if the parents can be assisted to perceive Jimmy's behavior in other and more adequate terms, their behavior will be quite different. Even their future perceptions may be vitally affected. This is exactly what the clinician attempts to do. If the parents can be helped to regard Jimmy's behavior as that of a child who is "upset," for example, a whole new series of differentiations and, thus also, of behaviors becomes possible. Viewing his trouble as a result of being upset is likely to lead, for instance, to differentiations as to the nature of what is upsetting the child and may even lead to new perceptions by the parents of their own behavior toward Jimmy. Such changed perceptions make more adequate behavior possible.

The effectiveness of behavior is a direct outgrowth of the differentiations the behaver can make in his perceptual field at the moment he is called upon to act. People cannot behave in terms of perceptions they don't have. We have seen in previous chapters how the phenomenal field is affected by the individual's fundamental need as this need is expressed through the phenomenal self, goals, and values. In the remainder of this chapter we shall examine further some effects of need on the availability of perceptions in the field.

NEED ORDERS PERCEPTION

The phenomenal field is continuously ordered by need. Any event which seems to the individual to be related to the satisfaction of need will have a strong effect upon the rest of the perceptual field. This change in organization normally has the effect of increasing the availability of perceptions related to the need. What affects need satisfaction compels attention and cannot be overlooked. All of us have experienced the way in which our attention becomes narrowed to some pleasant event which we may be experiencing or, perhaps, only anticipating. It is well illustrated by the ordering of our perceptions when we are preoccupied. Under a very high degree of concentration the area of the phenomenal field open to differentiation may be quite narrow, and perceptions will be confined to this fairly limited area. A commonplace example may be seen in our failure to differentiate the clock's ticking in a quiet room. As attention wanders from the book we are reading we may suddenly become aware of the ticking, which has certainly been available for differentiation all the time. As we narrow our field again to resume reading, the perception of the clock's ticking is no longer a major part of our field. This narrowing of the field can often be observed in clinical work as well. Clients are often found to be so anxious to achieve a particular goal that they repeatedly rush blindly straight for it, being unable to perceive any more adequate manner of approach. They are like the chicken, so intent on reaching the food dish on the other side of the fence that it keeps sticking its head through the wire instead of going around the barrier. In the same way, people who strongly desire respect may brag too much and so lose the very acclaim they seek. Had such persons been under less pressure they might have been able to perceive more effective although perhaps less straightforward techniques to achieve their goal.

Tunnel Vision

This narrowing of the phenomenal field when need is strongly affected has been called "tunnel vision," because the effect upon perception is very much like looking at an event through a tunnel or tube. The events at the end of the tunnel are clearly seen while surrounding events are blocked out of the field of vision. Because of this effect some perceptions are very clearly experienced. Other perceptions one might make in the periphery of vision if attention were not so closely oriented, however, become unavailable. While it is often a desirable and necessary thing to be able to concentrate upon a particular perception or series of perceptions, the narrowing of the field can also make it more difficult to perceive events from a broader perspective. A good example of this is the famous story of Archimedes' discovery of the principle of specific gravity. According to the story, Archimedes was commissioned by his ruler to discover whether a crown was truly of pure gold as it had been represented by the goldsmith. Archimedes was furthermore instructed that he must not harm the crown in the process of his investigations. This was a difficult problem and Archimedes wrestled with it for days trying to discover a solution, but to no avail. Finally, after long efforts he gave up the search. Then, suddenly, while he was relaxing in his bath, the solution to the problem came to him—he could weigh the crown in water and measure the amount of water it displaced! Archimedes had discovered the principle of determining specific gravity. While working intently his attention had been so narrowed he could not perceive the solution to his problem. Relaxed in his bath, his perceptual field was more open and he was free to perceive a new relationship of matter not understood before his time.

When Archimedes discovered the solution to his problem, the story goes on to tell us, he was so excited he jumped from his bath and ran naked through the streets crying, *"Eureka"* (I have found it!). Apparently any situation in which we are deeply involved tends to cause a narrowing of the perceptual field.

This narrowing effect of perception when interest is high and widening of perceptions when we are relaxed is not restricted to scientists alone. Almost anyone has had similar experiences wherein during periods of much straining to find an answer, no answers would seem to come, only to find that they popped into figure in our perceptual fields at some later moment when, perhaps, we no longer had need of them. This often happens when one is trying desperately to think of a name. The harder one tries the more restricted become the possible names that come to mind. Later, when we are no longer trying, the name may come to us with no trouble whatever.

A fascinating example of the organizing effect of need on perception is to be seen in a study carried out at two of our universities. Following a particularly rough football game between Dartmouth and Princeton in which some spectators believed they saw a number of evidences of "dirty" play, Hastorf and Cantril carried on an investigation in each school as to the ways in which the game was perceived by the respective student bodies. On each campus editorials appeared in the student papers deploring the "dirty" play of the other school while praising the home team for its sportsmanship and restraint "in the face of great provocation." Movies of the game were shown in fraternities on each campus and the men attending were asked to record infractions of the rules made by each team. As with the editorials, each side saw what it was prepared to see! There are, of course, limits to the individual ability to distort any specific datum, but in such a case the organization of the perceptual field tends to be maintained by distortion elsewhere. Members of a Midwest alumni chapter, failing to find evidence of the atrocities they had expected to see, complained that they had been fobbed off with a censored film!

ENHANCEMENT VALUES OF RESTRICTION OF THE FIELD

It should not be supposed that the restricting effect of need on perception is all bad. On the contrary, the ordering of perception has an important value to the organism, making it possible for him to achieve need satisfaction. When a speeding car is bearing down upon us as we cross the street, it is no time for us to be musing about the beauties of spring. We need to be keenly aware of the threat to our existence and to deal with it precisely and quickly. Concentration on a limited part of the field under threat often helps us to cope more effectively with emergency situations. But the same effect can also be a severe handicap to adjustment in our society. Many of the adjustments we must make in our daily lives are not simple or direct problems of our physical relationship to things. Rather, they often involve highly subtle and complex relationships, frequently not clearly or directly discernible. Our forefathers could become angry at a stalled mule and might even get results by kicking him. The angry driver who kicks his stalled automobile, however, may gratify his feelings but is unlikely to improve his transportation.

If perceptions were not organized we would be at the mercy of every momentary shift of attention. Our fields would make no sense without organization. We would be so continuously distracted by the myriad changes in the external environment to which we are exposed at every moment of our waking lives as to make it almost impossible for us ever to accomplish anything. Restriction of the perceptual field *may* have adverse effects upon our capacities to behave effectively. More often than not, however, it facilitates our adjustment and assists us in coping with life by ordering and organizing our perceptual fields so that we are not will-o'-the-wisps at the mercy of every fleeting perception which comes to us. Ordering and restricting the field makes concentration possible and assists in the achievement of need satisfaction. Some degree of organization of the perceptual field is an essential to the development of an adequate self.

It is, of course, possible that the selecting effect of need upon perception *can* be inefficient and harmful. Many good things become harmful when taken in overdoses. There are people in our society who seek so strongly for money, prestige, or power over other people as to overlook more important and lasting values. Absent-minded professors may be concentrating so much on a paper they are writing as to overlook the importance of their students' problems. Some men may be so busy making a living for their families that they never have time to get acquainted with them. Others may be so intent upon achieving power and prestige among their fellows that they unthinkingly grind other people beneath their onrushing wheels.

Restriction of Perception and the Experience of Threat

Perhaps most destructive to human personality is the restrictive effect upon perception brought about by the individual's experience of threat. We have seen that whatever seems to the behaver inconsistent with his existing perceptions of self may be experienced by the individual as threat. Whatever seems threatening to an individual in turn, demands attention and produces a degree of tunnel vision in the perceptual field.

Everyone has experienced this narrowing effect on perception under threatening circumstances. It is commonplace to hear one's friends report: "For a minute, I couldn't think what to say to him!" "Honestly, that truck looked big as a house!" "I just kept doing the same thing over and over. I couldn't see anything else to do." "I kept looking and looking and couldn't find it and later on, when I found it, I saw it had been right under my nose all along!" The author recalls even at this date, years later, the threat he experienced one evening during his college days. I was driving back to town at the end of a delightful evening with my "date" and another couple when suddenly one of the tires blew out and the car began to career wildly about the road. I can still recall, with much of the clarity it had when the accident happened, the picture that came to mind in those few moments fighting for control of the car. The perception I had most vividly in the moments following the blowout was a picture of myself standing before the father of the two girls, telling him his daughters were dead! The behavior of the car was far less threatening than facing the irate father! Fortunately, no smash-up occurred, but this was not due to the skillful handling of the car by the driver, for I made a number of serious mistakes. For example, though I "knew" better, in the stress of the moment I stepped hard on the brake, causing the car to swerve about the road. I had had blow-outs before, but with perceptions restricted to the relationship between myself and the father of my date, I was in no condition to behave in terms of more adequate understanding!

We do not need to rely upon testimonials concerning the effect of threat, however. The effect has been amply demonstrated in a large number of interesting psychological experiments. In a series of frustration experiments Hamilton found that both animal and human subjects under stress often were unable to perceive more than one line of behavior and this they used in rigid fashion despite the fact of its inappropriateness. Apparently, under great stress perceptions were so narrowed as to make it impossible to perceive better or more effective solutions. Other experiments have demonstrated that the experience of threat is accompanied by decreased efficiency and adaptability to a task, by adverse effects on learning and problem solving, and by perceptual inadequacy.

A vast majority of the threats we experience in modern life are not physical but social. We are less often threatened by things than by people. Such threats, furthermore, are seldom effectively dealt with by direct concentration on the threat itself. When one is threatened by his boss it seldom pays to tell him so. Direct attacks upon many of our modern threats often serve only to jam the machinery and increase the likelihood of our making further errors. In addition to increased errors and lowered efficiency, the experience of threat seems also to be accompanied by rigidity and intolerance of ambiguity. That is to say, under threat the ability of subjects to adapt readily when changed conditions are called for or to tolerate unsolved problems is seriously impaired. Paratroopers, for example, show impaired efficiency in perceiving before jumping, but after the jump has been successfully completed and anxiety is lowered, perceptual efficiency improves. Under threat, behavior becomes rigid and less fluid or adaptable to changing requirements. People under stress seem less able to cope with ambiguous or unsolved problems. They feel a need to have things definite and sure and in clear figure even though this may mean sacrificing accuracy.

Unfortunately, the restricting effect of threat in the phenomenal field simply complicates the resolution of problems. For adequate perception we need, not a narrow field of differentiation, but a broad one. Too narrow a field from which differentiations may occur results in repetitions of the same behavior time after time. This produces a characteristic behavior of threatened people often described as "compulsive" behavior.

Further Restrictions of Self Defense Upon Perception

In addition to the effect of "tunnel vision" upon the perceptual field, a second major factor restricting perception is brought about by the fundamental need to defend ourselves against attack. In the search for adequacy we have pointed out the need of each of us to maintain and enhance the phenomenal self. Under threat, then, we have no choice but to defend our self concepts when they seem to us to be severely threatened. Our phenomenal self after all is the only self we know. It is not just our dearest and most priceless possession. It is ourself. Without it we have no identity at all. Small wonder then that under threat we rush to its defense. We make excuses for our weaknesses, defend ourselves from criticism, and if pushed far enough, may strike out violently in retaliation against those who seem to be threatening us. One needs only to look about him to see numerous examples of self defense occurring in people everywhere. The child confronted with his misbehavior insists with vehemence upon his innocence, though we and he both know he did the act he is accused of. Husbands may defend with vigor threats to their concepts of self when wives cast aspersions about thinning hair or rounding figures. Wives are equally defensive of concepts of self as good shoppers, tasteful dressers, or fine cooks. Teachers are likely to be defensive when confronted with suggestions that they might be unfair or incompetent.

Attempts to defend the phenomenal self are not restricted to the individual's own self alone. People seek to maintain not only their immediate selves, but also those selves with whom they are identified. I defend not only me, but *my* child, *my* wife, *my* town, *my* country, *my* church, and those who are identified with these institutions or ideas. Indeed, these are all but extensions of myself, and in defending them I am but attempting to defend myself. In an interesting experiment on this question, Levanway asked subjects to rate themselves and others before and after a stressful situation. He found his subjects rated both themselves and their friends better under threat than when they were not under stress. Under threat we tend to "close ranks" and gather about us whatever strength we can.

This defense of the self concept provides a degree of stability to the self and makes the maintenance of identity possible. In this way self defense plays a vital and important role in need satisfaction. In the kind of world we live in, however, it can and often does have negative and destructive effects as well. The two factors, tunnel vision and the necessity for self defense under threat have far-reaching implications for human adjustment. Both factors contribute to making behavior static and unresponsive to the changing requirements of the world in which people live.

This nonadaptive, inflexible kind of behavior under stress has come to be known as "rigidity" and has captured the attention of many research psychologists in recent years. They have repeatedly demonstrated that rigidity is a concomitant of the individual's experience of threat and shows itself in decreased efficiency on intellectual tasks, an intolerance of ambiguous situations, and an inability to "shift gears" appropriately in moving from one situation to another. Some experimenters have even found rigidity to be closely associated with authoritarianism, dependency, and ethnocentrism. Apparently, threatened people have need to defend themselves by identification with strong institutions and figures, building up the prestige of their own groups and weakening that of others.

It must be apparent that this kind of rigid behavior produced by tunnel vision and the necessity for self defense is a far cry from the kind of behavior required for a great deal of modern living. Much of our adjustment to modern life requires not self defense, but self change. To live effectively in a technological, shifting, mobile society like ours requires of each of us the maximum of adaptability and resourcefulness to meet changing requirements. The achievement of a democratic way of life requires a free and open field of perceptions, untrammeled and unrestricted as can be. This will be true whether we are talking about an individual's adjustment to home, school, society, the world of work, or international relationships.

THE VICIOUS CIRCLE

The two effects of threat about which we have been speaking often lead to the permanence of behavior patterns in what has been called "The Vicious Circle." A phenomenal self which is incompatible with the demands of a social situation, for example, often leads to behavior not acceptable to the culture. People respond by rejecting or attacking the behaver, and this in turn forces the organism to greater defense of its position. The more violent the perceived attack the keener is the necessity for defense of the self. Furthermore, since it is often true that "the best defense is attack" the aggression of the society against the individual may result in aggression of the individual toward the society or its members, so that an unhappy state of attack and counterattack becomes established. This happens so frequently that in social psychology the principle that aggression results in return aggression has become almost a law of behavior.

One of the clearest examples of this vicious circle in operation may be observed in children who feel more or less rejected by parents. The child who has developed a concept of himself, whether justified or not, as unwanted, unloved, and unappreciated becomes aggressive toward his parents and seeks to regain his self esteem by punishing them or in some way demonstrating mastery over them. In this process he may utilize a very wide variety of techniques like temper tantrums, negativism, or any one of a thousand other fiendish devices. Parents, however, may be disgusted, shocked, or angry at such behavior and punish the child in an attempt to make him conform to the patterns of behavior they expect. From the child's point of view the threat inherent in his perception of his parent's behavior does not permit him to see the situation as they do. Their punishment is likely to appear only as further proof of what he already feels. This threat to self forces him to defend his position and his concept of himself is more firmly entrenched than ever. Thus he is driven to greater efforts in his attempts to gain a feeling of self esteem, which again may result in punishment, and so the cycle may be repeated over and over.

The resolution of this vicious-circle situation appears to lie either in some shift in the situation which reduces the threat to the phenomenal self or in aiding the individual to make some change in his self concept which will make him more adequate to deal with the present situation. Thus a delinquent may be treated by placing him in the more or less psychologically sheltered atmosphere of a foster home or by helping him to a new concept of himself capable of accepting his parent's behavior.

People under threat need the broadest possible field of perceptions from which to select appropriate behaviors. Yet the effect of threat is to make this kind of broad perceiving difficult, if not altogether impossible, so that the threatened personality may be reduced to repetitive unreasoning kinds of nonadaptive behavior under stress which, instead of relieving and solving the problem, may only serve to make it much worse. The delinquent, threatened and afraid of the police, is unable to communicate with the "cops" or to make an adequate adjustment to them when he confronts them. As a result he is quite likely to behave in ways that cannot fail to get him in trouble with the law. In the policeman's terms, "he seems to be asking for it."

Distortions upon perception may even have the effect of producing a feeling of threat where none exists. The child's feeling of guilt may cause him to behave in so guilty a fashion as to create suspicion in the minds of the adults who surround him. It is a commonplace observation that threatened personalities often behave in so exaggerated a manner as to call the attention of others to the very aspects they feel threatened by. This common behavior was illustrated by one of the writer's clients in psychotherapy, who said: "There are some things I sometimes don't want to tell you, so I try to hide them, but it's like trying to hide behind a tree. I sneak behind the tree so far I come right out into view on the other side!" "The wicked flee when no man pursueth." Threatened people with narrowed perceptions often bring upon themselves the very events they fear. They do, indeed, seem almost to be seeking their own destruction. In the complex society we live in a great many of the threats we encounter are not effectively met by direct, vigorous, or self-defensive action, and the utilization of such approaches may serve only to aggravate the problem.

The Intensity of the Experience of Threat

The important effects of the experience of threat upon the individual's perceptual field which we have been discussing occur not only when threats are perceived as violent or traumatic. Combs and Taylor, for example, have demonstrated that even with the mildest of threats to self, performance is measurably impaired. Any experience of threat, even of the mildest sort, seems to have its effects upon perception and produces an impairment of the efficiency of behavior. However, other things being equal, the more serious threats are likely to produce the more drastic and damaging effects. In general, the degree of threat experienced appears to be affected by at least the following four factors:

1. *Importance of the threatened concept of self.* You will recall

that the self concept is composed of many more or less discrete concepts of self. These concepts of self, moreover, vary widely in the degree of importance they hold in the particular economy of any individual. The degree of threat experienced by the person will be in part a function of the peculiar importance of the particular aspect of self under fire at any moment. The more important the aspect of self to the individual, the greater will be the experience of threat.

It is important to recall here that we are speaking of the danger to self *perceived by the behaver* and not that perceived by the outsider. From the point of view of the external observer an individual may appear to be under no threat whatever; yet from the behaver's own view he may be extremely threatened. A great many of our difficulties in human relations seem to stem from a failure to realize this important fact. The upper-middle-class female schoolteacher lives in a different world from her pre-teen-age boys. The values placed by upper-middle-class women on politeness, furthermore, are by no means shared by gang-age boys. Thus the teacher who calls a child before the class to learn to make introductions may, from her point of view, be "helping" George to get along in life. From George's view, however, this situation may appear as an excruciatingly painful threat to himself as a "regular guy," who is no "sissy"! The threats we feel are personal matters, the products of our own perceptions, and the degrees of threat we experience will be directly proportional to the importance of the peculiar aspects of self which seem to us to be threatened at any moment.

2. *Immediacy of threat.* A second factor affecting the degree of threat experienced will be the immediacy or closeness of the threatening event to self. Generally speaking, the closer, the more immediate the danger to the self perceived by the behaver, the greater will be the degree of threat he experiences. The examination coming next month seems much less threatening than the one tomorrow morning. The closer the event to self in time or space, the greater is the degree of threat which the individual is likely to experience.

The above statement seems a simple enough axiom, but it should be recognized that we are speaking here of psychological rather than objective immediacy. Objective evaluations of immediacy measured in terms of years, days, hours, minutes, or miles, yards, feet, or inches have little to do with psychological immediacy. Psychological immediacy does not refer to the external evaluation of distance or time, but to the individual's own experience of it. The cobra behind the glass in the snake house at the zoo is only a few inches from my nose, yet seems no great threat to myself. The same snake loose in a room with me, though 20 feet away, is a horrible and frightening threat to my being. Similarly, the man who is told today that he has only a few months to live may be more threatened by that fact at this moment than he will be two months from now on his deathbed. The immediacy of threat to self is a function of the individual's own unique perception of the situation, not the externally observable "facts." To understand the threat experienced by the individual it is necessary for us to perceive the world not through our eyes, but through his.

3. *Clarity of perception of danger: fear and anxiety.* Events perceived in clear figure are sharply experienced, while events differentiated only vaguely or as part of the ground of the perceptual field are less precisely experienced and result in vaguer, more diffuse kinds of behavior. Other things being equal, the experience of threat will be roughly proportional to the degree of clarity with which the disturbing event is perceived. Events only vaguely perceived as dangerous to self seem less threatening than those perceived precisely and sharply.

This relationship of the clarity of perception to the degree of threat experienced can perhaps best be illustrated in the distinction between fear and anxiety. Both of these words refer to the feelings we have when we are confronted with some sort of threat to our phenomenal self. People say they are "afraid" when the event which threatens is differentiated clearly and sharply in the perceptual field. Thus, we speak of being afraid of that car or that angry dog blocking our path, or of Joe Smith or Helen Jones. Fear is the word we use to describe those situations in which the object which threatens is clearly and sharply in figure. When the threatening perception cannot be so clearly differentiated, people speak of being anxious. Anxiety is thus a state of being threatened, but in which the object which threatens cannot, for one reason or another, be clearly and precisely differentiated. It is characteristic of people feeling anxious that they are unable to define precisely what it is that concerns and distresses them. They feel threatened, but they do not know by what.

This undifferentiated aspect of threat when people feel anxious is the very thing which makes it most difficult to deal with. Anxious people do not know what it is that threatens them and, as a result, cannot deal with the threats they feel with any degree of success. Helping people who feel anxiety clearly and sharply to see and understand the threats they feel is, in fact, a basic task of psychotherapy. One of the important things the psychotherapist does is to assist his client to explore his feelings and attitudes with great care until the client is able to pinpoint the cause of his distress, to bring the threat he feels into sufficiently clear perspective so that it can be dealt with. This is likely to be a painful process for the client, for the more clearly the individual perceives the danger to self, the greater is the degree of threat he is likely to experience. No wonder that therapy is often an extremely painful experience! Yet so long as the threats one feels remain undifferentiated and vague, they are difficult, if not impossible, to deal with effectively.

When the dangers to self are clearly and sharply in figure in the perceptual field, we say we are "afraid," and the threat we experience is likely to be similarly sharp and clear. When the dangers we perceive are only vaguely or diffusely differentiated in the perceptual field, we say we feel "anxious," and the threat we experience is similarly vague and diffuse. These two states represent the two ends of a continuum, but of course it will be recognized that there may be all stages of clarity of differentiation between these two positions, and the threat experienced by the individual will, other factors being equal, depend upon the degree of clarity with which he is able to differentiate the dangers to which his phenomenal self is exposed.

4. *Degree of threat as a function of personal adequacy: challenge and threat.* Finally, the degree of threat experienced by the individual will be a direct outgrowth of how strongly he sees himself as able to cope successfully with the emergency with which he is confronted. Other things being equal, people who see themselves as adequate are likely to experience threat less strongly than those who feel inadequate. Threat is the product of an inadequate definition of the self. When the phenomenal self seems adequate to deal with the situations with which it is confronted, there is no threat. Threat only exists when there is some feeling of inadequacy to cope. The degree of threat experienced will be an inverse function of the amount of adequacy felt by the behaver.

It is this degree of feeling of personal adequacy that distinguishes threat and challenge. When people feel completely adequate to deal with the problems that confront them, there is neither challenge nor threat. Behavior is likely to be quite perfunctory or carried out as routine. When the situations with which we are faced have not great possibilities for contributing meaningfully to our need for adequacy, they neither threaten nor challenge us. We do not ordinarily feel threatened or challenged by the breakfast set before us. We are not very hungry anyway, so there is little about it to enhance us. It is the same breakfast as yesterday and does not even have the interest of difference. There is no question of our adequacy to deal with the matter, and we behave toward it with little feeling of any kind.

We feel challenged when we are confronted by situations in which we feel fairly adequate, but in which we also see some opportunities for testing and enhancing our adequacy. There may even be some small degree of threat involved in the possibility that we might fail. This situation is exciting and challenging because the problem is perceived as one within our capacities and having inherent in it important opportunities for self enhancement. Let us take the example of a person asked to make a speech. When one is asked to make a speech and *feels fundamentally adequate* to the task, the request to make a speech may seem like an exciting and challenging opportunity to test one's adequacy, even as a means of building that adequacy further. There may also be a tinge of threat involved in the possibility that "it might not go over." Feeling fundamentally adequate to the task, however, the individual sees it as an opportunity for enhancement and further experience of adequacy. Hence he is challenged by the opportunity afforded him. Chances are, that feeling so, he will behave in a confident manner, will feel unthreatened by his appearance, and carry it off well.

People feel threatened when they are confronted with situations or ideas they feel fundamentally inadequate to cope with. The person who feels deeply inadequate when asked to make a speech perceives this request in a far different manner from the person we have just been describing. Feeling unequal to the task, the necessity to perform publicly holds nothing but threat for him. The more inadequate he feels, the stronger and more paralyzing is the threat he experiences. He tries to escape from the necessity of appearing through one excuse or another. If not successful in this, he approaches the speech with fear and horror. He may even be so frightened by the threat to which he has exposed himself as to be immobilized by his fear. We say, then, that he is a victim of stage fright. This failure may only serve to cause him to feel more inadequate than ever.

This same relationship seems to hold true not only for individuals, but for the societies they compose as well. Toynbee, the historian, points out that societies produce and progress when they are challenged, but make little progress when they are not confronted with problems or when the problems they confront are too overwhelming to be dealt with. Those societies, Toynbee points out, which are moved to action because they have problems to solve, yet which have sufficient adequacy to deal with the emergencies they confront, show the maximum progress. It would appear that societies, like individual people, respond to challenge but are paralyzed by threat.

What makes a matter challenging or threatening to a particular individual, it must be recalled, is a function of his own particular, unique ways of seeing himself and the situations in which he is involved. How it seems to some outside observer is irrelevant to the experience of threat. It is a failure to recognize this important fact that causes many of the breakdowns we encounter in dealing with other people. The teacher in the classroom, for example, may believe she is challenging a particular child to learn some aspect of a subject when in reality the child may be strongly threatened by the teacher's behavior. Or, the employer who gives his employees a "quota" of work to be completed in the belief that he is challenging them to greater efforts may be surprised to find that his workers do not see it that way at all. What seemed to the employer as a challenge to greater production and greater pay may seem to the workers only a threat to their dignity and integrity, a device to enslave them or make them produce beyond a reasonable level. Whether people feel challenged or threatened by a particular situation or event is a personal matter; a function not of the perceptions of an outsider, but rather of the behaver's own perceptions of adequacy or inadequacy.

The Sources of Threat

As we have said, people feel threatened when they perceive themselves as inadequate to deal with the situations in which they are involved. This feeling of inadequacy is a product of how the individual sees himself, the situations in which he is living and the interrelationships of these two. People may experience threat as a product of the inconsistency between self and the experience of the external world, or as a result of inconsistencies between two aspects of self. —

THREATS ARISING FROM THE PERCEPTION OF THE SITUATION. A phenomenal self developed in a particular group situation, over a period of time, is an expression of the experiences of the individual in that group.

Threat to the individual may arise when, for one reason or another, the social group begins to treat him in ways incompatible with the ways in which he has grown to perceive himself. This failure of expectancy may occur slowly as in the case of the young man who conceives of himself as a "great man with the ladies," but who in reality is not. He may be led to act, because of such a self concept, in ways extremely obnoxious to the fairer sex. His tales of his conquests, his condescending air, and his "freshness" may even eventually turn the eligible women from him. After numerous attempts to get dates and a sufficient number of cool refusals coupled with a few occasions in which he is unable to find any companion for himself at all, our young man may begin to become quite conscious that something is wrong. He feels tension and threat. Almost everyone has had experience with this sort of slow change in perception of life situations. The adolescent's changing perception of the reaction of those about him toward himself is a type of experience through which all of us have lived more or less successfully. —

People may also be threatened as a result of very rapid changes in the world about them. The loss of a marriage partner in an accident, for example, may suddenly confront the individual with perceptions extremely inacceptable and threatening. Threats may also occur when we change our jobs from one place to another. The present writer well remembers the shock of returning to graduate school as the lowliest of graduate students after a position of responsibility and authority in his home community. Such changes in the perception of life situations may suddenly present the person with concepts he cannot accept into his existing organization. We shall see later some of the ways in which the individual attempts to deal with such perceptions.

For the moment, however, it is important for us to recall that the production of new and inconsistent differentiations does not depend upon change in "real" situations alone. It is quite possible for such differentiations to arise although society continues to accept the individual on the same familiar basis. The pain experienced by many college students going home for the first time after a long period at college is a case in point. The treatment one gets from parents and friends is apparently no different than it has ever been, yet, since it is threatening to the student's new concept of self as an adult, the perception of this treatment may be radically changed and result in considerable anguish for the student. Similarly, the differentiation of a new idea may be extremely disturbing and even threatening to the individual. Many a student raised in a fundamentalist home has found the idea of evolution extremely disturbing because it is perceived by him to be inconsistent with previous ways of thinking about self and his relation to the universe. This is likely to be even more disturbing when others whom one considers to be important accept the idea without batting an eye.

Our culture values change much more than some others, and the attempts of our culture to "help" other less fortunate people have sometimes been more threatening than aiding. In parts of China, for example, where the population exists very largely on a rice and vegetable diet, it is customary for pregnant women to shift to a diet of fried chicken when they can get it. Small wonder then, that they rejected the public-health nurse who tried to persuade expectant mothers to eat vegetables. Vegetables indeed, when they had looked forward to special diets and special status for this mark of their maturity! Among people who feel it important that the body remain whole, surgery may seem worse than the disease it hopes to cure. Change can apparently be highly threatening, particularly when it runs counter to fundamental beliefs about self.

People may also feel inadequate because the circumstances they find themselves in suddenly seem overwhelming. Like the child lost in the city streets, people may sometimes feel threatened because the world they perceive is just too big and inexorable. This may be because the concepts they have of themselves are inadequate, or it may be that the situation to which they find themselves exposed will permit of no other interpretation. Like the psychiatrist in the *New Yorker* cartoon who diagnosed the young man, "As a result of my investigation, I can only conclude that you feel inferior because you are!" there are situations to which any of us may be exposed that permit of no other perception but that of our own inadequacy—at least at the moment we are called upon to respond. Without time for preparation most of us feel inadequate to deal with such cataclysmic events as hurricanes, earthquakes, epidemics, for example, or with such less wholesale dangers as speeding cars, falling objects, or others among the myriad emergencies of everyday life.

THREAT FROM THE UNKNOWN. People may also feel inadequate, not because things seem comprehensibly dangerous, but sometimes precisely because they are unable to comprehend whether they are dangerous or not. Some feelings of inadequacy occur because the individual is unable to determine the meaning of the situation in which he is involved. It is commonplace that what is unknown is often more frightening or threatening than that which is clearly perceived or understood, particularly when the individual is under the necessity of dealing with it. It is difficult or impossible to feel adequate when the expectancies of the situations in which we are involved are unclear to us.

To cope with life effectively, one needs to have a clear picture of the situation to which it is necessary to make an adjustment. The infant who is placed on the toilet and demanded to produce may be quite unable to comprehend the strange behavior of the adults who surround him or what it is that is expected of him. Putting pressure on him to respond only increases the feeling of inadequacy, and the whole process of toilet training may fail because the child is made to feel inadequate through inability to comprehend what is demanded of him. Adults, too, feel inadequate when they are unable to grasp the meaning of the situations in which they are involved. People in an office may feel threatened and inadequate when they do not know what is going on in the conference in the employer's office. Students feel threatened when they are unable to determine whether they have passed or failed the examination. It is a common experience to be "afraid of the dark," for it is difficult to deal with the unknown! It makes one feel inadequate. Throughout history, men have sometimes sought to escape this kind of threat by giving unknown events *some* kind of meaning, almost any kind of meaning, rather than be faced with the threat of the imponderable or incomprehensible. Thus lightning was attributed to the gods, and insanity to possession by the devil. Events without meaning or whose meaning is vague and unclear may cause feelings of inadequacy and threat in the perceiver.

Situations sometimes seem incomprehensible to the perceiver, not because meanings are unclear, but because meanings which do exist are too vacillating or rapidly shifting to make it possible to deal with them. The fulfillment of need requires an organized perceptual field. We feel more adequate when things stand still long enough for us to be able to comprehend them. The substitute teacher who must "fill in" for another in the middle of the semester often runs into this problem. The children, not comprehending the meaning of this new teacher, begin to try her out. They seek to discover the limits to which they can go. They try getting away with first one thing, then another. They keep on testing the limits until they have discovered where this teacher stands. When the substitute teacher helps the children to understand quickly and precisely what kind of person she is and how far they can go with her, she

soon establishes an effective working relationship, the children feel secure, and the class gets under way again. If, however, she is vacillating
and indecisive, if she permits things one day and "cracks down" on them
the next, it becomes difficult for the children to discover the meaning of
the situation and they feel inadequate to deal with it. Not knowing what
to expect, they feel threatened and tense and so continue their explorations in an attempt to find out where the teacher is *now*. It has sometimes been said that people can adjust to almost anything so long as it
stands still, and indeed there seems to be much truth in the statement.
People feel inadequate and threatened when they are confronted with
situations too vacillating or confusing to permit the discovery of meaning.

THREAT FROM INCONSISTENT PERCEPTIONS OF SELF. The effective satisfaction of need requires an organized self. The fact that the phenomenal
self has many aspects, however, frequently makes the achievement of
self consistency a difficult matter. Differentiations leading to enhancement of one aspect of the self may at the same time threaten other
aspects. The individual may thus be placed in a position wherein his
perceptions of what he has done as an expression of one aspect of self
are seriously inconsistent and hence threatening to another concept of
self. As a consequence he may show signs of tension arising from the
threat he perceives. The more seriously the self is threatened by such
differentiations, the greater will be the individual's feeling of threat and
distress. As Murphy has observed, "the very activity which brings us
one satisfaction reminds us constantly that it is depriving us of another—
and this is especially true of ego values." Threat may arise from inconsistencies within the self even when two aspects of self are fundamentally
enhancing.

THREAT FROM MULTIPLE ENHANCING PERCEPTIONS. A young minister we
have known came to conceive of himself as a successful preacher and as
a scholar. He made a very brilliant record in theological seminary, and
indeed at the seminary he was both an excellent preacher and scholar.
When he came to accept his first charge at a small community, however,
he was almost a total loss to his congregation. His talents as a scholar
were completely unappreciated. His most eloquent addresses went for
nothing. In that community to be considered an excellent preacher required a homely, nonscholarly approach. When he was a successful
preacher, he was most unscholarly; when he was most scholarly he was
a total failure as a preacher. The poor man became more and more dis-

traught at his lack of success and was at a loss as to how to deal with it. Unfortunately, his concept of himself as a scholar brought about a reaction to him in that community which belied and threatened his concept of himself as a speaker. Similarly, if he had been a good preacher in that community, his concept of himself as a scholar would have been threatened.

Threats arising from such inconsistencies are sometimes described as "conflict." It should be pointed out, however, that the term "conflict" is a term of external description. It is an outside observer's description of what he observes. The behaver himself does not experience conflict. He experiences threat to need satisfaction. He experiences threat to self maintenance from one or more differentiations of his self which he is unable to accept at that moment. This is Lecky's principle of Self Consistency. Such threatening differentiations may occur in rapid sequence and even be described by the individual as "conflict." In so doing, however, he is making an external observation of his behavior just as any outsider would. To state that the minister, in the example above, is in conflict with himself leads us to a ridiculous state of affairs. There is nothing conflicting about differentiating oneself as a good speaker and a scholar. Some of our most successful clergymen are both! Even in cases where two aspects of self appear to be in conflict, it will usually be discovered that one of these aspects is considered momentarily to be *not self* threatening self. Where inconsistent definitions of self exist in the same individual, it will usually be observed that one of these exists only at a low level of differentiation. Antagonistic concepts of self cannot exist at high levels of differentiation at the same time unless one is regarded as *not self*.

When two differentiations are perceived to be enhancing to the individual and can be achieved simultaneously, or in rapid order, little or no feeling of threat is likely to be experienced by the individual and he operates to realize the enhancement perceived. If, however, the realization of the two differentiations about self are not simultaneously or in quick order capable of realization, a very great degree of threat to need satisfaction may ensue. This is especially true where the realization of one may force the abandonment of another. The instant one is abandoned, it becomes threatening to need satisfaction and demands attention. The enhancing differentiation which is realized satisfies need, but the enhancing differentiation not realized threatens the self greatly. A good example of this is to be observed in the young woman in love with two men. Conceiving of herself as being loved by A and loved by B is enhancing to self. The decision to marry either A or B, however, immediately threatens self with a loss of the other. When adequacy can be achieved equally well through either of two goals, movement toward goal A means abandonment of goal B. The instant goal B is relinquished, however, the woman is threatened by its possible loss. Since she desires goal B, however, she moves to recapture it and now may find the same situation reversed. As a result, she may vacillate back and forth between her two suitors, unable to settle on either because of the threat of the loss of the other, until such time as either A or B is perceived as more enhancing than his rival.

MULTIPLE THREATENING PERCEPTIONS OF SELF

An even more threatening situation exists when the individual has two or more differentiations, all of which are highly threatening. For the sake of simplicity, let us suppose that only two such perceptions occur. In this situation the individual has no opportunity for self enhancement whatever. This is the state characteristic of many neurotics. An excellent example is to be observed on any college campus in what is sometimes called, "term-end-neurosis." The student who begins to feel failure bearing down on him is faced with two negative differentiations each of which is threatening. To stay at college and fail is unthinkable. It threatens his concept of himself. On the other hand, to withdraw from college and go home to face his parents and their expectations is also inacceptable. He is a failure if he remains; he is a failure if he leaves. Either situation is intolerable and threatening, but what is even worse, one or the other is inevitable. As the term progresses and the full realization of his jeopardy becomes greater, the necessity for defense of self becomes more pressing, and the student's activity becomes wilder and wilder. He engages in frantic behavior. Effective study becomes impossible. Finally, he may literally wear himself out and collapse before exams in "nervous exhaustion," and the school physicians send him home. This exhaustion is usually short-lived, because the moment the student arrives at home he is met with the sympathy of parents, the reassurance of relatives, and exclamations of "Poor boy, he worked too hard!" The threat and tension under which he has been operating disappears. He feels quite adequate once again and with a little rest he makes a quick recovery.

Another seriously threatening situation may arise when one aspect of self becomes differentiated and is recognized as inconsistent with another highly differentiated aspect. We have seen that inconsistent concepts of self may exist in the same phenomenal field so long as both are not simultaneously in clear figure. Antagonistic or derogatory perceptions of self produce feelings of threat and consequent defenses against such perceptions. Such inconsistent concepts of self may be kept from confronting each other in two ways. In the first place, the two concepts may be differentiated as applying to two different social situations. This is characteristic of the man who conceives of himself as a "good" and a "religious" man on Sundays, in deacons' meetings, and on religious holidays, but conceives of himself as a "good businessman" on weekdays. Sharp business practices, dishonesty, and even gambling may thus comfortably be engaged in on weekdays, while Sunday finds the same person sitting in a pew and piously following the dictates of his Sunday self concept. To conceive of himself in his Sunday self concept on Monday would prove extremely threatening to the weekday self concept and so must be strongly resisted. He may also be deeply disturbed if his minister calls on him at his place of business during the week, for this brings into figure concepts of self and of role out of touch with present experience.

THREAT FROM LOW-LEVEL DIFFERENTIATIONS OF SELF

A second way in which inconsistent self concepts may be prevented from confronting each other is through keeping one concept at a low level of differentiation so that it never appears in very clear figure. So long as one perception remains at a low level of differentiation, it may not greatly disturb another. We have seen that differentiations may be kept at a low level if they appear too threatening to the individual. This is true of perceptions regarding the self as well.

When one concept of self exists at a low level of differentiation and is antagonistic to another clear definition of self, the potentialities for threat are tremendous. If the individual behaves at some time in terms of his low-level differentiation, he may find that he has committed an act extremely threatening to a more clearly differentiated aspect of self. Such an act may bring an inconsistent concept of self into clear and inexorable figure, resulting in violent shock. The following case illustrates how this may occur. A young woman considered herself a "good Catholic" and conscientiously observed the rules of her religious faith. As she grew older, however, she desired more and more to marry but had very little opportunity to realize her goal. Finally, she met a man of her own religious faith who previously had been divorced. When he proposed she was delighted, and although she understood the ban of her church against marrying a divorced person, she was so intent upon her objective that this disturbing thought never appeared in very clear figure. For a while after marriage things went well, until one day a priest pointed out to her very clearly the position of the church. This brought the entire question into clear and inescapable figure in which both aspects of self were threatened by what she had done. To give up her husband was a threat to her concept of herself as a married woman, and to keep her husband was a threat to herself as a good and conscientious Catholic. For a time she vacillated desperately back and forth between these two concepts of herself. Finally, unable to find an acceptable solution, the poor woman collapsed and had to be hospitalized.

A self under threat has no choice but to defend itself. What is more, the very existence of threat makes the solution of problems more difficult. To resolve a threatening situation requires exactly the opposite of suppression and tunnel vision. It requires freedom to examine and to differentiate any and all aspects of the field in the search for a more adequate self.

Behavior Change Under Threat

While it is true that behavior under threat is likely to be rigid and narrow and defensive, this does not mean that under threat it is impossible to change another person's behavior. Far from it. Throughout history, man has discovered that threatening people is an effective tool for changing behavior. Since time immemorial many parents, teachers, priests, and political leaders, to say nothing of businessmen and military leaders, have used this method of dealing with people.

We have seen that threat leads to tunnel vision and the defense of the self. The effect of threat, then, is one of concentrating and restricting the area of the perceptual field to which an individual is responding at a particular moment. People under threat are likely to behave rigidly and unquestioningly and with a direct (perhaps even violent) response to the threats they perceive. This characteristic makes threat a most effective device for dictators. People under threat are likely to be so busy responding to obvious threats that they have little opportunity to explore those which are less obvious or which are purposely obscured by those in power. Every dictator has been keenly aware of the importance of giving people a clear-cut enemy.

People can and do learn under threat. People always learn when their need is seriously affected. Unfortunately, what people learn under threat is likely to be narrowly focused on the nature of the threat to which they see themselves exposed and may even lead to seeing threats where they do not really exist. The effect of threat is to concentrate attention on the threat perceived rather than upon the broader circumstances to which the threat is attached. A child we know was asked by her father what she "had learned in school today." "Oh, nothing," was the child's reply, "but was our teacher mad! Wow!" Clearly, this child *had* learned something. But also clearly, it was not at all what the teacher thought she was communicating! Under threat this child's attention was riveted upon the object which threatened her and she was in no condition to perceive from a wider frame of reference. What she learned was related to the nature of her angry teacher, a matter of concern to her at the moment of much greater importance than the structure of the United Nations, the physical geography of Wyoming, or how to do subtraction.

Threat lends itself well to dealing with people where it is desired to control and channel behavior. It may, for example, prove a useful device in teaching a child *not* to cross the street. It does not help much, however, in teaching him *why* he should behave so. Indeed, one of the important effects of threat is that it restricts "looking." It is the perfect device of the manipulator, for it provides a means by which human beings can be prevented from exploring widely while at the same time attention is held rigidly and unquestionably to those events the manipulator desires people to look at. It is the perfect tool for a regimented society.

A free society requires independent, thinking people of wisdom and perspective; it requires unthreatened citizens, people who are challenged but not threatened. A complex, interdependent society like ours requires people who are flexible, not rigid; who can perceive broadly rather than narrowly; who are not so bound to the necessity of self defense as to have little time or energy to devote to the problems of their fellow human beings. In our kind of society not all possibilities can be readily foreseen, and it is necessary for us to be able to rely not on the brains of a few, but on the interacting creative efforts of millions. Rigidity, narrowness and preoccupation with self defense are the very antithesis of what a fluid, open, dynamic modern society requires. Fear and threat have no place in such a society.

CHAPTER 10

Learning, Forgetting, and Problem Solving

EFFECTIVE, efficient behavior requires that individuals be able to learn new things, to retain this learning over long periods of time and to solve new problems when confronted with them. Learning, remembering, and problem solving, however, are, like any other behaviors, the products of the individual's perceptual field. In particular, they are the direct outgrowth of the process of differentiation we have discussed in an earlier chapter.

Learning as Differentiation

When we speak of learning we mean the process by which an individual is able to change his behavior, usually in some more constructive fashion. Such changes are brought about by differentiation within the perceptual field. All learning of whatever variety has as its basic characteristic a progressive differentiation from a more general perceptual field. This is perhaps best illustrated by observing changes in the drawings of young children. Children draw what they know; that is to say, what they have learned. Observing their drawings, therefore, can provide us with interesting insights as to what is probably going on in the child's perceptual field. The differentiation characteristic of child learning is perhaps best illustrated in the child's drawings of a man. The earliest of such drawings are likely to be composed of little more than a head with appendages attached. Later, as the child grows and apparently differentiates more and more detail with respect to the adults who surround him, his drawings mirror this increased detail and we may find him adding fingers to arms, a trunk between legs and head, and the addition of feet, hair, and ears. Still later, when the child has differentiated still more details about adults, he may draw a man with a neck between head and trunk and various details of clothing. See Figs. 17, 18, and 19.

Fig. 17. Typical Early Drawings of Man. *Left:* Drawn by Alice K., age 5 years, 11 months, a shy retiring child who accepts adults only very cautiously and fearfully. *Right:* Drawn by Bill J., age 6 years, 5 months, born prematurely who shows lack of stable adult contacts and feels deeply rejected.

Fig. 18. More Mature Drawings of Man. *Left:* Drawn by Albert M., age 5 years, 10 months, a tense introverted child who accepts adults only very slowly and fearfully. *Right:* Drawn by George R., age 5 years, 10 months, a happy, active, relaxed child who shows little dependence on adults, and who had seldom held a pencil until this point.

Fig. 19. Drawings of Man Produced by Very Mature Children. *Left:* Drawn by David B., age 6 years, 0 months, well coördinated and almost too mature for his age, who prefers relationships with adults to peers. *Right:* Drawn by Helen S., age 5 years, 2 months, a very mature, adequate little girl who is a leader in her group.

The same development of differentiation and growth from a total field to a more and more precise kind of performance may be observed in handwriting, number concepts, reading, and vocabulary, to name but a few areas of a child's learning.

Learning at all levels at which psychologists have studied the problem is characterized by this process of increasing differentiation from a more general field. This is true whether we are speaking of the highly controlled laboratory experiments on "conditioning," "trial and error learning" on a less carefully controlled level, or "insight learning" of a problem-solving character where subjects are given a maximum of freedom. Pavlov noted in his famous experiment on the salivation of dogs that his subjects' first responses were highly irregular and vague, but as the experiment continued his dogs responded with ever-increasing regularity and precision as they were increasingly able to differentiate from the general field the most efficient response required. This differentiational character of learning in conditioning experiments has been illustrated repeatedly with many other animals, including man himself.

Experimental subjects who seem to learn by "trial and error" in running a maze or finding the proper means of escape from a puzzle box also show this differentiational characteristic of learning. Behavior which is quite general and vague at the beginning of the experiment becomes increasingly precise as the animal is able to perceive with greater and greater accuracy the "proper" solution to the problem. This will be true whether we are speaking of ants, rats, or men. The process can be clearly observed in examining the day-by-day productions of a child who is learning to write. Little by little over a period of time, as he is able to differentiate more clearly what is required and how to operate his muscular system to achieve those ends, his writing becomes increasingly precise. Most of us have forgotten how difficult a process this was. We have lived so long with an accepted ability to write that we have forgotten how slowly and painfully the process of achieving these new differentiations was at the time we originally learned them.

The reader can relive some of this early difficulty in learning to write and at the same time observe the differentiational characteristic of his own learning in action by learning a new skill such as mirror writing. This can be done by setting up a bridge of books, as in Fig. 20, in such a way as to make it impossible to see what one is writing unless he looks in the mirror. Now, if the reader will make four dots on a sheet of paper in the form of a diamond, he can place his paper in such a posi-

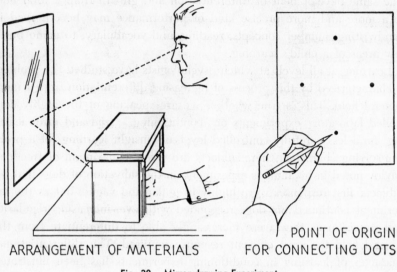

ARRANGEMENT OF MATERIALS   POINT OF ORIGIN
                                   FOR CONNECTING DOTS

Fig. 20.   Mirror-drawing Experiment.

tion that it can be seen only by looking in the mirror and can proceed to
try to connect the dots he has made and so to complete the diamond.
At once the experimenter will observe that he is behaving very much
as the young child who is learning to write. He may, for example, find
himself gripping his pencil for dear life, trying desperately to push it
in directions it does not seem to want to go. He may even find himself
chewing his tongue and making grimaces just as the young child does.
His performance record, indicated by the pencil marks on the paper,
can also be observed to be hesitating and tentative as he seeks to differentiate the proper solution to the problem (unless, of course, he goes
through this process symbolically in his field without moving his pencil).
With a little practice, however, the ability to carry out this task becomes
rapidly more precisely differentiated and can shortly be done with a
high degree of accuracy. This is a much quicker process than the way
we originally learn to write, but then we are now adults with a great
deal more experience to call upon than we had in those early days.

Some learning, at first glance, seems to occur "all at once" as a kind
of sudden "insight." This seems to happen, for example, when we suddenly become aware of the solution to a problem with which we have
been struggling for some time. On closer examination, however, it can
be observed that this kind of learning, too, is a product of differentia-

tion. What is happening here is the kind of differentiation producing synthesis and generalization, which we discussed earlier. A new principle or relationship is differentiated on an overall, generic level providing new meaning or relationship between two events not previously observed as related. The ape suddenly differentiates the box in his cage as something to stand upon to reach the banana hanging from the ceiling. The scientist differentiates a new relationship in the complex data with which he is dealing and experiences what the French have called an "ah-ha moment," in which previously differentiated perceptions are suddenly seen with a new meaning.

Actually, such sudden differentiations are the end product of long series of previous differentiations. This is perhaps best illustrated in the protocols of psychotherapy, in which it can be observed that the client's, apparently sudden, insight is really only a new differentiation of the interrelationship of two series of differentiations. A client may spend hours exploring his perceptions concerning his father and more hours exploring his perceptions concerning himself and his behavior, and then suddenly come to the "insight" that his own behavior has been caused by the kind of person his father was. Such an insight, however, although sudden and highly meaningful to the client, could only occur at the end of a long sequence of previous differentiations.

Learning as a Function of Need

Perhaps the most important contribution of the personalistic point of view to the psychology of learning is the recognition that learning, like all other experiencing and behaving, is an active process which results from the efforts of the individual to satisfy need. Whether we like it or not, people are always striving for the satisfaction of need; they are always learning. If they are to learn the attitudes, skills, and facts that are socially desirable, the situation must be arranged so that they can further their own ends by such learning. Mere presentation of material by repetition or drill is not sufficient. Habit and repetition are not, from the behaver's point of view, causes of behavior. As he sees it, he performs the act for the thousandth time for the same reason he performed it the second time, because it is the most effective way he knows of satisfying his immediate need. What any individual learns (differentiates) in a given situation is determined by the need of the moment. A child practicing the piano *may* be learning to play the piano better. He may also be learning how to give the appearance of practicing with the least possible effort. This relationship of learning to need raises difficult problems for educators. What teachers teach and children learn can often be maddeningly different because the immediate goals of teacher and child may be worlds apart. The best, most elaborate efforts to induce learning may thus come to be frustrated.

THE PROBABILITY OF LEARNING. We have already seen that the degree and direction of differentiation are always determined by the need of the behaver and the opportunities for differentiation that are available. Since the selections made by the individual in his perceptual field are always a function of his fundamental need, whether or not there is any learning at all will be dependent upon the operation of this need in the situations where learning is expected. Rats will not run mazes with any degree of precision without some need to do so. As a consequence, the experimenter usually makes certain that his rats are hungry and that their need is satisfied at the conclusion of the maze. In a similar fashion education had traditionally established a grading system by means of which students could be punished or rewarded for performance. Learning is always a function of need. But the need we are talking about is need from the behaver's point of view, not that of an outsider. Even hungry rats will not run mazes if their need to sleep is greater. Children with a desperate need to be accepted may find it more important to play with their neighbors than to pay attention to the teacher's lesson.

THE SPEED AND ACCURACY OF LEARNING. It is well known that the rate of learning may be accelerated by increasing the strength of the subject's need. It can also be accelerated by increasing the opportunities for the differentiation of essential cues and solutions. In general, the hungrier the rat, the more likely he is to learn the maze, providing the opportunities for making differentiations are not too limited. The effect of increased need upon learning has to do with increasing the intensity of effort and exploration. We can check this principle by observing our own behavior. When need is greater, we search harder and longer, and hence we are more likely to find solutions. Whether or not this exploratory activity pays off in increased learning, however, will of course be determined by whether or not the opportunities are such that the necessary differentiations can be made. No matter how hungry a rat may be, he will not learn the maze while sitting in his cage. Nor will a human being longing to sail a ship learn to do this effectively while plowing a field in Iowa.

Of course, there are limits to the degree to which the strength of need will affect the accuracy and speed of learning. If the individual's need is too great, his awareness of the need may become so acute and detailed that all other parts of the perceptual field fall into ground and further differentiation of those parts ceases. Under these circumstances the behavior loses its effectiveness or may even stop completely. Examples of this may be observed in people under panic when persons feel so threatened they become the victims of "tunnel vision." It is a common thing to find reports in our newspapers of persons being killed in panic because perceptions become too narrowed to make it possible for them to see the obvious solutions to their predicament. The drowning swimmer may be so intent upon keeping his head above water that he cannot permit himself to sink momentarily while he removes the heavy shoes which make swimming impossible. The frightened driver "freezes" to the wheel and cannot perceive what to do next. The person with clothing on fire seeks to run from the threatening flames and so fans the flames he seeks to escape.

THE LEVELS OF LEARNING. Aspects of the perceptual field may be differentiated in varying degree from ground to clear figure. As a consequence, learning may occur at any level of awareness, from a level so vague that the individual may not be able to report his experience to a level so clear and precise that the individual can report his learning with great keenness and certainty. Learning can occur at any level at which differentiation is possible. Many of the things we learn in life are never differentiated in sufficiently clear fashion that we could report them to other people. This can be demonstrated in such experiments, for example, as those on "unconscious learning," wherein it is possible to teach a subject to blink his eyes to the sound of a buzzer so faint that he is not able to report that he heard anything at all. The principle of learning at low levels of differentiation has been commercially exploited in the development of a record player with an under-pillow speaker which makes it possible for an individual to hear music, the lines of a play, or even factual information of various sorts while he sleeps. Later, when he seeks to learn these in a waking state, they seem easier to bring to clear figure apparently because they have already been perceived at a lower level of awareness.

THE PERTINENCE OF LEARNING. We have already seen in an earlier chapter that the degree to which any perception will affect behavior is a function of the relationship of that perception to the self. Events perceived as having little relationship to self have little effect upon behavior, while events perceived as being closely related to self affect behavior in marked degree. Even an event which is clearly and precisely perceived may have little effect upon the behavior of the individual if it is not also differentiated in some manner as having a meaning to the individual himself. The pertinence or applicability of learning will be a function of the perceived relationship to self.

There is a difference between knowing and behaving. It is familiar to any of us when we find ourselves saying, "Now I knew better than to do a thing like that!" A great deal of what people learn in school is of this character. Although concepts have been clearly perceived, the further differentiation of the relationship of these concepts to the individual's own need has not been perceived and as a consequence the individual does not behave in terms of what he "knows." Any student is aware that when he "needs to" he can learn a set of facts with sufficient clarity to be able to report them back to his professor on an examination, yet behave the following day as though he had never heard of the concept in his life. Learning proceeded as far as the student saw a need.

Differentiations may occur in any area of the perceptual field: in the self position, the not-self position, or at any point between. We can learn about events having little to do directly with self if we develop the desire to know about such matters. The objective observations and disciplined experimenting of the physical scientist are attempts of this sort to explore matters of interest with the least possible distortion from self reference. He "needs" to rule self out of the picture and so confines his differentiations to the not-self aspects of his field. In this fashion, the existing body of "fact" in a science may be built up. Such differentiations made in the not-self portion of the field, however, may never be perceived by the learner to apply to "real" problems of life. The author recalls some years ago congratulating a well-known child psychologist on the birth of his first child, then jokingly adding: "Now, John, you can talk like an expert." He was quite unprepared for his friend's reaction. John drew himself up and replied with icy coolness, "I don't think that will make any difference!" Apparently the learning of this eminent scholar was not perceived as having a practical bearing upon his own life and family. Differentiation is a function of need, and if the need is only *to know,* the effect of differentiation upon *behaving* may never progress beyond an esoteric level of abstraction.

Although differentiation can be made in the not-self portions of the field, it should not be supposed that learning can ever escape from the personality of the learner. Since the perceptual field is always organized with respect to self, differentiation and learning may occur with more or less reference to self; it can never occur unrelated to self. Even the disciplined scientist, making his observations with meticulous care to rule out self, is seeking by this very behavior to satisfy his very personal need for self adequacy as a scientist! Though it is helpful, even essential, for the solution of some of our problems that learning progress in these not-self areas, sooner or later they must be differentiated with relationship to self if they are ever to make a difference in the behavior of individual people.

The Economy of Learning

The major determinent of the kind and degree of differentiation which is immediately possible in any situation is, of course, the character of the existing perceptual field. A limiting factor, therefore, is always the degree of differentiation already attained. In our society, children differentiate the wheels from the rest of vehicles rather early and their drawings begin to show an awareness of how they are attached to vehicles at 5 or 6. An adult Australian aborigine from an island off the north coast where no wheeled vehicles existed, lumped all the vehicles he saw in Sydney as "houses that ran around." His reason for classifying them as houses was the fact that he saw people looking out of the windows. He showed no evidence that he had even seen the wheels, much less their mode of attachment. The same individual had very high skills as a hunter and tracker, which required a high degree of differentiation and observation of details.

The process of differentiation is quite regular and proceeds step by step, and it is futile to attempt to teach a pupil any detail for which he is not ready. An advanced 5-year-old who had noticed the wheel-and-axle relation was met by incomprehension and, finally, resistance when he attempted to get his kindergarten classmates to revise their less-differentiated pictures which showed the wagon box resting on the tops of the wheels. They were unable to see the difference between the two positions, and could not understand what he was excited about. It is quite probable that the lack of confidence in their drawings that appears in most children about the time they enter the third grade, is the result of misguided efforts by their teachers to get their drawings to conform to the phenomenal field of the teacher rather than that of the child. He learns that he is not making an accurate picture but is not able to see why it is not accurate. Schools where the teachers do not insist on their own personal adult "realism" do not produce this effect of discouragement and frustration.

The effective satisfaction of need is best achieved with the greatest possible accuracy of differentiation. Accordingly, learning proceeds to the point of ever more precise figure in the least amount of time. Need satisfaction does not stop here, however. Human need is insatiable and, once satisfied by events differentiated only a moment ago, continues the process of differentiation in ever new and more productive directions. Events learned to the point where they are differentiated in clear figure soon fade into the ground of the perceptual field, being replaced in figure by some new or more extensive differentiation. In Bryan and Harter's classic experiment on learning telegraphy a half century ago, beginning operators were found attempting to differentiate letters. As this was achieved, they began to "go after words." Following this, fair operators were able to differentiate phrases and even short sentences. The real expert, they found, finally reached a point where he had differentiated all of these aspects with such clarity that they became ground in his perceptual field, and he gave them practically no attention at all, which is to say, he did not find it necessary to call them into clear figure again. The expert operator even preferred to keep ten or twelve words behind his instrument, where he could perceive the larger, more meaningful pattern.

The economy of the organism requires that we be able to drop what has been differentiated in clear figure further and further into the ground of the field. If every event had to be new and clearly differentiated at every moment, need satisfaction, even the very existence of the organism, would be impossible. We are all familiar in our own experience with this movement of what has been learned from clear figure into the total field of our experience. In learning to drive a car, for example, starting, shifting, accelerating, and steering are each at first done painstakingly and with great concentration of effort. Later, as we learn to do these things effectively and smoothly, they become more and more a part of the total situation with which we are concerned. At first our need in driving the car was to differentiate how to turn it on. Having mastered this, the next problem became how to make it go. Later, when we had learned to drive very well, the whole business of driving became mere ground for the more important figures of where we want to go and how do we get there. What emerges into figure at one time may become ground for new figures the next.

DIFFERENTIATION AND HABIT

The apparently automatic behavior as a result of differentiations no longer in clear figure is called, in external approaches to psychology, "habit." Although such behaviors seem automatic, it should not be assumed that they ever occur without meaning or without some degree of awareness. Behavior is always a function of the total field and never exists without meaning. Habits in a perceptual sense are behaviors resulting from low-level perceptions in the phenomenal field. The assumption that habits are automatic and without meaning has probably come about because of the fact that the individual often does not seem to be keenly aware of his behavior at the moment it occurs. A confirmed smoker may suddenly find himself with a lit cigarette in his hand without having been consciously aware of, that is, able to report, the sequence of behaviors that have brought him to this condition. What has happened is that smoking, orginally a series of techniques for the satisfaction of need in clear figure, has now become part of the ground of his perceptual field as more immediate problems of need satisfaction arise into figure. The confirmed smoker's "habit" is a lower-level differentiation in the perceptual field. Its presence in the ground of the field, however, necessarily affects behavior even though it exists at a lower level of differentiation than the immediate events in figure for the individual at the moment.

The operation of this figure-ground relationship of habit is neatly illustrated in Dunlap's fascinating method of breaking a habit by practicing it. Dunlap observed that in typing he had developed a very bad habit of typing *hte* when he meant to type *the*. When he attempted to break this habit by practicing writing *t-h-e*, he found that his habit persisted. When, however, instead of practicing *t-h-e*, he practiced writing *h-t-e*, his unfortunate habit quickly disappeared. What apparently happened in this case was that Dunlap had developed perceptions which resulted in his writing *hte*. These perceptions at a low level of awareness in his field caused him to continue writing *hte* as he typed his manuscripts. The attempt to break his habit by practicing *the* did not help matters any, because it served to bring into figure the differentiation *t-h-e* instead of the differentiation *h-t-e* which was the real source of his difficulties. When, however, he practiced *h-t-e*, thus bringing this differentiation into clear figure, he was able to change it and the habit was broken. Behaviors operating from low-level perceptions often continue to persist until they are somehow brought into clear figure where they can be dealt with in a new fashion. Nail biting or thumb sucking are "habits" which may sometimes be dealt with effectively by practicing them directly and openly for a certain length of time each day. This brings the low-level differentiation into clearer figure where it can be dealt with. Events can be much more effectively dealt with in clear figure than when they remain as part of the ground. The same principle operates in psychotherapy when the counselor seeks to help his client to bring his anxieties into clear figure where they can be more effectively dealt with.

Remembering and Forgetting

Remembering and forgetting, like any other behavior, are functions of the differentiations the individual is able to make in his perceptual field. When a person is able to recall into figure differentiations he has made on a previous occasion, we say he "remembers." When he is unable to call again into figure differentiations he has previously made, we say he has "forgotten." Thus, we may define remembering and forgetting as functions of the ability of an individual to recall into figure events he has previously differentiated. As products of perception, remembering and forgetting will be affected, just as learning is, by those factors which control the processes of perceiving we have discussed in the previous chapters of this book.

Earlier in our examination of the nature of the perceptual field, we observed that differentiations once made are permanent. That is to say, perceptions once made have been made forever. Perception and differentiation are a one-way process and one cannot *un*differentiate or *un*perceive. A perception or differentiation has presumably been made forever. There seems ample evidence to demonstrate this permanent character of learning. Burtt found, for example, that Greek passages read to his infant son were "learned" more quickly at later periods in his son's life than similar passages which the young man had never heard before.

Other evidence for the permanence of learning may be found in the remarkable ability which many people show under hypnosis or under the influence of hypnotic drugs to remember with great detail events occurring at extremely early periods in their lives. Similarly, a large portion of the time of a client in psychotherapy is spent in recalling events he has long since thought he had forgotten. If what is once differentiated in the field is differentiated for all time, how then shall we explain the varying degrees with which we seem able to recall previous events?

Before looking at some of the factors which affect the degree of remembering and forgetting, it is necessary for us to recall that the perceptual field is differentiated in terms of the individual's unique and personal experience. The perceptual field is differentiated, not in terms of the experience of the outside observer, but as events are perceived by the behaver himself. Failure to understand this point may sometimes result in an assumption of a failure in memory which is really no more than a difference in perceiving as seen from the point of view of the behaver and the observer. Two people exposed to the same situation perceive this event in quite different fashion. On a later occasion person A may discover that person B reports quite a different picture of what happened. Since A assumes that his field is correct, he may then conclude that person B has "forgotten" what is quite obvious to A.

What can be remembered can only be that which was once perceived. To ask an individual to remember what he has not perceived is asking of him the impossible. Some of the frustrations adults suffer in attempting to deal with young children often arise from a failure to understand this fact. What adult has not experienced the frustration, for example, of asking a child "What happened?" and getting for an answer, "I don't know!" In the adult's world it seems inconceivable that anybody should have forgotten so soon what happened to him. We are likely to forget that the perceptions of children are far different from those of adults. A child confronted with a highly threatening situation, for example, may have differentiated little more than the overwhelming enormity of the threatening object and his own inadequacy to deal with it. Little wonder, then, that he finds himself confused still further by adult demands that he describe with accuracy and precision the what, why, how, who, and when of the situation in which he has been involved. What is going on here is not so much a failure of a child's memory as of an adult's understanding.

The perceptual field at any instant is, from the point of view of the behaver, his whole universe and consequently includes what he knows of the past at that moment and what he infers about the future at that moment. Like all other parts of the field, these memories of the past or expectations of the future will emerge into figure or lapse into ground in conformity with the needs of the individual and the activity he is pursuing. Like all parts of the field they are subject to distortion and modification by the major variables of perception we have discussed in Chapters 3 to 8 of this volume.

THE CLARITY OF AWARENESS

We have already observed that perceptions exist in the phenomenal field at all levels of awareness, from those so vague and indistinct as to be forever in ground to those, on the other hand, so sharp and precisely in figure that it becomes possible for us to express them even to other people through the symbolism of language. Other things being equal then, memory will be dependent upon the level of awareness of a given event in the individual's perceptual field. Generally speaking, we will be able to reproduce on demand most effectively and efficiently those events which have become, as a consequence of our experience, sharply in figure. Events in the ground are always more difficult to bring again into figure. This creates some serious problems for our courts and the legal profession. Two men standing on the street corner talking with each other, for example, may be aware of the traffic patterns surrounding them only as vague and indistinct movement. When suddenly two cars collide, their attention is immediately drawn to the collision and the events surrounding. Later, on the witness stand, they can give quite precise accounts of the position of the cars, their condition, and perhaps the behavior of the passengers immediately following the impact. Their perceptions of the events leading up to the accident, however, may be far less clear, even highly confusing, as this calls for differentiation of events never really clearly perceived. Unhappily, it is these very events leading up to the causes of the accident that are of most concern to the judge, jury, and attorneys involved in the case.

Several "laws of memory" have been developed as a result of extensive experimentation with problems of memory. Among these are the observations that memory is a function of frequency, intensity, and recency. That is to say that, other things being equal, what is likely to be remembered most easily will be that which the individual has experi-

enced frequently, with greatest intensity, or most recently. These observations seem to hold true with respect to the differentiations an individual is able to make, providing we prefix each of them with the statement
"other things being equal." Whether or not these principles apply in a
given case will of course be dependent upon what has been previously
differentiated in the field. Almost any of us have had experiences which
illustrate that frequency of exposure to an event is by no means enough
to guarantee adequate differentiation. For years we may walk the same
street to work and never observe important details in the buildings along
our way until we make a point of it. Similarly, it is possible in listening
to a symphony orchestra almost to ignore the intense sound of the per-
cussion instruments as we strain to hear the soft melody of the wood-
winds.

THE EFFECT OF NEED ON MEMORY

What is remembered is always a function of the individual's basic
need. As in all field change, the subject matter and degree of differentiation are determined by the need of the behaver and the opportunities
for differentiation that are available. Like all items of awareness, memories are characteristically pertinent to the immediate problems of the
individual and are not fortuitous or random. If we are distracted from
our work by vagrant memories, it is because the work itself does not
promise adequate satisfaction of our need. We are not always able to
remember what we need but we do need what we remember.

The same characteristics of purpose and direction which select our
memories also determine the relations within the remembered material.
As in all cases of differentiation of the field, the sequence is from a
relatively large and homogeneous figure, which usually cannot be verbalized, toward a more detailed but restricted figure, the process ceasing
when the need is satisfied or the activity is abandoned. As a general
thing, the first emergence in remembering is not of isolated objects or
individuals but of generally meaningful events which are then differentiated into their necessary details. For instance, a freshman student remembers his fourth Christmas because he then got the sled which led
to the accident he remembered.

Whether or not an individual can differentiate on a later occasion
what has been previously differentiated will be affected by his need both
at the time of the first experience and at the time that recall is demanded.
We have already seen above that the individual's need at the time of

the occurrence of an event will determine what is differentiated in clear figure at that time. In the case of the auto accident cited above, the need of the men on the street corner to talk with each other may have caused each to be in such clear figure to the other that neither participant could perceive with any degree of clarity what was going on about him. With a shift of interest to the actual collision, differentiations having to do with that event could occur with much greater clarity and precision.

The individual's personal need will also determine in large measure what is remembered on the occasion when it is later demanded. In general, we recall what we have a need to recall. When I need a drink, I recall where the drinking fountain is located. When I need a plumber, I recall the whereabouts of his shop. It should not be supposed, however, that simply because an individual verbalizes a need to remember that such a statement constitutes his real need. It may represent only that he needs to have us believe he is making an effort. We have already seen in our discussion of threat that events perceived as threatening to the individual may be refused admission into clear figure. Clients in psychotherapy, for example, may often be observed to be making what seems on the surface like a very intense and painful attempt to remember an earlier experience without success. They may even complain quite sincerely, "I need to talk about that. I wish I could tell you about it." The counselor, however, knows that what his client is expressing is not so much a need to remember as a need to be strong enough to deal with the event. What he is saying is "I wish I were adequate enough to permit myself to confront this question." The individual's statement of what he needs cannot always be relied upon as an accurate representation of the need he really feels.

Since only one event can appear in figure at a time in the perceptual field, the effect of need in focusing attention in one direction may make it impossible to perceive some other aspect of the field at that moment. This is what often happens in stage fright, when the individual's concern about himself and his performance become so clearly in figure that he cannot perceive his lines and later claims that he forgot them. If he has been well trained, this proves only a temporary lapse and he is soon able to turn his attention again to his speeches and get on with the play.

An intense need of any kind has this sort of ordering effect upon the perceptual field and may make it difficult for differentiations to occur. This happens not only with threat. It may also occur in periods of high anticipation. The joy of reunion with a loved one at the station may sometimes cause us "to forget" where we are and so behave in ways usually not appropriate for public display. Much forgetting and failure of memory is the product of this kind of focus of attention on aspects of the field determined by need at the moment.

OTHER FIELD EFFECTS UPON MEMORY AND FORGETTING

Since behavior is a function of the total perceptual field, what is remembered is always a product of the field state at the instant recall is demanded. We have already observed above how the level of differentiation in the field affects memory. Various factors having to do with other aspects of field organization will also determine what is remembered or forgotten.

What is remembered is always a product of the phenomenal field. As a result, a good deal of distortion may sometimes be imposed on memory either by the field existing at the time of the original event or, later, at the time it is to be recalled. Things are not always experienced in the same way by children and adults, for example, and thus the experience remembered may be quite different. The reader can test this for himself by discussing some of his childhood memories with the adults who were there. One can usually discover that some things he remembers never really happened at all. What is remembered can only be our experience of an event. This experience, moreover, is not equivalent to the physical occurrence but is perceived in terms of the individual's need and the state of his field at the time the event occurred. Unnecessary details are omitted and details necessary to the phenomenal event are added and "remembered" even if they were never seen or never existed.

Just as the existing field affects the perception of the event at the time of its original occurrence, so also does the need of the individual and his current field affect perception at the time of recall. It is a common experience to discover we have inaccurately remembered a name, a place, or idea on later occasions.

What the individual experiences when he is first exposed to an event is always a function of the total field at that instant. What he perceives is what best fits the existing field at that time. This is also true of what is remembered. The perceptual field is always meaningful and what is remembered is affected by the existing meanings in the field. It thus happens that a person reporting upon a previous experience may often be observed to distort his report in terms of what he now knows to be meaningful. This raises some additional problems and new causes of error for the psychology of testimony we mentioned earlier. Since the individual's field always has the feeling of reality, it is sometimes difficult to distinguish between an event that really happened and an event which now seems *reasonably to have happened*. Some things we remember not because they occurred but because it seems to us that they *must* have occurred.

This experience of the perceptual field in terms of what is meaningful is illustrated in the phenomenon of paramnesia or *déjà vu*, the feeling of having been in a place before although we know that fact is impossible. Almost everyone has experienced this feeling at some time or another. It may occur walking down the streets of a city in which we have never been before: we suddenly get the feeling of great familiarity with this street, even to the extent of being certain that we could describe what is around the next corner. Such feeling seems to come about in this way: traveling often over a particular street in our home town, we may differentiate, usually very vaguely, a pattern or series of houses or stores or whatever. Later, on a new street in a new city where we have never been before, if the pattern or series of stores or houses in this neighborhood has a degree of similarity to those in the old one, the total field response we may get includes the feeling of familiarity characteristic of the old setting. Ordinarily, an attempt to differentiate more precisely the cues to which we have been responding in the two situations will quickly make it apparent that they are not by any means alike.

The perceptual field is always meaningful and related to the satisfaction of need. Need, however, cannot be efficiently and effectively satisfied if it is only possible to deal with events that are in clear figure. As a consequence, much of our forgetting actually contributes to the efficiency of our behavior. For example, I need to know the names of the students in my classes and, if the class is not too large, within a few weeks I can manage to differentiate the names of most of the people in the group. When the semester is over, however, I have often been embarrassed by meeting a student whose name I could easily have called last week but now find myself quite unable to do so. The reason for this seems to be that with the end of the semester I no longer "need" to know the student's name. As a consequence these differentiations are difficult to make again when my perceptual field has become organized in a new direction. I have even been fascinated to discover that within a week or two after a class was completed I found great difficulty in calling the names of individual students whom I met about the halls of the university. At a reunion with the same class several years later, sitting about the table as we did on earlier occasions, however, I was delighted to find that I knew their names as I had during the days when the class was actively in session. Apparently the most important factor affecting memory is the need of the individual himself. Some politicians with very intense need to call people by name have been able to develop phenomenal abilities in this direction.

Reasoning and Problem Solving

Just as perception and learning differ only in the complexity of the differentiation required, so "problem solving" and "reasoning" also appear to be functions of differentiation. As an example of reasoning let us take the solution of the following problem. Dr. S. had rented a garage in front of which was an electric-light pole, about fifteen feet from the entrance. When he got into his car at 6:55 the next morning and began to back out to the street on his way to a seven-o'clock class he discovered the light pole by crumpling his right rear fender against it. The following morning he was very much aware of the pole and cut his car sharply to the left to avoid it, with the result that the right front fender scraped against the open garage door. Two major obstacles had now emerged from the ground, the pole and the door. A fence made it impossible to push the door farther out of the way and the pole could not be removed; so it was necessary for him to discover a path by which he could back his car from the garage to the street without striking either obstacle. It seemed quite likely that, by continuing to do the best he could to avoid these obstacles as he backed out, he would eventually learn (by differentiation of visual, temporal, and kinesthetic cues) to do so. However, such a course might require a considerable amount of time and cost more money than he could afford for repairs to the car. He was accordingly impelled to solve the problem more directly. Since he could drive into the garage without damage (because in driving ahead the field was more highly differentiated in terms of both visual and kinesthetic patterns), it was only necessary for him to discover some way of backing out along the same path. By noting (differentiating) two or three landmarks as he drove in at night it was only necessary for him to observe these points when he backed out the next morning. He had no more trouble during the rest of the summer, except for one morning when his alarm clock failed to ring. While he was backing out of the garage at 7:02 in a vain effort to reach a seven-o'clock class on time, the urgency of the situation became the figure in his field, the landmarks dropped into ground, and he backed into the light pole.

As in learning and perception, the first awareness was of the gross situation, and the essential cues and orientation points did not emerge into figure until the behaver became aware of his need for such details. The factors determining the degree and direction of differentiation were, again, the goal or need of the behaver and the opportunities for differentions that were available. Reasoning and problem solving, it would appear, are not something different. All behavior is in a sense problem solving. The important question is, what is the nature of a superior ability in this direction? How does one become more skillful or efficient?

Problem solving has to do with the individual's ability to perceive new, different, or more efficient aspects of a complex situation. Even the lowest animals are able to differentiate in this fashion in some degree. The ability to differentiate in this way on a symbolic level available to us as human beings, however, opens vast new horizons for effective and efficient differentiation, and hence need satisfaction. Operating on a symbolic level gives us a kind of shorthand in terms of which we have an immensely increased mobility of action.

As a consequence of the experience of past generations of thinkers, techniques of inductive and deductive reasoning have come to be formalized as particularly fruitful approaches to problem solving. The experience of more recent generations living in the midst of the marvelous accomplishments of the physical sciences have added the "experimental method" of hypothesis, experiment, and conclusion as the "right" approach to reasoning. Certainly these methods are useful devices by which it becomes possible to bring order and meaning out of large bodies of data. The attempt, however, to teach problem solving and reasoning by the use of such formal devices usually fails. What is logically reasonable is not always humanly practicable. The attempt to utilize some of these formal techniques of problem solving may even, sometimes, interfere with the process of reasoning by turning attention away from the aspects of the perceptual field in which the solution must be found. The field in which a problem must be solved is a field organized with respect to the problem. Preoccupation with a *method* of solving problems brings into figure aspects of the field having nothing to do with the actual solution of the problem. The solutions to problems after all can only be found in the field pertinent to those solutions. Two things cannot be in figure in the perceptual field at once, and when methods are in figure, concepts cannot be.

Improvement in reasoning and problem solving, it would appear, is not likely to be effectively brought about by formal methods. What improves capacity in problem solving are the same things which produce richness, variety, and availability of perceptions in the perceptual field. What improves reasoning and problem solving are the same factors which produce creativity, spontaneity, and the kind of free and open perceptual field which we have found is characteristic of the adequate personality. In later chapters on the problem of human capacities and the nature of the adequate personality we shall consider in much more detail the kind of perceptual field necessary for most effective reasoning and problem solving.

CHAPTER 11

The Nature of Capacities, Emotion, and Feeling

WE began this book with the premise that all behavior is a function of perception. To understand behavior, we said, it is necessary to understand how things seem to the person who is behaving. Accordingly, in the past eight chapters we have been systematically examining the factors which influence perception. In particular we have given a good deal of attention to seven variables having important effects upon perceiving:

1. The physical organism
2. Time
3. Opportunity
4. The effect of need
5. Goals and values
6. The phenomenal self
7. The restriction of the field

The first three are well known to us in our common experience and have also been extensively explored in the psychology of the last 50 years. These are factors affecting behavior that lie very largely outside the individual and are open to manipulation by those who surround the individual. Throughout man's history they have provided the primary bases through which people have sought to control or affect the behavior of their fellows. The latter four are factors inside the behaver and are open to external manipulation only indirectly and in limited degree. These four are functions of the phenomenal field and have only in recent years been greatly appreciated for the vital bearings they have upon behavior. All seven of these factors we know have important effects upon how people perceive. There may be others of which we are not now aware, for perceptual psychology is not very old, and it is only in fairly recent years that the problems of perception have been intensively or widely studied. It is conceivable that in the years to come we may discover still other important variables which will help us to push forward the frontiers of our understanding.

In the preceding chapters we have had to look at these variables of perception one by one; but, of course, behavior is never the product of any one of these variables operating alone. Behavior is always a function of the whole perceptual field at any moment, and the perceptions available to the behaver in his perceptual field will be the product of all of these factors.

All behavior, we have said, is determined by the perceptual field of the behaver at the moment of his behaving. How effectively a person is able to behave at any moment will depend upon the perceptions available to him at the instant he is called upon to act. Let us go back and look at that statement again. If the statement is true, it means that human capacities and abilities to behave are a function of the perceptual field, and the factors controlling human capacities will be the same factors as those which govern the process of perceiving! If behavior is a function of perception, then, the factors which govern perceptions will also determine the nature and degree of the abilities which any individual possesses.

Historically, we have been accustomed to think of human capacities and abilities as the direct products of heredity or of the strength, agility, or health of the physical organism. And, of course, when we are thinking of purely physical potentialities these observations hold true. One cannot jump, for example, without legs, and how far he can jump with legs will be dependent upon the strength and health of the organism which is doing the jumping. There must, of course, be a physical organism to operate, and the physical operation of that organism will be dependent upon the kind of structure it possesses.

We have already seen (Chapter 4), however, that human behavior cannot be understood solely in terms of physical structure. Our physical bodies provide the vehicles for perception and behavior and set important limits upon some types of behavior; they do not provide a sufficient cause for the understanding of *all* behavior. One must have the necessary structure of the throat in order to speak, but *what one says* is not to be understood in terms of the laws of heredity or the physiological make-up of the individual alone. Although the physical organism is essential for behavior, we must search elsewhere for a comprehensive understanding of the nature of behavior or of human capacities for behaving or misbehaving.

Previous generations of psychologists were deeply impressed by the successes of the physical sciences and often pined for the kind of precise measurements which those sciences found possible. It seemed only reasonable to them that human behavioral capacities must be limited in the same fashion as physical capacities, since both occurred in the same physical organism. To conceive of a limited organism capable of almost unlimited behavior seemed too mystical for scientific belief. Accordingly, the psychologists of 30 years ago were almost unanimous in describing human capacities as the direct product of the individual's heredity and physiological structure. It was thought then that children were born with certain specific potentialities of intelligence or aptitude. This potential, moreover, was conceived as fixed and immutable. A child could fail to achieve his inherited capacity, but he could certainly never exceed it. Many human abilities were conceived as inborn and, hence, as unchangeable.

In more recent years many psychologists have come to have grave doubts about this fatalistic conception of human abilities. Human abilities seem capable of far more change than had previously been thought. Numerous instances have now been reported which demonstrate that considerable changes in general level of achievement are possible. Programs enriching the environments of children deprived of affection and evidence of personal worth, for example, have shown measurable improvements in intelligence. Intelligence ratings have also been found to change positively following play therapy, and negatively with long periods in restricted environments. Human abilities no longer seem so exclusively the product of the behaver's genes as we once thought. It seems necessary now to consider a large number of psychological factors in addition to physiological ones.

This is not a denial of the importance of our physical beings in behavior, but a matter of seeing the contribution of our body structure in better perspective as one of a number of factors rather than the sole determinant of capacity. The contribution of physical factors to any behavior will vary widely from act to act, never reaching zero, but never serving as the full and sufficient explanation for behavior, either. We have attempted to diagram this in Fig. 21. The three bar graphs in that figure each represent a typical behavior. The shaded area of each graph represents the contribution of the physical organism to the behavior. Bar A might be such a behavior as climbing a rope, in which the physical strength and agility of the behaver will play a very large part. In this

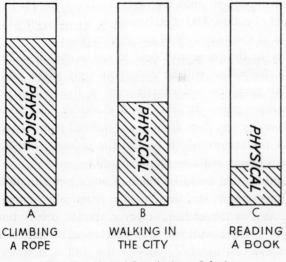

Fig. 21. Physical Contribution to Behavior.

instance, the physical condition of the subject determines in very large measure his capacity to behave effectively. Bar *B* represents a behavior in which the physical organism plays a lesser role as, for example, walking through a city. Here is a behavior which requires some degree of physical fitness, but not so much as climbing a rope. In Bar *C* we have represented a behavior like reading a book or making a speech, in which the physiological potentialities of the individual play a relatively minor role. By far the greatest portion of the things we do lie well within this latter sphere of operation, in which our physical bodies provide only the vehicle for behavior. How we behave, given the necessary vehicle, is a function of psychological or experiential factors like those we have been exploring in this book.

Intelligence as a Problem of Perception

By the term *intelligence* we ordinarily refer to the effectiveness of the individual's behavior. Intelligent behavior is behavior which effectively and efficiently satisfies the need of an individual and his society. Whether or not such behavior can occur, however, will depend upon the differentiations the individual is able to make in his perceptual field, which we have defined as "the universe of experience open to the individual at the moment of his behavior." In other words, the behavior of the individual will be dependent upon the perceptions existing for the individual at the moment of action. The effectiveness of his behavior will necessarily be a function of the adequacy of those perceptions.

If an entity in the perceptive field is vague and ill defined, the behavior of the individual will be correspondingly vague and lacking in precision. The precision and effectiveness of the individual's behavior will be dependent upon the scope and clarity of his personal field of awareness. Intelligence, then, from a perceptional point of view becomes a function of the factors which control the richness, extent, and availability of perceptions in the perceptual field.

The perceptions that could be made of any given situation, such as a stone wall, for example, are, theoretically, practically infinite in number and quality. As a matter of fact, however, we are strictly limited in our perceptions of a stone wall to those which we, as human beings, can make. We cannot, for instance, perceive the wall as it would appear to a man from Mars, or from the interior of an atom, or as it would appear to a centipede. What is more, we cannot even perceive it as it would appear to all people. Different people will perceive different aspects of the wall differently, even at the same instant. I can only perceive the wall, and hence behave toward it, in terms of the perceptions that I, as an individual, can make regarding it. I may, for instance, perceive it as a fine, sturdy fence enclosing my property, while a stonemason friend might perceive it as having been poorly designed or as having been built with too little cement in the mortar mixture. The perceptions open to my mason friend are the result of his unique experience. I, not having such experience, am incapable of those perceptions at this moment. Each of us is limited in perceiving by the richness, extent, and availability of perceptions in his unique perceptual field.

THE EXTENT OF PERCEPTIONS IN THE PHENOMENAL FIELD

At the instant of their behaving, people can only behave in terms of those perceptions which exist for them. In the example above, it might be possible for me to acquire the same kind of perceptions about stone walls as my mason friend. I could increase my own perceptions by a period of study or apprenticeship, for example. At the moment of behaving, *now*, however, I am limited by those perceptions which exist in my field. I cannot behave in terms of perceptions I do not have at that instant.

THE QUALITY OF PERCEPTIONS AS A LIMITING FACTOR

At any instant behavior will also be limited by the quality of the individual's perceptions. In the example above, the perceptions open to the writer and to the mason are by no means equal in quality. Even if these people had the same number of perceptions, the perceptions available to each would vary greatly in detail, richness, and meaning. The artist and the novice looking at the same picture might conceivably have the same number of perceptions, but the meaning or quality of these perceptions would be vastly different for the two observers.

THE AVAILABILITY OF PERCEPTIONS IN THE FIELD

Finally, the behavior of the individual at any instant will be determined by the availability of perceptions in his personal field at the moment of his behaving. The existence of perceptions in the phenomenal field is no guarantee that they will be available at a high enough level to affect behavior significantly at the instant they are required. Some perceptions may exist in the field only as *potential* perceptions. By this we mean those perceptions that exist in the individual's unique field of awareness and that, given the right circumstances at any particular moment, *could* rise into figure. The fact that a perception is potentially possible to any individual does not mean that it will occur at the moment of action. Even those perceptions that I can make potentially may not be active for me at any given moment. Potentially, I might be able, for instance, to perceive the wall in our example as a barrier to be gotten over, as an eyesore to be beautified, as composed of 687 bricks costing $80.27, or as providing pleasant shade on a hot day. These are all potential perceptions I am capable of making about the wall. They will affect my behavior, however, only when they are active or functioning in my field of perceptions. When I am beating a hasty retreat pursued by a neighbor's angry dog, perceptions about the shade, beauty, or cost of the wall, though potential, are not functional in affecting my behavior. I behave only in terms of my functioning perception of the wall as something to get over—and quickly.

The fact that particular perceptions may be potentially available in the field of an individual is by no means a guarantee that they will exist functionally at the moment of action. The capacity of the individual to behave at any moment will thus depend upon the extent and richness of his perceptions and the availability of those perceptions at the instant they are required. This extent, richness, and availability will in turn be dependent upon the seven variables of perception we have explored in earlier chapters (3-9). We have already observed how each of those factors controls the perceptual field.

The Maximal Limits of Behavior

What are the maximal limits of human capacity? At the lower level of these limits we know there are some unfortunates who have little more capacity for behaving than the bare minimum required to keep alive. Examples of this extreme degree of limitation would be the so-called "crib cases" to be found in many of our institutions for the mentally retarded. These are persons born with such drastic physical deficiencies as to be capable of little or no perception. They live out their lives in little more than a vegetative condition.

At the opposite extreme, what are the upper limits of human capacity? This is indeed a difficult question, for so far as we know no one has ever remotely approached the upper limits of perception. Indeed, the possibilities for human perception seem almost infinite. Given a healthy physical organism to provide the vehicle for perception, enough time, a stimulating environment, challenging and fruitful problems, and a nonrestrictive self concept, there seems no end to the perceptions possible to the individual. Given eyes capable of seeing, who can say what are the limits of what may be perceived? Presumably one could perceive whatever one looked at, and there are no end of things to look at! Unlike the limits imposed on the physical organism by our physical structure, the limits of what *might* be perceived by a particular individual seem practically nonexistent. The potentialities of perception are infinite.

Apparently, people can go on differentiating new perceptions in their phenomenal fields from conception to death. Their perceptions during this period seem limited only by the seven variables of perception we have discussed earlier. One of these variables, of course, is the state of the physical organism, and with advancing age, failures of the physical organism may contribute to a reduced ability to perceive. Students of the aging process now believe, however, that the intellectual, behavioral capacity of the elderly need not deteriorate with age simply because the body is less capable of the kind of reactions it could deliver in its younger days. Indeed, they have collected many remarkable case histories of persons, like Oliver Wendell Holmes, who remained remarkably keen and productive to extremely advanced ages, sometimes even in spite of great physical deterioration. It would appear that some of the rigidities of aging are not so much questions of a slowing down of the physical organism as limitations on perception brought about by some of the variables of perception. Some elderly people seem limited by their perceptions of self. Seeing themselves as unable, unacceptable, or useless, they behave as though they were, though they may be enjoying perfectly good health. Some seem limited by their own feelings of threat at anything which resembles change in their accepted pattern of life, and they avoid exposing themselves to the necessity for change as much as feasible. Still others seem to have become the victims of their own goals and values, so that new events and new ideas have no place in their perceptual fields. Although deterioration of capacity may come with advancing age by reason of a failure of the physical organism, it now seems clear that this is not a necessary occurrence if other factors affecting perception can be kept operating in positive constructive ways rather than contributing to rigidity and narrowness of the perceptual field.

THE DEVELOPMENT OF SPECIAL CAPACITIES

In the course of differentiating perceptions throughout a lifetime each of us develops a unique field of perceptions richer or more extensive in some areas than the fields of our friends and neighbors and poorer and narrower in others. This unique pattern in the content of our field is brought about by the action of the variables of perception during the years of our growing up. The particular field we develop represents our own specialization, our own peculiar know-how, skill, or understanding. No one can respond to everything, and as a result our perceptions become more or less differentiated in these fields depending upon the kinds of experiences to which we have been exposed. Even the decisions we make from day to day have a directing and selecting effect upon the kinds of perceptions we can have and will have thereafter. If a young woman should decide to enter nurse's training, for example, it is unlikely that she will have many perceptions about calculus and topology during the next four years. Our perceptions become specialized by the very nature of the decisions we make.

For some people, this specialization of perception may proceed to extraordinary lengths so that they seem to have capacities far beyond that of ordinary mortals. A young man whom the writer tested at an induction center during the war illustrates the point very well. This young man was a newsboy on the streets of a West Virginia city. Although he had failed repeatedly in grammar school and was generally regarded as "not bright," he appeared on a national radio hookup as "The Human Adding Machine." He was a wizard at figures. He could multiply correctly such figures as 6235941 $\times$ 397 almost as fast as the problem could be written down. He astounded our induction center for half a day with his numerical feats. Yet on the Binet Test he achieved an IQ of less than 60!

People in his home town, who bought his papers, amused themselves by giving him problems to figure. When not so occupied, this young man entertained himself by adding up the license numbers of cars that passed his corner! He was a specialist in numbers. Apparently as a result of some early success in this field, he had been led to practice numbers constantly, eventually to the exclusion of all else. This was one area in which a poor colored boy could succeed and he made the most of it. His number perceptions were certainly rich and varied, but other things were not. Although he was capable of arithmetic feats not achieved by one in millions, he was classified on the intelligence test as dull. Such specialization or unusual richness of perception in a particular area of behavior is not magical. It is produced by the operation of the same factors governing perception as exist for the rest of us. In fact, most of us could probably duplicate the boy's feat if we were willing to give up most of our other goals as he did.

What Do Intelligence Tests Measure?

Intelligence tests are basically tests of achievement. No one has yet devised a means by which we can approach the measurement of capacity directly. Instead, we are forced to approach this problem indirectly by means of inferences from what we can observe. Intelligence tests are based upon the fundamental assumption that all people taking the test have had an equal opportunity to learn the things the test measures. Accordingly it is assumed that people who have learned more must have had more basic ability or capacity for learning. For example, if John and Mary, two children of equal age and the same general culture, are each given an intelligence test and John makes a better score than Mary, the test administrator would infer that John probably had somewhat more ability than Mary. How accurate the inferences made from such tests are is, of course, dependent upon the degree to which this fundamental assumption holds for the individuals being tested.

A great deal of research has gone into the development of adequate intelligence tests over the past 40 years, and test makers have sought continuously to refine their instruments, primarily through an attempt to find more valid items for these tests, items which could accurately be presumed to be part of the experience of all people taking the tests. This search for common items has been most successful for those age ranges during the school years. Earlier, during infancy, it is difficult to find common items of experience, but our public schools provide a considerable area of common experience (at least as it is seen by an outsider) for children. Consequently, during these years intelligence tests seem to have their greatest validity. After the school years when individuals are free to go their own ways as adults, this modicum of comparable experience rapidly disappears. As people grow up, marry, and embark in the infinitely diverse field of work, it is no longer easy to find common experience upon which intelligence tests may be constructed. The older one gets, the more unique he becomes. Intelligence tests, therefore, based largely upon materials drawn from the school years, sometimes show a leveling off or even a decrease in intelligence after age 16 to 18, the years when children characteristically quit school. Observing this drop, it was once assumed that intelligence ceased to develop after age 16, but we know better than to make such assumptions these days.

From a perceptual point of view, what intelligence tests measure is the phenomenal field. They do not measure this field directly, of course. Instead, they provide us with a sample of the individual's perceptions as these are expressed in the behavior of the individual taking the test. Since behavior is a function of the perceptual field, it becomes possible to infer the nature of the perceptions existing in a person's perceptual field from his behavior. This is exactly what intelligence tests do. From the behavior of the individual on the tests we infer the quality and extent of the perceptual field from which that behavior originated.

We have already defined intelligence in this frame of reference as a function of the quality, extent, and availability of perceptions in the perceptual field. Intelligence tests, then, sample these three aspects of the field. From the sample we may conclude what the whole field may be like. This sample, it should be recalled, is a sample of the state of things in the *current* perceptual field. It gives us an indication of the individual's present perceptions. Ability in this sense is a developmental characteristic, not an immutable or inherent or never-changing trait. In the degree to which the perceptual field is stable and unchanging, so our assessment of an individual's capacity will similarly be stable. We have already seen, however, that the perceptual field is characterized by some capacity for change, and in that degree intelligence or capacity will also be open to change.

In our culture many people have come to accept intelligence-test results almost as trustingly as a prescription from the family doctor. Important decisions are often made as a result of such tests. It is important, therefore, that we have a clear understanding of what tests measure and of the degree to which the results they provide us are accurate assessments of the capacities of people. We need, for example, to be very sure the sample of the perceptual field is indeed an adequate sample of what is there. It is conceivable, for example, that a test might sample so narrow a portion of the perceptual field as to cause completely erroneous conclusions about the individual's perceptions. Tests designed to sample a subject's perceptions about music or art, for example, might be totally inadequate as samples to determine the probable effectiveness of the individual in flying an airplane.

A second possible source of error in sampling has to do with the determination of what is worth sampling. Our own perceptions always seem the "right" ones to each of us. By whose standards, then, shall we take our sample—yours, mine, society's, the subject's own? For the most part our intelligence tests are based on the assumption that academic, upper-middle-class, intellectual perceptions are important. But are they? Can we assume that the expert machinist, who can perceive things "out of this world" for most of the rest of us about a piece of stock on his lathe, is less intelligent than a diplomat who perceives many things about foreign affairs? Can we be so sure of our values as to call one bright and the other dull? Can we blame the machinist for his lack of perception about foreign affairs without asking the diplomat to be equally skilled in the machinist's field of perceptions? In the past it has sometimes been assumed that primitive people are incapable of abstract kinds of perceptions. After studying the capacities of Tepehuan natives to deal with abstractions, McConnell comes to this conclusion; "It is far too easy to read simple mindedness into simple behavior. Merely because some primitive cultures may not demand complex abstract modes of behavior from their members does not necessarily mean that the primitive may not be able to function on a higher level whenever called upon to do so."

Intelligence, we have said, is the capacity for effective, efficient behavior. But who is to determine what is effective and efficient behaving? To a very large degree we adhere to an upper-middle-class definition of values in creating intelligence tests. Since middle-class professional people construct these tests, it is not surprising that the items they choose to test their subjects are derived from their own values. It is probably no accident that, almost without exception, psychologists make the highest scores of anybody on intelligence tests as compared with other professions. They should. They made the tests and included the items that are important to them.

IS THE CAPACITY FOR INTELLIGENT BEHAVIOR OPEN TO CHANGE?

It will be noted that all of the factors we have spoken about which affect perception are capable of some degree of change or manipulation. Even the effect of the physical organism upon perception is capable of variation within certain narrow limits, although, to be sure, it cannot be drastically shifted. The remainder of the factors in our list, however, seem open to fairly wide degrees of change. If this is so, it would appear to follow that the capacity for intelligent behavior can be created! This seems to be true within the limits to which the perceptual field itself is open to change.

Although it is well within the realm of possibility that the perceptual field and, hence, the capacity for more intelligent behavior, may be changed, it should not be assumed that this is either easy or quick. The field has a degree of fluidity and within the limits of that fluidity change is possible. We have already seen, however, that a major characteristic of the perceptual field is its stability, its resistance to change. The factors affecting perception vary in the degree to which they may be manipulated and controlled. There are ways, for example, in which we can provide people with different kinds of opportunities to perceive. There are things we can do to help people discover new and more adequate goals and values or concepts of themselves. It is even possible to deliver many people from the unhappy and restricting effects of threat. To make such changes, however, is neither simple nor easy.

Perceptions of long standing do not change rapidly. The child who has come to define himself as a person who cannot do mathematics as a result of ten years of failure does not change his ways of seeing himself in a moment. It took a lot of experience to build this self concept as a part of his perceptual field, and to organize the rest of the field to fit it; and it is quite likely to take a large amount of a different kind of experience to counteract it. The man who has believed for 40 years that his methods of farming or teaching are the "right" methods cannot be induced to change his goals and values in a moment. Perception is a function of experience. Long established and deeply meaningful experiences have a high degree of stability and resist change. As we have seen, the individual's need tends to produce behavior which corroborates his already existing concepts. Once perceptions have become firmly established in the field they tend to perpetuate themselves and this, of course, adds further to the difficulties of inducing change in the field.

The perceptual view of capacity we have been discussing in these pages is consistent with the position many psychologists have taken in recent years: that intelligence is open to a degree of change. They believe it is not so unchanging or limited by our physical heredity as we once thought. Several studies indicate that intelligence is capable of change, but that this change is not something which can be brought about quickly or easily or in unlimited degree. To produce such changes, however, requires major changes in the experience of the individual whose capacity is being studied. They have found, for example, increases in intelligence levels when children have been moved from the restricted environment of an "orphanage" or "children's home" to the richer experience of living with adopted parents. The reverse has also been found: that children committed to the restricted environments of some types of institutions show a gradual decrease in capacity. It has been found, too, that major changes are increasingly difficult as the person grows older. Intelligence levels then seem open to some degrees of change depending upon the experience of the individual. The point of view with respect to intelligence or capacity we have been discussing here is consistent with such observations and suggests, further, some possible reasons for the phenomena these psychologists have observed.

From a perceptual point of view, intelligence is not something static and unchangeable. But neither is it so fluid as to be open to rapid manipulation. Capacity, in this frame of reference, is a developmental characteristic affected and controlled by at least the seven factors of perception we have been exploring in this book. It is a function of the richness, extent, and availability of perceptions in the perceptual field and is open to change in the degree to which the phenomenal field itself can be changed. This view by no means offers hope that every child of low intelligence can be made normal. The perceptual field is not that fluid. On the other hand, we need to explore every possible avenue to the creation of intelligence and to push as far as we can go up every avenue that is open to us. The perceptual point of view may not be able to reverse the trends of a lifetime, but it can point the way to some challenging routes to explore.

SOME IMPLICATIONS OF THIS CONCEPTION OF INTELLIGENT BEHAVIOR

If the conception of intelligence we have been discussing is accurate, it raises serious questions about some of our common assumptions about intelligence and, at the same time, opens some exciting new possibilities for the treatment or education of persons we have often assumed to be beyond help. Perhaps we have been too impressed with the limitations upon growth and development which we observe in physical maturation.

We should explore to the very fullest the possibility that in those cases where we cannot demonstrate biologic impairment, the limitations upon intelligence may be psychological. If it turns out not to be true, we shall find out in time. We cannot afford to limit the places where we look by the preconceptions we have about the matter. Our responsibility here is too great. Education, to name but the most obvious of our social institutions, has in large measure predicated its goals and methods on a concept of humanity with certain static limitations on intelligence. If these limitations are not static, educators need to know that as soon as possible. The task of the scientist is to question, not to be content with answers. We cannot afford to accept an undemonstrated point of view that prevents us from asking questions.

Who can say, for example, what results we might be able to achieve by a systematic effort to remove or decrease the effectiveness of the limitations on perception discussed in this chapter? It is fascinating to speculate on the possibilities one might try in constructing a situation for a child, or adult, consciously designed to minimize the limitations imposed on perception by physical condition, environment, goals, the individual's self perceptions, and the effects of perceived personal threat.

If the position we have taken is accurate, it would suggest that there is much we can do (a) to free individuals from the restraints upon perception and (b) to provide the opportunities for perception to occur.

1. First and most obviously, we should be able to discover and make available to far more people the means to achieve better physical condi-

tion. We have already done a good deal in this area, but much needs yet to be done. Who can say, for instance, what completely adequate medical care for all our people or a more adequate diet for many might mean a generation hence?

2. If this discussion has merit, there lies the possibility of providing experiences for people that will make adequate perceptions possible. We have tried to do this in our schools, but have not always accomplished it. Can it be that the decreases in school success with advance through the school years is more a function of lack of meaning for students than lack of intelligence? Is it enough to assume that experience provided by us to the student is truly provided when he is free to experience it? Has the school child who is so worried about his relationship with his peers that he cannot perceive what his book is saying, truly been provided opportunity to perceive?

In our training of children of "low intelligence," we often provide situations wherein they are carefully taught to perform repeatedly a simple act. Is it possible that in so doing we may be further narrowing their fields of perception and building phenomenal selves that produce even narrower perceptive fields?

What kinds of environments could we construct that might more effectively result in increased perception? Such experiments as Lippitt and White have carried on with democratic and autocratic environments suggest some possibilities, but we need to know much more. Perhaps we could learn to build such environments from observing with greater care and understanding the methods of good teachers.

3. Who can say what possible effects might occur from a systematic release of the individual's perceptions by the satisfaction of his most pressing needs or goals? College professors insist they can produce more, which is another way of saying perceive more, when they have the leisure time to do so, when they are freed from the necessity of spending their time satisfying their needs for sheer existence. Can this be less true of others? It is possible that the child with strong desires for love, affection, status, prestige, or friendship might also be freed to perceive more widely and richly, if we could but find ways of helping him satisfy his need. Ordinarily we pay a good deal of attention to the physical needs of a child, understanding that with these needs unfulfilled he makes a poor student. Is there any good reason to suppose his psychological need is less pressing or less important in freeing him to perceive widely and accurately? We spend much time and energy trying to find ways of

"motivating" people or blaming them for not being motivated to do what we need them to do. We assume that if permitted to seek their own ends, people will not satisfy ours. Perhaps we should get further by helping them satisfy their need; they might then be free to satisfy ours.

4. Most of our educational methods are directed at the provision of perceptions for the student. He is lectured, required, shown, exhorted, and coerced to perceive what someone thinks he should. It seems possible that with equal energy devoted to the matter of creating new goals, and values in students, rich and varied perceptions might be more efficiently produced.

5. What effects might we be able to produce by providing experiences that build adequate concepts of self in children and adults? What differences in the richness and variety of perception might result from a generation of people with "I can" rather than "I can't" conceptions of themselves? What possibilities of increased perceptions and hence of increased intelligence might accrue to such a program? Clinical experience has demonstrated frequently how a changed perception of self as a more adequate personality can free children for improved school performance, for example.

What would happen if we were consciously and carefully to set about the task of providing experiences that would lead people to perceive themselves as adequate, worthy, self-respecting people? The child who perceives himself as unwanted, unacceptable, unable, or unliked perceives and behaves in rigid, defensive fashion. It should be possible to reverse this process and produce more adequate perceptions by systematic efforts at producing more adequate definitions of self. The possibilities seem tremendous, but we have scarcely scratched the surface of this problem.

Finally, if threat to the individual has as important effects as seem indicated in this discussion, helping persons to perceive themselves as adequate would seem a most important factor to consider in the release of the individual to perceive more adequately. The work of Rogers and his students in client-centered therapy has already illustrated to some degree what possibilities freeing the individual to perceive more adequately may accomplish through the provision of a permissive, nonthreatening relationship between counselor and client. We have already mentioned the effects Axline has reported following a permissive, nonthreatening form of play therapy.

The Phenomenal Self and Emotion

[Psychologists have come to believe that there is some degree of emotion connected with every human behavior. Psychologists, however, did not always think this way.] Experimental studies of the causes of emotional behavior have been made only in fairly recent times. For a long time fear and anger, as well as other emotions, were assumed to be innate responses to fairly definite situations. This assumption, which tended to discourage any efforts to modify emotional behavior by training, was first questioned by Watson. From that point on the psychologist's concept of emotion has undergone a rapid evolution. Today most psychologists approaching the problem from an external view have adopted a description of emotion as being nonspecific—a "disorganized response" on the part of the organism irrespective of the nature of the stimulus which sets it off. They point out that any person will become excited, afraid, or angry when he is in a situation which he is unable to control.]

Most recently, a number of psychologists, perhaps best represented by Prescott and Leeper, have expressed disagreement with this view and have seen emotion, not as disorganized response alone, but as having an organizing and facilitating effect as well. These writers see all behavior as possessing more or less of the physiologic accompaniments of what is usually called emotion. They point out, for example, that even in slight emergencies there is some increase in all our bodily activities. Every human activity seems to be accompanied by some degree of emotional response.

It is probably the increased consciousness of personal power and effectiveness resulting from this heightened bodily activity that causes people to like excitement, adventure, and change, to ride on roller coasters, to travel for pleasure, and to go on blind dates. By placing ourselves in situations that automatically demand a moderate rise in body tonus, we secure a sense of well-being and physical power that is very satisfying to our fundamental need for enhancement.

In the presence of a problem of modest difficulty we raise our fuel consumption and output of energy above the "idling" rate which is sufficient for the maintenance of bodily temperature, and increase the activity of practically all parts of the body. With increasing demand for action on the part of the organism, the physiologic changes accompanying an emotional state are increased. This mobilization of the resources of the organism was described by Cannon as placing the organism "on a war footing." It results in making available the necessary energy resources required either for meeting or fleeing the threat confronting the individual.

It is interesting that the physiologic changes which occur under "emotion" are the same no matter how the individual may describe the emotion he is experiencing. A high degree of "emotion" is accompanied by a whole series of physiologic changes among which are the following: (1) sweating of the palms of the hands; (2) increased activity of certain glands, particularly the adrenals, which make it possible for the blood to coagulate more rapidly; (3) the release of blood sugar, which provides large stores of quick energy; and (4) the increase in heart rate and breathing, which makes great exertion possible should it be necessary. These changes occur, moreover, whether it is fear, anger, or the ecstasy of a first kiss that we are experiencing. Regardless of our description of the experience, our purely physiologic responses to "important" events is the same.

Our present view of emotion is thus to see it as a kind of acceleration of body processes, a mobilization of energy which makes it possible to meet the peculiar needs of the situations with which we are confronted. We might illustrate this by our behavior as we rise in the morning to go about our daily business. When we are asleep the energy output required of our bodies is very low. We need only to "keep our motors turning over," as it were. Now, when the alarm clock rings we are confronted with the necessity for more activity. We can no longer lie still. We have to move, and this movement requires more energy than we have been expending. Our body processes must be speeded up to take care of this new requirement. As we go through the accustomed activities of dressing, washing, shaving, eating breakfast, we need still more acceleration. Later on in the day, we may find ourselves confronted with exciting or threatening situations which call forth still higher degrees of acceleration of our bodily processes, as when we receive a letter from a sweetheart or narrowly escape being run down while crossing the street. At these times we may find our "heart pounding," our faces flushed, our breath coming faster. We "feel excited."

When our caveman ancestor walked down a forest trail and came face to face with a bear it was important to have available the necessary energy to deal with this sudden emergency. He needed accelerated body processes whether he fought with the bear or ran from him. Even in our modern life we have need for this kind of quick energy to make it possible for us to deal with emergencies like avoiding an oncoming car, getting out of the way of a falling tree, or running a race. Emotion in these situations has survival value. At other times, however, the effects of increased body tone may sometimes be more embarrassing than helpful. The student who is called "on the carpet" by the dean has little need for great acceleration of his body processes. Under the circumstances neither fighting nor running is appropriate. Similarly, in making a speech one needs some increase in bodily activity. Too much, however, can be downright embarrassing or may even be incapacitating, as sometimes happens in extreme fright. Release of large amounts of energy with no appropriate outlet can be a very exhausting experience. Accelerating an automobile motor on the open road gives a smooth, exhilarating ride. Speeding the motor with the brakes on shakes the car in unbearable fashion. Much the same sort of thing happens to human beings under the stress of great emotion.

It is even possible in a very high degree of acceleration that an individual may be immobilized completely. An observer may watch an approaching tornado with mild excitement. As the tornado comes closer, and it becomes clear that he is in its path, this interest may be heightened to even greater attention and activity as he seeks shelter. Finally, with the tornado upon him, it may even result in so great an emotion as to "paralyze him with fright."

EMOTION AND TENSION. In the past there has been a tendency to regard emotion as a cause of behavior. This appears to be a confusion of the symptom for the cause. Some writers have spoken of a child's aggressive behavior as being a *result* of its anger, or a mother's overprotection as a *result* of her love for her child, and it is extremely frequent to find references to behavior occurring "*because* the individual is afraid."

It is probably more accurate to say that emotion is a state of tension or readiness to act. This tension represents the reaction of the organism to the perception of the possibility of need satisfaction (self enhancement) or the perception of threat (maintenance of self.) Thus, emotion is a behavioral manifestation of the organism's attempt to satisfy need. As is true of any other behavior, tension, or emotion, may be regarded as an aspect of the activity of the organism in seeking adequacy.

What the individual describes as his emotion is actually his account of his personal relation to the situation. The greater the personal reference, the greater is the degree of emotional experience. It is well known, for example, that stage fright is a function of this personal reference. The greater the attention to self, the greater is the likelihood of crippling emotional reactions. If the speaker can use a common technique and "get his mind off himself" such emotional responses quickly disappear. Almost any school child is familiar with the stunt of getting another to blush by focusing the latter's attention on himself. The blusher may also be aware that he can quickly reduce his tension if he can turn his attention and that of others away from himself.

THE DEGREE OF TENSION EXPERIENCED. The person under tension is seeking satisfaction of need. The feeling of tension is the result of his awareness either of menace to his organization or to the possibility of self enhancement. The degree of tension experienced will vary widely dependent upon at least the following factors:

1. The perceived relationship of an event to the phenomenal self.
2. The psychological immediacy of the event.
3. The clarity of the perception.
4. The individual's feeling of adequacy to cope with the matter.

The first of these factors we have just been discussing. We might state it as follows: The degree of emotion or tension experienced by the individual will be roughly proportional to the perceived importance of the relationship of the event to the self.

PSYCHOLOGICAL IMMEDIACY AND EMOTION. The second factor affecting the degree of emotion or tension experienced will be the nearness in time and space of the threatening or enhancing object. Threats or enhancements occurring right now are perceived as much more menacing or flattering than those which are some time off. Atomic bombing ten years from now does not seem nearly as threatening as planes overhead today. The grade which comes at the end of the semester is not nearly so threatening in the first few weeks as it becomes during final exam week.

When we speak of the "nearness" of an event in time or space it should be clear that we are speaking of closeness as it appears from the point of view of the behaver, not an outside observer. This is a matter of "psychological" rather than physical immediacy. The tiger which I see through my binoculars a mile off will cause me much less concern than the one on the other side of that bush. In speaking of proximity in space it is necessary to think, not in terms of physical space, but in terms of psychological space. The tiger behind the bars at the zoo may be no further away than the one behind the bush, but in terms of my own perceptions he is, even so, at a very safe distance. This principle of the immediacy of threat is nicely illustrated in the neurotic whose anxiety increases markedly and whose attempts to escape become more frantic as he approaches in time and space the threat he perceives to himself. There are always more "nervous breakdowns" at a university just before final exams than at any other time.

All of the illustrations we have used here have been with respect to threat. The principle is just as true in terms of enhancement. When Christmas is six months away, the prospect of a picnic *today* is much more exciting to the child than the bicycle Santa Claus promises to bring next winter.

THE CLARITY OF PERCEPTION AND EMOTION. A third factor affecting the degree of emotion or tension will be the clarity with which the situation is differentiated by the individual as dangerous or enhancing to the phenomenal self. In newborn babies, for example, the awareness of environment is so vague that only extreme and sudden changes in it will arouse responses violent enough to seem emotional to others. As the child develops, differentiations become more precise, and sometime after he is six months old he may burst into tears at the approach of a stranger or when placed on the floor in a strange house. His parents may be quite at a loss to explain his behavior because he has never shown such reactions in similar situations before. The real reason for his behavior, however, is probably this: That he had not previously differentiated his environment with sufficient clarity to distinguish what was strange and different.

It is quite possible for an individual to be in the midst of a highly dangerous situation, yet feel no emotion or tension whatever. One can stand in the midst of a sunny field enjoying the country air without feeling in danger so long as one does not know that the field is impregnated with hydrogen-bomb "fall-out." An event unperceived is unexperienced and calls for no behavior in response. This is not just an all or none problem, however, for clarity of perception is a matter of degree and the emotion experienced is likely to be roughly equivalent to the clarity of perception, other factors being equal. Thus a vaguely perceived danger may produce a mild degree of tension. The clearer the perception of menace or enhancement, the greater is likely to be the accompanying experience of emotion.

THE FEELING OF ADEQUACY AND EMOTION. (The degree of tension experienced appears to depend upon the individual's evaluation of the amount of enhancement or threat to himself he perceives in any situation.) The novice at flying may be quite upset by the very thought of leaving the ground, while after such an experience he may even seek further opportunities to fly because he so enjoys the excitement. The pilot of his plane, on the other hand, may be quite bored with it all and find his job monotonous and dull. Since the threat or enhancement involved in any situation is for each of us a completely unique function, it is clear that the emotion we experience must also be different for each of us.

The amount of need satisfaction inherent in any situation will be dependent upon the relationship which the situation bears to the phenomenal self as observed by the individual. Obviously, the person who conceives of himself as a very effective and popular public speaker will have a very different approach to an invitation to speak before an audience from one who conceives of himself as inadequate or of queer appearance. For the accomplished speaker it can be truly said that the idea of anyone's laughing at him on the platform "never enters his head," while for the novice this thought may be very nearly paralyzing in the emotional response it calls forth.

The degree of emotion or tension experienced will be determined very largely by the individual's feeling of adequacy to deal with the event he perceives himself confronted with. The things we feel adequate to cope with do not have an emergency character in our perceptions. They seem far less frightening and distressing than those things which seem beyond our control or capacities. Individuals who feel generally adequate suffer much less the incapacitating effects of emotion than persons who feel generally inadequate. Persons with concepts of themselves as generally unliked, unwanted, unacceptable, unable, and unworthy often find the tension they experience so great that they may be unable to operate effectively and efficiently. Instead, they are in a continual state of emergency, and the emotions they experience are destructive rather than helpful in maintaining and enhancing themselves.

The Phenomenal Self and Feeling

Most of us in the course of our daily lives make no distinction between our "feelings" and our "emotions." In attempting to communicate with other people we talk about our feelings or emotions of hate, anger, love, fear, anxiety, appreciation, or grief without stopping to define more precisely what it is we mean. Other people in turn grasp pretty effectively what we are trying to say. Whether we talk about feelings or emotions is, in everyday life, a matter of no great moment. The important thing is that we be able to communicate effectively with other people so that they understand something of what it is we are experiencing. The psychologist, however, trying to understand the nature and dynamics of behavior, cannot be content with so free and easy a use of terms. To shed light on the problems psychology is attempting to deal with, it is necessary to distinguish more clearly and precisely the concepts we use. This does not mean that the layman is wrong and the psychologist right or vice versa. It means only that different degrees of exactness in description are required for different purposes. The layman uses terms in his way for his purposes, and the psychologist uses terms in other ways for other purposes.

From the psychologist's view, what are these things we call our "feelings"? When we speak of our feelings, we are seeking to convey the personal meaning of an event for us. When we say we are "so mad at Jim," we are trying to communicate to someone else the particular meaning our interaction with Jim has for us. This feeling, "so mad at Jim," is the best we can do to translate the full flavor of our perceptions about ourselves and our relationship to Jim at a particular instant. Similarly, when we say "I love you," "I was scared stiff!" or "I wanted to sink through the floor," we are attempting to communicate either to ourselves or to others the particular meaning of a particular situation as we experienced it. Feelings are a kind of shorthand description of our perceptual fields at a particular moment.

Feelings are our perceptions of ourselves, of the situations in which we are involved, and the interrelationship of these two. This is a great deal to attempt to express in a single word or two, and it is not surprising that most of us feel our spoken words never quite convey the full flavor of what it is we experience.

What we experience at any moment is, of course, our whole perceptual field. To convey this, however, is patently impossible. To manipulate our own perceptions or to communicate them to others we need a kind of symbol by means of which we can express our field state. To express these perceptions of ourselves and the state of our respective fields we have developed a large number of symbols to convey our meanings to others. We speak of feeling angry, tired, blue, gay, in love, anxious, afraid, grateful, and a thousand others. These represent our attempts to convey to others the personal meanings events have for us. They are our attempts to translate our own perceptual fields in a way that can be understood by others. The deeper, more pervasive the meaning for us, the less likely are we to be able to express it satisfactorily. Our perceptual fields are so complex and include such a myriad host of perceptions that it is a wonder we are able to convey as much as we do to an outsider who has not experienced it with us.

Since the individual's bodily self is always a part of his perceptual field, a very large part of what a person describes as his feeling is made up of his awareness of the bodily conditions he differentiates in the field at that moment. Our body states are always with us and always in some degree a part of the perceptual field. This includes, of course, awareness of our state of tension or acceleration, which we described as emotion in the previous section. Almost all of the feelings we express convey to our hearers some sense of our physical status. For example, when I say that "I feel fine," what I am describing is the nature of my field at that moment including the state of my body. This is my way of expressing to others the vague organization of physiologic conditions existing within me at the moment as well as perhaps my knowledge of having achieved something noteworthy. If I am pressed for further description I might say "I feel vigorous," "my body tone is up," or "I feel like I could lick my weight in wildcats." On the other hand, when I feel "blue," if pressed I would probably tell you that I feel "funny in the stomach," "feel tired," "heavy in the chest," etc. The more intense the feeling, the more of this awareness of body state is conveyed. The terms "rage," "hate," "fright," "love" all carry strong feelings of body state even to the listener. Some psychologists have rather plainly although inelegantly described these kinds of words as "gut words" because they seem to include so very large an experience of our visceral states.

What we attempt to communicate by our feelings, then, is the state of our perceptual fields including our state of tension or acceleration. Feelings differ from emotion, however, in that they symbolize *all* of the perceptual field. The degree of tension experienced would express very little to other people without some further description of what brought on this state. To say "I felt very tense" conveys very little until we add to this a description of the meaning of the tension for us. It makes a good deal of difference whether we are talking about a degree of tension brought on by another person as anger, fear, or love. Feelings always include the emotional condition as an important factor in the total perceptual state, but usually extend far beyond body status.

Since feelings always include emotion, we would expect that the intensity of feeling would vary in the same ways as emotion, and this is actually the case. Like emotion, the intensity of feeling is likely to be a function of: (1) the perceived relationship of an event to the phenomenal self, (2) the psychological immediacy of the event, (3) the clarity of the perception, and (4) the personal feeling of adequacy possessed by the subject.

Often feelings, which are really descriptions of perceptual field states, have been confused with causes of behavior. Actually they represent no more than the individual's differentiation of a part of his field in symbolic and often highly stereotyped terms. As descriptions it is clear they cannot be causes of behavior. When a person says "I did it because I felt like it," what he is describing in a vague way is his perceptual field at the moment of his act. When he says he "felt angry" and struck his assailant, or felt "afraid" and fled from the scene, his behavior was not motivated by the feeling but was a result of the perceptions existing in the perceptual field at the moment. In either case, his bodily state was probably identical, for we know that the physiologic aspects of any "emotion" are always the same in kind though they may differ in degree. As a matter of fact, if the threat to his organization was very great he probably was not even aware of his "feelings." It is a common experience that in moments of great stress we may act with extreme vigor and are often surprised to find we did not feel afraid till the moment of crisis had passed. This is probably due to the fact that we were not aware of our body state during the moment of crisis and only became so when sufficient leisure was reached for attention to be directed to body conditions. Being "afraid" is thus the individual's description of his state—his personal reference and has nothing to do with cause or effect of the behavior of the moment of action. The behavior is the result of the perceptual field, not the feeling which describes the field.

It should not be supposed, that the feelings *as reported by* an individual are necessarily the same as those he experiences. What an individual feels is an internal experience going on in his own private world. What he chooses to reveal of this sanctuary to an outsider may have a more or less accurate relationship to the feelings he really possesses. Even with the best of intentions, it is likely that he can never succeed in conveying the full flavor of his perceptual experience to another. It is even true that a large part of our time and effort is spent in preventing other people from knowing what it is we are feeling about particular matters. Most of us want to keep our private worlds intact, and even those whom we love and trust most can never be fully admitted to this inner sanctum. Feelings as experienced and feelings as reported to other people are by no means one and the same.

Some writers have made a distinction between "intellectual" behavior and "emotional" behavior. They point out that some things we do seem to be the result of our thinking about things, while other activities seem to be the outcome of how we feel about things. This is, of course, a false dichotomy. We cannot separate intellectual from feeling functions. All our behavior is always a function of the total perceptual field at the moment of behaving. Some events seem to us to be more closely related to ourselves and may be accompanied by more or less tension. In this sense, some events are more likely to be matters about which we have definite feelings than others, but no behavior can ever be purely intellectual or emotional. All behaviors are a product of our perceptions and all involve a greater or lesser degree of acceleration or tension.

In this discussion we have talked primarily of the individual's own feelings. We have said that the words he uses to describe his feelings are symbols by which he tries to convey something of the nature of his perceptual field to other people. Other people use similar words to describe the state of their perceptual fields in their turn. We thus become aware, not only of our own perceptual fields, but also to some degree of the fields of others through this kind of communication.

But language alone is by no means the only source of information about the fields of others. We are able to understand a great deal about how other people feel from the clues they give us through their behavior. Observing other people's behavior (including, of course, what they have to say, which is a kind of behavior too), we are able to infer something of what they are feeling and this makes it possible for us to understand something of the nature of the perceptual field which lies behind their actions. This ability to "feel like another" or to "place one-self in another's shoes" is called *empathy*. It is a talent possessed in some degree by all of us, although some of us have developed it far more than others. It is an important factor in communication and in effective human relations.

CHAPTER 12

The Adequate Personality

ADJUSTMENT AND MALADJUSTMENT

Our unceasing striving for feelings of worth and value places all of us under the necessity for adjusting to something at every moment of our lives. Some of us are more successful in achieving need satisfaction than others, but none of us is ever granted leave from the struggle for any length of time. In the course of this never-ending search we may behave in countless varieties of ways. Other people looking at our behavior may describe us as adjusted or maladjusted, depending upon the degree to which our behavior conforms to their peculiar values. From our own points of view, however, we do not describe ourselves as adjusted or maladjusted unless we are students of psychology or persons who are accustomed to trying to see themselves "objectively." Most of us describe ourselves in terms of our "feelings." We say we are happy or unhappy, satisfied or dissatisfied, angry or in love, depending upon the extent to which our need is being satisfied, and upon our progress toward the goals through which we are seeking to satisfy it.

The terms "adjustment" and "maladjustment" are terms from an external frame of reference. They are objective terms used to describe behavior as it appears to an outside observer. More often than not they are applied to evaluations of the extent to which an individual's behavior conforms to social expectancy. This approach to the nature of adjustment is a static one. It establishes a "norm" for behavior and thereafter judges individuals as "adjusted" or "maladjusted" depending upon their degree of conformity to such norms. Almost inevitably labels of "bad" and "good" also become attached to behavior of one variety or the other.

While the terms "adjusted" and "maladjusted" have a real usefulness in an external setting, they are likely to prove inadequate in helping us to understand the behavior of a unique human being. Many a "maladjusted" individual appears to be quite well satisfied with himself and many a seemingly "well-adjusted" person may actually be a desperately unhappy individual who conforms to others because he lacks confidence in himself. What brings the person to the psychological clinic is not the situation as it is seen by others, but the situation as he sees it himself. The case histories in any clinic reveal dozens of persons whom others would judge to be quite well adjusted, but who still feel so ineffective or unhappy that they seek the assistance of the psychologist. It even happens that persons tortured and driven by feelings of inadequacy have sometimes been pointed out with pride as examples of industry and perseverance for our children. On college campuses, homosexuals have been voted the "best-adjusted girl in our sorority." External observations are by no means adequate in understanding the particular human being.

Though the concepts of "adjustment" and "maladjustment" are useful in an external frame of reference for the classification of behavior, they have little value to the behaver himself. People behave according to their feelings or perceptions at any moment and it is seldom that "adjustment" per se is the goal toward which an individual strives. Who, after all, wishes to be average? Most of us may have to settle for such a state, but few of us are content to remain there if any other possibilities seem open to us. Adjustment in the normative sense is hardly desirable as a goal for society either. A society all of whose people were busily engaged in seeking to be average would soon find itself hopelessly outmoded and sitting still while the rest of the world passed by. We need a concept of adjustment which represents an achievement to strive for; a concept which defines the *best man can be* rather than the average of what he has been.

Actually, the best he can be is what each one of us is striving for in everything he does. The goal of all behavior, we have seen, is the achievement of personal adequacy. The search for the maintenance and enhancement of self is never ending. It is a dynamic, active search, a continuous striving to become the ultimate of which one is capable. Other authors have called this active "seeking to become" by such names as: "growth tendency," "self-consistency," "self-realization," "self-actualization," and "self-fulfillment."

Though each of us strives continuously to achieve an adequate personality, it should not be supposed that such an end is ever reached. On the contrary, this is a goal toward which all of us struggle but at which none of us ever arrives. Adequacy is a mark we can achieve only in degree; some of us more, some of us less, but none of us ever completely. Some unhappy people live out their lives with little or no feeling of adequacy, while other people achieve high degrees of satisfaction and pleasure from feelings of adequacy in very great measure. But not even the most adequate man who ever lived was able to achieve the fullest possible extent of adequacy. So long as life exists there is room and need for further effort.

READ What Is an Adequate Personality?

There are two ways in which we can attempt to examine the adequate personality. We can look at such a personality in terms of his observable behavior. We can ask, "How does such a person behave?" or "What are the particular behavioral traits that characterize an adequate person?" This is the approach taken by Maslow, who has attempted to study a number of self-actualizing persons with an eye to discovering the kinds of behaviors typical of such people. Since behavior is a function of perception, we can also approach the study of the adequate personality by an exploration of how such persons perceive themselves and the world in which they live. This latter approach is more consistent with the point of view of this book, so let us begin our exploration by examining how the adequate personality sees himself and the world. Having examined the ways in which adequate personalities perceive we may then take a look at the kinds of behaviors characteristic of such people.

READ The Perceptual View of Adequacy   WHOLE

Generally speaking, we could describe the adequate personality in perceptual terms as one who has achieved a high degree of need satisfaction. These are people who feel generally capable of coping with life, who have developed phenomenal selves so defined as to be highly successful in the achievement of effective maintenance and enhancement of self. They see themselves in essentially positive ways and as a consequence are free and open to their experience, able to accept both themselves and others and to identify strongly with their fellow men. Adequate people feel strong enough and safe enough to cope with life openly and directly with a minimum of threat and fear. They see themselves and the world in which they live more often than not as exciting and challenging. Life does not seem too much to such people. Events seem

to them to lie well within their own capacities, and they feel capable of
dealing with life effectively and efficiently. Indeed, they might almost
equally well be called nonthreatened personalities.

Examining more closely the perceptual fields of adequate persons it
seems possible to differentiate three major characteristics: (1) Adequate
persons perceive themselves in generally positive ways. (2) Adequate
persons are more capable of accepting and integrating their perceptions
in the phenomenal field. (3) Adequate persons are capable of wide
identification of self with others. It should not be supposed that these
are discrete characteristics capable of operating by themselves. On the
contrary, the perceptual field is a unitary organization, and the operation of these three factors is so mutually interdependent as to remind
one of the old adage about "which came first, the chicken or the egg?"

POSITIVE SELF PERCEPTIONS

The self concept as we have described it is an organization of self
meanings or ways of seeing self, varying in importance or centrality in
a given individual. The basic need of each of us, moreover, is to maintain and enhance this self. Adequate personalities have achieved a considerable degree of such need satisfaction. They see themselves more
frequently in enhancing than in destructive ways. In our society this
usually means that adequate people see themselves, among other things,
as liked, wanted, acceptable, able, and worthy. They perceive themselves as persons of dignity and integrity who belong and contribute to
the world in which they operate. Their phenomenal selves are, for the
most part, defined in positive ways as adequate to deal with those
aspects of life important to the achievement of need satisfaction in their
culture.

In another culture, to be sure, adequate people might perceive themselves differently. Most of us would feel woefully inadequate in a society which valued skill in the war dance, for example. Within the confines of the society important to him, however, the adequate personality
perceives himself as capable and effective. The majority of the concepts
of self which go to make up his peculiar phenomenal self are positive
and appropriate to the culture in which he lives out his days.

This is not to say that adequate personalities are incapable of negative
self perceptions. On the contrary, they may very well have negative
concepts of self within the total organization of the phenomenal self.
An adequate person might conceivably have within his self organization

such concepts of self as: "I am not a very attractive person, I am thoroughly disliked by my father-in-law, I am a terrible golfer, joke teller, and typist." Negative concepts of self are not absent in the total organization of the adequate personality. They are present, but do not color and distort the entire organization. Such percepts maintain their proper perspective as parts of the self concept, but do not overbalance it. A very large part of the assistance rendered to people in psychotherapy consists primarily of helping them to gain a new perspective of self so that negative self perceptions do not exert an undue influence upon the organization of the phenomenal self. Adequate personalities have essentially although not exclusively positive concepts of self.

Concepts of self, we have seen, vary not only in number but also in centrality or importance to the individual. Adequacy is not simply a function of the *number* of positive perceptions; it is a function of the *importance* of the concepts of self possessed by a given personality. The important or central aspects of self have a greater effect on the total economy of a personality than do peripheral or marginal self percepts. It is being spurned by *the* girl which depresses the lover, although he may be attractive to dozens of others. A thousand good acts may be insufficient to counteract the feeling of guilt from a single act of years past. The child's perception of what his playmates say of him may be of far more importance than his teacher's good opinion. A plumber coming to fix the radiators in our play-therapy room was shocked to discover the freedom permitted our young clients. The idea of permitting a child to wet on the floor was completely repugnant to him, and he criticized our "damfool" notions in no uncertain terms. This attitude on the part of the plumber bothered us very little. Had the same ideas been expressed by an honored and respected colleague, our reaction would have been very different. We do not care much what a plumber thinks of our professional techniques; we care very much what some psychologists think.

A self concept organized of many positive self definitions provides the individual with a great resource for dealing with the vicissitudes of life. Many positive self perceptions give the individual a feeling of adequacy and confidence, so that he approaches the events of life with an essentially positive, assured bearing which, in itself, is an important head start. Research on leadership suggests that leaders generally possess more favorable attitudes toward self and others. The very presumption of success is likely to make success more likely. Moreover, positive self perceptions are conducive to still further perceptions of the same order.

This is a common observation which finds its place in our folk sayings: "Nothing succeeds like success," "Them as has, gets," "The rich get richer and the poor get poorer."

The positive self perceptions characteristic of the adequate personality act also as a reservoir against which negative, damaging experiences are perceived in a more accurate and realistic perspective. Because the self is overwhelmingly defined in positive terms, most negative self perceptions can be readily assimilated in such a reservoir with little or no disturbance to the whole structure. Negative events can be accepted and taken in stride. Feeling fundamentally self confident, the adequate person is less ruffled by unhappy events. He finds it possible to take criticism calmly and to evaluate it clearly. Instead of being disorganized by minor self-damaging experiences, negative percepts are evaluated against the larger mass of basically positive experience, in which perspective they seem far less important or overwhelming.

Since adequate personalities do not feel deprived, they have far less need to defend the self against external attack. Assaults upon self do not seem crucial or overwhelming. Rather, they seem well within the capacities of the self to cope with and even, if they are minor attacks, may be perceived by the adequate personality as exciting and challenging opportunities to test his mettle. For adequate persons, self testing can itself be an exhilarating experience to be met with interest and joy. For such people the trying is often more exciting and enhancing than the achieving. The possession of a large reservoir of positive experience of self provides the individual with a vast security to be used as a base for adventure and a firm foundation for meeting even the more difficult aspects of life with courage.

This fundamentally positive self organization seems characteristic of "well-adjusted" people seen from an external frame of reference as well. Numerous studies of "adjustment" have demonstrated that well-adjusted persons have essentially positive attitudes toward self and others, while the reverse is true of "poorly adjusted" people. Psychological health seems basically determined by the adequacy of the individual's self definitions. Effective living is closely allied to personal feelings of dignity and integrity, to feelings of worth and self actualization.

ACCEPTANCE AND ADEQUACY

A second major characteristic of the adequate personality is his ability to accept any and all perceptions into his awareness. As Rogers has pointed out, an individual confronted with a particular event may deal with it in any of three ways. The experience may be: (a) symbolized, perceived and organized into some relationship to the self; (b) ignored because there is no perceived relationship to the self structure; (c) denied symbolization or given a distorted symbolization because the experience is inconsistent with the structure of the self. The first of these methods of dealing with perceptions is what we mean by acceptance. An adequate personality is one capable of admitting any and all experiences and of integrating this experience into his existing self structure. Such a person can acknowledge his experience, allow it entrance to his consideration, and relate it in some fashion to the existing concepts he holds of himself and the world about him.

This characteristic is so important a factor in the perceptions of adequate personalities that in the earlier edition of this book the adequate personality was defined solely "as one capable of accepting into its organization any and all experience of reality." While acceptance is certainly an outstanding characteristic, it is hardly sufficient to define the adequate person in those terms alone. Acceptance is, itself, a function of the extent and nature of the already existing perceptions in the field. In the section just above we have seen that the adequate personality has a phenomenal field containing many positive self perceptions. The very existence of these perceptions makes acceptance more likely. Acceptance is thus a characteristic of adequate personalities derived from and largely made possible by the individual's positive experience of self. Because such persons have a reservoir of positive experience they are able to accept. Acceptance, in turn, makes possible even greater adequacy.

Adequate personalities do not feel a great need to defend themselves against their experience. They have an openness or readiness for new experience and are capable of reorganizing the phenomenal field to make most effective use of it. This willingness to confront experience has sometimes been confused with resignation. Adequate personalities, however, are by no means resigned. On the contrary, they are quite likely to be among our most important agents of social change. A readiness to admit the *existence* of an idea by no means implies its adoption. The acknowledgment of the presence of an event must be the first step to effective action. The readiness to receive and consider the facts about Communism, for example, does not mean a whole-hearted or even a faint-hearted conversion to such ideals. The acceptance of the facts may actually be the first step in a vigorous defense against such concepts. Acceptance refers to the admission of evidence, not a commitment to a line of action.

Clearly acceptance, in the sense we have used it here, is a *sine qua non* for effective, efficient, satisfying behavior. The individual able to accept is open to all experience. He has fewer limits imposed upon what he can explore and examine. He has less need to defend or distort his experiences and so is capable of examining even that which is too frightening or unpleasant for less adequate personalities to consider. This straightforward, uncomplicated kind of relationship to his experience gives the adequate personality a tremendous advantage in dealing with life, for behavior based upon more and better evidence will almost certainly be more effective, efficient, and satisfying in the long run.

This open, "all-the-cards-on-the-table" kind of relationship to events occurring about him is just as characteristic of the adequate personality's approach to perceptions about himself. Adequate personalities are just as capable of accepting their experience of self as of events in the not self. Maslow has expressed this relationship as follows:

> They can accept their own human nature with all its shortcomings, with all its discrepancies from the ideal image without feeling real concern. It would convey the wrong impression to say that they are self-satisfied. What we must say rather is that they can take the frailties and sins, weaknesses and evils of human nature in the same unquestioning spirit that one takes or accepts the characteristics of nature. One does not complain about water because it is wet, or about rocks because they are hard, or about trees because they are green. As the child looks out upon the world with wide, uncritical, innocent eyes, simply noting and observing what is the case, without either arguing the matter or demanding that it be otherwise, so does the self-actualizing person look upon human nature in himself and in others.

Taylor and Combs, for example, found this ability to accept self to be highly related to adjustment. They asked a group of fifth grade children to indicate on a list of 20 unflattering statements, probably true of all children, those which each child believed were true of himself. When these results were next compared to the same child's scores on a test of adjustment, highest scores were found among the best-adjusted children and vice versa. The better the child's adjustment, the more unflattering truths he was able to accept about himself! The admission of the existence of unflattering truth about self is often the first step toward more effective behavior. Indeed, many churches recognize this age-old principle, and utilize it in the confessional in the belief that confession (acceptance of the fact) of sin is the first step toward reformation.

Acceptance of self should not be confused with "liking." Some experimenters, for example, have attempted to measure self acceptance by asking subjects to indicate the degree to which they liked certain characteristics about themselves. But acceptance is no more related to liking than it is to resignation. Acceptance has to do with the admission of fact, the acknowledgment of existence, and has nothing to do with liking. The adequate personality may accept the fact, for example, that he is sometimes nasty to his children, but this hardly means that he likes himself so! Liking and disliking have to do with judgments about self, while acceptance is nonjudgmental. It has to do with the consideration of evidence, not its evaluation. The adequate personality neither overvalues nor undervalues self. He is maximally able to put his "self" on the block for examination and scrutiny like any other datum. Research on the outcomes of psychotherapy corroborates this characteristic of adequacy. The data show that as clients get better (and presumably more adequate) their capacity to accept both self and others increases markedly.

While acceptance is most notably characteristic of the perceptions of adequate persons, it is also characteristic in more or less degree by every human being. It is only through some degree of acceptance that any individual is able to profit from his experience. What distinguishes the adequate personality from his fellows is that he has achieved this ability in greater degree than the rest of us. The effect of a capacity for acceptance, furthermore, is cumulative. The wider, richer experience made possible by acceptance contributes to an ever more adequate phenomenal field and phenomenal self. In turn, the kind of self assurance possessed by the adequate person places him under less need to deny or distort his experience and thus leads to still further achievements of adequacy. A phenomenal self becomes adequate in part by acceptance; and the more adequate a person feels, the more acceptant he becomes.

THE ADEQUATE SELF AND IDENTIFICATION

We have constructed so far a definition of an adequate self from the individual's own frame of reference. But no individual in our society lives in isolation. Whether or not any person achieves need satisfaction does not depend upon himself alone but upon his interaction with his environment and the society he lives in. Presumably an individual could get along for a time on a desert island without other people, but few of us would choose such an existence. The concept is in large part a definition of the relationship between the self and society and must be in harmony with that portion of the culture important to the individual. We are so entirely dependent upon the good will and coöperation of others in our society that it would be impossible to achieve feelings of adequacy without some effective relationship with them. The adequate personality must be capable of living effectively and efficiently with his fellows.

The self, we have seen, is not a static and unchangeable organization. Rather, it is a more or less fluid organization capable of change and redefinition in the light of the individual's experience. The self may, for example, be so narrowly defined as to exclude some aspects of self which are apparent to others. It sometimes happens, for example, that handicapped persons may define themselves in such a way as to disown their handicaps. Similar physical manifestations of a restricted self definition can be found in hypnosis when a subject is told he cannot feel what is happening to him. With such a restricted self definition, he may not respond at all to a cigarette burn, for it does not seem to him to be happening to him. All of us are familiar with persons who have defined themselves in such a way as to deny some of their less pleasant characteristics.

Fortunately, the self may also be defined in ways that extend beyond the confines of self, so that one may, almost literally, rise above himself. We may extend the physical confines of ourselves when we point with a stick and we have a feeling of touch, not in our fingers but at the end of the stick. We may extend ourselves also by the use of a gun, a telephone, or a letter. Having written to another person, we say: "I told him . . . ," although it was the letter that did so. The business world is dependent upon the extension of self we achieve by signing our names to a contract. Most important of all, however, is the kind of self extension we achieve through identification with other people. In the course of growing up, each of us becomes more or less identified with large numbers of people and events, sometimes only remotely, but sometimes, too, so closely as to make it almost impossible to distinguish between "me and thee." People become identified with parents, husbands or wives, teachers, institutions, towns, races, nations, and a million other categories. These identifications become basic parts of self and we therefore speak of *my* daughter, *my* country, *my* fraternity, *my* race, *we* Southerners, or *us* Texans. Whatever the identification, it becomes part of an expanded self.

What is more, since the fundamental need of the individual is to maintain and enhance the phenomenal self, whatever the self is identified with must also be maintained and enhanced. Praise heaped upon those with whom we are identified is received as though it were personally earned. We rejoice at the winning of *our* team, the happiness of *our* wives or husbands, and we share the tragedies of *our* friends and neighbors. The individual behaves toward those things, people, or places with which he is identified as though they were, in truth, himself. The doctor cannot operate on his daughter any more than he can on himself. The psychologist can understand somebody else's children with greater objectivity than his own. The maintenance and enhancement of self becomes extended to those with whom we are identified, and the satisfaction of our own need becomes almost indistinguishable from the satisfaction of theirs, too.

To some people first exposed to the idea that each human being is insatiably seeking the maintenance and enhancement of self, it appears that people must indeed be extremely selfish beings intent only upon self gratification. This is only true, however, for the isolated personalities, the rejected hangers-on of our society. The stronger an individual's identification with others, the more certain it is that in seeking his own maintenance and enhancement he will be seeking that of others as well. He must, for they are one and the same. The need for adequacy in the individual extends to the people, things, places, events, and ideas with whom and with which he becomes identified. The more adequate the personality, the broader and deeper will be the relationships he has discovered between self and others. The more adequate the personality, the more likely he is to feel a sense of oneness with things and people about him. Adequate personalities behave in ways beneficial to all of us, not because it is a good thing to do, but because behaving so is a normal and natural expression of themselves. It is not the adequate people we need to fear in our society; they are likely to be so closely identified with us that they seek our needs along with their own. It is only the people that do not feel they belong who see no need to consider the good of others and to abide by the rules. It is the inadequate persons, the deprived, the rejected, the alone in our society who, seeing themselves apart from the rest of us, can behave in ways that are dangerous and destructive.

Psychology has long pointed out that the development of the child is from a state of egocentricity as an infant to altruism as an adult. That is, the very young child is primarily concerned with gratification of his own personal need. He wants what he wants when he wants it! Nothing is more tyrannical than a newborn baby. Even a child's parents are only objects to him at first, and it is only with time that he learns to identify himself with a particular person as *Mother* and a particular person as *Father*. Later he comes to identify himself with others of his family, then his neighborhood, his school, and after a time, with his town and country. The growth of an adult human being is a process of increasing identification with the world about him. Little by little over the years of his existence each human being discovers his unique relationship to people and events. Some people, like the saints, have developed this feeling of identification to a degree wherein they could feel at one with all mankind or even with all life. Some, like the criminals or the insane, live out their lives in isolation. Most of us lie somewhere between in our capacity for identification.

The more adequate we become, the greater the identification we achieve. Acceptance of self is closely related to acceptance of others. The modern closely interrelated society requires that effective citizens be deeply aware of their fellows and behave responsibly toward them. Adequacy requires both the discovery of self and the discovery of others.

The Trait Versus Perceptual Approach to Understanding Adequacy

It is the basic premise of this book that all behavior is a function of perception. It would follow, then, that the perceptual characteristics of adequate personalities should have their counterparts in behavior. And indeed this seems to be true. We have described adequate personalities as those who: (1) perceive themselves in essentially positive ways, (2) are capable of acceptance of self and others, and (3) perceive themselves as closely identified with others.

The more adequate the personality, the more these ways of perceiving self and the relationship to the world about him will be characteristic of the individual's phenomenal field. Such perceptions in turn will often cause such persons to behave repeatedly in certain ways. Behavior may even become so predictable and characteristic as to be described by the external observer as "personality traits." Similarly, because they perceive in more common ways, the behaviors of several different adequate persons are likely to be highly similar. Thus, certain kinds of behavior seem fairly generally characteristic of adequate persons. It should not be presumed, however, that these common kinds of behaviors are *always* present in every adequate personality. Nor can they be used as criteria to determine the degree of a given person's adequacy. Behavior is always a function of the individual's total field at the moment of action, and similar perceptions in the fields of different people will not necessarily result in identical behaviors. A way of behaving which deals satisfactorily with one problem may be totally inappropriate for another. Therefore we cannot judge adequacy solely on the basis of the presence or absence of particular traits. Truly adequate people are not rigid personalities. They have sufficient fluidity of perception and action as to be maximally effective in the situations to which they are exposed. This kind of effective interaction requires a high degree of sensitivity and openness to change when such change is necessary. As a consequence, the behavioral traits of such people cannot be employed as guides for the behavior of everyone else.

Those people in our society charged with the responsibility for helping others to grow and develop into effective, adequate citizens need to understand very clearly the difference between an external trait approach to the question of adequacy and a personal, perceptual approach. The achievement of adequacy is the fundamental need of both the individual and his society. Whatever we believe about the nature of the adequate personality, therefore, sets the goals for our personal growth as well as the goals toward which we strive in helping others to achieve adequacy in our homes, schools, or community life. An understanding of the nature of adequacy solely in terms of the ways adequate people frequently behave leads directly to attempts to catalogue "good" ways of behaving, and then to an attempt to teach these ways to others.

Such a trait approach to helping people often fails because it is exclusively concerned with *what people do.* What people do, however, is only a symptom or the expression of the dynamic factors within the individual that produce his unique ways of behaving. Assisting others to achieve adequacy, therefore, by means of telling, exhorting, or "teaching" people how they should behave ordinarily has little chance of success. What seems appropriate to do in a given circumstance is always dependent upon the individual's need and the state of his perceptual field at the moment. Few of us behave inadequately because we do not know better. Mere knowledge of how adequate people behave is of little value to other people because it seems to have little relevance to their own peculiar needs and problems. Much as we may admire what our heroes have done, such action may seem too difficult, impossible, or irrelevant and inappropriate to the situation *we* perceive ourselves to be confronted with.

It is the fundamental thesis of this volume that behavior is a direct function of the individual's perceptual field and change in behavior can only occur when some change has occurred in how people perceive. In the following pages we have tried to describe some of the characteristic behaviors which seem typical of many adequate personalities. These "traits of adequacy" are interesting observations about adequate personalities made from the point of view of the external observer, and they give us clues to how adequate persons are likely to behave in our society. Interesting as these traits may be, it should be kept in mind that they do not provide satisfactory or effective direction for helping others to achieve greater adequacy. They are products, not causes. The perceptual characteristic of adequate personalities we have outlined above will provide us with far more dynamic and applicable guides to effective action. When people can be helped to see differently, they will behave differently. If people can be helped to perceive themselves and the world they live in more adequately, they will behave more adequately as well. With this reservation in mind, let us now look at some of the characteristic ways in which many adequate people behave.

Some Behavioral Characteristics of Adequate Persons

MORE EFFICIENT BEHAVIOR

Adequate personalities behave more effectively and efficiently than their less adequate fellows. The great reservoir of positive perceptions and the capacity for acceptance of self and the world gives the adequate person a tremendous advantage in dealing with life. Being under no great necessity for self defense he has less need to distort his perceptions or to select them in terms or his peculiar unfulfilled goals or desires. He is able to behave more effectively and efficiently because he behaves in the light of more and better data. Being more open to experience, he has a wider phenomenal field on which to base his behavior. He is able to behave more often from choice than from necessity.

Maslow, in a study of self-actualizing persons, has described such people as follows:

The first form in which this capacity was noticed was an unusual ability to detect the spurious, the fake and the dishonest in personality, and, in general, to judge people correctly and efficiently. In an informal check experiment with a group of college students, a clear tendency was discerned for the more secure (the more healthy) to judge their professors more accurately than did the less secure students.

As the study progressed, it slowly became apparent that this efficiency extended to many other areas of life—indeed *all* areas that were tested. In art and music, in things of the intellect, in scientific matters, in politics and public affairs, they seemed as a group to be able to see concealed or confused realities more swiftly and more correctly than others. Thus, an informal experiment indicated that their predictions of the future from whatever facts were in hand at the time seemed to be more often correct, because less based upon wish, desire, anxiety, fear, or upon generalized, character-determined optimism or pessimism. . . . They are, therefore, far more apt to perceive what is "there" rather than their own wishes, hopes, fears, anxieties, their own theories and beliefs or those of their cultural group.

In the dynamic relationship of perception to behavior, more adequate perceptual fields must necessarily result in more adequate behavior. People who perceive more efficiently will behave more efficiently. The individual who is able to behave from a phenomenal field open to more data has a great advantage over the rest of us. He is able to play a better game because he holds more and better cards. With more data available, adequate personalities are able to penetrate more directly and sharply to the heart of problems. They often possess an uncanny ability to place their finger on the core of issues and are thus able to deal with matters more precisely and appropriately. Their perceptions are less complicated by extraneous events, personal goals and values, or the necessity for immediate self gratification.

Because adequate persons feel fundamentally secure they are able to evaluate themselves more accurately. Their levels of aspiration are far more likely to be realistic and attainable. They are able to deal with events, and with themselves, with greater objectivity and equanimity. Feeling secure within himself, the adequate person has less need to hide from the unpleasant and can feel more comfortable with himself even when under attack. This fundamental security makes it possible to deal with events with less "personal axes to grind." It even makes it possible for the adequate person to risk himself. He is capable of placing himself in a poor or unflattering light if necessary, and this makes possible the consideration of evidence not open to the individual who is fearful and defensive of self. Adequate people are able to be and to give of themselves with courage and conviction.

Adequate personalities do not *need* to have an immediate answer to problems. They are capable of what Frenkel-Brunswik has called "toleration of ambiguity." That is, they are able to live comfortably with an unsolved problem. They do not *need* to have an answer at once. Consequently, they are less likely to accept partial solutions to problems as sufficient or final. With a backlog of security in their own feelings of adequacy, they are not easily upset when confronted by events whose meanings are not immediately apparent. They do not ignore such events in the hope that "if I don't notice it, it will go away." They do not find it necessary to deny that an event has happened, nor do they find themselves compelled to "explain it away." Because they do not *have* to have an answer, they are able to consider wider samples of evidence and to deal with events with far more patience than the rest of us.

The individual who is capable of seeing in broader perspective and with less necessity for arriving at foregone conclusions obviously has a wider choice of action. He can deal with matters more objectively and leisurely because there seems to him less at stake. As a consequence, such people are likely to make fewer mistakes and run up fewer blind alleys. The value of this capacity for society can hardly be overestimated. We need such talents to prevent our becoming the victims of unfortunate concepts adopted because they are convenient or fit the existing patterns of thought.

SPONTANEITY AND CREATIVITY

Closely associated with the greater efficiency of behavior of the adequate personality, and growing out of the same basic characteristics of the phenomenal field, is the capacity for spontaneous creative behavior. The reservoir of positive perceptions and the ability to accept new experience provides a firm basis from which the adequate person can launch into new and different areas of experience. It is the secure people who can take chances. They do not have to maintain rigid, narrow lines of operation. A rich self can afford to be extravagant, a poor one must shelter and protect his investments with scrupulous care and conservatism. Adequate people have far less need to defend themselves and consequently are able to devote much greater time and attention to wider fields of experience. Feeling fundamentally secure, they are capable of experimenting, branching out, extending themselves to the limit. They are even capable, when necessary, of placing themselves in jeopardy for the sheer joy of testing their own limits. As a consequence such people are to be found among the most spontaneous and creative people of every generation.

It is, of course, possible for people to break with the conventional from motives of weakness or fear. It has happened that people have made important contributions to human advance out of motives that were purely hostile. A man may, for example, develop a new technique out of anger at a supervisor or a desire to embarrass his foreman. People may also be creative out of an attempt to rebel against the existing system or from a desire to break out of the sheer monotony of existing patterns. The creativity of the adequate personality, however, does not seem to stem from this kind of rebellion. Rather, the spontaneity of adequate persons seems an outgrowth of their basic security and courage to break with tradition and orthodoxy, not because they feel deprived or deficient, but out of an opposite feeling of inner strength and security which permits them to risk themselves in experimentation.

This originality of adequate persons is what one would logically expect as a consequence of the broader, richer phenomenal fields characteristic of such people. With wider fields available and less need for self defense, adequate people sometimes seem to fairly "pop with ideas." They are capable of seeing relationships not seen by others. Their more efficient perceptions make it possible for them to penetrate more effectively to premises while others are still muddling about with techniques. Persons dealing with the *essence* of ideas rather than their forms are far less likely to confuse means and ends. They can concern themselves with problems and issues and avoid being so bogged down in detail as to miss the major aspects. Because they operate from more inclusive frames of reference, they can often perceive more adequate, creative, and original solutions to life problems.

The kind of openness to experience we have been discussing has another effect upon the behavior of adequate people. It makes possible a capacity for wonder and a sensitivity to events that makes a thrilling experience of much that may appear humdrum and ordinary to others. Maslow speaks of this as a continued freshness of appreciation and describes it as follows:

Self-actualized people have the wonderful capacity to appreciate again and again, freshly and naively the basic goods of life with awe, pleasure, wonder, and even ecstasy, however stale these experiences may have become to others. Thus, for such people, every sunset is as beautiful as the first one, any flower may be of breath-taking loveliness even after he has seen a million flowers. The thousandth baby he sees is just as miraculous a product as the first one he saw. He remains as convinced of his luck in marriage thirty years after his marriage and is as surprised by his wife's beauty when she is sixty as he was forty years before. For such people, even the casual workaday, moment-to-moment business of living can be thrilling, exciting, and ecstatic.

It will be recognized that the freedom of the phenomenal field characteristic of adequate personalities, their clearer, more accurate perceptions of events, and their capacity for originality are synonymous with what we usually mean by intelligence. In Chapter 11, we define intelligence as a function of the richness, extent, and availability of perceptions in the phenomenal field. The acquisition of such a phenomenal field is enormously enhanced when people feel adequate.

THE AUTONOMY OF ADEQUATE PERSONALITIES

(Adequate persons often seem characterized by a much higher degree of independence of the social and physical forces which bind many of the rest of us. They seem less in the grip of external events and respond more to inner wellsprings of understanding and motivation.) They have a profound respect for the dignity and integrity of themselves as well as of others and so utilize themselves and their experience as the basic frame of reference for much of their behavior. As a result, they are able to break loose from many of the petty tyrannies of their surroundings to deal with events straightforwardly and uncomplicatedly. (This autonomy seems a direct outgrowth of the individual's openness to experience and trust in self.)

We have already observed that the characteristic openness to experience of adequate personalities provides such people with a much wider, less complicated, more precise and accurate perception of events. As a consequence the behavior of adequate people is likely to be more effective and efficient than that of his less gifted fellows. This greater accuracy of perception produces more effective behavior and need satisfaction and is likely to cause the individual, over a period of time, to have an increasing trust in himself and his own capacities and perceptions. Such a trust is likely to be fostered further by the appreciation and admiration of other people who perceive and react to his behavior. The adequate personality discovers in one fashion or another that his self is a highly trustworthy, effective instrument. As a result he comes increasingly to trust his perceptions of self and the world about him. He discovers that his feelings, attitudes, beliefs, and understandings are more often than not effective and efficient guides to behaving. He utilizes himself and his experience as the frame of reference from which to observe and judge other events. He learns to appreciate himself as an ongoing, sensitive, trustworthy process. Instead of defending himself against his experience or dealing with life at arm's length, he finds he can immerse himself in events, confident of his ability to assimilate and grow with interaction. This straightforward, uncomplicated relationship to life and to self makes possible a greater awareness, a quicker perception, and a more accurate judgment of all aspects of experience, including self.

It is this greater openness of experience and trust in self which seems to provide the adequate personality with a high degree of personal autonomy. He learns to use himself and his experience as his frame of reference for dealing with life and is far freer from the pressures and demands of his environment. Flowing smoothly with life, he finds it less necessary to utilize his energies in purely "coping" activities. Being closely in touch with events and able to trust his own experience, the adequate personality finds living far less complicated. He does not have to "deal with" life so often. Rather, he discovers that need satisfaction can be attained effectively and satisfyingly through simple expression of self in response to events, with little need for the complications of coping or manipulating.

Maslow has described this autonomy as a matter of "growth" rather than "deficiency" motivation:

One characteristic of self-actualizing people which to a certain extent crosscuts much of what we have already described, is their relative independence of the physical and social environment. Since they are propelled by growth motivation rather than deficiency motivation, self-actualizing people are not dependent for their main satisfactions on the real world, or other people or culture or means-to-ends or, in general, on extrinsic satisfactions. Rather they are dependent for their own development and continued growth upon their own potentialities and latent resources. Just as the tree needs sunshine and water and food, so do most people need love, safety, and the other basic need gratifications which can come only from without. But once these external satisfiers are obtained, once these inner deficiencies are satiated by outside satisfiers, the true problem of individual human development begins, i.e., self-actualization.

This independence of environment means a relative stability in the face of hard knocks, blows, deprivations, frustrations and the like. These people can maintain a relative serenity and happiness in the midst of circumstances that would drive other people to suicide They have also been described as "self-contained."

The feeling of adequacy to deal with external events makes such events less urgent. This in turn makes possible a high degree of concentration. Adequate personalities are, therefore, likely to be far less distractable. Their capacity for detachment from external demands makes it possible for them to devote their attention to problems with an intensity and devotion seldom achieved by less well-actualized persons. Indeed, so intense is this concentration that it sometimes seems to outsiders to indicate a lack of concern for human values. While adequate personalities do seem to have less "need" for other people on occasion, it would be a serious mistake to conclude that such people are disinterested in human affairs or human values. Quite the contrary is true.

THE COMPASSION OF ADEQUATE PEOPLE

The capacity for acceptance does not apply solely to impersonal events. Adequate persons are equally acceptant of people. Their perceptions of human beings are admitted to awareness with the same lack of defensiveness and distortion as any other perception. Having little need to be defensive, adequate persons find it possible to perceive and behave toward their fellows with a minimum of hostility. They accept people for what they are: human beings with interesting individual quirks and characteristics, to be comprehended without fear, hatred, or distortion.

When the factor of identification is added to the acceptance characteristic of adequate persons, another quality is produced. Identification, combined with a capacity for acceptance, gives adequate persons a deep and extensive feeling of being "one with" their fellow citizens. This feeling of oneness, or empathy, makes them capable of great understanding, for, in a sense, they share in the experience and feelings of others far more surely and intensively than less adequate persons. This ability to "place oneself in another person's shoes" makes it possible for adequate persons to understand their fellows and to communicate with depth and intensity of feeling. It also facilitates the achievement of a broad feeling of oneness with mankind in general. In a study of self acceptance, Berger found, for example, positive correlations between these feelings about self:

1. Relies on internalized values and standards.
2. Has faith in capacity to cope with life.
3. Assumes responsibility for and accepts causes of own behavior.
4. Accepts praise or criticism objectively.
5. Does not deny or distort feelings, motives, abilities in self.
6. Sees self as person of worth on equal plane with others.
7. Does not expect others to reject him.
8. Does not regard self as queer or abnormal.
9. Is not shy or self conscious.

And these feelings about others:

1. Does not hate, reject, or pass judgment on others when different from self.
2. Does not attempt to dominate.
3. Does not assume responsibility for others.
4. Does not deny worth or equality of others.
5. Shows desire to serve others.
6. Has active interest in others, desires to create mutually satisfactory relationships.
7. In advancing self is careful not to infringe rights of others.

The feeling of identification has a further effect. When one is strongly identified with others, what he does to actualize self is likely to contribute also to the actualization of those with whom he is identified. Adequate persons have much concern for other people, which shows itself in humanitarian interests and in close association with some of our great attempts at social welfare. Adequate persons are often motivated by love, understanding, and compassion for their fellow man. With less pressing need to demonstrate their adequacy or to strive desperately in areas in which they feel deprived, adequate persons are free to accept, appreciate, and love other people. They do not find it necessary to use others for solely personal gratification and, as a consequence, can devote themselves more fully to other people. They have the capacity to "give of themselves."

The capacity for compassion characteristic of adequate persons extends to themselves as well. Adequate persons have less feelings of guilt and failure, in part because they are more successful, effective people, but also because they are more realistic and accepting. They do not expect themselves or others to be what they are not. They accept their fundamental humanity and forgive themselves as well as others for the limitations of human frailty. Such compassion for self releases the individual and makes possible an open, accepting relationship with the world about him.

One outgrowth of the combination of acceptance and identification in adequate personalities is a greater responsibility and humility where others are concerned. With less pressing need for self aggrandizement they can be content with secondary roles. They are under less compulsion to prove themselves at the expense of others. On the contrary, with strong feelings of identification they behave with characteristic concern for their fellows. For these people the golden rule is not an ideal human relationship to be achieved, but a way of living that occurs as a normal outgrowth of the nature of such personalities. Compassion, understanding, responsibility, and humility are not blindly sought as desirable goals for behavior. Rather, such characteristics are a natural outgrowth of the capacities for acceptance and identification typical of their processes of perception and the fundamentally positive phenomenal selves they possess.

The Adequate Self and His Society

Since each of us lives inescapably embedded in one or more societies, it is necessary that people satisfy both their own and society's needs. The adequate self from *both* the individual's point of view and society's must necessarily be in touch with the expectancies of the members of the society in which he operates. These expectancies will vary considerably within a particular culture. What is expected of a child is considerably different from what is expected of an adult. Expectancies for men are different from those for women. What is expected of the banker is different from what is expected of the dog catcher. What is more, the amount of deviation permitted an individual before he is brought under social controls will vary widely within a particular culture. Women in our culture are permitted a good deal of experimentation and license in choosing clothing, but far less in choosing sex partners. The adequate differentiation and acceptance of such aspects of his world into the organization of the self is a necessity if the individual is not to find himself threatened by his environment and so made unhappy, uncomfortable, and ineffective in dealing with it.

Interestingly enough, an adequate self in the terms in which we have described it will produce an individual who not only satisfies his own need, but will operate to the ultimate satisfaction of his society as well. Every individual lives in and is dependent upon society. So long as his behavior is consistent with the expectancy of the members of society he operates smoothly and effectively and with a minimum of threat to himself from that society or to the society from himself. Adequate personalities, we have seen, are maximally open to experience. The individual with an adequate phenomenal self will react quickly and easily to his society. Since he is dependent upon his society in large part for his need satisfaction, he cannot operate in ways which would be destructive to it. When threats do occur from his society, he is capable of accepting them and modifying himself accordingly.

For every antisocial act there is a penalty imposed either by society or, worse still, by the individual himself. If he is free to make all differentiations, these penalties must necessarily be examined by him. Since need satisfaction requires the absence of threat, the likelihood of action being taken which results in greater threat is impossible. Note in the following transcript from counseling how in her attempts to find a solution to her problem a young woman examines and rejects behaviors inacceptable to herself and to society.

A college student who had not been doing as well as she expected had sought all sorts of answers in the course of her counseling. She consciously and clearly examined the possibilities of quitting school, of developing a "nervous breakdown," or of running away, and eventually rejected all. Finally she came to the counselor's office elated over a solution which went roughly as follows:

STUDENT: I'll drop some of the work I'm doing now. That will give me time to get good grades in the rest. Then, I'll come back this summer and make it up and be right up with my class in the fall.

(Examining the plan from every angle, she left, still elated. Six days later she was back.)

STUDENT: I felt so good about that plan and then I didn't want to do it at all after I saw you. So, I decided, I'm going to get my work done—all of it.

COUNSELOR: You discarded your plan?

STUDENT: I feel more confident now. I'm going to get it done. That other decision—I really had a guilty conscience after I left you. I thought, maybe I'm just making excuses. That decision was just a way out. Just making the decision helped me. It affected me just the opposite. I felt terribly guilty.

COUNSELOR: You felt you were not being honest with yourself.

STUDENT: It taught me I'm no different if I'm slow. It's better that I do what I can and take the consequences. I decided that the next day and I haven't had the jerks since. (Client had had a severe shoulder tic diagnosed by her physician as chorea.)

COUNSELOR: You feel you must accept yourself then.

STUDENT: I do. I'm slow and average. Now I'm utilizing time I never did before. I feel more confident. This is the most difficult adjustment I've ever had to cope with. That other decision was just making excuses. It's unfortunate I'm slow but I'll just have to work harder. Since I've gotten through this, I'm sure I can get through anything.

A similar excerpt involving possible suicide is presented on page 49. Note that differentiation and acceptance in both cases includes the social situation and that even the possibility of suicide, which removes the person from society, does not remove him from its controls. A social being must necessarily adjust to the demands of society or remove himself from it. If he identifies himself with society he cannot deny it, for to do that is to deny himself. Since he lives in and is dependent upon society for his welfare, his own maintenance and enhancement will lead to that of the members of society as well, providing he is free to make adequate differentiations and to accept these into his concept of self. Persons unable to differentiate freely or with an inadequate self concept are unsatisfactory to themselves and to society. The high degree of identification of adequate people with their fellows assures a relationship between self-actualizing people and their societies of mutual enhancement with a minimum of friction, hostility, or destructiveness.

ADEQUACY DOES NOT DEMAND CONFORMITY

It should not be supposed that because adequate persons have a close and sensitive relationship to their societies that they must necessarily be conformists. The adequate personality is so open to his experiences that his adjustment is often to a larger society rather than to a restricted subgroup. Thus, he might be out of harmony with a smaller group but in a closer relationship to broad human goals. The spontaneity and creativity of self-actualizing people would not permit complete conformity. Adequate persons are possessed of great dignity and integrity. Their characteristic goals have little or nothing to do with conformity or its lack. Conforming or rebellious behavior is for these people merely a by-product of their movement toward goals satisfying both to themselves and to their fellows in the long run. In the process of seeking such goals adequate persons may be conventional or unconventional as demanded by the situations they encounter in their search for mutual self enhancement. Conformity as an end in itself may never enter their phenomenal fields at all.

As we have said, society has little to fear from adequate personalities. It is not the people who feel liked, wanted, acceptable, and able who cause difficulties for the rest of us. The individuals in our culture who represent an ever-present danger are those unfortunates who see themselves as unliked, unwanted, unacceptable, and unable, who are incapable of acceptance and who have little or no feeling of identification with the rest of us. Adequate persons provide leadership and the dynamic force which makes possible both their own good as well as that of their fellows. They often become the focal points around which many of the rest of us can rally to combine our efforts toward the achievement of important social goals. In a very real sense such people provide the backbone of democracy. They are the kind of people a democracy seeks to produce and are at the same time the kind of people upon whom the success of a democracy depends.

How Adequate Selves Develop *READ*

In Chapter 7 we have seen something of how the self concept develops as a result of the perceptions of the individual while he is growing up and particularly of his perceptions of the people who surround him in his formative years. Adequate personalities develop their concepts of self in the same fashion as their less adequate fellows, from the experiences they have throughout their lives. Adequate people, like any others, learn who they are and what they are from the things that happen to them. What makes an adequate person seems to be the peculiar kinds of experiences he has had.

Important as the question is, we have little precise experimentation leading directly to answers to the problem of how to produce adequate personalities. However, much of the great body of research already accumulated in the field of human growth and development sheds light on this question. From that research we can discern certain guide lines which give us clues to the probable production of adequate personalities. These clues are closely related to the three characteristics of the perceptions of adequate people we have been discussing in this chapter.

THE POSITIVE EXPERIENCE OF SELF AND THE WORLD

Adequate personalities, we have seen, have generally positive perceptions of themselves and the world in which they live. They see themselves as people who are liked, wanted, acceptable, and able, living in a world with which they can cope. Such concepts of self do not arise in a vacuum. They are the product of the experiences of the individual in his development. Nor does one have to be an expert to design a kind of program which would be likely to lead to such a characteristic way of seeing self and the world. The kind of experience needed to produce this kind of self definition is apparent from the definition itself. One needs only to ask:

How shall a child feel liked unless somebody likes him?
How shall a child feel wanted unless somebody wants him?
How shall a child feel accepted unless somebody accepts him?
How shall a child feel able unless somewhere he has success?

In the answers to these questions lie clues to ways in which it may be possible to construct life situations more likely to lead to adequacy.

Positive self definitions can arise only from positive self experience. Similarly, a positive view of the world is likely to be found only in those who have found their own experiences with the world to be generally enhancing.

THE CAPACITY FOR ACCEPTANCE

The capacity for acceptance, we have seen, is in large part a function of the existence of a generally positive phenomenal self. Positive self concepts make possible greater acceptance. Acceptance seems to be a capacity one can "learn" given the right kinds of circumstances. We know, for example, that people can be more accepting of themselves and other people in the absence of threat. As a result, many teachers and counselors have learned to create warm, permissive, nonthreatening atmospheres for their students and clients, and this kind of atmosphere in turn makes possible a greater degree of acceptance by the subject. Whether or not acceptance is possible is very largely a question of the degree to which one feels safe and secure. The greater the degree of personal security felt, the greater the degree of acceptance.

There is research evidence which indicates that people can, indeed, learn to be more accepting as a result of being given the right kinds of opportunities. The experience of being accepted in therapy has been found to be followed by an increased ability of the client to be accepting in his turn. Similarly, teachers know that when they are successful in creating situations where children feel free to talk and to look at controversial matters without fear or censure, the children become better able to deal with people in a similar manner in other settings.

IDENTIFICATION CAN BE LEARNED

Finally, the identification characteristic of adequate personalities seems open to considerable modification. People can "learn" to identify with wider groups of people. Experiences can be provided for them which make a high degree of identification possible. Many a Southerner forced to work side by side with Negroes in the armed forces during the war came to appreciate his colored "buddy" in a way that would never have been possible had he spent those years in his home community. This is only one of many instances which could be cited of persons learning to identify with people of different races, creeds, and religions in all parts of the world. The literature of social psychology is particularly rich with examples of situations in which people learned to identify with one another.

Interesting techniques have been devised by some workers to provide people with experiences of identification and increased understanding of how things look to others. Rachel David Du Bois, for example, has developed a method of inducing people to share one another's fields through remembering a common experience they have had. People interested in group process have developed other methods like role playing and psychodrama. Psychotherapists have found ways of teaching themselves to empathize with their clients.

🗶 The Adequate Person in Crisis *READ·*

Throughout this chapter we have seen that the adequate personality has more effective, efficient, and dependable relationships with the world about him. Nevertheless, there are those who loudly proclaim the virtues of failure, rejection, and humiliation as devices to be liberally used in the training of the young on the theory that the intense experience of failure and indignity "toughens" the individual and makes him strong in the face of later adversity. Nothing could be further from the truth. The idea seems to have arisen from the fact that successes, to be enhancing, must be over great difficulties. The uncritical observer, seeing the difficulty as the common element in the development of great people, advocates difficulties without worrying about success. This is like the man who, having acquired hang-overs from Scotch and soda, bourbon and soda, rye and soda, and gin and soda, gave up soda. The best guarantee we can have that an individual will be able to deal effectively with crises lies in the degree of his personal adequacy. Even those who most staunchly defend the "school of hard knocks" mostly advocate it for other people's children.

Adequate personalities are the products of positive experience. What is destructive to human dignity and integrity, what indoctrinates people with false perceptions of themselves as people of little worth, respectability, or capacity represents a tragic waste of human potential. Worse still, it produces people who constitute an ever-present danger to the rest of us in the interdependent, coöperative environment of modern society. Adequate personalities are not a luxury in our society, but a continuously increasing necessity. Indeed, it can be argued that societies themselves are no more than means by which people may band together to achieve greater personal adequacy. As a consequence, it is necessary for us to search always for new and better ways of providing people with the kind of positive experiences and relationships which contribute to their adequacy. The best guarantee we have that people will operate effectively to fulfill their own and other people's needs is that their own need for feelings of worth and value has been adequately filled in the past. This principle has vast implications for every phase of human relationships, whether we speak of child-rearing practices, educational method, labor-management relations, or the relationships of nations with one another.

CHAPTER 13

The Inadequate Personality: The Dynamics of Failure

I T would be nice if we were able to construct in our time a society all of whose members were adequate personalities. Unfortunately, we have not yet progressed that far. There still exist in our culture inadequate personalities who eke out an existence with little or no satisfaction either to themselves or to anyone else. Some of these attract our attention by careers of violence and revolt. Others live out their lives in silence and despair. The most inadequate we call mentally retarded, criminal, or mentally ill; and these fill our institutions, our jails, and our mental hospitals to overflowing. Such unhappy people represent a drag upon the rest of us and a pitiful waste of human potentialities.

Inadequate personalities are those who regard themselves as unable to achieve need satisfaction. They are people who feel unable to cope with life in one or more important respects. Inadequate personalities develop in the same manner as adequate ones, as a result of the peculiar experiences they have had in the process of their growing up. Whereas adequate persons see themselves as capable of coping with life, inadequate people have grave doubts about their capacities to deal with events. Their experience has taught them that they are more often than not unliked, unwanted, unacceptable, or unworthy. Seeing themselves in these ways, inadequate personalities find living a difficult and hazardous process in which they must constantly be prepared for emergencies. They feel threatened so much of the time that we might well use the term "threatened people" as synonymous with inadequate personalities.

The problem of inadequacy, however, is not just a matter of the very inadequate, nor is it a matter involving only the other fellow. Most of us are more or less inadequate from time to time, just as most of us are more or less adequate. Adequacy is a continuum extending from very little to very much. (See Fig. 22.) Though all of us are continuously and insatiably striving for adequacy or self actualization, none of us

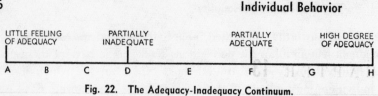

Fig. 22.   The Adequacy-Inadequacy Continuum.

ever achieves this goal entirely. Most of us exist somewhere on the continuum schematically represented in Fig. 22 between *D* and *F*. A few people in our world, like the Lincolns, Gandhis, or Albert Schweitzers, achieve a high degree of self actualization and manage to reach such high plains of adequacy as indicated by the general area *G* to *H* on our continuum. At the opposite end of the scale are those people with little or no feelings of adequacy, the neurotic, the criminal, and the psychotic. The "neurotic" personality might be represented on our adequacy rule in the neighborhood *C* to *D*. Although they feel severely threatened, such people nevertheless feel a sufficient degree of adequacy to make it possible for them to go on struggling and fighting for better things. At the very lowest levels of adequacy in our society are the psychotic and the violently criminal personality, represented on our chart at points *C* to *A*. These are the people so severely threatened and inadequate as to be driven to extreme devices to achieve even the smallest measure of adequacy.

It should not be supposed that the above chart represents a discrete classification of adequacy and inadequacy. None of us ever achieves a full measure of adequacy, on the one hand, or escapes from some measure of inadequacy, on the other. In the previous chapter we described the adequate personality and some of his characteristics. In this chapter, we shall turn our attention to the other end of the continuum to examine the nature and characteristics of inadequacy.

Perceptual Characteristics of Inadequate Persons

We have seen that the perceptions of adequate people are characterized by: (1) an essentially positive phenomenal self, (2) a capacity for acceptance, and (3) a high degree of identification with others. We would expect to find that the perceptions of inadequate people were characterized by the reverse of these criteria, and this is exactly the case.

A FUNDAMENTALLY NEGATIVE PHENOMENAL SELF

Inadequate people see themselves in generally negative ways. As a result of their past experience they have come to define themselves, for example, as unworthy, unwanted, unacceptable, and unable. This is, of course, not true of all of the perceptions such people have of themselves. It is, however, likely to be true of those aspects of self which seem to the individual most important or central to his self structure.

A self defined in negative terms is a poor instrument for dealing with the vicissitudes of life. It leaves one helpless and fearful before the demands of living. It provides but a shaky and tenuous foundation for effective existence. The smaller and more insignificant the self, moreover, the larger, more overwhelming, and threatening are the problems with which such a person sees himself confronted. Life need not be threatening to the adequate individual with a strong and positive phenomenal self. The self concept made up of many negative self definitions, however, finds itself in constant danger from external events. Such a self lives in perpetual jeopardy.

The inadequate self may find it necessary to live a life of continuous, belligerent, aggressive seeking for self enhancement in a desperate effort to demonstrate to himself and all the world that what he feels to be true is not so. This is characteristic of many criminals and neurotics. Such people find no rest or contentment, for life is a continual contest in which they daily run the risk of destruction. If the self is defined in too negative a fashion, the individual may even give up in despair. He may accept himself as defeated and incapable of dealing with life, and content himself with a lackadaisical existence pushed about by whatever forces are exerted upon him. Many psychotics and mentally retarded people show this kind of reaction. This intimate relationship between the individual's feeling of adequacy and violence of behavior was demonstrated by Balester in a study of the self concepts of delinquents. He found adults had more positive self concepts than juvenile nondelinquents, nondelinquents perceived themselves more positively than first-offender delinquents, and these latter, in turn, possess more positive self concepts than "repeaters."

Human need for personal adequacy is insatiable, and threat to the self must be met with some kind of response. Much of what we describe as "maladjusted" behavior is the individual's "loud protests against the crushing of his psychological bones, of one's true inner nature." What is more, the greater the threat, the greater will be the response, so that threatened people almost always overreact and behave in exaggerated ways. They smile too broadly, try too hard, compliment too much, protest their innocence too forcefully, brag too blatantly, give too little or too much, because they are continually faced with the necessity for proving their adequacy.

We have seen in an earlier chapter that when individuals feel threatened their perceptions are affected by two phenomena: tunnel vision and the necessity for self defense. Unfortunately, each of these effects markedly reduces the individual's ability to perceive effectively and efficiently. Tunnel vision reduces the field from which behavior may be selected, while the necessity for self defense makes change difficult or impossible. Adequate behavior requires not a narrow, restricted phenomenal field, but an open, rich, and maximally free field of perceptions. The experience of inadequacy provides a poorer, more restricted field from which the individual must select his behaviors. It is not surprising, therefore, to find that inadequate personalities are often characterized by rigid, inflexible patterns of behavior or that they are quite likely to be inaccurate in their assessment of themselves and the world about them.

LACK OF ACCEPTANCE

The necessity for self defense imposed upon the phenomenal self by the experience of threat makes difficult or impossible acceptance of new or conflicting perceptions into the perceptual field. Most of us have experienced this phenomenon when, perhaps in the heat of an argument, we found it difficult to understand or even to hear what our antagonist was trying to express. The fundamental need to maintain and enhance the phenomenal self requires self defense. As a consequence, threatened people reject unflattering or self-damaging perceptions and seek those which assuage wounded self perceptions or help to bolster the self against the threat experienced. When this happens, many important differentiations may not be accepted into the phenomenal field or, if they already exist in the field, may not be accepted into clear figure.

This inability to accept important aspects of his experience has unhappy effects upon the individual's capacity for effective behavior. He is forced to behave on the basis of restricted or partial evidence. Behavior originating from only part of the data must necessarily be less precise and effective than that arising from a wider, more inclusive frame of reference. Like trying to build a house with but part of the necessary lumber, the product is unsatisfactory to everyone concerned. Inability to accept the data of their experience often produces a rigid, vicious-circle kind of behavior which seems only to prove to inadequate persons their own inadequacies. The pattern goes something like this:

1. A person behaves in terms of his phenomenal self.

2. This behavior is rejected by those with whom he comes in contact.

3. Rejection, in turn, may so threaten the individual that he is forced to defend himself with great vigor and is unable to accept the evidence of his rejection. As a consequence, he behaves even more strongly in terms of his existing phenomenal self.

4. Such behavior, of course, only intensifies the rejection of his fellows, bringing more threat to himself, an even greater need for self defense, and progressively less ability to accept the facts of his situation.

Just such patterns of perception and behavior cause many inadequate personalities to behave in ways that produce the very reactions in others which corroborate their own already existing beliefs. Thus the delinquent may attempt to force people to respect and notice him by an attitude of toughness or belligerence which only intensifies the wrath of society against him. Some psychologists have seen this, erroneously we believe, as a drive toward self destruction.

The inability of inadequate persons to accept threatening perceptions does not apply only to perceptions of the situations in which they find themselves. Lack of acceptance also distorts their perceptions of themselves. For effective behavior, people need to change their concepts of self on occasion as demanded by new experience, new times and places. Threatened personalities find this extremely difficult. The dire necessity for self defense may preclude the acceptance of new concepts inconsistent with existing self definitions. Common examples of this effect may be observed in the woman who cannot accept her fading youth, in the child unwilling to accept the responsibilities involved in growing up, in the worker unable to change with changing methods and techniques, or in the student so unable to accept the evidence of his inadequacy that he must maintain his failures are due to teachers who "had it in for him." This tends to keep the phenomenal self a static and rigid organization, a characteristic which only increases the likelihood of its being threatened by the changing world in which all of us live. A phenomenal self incapable of accepting change in itself is practically certain to become increasingly out of touch with the world and therefore increasingly inadequate and threatened.

INABILITY TO IDENTIFY BROADLY WITH OTHERS

Inadequate persons do not possess strong feelings of identification. Indeed, it has often been observed that severely threatened people, like criminals and the psychotic, are fundamentally lonely people. Often they do not have so much as a single person in their lives whom they feel really respects them. Mostly, they have been unsuccessful in their relationships with others. Extremely threatened people, like hardened criminals or certain kinds of psychotics, may even attempt to destroy any possibility of developing such identification. Other people are perceived only as dangerous and so to be avoided, or as victims to be manipulated and used.

Threatened people are likely to be selfish or egocentric. The experience of threat focuses attention upon the self and its maintenance and enhancement, so that there is little opportunity for broader, more outgoing kinds of perceptions like those required for identification. What is more, the poorer, more meager the phenomenal self, the greater will be the necessity for its defense and the less likely is there to be any extensive feeling of oneness with others.

Just as each individual grows up with a self concept which is in large part the product of how he has been treated by those important to him in his growing years, he also develops perceptions of what other people are like. Depending upon his experiences of them, he comes to feel that other people are essentially friendly or unfriendly, warm or cold, interesting or frightening, pleasant or unpleasant. It is characteristic of deeply inadequate persons that their early experiences with others have been unsuccessful. The same unhappy relationship with an adult from which a child learns that he is unacceptable or unable may teach him also that people are unfriendly, dangerous, or untrustworthy. Small wonder then that inadequate people have little feeling of identification with others. A low opinion of self is likely to be associated with a fear and distrust of others. To feel unacceptable is to perceive others as unaccepting, as unfriendly. The inability to accept self is therefore strongly correlated with inability to accept others. This relationship between self acceptance and ability to identify with others is also demonstrated in the progress of psychotherapy, where it is repeatedly found that as persons are aided to greater acceptance of self they show a concomitant increase in positive feelings toward other people.

People with little feeling of identification with their fellows are unlikely to be deeply concerned about them. This is perhaps observable in its most extreme form in the case-hardened criminal, who feels not the slightest compunction at harming another human being. He may even enjoy it. After all, when you don't belong to the club, you don't have to abide by the rules, pay your dues, or defend the membership! And when the club has blackballed you, you owe them no sympathy. Inadequate personalities do not develop in a vacuum. They are produced from interactions of the individual and the world in which he lives.

Techniques of Dealing with Threat

The experience of threat is an event which cannot be ignored. Threat to the self requires some sort of action, some technique for dealing with the experience. Many of these techniques are familiar to all of us and can be seen in daily behavior. They may be simple and transitory devices used only on rare occasions by mildly threatened individuals, or they may be fixed and permanent methods of dealing with life employed by the deeply disturbed personality. These techniques have often been described by psychologists as "defense mechanisms," a term which itself implies the attempt of the organism to deal with a threatening situation. Such techniques seem to fall in three general categories:

1. The phenomenal self may be reorganized to include the threatening perception.

2. Perceptions may be denied acceptance into the organization of the phenomenal field.

3. Perceptions may be so selected or modified as to be consistent with the existing organization.

REORGANIZATION OF THE PHENOMENAL SELF

We have seen that the adequate personality is characterized by an ability to accept any and all differentiations into the phenomenal field. When a threatening differentiation can be so accepted, threat no longer exists. It is only those perceptions refused acceptance which continue to appear threatening. The inclusion of a new differentiation into the field, however, will necessarily result in some degree of reorganization of the existing structure. Sometimes this will be very great, sometimes only slight. The individual confronted with a personal criticism by his employer, for example, may find himself faced with a disagreeable threat to self. The appropriate thing to do in these circumstances is to accept the perception, evaluate its accuracy, and modify one's behavior if necessary. This is what the essentially adequate personality does. Unfortunately, this kind of reorganization of the self is not so easy to accomplish if threat is very great or the personality fundamentally inadequate.

The acceptance of all pertinent evidence leaves the individual in a far stronger position to deal with life. It leaves him open to adjustment and the possibility of change to meet the shifting exigencies with which he is bound to be faced from time to time. Reorganization of the self permits the inclusion of new data and a relationship with the outside world characterized by a maximum degree of accuracy and realism. One is always able to deal more effectively with life when he is in possession of more evidence. The reorganization of self in the light of one's experience keeps the self in closer, more intimate contact with the world in which one lives and moves.

This method of dealing with threatening perceptions is likely in the long run to offer the greatest satisfaction to the individual. Unfortunately, it is not always possible, particularly for the threatened, inadequate personality. Acceptance of threat and reorganization of the self are the very events the threatened personality seeks to avoid. Inadequate personalities are characteristically incapable of acceptance. The more inadequate the individual feels, the less he is able to utilize this approach to dealing with his threatening perceptions and the more likely he is to be driven to the use of some less productive but, from his point of view, safer technique of dealing with threat.

DENIAL OF THE RELEVANCE OF THREATENING PERCEPTIONS

A second, but less happy means of dealing with threatening perceptions is simply to deny their relevance to self, thus escaping the necessity for dealing with them at all. This may be brought about in three general ways familiar to all of us in their milder forms. The threatened person may deny the relevance of a threatening perception by:

1. Denying its existence completely. "It isn't so!"

2. Accepting the possibility of its existence, but denying the relationship to self. "It doesn't refer to me!"

3. Postponing the matter in space or time. "I don't have to deal with it now."

DENIAL OF THE EXISTENCE OF THE EVENT. This method of dealing with threat is accomplished by insisting that the threatening perception simply does not exist. Galileo, for example, was persecuted for his insistence that the earth revolved around the sun. The scholars of his day found this idea so repugnant and so threatening to their way of life that they dealt with the matter by insisting that the event was not so. What was more, because Galileo threatened them so by insisting that it was true, they found it necessary to bring him to trial and to force him to recant his idea. Man's history has been replete with examples of this "ostrich-like" method of dealing with threatening events. People found great difficulty in accepting Darwin's ideas about evolution, and Einstein's concepts of relativity, time, and space were laughed at and ignored by many when they first appeared.

Such methods of dealing with threatening events are not limited to earth-shaking discoveries or to deeply threatened people. Almost any of us, even the most adequate, may utilize such a method of dealing with threat, at least momentarily, if the threat we experience is sufficiently great. Any of us might find ourselves on occasion refusing to admit the death of a loved one or the approach of our own demise. The technique is also common among children who may find it necessary to object violently to the idea that "there is no Santa Claus"! Matters which do not exist do not have to be dealt with, and an inadequate phenomenal self may find it necessary to ignore the existence of threatening events.

We may even anticipate the possibility of such events and avoid or resist entering the situation where they may occur. One of the most common examples of this method of dealing with threat may be observed in the mechanism psychologists call *negativism*. It is particularly common among children, but often exists in adults as well. Negativism can often be used as a positive device for controlling other people. Thus a threatened self may be able to forestall the necessity of experiencing a disturbing event and may even be able to restore the self to a feeling of personal worth through forcing others to give in. In this way, a feeling of mastery may be obtained from one element of the situation while at the same time avoiding the necessity for dealing with another. For example, before going to bed one evening a young boy complained that it was much too early to retire. This was threatening to his concept of self. He attempted to point out to his father that it was unfair to expect him to go to bed when it was still light, especially for such a big boy as he. When these arguments proved of no avail he rebelled and said "No!" to brushing his teeth, washing his face, taking off his clothes, and picking up his toys. He even went so far as to say "no" when asked if he wanted to be read to (a decision he quickly regretted and only saved face at the last moment by changing his "no" to refer to his father and not his mother). Having been threatened by his parents' failure to regard him as he regarded himself and being overpowered by the might of adults, he sought a means of restoring his feeling of self esteem by mastering his parents through negativism. Even as he said "no" while standing with his back to his father at the basin, his father could observe in the mirror the delight written all over the child's face. The enhancement of self achieved by such tactics is often far more pleasurable than the minor losses one may sustain by the negativism. This is true of adults as well. Strikers out for weeks for an extra cent per hour count nothing lost if in the end their tactics of refusing to coöperate achieve their goal, even though it may take years to recoup their losses on the new pay scale.

DENIAL OF THE RELATIONSHIP TO SELF. A variation of the denial of relevance may be found in the relegation of threatening perceptions to the not self. This is a common device seen in daily life in the bland assumption that new rules and regulations, "of course," do not apply to us. It may be observed, too, in the phenomenon pointed out by Freud, that we discover in others the characteristics we deplore in ourselves. We may also find it possible to deal with threats in this fashion by the common excuse that "it was not our fault."

Techniques of denial may often be extremely effective for a while. Sometimes, too, they are extremely useful devices which protect us against minor upsetting perceptions. When we "forget," for example, it may be that after a time the situation will change and it will no longer be necessary for us to remember anyhow. Or, when some unacceptable aspect of ourselves is relegated to someone else, we may discover at a later date that we have changed in the meantime and the threatening perception is no longer applicable. In either event, the situation has been met with a minimum of difficulty. The self has been successfully maintained intact. Though such methods of dealing with threat have momentary value to the individual, they may sometimes only make things more difficult to deal with on later occasions. When perceptions are very important they are likely, sooner or later, to be forced upon us in one form or another. Society will usually see to that.

Another method of dealing with threat by denying relationship to self is nicely illustrated in the technique of *projection,* in which the threatening experience is avoided by relegating it to someone else. Mr.

Allen may have extremely aggressive feelings toward his wife and children, which if brought into clear figure would shock and frighten Mr.
Allen himself. One way of dealing with such feelings may be to disso-
ciate himself from these ideas by attributing them to someone else. Indeed, if he can manage to attribute similar feelings toward him on the
part of his family, he may even be able to justify his own ill will. Still
another way of dissociating himself from his threatening feelings may be
to express exaggerated concern for his family's safety and comfort. If
we place Mr. Allen in a situation where he is under no threat from those
around him or in which he may behave without restraint, however, it
is likely that he will reveal much more of his real feelings to the eyes of
a practiced observer. Thus he may be able to "let himself go" in a play,
because a play is "only an act," or in telling of his childhood, for "you
can't blame a man for what he did as a child," or in telling a story, for
then "it is only a story." It is just this release from the restraints of
objective reality that makes projective instruments so revealing of the
fundamental motivations of the person's personality.

But projection occurs not only on projective tests. It is often utilized
by the individual in daily life. Through identification with others (and
thus protection to the self) it may be possible to find vicarious pleasure
or self esteem in blaming others who do those things he would like to
do himself. It has been reported, for example, that the founder of a
famous society advocating kindness to animals used to walk the streets
of New York with a horsewhip to use on drivers who beat their horses.
The guilty are often the most avid reformers. Criticizing behavior of
others, they absolve themselves from feelings of guilt and, as fighters
against evil, justify their use of techniques differentiated as shameful
or evil when used by others. Projection gives the individual self justification for operating free of normal social controls.

POSTPONEMENT OF THE THREATENING PERCEPTION. The relevance of
threat to the self may also be reduced by postponing its effects in time,
in space, or in clarity. We have seen in a previous chapter that the experienced magnitude of threat is a function of its psychological immediacy. Generally speaking, the more immediate the event to self, the
greater is the experience of threat. One means, then, of reducing the experience of threat is to postpone it in one fashion or another. This postponement may be affected in time by putting off the critical event until
some later occasion. The failing student may thus reduce the imme-

diate distress of facing the dean by putting off seeking an appointment till "tomorrow" or "after the week end." Procrastination is a time-honored device by which the threats of decision making can be alleviated, and it has been used at one time or another by almost everyone.

One of the most interesting and important of these techniques in the psychology of human adjustment is suppression. This is a method of dealing with threatening perceptions by holding them at a lower order of differentiation. Perceptions which would require too great a change in the self cannot come into clear figure. The need of the organism for self maintenance will not permit this, and the perception may be held in the field at a low level of differentiation. This does not eliminate the threat, however, for a suppressed differentiation is still in the phenomenal field. Nor will the need of the organism permit a threat to exist without action on the part of the individual. As a result, the threat, although not clearly differentiated, keeps the organism continuously in a state of tension or distress. This produces the state we have previously described as "anxiety," in which the individual feels threatened but is unable to clearly discern the threatening object or event. This is particularly characteristic of the neurotic who complains of being afraid, anxious, and uneasy but is unable to tell us what he is afraid of.

The failure of threatening events to emerge into figure is not surprising, since if the threat is very great clear perceptions may be too frightening to accept. A good example of such failure of differentiation is to be seen in the young child's insistence on his parent's goodness and power, often, in spite of many obvious proofs to the contrary. To conceive of his parents, on whom he is dependent, as being confused and weak in a terrifying world may be just too much for the child to take. Accordingly he is forced to deny or protest suggestions which imply his parent's weakness.

Persons who feel threatened by poorly differentiated experience often seek one activity after another in a frantic effort to keep from giving attention to themselves and their problems. Such an approach may be observed when we attempt to "snow under" a threatening perception by a series of enhancing techniques that reinforce a damaged phenomenal self. This is the sort of thing that occurs when a man who has been insulted by his wife at breakfast, drives to work at breakneck speed, gets in an argument with his foreman, or "tells off" his best friend. He attempts to reëstablish his feeling of self esteem by wildly seeking momentary superiority over people or objects most available at the time.

It is comforting and reassuring—and sometimes necessary—to emphasize our strengths in moments of weakness or inadequacy. This seems to be an attempt to prevent low-level differentiations from becoming clearly (and so, more threateningly, defined. By maintaining a high degree of attention on other things, it is possible momentarily to avoid the threatening perception. When vigilance flags, however, the need of the individual to maintain and enhance himself tends to bring these differentiations into clearer figure. Persons caught in this merry-go-round remind one of the policemen at the parade, who keep pushing the spectators back only to have them press forward again sometimes one at a time and sometimes in whole batches at once.

The following case of Nancy summarized from the files of a mental-hygiene service illustrates this effect. As a girl, Nancy was very tall and not very attractive to boys. In addition, her family were well-known "intellectuals" who taught their children the importance of being *controlled*. As a result, Nancy grew up with the idea that she was something very special in womanhood, destined for great things and as a professional person several cuts above the ordinary female. This concept of herself was very reassuring and gave her a good deal of self esteem while she was growing up. Nancy married a man who was also an intellectual and who was very proud of her in her job. All went well with this sort of arrangement until Nancy discovered she was pregnant. This was a very threatening perception, and she refused to accept the idea because it did not fit her existing concept of self. Up to the day the baby was born, Nancy never mentioned her condition or made any attempt to prepare for the baby; she merely redoubled her efforts on her job. But babies have a way of arriving in time and she could not forever deny its existence. With the coming of the baby she was faced with an even worse threat to her concept of herself and to her hopes of enhancing it. She had to give up her job to care for the child. Who ever heard of intellectuals who washed dishes, or nursed babies, or made beds? Such ideas were completely foreign to the kind of person she thought herself to be. As a result, Nancy rejected her child and began a whirl of activity that kept her busy from morning till night. She could not stand being with other women who talked about their children. She no longer had her work to give her self esteem, and she could not achieve it at home. So Nancy neglected her housework, put her child in a nursery school, and became a well-known public speaker in her community. She became a veritable dynamo of energy, racing about from meeting to meeting until at last her physical resources gave out and she collapsed in "nervous exhaustion."

SELECTION OF PERCEPTIONS CONSISTENT WITH THE SELF

A third class of techniques for dealing with threatening perceptions is the selection of perceptions in such a way as to be consistent with the existing phenomenal self. Perceptions threatening to self may be so selected as to appear, not threatening, but even enhancing to the phenomenal self. This is the sort of thing that occurs when an insult is taken as a compliment. All of us use this technique day after day, so smoothly that we succeed in fooling ourselves. The reason a student leaves his work until the last minute is not that he doesn't want to study. Perish the thought! He leaves his work till the last minute because "there was just too much to get done," because "the fraternity had a house meeting," or because of any number of other more satisfying reasons. And this is true of professors as well. Students' papers may not get marked, not because the professor hates to grade papers, but because of the pressure of "important" work to be done, or the "need to take a day off now and then," or even because it doesn't really matter, "the students don't mind."

This distortion of perception to bring about greater consistency may (1) be applied to the threatening perception, so as to reduce the degree of threat it poses, or (2) the threatened person may select his perceptions of self in such a manner as to increase his feeling of adequacy and reduce the threat experienced in that way.

THE DISTORTION OF EVENTS. It has sometimes been said that there are two ways in which a person may react to a new idea: he may discount it by saying, "Why, there's nothing new about that. We've known that for twenty years!" or he may minimize it by saying, "It's just a silly new fad. It will soon pass away!" Either way it is no longer necessary to deal with the concept, and the threat has been dealt with, at least for the present. Distortion makes events seem less threatening by bringing them in line with existing concepts of self, and results in certain types of adjustive behavior which psychologists call the *sour-grapes reaction, rationalization,* or *compensation.*

The amount of distortion shown by an individual is proportional to the degree of adequacy he feels. The greater the feeling of inadequacy the greater the incidence of distortion. An interesting study by Friedenberg of student perceptions of self and the university demonstrates, for example, that successful and unsuccessful graduate students see themselves and the university quite differently. The successful students showed much self determination and acceptance of self and saw the university's purposes as consistent with their own. Unsuccessful students, on the other hand, had less self acceptance and less self determination, and saw themselves as cash customers of the university frustrated in the legitimate pursuit of their goals.

The sour grapes reaction is a technique of dealing with threat which gets its name from Aesop's famous fable of the fox and the grapes. Like the fox in the fable, persons may console themselves over prizes they cannot win by concluding they weren't worth having anyhow. People may thus assuage their disappointment by deciding that the more expensive house "would probably have cost more to heat," or that the missed play "was probably no good anyhow," or that the lost opportunity "would probably have turned out to be a dud." By belittling the importance of the goal, the failure to achieve it ceases to be a sign of failure and inadequacy.

A similar method of dealing with threat is that of *rationalization*. It represents a selection of perceptions in such a fashion as to be consistent with existing concepts of self. We are ordinarily aware of our rationalizations only after the need for them has passed. We may perceive a threatening concept as consistent with the self by selecting those aspects which are self enhancing and ignoring those which are not. The individual finds "good" reasons for the "real" reasons for his behavior. For instance, a woman goes shopping and finds two dresses in which she would be very attractive. She buys both dresses and thus achieves an enhancement of self. When friends remark, "Oh, you bought *two* dresses," this may represent a threat to her concept of herself as thrifty, and our shopper replies, "They were such a bargain, I couldn't resist them." Thus she achieves not only a dissolution of the threat but even an enhancement of self as a thrifty shopper who knows how to take advantage of a bargain!

Rationalization is so common that most of us are not aware of the existence of such distorted perceptions. Even when they are brought to our attention it may be very difficult for us to accept them as rationalizations, for to do so may threaten our existing organization. The man who buys a new car, for example, and gives as his reason for this behavior that the old one was beginning to use too much oil, will probably object to our pointing out that the expense of 20 quarts of 40-cent oil in a year's time hardly justifies an expenditure of several thousand dollars in turning the old car in. Such an admission is likely to be a threat to his concept of himself as a smart businessman and, furthermore, may force the admission that the real reason for getting the new car is because it increases his self esteem. To increase one's self esteem is not a socially acceptable reason for buying a car. Such selective effects of the phenomenal self upon perception may be seen in thousands of daily acts illustrated by the following statements:

"Let's go to the movies. A fellow gets stale when he studies all the time."
"Who wants to be a Phi Beta Kappa—a bunch of greasy grinds."
"A little nip now and then is a good thing for a man."
"Nobody really pays any attention to those silly speed limits."

In *compensation* the individual may make quite open and unrestrained attempts at mastery, often with the full support and encouragement of the culture. In fact, in America we take much pride in the great compensators. We point out to our children from the earliest days of schooling the examples of Steinmetz, the hunchback; Cunningham, of the burned legs; Edison, the deaf; Lincoln, the poor; Demosthenes, the stutterer; and Roosevelt, the cripple. These we delight in setting up for our children as guideposts to great achievement, and the implication is clear to "go thou and do likewise." We have succeeded so well in implanting this concept of compensation that it has even become a common notion that anyone who accomplishes something must certainly be a bit queer!

Compensation may appear in either of two common forms, known as direct and indirect compensation. In direct compensation the individual attempts to achieve self esteem or mastery by refusing to accept the threatening differentiation. He denies that any handicap exists, and acts accordingly. His phenomenal self is defined as though the handicap were not a part of himself. In so doing he must deny the proof to the contrary which appears in the reaction of others toward him. A young woman in a small Ohio town who severed the major nerves leading to her legs in an automobile accident the night before she was to have been married, refused to accept the idea that she could never walk again. The author vividly remembers this girl's pathetic efforts to force herself to walk in spite of her hopeless condition. She had a pair of parallel bars built on her porch and daily spent hours dragging her legs behind her as she went hand over hand along the bars. She refused to give up her fiancé because she could not accept the notion that she would never walk. Nor would she marry him, for that would not be fair to him until she was able to walk again. This state of affairs continued for several years until finally she released her fiancé from his promise, gave up her attempts to walk, and died a very short time after. Not all cases of direct compensation end so tragically. Many people, like Glenn Cunningham or Theodore Roosevelt, find it possible to make such improvement through the extreme efforts which such a technique can produce that eventually the threatening handicap is, in fact, overcome.

In indirect compensation a person possessing a handicap may be driven to seek self esteem in other areas entirely. Thus, a child who feels incapable of participation in the usual playground sports may find satisfaction in being the brightest child in class—or the worst. Oftentimes, such compensatory behavior may be far more potent than behavior not so driven, for much more is at stake. It is probable that the amount of energy expended in compensatory activity will depend upon the importance of the threatening self perception in the economy of the individual's particular organization. So long as the perception cannot be accepted into his organization it remains threatening and disturbing to him. He must defend himself at all costs against the threat which he perceives. Nor does it matter whether the handicap is real or imagined from an outsider's point of view. If the perception exists in the field, it is real to the behaver and that is the only point that matters to him. The more threatening the perception, the greater the amount of energy which will be expended in attempting to deal with the problem.

In indirect compensation the individual has given up attempting to deal with the self-threatening perception directly. He recognizes that he is helpless before it, yet cannot accept it as part of his organization. He attempts to rehabilitate his damaged concept of self by "snowing under" the threatening perception with a series of other enhancing perceptions. The girl who is homely may find solace and comfort in extraordinary achievements as a student, as an athlete, as a comic, or in any of a thousand other ways. Since the fundamental perception cannot be accepted, however, it remains in the field and continues to threaten, requiring ever new heights of accomplishment to give a feeling of adequacy. It is only with continued success that the threat can be prevented from arising into figure. It is interesting that society often profits greatly from the tremendous efforts put forth by such persons. Many compensators make great contributions in all walks of life. In spite of the external evidences of success, however, the compensating individual may feel extremely unhappy and inadequate in the very midst of his successes. It is only with the acceptance or elimination of the original negative self perception that real "peace of mind" can occur.

DISTORTION OF THE PERCEPTION OF SELF. Threatened personalities may sometimes be observed to deal with the threats they perceive by selecting perceptions of self which help them feel more adequate. This is, of course, characteristic of all people, but the greater the threat experienced, the greater the necessity for selection. In a previous chapter we have seen how this may be accomplished through the use of drugs or alcohol, which give a spurious, but satisfying, feeling of adequacy at least temporarily. Under these circumstances, the self may be perceived as stronger or more adequate, and the world seems therefore less frightening and more nearly within the capacities of the individual. One can also make himself feel more adequate to deal with certain kinds of threatening situations by arming himself with a knife, a gun, or a club. Another means of increasing one's feeling of adequacy is to identify oneself closely with some other stronger personality or group. In this way it is possible to add the adequacy of others to one's own perceptions of self. Exaggerated needs to conform, for example, have been shown to be closely related to feelings of inadequacy.

Simple regressive techniques are often used in much the same way to increase feelings of adequacy. When perceptions are threatening, many of us fall back upon concepts and techniques which have helped us to feel adequate in former situations. The housewife who formerly found her tears could change her mother's mind may utilize these again in moments of stress when her husband does not treat her in a manner to which she feels she is entitled. Such techniques are not labeled by the individual as regressive, however. That description would be much too threatening. They are labeled as "regressive" only by outside observers who realize that they are not appropriate in the new situation.

Children, faced with the necessity for growing up, sometimes find the business of maturing extremely threatening. This may be particularly true when the child is subjected to a great many demands which are difficult for him to meet. The resulting feelings of inadequacy are threatening, and the child appears to adopt a self definition at a younger age as a means of excusing his behavior to himself and achieving the self enhancement characteristic of former times. When one is younger he cannot be expected to do so much and the demands being imposed upon him appear less threatening. By defining oneself at a lower age, the threats perceived can be given up—they no longer apply. The child who finds going to school threatening may thus regress to an earlier age level where one is not expected to go to school. At such a level he can feel adequate again. The toilet-trained child may lose his newly mastered skills with the arrival of another child or when subjected to such an upheaval as moving from one home to another. It may often be seen that children subjected to a great many demands in the early school years may show such "regressive" behavior. They may want to be rocked or sung to as a means of gaining comfort and reassurance that had value in other days. When demands become too heavy there is much comfort and reassurance in such redefinitions and many threatening situations can be avoided.

Various forms of fantasy may give similar feelings of mastery and offer opportunity for the self concept to operate without the disillusioning impact of threatening differentiations. Daydreaming, moviegoing, some types of reading—all offer avenues for temporary enhancement which the actual situation does not appear to provide. Such flights of fantasy are common to all of us and appear to be motivated by our attempts to achieve some feelings of self esteem or self enhancement. In daydreams we may be anything. We are relatively free from the impact of immediate external events and are free to manipulate ourselves and the world pretty much as we please. This manipulative function also makes fantasy extremely useful to us. As we bring external reality more and more into the phenomenal field, fantasy shades almost indistinguishably into planning, so that the fantasies of yesterday become the actions of today and the achievements of tomorrow.

Children frequently employ fantasy as a means by which the environment can be manipulated and controlled, and it is helpful to many children in assisting them to find meaning in the world about them. In play therapy, for example, a child may be observed to spend hours manipulating various elements of his environment with which he may be having unusual difficulty. In the process he may discover new ways of dealing with his environment or new definitions of self more adequate to deal with the environment he faces.

While fantasy has value as a device for manipulation and for the achievement of self esteem, it may also represent a clinically undesirable type of activity, and it is necessary for the clinician to have some measure by which it is possible to determine when this "danger point" is reached. From a phenomenological point of view, that point is reached when the individual finds the world of fantasy more real than his experience in an external world. The critical point is thus a matter of the attitude taken by the individual toward his fantasies. In extreme cases the threat resulting from the individual's perceptions may sometimes be so great as to leave him no other recourse but to cut himself off from external reality entirely to seek a more friendly environment in a world of dreams. There, he may divorce himself from threat and create a world which is far more pleasant.

But not all daydreams are pleasant. Sometimes they are reported as fantasies in which self punishment is the major consideration. At first glance it would seem difficult to understand how such fantasies could contribute to the maintenance or enhancement of the phenomenal self. Yet this is exactly what seems to occur. In such apparently self-destructive fantasies we may often find the self concept defined in a way which might roughly be described as "I am guilty." With such a self concept it is not surprising that the individual may find real satisfaction in berating himself in fantasy. It is what he deserves in his eyes. By atonement he achieves enhancement of self! Furthermore, there are certain advantages in such self punishment in fantasy, for one can be punished to one's heart's content with a minimum of real danger to the self, whereas if one sought punishment in the world of reality it is quite likely he would find his experience too threatening and out of control. The recognition by the individual of guilt and shame are ways in which he rises above his self. By such recognition he is enabled to feel superior to what he once was or has been. He achieves enhancement of self by thus dissociating from guilt and, by punishing himself, becomes the punisher rather than the punished. Thus behaviors which appear to the external observer to be operating against the individual's own best interests may be, from the behaver's own point of view, enhancing to self.

The Frightened Ones—The Anatomy of Neurosis

To adjust successfully to the varying problems of life requires of the individual a phenomenal field maximally open to experience. Adequate people are able to differentiate themselves and the world about them with accuracy and efficiency. Unfortunately, when people are severely threatened this optimal relationship with experience is no longer feasible.

For the severely threatened, inadequate personality the processes of differentiation and acceptance break down. The ability to perceive and to reorganize the phenomenal field becomes seriously hampered. The more inadequate the personality, the less accurate are his perceptions of self and environment. This does not mean that threatened persons are unable to differentiate *all* events accurately. Actually, even the most seriously disturbed person is able to perceive many events about him with sufficient accuracy to make some degree of operation possible. Things in which he is not deeply involved, for example, may be perceived quite effectively. His difficulty arises primarily with respect to perceptions in which he feels his own adequacy is at stake.

The outstanding characteristic of the inadequate or severely threatened personality is the inability to accept perceptions. Neurotic patients, for example, are always the victims of a distorted perspective. The neurotic mother believes she is a "bad" mother because she has made some mistakes with her children. The neurotic typically overreacts to situations. He suffers great guilt over some act which would have bothered other people very little. He feels *totally* guilty although the rest of his life experience may be spotless. Almost without exception the neurotic clients of the psychotherapist turn out to be people who see themselves in exaggerated and distorted perspective. They feel that as they are, they are unacceptable, unworthy, or unable to an extent completely unjustified by an outside appraisal. Distorted perceptions, it is clear, are unlikely to prove effective in helping individuals to new and better adjustments. To deal effectively with life requires the clearest possible perceptions of oneself and his relationships to the external world. The failure of adequate perception is the most obvious of the characteristics of inadequate personalities, and at the same time, the most vital factor in serving to keep them inadequate.

Strong feelings of inadequacy are likely to be accompanied by more or less violent attempts by the individual to achieve a greater feeling of adequacy. So long as these struggles for adequacy operate within the individual or result in behavior within the limits of tolerance established by his society, the inadequate person is considered "neurotic" or "maladjusted." When, however, the individual's search for adequacy leads him to behavior threatening or destructive to persons or property, he may be considered delinquent or criminal and subject to the penalties of an outraged society. Both delinquent and neurotic, however, are motivated by the same basic feelings of inadequacy. Each seeks in the best ways he can to achieve a more adequate self. Though the behavior each manifests differs markedly, each suffers the same fundamental complaint, a frustrated, limited self. Where once the criminal and delinquent were regarded only as dangerous or bad and locked up to isolate them from society, modern approaches recognize such disorders as requiring treatment rather than punishment.

Neurosis, maladjustment, delinquency, and criminality are personality problems occurring in human beings unable to find more effective and satisfying means of achieving self actualization.

ANXIETY AND INADEQUACY

Whenever the self is perceived as endangered, the organism is placed on a "war footing," and this will be true whether the threat which the self perceives is clearly differentiated, as in the case of fear, or when only vaguely differentiated, as in the case of anxiety. Anxiety and its accompanying tensions are the inseparable partners of inadequacy feelings. Indeed, anxiety is so constant a characteristic of neurosis that it has sometimes been treated as though it were a cause of such behavior. Anxiety, as we have used the term, however, is not a dynamic, but a feeling which the individual experiences when confronted by a vaguely defined threat to his phenomenal self.

The anxiety feeling experienced by the individual may be more or less clearly attached to some perception or may be vague and unattached to any perception. The former is the kind of anxiety found in a phobia, in which it seems to accompany some specific object or event. When it is experienced without any apparent reference to a specific object or situation, it is sometimes called "free-floating" anxiety and is likely to be found in more generally threatened personalities. Let us examine the dynamics of a phobia as an example of how this kind of perceptual failure operates in producing threat and anxiety.

A young man had a very severe phobia for knives. The very sight of a knife in the hands of another person was enough to make him extremely uneasy, sometimes to the extent of begging others to put the knife away. This fear was extremely embarrassing to him and often made him the butt of unpleasant jokes among his friends. The young man himself recognized that his fear was quite unnecessary and even extremely silly, but at the same time he could not help feeling upset and frightened by the sight of a knife. He could not remember any good reason why he should be afraid of such things. This is a typical picture of a phobia.

Such fears are characterized by an unreasonable dread or anxiety attached to one or more fairly specific kinds of situations. Almost always, they are regarded as silly and unreasonable by the person who has the phobia, and it is characteristic that he is quite unable to recall the origins of his behavior.

In the case of this young man, the feared object has been strongly differentiated as an object to be avoided at all costs. The threatening aspects of the situation, however, are not so clearly differentiated. He feels anxious but cannot tell why. The reason for this failure of differentiation usually lies in either or both of two possibilities. First, the origin of the fear may have occurred so early in the life of the individual that he did not possess the necessary symbols which would make its differentiation possible. For example, a child who is frightened by some object might perceive it clearly but have no symbols with which to differentiate it from the guilt feelings which existed in the situation. The differentiation of "guilt" clearly requires an ability to deal with abstract symbols not possessed by young children till a later period. Later in life the individual may feel unreasonably fearful or anxious about the object long after familiarity with it should have taught him there is no need to fear it. The object can be clearly identified but the guilt feeling is still an aspect of the total situation.

A second possibility which may cause a threatening situation to fail of clear differentiation on a later occasion may be that the perception is too threatening. As we said in discussing "suppression," threatening perceptions may not be clearly differentiated because their acceptance into figure would require too great a reorganization of the self. As an example, a child whose parents have severely threatened him with loss of their love and affection may find this idea so painful and threatening to his organization that he resists any tendency for that aspect of the situation to rise into clear figure.

Let us see how these points apply to the case of the young man we mentioned above. In therapy the young man with the phobia for knives revealed this story of the origins of his strange behavior: As a young child he felt deeply rejected by his mother and felt a very great need for her love and affection. Unfortunately, this was not always easy to obtain, because his mother was extremely critical, unpredictable, and often very "nervous." He had been repeatedly warned by his mother that under no circumstances was he ever to touch a knife. One day, however, this youngster overheard his mother complain that she did not have a sharp knife in the house. Desperately seeking to please her, he took several of her kitchen knives to the curb in front of the house to sharpen them. He looked forward to the commendation he would receive for his act. In the process of sharpening the knives, one of them slipped and nearly severed the child's finger. Attracted by his cries, his mother rushed from the house in a panic, picked up the child and rushed him into the house, spanking him on the way and making it evident he was a *very bad boy*. She pointed out in no uncertain terms that this would never have happened had the child done as he was told. All this was terribly threatening. The child felt he had committed an unforgivable sin which caused his mother to reject him. From this incident, knives were differentiated strongly as objects to be avoided at all costs, but the concept of himself as guilty was by no means so clearly differentiated, probably because he had no symbols in which it could be brought to figure and (or) because bringing such feelings clearly into figure would have represented an intolerable threat to his phenomenal self. In later life it was often necessary to use knives for one purpose or another, and the young man was able to do this but never without a vague feeling of anxiety. Although he regarded his fear as silly in a grown man, he could not avoid his uneasiness and was often driven to certain impulsive behaviors which he was quite at a loss to explain. When, in the course of therapy, he was able to examine this early situation carefully and come to a clear differentiation of his feeling of guilt, he was able to reorganize his perceptions so that he no longer felt unworthy and unacceptable in the presence of a knife. As an adult he felt adequate to deal with the knife, and when he had clearly differentiated the threatening aspect he was able to accept this too into his organization. When this had occurred he lost his phobia completely.

NEUROSIS

The undifferentiated threat we have been discussing as characteristic of phobias is also the major characteristic of the neuroses. In fact, the primary difference between a neurosis and a phobia seems to lie in the fact that the threatening perception in a phobia appears primarily attached to one or more fairly specific objects or situations, while in neurosis the undifferentiated threat may be quite general and catastrophic. A very neurotic middle-aged schoolteacher came to a psychological clinic for assistance. She complained of constant tension, inability to sleep, and vague aches and pains for which her doctors could find no physiologic reason. She found it necessary to dose herself with all manner of medicines and complained of being in constant dread of something which she could not define. She was unable to concentrate on her work and found herself extremely overemotional, laughing or crying almost uncontrollably on the slightest pretext. Under therapy the following facts began to emerge.

She had always been a very popular and good-looking young woman, but was also under the domination of her mother to an extreme degree. As a result, although she had had numerous offers of marriage she was never able to bring herself to make the break from home. This state of affairs continued for some years until she began to be less attractive to men and her chances of marriage became fewer and fewer; finally she found herself 40 years old with no potential suitors left. About then, her mother began to show definite signs of age and it became apparent to the teacher that the time was not far off when she would be all alone in the world. She began to feel vague dreads of something she could not quite discern. Her behavior became compulsive and erratic and she felt constantly tense and uneasy. About this time her principal, a married man of her age, began to show her marked attention and finally asked for a date. The two became more and more intimate. Other people began to become suspicious and the threat of scandal and loss of position made matters even worse. The teacher became more and more frantic and more and more "neurotic" in her behavior.

In the course of counseling with this teacher it became clear that she reveled in the attentions she received from her principal although she knew full well the price she might have to pay for her clandestine affair. These aspects of her situation were clearly and sharply differentiated. Her feeling of guilt with respect to the possibility of breaking up her principal's family was similarly clearly perceived. In spite of this, she still felt that she could not give him up and continued to feel anxious and tense, although somewhat less than previously. She acted like a schoolgirl. She was radiantly happy in her intrigue and her mannerisms and affectations were those of a woman of 20 although she was twice that age. She was violently opposed to revealing her true age and went to football games and parties with teachers half her age, while at the same time speaking of people of 40 as "old-fashioned" and severely criticizing her contemporaries on the job. She acted 20 because she needed to regard herself as 20. She conceived of herself as still young, attractive, and desirable, and this led her to behave in ways often ludicrous to external observers. With such a concept of herself she could not give up her lover, for he probably represented her very last chance. To give him up would mean resigning herself to being an "old maid," would mean acceptance of herself as growing old. This was the vague dread that she could not face. With such a self concept she was beset on all sides with proof from the world about her that her concept of herself was just not so. She was kept so busy defending herself from the various onslaughts on her established position that change became impossible while threats became more and more pressing. The threat became larger and larger, becoming so much a part of her field that she acted fearfully in many situations, even those having no apparent connection with her dilemma.

To examine the dynamics involved, let us reduce this case to its basic elements. This woman conceived of herself as a teacher, which occupation was absolutely essential to her as a means of making a living. She regarded herself, also, as desirable, as young, as marriageable, and as essentially moral. She needed to maintain and enhance all these self definitions. But behavior which led to enhancement of one important aspect of self as young and desirable faced her at once with the terribly threatening perception of being immoral and unemployed. To give up her man was equally intolerable and threatening. At the same time external events were pressing for a showdown. She felt more and more threatened. What is more, the threat she felt made the broader examination of her field impossible, so that no solution was perceptible anywhere. She suffered from extreme anxiety. Since the perception of a solution was impossible, obviously, none could occur.

The major characteristics of this case are almost identical with the picture presented in the results from "experimental-neurosis" studies with animals. Shaffer, for instance, summarizes these results as follows: "First, the animal becomes unable to discriminate, losing even the older more habitual differentiations that have been formed previously. Second, he shows an irrational spread of response salivating for stimuli only incidentally connected with his training. Third, the animal gives evidence of tension and of emotional responses. . . . The same characteristics are seen in persons who are neurotic, unintegrated and predisposed to maladjustments." It is probably no accident that all of the work in "experimental neurosis," from Liddell's sheep and Pavlov's dogs to Krasnogorski's children, shows "neurosis" occurring when differentiation of adequate response is impossible.

DYNAMICS OF NEUROSIS

The dynamics of a typical neurosis seem to follow a pattern somewhat as follows:

1. One or more aspects of the phenomenal self become severely threatened either (a) by the perception of external events or (b) by the perception of the individual's own behavior motivated by another aspect of self.

2. These threatening perceptions cannot be accepted into figure and are maintained at a lower level of differentiation. This keeps them vague and diffuse. But they do exist in the field and so affect behavior.

3. Such "suppressed" differentiations continue to threaten the self although vaguely and unprecisely. The individual experiences anxiety.

4. The need of the organism to maintain its phenomenal self will not permit threatening perceptions to exist in the field without solution. Even low-level perceptions continue to motivate the individual, and if these cannot be fitted into the organization they keep him in a continual state of emergency so that he feels tense and emotional.

5. The individual's behavior proceeding from these vague and diffuse low-level perceptions will be similarly vague and lacking in precision. This inefficient behavior is unlikely to provide adequate solutions to his problems. Indeed, it is even likely to make things worse or more complicated than ever, bringing on a kind of vicious circle in which the experience of threat makes precise differentiation impossible, which in turn makes effective behavior unlikely, which does not resolve the threat and only increases the likelihood of ineffective perception. Such a circular pattern of perception and behavior may go for years without resolution. Large numbers of unhappy and maladjusted people in our society are caught in just such a cycle as we have been describing above. Having come to see themselves, for one reason or another, in inadequate ways, they become deeply threatened and frustrated, living large portions of their lives in grim attempts to achieve a measure of adequacy they do not feel. The pattern of a neurosis we have just been describing would serve equally well to describe the dynamics of delinquency. In the case of the teacher described above the same feelings of inadequacy that led to "neurotic" behavior produced a number of delinquent acts as well.

If neurosis and maladjustment, delinquency and criminality are, as we have suggested, the product of inadequate perceptions of self and the world people live in, it would seem to follow that the treatment of such disturbances must be based upon helping inadequate personalities to new and more satisfying perceptions of themselves and their relationships to the world. This is exactly what modern methods of psychotherapy seek to accomplish for all of these disturbances. Although there are a number of different schools of thought about how to treat extremely threatened personalities, all schools agree on the necessity for producing some kind of change in the ways in which the individual sees himself and his world. Psychotherapists help their clients to explore their perceptions of themselves and the worlds they live in to the end that they may discover new and more satisfying definitions. Since the experience of threat looms so large in the dynamics of inadequate personalities and serves to complicate the problem of adjustment, most psychotherapies also include one or more methods by which clients seeking treatment can be at least temporarily protected from threat.

The Desperate Ones—The Dynamics of Psychosis

The existence of threat in the individual's phenomenal field cannot be ignored. It must be dealt with. The greater the experience of threat, the greater must be the attempts of the organism to find resolution. Mild threats may require only mild kinds of behavior, but extreme degrees of threat are likely to call forth increasingly bizarre and violent behavior on the part of the individual attempting to seek adequacy in a too threatening world. Severely threatened persons like neurotics may act in ways that sometimes seem to us to be odd or unnecessarily intense. Such people are not the most inadequate persons in our society, however. Though they feel inadequate in ways important to them, they do not feel totally inadequate or defeated. Consequently the methods they use to achieve feelings of adequacy are likely to remain within the tolerance of people around them. Persons who feel more deeply inadequate and threatened are likely to use much more extreme ways to achieve a measure of adequacy. At times these methods may even become so upsetting or dangerous to themselves or to the rest of us that such people have to be isolated.

The most threatened, desperate individuals in our society are those we describe as psychotic, mentally ill, or the more violent and dangerous criminals. These are the desperate ones, the people unable to find more than a modicum of need satisfaction. They differ from the neurotic in the degree of inadequacy which they feel and the techniques they use to deal with the threats they experience. They feel so deeply inadequate for one reason or another that they live almost constantly (from their point of view) in the shadow of destruction. They feel desperately unable to cope with the threats they perceive and find little opportunity for successful or satisfying fulfillment of need. The extremity of the threats which they experience, moreover, calls for heroic measures in coping with life.

It is not our intention to enter upon an extended discussion of the psychology of psychosis here. The variety of techniques used by deeply inadequate personalities are almost limitless. In kind, they extend all the way from simple techniques of rationalization to some of the most bizarre and imaginative devices of which the human mind is capable. The particular symptoms of a particular individual may range from a single repeatedly used technique to a wide variety of techniques used in rapid succession. To deal with these extensively would be beyond the scope and purpose of this volume. Instead, we shall content ourselves with a few illustrations of how some common techniques of dealing with threat are utilized by extremely threatened, inadequate personalities.

The particular symptoms observed by outsiders examining the behavior of extremely inadequate personalities are the outward manifestations of the individual's attempts to deal with the threats he perceives. They are the techniques he uses as his peculiar means of achieving need satisfaction under great difficulties. He may use them in the same ways less threatened people do or he may use them in much more extreme degree or with variations undreamed of by more adequate persons. Desperate feelings, after all, require desperate measures, and what seems quite normal in a minor degree may become bizarre and outlandish when pushed to an extreme. Punishing others by failing to speak to them is usually permissible; punishing others by murder is seldom tolerated, at least in our society. The mildly threatened individual may find it assuages his wounded self to find a "good excuse" for failure. He explains that he "wasn't feeling well," "forgot," or "someone interfered" in his achieving his goals. The more threatened individual may do exactly the same thing in extreme form when he explains that "someone is controlling him against his will," he "was in Afghanistan on a secret mission for the President" at the moment he was called on to perform, or perhaps he may explain in great detail how "certain persons have cunningly arranged" just this sequence of events for his discomfiture.

In general the peculiar techniques of dealing with threat used by the psychotic may be classified in two of the categories we described earlier in this chapter, namely, (1) threatening perceptions may be denied relevance to the self in one form or another, or (2) perceptions of self or the world outside may be so distorted as to fit the existing organization of the phenomenal field. Let us examine some of the ways in which such techniques may be used in extremely inadequate personalities.

DENIAL OF THE RELEVANCE OF THREAT

The experience of threat may be dealt with by denying its relevance to the self. This may be accomplished, we have seen, either by relegating it to someone else or by denying its existence at all. This is typical of some forms of schizophrenia. Many such patients appear to feel so inadequate that any event, no matter how insignificant to the outside observer, is perceived by them as extraordinarily threatening. The slightest word or phrase, even the lift of an eyebrow in those important to them, may be interpreted as threat. The whole external world seems just too threatening to tolerate.

Some schizophrenics solve this problem by retiring within themselves and relegating more and more of experience to the not-self aspects of the field. Although Maslow has approached this problem from a different frame of reference, his description of the schizophrenic lies very close to our own conception of these states. He describes them in part as follows: "The evaluation of reality, as regards both social customs and perceptions, is disturbed partly because . . . the patient seems to follow a formula which implies: 'Reality does not matter; only what I desire matters.' This results in the absence of shame and the disregard of restriction common to normal human beings." From the patient's own point of view, of course, he is not denying reality. On the contrary, so far as he is concerned, he is living in the only reality: that of his phenomenal field.

In its milder forms this withdrawal from life may be observed in simple schizophrenia, in which the person adopts an attitude of "it doesn't concern me" and often becomes apathetic and dull. Many hobos present this picture. A young man known to one of the authors showed an interesting pattern of this type. All his life until he came to college he had been protected and petted by an oversolicitous mother. He became almost entirely dependent upon her, and in his college years he made a remarkable academic record. All his out-of-class time was spent at home with his devoted and adoring mother. In his last year of college she remarried, and the young man set out after graduation for his first teaching position. Within a few days he walked out of class and never returned. He was picked up wandering the streets of a town some distance away. In the hospital he was coöperative and pleasant and when attention was paid to him he would converse intelligently on a wide variety of topics, always on a high intellectual plane. The moment the topic of conversation was steered toward himself he would skillfully avoid the reference and skip off to another topic with less personal reference.

When put to work on the farm, this young man would go along willingly, would start hoeing at the beginning of a row, but when he reached the end would lie down. He was through for the day. No amount of urging could induce him to work any longer. When he was discharged from the hospital to a job in a gas station he worked three hours, then wandered off for several days. He was picked up some distance away. When returned to the hospital he sat by himself with a fixed smile for hours until someone stirred him enough to get him talking on some subject. He delighted in talking to groups of students touring the hospital and discoursed at length with them in their own campus language. Thus, when opportunities were presented to him for self enhancement without overt effort, he would rise to the occasion and was willing to remain in contact with external events. However, the moment that he was thrown in any degree upon his own resources, or when it became necessary to react more than passively to his environment, he retreated into his apathetic and disinterested pattern of behavior. When he felt adequate, he acted normally. When he felt inadequate, he retreated into his protective shell. It seems likely that the loss of his mother's protection and aid left this young man so poorly equipped that the necessities of assuming personal responsibility became a very real and violent threat to his existence.

Perhaps the most extreme example of this withdrawal of the individual and refusal to operate in external reality is to be observed in catatonic types of schizophrenia. In this state, denial of the relevance of threat may even involve separation of the self from the physical body. It becomes possible to stick the patient with pins, to mold him almost at will without his slightest response. He behaves as though he felt "it doesn't concern me in the least." He acts like an innocent bystander with respect to his own body conditions. The catatonic behaves as though his phenomenal self were completely apart from this world. He treats outside

events as irrelevant and immaterial. He may sit quietly while his room
burns. He sees the fire but, since it has no relation to him, it does not
spur him to action. Occasionally, however, he may suddenly return to
contact with objective reality with violent excitement and impulsive activity. Such returns appear to occur when the individual shifts his techniques from a withdrawal from threat to an attack upon it. Such sudden
returns to contact seem to be associated with increased feelings of adequacy.

It will be recognized that the denial of the relevance of threat is a
major characteristic of criminals as well. The assumption that the normal controls of society do not apply to him leaves the desperado free to
behave as he desires. Or if he is really threatened and has little sense of
identification, some threats may be eliminated by eliminating the persons
who produce them. The methods he uses to deny the relevance of threat
are often the very factors which cause some individuals to be considered
criminal rather than psychotic.

DISTORTIONS OF PERCEPTION TO FIT EXISTING FIELD ORGANIZATIONS

Like all people, seriously inadequate personalities attempt to deal with
threat by distorting their perceptions of themselves or the world they
live in in such a manner as to be consistent with the existing field organization. Many psychotic states are characterized by such distortions.
They exist as hallucinations, delusions, and obsessions of one variety or
another. Though we describe such distortions as false or unreal, it should
not be thought that they seem so to the persons who experience them.
Quite the contrary, to the individual at the moment of having such perceptions, the experience is real and vital.

Perhaps the best illustration of the distortion of external events is to
be observed in paranoia. This is a psychotic state characterized by great
suspicion of others and often highly fanciful delusions of persecution.
Here the threat to the individual's phenomenal self may become so great
that it is involved in every slightest activity in which he is concerned.
He perceives threat in everything; the letters he receives are summonses
to court, his friends are out to "get him," all the world is lying in wait
for him. His feeling of being threatened colors a very large share of his
perceptions. It appears to him that he is threatened by even the smallest
details of his surroundings. Alone in this threatening world, the paranoid
patient often spends much time in scheming to get the better of the
host of enemies by whom he feels he is surrounded. Everything must be

given an explanation and even events having nothing to do with him are seen as oriented toward self. He suffers delusions and hallucinations and, to all intents and purposes, he is indeed alone against the world.

Unlike some of the other psychotics, the paranoid patient lives in the midst of his threats instead of withdrawing from them. He often remains more or less in touch with many aspects of external reality but builds a keen and often highly logical defense against those perceptions which appear to him most threatening. Some paranoid patients may be quite normal with respect to much of their daily living and feel threatened only when some event is perceived as relating to those areas in which they feel vulnerable. Paranoids frequently organize their field so completely that they are able to pluck enhancement out of the threat. Once they have explained their failures and feelings of inadequacy by believing that they are surrounded by enemies, it is almost necessary for them to ask themselves: "Why am I so important that so many people spend their lives conspiring against me?" It should not surprise anyone that many paranoids come to believe that they are God.

MULTIPLE PERSONALITIES

Distortions which maintain the organization of the phenomenal field may affect the individual's perceptions of self in other ways. Behavior resulting from one concept of self may be unacceptable and threatening to another aspect of self. Under these circumstances perceptions of self may be so distorted as to keep such diverse self perceptions from existing simultaneously. This appears to be illustrated in an extreme form in what are often described as *multiple personalities*. In a mild form this separation of self was illustrated in the case of Helen, a little girl known to the author. Helen had developed another personality, Marie. Helen was an extremely "good" child who always did as she was told. She was in every way a delight from an adult point of view. Marie, on the other hand, was a "naughty" girl who said "bad words," who sometimes wet her panties, who slapped her little brother, and who was generally responsible for most of the quarrels among the children of the neighborhood. This dual personality had been brought on by the birth of Helen's little brother and the child's consequent attempts to gain self esteem. Finding herself no longer the "apple of her parent's eye," she sought to achieve self esteem in new ways. These attempts were met by her shocked and horrified parents with many statements that she was a "bad" girl and were accompanied by moralistic reproof and severe punishment. Such proof of her immorality could not be accepted by Helen, who had always regarded herself previously as a "nice" girl. Yet the proofs could not be done away with. Her own parents in whom she trusted *insisted* that she was a bad girl! Her "naughty" behavior, moreover, was extremely satisfying and made it possible to regain a feeling of enhancement necessary to her. She could neither accept her behavior as bad nor go on believing herself good. A multiple personality solved the problem for Helen. Helen did not have to feel guilty at what Marie did, while Marie could do things that gave the child immediate satisfaction without threatening Helen. When the child's parents were helped to remove the threats and pressure from Helen, when they had accepted their little girl's behavior, and when they had provided new ways in which Helen could gain self esteem, Marie disappeared and has never been heard from since.

T. W. Mitchell and Gardner Murphy have made a distinction between two general types of multiple personalities. In Type I, the two or more personalities are widely separated, and the individual operating in either frame of reference has little or no apparent knowledge or memory of the activities of the other. This state of affairs appears to exist when both A aspect of self and B aspect of self are inadequate, that is, too threatened by the perception of their counterparts to be able to accept their perceptions into the organization. In this case, A will not even "know" what B has been up to. Nor will B have any apparent knowledge of A's activities. It should not be imagined, however, that this is a "real" difference in personalities, for under hypnosis or some other method by which the individual can be made to feel unthreatened, both personalities can be recalled and described by the individual.

In Type II, personality A is able to recall the activities of personality B, but B is apparently unaware of the activities of A. Murphy summarizes Morton Prince's "BCA" case as follows: "[BCA] after recovery wrote her autobiography as a double personality. . . . A was sober, serious, reserved, afraid of life, and of herself, 'full of metaphysical doubts and fears, full of scruples.' B was jolly and carefree, healthy and vigorous. When B suddenly disappeared, A was often shocked to find herself confronting a wineglass or a cigarette. B, however, knew all about A, pitying and despising her thoughts and attitudes, of which B always had complete and direct knowledge." We have here what Murphy has called a "restricted" and a "relaxed personality." In perceptual terms we would call them threatened and nonthreatened, respectively. The already threatened personality cannot tolerate new threatening perceptions, while the less threatened personality finds it possible at least to accept new threats into figure, even though they may be rejected and despised. Whereas in Type I we have been discussing two aspects of self each highly threatening to the other, in Type II we have a highly threatened self definition and a less threatened one.

This restricting effect of threat is nicely illustrated in W. F. Prince's classic case of Doris Fischer. Over a period of time Doris developed four fairly distinct personalities. The original Doris was a "good" girl who ordinarily did quietly what was demanded of her. She was a restricted, introverted personality deeply attached to her mother. The second of Doris' personalities appeared when she was about 3 years old, following a traumatic experience in which she was brutally thrown to the floor by her drunken father. Following this experience, Doris developed a second personality, Margaret, Margaret was quite a different person than Doris. She was active, carefree, mischievous, and constantly engaged in aggressive behavior of one sort or another. Margaret knew about Doris, disliked her intensely, and even punished Doris on occasion for playing with Margaret's possessions. Doris, however, apparently knew nothing of the existence of Margaret. The third personality came into being when Doris was sixteen. Doris' mother died then, quite suddenly. This was too much for the young girl. She was deeply shocked and distraught, and "Sick Doris" appeared on the scene. This new personality was an extremely threatened one, a highly restricted drudge who went about her tasks without imagination and little or no response. "Sick Doris" seemed to know nothing of her other selves.

At the time Prince worked with this patient then, she had three distinct personalities—Sick Doris, Doris, and Margaret—arranged in order of the increasing freedom of the personalities. It is interesting that the more threatened personalities "did not know" of the less threatened ones but the freer personalities were apparently aware of the more restricted ones. Finally, under hypnosis, a fourth personality made its appearance. This was "Sleeping Margaret." Sleeping Margaret was the most unrestricted and unthreatened of the four personalities. She knew all of the activities of her other selves and was able to converse at length, in detail, and with much objectivity about each of the other three. Thus the multiple personality seems to be an attempt to maintain the phenomenal self through acquiring another self, adequate and able to do what is impossible or inappropriate for the original. Extremely threatened personalities may find it possible to achieve a degree of adequacy by assuming a different identity.

Closely related to such distortion of self perception is the assumption of new, more adequate personalities unrelated to the original self. Many mental patients appear to find another solution to the problem of threat in various "delusions of grandeur." Feeling inadequate to deal with the world as themselves, it is sometimes possible for them to achieve a feeling of adequacy and even of invincibility by adopting a ready-made and proved self from history, religion, or mythology. Thus, if George Smith is not adequate to deal with life as Smith he may become George Washington instead. There is no doubt in either his mind or those about him of Washington's adequacy.

Perhaps the most extreme distortions of self perceptions are to be observed in some types of psychosis in which the organization of self seems shattered, or so wildly fluctuating as to leave the individual completely confused and with little or no frame of reference from which to operate. This kind of disorganization of self perception may be seen in some types of schizophrenia generally characterized by disorganization of thinking and often by rapidly shifting and changing behavior on the part of the patient. These patients seem characterized by self concepts which appear to have lost the stability characteristic of those of the normal individual. They appear to feel threatened in many aspects of self, so much so that they cannot accept any consistent evaluation of self. They appear to be confused as to who and what they are, and feel inadequate in many ways. The definition of the phenomenal self seems almost to be shifting and changing quite out of the patient's control, and his ideas and actions may shift rapidly from moment to moment. Often it is possible to observe in the so-called "word salads" of such patients a train of coherent thought which appears to rise to the surface and then disappear in a jumble of other ideas only to return again later in the passage. This sometimes appears as though the patient's field had a momentary organization which slipped away, and returned, and slipped away again, over and over.

CHANGING FEELINGS OF ADEQUACY

It is interesting to note how the techniques used by very inadequate personalities change with varying degrees of feelings of adequacy. With increased feelings of inadequacy, techniques become increasingly violent, bizarre, or withdrawn. As feelings of adequacy increase, techniques become more socially fitting, acceptable, and active. This is nicely illustrated in the following case known to the author. Bill Johnson was an extraordinarily successful businessman. He was known in his community as a veritable dynamo of energy. He was athletic, hearty, and a rather dominating sort of person. He seldom listened to other people but usually had good ideas of how things could be accomplished and the energy with which to follow them through. By virtue of his tremendous energy and frequent flashes of brilliance he rose rapidly in the X Corporation through a whirlwind development of the sales department. He finally became vice-president of the corporation. He was a promoter of no mean ability. His family was inclined to breathe a sigh of relief when he was away from home, for even in the family setting he continued his whirlwind methods of operation. He seldom slept more than four hours a night. He looked like a very promising young man until the president of his corporation began to feel threatened by the extraordinary rise of his junior officer. The corporation president began to block Bill Johnson's ambitious efforts at every hand. Bill became wilder and wilder in his efforts to achieve his ends and finally precipitated a showdown with the board of directors. He lost, was forced to resign his job, and retired to his home a very sick man. For many months he was in the depths of despair, feeling himself a complete failure. He felt inadequate to attempt the simplest thing and slept 12 or 13 hours a day.

A few months later he was offered an important position with a government agency in a distant part of the country. Almost overnight he was a different man. He packed up his family and was off to the new location. He had hardly arrived before the same cycle began all over again. Once more he was a dynamo of energy involved in all of the affairs of his community. Again he rose rapidly to a position of considerable responsibility in the new agency until he had reached the top. It was impossible to go further in this job, after three or four years, without participating in politics and being elected to the next highest office. Without batting an eye he became a politician overnight and ran for election. Unfortunately, he lost by but a few votes. Immediately after election he collapsed and was hospitalized for almost a year in a deeply depressed state.

The dynamics of Bill Johnson's case appear to be as follows: Bill Johnson is possessed of a concept of self as inadequate. This concept, however, is intolerable to him and he strives in countless ways to "snow under" such threatening perceptions by a ceaseless round of activity.

He attempts to prove to himself that he is better than he feels he is. Often he is successful at this sort of thing for long periods of time. So long as he remains physically healthy and has reserves of energy to call upon, he continues his wild course of behavior. He literally runs away from his problem by doing things, *anything*. When his physical resources collapse, however, he no longer feels adequate. He has not the energy with which to carry on his frantic behavior. He is forced to slow down in spite of himself and is, at once, faced with the very threatening perceptions he seeks to avoid. In a very real sense his immobility robs him of his best defensive technique. He feels depressed and woefully inadequate. Such depressions are often their own cure, however, for they prevent him from being active and over a period of time his physical resources may return. Now he can feel adequate again, and some little success sets him off on the business of convincing himself once more that what he believes to be true is "just not so." When Bill Johnson felt more adequate, he behaved more adequately. Unfortunately, even when he was operating in high gear, he still felt basically inadequate.

TREATMENT OF PSYCHOSIS

Even the most threatened, withdrawn psychotics can sometimes be induced to come out of their protective shells and return to fuller "contact" with the outside world when they can be helped to feel more adequate and secure. When such patients are treated in a warm, non-threatening atmosphere for long enough periods, they can sometimes be induced to carry on conversations with others or to make halting attempts to renew relationships they have rejected for years. Many mental patients seem to get well when they are hospitalized, even though they have had no formal treatment whatever. Sometimes the very fact of hospitalization removes the patient from the threatening relationships of his daily life. In the sheltered atmosphere of the hospital he then is able to feel more adequate and, temporarily separated from his inadequacies, may find it possible to relax and differentiate new self definitions more satisfying than those he held before. Unhappily, this does not always occur. Frequently the patient improves in the sheltered atmosphere of the hospital only to suffer a relapse when he is plunged back into his normal setting and finds himself once more confronted with threats that seem just too much for him to bear.

Once it was customary to treat inadequate personalities as the psychotic or criminal by locking them up or subjecting them to various forms of punishment or horrible experiences of one sort or another in the hope of frightening them back to a semblance of normality. Occasionally these methods worked, but more often the patient became worse if he succeeded in surviving at all. This is what we would expect in the light of our current knowledge of the effects of threat. Modern treatment of seriously inadequate personalities is a far cry from the primitive techniques of a generation ago, and the past 20 years has seen great changes in the operation of our institutions for the criminal and the psychotic. New understandings of the psychology of these desperate ones has made it possible to devise new methods of treatment for severely inadequate persons with far greater chances of success than formerly. The most successful of these new methods assist the individual in one way or another to differentiate new and more adequate concepts of himself and the world in which he lives. This is, of course, neither simple nor easy. Rather it is often a long, painful, and difficult process of self redefinition requiring patience and skill on the part of the therapist and his coworkers as well as a high degree of courage and perseverance on the part of the patient. Given a chance, however, the individual's own need for adequacy will impel him toward better health if the ways seem open to him. In recent years we have found better and better ways to help such desperate persons to find greater adequacy and to achieve a larger measure of self actualization.

PART II

The Perceptual Approach Applied

So much of our lives is concerned with human relationships that any change in our beliefs about the nature of man and his behavior must, of necessity, have tremendous implications for all aspects of our social existence. This has always been true throughout man's history and is just as true today. Whatever we believe about people must inevitably affect the ways we behave toward them. In the previous chapters of this volume we have developed a frame of reference for the understanding of behavior. It is time now to look at some of the implications of these concepts for dealing with the great human problems of our generation. Practice provides the test of theory. Theory opens the doors to new possibilities in practice. No matter how consistent and plausible a theory may be, it is of no value if it does not contribute ultimately to the improvement of practice. If the point of view presented in the preceding chapters has any value, it should be manifest in a contribution to improved understanding and action.

What, we need to ask, has this view of behavior to offer for dealing with some of the practical problems of man's relationships with his fellows? In the pages to follow we shall attempt to answer this question by exploring the implications of a perceptual view of behavior as they apply to several important areas of human action.

CHAPTER 14

Some General Implications for Human Relations

The Facts of Human Relationships

The facts of human behavior, we have seen, are not the facts that exist for others but the facts that exist for the behaver. If it is true that people behave according to how things seem to them, then it is the things people believe which are the facts of human relationships. In this sense, seeing is not only believing; seeing is behaving! A fact is not what is; a fact is what one *believes!* The data with which we must deal in understanding and changing human relationships, then, are feelings, attitudes, beliefs, and values. The citizen who voted for the Democratic candidate did so in the belief that he was the better man. Millions of Republican voters disagreed. Each voter behaved in terms of what seemed to him to be so. Which voter was correct we shall never know, but each behaved as though his own *belief* were the fact of the matter.

Many Russians believe we are a nation of "capitalistic warmongers bent upon world domination." Many of us, on the other hand, believe the Russians to be "fanatics who will stop at nothing to achieve world domination." Each nation behaves as though its assessment of the other were an inescapable fact. We are shocked by Russian perceptions of us and deeply hurt that we are regarded with such suspicion. How people perceive, however, is not a matter to be ignored or to feel hurt about. Perceptions are not matters to deplore. If it is true, as we have postulated, that behavior is a product of perception, then they become the basic data of human relations and the facts with which we must learn to deal.

To regard the facts of human behavior in this way is likely to prove extremely distressing or difficult to some people. Though the idea that people behave according to how things seem to them is simplicity itself, there are strong factors both in ourselves and our society that make this quite difficult to accept. We have been so impressed, for example, with the magnificent achievements of the physical sciences in our society that many of us have come to regard the "objective" world of the physical sciences as equivalent to reality itself. This view of events has served our society so well in dealing with the problems for which it is appropriate, that many people have come to believe the objective approach is the only possible method of observation worthy of consideration.

It is a natural thing to attempt to apply the methods with which we have been successful in the past to problems we meet in the present. There is a glorious definiteness about dealing with "things." They stay where they are put and behave in comfortable, predictable ways, and we would like people to behave so too. Because of this former satisfying experience it is a temptation to extend the methods we have found so useful to the new area of our interest. We fail to understand that different problems require quite different approaches.

It is difficult for us to approach human relationships from a perceptual view, for another reason. Our own perceptions always have so strong a feeling of reality that it is easy to jump to the conclusion that they must be real to others as well. If others do not see as we do, we may even regard them as stupid, stubborn, or perverse. It is hard to set one's own experience aside, yet it is difficult to see how effective human relationships can be built without a clear recognition of the personal character of perceptions. The first step toward the solution of our human problems seems to require a willingness to grant that "How it seems to me may be different. I, too, could be wrong!" Humility, it would seem, is more than a nice idea. It is an essential to effective communication!

Still another factor makes the perceptual approach to human relationships difficult. That is, the widespread feeling in some quarters that the admission of human feelings, attitudes, and perceptions as behavioral data flirts with the mystical and runs the risk of being "unscientific." No real science, however, can afford to ignore data relevant to its purposes simply because they are difficult to measure or do not lend themselves to treatment by orthodox means. If behavior is a function of perception, then a science of human relationships must concern itself with the meaning of events for the behaver as well as for the observer. Human feelings, attitudes, fears, hopes, wants, likes, and aversions cannot be set aside while we deal with objective events. The subjective aspects of human experience cannot be suspended from operation. Perceptions are the very fabric of which human relationships are made. They are the crucial facts with which we must deal in attempting to solve our most pressing problems. If we do not currently possess the means of studying perceptions effectively, then we need to get about the business of finding out how without further delay. Time presses upon us.

Man as Responsible Agent

A second broad implication of the perceptual approach has to do with the way in which we regard man and his relationships to the world in which he lives. One of the earliest conceptions of the nature of human beings held that man was a completely independent and responsible agent. People in those times, looking at themselves and their fellows, observed that human beings made decisions. They concluded from these observations that man was, therefore, a creature entirely responsible for his behavior. Whatever he did arose entirely from within himself. If a man misbehaved, it was his fault that he did so. He was thoroughly and inescapably to blame for his acts.

With such a conception of what man was trying to do, it is not surprising that education in those days was a gloomy, coercive affair in which children were "taught," *made* to behave. And no wonder—salvation was at stake! Nor is it surprising that adults believed quite thoroughly that people deserved what happened to them. Since man was utterly responsible, punishments were harsh and severe. Little sympathy was wasted on the criminal, the sick, or the insane. Indeed, that such misfortunes befell a man only served to prove how bad he must have been! Parents were blamed for their failures to correct a child or to force obedience, not for their failures to provide a child with love and affection. When a child misbehaved it was because the child was bad and parents were sympathized with or pitied. If they were blamed at all, it was for failure to force obedience, teach manners, or "bend the twig properly." We still have in our society people who believe that criminals and even nations should be punished severely for their misbehavior.

Whereas the concept we have just been speaking about held that man was completely responsible for what happened to him, another concept commonly held even today sees man as the *victim* of his environment. He is what he is because of what has happened to him. Unfortunately, this point of view, while making possible great strides in some aspects of human living, has, at the same time, made it difficult for us to understand some of our most pressing problems. It has given rise to a mechanistic conception of human beings as physical objects whose behavior is the result of forces acting upon them. It has largely dehumanized psychology, making of human beings little more than objects to be manipulated at will. In this view human beings are often compared to steam engines, automobiles, or other pieces of machinery. Man is thought of as a passive automaton, buffeted about by the circumstances surrounding him.

·Such a view of behavior places the responsibility quite outside the individual himself. The implications of this view are widespread throughout all phases of our society. Perhaps no group is more affected, however, than our defenseless, unorganized parents. As low man on the totem pole, the responsibility for all our social ills is laid squarely at their door. Whatever institution is criticized for its failures to deal with people effectively sooner or later ends by blaming the parent. The parents, having no one to whom to "pass the buck," are stuck with it! The best a poor parent can do is to blame it all on his spouse's side of the family. But if behavior is truly a function of environment only, then parents can no more be held responsible than other agencies in society and the people *really* responsible are our forefathers clear back to Adam or the first living organism!

The view of man's behavior we have adopted in this volume helps us to resolve this dilemma. We have seen in Chapter 3 that man is continuous with his environment, but we have also seen that he is never free from the dynamic, creative force of his fundamental need for adequacy. This gives us a view of man neither so completely responsible for his behavior as the first view we have cited above, nor on the other hand so willy-nilly at the mercy of his environment as the second would lead us to believe. He is part controlled by and in part controlling of his destiny. It provides us with an understanding of man deeply and intimately affected by his environment but capable also of molding and shaping his destiny in important ways. Such a view fits more closely our own experience and is an understanding broadly significant in helping us find solutions to some of our great social problems.

Two Approaches to Dealing with Human Problems

THE FENCING-IN APPROACH

The differences between the environmental and perceptual views of behavior are nowhere so clearly marked as in the kinds of methods they lead to in dealing with human relationships. The environmental approach to behavior has led us to believe that almost anything can be accomplished in dealing with people if we are sufficiently skillful in the manipulation of the proper forces at the proper times. Its adoption results in an approach to human problems based upon control of environment and has produced a way of dealing with people familiar to anyone who has ever visited a stockyard or driven the cows home from pasture. One goes down the lane from the barn and carefully closes all the gates where he does *not* want the cattle to go and opens the gates where he *does* want them to go. In the pasture the cattle are set in motion by creating an annoyance behind them, thus driving them forward up the path prepared for them.

While the fencing-in technique works fine with cattle and sheep, it often breaks down with human beings. People, being somewhat smarter than cows, have a disconcerting way of discovering that the "right" way often leads to places they would rather not go. They are just as likely as not to jump the fence, open gates that were overlooked, and generally behave in the most unpredictable and "uncoöperative" ways. In spite of its frequent failure, however, this fencing-in philosophy of human relationships is applied in dealing with people throughout our society: in advertising and selling, in labor-management discussions, in administration, in our legislatures, and even in our diplomacy of power politics, buffer states, and vetoes. It is common practice in our schools, our churches, and our homes. If we believe that human behavior is alone a function of the forces exerted upon people, a philosophy of force and coercion naturally follows as the appropriate means of dealing with our fellows. Such force may be expressed as naked power. It may also be clothed in a velvet glove as "friendly" advice, reward for "proper" behavior, or various more or less subtle forms of reward or punishment.

The fencing-in approach moreover, raises an additional serious problem, for it requires that someone must know what the "right" goal is in order effectively to manipulate the required forces. Someone must know where the people *should* go. This calls for a leader or great man, to chart the proper path for the common people. Such an approach sometimes works fairly well when the right answers are known and leaders are essentially benevolent. Unfortunately, right answers to human problems are remarkably elusive and great men are as often wrong as right. Despite the fact that this essentially manipulative method of dealing with people seems hardly compatible with our democratic ideals, it nevertheless may be found operating even in some of our most "democratic" institutions.

THE GROWTH APPROACH

If the view of human behavior we have been exploring in this book is accurate, it calls for a very different approach to human problems from the one above. How people perceive themselves and the world in which they live is an internal, personal matter. What people believe about themselves and their environment is not directly open to manipulation. A man's perceptions arise within himself. We cannot *make* people perceive. Effective, satisfying human relationships can only be developed through helping ourselves and others to perceive more freely and accurately. Man is not a puppet bandied about at the mercy of the forces exerted upon him. On the contrary, he is a creature of discretion who selects his perceptions from the world he lives in. He is not the victim of events but is capable of perceiving, interpreting, even creating events. Such a conception of human beings requires a very different approach to working with people than the "fencing-in" technique we have outlined above. It calls for the development of understanding rather than manipulation; for freeing communication, in place of coercion; for stimulating mutual exploration and discovery of goals and means, as opposed to servile dependence on an elite.

The perceptual view sees man as a growing, dynamic, creative being continuously in search of adequacy. Instead of an object at the mercy of environment, he is, himself, a purposive agent engaged in a never-ending business of becoming. People in this sense are processes rather than objects, growing rather than static, and call for the same kind of treatment we accord other growing things. To grow a good plant, for example, we acquire the best seed we can get, plant it in the best ground we can provide, surround it with the very best conditions for growth we can produce; then we get out of its way and let it grow! In a similar manner, the perceptual view leads to methods of dealing with people which recognize the internal character of perception and seek to affect behavior through processes of facilitation, helping, assisting, or aiding the normal growth strivings of the organism itself.

Since perception is an internal process not open to direct manipulation from without, change in behavior cannot be brought about directly but only through the kinds of experiences people are exposed to. From a perceptual frame of reference therefore, the emphasis in dealing with people is upon the creation of *kind of situations which facilitate or assist the process of perception change.* Good teachers know, for example, that children cannot be *made* to learn. Children, however, can and will learn when teachers are successful in creating experiences which encourage and assist the learner in his search for adequacy. Our frame of reference calls for an approach to human relationships which seeks change in behavior through change in perceiving rather than through a direct attack on behavior itself. It emphasizes in practice techniques of communication, persuasion, learning, and discovery rather than the employment of force, coercion, or various forms of manipulation.

Since perceptions are more directly causative of behavior than environmental manipulation, methods of dealing with people dependent upon changing perception rather than controlling and directing behavior are likely to be more permanent and trustworthy on later occasions when pressure and coercion are no longer present. Although it is of course possible to make people behave as desired by the application of sufficient force at the right time, such behavior cannot be counted upon to occur at times when the force is no longer applied. What people *believe* they carry about with them, but environments are external and therefore can be left behind.

The perceptual approach seems particularly effective when applied to problems of human relationships in group settings. Because it recognizes the unhappy effects of threat upon perceiving and seeks to challenge people without threatening them, conflict among the members of the group and with outsiders as well is likely to exist at a much lower level. Conflict is heightened when people feel frustrated, inadequate, or coerced into moving in directions they do not wish to go. As a consequence resistance is likely to be high and change occurs only slowly and painfully, if at all. A philosophy of group operation based upon helping, aiding, assisting, however, keeps frustration at a minimum so that conflict is not so likely to occur. Even when it does occur, the elimination of threat provides little to support it and it soon fails of its own weight.

Such approaches to human interrelationship, furthermore, actually create leadership in groups rather than being dependent upon leadership provided from without. Where human dignity and integrity is respected and valued, when people are treated as though they were able, given assistance and help in their search for adequacy, and confronted with challenging tasks, creativity and spontaneity result. It should not surprise us either that under such circumstances the solutions people find to problems are likely to be of superior quality. And why not? Groups operating on a growth philosophy are not restricted to the solutions which occur to a single leader; the groups themselves create leadership and release human potentialities. What is more, persons who have experienced these kinds of human relationships are far more likely to have faith and trust in their fellows and to be capable of identifying and empathizing with others.

To some this approach to dealing with human problems as a process of facilitation of perceptions seems highly disappointing and much too slow to be capable of solving important problems. A helping, assisting, freeing approach seems somehow to smack of anarchy and laissez faire. They have little assurance that people will arrive at the "right" answers to problems without someone to decide what these are and arrange matters in such a fashion as to make sure that everyone gets there. As a matter of fact, the emphasis upon processes and facilitation in the long run seems much more likely to supply us with better solutions, for it has the advantage of producing an open, rather than a closed, system of thought. Whenever we choose a particular set of goals or values for people and then set about deliberately to achieve these ends, we are operating in a closed system. Such systems seriously restrict the field from which we can make our selections. Rogers, in a discussion of this principle applied to the science of human relationship, has described closed systems as follows:

. . . If we choose some particular goal or series of goals for human beings and then set out on a large scale to control human behavior to the end of achieving these goals, we are locked in the rigidity of our initial choice, because such a scientific endeavor can never transcend itself to select new goals. Only subjective human persons can do that. Thus, if we choose as our goal the state of happiness for human beings (a goal deservedly ridiculed by Aldous Huxley in *Brave New World*), and if we involved all of society in a successful scientific program by which people became happy, we would be locked in a colossal rigidity in which no one would be free to question this goal, because our scientific operations could not transcend themselves to question their guiding purposes. And without laboring this point, I would remark that colossal rigidity whether in dinosaur or dictatorships has a very poor record of evolutionary survival.

Implications of an Immediate View of Causation

The perceptual frame of reference provides an immediate rather than a historical understanding of the causation of behavior. It suggests that, since perceptions exist only in the present, it should be possible to deal effectively with behavior through an understanding of present perceptions even if we do not know anything about the individual's past! If true, this notion has vast implications for our methods of dealing with people everywhere in our society. On the surface this statement seems quite contrary to the widespread belief that any attempt to deal with a human being must be preceded by a detailed analysis of his previous history. Actually, both immediate and historical views are quite accurate descriptions of human behavior and not at all antagonistic. Although the perceptual view of behavior is concerned primarily with present perceptions, this is not to suggest that the past is unimportant. On the contrary, one of Freud's great contributions to our understanding of behavior was his observation that behavior is a product of past experience. The principle seems just as true today as it ever was. Behavior is *historically* a function of what has happened to us in the past but *immediately* a function of our present perceptions. A child brought up in a family where he was often rejected and treated as unimportant may grow to manhood with deep feelings of unworthiness or inferiority. These feelings (ways of seeing) may in turn motivate much of his present behavior. What has happened to him in the past has produced his present ways of perceiving. A knowledge of his past thus *explains* his present perceptions. It is possible for us, however, to interact effectively with him even if we have no knowledge of his past whatever, providing we understand how he is presently perceiving.

For several generations Freud's observation provided the principal direction for hundreds of experiments and investigations into the nature of behavior. As a result of these studies, we have acquired a vast store of information about the ways in which human beings grow and develop, become adjusted or maladjusted, effective or ineffective. Workers in the helping professions like social work, psychotherapy, education, and counseling were particularly affected by this observation and many came to feel that careful studies of the life span of their clients was an indispensable requirement for properly carrying on their functions. The case study, the anecdotal record, and free association became fundamental tools for carrying out their roles.

There can be little doubt of the essential accuracy of Freud's principle, but it has severe limits when applied to problems of treatment or learning. An understanding of how an individual got the way he is today is not always helpful in guiding us in the determination of where to go from here. Gordon Allport once suggested, "People are busy living their lives forward, while psychologists busily trace them backward!" The perceptual view makes it possible to break away from this unhappy preoccupation and opens vast new avenues for understanding and dealing with human interrelationships. It releases the applied worker from the necessity of accumulating quantities of information formerly thought essential. There is, after all, very little we can do about a person's past. There is a great deal we can do about people's present perceptions.

PERCEPTION AND ENVIRONMENTAL CHANGE

A second significant implication of the immediate view of causation is the freedom it gives us to deal with human problems without the necessity of environmental change. Environments are not always amenable to manipulation. There are serious limits to the degree to which they can be changed to suit the need of individuals. A way of dealing with human problems which is not dependent upon environmental change therefore opens vast new possibilities for solving some of our most knotty social problems. We are beginning to discover that when we find ways of helping people change the ways they see themselves and the world in which they live, it may not be necessary to change their environments. For instance, parents who see the need for better schools are more likely to get them through their own efforts. Children aided to see themselves more adequately can live effective lives even though outsiders may be unable to make basic changes in distressing family situations. Following play therapy, for example, in which children have been helped to perceive themselves and their parents more adequately it is not uncommon to find changes occurring in the child's family despite the fact his parents have not been involved in treatment themselves. Apparently, as the child feels better he behaves better and this in turn affects the feelings toward him of those who surround him.

This is not to suggest that improvements in housing, parent education, or the provision of food, shelter, and clothing for the needy are either unnecessary or undesirable. Such devices will always be important approaches to social problems. In fact, it frequently happens that changes in environment will be accompanied by important changes in perceiving. The understanding that people behave according to how things seem to them does not discard other approaches. It simply opens another avenue by which we may contribute to human happiness and development.

If behavior is a function of present perceptions, however, then there is something that can be done about *any* individual, even those from the worst backgrounds. It means that whatever we do in interaction with other people is *always* important. The behavior of people toward each other can be helpful or hindering, constructive or destructive in greater or lesser degree. We need not throw up our hands in despair over inability to change the past or control all aspects of present environment. The interactions of people need not be trivial and unimportant no matter what the previous experience of an individual may have been. Fritz Redl once commented in a speech that the distance between a naughty boy and a hardened delinquent was a very long way. Redl then went on to exclaim, "If we could just keep 'em naughty, what a wonderful thing we have done!" Although we may not always be able to produce deep and meaningful changes in those who surround us, whatever we do is worth doing, even though it may be sometimes too little or too late to make the kind of difference we should like.

THE IMMEDIACY PRINCIPLE IN PROFESSIONAL WORK

The importance of this principle is nowhere so appreciated as in the professional work of teachers, social workers, and psychotherapists. To many teachers, for example, this idea opens the doors to vast new possibilities for helping children with problems. It means no child is hopeless. There are things which can be done to help even the most unhappy and maladjusted child right in the classroom. To many discouraged teachers it brings new hope that their jobs are important, that they can be, and often are, effective in helping children grow. It means teachers can help children in school even though they have no control over the child's outside environment.

This is no small matter. Teachers for a generation have been made to feel they are powerless to help children who come to them too late or who are present victims of unfortunate home environments. The perceptual view of behavior emphasizes that present experience in the classroom can affect a child's perceptions in the same fashion as his experiences outside the schoolroom. The child who sees himself as unliked, unwanted, unaccepted, or unable can be helped by the teacher's own behavior toward him even though neither he nor his teacher may have any idea whatever of how he came to feel as he does. You do not have to be an expert to know what to do with a child who feels unliked, unaccepted, or unable!

The principle that behavior can be changed without full knowledge of the past seems equally promising for the field of social work. Much of the social worker's time and energy, to say nothing of shoe leather and carfare, has often been spent in the painstaking collection of mountains of data about the histories of clients. While much of this is necessary, much, too, is not. Such collection of data is often regarded by the social worker's clients as unwarranted and malicious snooping, and such attitudes immeasurably increase the difficulty of establishing a helping relationship. Seeing behavior as a function of present perceptions makes it possible for the modern social worker to dispense with much of this. As a result he appears in the eyes of his client far more understanding and sympathetic.

Like the teachers, social workers have often felt themselves powerless to help clients enmeshed in harmful environmental circumstances. Frequently they have become depressed and discouraged because so little could be accomplished in changing the conditions they observed. With this point of view, however, new possibilities are open to the social worker for helping clients to change their perceptions even though it may not be possible immediately to change their present conditions. Indeed, it often happens that when clients change their perceptions they find more ingenious and effective ways of helping themselves than any outsider could contribute.

The emphasis upon present perceptions rather than past experience has also produced changes in our approaches to counseling and psychotherapy. Once it was considered impossible to help a disturbed child without first producing fundamental changes in his parents. This is not always possible, however, and in the past such children often had to be charged off as bad risks. The perceptual point of view opens new possibilities. Psychotherapists are now finding it possible to help children to new adjustment and happier lives even when there is little opportunity to make fundamental changes in family structure. Methods of play therapy, for example, dependent solely on assisting children to explore present perceptions of themselves and the world they live in, have produced startling results in aiding disturbed youngsters.

The principle has proved equally effective in assisting adults with their problems. About 1942, Dr. Carl Rogers proposed a method of psychotherapy based on helping his clients explore their present ways of seeing themselves and the world in which they live. These methods have since been subjected to much research and have proved remarkably effective in a wide variety of cases. The method is based upon helping the client to explore his ways of seeing himself and his world in an atmosphere of warmth and understanding. The therapist avoids probing and exploring his client and instead assists his client to explore himself. The method is known as client-centered therapy because of this emphasis upon the client's rather than the therapist's understanding. Using such methods, it seems possible to help many clients without extensive delving into the past. To many, the idea of helping people to better adjustment without a thorough understanding of the client's past history seems highly unorthodox, even irresponsible. Viewed from our former ideas about the nature of human behavior, such objections appear sound. From the perceptual view of behavior, however, such methods make good sense.

Implications of the Need for Adequacy

In Chapter 3 we have described the basic human need as the search for adequacy. In later chapters we have examined in some detail how this need operates in the insatiable striving of the organism for maintenance and enhancement of the self. We have seen, too, how it may be fulfilled in the adequate personality or frustrated in the inadequate one. Such a view of human need has important implications for the ways in which we view our common human problems and the kinds of ways we choose for dealing with them. If it is true, for example, that all human beings are motivated in all times and places by a need to be adequate, then much of the blame we are accustomed to heap upon other people for the stupidity, perverseness, or viciousness of their motivations is completely futile. Who, after all, can blame a man for seeking to be adequate?

People are always motivated from their own points of view. What we mean when we complain of the goals sought by some of our fellows is really that they are not motivated to seek the goals we *happen to think are important.* Even the neurotic, the criminal, and the insane are seeking in their own desperate ways to achieve the greatest possible degree of adequacy that *seems open to them.* The murderer at the moment of his act perceives what he is doing as the very best thing he could do under the circumstances, perhaps, even, the *only* thing he could do. The problems of human relations, then, are not so much a question of motivation as a problem of helping people to perceive more clearly. When people are able to perceive more adequately they will behave more adequately, too.

The basic character of human need is essentially positive rather than negative. Given a decent break, the need of the individual will drive him toward essentially positive goals and values. We have already seen that the truly adequate personality cannot behave in ways that are destructive either to himself or to his society in the long run. So long as people live in society and are dependent upon other people, the search for adequacy must include the adequacy of others as well. Whether the behavior it produces is "good" for the individual and those about him will depend upon the ways in which he has learned to perceive himself and his fellows as a result of his past experience and the richness, scope, and availability of perceptions in his present phenomenal field. A positive view of human motivation leaves little room for wasting time on futile blame and castigation and turns attention to the importance of human compassion and understanding.

That the essential character of human motivation is positive by no means guarantees that it will only result in positive kinds of behavior. The ways a dope peddler uses to seek adequacy are certainly destructive. The problem is not with the nature of his need, but the means he has perceived to achieve it. Negative acts may of course be produced by inadequate ways of perceiving. The problem of human relations becomes one of freeing people to perceive themselves and the world they live in in more adequate terms.

MOTIVATION AND ETHICAL VALUES

This essentially positive view of motivation has another important implication for human relationships. It means the faith in our fellows demanded by our democratic society is not an idle dream but finds its justification in the nature of the organism itself. Faith in others is justified, even demanded, if the basic motivation of people is for adequacy. Our democratic credo holds that when men are free they can learn to rule themselves. We could not afford to grant men freedom in the kind of interdependent society we live in if the basic human need was not for adequacy. It is because men fundamentally seek adequacy that we can afford to trust them with freedom. When the credo fails, it is not because men's motivations are bad, but because we have not been successful in finding ways truly to set them free.

Like the concept of faith, other ethical values we are accustomed to think of as "good" arise out of man's need for adequacy operating in an intensely interdependent and coöperative society. Living alone on a desert island, an individual might seek adequacy with no concern for such human values as love, respect, or the dignity and integrity of others. Living in a modern interdependent culture like ours requires strong feelings of identification with others, for adequacy cannot be achieved alone. As a consequence man's experience has led him to exalt those values like brotherly love, respect for one another, charity, justice, and friendship which facilitate human interaction, while condemning those which debase individuals or impede the achievement of adequacy. Ethical values are no accident but the product of long and painful experience. Our world would be in chaos if ethical values were held in low esteem by any large number of persons. In the kind of world we live in and with men motivated toward the maintenance and enhancement of self, love, respect, and the dignity and integrity of man become more than fine ideals to be sought after; they become absolute essentials to the very existence of life.

The Attack-Appease Dichotomy

Finally, if the concepts of this point of view about people and their behavior have any validity, they give promise of helping us to perceive some reasonable alternative to the horrible choice of attack or appeasement we are usually offered as modes of dealing with human problems. Ever since Munich we have behaved as though there were only two possible ways of dealing with human problems—attack or appease. These are the choices that usually occur to us for dealing with the great issues of our day. Appeasement, however, has become a word of scorn, a new "cuss word" of our generation. We were all so badly burned by the Munich Conference and its disastrous consequences that we have firmly resolved never to be caught in that way again.

But much as we despise appeasement, we are equally repelled by its opposite. Though we are willing to defend ourselves with vigor and determination, attacking others without provocation is as repugnant to us in one direction as appeasement is in another. We are essentially a peace-loving people. Attack seems the method of the bully or the desperado and its use seems morally indefensible. In agreement with other nations, we have decided that attackers are aggressors and aggressors are outlaws.

If it is true, as many would have use believe, that we can only attack or appease, then indeed we are in a fearsome dilemma. Appease, and we lose all we stand for. Attack, and we become outlaws in the eyes of the world. Either way we lose. This is the Hobson's Choice we are offered for dealing with the great problems of our time. What is more, there are many who would have us believe there is no alternative. Any slightest gesture of good will toward nations or people with whom we disagree, or acceptance of a point at argument, runs the risk of being hysterically labeled appeasement. You either attack or appease, they tell us, and it soon becomes clear that there is no middle ground; appeasement is anything less than outright attack!

If attack and appeasement appear in our eyes as the only approaches available, we must perforce choose one of these as the appropriate method of coping with our problems. We can only behave, after all, in ways that occur to us. If there are other and better approaches to our problems, we need to be clearly and sharply aware of their existence lest we become the unwitting victims of our own misconceptions.

Is there an alternative to this fearsome dilemma? Out of the understandings we have been developing in this volume about human behavior, I believe there is. Essentially, it is an approach to human interaction which says in effect: "I am a person of dignity and integrity. I believe you are too. I have no need to attack you nor will I permit you to attack me." This is a position which is neither attack nor appeasement. It is not concerned with winning or losing. It is solely concerned with the maintenance of human dignity and the preservation of freedom for people to grow and develop to greater adequacy.

Appeasement interferes with the achievement of adequacy. It destroys the dignity of the appeaser. Attack violates the integrity of others and brings into being the negative effects of threat. The position we speak of maintains the dignity and integrity of the behaver without either violating the rights of others or relinquishing one's own in the process. It is a position of strength and security which stands *for* something as well as against something. This is a position consistent with man's fundamental need for adequacy. It is consistent too with what we know about threat and its resolution. It accepts the fact of differing human perceptions and seeks to avoid as much as possible the negative effects of threat on perceiving. It is a position equally applicable to relationships between individuals or nations.

It will be recognized at once that this position is by no means new.

It has been practiced by many throughout our history. It is the way of life advocated by the great religions. It is the method of Schweitzer and Gandhi and in lesser degree of all of us in our better moments. Each of us knows of people who behave this way. We even behave so ourselves sometimes, and now and then we rise to our full stature collectively and behave so as a nation as well.

Strangely enough, in spite of its simplicity and age this method of dealing with people is an approach without a name. We do not have an adequate word to describe it. This is a great tragedy, for it is difficult to deal effectively with matters without clear and precise terms by which we can refer to them. We can, after all, only deal with events in ways that occur to us, and ways that are clearly symbolized come much more readily into figure. *Attack* and *appease* are unequivocal and easily understood. As a result they come easily and quickly to mind when people are confronted with problems. We need an equally sharp and distinctive term for the kind of relationship we are speaking of here. Perhaps it is because we do not have a proper name for this approach that it seems so little understood and is so often overlooked as an alternative.

The alternative to the devil's dervish of attack-appease, we have suggested above, is a position which declares the dignity and worth of all people, including the self. It seeks the achievement of adequacy for all instead of the achievement of adequacy for some by the humiliation of others. It requires behaving in ways that are at the same time nonthreatening to others and expressive of the value of self. To be able to accept ourselves and other people in this way requires a high degree of personal security. It calls for a deep feeling of one's own worth and integrity. It requires of us both as individual people and as nations that we keep physically fit to resist aggression and to provide us with a healthy vehicle for our beliefs. Equally important, it demands a willingness to examine and reëxamine fundamental convictions and beliefs, making them ever clearer and more precise. To accomplish this we will need to appraise ourselves and our understandings with precision and courage. Doubt and vacillation will leave us wide open to threats from without. Firm beliefs and convictions, which is only another way of saying personal meanings or perceptions, are the best guarantee of consistent behavior toward other people as well as courage and determination in self. Persons with convictions and beliefs will not be easily panicked by show of force, nor will they be push-overs for false propaganda.

To behave in this way is not easy. It calls for a high degree of personal security, acceptance of self and of others, and a wide identification with other people, all characteristics of the adequate personality we discussed in an earlier chapter. The more adequate people we can produce, the more likely we are to find adequate solutions to our human problems. Attack and appeasement are methods of desperation and resignation, approaches to human problems of the threatened and the weak. To behave in the alternative fashion we have described above requires that we seek, on the one hand, the production of the largest number of adequate personalities possible in our generation and, on the other, that we be keenly and continuously aware of the existence of better methods of dealing with human problems than appeasement or attack.

CHAPTER 15

The Individual and His Society

THE ideas we hold about what people are like will have particularly far-reaching consequences in the ways we attempt to solve the great international and social problems of our generation. Theories of history or economics which are based upon inadequate principles of human motivation and behavior can have catastrophic results if they become part of national policy. An example is the theory of Aryan superiority, which not only helped plunge Germany and the greater part of the world directly into World War II, but was doubly disastrous to Germany by causing its leaders to underestimate Russia and conduct a war in such a way that they turned a potential victory into an overwhelming defeat. The ideas we hold about the nature of people inevitably affect our dealings with them. Even with the best of intentions inadequate concepts of what people are like can lead us to the adoption of techniques of dealing with them that may delay or defeat the very ends we hope to achieve. Well-meaning people have sometimes been led, for example, into action on matters of racial integration, labor-management disagreements, or community reform which, instead of moving matters forward, only served to inflame feelings and push people into defensive positions that slowed down the achievement of the very goals they sought.

Effective methods of dealing with human problems must be predicated upon accurate observations of what people are like and why they behave as they do. In this book we have set forth a way of looking at behavior. If this way of looking at human beings is accurate at all, it should have important implications for problems of human society and social action. Let us examine briefly the nature of some of those implications in this chapter.

The Personification Myth

It is a common practice among many people in our society to think of groups or other societies as if they could be understood as single persons. We think, for instance, of America, Britain, Russia, of labor, and capital, of the American Legion or the Knights of Columbus, the Catholics, the Baptists, etc. Each social unit then tends to be thought of as motivated by needs and motives for self preservation and aggrandizement which frequently have nothing to do with the needs and motives of its individual members. On the basis of the observer's bias and experience each group unit is endowed with a characteristic personality, and predictions of its future behavior are based upon this personality. Unfortunately, these group personalities are necessarily oversimplified. Any foreign statesman who predicts the behavior of the British government by thinking of the British empire as either "Honest John Bull" or "Perfidious Albion" is sure to make grave and serious errors. Neither the concept of America as the "unselfish good neighbor" nor as the "hypocritical Yankee imperialist" is adequate for predicting the behavior of the United States in world affairs.

On a consciously superficial level of speech such personification of groups is convenient and permissible, but if we are looking for a frame of reference which will allow us to predict changes in the way a group behaves, the device of group personification is a complete failure. When the entire group is treated as a unit the dynamics of action within the group are ignored and obscured, and, as a consequence, there are no means of studying or predicting the changes within the group which lead to changes in its behavior. In order to appreciate the disadvantages of thinking of "the Russians," "the English," or "the Arabs" as a monolithic unit, it is only necessary to think of the difficulties which are encountered by a foreigner who thinks of "Americans" as an undifferentiated group, all the members of which have the same characteristics and motives. Although societies are, of course, composed of persons with more or less common motives, the attempt to deal with groups as though they were single people is almost certain to lead to chaos.

Societies are formed as the products of human interaction in seeking need satisfaction. Recognizing this fundamental characteristic of societies, Adam Smith observed that men seemed to have deep needs for food, clothing, and shelter. Beginning with this assumption about human needs, he then proceeded to derive the basic principles of classical economics by deciding how such an hypothetical "economic man" would logically behave. In this way Smith was able to derive a system of causal principles which were to a considerable degree transferable from one situation to another. Unfortunately, his fiction that the only motives of behavior are economic does not correspond to the facts. As a consequence, the predictions of conventional economics are reliable only in those circumstances where people are seeking financial profit to the exclusion of all else. Note the frustration of conventional economists, for example, in dealing with labor-management problems when the real goals are mastery or power rather than food, shelter, or clothing. However, within the field to which he limited himself, the deductions Smith made in *The Wealth of Nations* constitute an internally consistent contribution which made it possible to predict, with fair accuracy, the behavior of people under certain restricted conditions.

In the nearly two centuries since Adam Smith published *The Wealth of Nations* a great deal of psychological research has taken place. If the picture of human motivation and behavior which we have presented in this volume is more accurate than that used by Adam Smith, it should be possible for social scientists to derive, by methods similar to those he used, causal principles of social behavior which will be more inclusive and more accurate.

Smith's approach to understanding his society by beginning with the fundamental needs of human beings seems like a fruitful and useful approach. The weakness of his approach lies not in his method of dealing with the problem but in the unfortunately narrow conception of human needs with which he began. What people need, we have seen, runs far beyond the material things of food, clothing, and shelter. What implications does a more inclusive conception of human motivation have for understanding human societies or the relation of the individual to the social group?

Principle I

Individuals tend to seek adequacy through identification with people seeking need satisfaction in ways similar to their own. It is this discovery, that by banding together with other people one's own need satisfaction can be more adequately attained, that is responsible for the formation of groups. The principle is true in all societies, but it is particularly active in highly coöperative, interdependent societies like our own. In our world it is practically impossible for individuals to achieve much in the way of need satisfaction except through the medium of some kind of group membership. The importance of people and of groups is one of the earliest concepts we teach our children.

The mere existence of common goals, however, is not a sufficient explanation for the formation and continuance of a group. Groups form and continue only so long as the association seems important to the individual in the satisfaction of his need. Millions of children, but almost no adults, have eaten spinach to be like Popeye. Popeye can be a hero to a child, but he is only an amusing character to most adults. People do not join *just any* group. They identify with those people and those groups which seem to them important and which most effectively contribute to the individual's own achievement of greater feelings of adequacy. The gang of the juvenile delinquent provides him with feelings of adequacy which he cannot achieve in other more established institutions of his society. As a consequence the delinquent associates himself with those people most likely to provide him with feelings of self enhancement and status, even though from some outsider's point of view such action may seem to be leading to an end directly the reverse. People come together in groups which provide them with increased opportunities for achieving adequacy.

Although persons band together for the more effective achievement of need satisfaction, and may even sacrifice some minor goals for the greater adequacy afforded by group membership, need satisfaction is always an individual matter. The individual search for need satisfaction is never totally surrendered to the group. Even when persons have become important members of a group, the need for personal adequacy may cause them to behave in highly individual fashion when it seems to them that adequacy is affected. This is particularly well illustrated in some of the reports about human behavior arising out of the experiences of World War II. Under the great stress of war, people may move in highly individual directions if this seems more likely to produce personal adequacy for them. Following the war, for example, thousands of young German women who had been raised in highly moral middle-class families turned to prostitution when this seemed the only method of escape from starvation. In the stress of prison conditions group structure and discipline often broke down as individuals desperately sought to remain alive even at the cost of rejecting lifelong ties with other people. Although need for adequacy may sometimes cause us to move in directions at odds with a group we belong to, most of us find our major sources of need satisfaction in some kind of group setting.

Principle II

Persons banded together in groups for the mutual satisfaction of need find their group purposes most effectively advanced by the development of group organization. Persons coming together for need satisfaction soon discover that their ends are best achieved through the development of some kind of organization and structure. At first this organization is vague and not highly crystallized. It may be no more than a highly informal kind of structure in which various roles and functions are simply understood by group members.

As time passes, different people within the group soon acquire roles and responsibilities as a result of the experience of group members with each other. Certain members characteristically behave in certain ways, and other members of the group observing this develop a kind of expectancy for such behavior. This expectancy in turn calls for certain kinds of behavior on the part of the individual. Eventually this kind of differentiation of the membership may develop into a much more complex kind of organization in which various kinds of status positions and group structures are spelled out in great detail.

As a result of the movement of individuals toward common goals and the group members' interaction with each other, groups also develop values and norms which become quite characteristic of the group. As group members seek for the satisfaction of need in the group and, particularly, as they interact with each other, common values, goals, beliefs develop. At first, these may be quite informal "understandings." Gang members develop a common abhorrence of "squealing." Workers on a job may set quotas for production levels. After a while such common values and standards may even become crystallized into passwords, slogans, customs by which group members can be distinguished from those who are not members of the group. Eventually, common values within a group may be written down as laws, regulations, or rituals.

Principle III

People tend to withdraw from groups whose approval they are unable to win or which no longer satisfy need. So long as membership in a group continues to provide the individual with need satisfaction in important ways, people tend to remain members of groups. When, however, membership in a group no longer satisfies need or when membership in a group becomes frustrating to individual goal satisfaction, groups disintegrate or evolve into some other kind of group which more effectively satisfies need. Toynbee points out that new civilizations arise when the previous civilization is abandoned by its proletariat. The origin of Western civilization, for instance, came in the adoption of Christianity by the oppressed proletariat of the Roman world. This principle functions just as effectively on the levels of the family, the social club, or the casual conversational group. An example may be found in children who find themselves unable to live up to the expectancies of parents and so violently reject the goals of social groups their parents value. It may also be observed in the loss of interest in the sorority or fraternity characteristic of many college students upon graduation.

Mere membership in a group does not guarantee that an individual necessarily possesses a high degree of identification with that group. Experience following the Korean conflict seemed to show that many young men who succumbed to so-called "brain washing" were young men who had never had any real understanding of the nature of democracy or any high degree of identification with the principles and morality of a democratic system. By purposefully breaking down group organization and group loyalties in the prison camps and encouraging individual search for need satisfaction, American soldiers could be made easy prey of propaganda, particularly when presented by earnest, sincere teachers speaking from deep conviction. Stripped of group support and with few firm convictions of their own, many young men accepted the "good" explanations offered them because they had no better ones of their own. Having little identification with their home group to begin with, they were fair game for the adoption of ideas and values espoused by people of another group who believed what they were saying with sincerity and conviction.

People do not move in single groups. Each of us lives and operates in many groups, moving in and out of varying spheres of influence from one group to another throughout our daily lives. Thus we may have membership in a family, a neighborhood group, a church group, a play group, a political party, a club, fraternity, profession, nation, civilization, etc. In each of these groups, what is more, we are expected to espouse differing values, standards, traditions, customs, and the like. Each group will allow differing ranges of permissible deviation from the values they hold dear.

The group with which we play tennis may be quite uninterested in our religious beliefs and quite willing to permit us a great deal of latitude in questions of morality, providing only we do not cheat at keeping score. Our church group on the other hand may be little concerned with our sportsmanlike behavior but very much concerned with the problems of basic morality which we evidence.

The mere fact of existence in these multiple groups creates interesting problems for the individual, since one of the necessities for adequacy is a degree of consistency in our personal beliefs, attitudes, and convictions. Membership in a number of different groups makes it almost a certainty that sooner or later the individual will run into some kind of conflict among the beliefs and values of his various groups. Sometimes antagonistic group values can be held successfully apart by a kind of compartmentalization, as when our prejudices and our religious beliefs are held safely apart by avoiding the consideration of problems of prejudice when we are in church and failing to apply the teachings of a church in dealing with persons of other races or religions when we act in public.

Conflicting norms and beliefs, we have seen in an earlier chapter, are likely to prove highly threatening. When the standards and norms of the groups to which we belong are brought into serious conflict, therefore, the experience is likely to be painful. Under these circumstances the norms the individual adopts and the groups with which he remains will be those which satisfy his basic need most strongly. Confronted with conflicting values the individual is most likely to stick to those which seem to him to be most meaningful. More often than not these are also likely to be those he has held for the longest periods of time, other things being equal.

Principle IV

Identification of an individual with a group leads him to adopt and defend the standards and behavior of that group. To think well of himself it is necessary for a person to think well of his group. This introduces a measure of distortion to the individual's perceptual field and becomes an important factor in breakdowns of communication. An attack upon the group is an attack upon self, and the strength of reaction to the attack is a function of the degree of threat. Criticism of the group by a fellow member stirs much less violent response than attack of the same

sort by an outsider, who is presumed to be hostile to the whole group.
A teacher, for instance, who has himself criticized features of the educational system, may resent such criticism from outsiders because he
feels he is part of the system. Criticism by foreigners is universally resented. Similarly, aggrandizement for the group is aggrandizement for
self. *My* team's victory is mine too. The accomplishments, prestige,
and glory of those with whom we are identified are fulfillment for us as
well.

Since each individual accepts the reality of his own perceptual field,
the customs and attitudes of his own group are judged as objectively
superior and other people and other groups are judged by these standards. Each must think well of his group. Americans, for instance, commonly place a high value upon houses with modern plumbing. As a result, many American soldiers consider that the Germans are superior
to the French, who are less able to afford such luxuries. The boy who
has identified himself with the predelinquent gang has a different system of prestige values from the boy who has identified himself with the
Boy Scouts or who thinks of himself as a responsible citizen. They admire
not only different institutions but different individuals and types of success. As a consequence they are not responsive to the same social controls.

When an individual becomes identified with a group he tends to adopt
the standards, customs, traditions, etc., of the group as the bases for his
own judgments of events occurring thereafter. Existence in a particular
group sets many expectations for the individual and in large measure
determines his levels of aspiration. Such bases for judgment and evaluation adopted with membership in a particular group become the standards by which the individual judges persons outside. Members of a
group accept and approve those individuals who seem to them to be
important. That is, an individual who is able to behave in ways admired
by members of the group will be sought as an associate, providing his
acceptance will enhance the self concepts of the members. Individuals
who behave in ways condemned by the group are avoided and rejected.

Other groups are likely to be judged good or bad depending upon
the degree of likeness which those groups have to the values and standards of one's own group. This social distance is well illustrated in the
class structure of many societies. Social classes are distinguished primarily by the behavior of their members. Individuals who are able to
behave in conformity with the standards of the group are accepted, and

individuals considered uncouth are rejected. Contrary to popular opinion, money does not automatically give advancement to a higher social class. It merely makes it possible with training to behave in ways that are admired by such a class. In Yankee City, for instance, the upper-uppers were almost exclusively members of families which had had two or three generations to perfect and master the class behavior. The wealthiest man in town was upper-middle class because he did not wish to change his behavior and insisted that his children conform to middle-class standards as well.

It is readily apparent that these principles confer a continuity, consistency, and conservatism upon the behavior of groups, which agree with empirical observations. This consistency is acquired, not from some mysterious quality of a group *per se*, but through the dynamics of the efforts of individual members to achieve adequacy. The effective factors in determining the individual's behavior toward society are, as for all behavior, his need, his perceptual field at the moment of action, and the potentialities for differentiation that exist in the field.

The Psychology of Culture Change

The same principles that govern the relation of the individual to the groups and institutions he encounters also govern the transfer and adoption of culture elements and techniques. Linton has pointed out that the factors most important in determining the introduction of cultural novelties are: (1) the prestige of the individual under whose auspices the novelty is introduced, (2) the prestige of the inventor or donor society, and (3) the effectiveness of the trait or techniques in the local environment. In other words, an individual in one culture adopts those aspects of another culture which make possible the enhancement of his phenomenal self. These are selected in terms of his existing field. Alcohol, for instance, was a boon from heaven in the eyes of the Plains Indians, who lived in a world where men became great and found power in dreams and delirium. The Hopi, on the other hand, living in a field of complete but fragile order and regularity, where a single mistake in the ritual dance might shatter the universe, saw alcohol as a tremendous menace and rejected it.

It is a well-established principle of anthropology that cultural elements which fit the pattern of the recipient culture are transmitted without obstacle, and that elements that do not fit the pattern are rejected or accepted only after modification and distortion. For instance, firearms are immediately transmitted to hunting societies which have a surplus for barter, printing presses are rejected, and alarm clocks are accepted only as ornaments. This is a normative application of the psychological principle we have cited earlier, that new entities or characters are selected in accordance with the individual's need and are modified or distorted by their relation to other parts of his field.

THE PSYCHOLOGY OF INTERGROUP RELATIONS

Since each individual customarily regards his own view of the world as true, just, and real, he is apt to regard the behavior of other people as more or less mistaken and in error. This is especially true if he is observing people of a markedly different culture, since by their failure to conform to his standards they inevitably stamp themselves as ignorant or evil or both. Contacts between different cultural groups are almost always uncomfortable because of the difficulties of communicating which tend to make individuals on both sides feel frustrated, inadequate, and often suspicious, unless one group is so clearly superior in power that the question of comparative force is not even considered. It can be taken as a basic principle that no minority group is the object of attack until it becomes large enough or powerful enough for the majority group to feel threatened.

Communities and schools which pride themselves on absence of intolerance and prejudice almost always prove to have only a few members of the minority group in residence. Under such circumstances the minority members may even have added prestige as exotic individuals. When minority groups become threatening to majority groups it is not of course necessary that the minority should be the actual source of the threat; but it is necessary that the minority group be large enough or powerful enough for the members of the majority to believe that it is a threat, so that it can become a reasonably convincing scapegoat. If the minority group is small, its members are more easily differentiated from one another and tend, therefore, to be treated as individuals rather than as group members.

Under threat the members of groups tend to respond by an accentuation and idealization of the group characteristics. It is only by placing emphasis on their differences from the other group that they can feel superior to it. See, for example, the great upsurge of Zionism after the horrors of Nazi atrocities and the glorification of color in the Negro press. Despite the insistence of social scientists on the fallacy of white supremacy, when racial tensions are aroused the old arguments of Negro inferiority are sometimes paraded anew in the public press.

The claim to be a master race is an effort to enhance the threatened phenomenal selves of group members. Propaganda stressing "encircle-ment" is a common technique of governments wishing to create a greater feeling of unity in their own group. Both Hitler and the Russian Communist leadership have used it with conspicuous success, and it is not unknown in America. It is most eagerly accepted by those members of the group who are most in need of self enhancement. As a general thing, group conflict is at its maximum between the lower levels of the conflicting groups, especially if these levels are the victims of aggression and domination within their own groups. In our own South, for example, the most violent reactions to the threat of school integration have oc-curred among the "poor whites," while middle- and upper-class whites with less need for self enhancement adopt a more moderate view.

The Resolution of Group Conflict

In thinking about problems of group conflict it is always a temptation to fall into the error of believing that the responsibility for such conflict is exclusively a responsibility of sick leadership. This is rarely ever the case, however. Individuals become leaders in groups because they seem to the members to be capable of leading the group to those goals which it holds dear. Leaders could seldom remain very long in positions of leadership if they did not represent the fundamental needs and desires of their group members. The abhorrence of dictatorship, characteristic of much of our thinking in this country, leads some people to the dan-gerous assumption that societies operating under a dictatorship are doing so totally without the support of the people in that society. Because we find this form of government unacceptable ourselves, it is easy to jump to the conclusion that persons living under dictatorships do not like them either. It is necessary for us to understand, however, that even a dictatorship exists because it supplies need satisfaction to its people. It is a temptation to believe that the Russians do not like their form of government and would not fight for it. To build a national defense on any such assumption, however, could conceivably prove to be disastrous. Although the Russian standard of living may be considerably below that of our own, it is probable that the average Russian today is better off than he has ever been in his previous history. From his point of view, his government is meeting his needs.

The goal of society is to meet the need of its members. Whether or not it is successfully meeting need, however, can only be judged by those persons having membership in the society. Even though a society may seem to some outside observers to be less adequate in providing need satisfaction for its members than some other society, this information is irrelevant and immaterial insofar as the members of a given group are concerned. People can, after all, only behave in terms of that which they know.

THE GOALS OF CONFLICT RESOLUTION

In earlier chapters of this book we have seen that when individuals are threatened, two negative effects upon perception ensue: (1) perceptions become narrowed to the object of threat, so that it is difficult for individuals to see broadly and clearly, and (2) individuals are forced into more and more rigid defenses of their existing perceptions. These unhappy effects of threat and counterthreat are bad enough applied to individuals in interaction. When these same effects occur to large numbers of people acting in groups, societies, or civilizations they carry implications of possible death and destruction too devastating to comprehend. Once war could be regarded as a kind of gentlemanly pastime in which comparatively small numbers of people were hurt. With the destructive power available to groups in our generation, however, the prevention of group conflict once it has occurred, or the resolution of such conflict, represents a major problem of our generation. In the light of the principles of behavior developed in this volume what can we say of the resolution of group conflict?

Once the threat-counterthreat spiral has gotten well under way the process is difficult to reverse. In the long run there seem to be only two alternatives to the resolution of such deep-seated conflict. One of these is the dissolution of conflict through assimilation or amalgamation of the conflicting groups. This may occur through the assimilation of one group by the other or through the development of a third group in which the conflicting groups can find similar goals and values. The United Nations represents this kind of a group. A number of examples of the assimilation of conflicting groups may be seen in our own history. At one time the Irish were regarded as uncouth and distinctly undesirable. On occasion these feelings even broke out in open violence. With the assimilation of the Irish culture into the American culture, however, St. Patrick's Day and the idealization of Ireland have become American traditions. As soon as the Irish were accorded a respected status, amalgamation could take place without loss of self esteem on either side. Such amalgamation of groups, it would seem, must be the eventual long-term outcome of the resolution of group conflict.

When groups amalgamate, the smaller group will ordinarily move farther and make more modifications of culture than the larger group. The comparative degree of shift may be roughly considered as inversely proportional to the population ratio of the two groups. If group A makes up one-fifth of the population and group B four-fifths, in a condition of nonselective movement and intercourse members of group A will have to adjust to members of group B four times as often as individual members of group B will meet and adjust to members of group A. If, as actually happens, the personal relations are selective, the process is slowed but the ultimate result is not affected unless contact between the groups is cut off altogether. This principle is only normative, like the others we are deriving in this chapter. What will actually happen always depends upon the phenomenal fields of the particular individuals involved. For instance, if the minority group has superior power and prestige in the eyes of a substantial number of the majority, the majority culture will shift farther because their members will move more than halfway in their contacts with minority members.

The second way in which group conflict can end is by reducing one group to impotence. This may be accomplished by destroying one group or by so reducing its size or importance that it no longer threatens. This is what wars have attempted since time immemorial. It is what Hitler attempted with the Jewish minorities. It is basic to the concept of "divide and conquer."

This is a hard alternative to contemplate, and it may appear to some that there might be an intermediate stage between the two long-time solutions to conflict, based on continued separation with avoidance of conflict through mutual respect and confidence. This is a desirable goal and one we should strive to achieve. Such a condition can be only temporary, however, since mutual respect encourages and makes possible the movement of individuals from one group to the other, and with such movement eventual assimilation of the two groups becomes inevitable.

MEANS OF REDUCING GROUP CONFLICT

Fortunately, while group conflict and suspicion are inevitable in some degree as long as groups exist, there do appear to be means by which the intensity of the conflict may be greatly reduced and eventual assimilation speeded. Conflict between groups is, in some degree, the result of aggressive and dominating behavior within one or both of the groups. Individuals who are unable to secure adequate satisfaction of need in their own society often seek such satisfaction by dominating and aggressive behavior against members of weaker groups. It is quite possible, therefore, that the most effective way of reducing group conflict would be the reduction of domination and aggression within the groups themselves. Individuals who achieve a satisfying degree of adequacy within their groups will find little need to dominate and harass other groups. Adequate people, as we have seen, are characterized by acceptance and identification, both antithetical with conflict. It would thus appear that an important means of eliminating conflict lies in helping groups to provide real opportunities for growth and need satisfaction for their own members.

Since conflict between groups is always carried on by individuals who think of themselves and their antagonists as group members rather than as individuals, group conflict can also be prevented by increasing the opportunities for the members of the two groups to differentiate one another as individuals. A major function of military training and indoctrination is to induce the individual to regard himself as a soldier rather than a civilian. Since a person's behavior is determined by his phenomenal field, it is impossible to get him to act as a soldier until he conceives of himself as one. Furthermore, if he thinks of himself as a soldier, acts which are taboo to him as an individual are not only permissible but, in many cases, mandatory. Europeans who have seen Americans only as soldiers may be expected to have a very erroneous picture of Americans, if by Americans we mean individual civilians. In the same way, a person who thinks of himself as a white in contact with a Negro will behave very differently than if he thinks of himself as John Smith in contact with Ed Jones.

The perception of other group members as individuals is increased when it is possible to encourage members of the minority to scatter themselves as widely as possible among the members of the majority. This is, of course, impractical where group feelings are already strong, since it is a step toward abandonment of the minority-group institutions and cannot, therefore, be taken under threat.

Another way of fostering the differentiation of members of the con- ◄ flicting groups as individuals is by increasing the possibilities for communication between them. Communication, however, is possible only when there is an overlapping of cultural fields so that there is a common area of meanings. From this point of view the practice by which books and motion pictures about foreign countries emphasize the strange and exotic can be expected to achieve little or nothing toward promoting tolerance and good will. The "Man Bites Dog" concept of news is of little help in fostering this sort of understanding. The emphasis of news-gathering agencies upon the bizarre and the different may even contribute to the intensification of group conflict.

On the other hand, a motion picture or story which shows the people at their daily work and children at their games promotes fellow feeling, if the work and games are those familiar to the audience. An interesting and effective means of promoting fellow feeling among members of different groups is that used by Rachel Davis DuBois. Instead of talking about the problems on which they suspect differences, they are asked to talk about their childhood memories—"talk about bread, for example." As soon as members of both groups have told about common experiences in making, tasting, or smelling hot, crusty bread they feel as if they have spent their childhood together and are members of a common group. Common experiences make possible a common feeling, and citizens of the same state, who would not stop to speak if they met at home, have a feeling of close kinship when they meet in a foreign land. A common language is a great advantage, especially if it is spoken with a common accent.

Another way of reducing conflict between groups is to provide them ◄ with a common objective or enemy. The need for action in the common cause makes all individuals in the previously conflicting groups important to one another through identification with the common cause. This technique of providing a common enemy is, as we have said before, often used more or less consciously by political groups and nations as a means of reducing tensions in their own ranks. Threat prevents disintegration of the group relationship, since all threatened individuals seek shelter and support from one another.

A more productive method of reducing group conflict lies in the development within a society of individuals who feel adequate to deal with their perceptions. We are afraid of that which we do not feel capable of handling. What we feel adequate to deal with does not threaten us. Thus the society which can produce adequate phenomenal selves in its members can tolerate or accept difference in others, and group conflict will thereby be reduced or disappear. A society composed of nonthreatened, nonthreatening personalities will not be in conflict. Such a society need not depend exclusively on attack or appeasement as the only solution to problems.

PROBLEMS OF GROUP AND INDIVIDUAL ASSIMILATION

Groups do not associate with another group as groups. The process of assimilation of groups really consists of the assimilation of separate individuals. An individual seeks admission to a new group, as we have said, if he so respects and admires the members that he would secure self enhancement through identifying himself with them, or if membership in the group will otherwise aid him in the satisfaction of need. Compare the complete and rapid assimilation of German immigrants in the United States, where the standard of living is higher than in Germany, with the unassimilability of Germans, even after hundreds of years, in eastern Europe, where the standard of living of the local culture is lower than that of the German culture. What the individual thinks of himself is the important factor in determining his search for assimilation and membership. Any person will seek membership in the new group more actively if he feels that he is acceptable to the members; and he is more apt to withdraw from his original group if he is threatened or humiliated within that group.

In the same way, an individual seeking admission to a group is assessed and accepted or rejected, not by an impersonal group but by individual members, each of whom considers the candidate in the light of his own need. If the membership of the candidate in the group will enhance the phenomenal selves of the individuals, he will be accepted. As a general thing, anyone advancing from an "inferior" to a "superior" group is handicapped by his previous membership in the "inferior" group so that he must have unusual qualities and abilities to gain acceptance. If he shows obvious physical or behavioral characteristics of the "inferior" group, he must counterbalance them with tremendous prestige in the eyes of the new group. He will be aided further by a personality that does not actively dominate or threaten the self esteem of the members of the group he seeks to join. It will not be a handicap and may even be an advantage if he threatens outsiders, provided he does it in a socially acceptable way. Artists, writers, athletes, and members of the professions, if successful, have unusual opportunities for social mobility because they are admired by so many people. The American public schools and, in particular, the high school athletic teams, by providing able individuals with opportunities for winning prestige, are an important factor in social mobility and group assimilation. It goes without saying that any society must provide opportunities for mobility if the most able individuals are to reach the positions where they will be of most benefit.

What Is a Good Society?

LACK OF AGREEMENT IN DEFINITION

As we have said above, one of the principal barriers to international coöperation among peoples, all of whom sincerely desire a better world and a better society, is the lack of agreement among the various groups as to what constitutes a good society. The representatives of each culture, considering their own version of society as fundamentally right and true, believe that the better society can only arise from a further development and modification of their own. This is true whether they be Iranian or Hindu, Russian or American, Berber or Eskimo. To the true representative of each, any other society is manifestly inferior to his own.

The United Nations must continuously struggle with this problem as it tries to achieve harmony and coöperation among individuals or nations which have as diverse pictures of the better world as do the various cultural blocs and groups of which it is composed. Such a conflict of ideals and values is almost certain to result in political conflict in which each bloc is chiefly interested in defending the integrity of its own society against the social reforms of the other blocs. To make matters worse, even when delegates may personally achieve a degree of understanding of other views they may be unable to act upon their changed perceptions because they are instructed rather than free delegates. Under such circumstances international conferences are chiefly concerned with obstruction rather than coöperation and often end either without agreement or in a mutually distasteful acceptance of the status quo. It seems likely that in years to come we may discover that the most truly effective work of the United Nations is not produced by the Security Council or General Assembly but by those backstage agencies which

operate with little fanfare to improve communication and raise standards of living and health.

Real coöperation for world betterment can arise only out of common
goals. This is to say, there must be mutual agreement on the ends which
are to be attained. All groups sincerely desire a better society. But there
can be genuine coöperation only among individuals who are able to look
beyond the particular devices and techniques used in their own societies
and focus their attention on the ends themselves.

THE GOOD SOCIETY SATISFIES NEED

What are these ends? We have already given two answers. The purpose of society and of social institutions, we have said, is the satisfaction
of human need. The basic human need is the preservation and enhancement of the phenomenal self. If these two assumptions are correct, we
have here a culture-free criterion by which the comparative goodness
of societies can be determined. A society is good to the degree that it
enables its members and neighbors to live with health, security, self
respect, and dignity. It is good in the degree to which it aids its members
to the development of selves adequate to deal with the world that
surrounds them. A society is bad to the extent that it fails to provide
these things for its members or removes them from its neighbors. The
inadequate self will feel threatened and will threaten others in turn.

The society must be judged primarily by the degree to which it satisfies the need of its least important members, since the nonsatisfied members of any society are, like cancer cells in the body, a source of danger
to their fellow members and to the social organization itself. For this
reason one criterion of a good society is the extent to which it makes less
necessary the use of techniques for satisfying need like domination and
aggression which give satisfaction to one member only by depriving
others. These are techniques of the inadequate phenomenal self. Socially,
such techniques may be thought of as attempts to lift the society by its
bootstraps; as the aggressor enhances his phenomenal self and goes up,
the victim goes down. When the domination is institutionalized on a
grand scale with a noticeable ruling class and hierarchy of domination,
the eventual result must be a revolt of the common man from within
the group or aggression against persons outside the group. A society
which fails to satisfy the needs of its members is therefore not only not
good for them; it is also a source of danger to its neighbors. In a good
society there can be no unimportant members. The criterion of a good

society is the amount of self actualization it succeeds in fostering in its members.

The good society must be dynamic. It cannot be described in terms of its institutions. All planners of Utopia, except More himself, have made a fundamental mistake in conceiving of a society which reaches an ideal state and remains unchanged thereafter. No static, unchanging Utopia can be the psychologically satisfying "good" society which we are seeking. The culture of such a society must be dynamic and flexible rather than static, because the individual's need for the maintenance and enhancement of his phenomenal self can never be completely satisfied. No matter how successfully he solves his problems and builds up his feeling of strength and security, no successes and no recognition can be enough to give him the permanent feeling of adequacy and self assurance that he seeks. Further achievement and growth are always necessary. As a result no society which attempts to remain static can adequately satisfy the needs of its members.

Since it is the function of societies to assist their members to need satisfaction, there can, of course, be many "good societies," almost as many good societies as there are ways of achieving self maintenance and enhancement. Furthermore, since human need is insatiable, "good" societies must be continually changing. Each must find ever new, more effective and satisfying ways for helping its members to achieve self enhancement.

In the previous chapter, we have contrasted the closed and open systems of thought in dealing with human problems. It will be recalled that the closed system is dependent first upon the determination of some manifest objective and thereafter upon the control of events to achieve these preconceived ends. The open system, on the other hand, had as its goal the process of growth and discovery itself rather than some more specific manifest objective. Its techniques of operation, furthermore, were concerned less with the control of events and more with the facilitation of growth, exploration, and discovery. This open system of dealing with human problems seems highly consistent with the kind of good society we have been describing here. The goal of a dynamic society is to create the optimum conditions for individual growth and achievement of adequacy. Such a society would avoid the dangers of a planned society, which sooner or later must find its plan no longer adequate in a changing world. A dynamic society, concerned fundamentally with setting men free, seems far more likely to evolve and change with the march of human events.

Culture Change—A Problem of Changing Individuals

What can be done to make society better? First, it will be necessary to recognize that there can be more than one "good" society. Any society which satisfies the above criteria is a good society, and it would be impossible to say that any society now existing could not develop into a good society. Very definitely, attacks upon other societies can not make them into good societies. People are not free to change under threat, and a group under attack simply accentuates its destinctive characteristics. A good society can only grow where there is a minimum of conflict between societies, so that the people of each feel free to move and change.

There are three ways of changing a culture. One way is to abandon it en masse, to give it up. Since we have mastered no alternative culture, such a course would cause the death of most of the members of our society as its institutions for the production and distribution of goods cease to operate. Another way to change a society is by revolution. Since people have learned to manipulate only the culture in which they have been living, human revolution results in surprisingly small changes in the culture pattern itself, although it often results in a more efficient and intelligent government. A good example of this may be seen in the Russian Revolution. Following an international period of westernization and democracy, the USSR has tended more and more to revert to the governmental and productive systems of czarist Russia, substituting the G.P.U. for the Cheka, a dictator for the czar, and the collective for the landed estate. It was apparently impossible for the new rulers of Russia to make a fundamental change in the culture of Russia because it was the only culture that they and their people had learned. Though revolutions can often produce changes, they rarely seem worth the price, owing to the high death rate during the initial stages. At this time sweeping changes in the society are being attempted and a great deal of disturbance and dislocation results.

The only alternative seems to be a continuation of the slow process of change in the ways individual people perceive. Since societies are composed of people and people only change when perceptions change, it follows that to change a society we must find ways of helping individual people change the ways in which they perceive. Individuals are often likely to feel weak and puny before the staggering requirements for changing a culture by means of revolution. Even if the price of change by revolution were not so exorbitant, it would still be true that very few of us would ever give up the struggle entirely. If, however, the most fundamental and permanent changes in society occur through the slow processes of evolution and changes in individual people, then every individual, no matter how great or small, has important effects upon social change.

The Individual as an Instrument for Social Change

Societies are the product of human interaction and every human interacting is part and parcel of the product. How effective any individual can be, therefore, as an instrument for social change will depend upon what kind of a person he is and the degree to which he behaves so as to contribute to the achievement of adequacy in others as well as in himself. It is a little disconcerting to find that the most effective means most of us have to change our societies is to change ourselves. It is so much more comfortable to change the other guy. An adequate society can only exist if its members are adequate people. One of the ways, therefore, in which we can contribute to social change is through the achievement of an ever greater degree of personal adequacy. Only then, when we have achieved some degree of self respect, dignity, and integrity in ourselves, are we likely to perceive and respect it in others as well.

Since societies are made up of people in interaction, we can also affect our societies through the impact of our behavior on our fellow group members. When our behavior contributes to the adequacy of others, it contributes also to making the group successful. Whether we behave in positive or negative fashion as a group member, however, will be determined by the way our own behavior is perceived by our fellow members. The ways we behave in interacting with our fellow human beings have a vital bearing upon the kinds of perceptions which make up their perceptual field. Not all of our behavior will, of course, be of equal value in producing changes in the perceptions of other people, but neither is our behavior ever entirely unimportant. Someone once observed that the only immortality any of us can achieve is carved out through the impact of our behavior on other people. While we cannot be responsible for the behavior of people who are dependent upon us, we ourselves can behave in ways that are constructive, destructive, or of no account at all in their effect upon others. We have a degree of choice in how we behave toward others and can learn to use ourselves effectively or ineffectively as instruments of social change.

To produce an optimum degree of effect upon our society we need to learn to behave in ways that contribute maximally to human adequacy and minimally in the production of threat. This relationship of the individual to his group has been diagrammed in Fig. 23. In this figure the

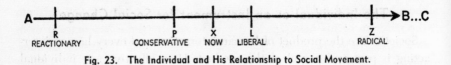

Fig. 23.   The Individual and His Relationship to Social Movement.

movement of society is expressed by the line *AB*; with society moving from *A* to *B* in the direction of some ultimate *C*. The present position of society in this diagram is indicated by the line *X*, also marked "Now." What then is the effect which an individual's behavior may have on this movement at varying points? The person who operates at point *P* is only in small degree behind the movement of his society. This is the position of the conservative. Much further behind society's current position is the reactionary (point *R*), who may be so far out of touch with the existing situation as to act as a considerable drag upon the process of change. If such people represent too great a threat to the societies to which they belong, however, these societies find ways of ignoring them and in some manner reducing them to a position of impotence.

Persons at the opposite end of the scale, operating at point *Z*, may be so far out of touch with the expectancies of their society in the other direction that their behavior may constitute a serious threat to the membership. Under these circumstances the society seeks to protect itself from such threats by reducing these people to impotence in one form or another, by walling them off, by counteracting their effect, or by outright destruction if the threat is great enough. A few persons operating at extreme positions may become martyrs and so serve an important function in dramatizing a concept or idea, sometimes at the price of their own destruction. Even so, if their message is to be at all effective it must eventually be carried by others more closely in touch with the realities of the social scene. More often than not the radical has a negative effect on his social group. By threatening his society he forces it to defend its position or even to retreat from its forward progress. Individuals operating at point L (the liberal position on our scale), while somewhat in advance of the current position of society, are nevertheless also sufficiently in touch with it so that they do not appear to the society to be seriously threatening. It is probable that persons operating at this position produce the maximum degree of progress in a society.

It should be clear that we have been talking about the relationship of the individual's *behavior* to his society's position. This does not place limits on how people may *think* or *believe*. The individual's impact upon the phenomenal fields of other members of his society occurs through the medium of his behavior as it is observed by those he comes in contact with. Individuals in a free society may think or believe as they please and do not become threatening to their society until such times as their behavior warrants. Thus, on our diagram a person may think far out at point B if he wishes, so long as he does not threaten his society by his overt acts. This is the position adopted by many pro-integration Southerners living in deeply prejudiced anti-Negro communities. They recognize that to work effectively for the principles they believe in, they must govern their behavior in terms of the tolerance levels of their communities. To stand on a soapbox in the village square and preach their beliefs would so deeply threaten many of their neighbors as to bring upon themselves social controls which would make it impossible to exert any further influence whatever. Accordingly, they adjust their behavior to the realities of the situation, learn to exert an influence toward the goals they espouse in ways less likely to threaten the social groups they hope to move. In such fashion they maintain their own integrity while at the same time exerting a maximum influence for change.

It will of course be recognized that the conditions we have been speaking of are relationships of the individual to a particular group. The same concepts may appear quite differently to different groups and what seems radical to one group may appear downright conservative to another. In moving from group to group, therefore, the individual must adjust his behavior in dynamic adjustment to the tolerances and expectancies of the groups he is in. Though operational levels may change, the optimal relationship for effective action remains a position in touch with the realities of the group yet moving onward at a pace with a maximum of challenge and a minimum of threat.

The "good" society is one whose members contribute maximally to the adequacy of their fellows. This means that effective action of individuals must be that which contributes to ever greater adequacy of self and others. We have described adequacy in this book as a function of positive self reference, acceptance, and identification, and intelligent action as arising from a perceptual field rich, extensive, and available. A free people can only remain so as long as they are able to perceive freely and broadly. All the more reason why we need to protect our freedoms with eternal vigilance, lest we become the prisoners of our own misperceptions. While there is in our environment unobstructed opportunity to see and understand, and within ourselves no fear of looking, progress can always be assured. A people can be held in bondage only so long as their perceptions can be limited or controlled, a fact well understood by any dictator. How any person behaves in moving toward such goals is necessarily a purely individual matter. There are no "right" ways for all people. Rather each person must discover those *best ways for him.*

CHAPTER 16

How People Can Help Themselves

WHAT are the implications of a perceptual view of psychology for the individual's own efforts at need satisfaction? How much control can an individual exert over his own destiny? In this point of view we have postulated that all behavior is a function of the perceptual field. We have seen, too, that perceptions are selected by individuals in the light of their fundamental need for adequacy. The fact of this selectivity makes possible a measure of control by the self over its own destiny. But how much control?

THE FALLACY OF REVOLUTIONARY CHANGE

The individual's basic need for adequacy requires a stable perceptual field. A perceptual field constantly shifting and changing in its basic characteristics would make it impossible for the individual to achieve any need satisfaction whatever. The basic need of the organism for the maintenance of organization forces each of us to protect ourselves against sweeping changes in self. We cannot "lift ourselves by our bootstraps" overnight. Nevertheless, it is apparent that people do change and, looking back, we can perceive that we, too, have changed. Such changes, however, are seldom ever violent or all-inclusive. Rather, clinical experience would indicate that even when major changes *seem* to happen, this evaluation of things is probably an artifact of the point of observation. When sweeping changes appear to occur they are ordinarily only the dramatic last step in a long series of many small changes.

The stability of the perceptual field is an essential to the achievement of adequacy. Changes in the self come about only slowly and over a considerable period of time. This is not to say, however, that there is not room in the perceptual field for movement and change to occur. As a matter of fact, the self is in a constant process of change throughout its existence. There is always a degree of freedom in the selection of perceptions, a certain amount of "slack" within which choice may occur. It is even possible that if this "slack" is consistently taken up in the same direction over a period of time, a considerable degree of change in the self may be brought about. As C. W. Hunnicutt once put it, "Even in the worst situation, there is always room to wriggle. If you would like to find out how free you are, try wriggling!" Dr. Hunnicutt's advice seems to apply very well to the perceptual field and the possibilities of self change. So long as there is opportunity for selection, there is room for change. The problem of self improvement becomes a question of maintaining a maximally fluid field, on the one hand, and making full use of the "wriggling room" permitted by such a field, on the other.

The Cumulative Effect of Selection

The perceptual field is the product of all the selections within the field that have gone before. As we have seen in an earlier chapter, the selections an individual makes in the process of his growth and development both narrow and expand the possibilities of his future perceptions. The decision to live in the country rather than in the city automatically eliminates certain kinds of experience which can only be gained in the city. On the other hand, it makes possible having the kinds of experiences which cannot be gained in the city but only in the country. The phenomenal field existing at any particular time is a product of all its previous selections. Its current rigidity or fluidity will likewise be a product of the individual's previous selections. The selections made today will similarly affect the rigidity or fluidity of the phenomenal fields of the future.

Effective self help is seldom a question of *making* oneself behave. This is a manipulative approach and is seldom likely to be effective because it deals with perceptions unrelated to dynamic events. For example, I may promise myself "next time I meet Mr. X I will not fidget around in such an impolite manner. Instead I shall listen to him carefully, even if he is a terrible bore." Such an approach to self change is almost bound to fail because it does not deal with the perceptions producing my behavior. The perceptions immediately producing my behavior are my perceptions of Mr. X, of what he is saying, of the situation in which we are involved, and a thousand other events. Indeed, if I persist in trying to change my behavior by concentrating on me, next time I see Mr. X I shall almost certainly convey to him my lack of interest in what he is saying by being preoccupied with what I am doing. I cannot respond effectively to him while perceiving exclusively me! The direct attempt to change behavior is seldom likely to be very effective because it does not deal with causes. The causes of behavior, we have seen, lie in the perceptual field, and the way to change behavior, it follows, must be through changes in perception.

Many people seeking to produce changes in self quickly find themselves bogged down in a morass of self evaluation, self analysis, self criticism, and self judgment, which is seldom very helpful in producing change. It seems a logical thing to do to begin the business of personality reconstruction with a careful diagnosis of the present state of affairs. This is the objective, "scientific" way. It is the approach we are used to in dealing with problems of physical health. It is the method we try to apply to our jobs and to certain intellectual pursuits. Although diagnosis, evaluation, and analysis seem logical, however, they often turn out to be of far less assistance than we might have hoped. This kind of approach to self help turns attention on the self as an object, but whenever people behave, the self is not an object but a process.

The factors affecting behavior, we have seen, are not the objective facts but the perceptual facts. The more closely events are perceived to self, the less objective people are able to be. I can be objective about your wife or your problem but not mine. When we deal with self we must be concerned primarily with those perceptions we call feelings, beliefs, attitudes, values, and convictions. Few of us, after all, misbehave because we do not "know" better. Important changes in the self are seldom brought about by deep introspection or highly critical self analysis. Like learning to dance, so long as one watches his feet he falls all over himself. When he learns to listen to the music and respond to its rhythm he gets along far better. In a similar manner preoccupation with self is seldom helpful.

Contrary to what the layman often believes, modern psychotherapy tends to avoid self evaluation and is concerned instead with the exploration of the client's goals, purposes, and perceptions of the world in which he lives. Indeed, one of the signs of successful therapy is increased acceptance of self. A great deal of psychotherapy is concerned with assisting clients to better perceptions, to appreciate and value self. The place to begin self help, it appears, is not with an exploration of "goodness" or "badness" of self but with questions of purpose and values: "What do I think?" "What do I believe?" "What seems to me to be so?"

The Willingness to Look

Long ago Freud pointed out that we never do anything unless we would rather. To accomplish some change in self, then, it is necessary for the individual to feel it is important and desirable to do so. To produce a perceptual field open to change, the first step required of the individual will, of course, be a willingness to look. The individual who is unwilling to look will almost certainly be unable to see. The first step in achieving a field open to change is the feeling that it is an important, enhancing, and desirable goal to accomplish.

Such a decision to explore one's field may even be highly painful. The need of the individual is for adequacy, and the perceptual field he has at the moment is the most adequate he is able to contrive. The development of a richer, broader, more fluid field means seeking new experience and new perceptions, confronting belief with belief, even placing oneself in predicaments for the risky joy of finding one's way out. It calls for valuing present adequacy less and future adequacy more. Such a program is not easy, for it requires placing oneself in jeopardy. This kind of flirting with inadequacy requires courage and determination, even willingness to put oneself in the position of being hurt.

Effective self help is dependent upon finding ways of seeing differently, with the understanding that when we see differently we will behave differently. It requires subjecting ourselves to new experiences not only of an intellectual character but at a deeper level of feeling and meaning as well. It is not enough just to know that something is true. It is also necessary to discover the meaning of that fact for oneself, and this is an active process of trying and failing and trying again and succeeding. Exploration, whether of strange lands or one's own personality, can seldom be accomplished by insisting on the status quo.

The Adequate Self: Goal of Self Improvement

We have already seen that each of us is continuously seeking to be a more adequate personality. We have also examined in an earlier chapter the characteristics of an adequate personality. In that analysis we found that three kinds of perceptions were typical of the adequate personality: (1) an essentially positive regard for self, (2) the capacity for acceptance of self and of others, and (3) the ability to identify broadly with other people. While, of course, no one can hope to begin perceiving like this all at once, each of these ways of seeing can be approximated by any of us over a period of time.

Each of us has it within his capacities to seek the kinds of experiences which will open and enrich his perceptual field and keep it essentially fluid and free. Each of us, too, can learn to avoid the kinds of experiences and events which narrow, restrict, or make the perceptual field more rigid. It is possible to seek experiences which will help us to feel more positively about ourselves, to accept ourselves and others more fully and completely, and it is, of course, possible for us to identify more closely with larger groups of people if it seems important for us to do so. Maslow has pointed out in connection with his study of adequate personalities that such people seem to be characterized frequently by what he calls "peak" experiences. Peak experiences, for Maslow, are those in which people live life to the hilt, sometimes only momentarily, sometimes for much longer periods of time. They are experiences in which people feel intensely, see broadly, communicate deeply, or respond completely. Apparently, the more often people are able to have these kinds of experiences, the stronger, more adequate, more self realizing they become.

Even though it is not possible for all of us to experience such peak moments in life with great frequency, we can learn to value and cherish them when they occur. Indeed, the very fact of valuing them is likely to contribute to their greater frequency. In addition, there are other, less dramatic but equally important, ways in which we can contribute to making our perceptual fields rich, varied and available.

Earlier in this volume we described a number of factors affecting the perceptual field and hence individual behavior. These factors, we have seen, provide valuable keys to the problem of behavior change. They also provide us with important hints as to ways in which we can exert some control over our own achievement of adequacy.

MAINTAINING A HEALTHY ORGANISM. One of the most obvious ways in which we can contribute to our own adequacy is through care of our physical being. While it is possible for a broken-down or outmoded vehicle to get us to the places we would like to go, other things being equal, an efficient, active body is far more likely to provide a minimum of restriction and a maximum freedom of movement for participation in new experience. Most of us already know a good many things we could do to improve our physical conditions. We are aware of the importance of diet, frequent checkups, exercise, and the like. Indeed, we are so continuously bombarded with information about the maintenance of physical health that one would have to be a hermit to be unaware of many things he can do to improve his physical condition. The problem is not a lack of information but a matter of valuing health sufficiently to make it seem desirable and enhancing to apply what we know to our own situations.

TIME AND ADEQUACY. Changing perceptions and hence behavior takes time. This is particularly true of perceptions of long standing or those which are closely related to the self. The more important or central the perception in the field, the more time it is likely to take to make any significant changes in it. A great many attempts which people make at self improvement fail for lack of understanding of this important fact. A human being is a growing, dynamic organization, and growth is a notoriously time-consuming process. Just as the teacher must pace the demands she makes on children to their existing levels of capacity and readiness for change, so too, as individuals, it is necessary that we adjust the demands made upon self to that which can be properly tolerated and assimilated. The attempt to hurry growth beyond a reasonable degree of acceleration may only contribute to frustration and failure.

A good deal of human unhappiness and maladjustment seems due to the individual's inability to accept the fact that it takes time to "become." The young mother must be a good mother *today*. The adolescent discovering religion is overcome with remorse because he is not as "good" as he should be, instead of seeing his church's teachings as something to strive for. Much remorse and guilt are produced by the individual's inability to accept his mistakes. Often he demands of himself that he be today what he can only hope to become some day in the future. One of the essentials for effective self improvement seems to be a degree of compassion for oneself, willingness to permit one's self to "be" while he goes through the process of "becoming." Just as the psychotherapist learns to accept his client and to move at a speed his client can tolerate, so the individual seeking to help himself needs a degree of compassion and self acceptance which will make it possible for him to move with maximum freedom.

Generally speaking, self improvement proceeds more smoothly and effectively when we do not attempt to move at too fast a pace or too far at a time. Attempts to move too far too quickly oftentimes simply result in increased anxiety, which can sometimes be even more crippling than the particular facet of self which we seek to change. Self help is most likely to be effective when we try what we can do easily and naturally. Whatever we seek to do needs to be consistent with the kind of person we are. The author recalls his first teaching job when, fresh out of college, he took over a junior high school class in the middle of the semester. Much of his course work in the teacher-training institution had convinced him that a good teacher was a "pal" to his students. The ensuing chaos produced by his attempts to deal with his classes in a way they could not accept, and which was not consistent with his personality structure, was complete. Like thousands of beginning teachers before him, he was soon disillusioned and discouraged by the complete failure of his attempts at teaching. In time, however, he came to perceive that he could be effective only when he was doing what "fitted." The attempt to change oneself too violently, too quickly, or too greatly in too short a time is responsible for a great deal of the disillusionment and despair of many beginners in whatever profession. The methods people use must be consistent with the kinds of people they are.

CREATING OPPORTUNITIES FOR PERCEIVING. Since perceptions are the product of experience, there is no more fruitful way of affecting or changing perception than through the medium of some kind of new experience. It is rare that we are successful in changing perceptions either in ourselves or others simply by a process of telling. Perceptions do not change simply by "willing" unless this process is accompanied by some kind of experience as well. Although individuals can seldom change their perceptions directly, it is possible for us to make changes in the ways in which we perceive through the kinds of experiences we seek. This can be done in two ways. In the first place, it is possible for us to change perception by exploring our old experiences to discover new meanings from them. This often happens in some kinds of group discussion. Engaging in successful group experiences, the members may discover that their perceptions of things which have happened to them in the past have changed as a result of bringing them out in the open where they can be explored and subjected to the impact of other personalities and other ideas. Old meanings can also be explored in solitary fashion. Many a fine new perception has been differentiated while people were quietly "musing" or permitting their fantasies to run riot as one often does in daydreaming. This sort of exploration of one's field can also be done more purposefully, as when we set ourselves the task to "think through" an idea. Many creative activities like painting or music or writing may serve to provide us with important and fruitful opportunities for perceptual exploration on a symbolic level.

Secondly, perceptions can be changed as a consequence of seeking new kinds of experience which will produce new kinds of perceiving. Perhaps one of the most important ways in which individuals can assure new perceptions is through the deliberate breaking out from accustomed patterns. The experience of thousands of white children in our South going to school for the first time with Negroes must inevitably affect the beliefs, values, and goals developing in their perceptual fields. Many adequate personalities seem to be possessed of a kind of *joie de vivre* or an attitude of open enthusiasm for new experience, new ideas, new problems. Such people seem to enjoy getting into predicaments for the sheer thrill of getting out of them again. The very valuing of such experience is likely to contribute to greater adequacy. Within reasonable limits the experimental approach of trying something new and different from time to time is a fruitful way of breaking out of old ruts and exposing oneself to the necessity for perceiving things in new ways. Often those instances when we have dared to thrust ourselves into new experiences may lead us into high adventure that adds new sparkle and meaning to life. This calls for a kind of campaign against rigidity and ossification. One can tear up last year's plans and start all over, take that trip one was always going to take and never did, meet those persons we have often thought would be interesting.

There is of course a limit to the degree to which we can uproot ourselves and provide ourselves with new experience. If such an uprooting occurs too violently, instead of challenging ourselves we may find that we have only threatened ourselves. New experience for ourselves, like new experience for any other growing, learning thing, is only of value when it is provided at a rate at which it can be assimilated. We rarely make progress in human personality by revolution. On the other hand, there is unlikely to be change if we fear it so much that we must sit at home surrounded by ever higher, tighter walls of protection.

In order to be free to seek new experience it will be necessary to shake ourselves loose from the very common fear of making mistakes. Some of us have been taught quite thoroughly in the years of our growing up that mistakes are reprehensible, perhaps as a consequence of being raised in a school system that values only "right answers." For some, the fear of failing may be so great as to immobilize or prevent them from having important experiences because they *might* make an error. Such an attitude is not likely to be conducive to seeking new experience. The fear of making mistakes is far more likely to produce a high degree of rigidity and ultraconservatism. When people are not permitted to make mistakes they may also be robbed of the very activities which make possible the discovery of new and better perceptions. One can learn responsibility, for example, only by being given responsibility. The individual who is given no opportunities to try because he, or those who surround him, feel too apprehensive of failure, may be robbed of the very experience through which he could discover new and more satisfying relationships.

It even seems helpful on occasion to foster an attitude of *expecting* to make mistakes, for the freedom this gives the individual to break loose from established patterns and to experiment and try. "Cap" Tracy was a woman of tremendous energy and deeply loved by all of the people in the slum section of Cincinnati in which she served for years as school principal. "Cap" Tracy spent her life serving the community and its children, many of whom were brought up under the most appalling of conditions. Several years ago she stood talking with the author and a bright young teacher who was having her difficulties starting out in her profession. As the young woman bewailed the enormity of the problems with which she was confronted, the older woman quietly suggested several things she might try. Finally, in despair, the young teacher burst out, "Oh, but I couldn't try those things. I'd be so afraid of making mistakes!" At this "Cap" put her arm around the girl and said, "My dear, down in my neighborhood I've seen God make so many mistakes that I'm sure He'll allow you a few." Perhaps it is an attitude something like this which we need to foster for maximum perception change.

THE FULFILLMENT OF NEED AND ADEQUACY. A fourth clue to self help may be found in the effect of goals and values upon the perceptual field. Those differentiated by an individual in his search for adequacy have a profound effect upon his later perceptions and upon the effectiveness of his behavior. While it is true that the individual's goals and values always seem to him to lead to need satisfaction at the moment of his behavior, the ones he selects from his perceptual field are by no means equal in their power to assist him to a feeling of adequacy in a longer view of things. The young delinquent who has differentiated "getting the best of the cops" as a means of feeling more adequate may indeed achieve a momentary feeling of adequacy, but if such a goal persists it is almost certain to result in a destruction of adequacy in the long run. Although any goal or value may conceivably contribute to an individual's feeling of adequacy momentarily, not all have equal potential for the achievement of need satisfaction in a broader perspective.

The human being's need for adequacy is constant and insatiable but the goals, techniques, and values differentiated by individuals, through which the need for adequacy is achieved, are open to change and modification. Unfortunately the goals men differentiate to satisfy need are sometimes confused with need itself. One may hear it said, for example, that another person "needs" to get drunk, to drive too fast, to be sexually promiscuous, to be rich, powerful, or eat too much. While it is of course true that an individual may achieve a momentary feeling of adequacy through any of these goals, seeing them as "needs" invests them with a kind of monolithic immobility which almost precludes the possibility of any change. The goals and values men differentiate are by no means synonomous with need. They are expressions of need and hence are open to change.

The very perception of this distinction between need and goals provides the individual with a key to self help. The mere fact of perceiving "I do not *need* to do this" or "I need to be adequate but not necessarily in this way" in itself provides a freedom to explore new and more satisfying means of achieving need satisfaction. The very perception that "I do not *have* to be married, or a doctor, or richer than my neighbor" in order to achieve adequacy, opens the doors for the consideration of new possibilities and new directions. The problem of changing goals and values is not one of seeking their control. Rather, it is a problem of seeking experience which makes possible the selection of new perceptions or the modification and extension of old ones.

THE DEVELOPMENT OF POSITIVE GOALS AND VALUES. While the individual's goals and values are not open to violent or sweeping changes, like any other perceptions they are open to modification and change with different experience. Although this change is not great, there is always "room to wriggle." Certain kinds of values themselves seem to contribute to the achievement of greater adequacy, and new possibilities for self help seem open to us when such values become part of the individual's organization. Certain kinds of goals and values, when differentiated by an individual, have continuing effects upon the nature of his phenomenal field. The mere fact of valuing change more than the status quo in itself leaves an individual more open to the possibilities of changes in perception. There are a number of such positive values which have an effect upon the selection of perceptions in such a way as to be more likely to produce greater adequacy than others. Some of these seem to be as follows:

1. The individual who values the testing of his own perceptions is far more likely to achieve changes in his goals and values that will lead to greater adequacy than the individual who holds his perceptions as a sacrosanct preserve which must be kept intact at all costs. An attitude of "willingness to look" is, itself, a first important step in the achievement of better, more satisfying values. One is after all unlikely to learn to swim if he is unwilling to get his feet wet. Goals and values can often be effectively changed and modified by confronting one with another in a search for ever greater consistency. The adequate personality is characterized by internal consistency, and such consistency is in part achieved as a consequence of confrontation of values. Unfortunately the confrontation of value with value within a particular personality is not always easy to achieve and may even prove highly painful. Sometimes it is far more comfortable to keep values and goals neatly pigeonholed where they cannot be trotted out side by side and seen together. It seems clear that little change in perceiving is likely to occur in the absence of a "willingness to look." Placing a high value on "looking" seems a first essential to the achievement of greater adequacy.

2. The achievement of adequacy in a changing world requires a perceptual field open to change. Rigid, restricted phenomenal fields, we have seen, are associated with inadequacy while breadth and fluidity of field are characteristic of adequate personalities and provide the basis for intelligent behavior. People then who value a fluid, open field are far more likely to be able to respond effectively and efficiently to the shifting demands of a dynamic society. Even scientists may sometimes succumb to the temptation to rule out data which may be uncomfortable or upsetting. It is often easier to deny the existence of events than to make the adjustment to them. Thus the chemist or biologist who carefully considers the variables involved in his field of knowledge may continue to utilize outmoded and inefficient methods of teaching his subject, even scoffing at the findings of educators about the nature of the learning process, although such findings may be supported by mountains of data.

There are two ways of approaching new ideas that may often be observed in people about us. One is to say: "There is nothing new about that. We've known that for thirty years!" The other is: "It's only a fad. It will soon pass away!" Either of these approaches permits ignoring the data and going about one's business undisturbed. Such behavior may often contribute to momentary comfort, but whenever we ignore data we do so at our peril. An open, fluid perceptual field is an essential to the achievement of maximum adequacy, and the first essential in developing such a field, it appears, is the possession of an attitude that it is important to do so.

3. The characteristics of the adequate personality provide some further clues to the kinds of values which may be likely to produce greater adequacy in ourselves. The adequate personality is characterized by a positive view of self, by the capacity for acceptance, and by a high degree of identification with other people. If, then, we can adopt these characteristics as desirable goals, they provide us with selective criterion for further perceptions which we may be able to make. Individuals who value acceptance highly are far more likely to be open to their experience. Similarly, the individual who values identification with his fellow men is much more likely to achieve this than one who finds it necessary to cut himself off from his fellows.

4. Finally, the individual who has determined which of his values and goals are most important to him and which are of lesser value has taken an important step forward in the achievement of adequacy. The goals and values we hold vary greatly. Not all are of equal importance, and the individual who persists in trying to treat them as though they were soon finds himself hopelessly bogged down in confusion. If he has an unclear conception of his values he finds himself buffeted about like paper in the wind by all of the forces impinging upon him from every side. Under such circumstances people do not become what they can be: they become what they are made.

When perceptions are vague and unclear, behavior is also. When we do not know what is important, behavior must be as haphazard and inconsistent as our perceptions. The failure of administrators, teachers, politicians, clergymen, and parents can often be traced to faulty perceptions of what is important. Thus, in dealing with those they are responsible for, they behave ineffectively and futilely. When what we believe to be important is out of touch with the realities of the situations in which we are involved, we can only flounder about like a ship without a rudder. Not all things are equally worth while, and human efficiency and the achievement of self realization require clear concepts of what is important.

THE PRODUCTION OF CHANGE IN SELF. Since the self is a perceptual organization, it too is open to a degree of change like any other perceptions. The central, all-pervading character of the self in a human organization, however, does not permit the kind of wide variations in perceiving that may occur in not-self aspects of the field. It is always easier to change what one thinks of others than to change what one thinks of oneself. Despite this resistance to change in the self concept, however, there is always some room to maneuver. Through an individual's experiences it is possible to bring about changes in the self organization in the direction of new and more adequate personality structure. This, of course, is not possible directly, but since the self concept is a function of experience it is possible to make important changes in the self by the kinds of experiences an individual is provided or provides for himself.

There is a common assumption that change in the self is often brought about by seeking to achieve an ideal self. Actually, this seldom turns out to be the case. The self ideal is nearly always a kind of report of what we might like to be which we provide for the examination of persons who have asked us about the matter. It is rare, however, that the self ideal has any very great dynamic effect in motivating the behavior of individuals. It seems logically true that if you want to get somewhere, the thing to do is to set up some clear-cut, manifest objective and go to work to achieve it. Actually, many such ideals are likely to have little effect on the individual or his behavior. Perceptions and behavior, we have seen, are immediate, whereas the kinds of self ideals we are encouraged to adopt are probably far removed from our present state in both time and quality. There is certainly nothing wrong with having lofty and distant goals for oneself, but unless such distant ends can be converted into more immediate and achieveable goals they will have little or not effect upon the individual. They may even succeed only in discouraging him entirely.

Most effective change is brought about in the self concept by more realistic and immediate perceptions. Clinical experience in psychotherapy would seem to indicate that maximum change in self is brought about not by the rejection of self, nor by longing for that which is beyond achievement, but through acceptance of self *as one is.* After all, we can only make changes in self by beginning where we are. The acceptance of self provides the platform from which it is possible to go somewhere else. In very large measure the difficulty of the neurotic arises from the very fact that he is unable to accept himself as he is and thus has no firm basis from which to move or frame of reference in which to interpret new events and directions. The psychotherapist knows that it is only when such a personality is more able to accept himself as he is that new and tentative steps toward becoming something else are possible. While it is, of course, not possible for the individual to accept himself just by saying he will, such an acceptance is more likely to occur if it seems a desirable growth-producing goal. So long as acceptance is seen as threatening and humiliating it is almost certain to be rejected.

Beginning from whatever self acceptance the individual is able to muster, change in the self concept becomes possible through the kinds of experiences he thereafter selects. We have seen in an earlier chapter that the self concept is a product of experience. We have seen, too, that the kinds of experiences individuals have are open to a degree of choice. However, just as it is necessary to begin with the self we are, it is necessary to select the experiences we would have in the light of what fits the people we are and the capacities we have. To force ourselves into experiences in which we are bound to fail will do little to increase our feelings of adequacy. In seeking new experiences it is necessary to choose those in which we stand a reasonable chance of success.

Effective change in self is a process of becoming involved in experiences or predicaments and working one's way out of them again. To do this successfully, however, requires a real appreciation of the personality in operation. The things we try must fit the selves we are. One of the greatest sources of discouragement in self help is the attempt to try to be what one is not or to do something in the way another person does it. The experiences we seek need to be selected in terms of our own personalities. To force ourselves into experiences in which we must be what we are not for any length of time is almost certain to result in increased feelings of inadequacy. Most people do not look their best in other people's clothes and even the best of mimics never becomes the person he mimics. To be successful in dealing with new events and new experiences we should expect to tailor them and remake them in the ways that fit ourselves most effectively and comfortably.

DEALING EFFECTIVELY WITH THREAT. Finally, for effective self help it will be necessary for us to deal with the unhappy effects of threat on the perceptual field. We have seen in several places in this book how the experience of threat forces self defense and narrows perception. To achieve self improvement it will be necessary then for us to eliminate these negative elements as much as we possibly can. While, of course, none of us can ever free himself from all threat simply by willing it so, like all other perceptions the perception of threat is open to some degree of modification.

In a sense, self change requires a kind of flirting with inadequacy, a willingness to open self to a degree of pain in the present in the understanding that greater adequacy may be achieved in the long run. The achievement of adequacy requires a degree of courage that makes it possible for a person to drop his barriers and venture outside his castle walls. Something must be ventured if there is to be any gain. This is, of course, not easy, for the fundamental need of the individual is the maintenance of self. But it is not impossible either. When individuals can perceive the possibilities of greater adequacy, the subjection of self to some degree of pain is seldom much of a deterrent.

Effective change in self requires a willingness to put oneself in the way of being hurt. This kind of courage and deliberate courting of threat, however, can also go too far. Indeed, it can even result in self destruction. Not all threats are worth seeking nor are all threats by any means equal in the degree of adequacy which they can provide for a particular person. In Chapter 10 we made a distinction between challenge and threat. People feel threatened, it will be recalled, when confronted with situations they do not feel capable of dealing with. People feel challenged, on the other hand, when they are confronted with situations lying within their capacities. Challenge offers opportunities for the experience of adequacy. Threat rarely contributes to the maintenance and enhancement of self. Individuals who value and seek for challenge contribute to an ever growing personal adequacy. With increasing adequacy many of the threats they formerly felt may even be experienced as challenges to be met with joy and excitement rather than with fear and dread.

The achievement of adequacy provides one with such strength and sureness of self that things outside seem far less threatening. The kind of continual testing of self we have been advocating is a far cry from the search for security which some people would have us believe is the mark of adequacy. It demands, in fact, a willingness to give up security, even to place oneself in jeopardy, for the experience of achieving a more adequate self. Security of self is achieved by a willingness, when necessary, to renounce the support of the familiar. To cross the street one must leave the security of the sidewalk. To achieve the security in self necessary to cross streets without fear, one must be willing to renounce the comfort and safety of what is for the greater achievement of what may be.

CHAPTER 17

The Goals and Purposes of Education

IN the complex interdependent world we live in each of us is increasingly dependent upon the intelligence and good will of an ever larger number of our fellow men. It is not surprising, therefore, that as our society has grown more interrelated and coöperative, education has also grown by leaps and bounds. From an institution once designed for the enhancement of a few in the leisure class we now seek an education "for all." It is no longer conceived as a luxury but as a stark necessity on which the welfare of all of us depends in greater and greater measure. Modern society simply cannot exist without a continuously increasing supply of more and more adequate people. The goal of education from society's viewpoint, then, is the production of adequate personalities, people who can be counted upon to behave effectively and efficiently and to contribute freely to the welfare of all. This is simply another way of saying that the goal of education is intelligent behavior.

This is a definition of the purpose of education which could hold true in all societies, for all times, and for all people. It is quite true that this statement of the desired result of education is more general than those which are usually given; but a more definite and specific description of the kinds of behavior which should result from education can be dangerous. Conditions change and any society which sets out to concentrate on securing a specific type of behavior from its citizens runs the risk of getting it under conditions where it is valueless or even undesirable. Other nations besides the Spartans have had this happen to them. For the good of our society and its members it is better to wish for intelligent behavior than for good penmanship, or the ability to diagram a declarative sentence, or any of the other limited objectives which may or may not be a valuable means of need satisfaction in the future.

Since education is always concerned with training a younger generation to assume responsibilities in an era the precise character of which we cannot foresee, its goals must always appear in general terms. To decide today in too specific terms what children should be tomorrow may run the risk of preparing them for a world that does not exist. So it is that we must be content with a goal of education concerned with the *production of intelligent, adequate people,* in the belief that if we can be successful in this general aim, the specifics can be solved as we reach them.

Advocates of all systems and goals in education agree on one thing: that, to be effective, it must result in a change in the behavior of the person educated. If no change results, the attempts at education have been unsuccessful. It is the primary thesis of this book that behavior is completely determined by the perceptual field at the moment of action. From this point of view, then, the process of education is fundamentally a process of change in the field. Behavior is determined by the field, and the way to change behavior is to change perceptions.

We have stated that the goal of education is the production of adequate, intelligent people. Earlier in this book we have defined adequacy and intelligence in perceptual terms. Let us stop here for a moment to review those definitions, because they will help us to define more precisely the goals of education.

The adequate personality we defined as one who (1) perceives himself in essentially positive ways, (2) is open to his experience or capable of accepting self and others, and (3) is strongly and broadly identified with others.

Intelligent behavior, we indicated, was the product of perceptual fields (1) rich, (2) extensive, and (3) maximally available when needed. These perceptual characteristics of adequate persons and intelligent behavior define more specifically the goals of education. An adequate educational system which produces these kinds of perceptual fields in its students is successful. A system which fails to affect these important criteria has failed.

THE INDIVIDUAL'S GOALS ARE PERSONAL

Fortunately, the individual himself is also seeking an ever greater degree of personal adequacy. Indeed, as we have seen, this is the basic need of the organism, motivating its every act. The problem of education arises, however, in the fact that while the student's goals are immediate and personal, the goals of education are frequently cultural and remote. This difference in perception of what adequacy entails accounts for much of the difficulties we have in the education of the young. A 10-year-old boy from a lower socioeconomic class intent upon the immediate satisfaction of need and a 30-year-old, middle-class woman teacher intent upon preparing the child for the future, for instance, are living in quite different worlds. The behavior which is of value to the teacher in the pursuit of her goals would be a positive detriment to the boy in the pursuit of his. For the middle-class schoolteacher it may appear important to be polite. Being polite, however, when one's adequacy depends on status and prestige in his gang could, from the child's view, prove dangerous to life and limb!

To control or change the behavior of any individual, it is necessary to change his perceptual field. The student's differentiations in his perceptual field, however, are not only directed toward the satisfaction of his need for maintenance and enhancement; they are directed toward the *immediate* satisfaction of this need. In the exploration of his field the differentiations which seem likely to achieve this end are continued and perfected, and the perceptions which seem less promising are abandoned as soon as their uselessness is perceived. People do work toward long-range objectives, it is true, but only in the general sense that these long-range objectives have determined the selection of the more immediate goals which they are currently trying to reach.

A student seeking self enhancement, for instance, decides to become a teacher. So he registers in a teachers' college. To graduate he must secure a passing mark in his educational psychology course. He comes to class. But he cannot postpone his need for self enhancement until he becomes a teacher. He must seek it in the immediate situation in the classroom in which his long-range efforts toward self enhancement have trapped him. Only to the extent that the situation in that classroom gives him immediate satisfaction of need will he become or remain an active participant. Lecturers who believe that their students are hanging on every word forget their own woolgathering at some of the lectures they attend. Children are no less human. A request to think about a problem the individual does not yet have rarely leads to serious or earnest effort on the part of anyone, child or adult. Even if he knows that he may have to meet that problem in the future there is little likelihood of active effort. We are all too much in need of immediate reassurance and enhancement to spend much time solving problems we do not have and pursuing "goals" we do not desire. Time enough for that later. Right now, we have to do the things which are important *now*. As a result children who do not own houses remain quite uninterested in the paper-hanging problems in arithmetic, and students who have elected psy-chology as a means to more and better dates are usually bored by lec-tures on learning curves or chronaxie.

Any given individual will differentiate from the field only that which helps him toward the satisfaction of need at that moment. When the student's immediate goal is reached, his differentiations in that direc-tion naturally cease. He learns no more about anything than he finds necessary. This "laziness" and "inattention" to the demands of the teacher and the school seems reprehensible to the teacher. It may even seem perverse and abnormal. But from the point of view of the individ-ual it is simply efficiency. Failure to learn what the teacher wishes does not mean that he has ceased to learn. It only means that he has turned to more promising objectives and is searching his field for ways and means of reaching them. If the subject matter presented by the school promises to assist him in the immediate satisfaction of need and is within his ability to differentiate, he will learn it. If it does not assist him or (the same thing) is beyond his capacity, he will discover how to evade learning it. Essentially the control of learning is in the hands of the student, not in the hands of the teacher.

The insistence of the child on pursuing his own immediate ends some-times arouses a great deal of indignation from his elders, who are apt to feel that the only way to behave is to conform to their plans and thus minister to their needs; but the point of view of the student is necessarily different. It is quite likely that much of the conflict between pupils and teachers which still occurs in schools is due to the fact that the schools are run by people who are chiefly concerned with preparing the student for his functions in adult life and are filled with students who want to satisfy their needs here and now. Each group is apt to find the other quite obtuse and unreasonable,

IMMEDIATE NEED VERSUS PREPARATION FOR LIFE

"Preparation for life" is good sense, as far as it goes. It is obvious that the way to have time enough tomorrow is to do part of the work today. Parents expect their children to do just that in school. But there is a catch. The catch is, as we have pointed out already, that people differ-entiate from the field only what is helpful to the attainment of their present goals. And school children have different goals from adults, partly because they are children and partly because they are in that special type of institution which we call a school. As a result they discover those techniques and make those differentiations which are most effective in securing their self enhancement *in the school situation* instead of discovering those techniques and making those differentiations which will be most effective in the adult situation for which they are "being prepared."

This is a problem peculiar to a culture in which childhood is put aside as a nonproductive period and in which children are not allowed to become productive members of society. In most primitive societies, where the economic and social contributions of children are needed and welcome, the problem does not exist. In such societies the work of adults and children is so much alike that the solution of childhood problems is often equivalent to the solution of adult problems. The child, in striving for satisfaction of his immediate need, is automatically "preparing for future life" as well.

In a complex and highly specialized society like our own we cannot go back to the educational practices of primitive times. To do so would bring our civilization to a speedy end. However, we would do well to bring our children into closer touch with adult society by giving them greater opportunities to become participating members. This cannot be achieved by make-believe activities such as Boys' States and Junior Governments, although they both, along with sociodrama techniques, are a long step in the right direction. Student governments, if they really govern, are of great value to the participants. As a step toward social membership, work-study plans have been very effective in many vocational schools; but for the purposes of general education a much wider program is needed. The best training in citizenship, for instance, is secured by children actively engaged in activities they have devised for the betterment of their community. The practices of some Southern schools whose students have contributed to their communities by reclaiming waste land, doing contour plowing, establishing canning centers, and finding new markets for community products are outstanding examples of effective education. The activities mentioned can be planned and carried out by young people in their teens; and in almost all communities even younger children can make real contributions to the public welfare. To the extent that they can gain recognition and acceptance for these activities they will inevitably develop concepts of themselves and their surroundings which will be very beneficial to them and to society in later life.

This does not mean that a school program is without value unless the child is making an immediate contribution to the community. Even when the school program is, from the point of view of adults, almost purely make-believe, it can be of great value in preparing the child for adult life if it allows and helps him to attack his own immediate problems, whatever they may be. A school program which emphasizes the value of the individual and helps him to make effective adjustments to other people is truly preparing children for the future. The school can best guarantee that a child will develop into a nonthreatened, nonthreatening, and socially effective person by providing him with success experiences and a nonthreatening, accepting atmosphere. Having self respect now will help him to develop a self which will be less threatened in the future and therefore more adequate in exploring his environment and dealing with other people.

As long as our schools persist in attempting to direct the child into activities which do not provide him with opportunities for immediate self enhancement, children will show great ingenuity in avoiding these activities. They must do so in order to concentrate on their immediate personal problems, which are the only things important to them. The traditional school has countered this refusal to deal with material which has no personal value by inventing the conventional system of marking and promotion. This gives the nonenhancing material an artificial self reference through requiring its mastery as a condition for avoiding censure or for securing a satisfactory mark. This makes the material a matter of concern to the pupils who have differentiated success in school as a means of self enhancement and it is, after a fashion, learned. However, the victim of this trickery does not allow himself to be put upon. He maintains his integrity by dropping the material from his field at the earliest possible moment, usually as soon as the mark has been assured. This state of affairs often results in the pupil's disregard of the subject matter entirely except as a vehicle for gaining approval or avoiding disapproval. And what he does or how he behaves toward it will depend on whose approval he is trying to gain.

What, then, is the solution to this impasse? Here is the student, on the one hand, intent upon the immediate satisfaction of his need and the school, and on the other, charged with the responsibility of assuring his adequacy in the future. Some teachers have attempted to resolve this impasse by designing educational practices entirely in terms of the immediate needs of the child. Other teachers have attempted to solve the problem by ignoring the needs of the child entirely and concentrating solely on "training the child for the future." The first of these approaches makes of the teacher a nonentity and ignores the goals of society. The second makes a nonentity of the child and glorifies the goals of society. Clearly, neither of these extremes is likely to result in an effective and efficient educational system. Effective education is not content with the fulfillment of immediate goals. It is concerned as well with the creation of goals. The truly great teacher does more than tell us what we want to know. He inspires us too to want to know what a moment before we had never dreamed of. To achieve such goals in modern education means that we must be deeply concerned with the meanings existing on the part of our students.

Education Must Deal with Personal Meaning

The important thing in the determination of behavior is not the objective description of objects and facts in the phenomenal field, but the meaning that those objects and facts have for the individual. This meaning is found in the relationship of the object to the phenomenal self, in the role which the object or fact is felt to have in the satisfaction of need. The work of Norman Maier indicates that objects differentiated from the field as a means to one goal may be correspondingly harder to experience with another meaning. In his experiments Maier's subjects were asked to solve a problem involving the principle of the pendulum and were given a piece of string and a pair of pliers. Many of his subjects were so used to pliers as pliers that it never occurred to them they could be used as pendulum weights. They were unable to see the new meaning pliers could have because they were so fixed on the old one. It is, therefore, very important that the fact or object emerge with a meaning which will make it most useful for the future satisfaction of need. If it is differentiated as something to be avoided, it becomes less available for future use. If it is differentiated with too narrow a meaning, it will also be less available.

Unfortunately, material forced upon students without consideration of their present need and immediate goals tends to acquire a meaning which makes it less useful in the satisfaction of need than if it had never been studied. Since it does not assist the satisfaction of need, its intrusion into the field simply creates additional difficulty for the student. The demand that he abandon his current problems and turn to the study of the required material is pretty sure to cause him to regard that material as an obstacle to self enhancement, as something to be avoided, a negative goal. If he remembers it at all after the examination is over he remembers it with this meaning and behaves toward it accordingly. If we wish a child to like a new food we give him the opportunity to eat it when he is hungry, when it will acquire the meaning we wish it to have. We do not, if we are wise, offer it to him when it will not satisfy his need; nor do we force it upon him under circumstances which humiliate or disgust him. Some parents, it is true, do make such mistakes, but teachers should be better trained.

MEANINGS CANNOT BE FULLY VERBALIZED

The meaning of any object or event is the relation which it has to the self of the perceiver. It is his perception of its effect upon himself and his efforts at self maintenance and self enhancement. As we have seen, however, not all meaning can be fully verbalized. Many meanings exist at such low levels of awareness as to be unreportable. It is quite likely that our inability to communicate and share meanings with more exactness is due to our inability to find verbal symbols for such low-level experiences. As long as they remain ground they are undifferentiated and therefore incommunicable. The result is that we rarely are able to communicate meanings fully and accurately. Students who are taught by verbal means alone are sure to behave as if most of the material they study is without relation to themselves, as indeed it is, until they actually experience the situations the books and teachers are talking about.

In general, the problem of communicating meanings is so difficult that it is often much more practical to help students discover the meaning of objects and events by actual experience than to try to convey them verbally. Furthermore, the meanings are bound to differ from one person to another because the object or event will play different roles in different fields. It will have different potentialities for different people.

MEANINGS DIFFER FROM INDIVIDUAL TO INDIVIDUAL

No two people ever share the same phenomenal field. In any objective situation and from each school subject the individual selects only those aspects which are pertinent to the achievement of his goals at that time. Because each fact and field of subject matter thus has very different meanings to different people, efforts to reform education by changes in the curriculum, although they may be helpful, are bound to fall short of expectations. We cannot reform education by this method alone, because the same curriculum means so many different things to different people. For example, the famous "hundred books" can be extraordinarily rich sources of growth and enlightenment to students who have identified themselves with their own society and are seeking to understand it and its problems. The same books, on the other hand, are mere compilations of irrelevant and boring opinion to people who read them "to learn what great men have thought," "to become cultured," or to acquire college credit. In the same way a student in a Latin class may learn a great deal about Roman politics, or about poetry, or about basic grammar. He may also learn how to cheat without being caught, how to avoid being called upon by the teacher, or how to wiggle his ears to entertain the people behind him.

THE FUNCTION OF SUBJECT MATTER

It seems obvious, therefore, that any system of education which concerns itself only with the formal presentation of standard subject matter without considering the individual student's point of view will affect different persons very differently. Subject matter and methods which have a desirable effect on the development and behavior of one student may have a very undesirable effect on the development and behavior of another. As a result any formalized system of education whether method-centered or subject matter–centered, is too unpredictable and erratic in outcome to be safely used by a highly integrated, democratic society. In such a society one ignorant, maladjusted, or disaffected individual may menace the life and happiness of people all over the world. No member is unimportant. As a voter, as a producer, as an inhabitant of the same world, the behavior of each citizen affects the lives of all. In such a society the education of no individual can safely be left to chance. To confine our educational effort to the production of change in the not-self part of the student's phenomenal field is to leave far too much to chance. The series of diagrams in Fig. 24 may illustrate the point. The top one schematically shows the entire phenomenal field of an individual. The middle shows the external part of the field only. This is the part accepted by traditional education as its entire field of action. The third shows the external field as it is divided among various fields of subject matter, each taught without reference to the phenomenal self and with many gaps and some overlapping. For several years educators have recognized the inadequacy of the bottom situation and have at-

The phenomenal field (the basis of behavior)

The phenomenal environment

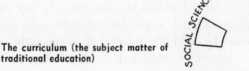

The curriculum (the subject matter of traditional education)

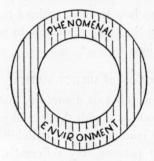

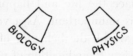

Fig. 24. The Phenomenal Field and the Curriculum.

tempted to remedy it by breaking down the subject matter boundaries and "correlating" the subjects to show the student their essential unity. If this could be done successfully, it would enlarge the field of education to the field shown in the middle diagram. But if our analysis of behavior is correct, even this would not help a great deal. To be really effective, education will have to accept the task of dealing with the whole phenomenal field of the individual, of producing changes in his perception of himself as well as in his perception of his environment.

This is necessary not only because of the dominant role which the phenomenal self plays in the determination of behavior but because of the organized and unified nature of the phenomenal field.

The Phenomenal Self

Since behavior must be appropriate to the phenomenal self, changes in the phenomenal self are invariably followed by changes in behavior. We have already cited instances of such changes in other chapters. Lecky has reported a number of cases of pupils who, after undergoing changes of the self concept, have made startling improvement in their level of achievement, often without tutoring: "A high school student who misspelled 55 words out of a hundred and who failed so many subjects that he lost credit for a full year, became one of the best spellers in the school during the next year, and made a general average of 91. . . . A girl who had failed four times in Latin, with marks between 20 and 50, after three talks with the school counselor made a mark of 92 in the next test and finished with a mark of 84. She is now taking advanced Latin with grades above 80."

The following case report, written by a teacher, further illustrates the important role played by the phenomenal self in behavior.

Roger is 12 years old, almost three years older than any other child in the class. He has failed three different terms in school and was passed into the sixth grade this year only because of his age. Achievement and other tests at the end of the year showed little improvement over what he accomplished on the tests given in September. He has had psychological tests three times: once when he was 7, again when he was 9, and once more this spring. Test results showed that he has normal intelligence and is abnormal in no way. He has never learned to read although there is no physical or mental obstruction to his ability to learn. He is far beyond the average child in his ability to converse and shows remarkable common sense and judgment for a child his age. He surpasses most of the class in reasoning out classroom problems not connected with schoolwork. He has a wonderful personality and is well liked by all the other children although the boys call him a sissy. Roger firmly believes that he was born without a brain and that it is impossible for him to learn. He will not attempt to do any kind of schoolwork which involves independent thinking and constantly attempts to foresee any challenge which might confront him before the school day even begins. Upon arriving at school he might say "If we do examples at the board today I'm not going up. I'll sit in my seat because I can't do them and only take up space at the board."

When Roger started to read in the first grade, the children laughed when he made a mistake and continued to laugh at his mistakes when none of his teachers corrected the other children. This occurred in more than the first grade. Roger at first laughed with them until he suddenly refused to read aloud any more. Since then he cannot even read silently. He dislikes school and has to be practically forced to school every day. His belief that he was "born without a brain" (and he sincerely believes this) excuses him from any thinking processes and so protects him from humiliation. He is no behavior problem as far as obeying rules, etc., and he is a very cheerful boy for, naturally, having no brain excuses one from the difficult things.

Roger was an only child until he was 7 and his mother did all the difficult things for him. When his brother was born, Roger demanded even more attention from his parents and, fearing he was jealous of the baby, the parents overworked themselves in showing their devotion. His mother tied his shoes until he was ten. I believe this dependence on someone to do all the hard things is one of Roger's problems now. Everything was made easy for him and all the difficult tasks taken over by his mother or father and now he is unable to do for himself.

He does not play with boys but prefers to play with girls. . . . The fear of failure in the boys' games undoubtedly keeps him from entering the sports. He can run faster than the girls and beats them at their games and to him this is better than being beaten by the boys. . . . Recently his mother called me to say that though he is signed up for two weeks at Boy Scout camp, he gets almost hysterical when it is mentioned and is begging to stay home. . . .

He is at the reading clinic on the Hill this year and there has been a decided improvement in his reading accomplishment. . . . The psychological tests have been bad for Roger, I think. These have naturally given him the idea he is different and that there must be something wrong with him, especially since he has had three. After his tests this spring (which his parents insisted upon) he came to school and said "Well, they gave me some more tests to see how dumb I was." His parents have never told him the results of the tests. . . .

We tried in school to help him gain more self-confidence but when his parents refused to let him take the bus to the city alone, would not allow him to go to the movies with a group of boys and girls on Saturday afternoon unless a parent was along, our work did little good.

The case of Roger illustrates quite well how the phenomenal self develops and how it affects behavior. This boy was treated as an incompetent by his parents, his classmates, and his teachers. He was placed in a situation where it was easier to accept this concept of himself than to reject it. As an incompetent at home he was waited on and protected. In school he found that the concept of himself as an incompetent was one which he could maintain because it was consistent with the way he was treated. His early efforts to behave as if he were competent were greeted with ridicule, so he fell back to a position he could maintain and became a boy "born without a brain," free from the responsibility of performing the tasks which led to humiliation. This self concept of incompetence as a student and as a boy not only caused his withdrawal from classroom activities and from competition with boys, it also became a determining factor in the further differentiation of his phenomenal field. Facts and experiences which threatened this self were rejected or were selected in conformity with it. His experiences at the psychological clinic, for instance, might have been a source of reassurance to another child. To Roger, however, they were supporting evidence which helped to maintain his phenomenal self and the stability of his field. This boy felt that to be able, to be normal, or to be masculine would be to be a failure because it would confront him with problems and responsibilities with which he felt unable to cope. It is no wonder that his teacher was unable to reassure him.

The case of Roger is unusual only in the clear-cut visibility of the mechanisms involved. It is easy to see in his case that the determining force which gave the individual character and direction to his behavior was the phenomenal self. Roger with a different perception of himself would have behaved very differently. So would any person.

This presents all schools and all teachers with a new responsibility. If we are to deal effectively with behavior we must consider what our students think of themselves. Indeed we must, if our assumptions are correct, frankly assume the responsibility for helping our students to perceive themselves in ways that will be more satisfactory to them and, through the resulting behavior, to others. The development of an adequate self by each student would seem to be a primary responsibility for us all.

THE ADEQUATE SELF AS A GOAL OF EDUCATION

In an earlier chapter we have seen that an adequate personality is characterized by three factors: (1) an essentially positive view of self, (2) the capacity for acceptance of self and of others, and (3) the ability to identify broadly with his fellow man. Since the self concept is a function of experience, what happens to students during their time spent in the educational system must be of vital importance in the development of the phenomenal self. Probably no other agency in our society outside the family has a more profound effect on the development of the individual's concepts of self. What happens to an individual in school is important to the production of an adequate personality. These learnings, furthermore, occur whether teachers plan for their occurrence or not. A teacher may ignore the effects of his behavior on a child's developing concepts of self, but the fact of his ignoring them does not eliminate the effect. An effective educational system can no more ignore the variables of behavior than the chemist can omit essential ingredients of his compound and expect to come out with the hoped-for product.

The ways in which the schools can assist their students in the development of satisfactory and desirable self concepts cannot be planned as a rigid syllabus of experiences or activities because the experiences and achievements which give self enhancement and confidence to a person at one stage of his life may be profoundly unsatisfactory to another person or to the same person at another time. Praise from the teacher, for instance, can represent either self enhancement or humiliation to different children or in different circumstances. It is possible, however, to make some assumptions about the general techniques that would be used by schools which deliberately set out to develop adequate self concepts in their pupils.

1. Such schools would provide each pupil with every possible opportunity to think of himself as a responsible citizen and a contributing member of society. They would see that he has the widest possible chance to identify with and be accepted by the socially desirable individuals and groups which he admires, so that he will feel accepted by and acceptable to society.

This seems to imply a need for democratic classrooms, where there is respect for the need, integrity, and potentialities of all members of the group and where all members feel free to express their opinions frankly and openly. It also implies an emphasis on coöperative activities which call for a wide variety of skills so that each student will have opportunities to gain a sense of self enhancement and personal worth from his contribution to the group. It implies a more appreciative attitude by adults, especially teachers, toward children's ambitions and achievements.

2. Such a school would provide its pupils with a wide variety of opportunities for success and appreciation through productive achievement. Under these conditions children would not only be able to gain self enhancement through the discovery of their talents and areas of strength, but would also be encouraged to discover their weaknesses and inadequacies under conditions in which they would feel adequate enough to acknowledge and deal with them.

3. It would provide its pupils with a maximum of challenge and a minimum of threat. It would stimulate and encourage the exploration of ever new fields of human thought, for nothing is quite as satisfying a contribution to personal feelings of adequacy than challenge successfully met and conquered. It need not be feared that children, in a situation where they are able to move freely toward self enhancement, will select activities which are "too easy" for them. Such activities do not lead to self enhancement and are chosen only when the individual is under threat. Under threat he attempts to protect himself from failure by reverting to an activity he has already mastered.

Other things being equal, more pupils will have opportunities for success and self enhancement if: (1) The achievements are evaluated by standards appropriate to the age and experience of the pupil. (2) The activity is chosen and planned by the pupils themselves. (3) The contributions of different members of the same class are so different in type that no comparisons are possible. (4) The activity is appropriate to the abilities, maturation level, and goals of the student.

The program of diversification of activities should not be prevented by the plea that the present subjects of instruction are of such unique importance that all must become proficient in all of them. Our society is one of coöperation among specialists. The United States census lists more than 35,000 occupations, each of which presumably calls for its own pattern of skills and abilities. It is to the advantage of our society that all of its members should think of themselves as responsible citizens and contributing members. It is not to the advantage of society that all have the same skills and items of information. Indeed, it is preferable that they do not.

The essential point is that the student, to acquire a satisfactory feeling of competence and acceptability, must grow up having success experiences and being accepted. Many students, it is true, do not win these experiences. But when we recognize that *every* student must have such experiences in order to become a happy and productive member of society, the defects of all but a few of our schools are at once apparent.

If it is important that students learn to perceive themselves as liked, wanted, acceptable, able, and responsible, then it follows that education must provide them with the kinds of experiences which help them see themselves so and avoid treating them in ways that destroy positive self feeling. If it is important that citizens grow up accepting themselves and others, then it is important that schools provide experiences of acceptance. It will be necessary to recognize that there are rejected children in schools as well as in homes. Finally, to achieve fully adequate people, education will have to aid young people in achieving the widest possible identification with their fellow men. This will require experience with others and interaction among peoples of a wide variety of race, color, and creed.

THE CREATION OF INTELLIGENCE AS A GOAL OF EDUCATION

The purpose of education, we have said, is the promotion of intelligent behavior. And in Chapter 11 we defined intelligence as a function of perception; the product of a phenomenal field rich, extensive, and maximally available. It follows that to produce an intelligent citizenry education must find ways of providing students with opportunities to become richly informed and fully free to utilize their perceptions to maximum advantage.

Human perceptions are the raw material with which education must work. How successful education is in accomplishing its goals will depend upon how effectively it deals with the problems of perception. The basic variables of perception which we have been discussing throughout this book thus become the raw materials with which the process of education must work. These variables, it will be recalled, are as follows: (1) the physical organism, (2) the effect of time, (3) opportunities for perception, (4) the effect of need, (5) the phenomenal self, (6) the effects of goals and values, and (7) the effect of restrictions on the phenomenal field. In the earlier parts of this chapter we have devoted a good deal of attention to discussing the effect of two of these variables upon the process of education, namely the effect of need and the phenomenal self. This is not to suggest that the remaining variables are less important. Rather, we have devoted so much space to them only because they are frequently overlooked and because they represent particular contributions of this frame of reference about behavior.

We do not have space here to examine in detail how each of the remaining variables is related to the problem of education. We have already discussed the operation of these variables at length in the early chapters of this book. In Chapter 11, we have raised a series of questions about ways in which our understanding of these variables might be related to the problem of creating intelligence. These questions are equally applicable to the problems of education in the creation of an informed citizenry. Educators and teachers in training may find it stimulating and exciting to attempt the application of these principles concerning perception to almost any aspect of education they choose. For the educator interested in experimentation with the teaching process, a perceptual understanding of these variables provides a veritable gold mine of hypotheses worthy of experimentation. Over the last ten years, for example, Combs has attempted systematically to apply some of these basic principles to understanding and practice in such areas as the construction of lectures, the training of counselors and guidance personnel, the development of group-discussion techniques, the solution of intergroup tensions, even, for a period, the task of a lobbyist in one of our state legislatures. Some of the thinking in the chapter to follow about the teacher and his relationships has grown out of this kind of attempt to apply what we now know of the basic variables of perception.

Similar experimentation on the part of Snygg has led to the following partial list of principles concerning the learning process:

1. In most schoolroom situations the chief motive of the children's behavior and learning is their need for self-esteem and a feeling of personal adequacy.

2. Activities and techniques which result in success and an increased feeling of self-esteem will be repeated; activities which result in failure or humiliation are avoided.

3. When children are confronted with a situation where the old techniques for satisfying their need for self-respect or security are not appropriate they will, if ready, learn new techniques for mastering the situation or, if unready, will use or discover methods for escaping from it.

4. Any child is ready to learn new techniques in situations which are not markedly different from situations he has already mastered. Any child is unready for situations which call for solutions quite unlike those he has already used and understood.

5. Attempts to teach children before they are ready are not only a waste of time but, by building up attitudes of avoidance, interfere with later learning.

6. Habit is not a cause of behavior. Acts and techniques are repeated only if they satisfy need. Habit is not the result of repetition but the result of success.

7. Repetition is not a cause of learning. It is true that some situations, such as those calling for the development of a new motor skill or a technique of solution completely new to the child, are ordinarily not solved at the first trial. In such circumstances most children must find themselves in the problem situation many times before they can find an adequate method of dealing with it. However, repetition sought by the child because he wishes to solve the problem has a very different effect from repetition forced upon him by the teacher. If repetition is imposed by the teacher in such a manner that the child is unable to notice progress or feels that he is failing, the result is invariably the discovery of a technique of avoidance.

8. Since the purpose of the schools is to develop each child to maximum capacity as a productive and happy member of society the real test of their success is not the degree to which the pupils can talk about desirable techniques or even the degree to which they are able to use them in school at the command of the teacher but the degree to which they voluntarily use them in their daily life outside of school. In other words, the attitudes which are acquired along with subject matter may be even more important than the subject matter itself.

9. The learning of any skill or item of subject matter is accompanied by the formation of attitudes by the pupil toward the subject, toward school, toward his teacher, toward teachers in general, toward adults, toward society, and toward himself which may be desirable or undesirable. As a result, how subject matter is taught may be even more important than what is taught.

10. Skills are better retained and more often used if they are learned under conditions similar to those in which they will be used.

11. Subject matter must be presented in such a way that each child shall secure a feeling of pride and satisfaction through its mastery. This involves an awareness of individual differences among children, not only in ability but in past experiences and present personality. It involves pacing the work for the individual child and it involves a wide and varied program of experiences in school so that each child will have an opportunity to feel successful in his work.

12. Since coöperation with others is a necessary feature of the work of all members of our society it seems desirable to provide many experiences where success can be obtained only as the result of the joint efforts of a group of specialized individuals.

13. The ideal program would be one in which the pacing of experiences is so appropriate that no experience ever needs to be repeated. It is not likely that this ideal will ever be attained but it is fair to assume that a program which requires large amounts of repetitive work is out of step with the normal development of the children and will result in techniques of avoidance rather than mastery. If a child fails to develop the desired attitude or skill as a result of an experience it should be assumed that what is required is a different experience.

The above statement of learning principles falls far short of completeness, since it only hints at the immense drive of the individual for self enhancement and self realization which makes him so unresponsive to the conventional methods and techniques of teaching. But it is not inaccurate as far as it goes. It can help us to decide what teachers can actually do to assist the education of their pupils. Such principles are only suggestive, and the interested reader may discover many more of particular interest and meaning for his own purposes and practices.

CHAPTER 18

The Teaching Relationship

IN former times teaching was conceived primarily as a business of gathering information and of imparting this information to students. The gathering process was accomplished through the collection of information in libraries, in museums, in research, and through bringing together in schools and colleges faculties of learned teachers. Education sought to impart information to students through such devices as books, lectures, demonstrations, art, and in more recent years, the vast field of audio-visual aids like film strips, movies, and television. Education has done very well in these gathering and imparting functions. It has done far less well in helping its students to discover the personal meaning of such information for their own lives and behavior.

This latter problem for education is comparatively recent. In a time when people were interested in educating only an elite, it was not necessary to worry about those people who came to the teacher wanting to know about things beyond what the teacher was prepared to teach them. It was enough to present students with information about the comparatively few subjects which then passed as marks of the educated man. The student's own desire to join the exclusive club of scholarship could be counted upon to produce the kind of active participation that would make learning effective. At about the beginning of the century, however, we decided to try something that had never been attempted before; we determined to educate everybody. Ever since we made that decision we have been faced with a very different problem, for the things *all* the people need to know about are so diverse that we can no longer restrict education to a few subjects satisfying to an elite. Nor can we be satisfied simply to gather information and make it available. Instead, we must now face the problem of how to help vast numbers of people translate a great variety of information into effective behaving. We must find better ways of helping people to *behave* better as well as to *know* better.

We are like the farmer who, when he was asked by the county agent why he did not attend local classes for the improvement of farming methods, replied, "Why man! I ain't farmin' now half as well as I know how!" Most of us know much better than we behave! We rarely misbehave because we do not "know" better. The translation of knowing into behaving is the most difficult and pressing task of education. Gathering and imparting of information can often be accomplished mechanically, but the business of helping people discover the personal meaning of information for them still requires a human interrelationship. This is the very heart of teaching, its reason for being.

Teaching: The Facilitation of Meaning Change

When modern education is criticized by the general public, it is most often for failures to present information. The presentation of subject matter, however, is so simple a problem that it offers comparatively little difficulty for most educators. Actually, both teachers and the public are concerned about the same thing; helping children to know and to behave differently as a result of their knowing. When young people do not behave in ways adults desire, the public often assumes it is because the proper subject matter was not taught. For the teacher, however, the problem is not one of presenting subject matter but of helping students discover and understand the *meaning* of subject matter so that it affects behavior. Teachers rarely fail for lack of knowledge of their subject. What most teachers feel a pressing need for is more effective ways of producing behavior change. "How," they as, "can I do a better job of affecting the *meanings* of my students?"

Modern education is probably doing a better job with these matters than it has ever done before, but the demands made by the public upon our schools have increased at an even greater rate. Modern society requires much more intelligent citizens than formerly. We need vast numbers of informed and dependable people, and modern education has been given the task of providing broader, deeper, and richer education to veritable tidal waves of students. The demands of society upon its teachers have temporarily outrun the supply of people able to fill the immense new demands of our age, but the job remains the same—helping people to discover the personal meaning of events for them.

In Chapter 8 we observed that information affects behavior in the degree to which the individual discovers the personal meaning of such information for him. We have seen how the same bit of information may have widely differing effects upon the behavior of an individual, depending upon the degree to which that information is seen by him as bearing a relationship to his self. The more intimately one perceives the relationship of concepts to self, the more certain, the more profoundly does information affect behaving. This discovery of the personal meaning of ideas, values, experiences, or the accumulated culture of the race is the very essence of learning and the art of teaching is in helping people to make this discovery.

OBSTACLES TO THE EXPLORATION OF MEANING

Though the exploration of meaning is the goal of teaching, it should not be thought that this process is either easy or quick. Many students have even been thoroughly taught to *avoid* the exploration of personal meaning. Past experience has led them to protect themselves against the revelation of personal meanings. Most of us, for example, have been hurt at times in the past when we have exposed our feelings, attitudes, beliefs, or convictions to other people, and many of us have learned as a consequence to surround ourselves with a kind of protective shell from behind which we can deal with life at arm's length. This can happen even in institutions presumably designed to "help" people. The development of this kind of protective shell was nicely but unhappily illustrated in the case of a sorority group with whom the author worked some years ago.

A group of sorority women found themselves about ready to graduate yet extremely unhappy because, as they put it, at the end of their college careers they "knew many people, but had very few friends." As this group of girls explored the whys and wherefores of this sad state of affairs with the author, it became clear little by little how the situation had come about. The sorority to which they belonged has as its ostensible purpose "helping" the sisters to become the best possible kinds of people. Unfortunately, this "helping" often had quite an opposite result. For example, the sorority sisters would sometimes attempt to "help" one of their members by pointing out to her that the clothes she was wearing were not quite appropriate, or that she really ought to do something about the kind of voice she had, or the way she laughed, etc. This mistaken notion of how to be helpful was a standard procedure in the sorority. It did not take more than a couple of experiences in which a girl was treated in this way before she learned to protect herself from her too helpful sisters. As a result, conversation in the house was primarily concerned with "safe" subjects and the girls became masters at the *forms* of "gracious living." Girls learned to talk about things at a comfortable distance from self. They talked about what had happened to them, but not about the things they felt, believed, or wondered about. This kind of experience is common to many of us and has often caused us to surround ourselves with a shell of protection which makes it extremely difficult to examine our personal experiences or feelings except under very special and protected kinds of situations. It occurs in the classroom too. Good teaching must find ways of overcoming this kind of resistance to the exploration of personal meaning.

A second obstacle to the exploration of meaning, strangely enough, is a product of previous teaching. Some teaching seems almost expressly designed to ignore or discourage the exploration of personal meaning. Our generation has been deeply impressed with the necessity for being scientific, which, in the minds of many, is synonymous with "impersonal" or "objective." Indeed, we have been so impressed with the importance of objectivity that we run real danger of "throwing out the baby with the bath water." Science is sometimes treated as a modern sort of witchcraft. Objectivity, in the minds of some people, requires a dispassionate, selfless consideration of events directly contrary to what is required for the personal exploration of meaning. It is not uncommon to hear teachers say "What are the facts? I am not interested, Helen, in what you think about this matter. Just tell us what he said!" This overemphasis upon the "facts" and the accompanying discouragement of the individual's own conceptions may even be one of the most important reasons for some of education's most glaring failures. An educational system which rules out personal meaning runs a grave risk of becoming a meaningless ornament to life rather than an effective and satisfying way of changing and improving it.

Getting an education is an important American goal, and most students assume that their teachers know what they are doing. Teaching, therefore, which glorifies objectivity and the separation of self from learning is likely to be accepted by students as the "right" way. They fall into the system and learn "objectively," as their teachers desire, but maintain a wide gulf between their "education" and living. If they discover or even explore the personal meaning of ideas for themselves it is often in spite of, rather than because of, their educational experience. The methods teachers use may actually make learning more difficult.

Some years ago the author had a vivid experience of this principle in operation. On the first day of a new semester he explained that the class would operate as a seminar with major emphasis upon class discussion and exploration of ideas. About three-fourths of the class quickly informed him they knew all about that kind of class because they had had a course just like it the previous semester with another professor. The instructor was happy to hear this, thinking he would have to spend little time teaching the group the techniques of group discussion. Actually, the class was one of the most frustrating he had ever experienced. Each class would start off as though at the crack of a gun with everyone wildly waving his hand and wanting to speak. Everyone acted as though it were a matter of life and death that he should be sure to speak at each session. When students did get the floor, their talk was almost entirely descriptive. They spoke of what they had read, what they had seen in the papers, what had happened to them, ad infinitum. Almost never did anyone speak about what he thought, believed, felt, worried about, wondered, or was puzzled about. The discussion never was able to get off a purely descriptive, intellectual level. Students spoke always of things outside themselves, but never of things having any relation to self.

After several frustrating weeks, the instructor began little by little to piece together the reasons for this behavior. These students had learned to behave in this fashion because of the kind of experience they had had the previous semester. In another class the professor had told them it did not matter whether they participated in class discussions or not. But at the end of the semester when students came in to discuss their grades he would say, "Yes I see, Miss Brown, you believe you should have a B but, you know, you really did not participate very much this semester and I am afraid a C is all I can give you!" Following this kind of treatment, students came to their new class determined to participate if it killed them! The same professor had another interesting technique for handling a discussion. When one of the members of his class expressed an opinion he would turn gravely to the rest of the group and say, "Now class, why do you suppose Mr. Adams feels this way about this question?" and for the next half hour the class would take Mr. Adams apart piece by piece! Under this kind of treatment it did not take students long to discover that it was a very dangerous thing to talk about anything in class that revealed a personal feeling. In their new class, therefore, they each had resolved, as one student phrased it, "to participate like crazy but not about anything important!"

Effective teaching must find ways of helping students escape from the unhappy effects of past experience in the exploration of meaning. The walls people build to shut other people out unfortunately shut the builder in. Exploring meaning requires freedom to move, and effective teaching must find ways of helping students break down their defenses and open themselves to new experience. We have seen that intelligence is a function of a free and open phenomenal field. It is increased by freedom to perceive and diminished by that which inhibits and narrows experience. Good teaching must begin with the creation of an atmosphere that makes exploration possible.

The Atmosphere for Learning

To aid students in breaking down their barriers, on the one hand, and actively to engage in the exploration of meaning, on the other, requires an atmosphere conducive to such ends. Atmospheres, however, are not accidental, nor are they matters of physical environment alone. Atmospheres are created out of the interaction of people with one another. The climate for learning is the product of the kinds of interactions students have with teachers. The fact that a teacher is unaware of or doesn't care about the atmosphere he creates with his students does not change the fact. Atmospheres provide the stage upon which learning occurs and arise out of the interaction of teacher and student. They can be ignored only at the risk of making the process of learning haphazard and inefficient.

Even eminent scientists may sometimes be found expressing impatience with the idea of being concerned with what seem like extraneous issues in the learning process. The idea of taking student needs or classroom atmospheres into consideration in teaching strikes them as unimportant. This is like recognizing that an automobile needs a carburetor in its motor and air in its tires but insisting on starting on a trip without these no matter what! A scientist cannot ignore the variables that affect his processes. He can only learn to control them effectively. This is true of learning processes as well. The factors controlling learning still operate whether we take cognizance of them or not. Modern psychology has supplied us with some cues to what the atmosphere for effective learning should be. The following are some of these cues.

FREEDOM FROM THREAT

People can learn under threat, but we have seen that the effect of threat is to narrow perception to that which threatens and to force the defense of self. For most learning situations these two effects of threat are directly contrary to what we desire in an educational experience. We do not seek to narrow perception; education hopes to broaden and open perception. We do not want to encourage self defense; we want to facilitate change of self. The effects of threat seem directly the antithesis of the goals of teaching. Modern research seems to indicate that the effect of threat is to produce autocracy, rigidity, and intolerance, all destructive to the development of free and independent personalities.

It seems clear that an atmosphere conducive to effective learning must be one as free from threat as can be. This requires of the teacher a sensitivity to his own relationships with students and of his students with each other, for threat is a personal experience and can only be understood through the perceptions of the people who feel it. Great teachers have the capacity for creating situations in which threats remain at a minimum and students are encouraged to drop their defenses and engage in the exciting business of growth and change. Because threat is eliminated from the atmosphere of learning does not mean, however, that the situation is also without challenge. It will be recalled that in an earlier chapter we made a distinction between threat and challenge. At that time we pointed out that people felt threatened when they felt inadequate to deal with the events confronting them and challenged when they felt the situations they were involved in were within their capacities. The elimination of threat from the learning situation does not mean that teachers must coddle or shield their students. Quite the contrary, the task of teaching is to continually encourage and challenge students, to help students stretch themselves to their utmost. Students who are truly challenged do not need to be coddled or babied. As a matter of fact they are likely to surprise us by the capacity they have to place themselves in jeopardy for the sheer joy of self exploration and the achievement of greater adequacy.

The genius of good teaching lies in the ability to challenge students without threatening them. To do this effectively means that teachers must be sensitive to the impact upon their charges of what they do and say, for the distinction between threat and challenge lies not in what the teacher *thinks* he is doing, but in what the students *perceive* him to be doing.

AN ATMOSPHERE OF ACCEPTANCE

Generally, the absence of threat we have been speaking about is best achieved in situations which treat each person as an individual of dignity and integrity; situations characterized by warmth, friendliness, and acceptance of the student as he is. In this kind of atmosphere students can and will explore their personal meanings more effectively. Such an atmosphere is not created haphazardly, however, nor can it be expected to occur when the leader of the group is not sensitive to the meanings of his own behavior and personality as these affect the people he must work with. It requires a kind of self discipline, understanding, and sensitivity to other people far beyond that required in some other professions.

Modern research seems to indicate that acceptance of others is a function first of acceptance of self. People who cannot accept themselves are unable to accept other people. In order for a teacher to create an accepting atmosphere for students, then, it would appear he must first accept himself. While it is possible for a short time to create an atmosphere strikingly different from the personalities we possess, this is a most difficult deception to maintain for any length of time. To create a situation that is truly warm, understanding, and accepting, we are beginning to understand, requires a certain kind of person; not just someone who *knows* he should be these things. Good teaching requires that the teacher himself has discovered who he is and what he is and what he is trying to do, just as he is attempting to assist his students in discovering these things for themselves. It is only when people are able to accept themselves that they are able to engage with any great degree of freedom in exploring themselves. To make this possible, those who teach the student must themselves be capable of acceptance.

The good teaching atmosphere should be accepting, but some people have confused this word with resignation and have assumed that an accepting situation is one in which students are allowed to follow whatever whims meet their fancy. Some teachers have practically abrogated their responsibilities in an attempt to please their students. This is not the sense in which we use this word at all. Acceptance, as we have used it, is a dynamic word to describe an attitude of willingness to look at and consider the facts. It has to do with admission of data to consideration. A willingness to examine facts does not imply weakness and passivity. Resignation is an attitude of defeat. Acceptance is understanding without judging. It requires an openness to experience which provides the only sound basis upon which to progress. It is an attitude of taking people as they are and moving forward from this point. It accepts students where they are and serves as a starting point for learning. Acceptance of where a person is does not mean we must be resigned to leaving him there. The task of teaching is to help people move, change, and grow, and this is an active process encouraged by the kind of accepting atmosphere we have been talking about. Acceptance is conducive to the exploration of personal meaning. It is not a substitute for it.

THE IMPORTANCE OF LIMITS

All life situations have limits and the teaching relationship is no exception. In fact, the very existence of limits provides the structure for the teaching relationship and makes the exploration of meaning possible. Limits make possible the definition of relationships and the development of stable frames of reference. Without them we become lost and uncomfortable and learning is seriously disorganized. Anyone who has ever acted as a substitute teacher is keenly aware of the manner in which children explore the limits of a new teacher in an attempt to discover where *this* teacher stands. Those who have not experienced this as teachers may remember how they tried out the substitutes assigned to them. The attempt to discover the limits of new situations is characteristic of everyone placed in an unfamiliar setting. Experienced teachers know that when people are made quickly and surely aware of limits, everyone is happier and the attention of the class quickly reverts to the daily tasks. When limits are not made clear, or when limits vacillate, students are likely to continue the exploration of limits to find out *where teacher stands now.*

Limits have important growth-inducing values for people, and the lack of limits makes adjustment to new situations more difficult. A stable structure has important positive values in providing expectancies against which to judge one's behavior. Clear and reasonable limits provide important security values. In recent years some educators have been so impressed with the unhappy effects of threat and coercion upon the learning process that they have sought to decrease threat through making classrooms more permissive. In the attempt to be "permissive," some teachers, unhappily, have gone so far as to behave as though *any* establishment of limits were coercive. Of course, limits *can* be coercive, but they can also provide important structure and security, facilitating learning. The problem is not one of eliminating limits but of establishing limits which are clear, reasonable, and related to the exploration and discovery of meaning.

Teaching is a relationship, but there can be no relationship with a nonentity. The good teacher is not a shadow but an important and vital part of the learning situation. His personality, as it is experienced by his students, creates the atmosphere for learning. Teachers cannot abrogate their responsibilities by withdrawal and self effacement. Neither can they create an atmosphere conducive to learning by threat and coercion. The effective teacher is one who has learned how to use his own personality in establishing limits for learning that will be clear, reasonable, and maximally helpful in the encouragement of exploration and discovery of personal meaning.

The Provision of Information

The traditional task of education since time immemorial has been to induct young people into the accumulated culture of their age. To live successfully requires information, and the provision of information is a basic task of the educational process. An informed people is particularly necessary in a free society which permits its citizens to make decisions, for good decisions can only be made in the light of the pertinent information. But information is not only important for societal and governmental reasons; people need information about all kinds of things in order to make personal decisions and personal adjustments for effective living as individuals. Information is necessary for the satisfaction of need.

The search for adequacy, we have seen, is insatiable, and the information people require for the achievement of adequacy seems equally infinite. What is more, each of us is so unique and individual that the information we require to work out our destinies is a highly individual matter. Even in those instances where we have common requirements for information, we are likely to need it at quite different times. The teacher is thus confronted with the problem of how to supply a vast amount of information to people with widely differing needs at the same time.

The matter is further complicated by the interests of the teacher in his subject. He "knows" there is beautiful order in his discipline because he has discovered its logic and organization as a result of his own experience. He would therefore like to present this material in the neat orderly way it has come to have meaning for him. He is quite likely to be frustrated in this attempt, however, by the maddeningly haphazard way in which students want to know about things. They are just as likely as not to want information at the beginning that "should" come at the end of a long road of learning. Teachers often forget that the systematic understanding they have achieved followed a similar highly personal search for understanding. As a consequence, teachers and students sometimes pass like ships in the night, one sailing a course for system, the other charting his course by personal need. Sometimes both ships may arrive safe in the same harbor, but this is risky navigation at best.

Before information can have an effect upon behavior, the individual must perceive its relationship to self. He must discover its peculiar personal meaning. This means that efficient and effective teaching must relate information to the need of the learner. It is a comparatively easy matter simply to provide data. It takes real skill, however, to provide information in such a manner as to assist students in discovering its meaning for them.

The discovery of personal meaning requires some sort of activity on the part of the learner. People will learn what they "need" to know. Some teachers achieve this "need to know" through the use of artificial motives like grades or other varieties of reward and punishment. Artificial motives are rarely as effective as those arising from the student's own interaction with his teachers, fellow students, and the subject matter itself. The exploration and discovery of personal meaning is more effectively achieved through the kinds of atmospheres teachers create through their personal relationships with students. Good teachers are able to *create* desires to know. They have the capacity to relate information meaningfully to the perceptions of their students. By their own enthusiasm, interest, and understanding of both their subject and their pupils they excite similar interest in students. Good teachers do not deplore the disinterest of their pupils; they have the power to create interest.

The Reorganization of Meaning

The provision of information in an atmosphere conducive to exploration is not enough to insure that effective exploration of meaning will occur. It is the task of the teacher to insure that this process of exploration occurs. He must point the way to the importance of personal meaning change, must set an example of how to explore meaning, and must actively assist his students to make such exploration. We do not have space here to discuss all of the thousands of ways master teachers have worked out to accomplish these ends, but we can look briefly at several of the principles involved in these processes.

The techniques developed by good teachers down through the ages to assist and encourage students in the exploration of meaning are almost limitless. The particular techniques found useful by teachers are a highly individual matter. Each teacher finds his own best ways of operating as an expression of his own personality, goals, values, experience, and perceptions of the situations in which he is operating. Despite this highly individual character of the teacher's techniques there are several important general principles that seem common to the process of encouraging and assisting the exploration of meaning.

EXPLORATION TAKES TIME

The discovery of personal meaning is a process which seems to proceed best in an unhurried, unharried atmosphere. We have seen in an earlier chapter that perceiving takes time and good teachers are keenly aware of this fact. They know it is possible that the pressure of speed may destroy the process of exploration entirely. The organization and reorganization of perceptions in the phenomenal field is an active process best accomplished through some form of interaction of individuals with problems. The value of a learning situation can be completely lost by such an emphasis upon speed that the learner is reduced to passivity while subject matter is poured forth at a rate he is unable to comprehend. Almost any student has at one time or another been exposed to the teacher in such desperate haste to "cover the subject" that he succeeded in burying it forever.

GUIDING EXPLORATION

Teachers can point the way to exploration of meaning by actively helping students to explore the crucial aspects of learning—the personal meaning of events for the student. They may do this in two ways: (a) by learning to listen intently to what students are expressing; and (b) by holding up for the students' examination the crucial aspects of the events he is exploring, namely their peculiar meaning for the student.

Intent listening is something that many people have never learned to do. For many of us, listening is no more than waiting till the other fellow gets through so we can get a chance to speak again. Intent listening is quite different. It is an active process, not passive waiting. It is a matter of striving to comprehend the meaning of what another individual is attempting to express. To get an idea of how difficult this is, the reader may like to try a procedure devised by a group of graduate students in training as counselors. To teach themselves to listen carefully they required that no member of the group could express his own point of view until he had first stated the gist of the previous speaker's ideas *in a way acceptable to the previous speaker!* In this way they sought to discipline themselves in the art of listening. Good teaching requires a sensitivity to what students are expressing and this requires accurate hearing of what others are trying to convey.

Understanding what a student is seeking to express is not enough, however. Students need help in exploring their perceptions as well. Students will do this quite naturally when the atmosphere permits and when teachers demonstrate their willingness to explore their own perceptions. In recent years educators have been experimenting with a number of promising new techniques for helping this process along. Some of these, like techniques of role playing and psychodrama, have been borrowed from the experience of psychotherapists. Others have been derived from the work of psychologists and educators interested in group process and the techniques of group discussion. Still others have been devised by teachers experimenting with a wide variety of methods for helping students bring into the open and explore their own feelings, attitudes, beliefs, and convictions about themselves and the world about them. All of these techniques are dependent upon active exploration of personal meaning, not only of cold objective fact but also of feelings, attitudes, beliefs, convictions, doubts, questions, and concerns. When people feel *very* safe they may even explore their loves, hates, and fears. By holding up for examination the individual's personal perceptions of events, in an atmosphere which makes this possible, the student is helped to examine his perceptions and to organize and reorganize his phenomenal field.

ACCEPTANCE OF MISTAKES

Since exploration necessarily involves trial, practice, seeking, striving, and pushing into the new and unknown, it is bound to result in frequent error. Therefore, a learning situation which regards mistakes as affronts against God and man is hardly likely to encourage the exploration of meaning. Personal meaning can only be discovered in settings wherein one has the opportunity, indeed even the right, to make mistakes. An educational setting which cannot tolerate or permit mistakes imposes severe limits upon the freedom with which students can explore their own perceptions.

When students are not permitted the luxury of making mistakes, they may by the same action be prevented from learning the very things their teachers hope to achieve. A teacher the author once knew had to leave her classroom one day to visit the administrative offices. On leaving her class she told her students: "Children, I must go down to the office for a little while. I want you to be very quiet and go on with your work while I am gone." When she returned to the room a short time later, she found the place a bedlam. Sailing into the middle of the group, she expressed her displeasure in no uncertain terms, ending her tirade by saying, "I will never leave you alone again!" By this last act, she robbed these children of their only opportunity to learn how to behave when the teacher is not there! How indeed can one explore the meaning of responsibility and learn to be responsible without the opportunity to try? Making mistakes is an essential part of learning and where errors are not permitted there is likely to be little learning either. Most effective exploration of meaning is likely to occur where mistakes are expected and accepted as a normal, necessary part of the process.

APPRECIATION OF THE NEW AND DIFFERENT

The discovery of personal meaning is vastly encouraged in an atmosphere which assists people to look at the new and the different. This is not always easy, for this can be frightening and threatening. This is all the more true when new events and ideas are closely related to self. Any psychotherapist knows of the tremendous threat involved, for example, when an individual is confronted with unacceptable perceptions of self. Such threats are destructive to the process of meaning exploration. Good learning situations must find ways of eliminating threat on the one hand and of encouraging the exploration of the new and different on the other.

This kind of situation is created, in part, by the elimination of threat and the creation of an atmosphere of warmth and friendliness. It is created also by the teacher's own demonstration that he is willing, able, and unafraid to explore his own personal meanings. It is also fostered by an attitude which approaches the whole process of learning as an exciting, challenging, enhancing activity well worth whatever effort is expended. To create this latter attitude the teacher must be skillful in interpreting his subject in a fashion that makes it seem valuable and worth while to his students. He must be skilled in transmitting to them a freshness of appreciation, an enthusiasm for the new and the different, and a wonder and delight in their exploration. To do this well, however, is not easy unless it is a vital aspect of the personal meanings of the teacher himself. It cannot be put on like a cloak, for this fools no one. The teacher who does not himself have a wonder and appreciation for the new and the different is unlikely to produce such attitudes in his students, who might well say, like the Indian, "What you do speaks so loudly I cannot hear what you say."

As we have already seen, our educational system has often emphasized goals which do not encourage the exploration of meaning. It has even operated sometimes to discourage and prevent such exploration. Intellectual, disinterested examination has often been glorified as the "scientific" and therefore desirable way of dealing with events in spite of the fact that even the scientist only behaves so in his professional life, never in his private affairs. It is the personal meaning of things which matter to people, and schools which do not value personal meanings run a grave risk of dealing only with unimportant things. Large numbers of children in our society have learned to make sharp distinctions between ways to behave and things to be concerned about in school and out. They have learned too often that "what you learn in school has nothing to do with life." Small wonder, then, if school learning has little affect on performance.

Educators have long been disturbed by the problem of "transfer of training," which is another way of asking: "How do you get subject matter to make a difference?" The answer, as we have suggested in this volume, lies in helping students discover the personal meaning of matters for them. An educational system which seeks to produce change in behavior must value the importance of meanings, and its teachers must be skilled in helping students to explore and discover them.

The Teacher as Instrument for Behavior Change

The kinds of learning situations we have been speaking about in this chapter cannot be produced by force and coercion. Teachers cannot make changes in behavior directly. They can only serve as agents or catalysts in the process of change. This does not mean that teachers are any less important to learning. The task of teaching is the creation of situations conducive to the effective exploration and discovery of personal meaning. In the carrying out of this task the teacher may call upon a vast number of teaching aids, but in the final analysis there is no substitute for his own personality, which serves as the medium through which all he does is expressed. The efficient production of learning experiences for others depends upon the skill of the teacher in using his personality as an instrument for helping others learn.

There is no *one way* of creating relationships with students. As a matter of fact, the kinds of relationships teachers have with students are as diverse as human personality itself. One needs but to think of his own school experience and recall how differently his teachers behaved in accomplishing their results. Good teaching can occur though teachers be sweet or tough, lenient or strict, reserved or out going. What makes an effective teacher, it seems clear, is not the possession of some particular list of traits. It is not a kind of garment which can be put on or off as the season requires, nor is it a bag of tricks to be performed from time to time. People seem able to learn from a variety of teachers and methods. This was illustrated for the author in the conversation of three little boys he overheard at the end of the school year discussing their next year's teacher.

First Boy: Hey, who ya got next year?
Second Boy: I got Miss Baxter.
First Boy: Wow! I feel sorry for you!

And he launched into a long tale of how "awful" Miss Baxter was. Finally, as he wound up his tale of horror, the third little boy spoke up.

Third Boy: Oh, that's all right, Jimmy. You'll get used to her!

And indeed, this seems to be true. Children seem able to adjust to almost anything if it stands still! There is no kind of personality that all teachers should have. Good teaching seems, rather, to be a matter of effective use of the teacher's unique personality. There will be as many methods of teaching as there are kinds of teachers.

People are used to believing that teachers know how to teach. They are inclined to follow the lead of the teacher in the process of learning. As a result, the way in which the teacher behaves and the things he believes important are quite likely to be regarded by his students as signposts pointing the way to those things which should be important to students as well. One has only to observe the ways in which students seek to outguess the teacher on the final exam. They try in every way possible to discover what he wants, then try their best to give it to him. What the teacher believes to be important has an inevitable effect upon his own behavior and hence upon the behavior of students. Teachers reveal what they believe is important in spite of themselves. The teacher who does not feel the importance of helping students explore personal meaning will almost certainly not encourage his students to do so.

Whether teachers are aware of it or not, their behavior and their effectiveness as teachers depend upon their perceptions about themselves and the situations within which they are involved; particularly upon their beliefs, values, and convictions. Some years ago one of the authors was taken on a tour of a new school building by its proud principal. He was taken to see the shops, the bus-loading docks, the three gymnasiums, the cafeteria, the swimming pool, the public-address system; even the school's own barbershop for rural children. Finally, he was brought back to the principal's office without ever having been shown a classroom. When he pointed this out, the principal apologized for his oversight and called his secretary to lead the author to a classroom in operation. It was clear from his behavior what aspect of his job seemed most important to him! This was further illustrated a short time later when a little boy was brought to the office by a bus driver, who entered with the boy in one hand and the broken arm from one of the bus seats in the other. On the way to school the youngsters on the bus had begun pushing each other. This child had been pushed against a seat arm and had broken it. Now, knowing what we do about this principal's values, it does not take a psychologist to predict how he would behave toward this child! It is a foregone conclusion that he would be very angry—and that is exactly what happened. The principal behaved as though the boy had broken the principal's arm, and in a sense, the child had!

Effective teaching depends upon teacher perceptions. In particular, it depends upon the kinds of perceptions they possess about these things:

1. What people are like
2. The goals and purposes of education in our society
3. The adequacy of the teacher's own personality
4. Effective methods of encouraging learning.

WHAT PEOPLE ARE LIKE

When doctors believed that illness was the result of bad blood, many a defenseless invalid was bled to death. Teachers, too, can make less serious but no less certain mistakes in dealing with people, when the ideas they hold about their charges are false or inaccurate. Effective behavior can only be predicated upon accurate beliefs about the nature of human behavior. The beliefs teachers hold about what their students are like and why they behave as they do define the teachers' own relationships to them. It has been the purpose of this book to set forth one approach to understanding the nature of human behavior. Since education is, in a very real sense, applied psychology, it is our belief that every principle about people and their behavior we have stated in this volume has important meanings for educational practice. We obviously cannot explore all of these here. Let us, however, examine just two of the more obvious implications for teacher behavior growing out of the basic concept that behavior is a function of perception.

Teachers who understand that behavior is caused by present perceptions behave quite differently from those who believe that the causes of behavior lie primarily in the student's past. Teachers who see people's behavior as solely the product of history, for example, will need to acquire vast quantities of information and records about their student's lives. They are likely to judge pupils' capacities on the basis of previous performance and establish expectancies for them at similar levels. The students they face may be seen as already immutably fixed in capacity and the teacher's own contribution as comparatively minor and trivial. Seeing behavior as primarily produced by the influence of others, they are quite likely to demand coöperation of parents and to complain bitterly about parents who do not or cannot respond "properly." Too strong a belief in such a concept of causation may even result in disillusion and discouragement, for if the causes of behavior all lie in the past, the teacher's present role becomes unimportant and of little consequence. One advantage of such a belief, however, is that it provides fine excuses for teacher failure. After all, if behavior is caused by past history, a student's failures are the result of what other people have done before the present teacher got him and teachers can bury their failures by explaining, "What can you do with a child from a home like that?"

On the other hand, teachers who see behavior as the product of present perceptions will behave quite differently. They will need less detailed and extensive information about their students' pasts and will be much more concerned with understanding their students as they are. For many teachers it will come as a great relief that they do not *have* to be amateur psychiatrists to carry on their jobs successfully. Seeing behavior as a function of perception makes human capacities much more amenable to change or modification, and the possibilities for education become immensely greater. Since perceptions are open to modification, there is hope for change and wider horizons for personal growth. Teachers are far less limited in what they can hope to accomplish with a particular student, and the role of the teacher is seen as a much more important one in human affairs. Seeing behavior this way, there is less need to feel discouraged or disillusioned and the possibilities for affecting human growth and development become far more exciting and challenging.

Teachers who see behavior as a function of the forces exerted on students will be led to seek ways of forcing and coercing their charges toward desirable goals. They will value "fencing-in" methods of guiding learning and techniques of reward and punishment. Argument and the weight of evidence will play a large part in their approaches to learning while emotion and feeling will probably be seen as disrupting and extraneous aspects of behavior having little to do with learning. Believing that people respond on the basis of the stimuli to which they are exposed, they must put much emphasis upon authority in their teaching, for someone will have to know where the students *should* go. Teachers who believe this way about human behavior will be heard making such statements as: "I told them . . . ," "I've got to get them to . . . ," or "You must make them see. . . ." Their concepts of "leadership" and "guidance" will often turn out on closer examination to be subtle techniques of coercion aimed at getting people to do what someone has already decided in advance "should" be done. Carried to an extreme, such a way of seeing behavior may even result in seeing students as things to be molded in some preconceived image rather than as independent people.

In contrast, teachers who see behavior as a function of perception are more likely to see themselves as "helpers" than "makers," and their stu-

dents as dynamic and growing rather than objects to be manipulated.
They are likely to value the process of learning as well as the product
and to see themselves as assisters and facilitators in a normal stream of
development. Students will be seen not as objects to do things to, but as
people to interact with. Recognizing "feeling" as a kind of perception,
attitudes and emotions, beliefs and conviction will play a much larger
part in the business of teaching. The perceptual view leads teachers to
be less concerned with reward and punishment and much more concerned with the motivational values of interest, challenge, and the creation of "new needs to know." Their speech will include much less of "I"
and "you" and much more of "we" and "us." They will be more concerned with experience and less with telling, with questions and problems rather than answers and dicta. They will see their own roles as
freeing and stimulating rather than directing and coercing. They will
value more highly discussion, doubt, and uncertainty. Teachers who understand behavior as a product of perception will seek to understand
their students as well as the subject, and the probability is that when
they see their students as people, their students will return the compliment.

Whatever we believe is so has its inevitable consequences upon behavior. What teachers believe about people and their behavior must of
necessity affect the ways in which they behave as educators. Effective
teaching requires an accurate and realistic concept of the nature of
human beings and the ways in which they grow and develop. The more
accurate and useful the teacher's understandings, the more likely he is
to behave effectively and efficiently. Some teachers develop such understandings as a result of experience and observation; others acquire their
understandings from more formal educational experiences; but wherever
they acquire them, no teacher is without them. Whether he is aware of
the fact or not, every teacher's behavior is a direct outgrowth of his
beliefs about what people are like. Accurate beliefs make possible effective teaching and satisfying experiences with education. Poor teachers
unhappily remain the victims of their false perceptions.

THE CLARITY OF TEACHER GOALS AND PURPOSES

Behavior, we have seen, is never without purpose. The goals and
values people hold have inevitable effects upon the ways in which they
behave. How teachers teach is likewise affected by the particular values
they espouse. Teachers who feel it is important to have a noiseless class-

room will behave quite differently from teachers who believe it important that children be active. A belief that democracy requires every decision be made by the entire group will cause teachers who feel "democratic" teaching is important to emphasize group decisions. On the other hand, teachers who believe democracy is "treating everyone alike" may decry group decisions and establish common standards for everyone. No one can escape the consequences of his own beliefs, and teachers are no exception. The effectiveness of teaching then will be dependent in part upon the kinds of goals and purposes the teacher has differentiated in his phenomenal field and which thereafter serve as the producers of his behavior. To complicate matters further, society expects teachers to have adopted and to be motivated by many of society's values as well. This is fine so long as the teacher's values and those of society are similar. When society's values are different from those of the teacher or when society's values are unclear, teachers have a difficult task to find effective anchors for their own behavior in the classroom.

When teacher values are clear, teacher behavior is similarly clear and direct. When teacher purposes are fuzzy, confused, or vague the teacher's behavior is likewise confused and inexact. When teachers are frustrated and tense, it is almost never because they do not have a grasp of their subject matter. When teachers fail it is far more likely to be the result of a lack of clarity in their own perceptions about what is important. When people are vague about what is important, behavior lacks direction and purpose. If such vagueness is long continued, a vicious circle of frustration and tension may be set up somewhat like this: the teacher is unclear about what is important, so everything that happens in his classroom must be seen as important! Important things cannot be ignored or overlooked; they must be dealt with. So the teacher deals with everything. Other people seeing him deal with everything are likely to assume that is how it should be, or how he wants it, and therefore expect him to deal with everything. This expectancy only adds to the teacher's pressures, and he may soon find himself so busy he has *no time to think about what is important!* So it is that the teacher who has not clarified his beliefs may become the victim of his own indecision and kept so busy dealing with crises that he has not time to discover what is really important.

The teacher without clear values is in the same position as a friend of ours who operated a small machine shop. His company was repeatedly approached by large manufacturers to make small items they needed for their assembly lines. Many of these contracts were so "juicy" that our friend accepted them even though the plant did not have the necessary machines to make the items. Having accepted the contracts, he then rushed out to acquire the tools to make them. After this had happened a few times and the contracted items had been delivered, his company found itself with large, expensive machine tools that had to be kept running. To keep these machines running the manager had to rustle up new contracts and soon found himself constantly on the road desperately scouting the country for new contracts to keep his machines operating. The contracts that had seemed so promising produced a Frankenstein. The shop had been "tooled up" with so little direction and purpose that management was kept frantically racing about trying to keep a wide variety of unrelated operations going. It was not until the owner collapsed in exhaustion and spent months in the hospital that he had time to think about his plant's directions and purposes and develop some guides to when to say "yes" and when to say "no." In a similar fashion teachers without clear purposes may find themselves "tooled up" for such conflicting ends and values as to defeat their own purposes.

Teaching, as we have said, is a relationship, but there can be no relationship with a nonentity. Teachers must stand for something. Confused purposes lead the teacher to such inconsistent behavior that students are unable to discover where he stands, what he believes, or even what it is he wants of them. Under such treatment students can find no clear guides for their own behavior. If such confusion is long continued students may come to feel frightened and anxious and will then seek to avoid or defend themselves against the teaching relationship in whatever ways seem possible. Thus the teacher's own confusions are conveyed to his students. Without clear purposes the teacher may destroy the very relationship essential to effective teaching.

The discovery of clear values and purposes is not always easy. Some teachers do not even make the effort, but nobody behaves without them. Having adopted, either knowingly or unknowingly, a set of values and purposes usually acquired from their own experience as students, some teachers proceed forever after to behave unswervingly in terms of those purposes even when they may be grossly inefficient. This is what often happens with the college teacher who acquires his Ph.D. in the study of a particular subject and assumes that "anyone can teach" and the sole purpose of teaching is "to get his subject across." His narrow view of purpose makes him dull and uninspired and may defeat the very goals of education. At the opposite extreme are those teachers whose search for goals and purposes is so confused and vacillating that they are like will-o'-the-wisps blown helter-skelter from fad to fad. They never light long enough in one spot to permit the development of any sort of comfortable relationship with students.

The discovery of stable values and purposes is further confused by the fact that the society which the teacher represents is itself sometimes confused. Societies, like everything else we know, are subject to change, and this change is reflected in the institutions designed to serve social goals. During the time such changes are coming about there is likely to be a period in which values and purposes become confused as varying segments of the population pull and haul in one direction or another. Sometimes this is the result of old purposes being called into question and new ones set in their place, as when several generations ago we decided to educate not just an elite, but everyone. Such a profound shift in purpose is necessarily attended by a good deal of confusion as more and more people come to appreciate the full significance of the idea and readjust other values and purposes to conform to this decision. Sometimes, too, the shift in social purpose may be the product of new needs arising out of new problems for society, as illustrated in our current need for ever greater numbers of highly skilled scientists and engineers, a need which has placed new demands upon our schools and necessitated new thinking about purposes and values.

Other shifts and changes of purpose are going on in our society with respect to such questions as: How much of an individual's development shall education be charged with? What is the responsibility of home and school? Of church and school? Shall schools seek to indoctrinate a given way of life or promote the seeking for better ways? Shall schooling be general, cultural, specific, or practical? In addition, there are the vast questions posed by the nature of our ideals themselves and the changes in our thinking with respect to them as we slowly learn to translate the essence of the democratic ideal into practice. These are but a few of the questions about purposes teachers must settle each for himself.

The goals and purposes of the teacher will be translated into behavior in dealing with students. When these goals are consistent with the nature of human beings and with the purposes of our society, teaching is likely to be effective and efficient. This will be true whether teachers are able to state their purposes clearly and precisely to others or not. Beliefs continue to affect our behavior even though we may be unwilling or unable to state them clearly to other people. Some teachers discover their goals and values by a kind of psychological osmosis as a product of their own experience and never clearly brought into figure or symbolized in words. Others have arrived at their beliefs as the product of study and discussion on a more precise and "formal" level of operation. Whether teacher purposes are clear or vague, implicit or explicit, however, they inescapably affect the ways in which teachers behave and determine in large measure the success or failure of the teacher's efforts.

THE TEACHER'S PERCEPTIONS OF SELF AND ROLE

A third factor governing the success of the teacher has to do with the teacher's own concept of himself and of his role as a teacher. How a teacher behaves in the classroom depends not only on how he sees his students and the situation in which he is involved, but also, upon how the teacher sees himself. Like everyone else, teachers are seeking personal adequacy and their behavior will be deeply affected by the degree of adequacy they have achieved. Students are responsive to teachers' personalities and there is much evidence to show that well-adjusted teachers produce better-adjusted students while poorly adjusted teachers have negative effects upon those they teach.

We have already discussed the adequate personality in another chapter. Generally speaking, the characteristics of the adequate personality are also the characteristics likely to produce a mature, effective teacher. Such characteristics as seeing oneself positively, the capacity for acceptance of self and others, and a high degree of identification with others are just as much desirable qualities of effective teachers as they are of effective personalities. In very large measure, effective teaching is a process of sharing self with others. Inadequate personalities find this very difficult to do. The ability to involve and to share self with others is highly dependent upon the individual's own feelings of his personal adequacy.

Setting the stage for the effective exploration of meaning requires that teachers demonstrate by their own behavior that this is the road to learning. To set such an example requires that the teacher himself be unafraid to make such explorations. He must show that he has the courage to look at himself and his beliefs without being defensive. He must be willing to explore his own perceptions just as he seeks to have his students explore theirs without fear, hesitation, or embarrassment.

He must show by his own behavior that he believes the search for meaning is profitable, exciting, and worth the effort. He cannot do this solely by exploring his students; he must permit his students to explore themselves and the teacher as well.

In addition to the general feeling of adequacy a teacher has about himself as a person, his behavior will be a function of much more specific concepts he may hold about himself as a teacher. Teachers who see their fundamental role as one of judging or evaluating students will behave quite differently from teachers who see themselves as friendly representatives of society. Similarly, the behavior of teachers will vary widely depending upon whether they see their role as one of telling or of helping to explore, as requiring control or effecting release. Some teachers see their task broadly as having responsibilities in all aspects of a child's life while others see their functions as related only to the imparting of a particular group of ideas or concepts. Whatever the role perceived by the teacher, it plays its part in producing the teacher's behavior and determines in large measure the kinds of results he gets.

Modern teacher-training institutions have recognized this close relationship between what the teacher thinks and believes and his behavior in the classroom. As a result many training programs now emphasize techniques of group discussion and individual participation in an attempt to help student teachers explore and discover themselves and their roles in the teaching process. They have recognized that the adequate teacher is more than a technician; he is a kind of personality. The teaching of subject matter, they have found, is comparatively simple. Helping student teachers discover themselves as people and as educators is a much more difficult task, involving the student's own exploration of himself as an instrument for helping people to learn.

THE PERSONAL DISCOVERY OF ADEQUATE METHODS

The achievement of understanding of the nature of people and of the goals and purposes of education, and the development of personal adequacy are all essential to effective teaching but not enough. Good teaching is also a professional matter involving the ability to utilize effective methods of teaching. Many of these methods may be no more than good human relationships that are the common property of anyone, and to the extent that good teaching involves no more than these, it is indeed true that "anybody can teach." Other techniques of teaching call for specialized kinds of experience less likely to be found in everyday life.

Some people learn these as a result of their own experience, some from special training. Some never learn at all. Regardless of where and how it is learned, however, (effective teaching is dependent upon the teacher's skill in the use of effective methods.)

Psychologists and educators often argue loud and long over "good" methods and "bad" methods of dealing with people, as though the methods we use to deal with people could be judged separate and apart from the people who used them. This emphasis upon "methods" as goals of behavior has sometimes led to unfortunate results. A generation ago, for example, many child psychologists deplored the spanking of children as evil and destructive. As a consequence many parents, who knew no other means of helping a child to learn, felt frustrated and helpless in the face of their child's misbehavior. If they spanked the child in spite of such teaching, they were no better off, for then they were saddled with the guilt of being "bad" parents. Similarly, there is a good deal of discussion in educational circles these days over the question of "homogeneous or heterogeneous grouping," by which is meant whether children of similiar characteristics should be grouped together or whether classes should include children of widely differing abilities. Advocates of one or the other of these methods have sometimes behaved as though the methods themselves were "good" or "bad." No method, however, is one or the other except in relationship to the three factors we have been discussing above, namely, the nature of the student, the purposes of the teacher and schools, and the personality of the teacher himself. A "good" method employed by a teacher who is unable to use it effectively may be a very "bad" method for student and teacher alike. If a teacher cannot deal effectively with wide differences in his classroom, it is probably better that he be given a homogeneous group of students with less variability than that he be left floundering with a heterogeneous group he cannot cope with. Even a good method is only good if people can use it effectively. Insistence upon a "good" method for people who do not understand it or cannot use it may even have a negative effect by undermining the teacher's self respect and confidence to operate as a teacher at all!

Methods of teaching are individual matters closely related to the personality of the teacher who uses them. What works for one teacher may not work at all for another. The kind of clothes we wear seem to us to fit our particular selves. We feel awkward and uneasy in someone else's clothes and the probability is that we do not look well either. In the same way, the methods some teachers use successfully fail miserably for others. A stimulating and inspiring lecturer whom we know is a complete dud in trying to operate a discussion group, while another friend of ours is exactly the reverse. Some teachers can joke and play with their students and do so naturally and effectively. Other teachers are more serious and remote from students and they too get excellent results. It is apparent that teachers need methods; it is also apparent that there can be no such thing as *the method* of teaching. Effective teaching requires the sensitive use of a human personality as an instrument for assisting other people to new experience and new discovery. It must always be a highly unique and individual matter.

CHAPTER 19

The Personal Approach to Treatment

THERE was a time when society could afford to ignore its inadequate personalities. They could be written off the books with hardly a second thought. But no more! The kind of interdependent society we live in cannot afford maladjusted, unhappy people. The very existence of desperate, inadequate, defeated people in today's world is a drag and a burden on the rest of us. Their presence in large numbers may even prove to be destructive of the institutions and values we hold most dear. These are practical reasons for concern about inadequate, unhappy personalities. But even if these practical considerations did not exist it would still be important to provide help for them on purely humanitarian grounds.

WHO NEEDS HELP?

The world we have created is often bewildering and complex. Few of us are so completely secure as to be immune from the possibility of suffering a more or less severe period of inadequacy at some time in our lives. No one is so strong as to be completely above such eventualities. Subjected to the proper combination of unhappy circumstances there is almost nothing which we might not do. Any one of us, on occasion, may find that our concepts of ourselves, for one reason or another, are no longer adequate to assist us in achieving optimal need satisfaction. In any of the ways we have discussed in Chapter 9, we may become threatened or inadequate personalities. Given time, most of us are able to achieve a reorganization of self and so return to greater harmony with the world we live in. Fortunately, most of our difficulties are minor or temporary and we shortly regain our equilibrium.

Some people, however, may be unable to arrive at new definitions of self so readily and may continue for long periods to be threatened, ineffective, and unhappy. We might take the position that society has often taken with these people in past generations and ignore them, quarantine them, or kill them off. But to do so is to lose their potential value for society and requires great waste of time, energy, and expense, while still more persons are removed from productivity to take care of those who are deeply inadequate. A much better and certainly more humane approach is to help threatened people to new and more adequate definitions of themselves which will make it possible for them to live effectively and productively in the social system. To provide such help we need persons with deep understanding of human behavior, who are trained in methods of assisting inadequate persons to a better life. People have been helping each other in one form or another ever since the dawn of man. In this sense psychological treatment has been carried on more or less effectively as a part of the functions of teachers, parents, and the clergy for hundreds of years. More recently, we have seen the development of a number of helping professions which employ professional counselors and therapists under such varied names as: counselor, guidance worker, psychiatrist, social worker, school psychologist, visiting teacher, play therapist, and family consultant, to name but a few.

In practice, counselors, psychotherapists, teachers, social workers, and others engaged in the "helping" professions are called upon to assist several types of threatened personalities. Sometimes threatened persons themselves will ask for aid. They may be so inadequate that they are perceived by outsiders as needing treatment or they may be unhappy and ineffective personalities whom society does not recognize as problems at all. Sometimes the therapist may need to deal with persons about whom society is concerned, but who themselves may or may not feel the need for assistance. This latter class will include a great many children who are unaware of the possibilities of any other life than that which they are leading. It will include, as well, those persons so limited in the development of an adequate self as to be unable to seek therapeutic assistance on their own initiative. Treatment methods must be capable of assisting each of these groups of threatened personalities as effectively and as economically as possible.

What Is Psychotherapy?

THERAPY DEFINED

We have seen that human beings are constantly, insatiably striving for ever greater adequacy. Sometimes, however, the organism is blocked in its striving by internal or external factors which prevent maximum achievement of this end. Such blocking may occur either in physiological or psychological terms. For example, the organism's need to maintain organization may be blocked physiologically by a germ, an injury, or impairment of its function due to aging, malnutrition, or the like. Psychologically, such blocks appear to be due to failures of differentiation, particularly those involving the self. The new field of psychosomatics is demonstrating that there are even physical effects of psychologic blocking, and vice versa. Since the need to maintain organization is all-pervading, the organism not only can but must move toward health if it is free to do so. It is this freeing of the organism to move toward health with which therapy of any sort is concerned. We might define therapy as follows: *Therapy is the provision of a facilitating situation wherein the normal drive of the organism for adequacy is freed to operate.* In medical therapy the physician or surgeon provides this "therapeutic situation" by eliminating or inhibiting the blocking factor, or by building up the organism itself so that it may operate as efficiently as possible. We shall find this definition describes the process in psychotherapy as well.

PSYCHOTHERAPY DEFINED

Psychotherapy is that branch of behavioral science concerned primarily with behavioral adjustment. Like all other therapies, it too is directed toward freeing the individual to operate effectively. Psychologically, the threatened person's need is impeded, not by physical obstacles but by inadequate differentiations of people, events, ideas, and concepts. The individual's satisfaction of need is blocked when for one reason or another his concepts of himself and his perceptions of the world about him are inadequate to make effective need satisfaction possible. We might define psychotherapy therefore, as follows: *Psychotherapy is a relationship consciously and carefully designed to assist persons to an exploration of themselves and the world in which they live so that they may arrive at new and more adequate relationships between themselves and the world in which they operate.*

The goal of treatment is the development of more adequate personalities, of individuals having personal worth and value. This goal of treatment is also the basic need of the individual. This makes treatment a coöperative project in which a client seeks for greater adequacy and personal worth and his therapist helps him to achieve it. Adequacy and personal worth are not things that can be *given* to people, they can only be achieved. Consequently, modern psychotherapy is not a battle be-tween an all-knowing therapist and a perverse, unwilling client; it is a process of assisting, helping, or facilitating the normal capacities of the individual for perceiving and differentiating. Although the goals of client and therapist are alike, it should not be supposed that psycho-therapy is easy or entirely pleasant. It may be the most difficult and painful experience of one's life. I have often felt that my clients in coun-seling are among the bravest people I have known. It is not easy to re-organize self, but the dividends may be very great.

How Psychotherapy Differs from Other Helping Relationships

The problems of human beings are the just concern of so many groups and agencies that it seems unlikely that psychological treatment can ever be made the exclusive perogative of any one. Psychotherapy is a human relationship, and human relations are engaged in by everyone. Aiding people to change perceptions is everybody's business in a sense, and the only excuse for a professional therapist is the presumption that because of special training, understanding, or skill he can help more effectively than most. Professional treatment differs from other helping relationships in three respects: (1) The ordered purposeful character of the therapeutic situation, (2) the intensity of the relationship, and (3) the data with which it is concerned.

THE DISCIPLINED CHARACTER OF THERAPY

Many human relationships we experience in our daily lives help us to explore and discover new meanings about ourselves and the world we live in. Even the most casual kinds of human contacts may serve to effect important changes in our ways of perceiving. Most of these ordi-nary interactions involve two or more people, each seeking to satisfy his own need. This is what happens at a tea, where each person stands about enhancing himself in a polite sort of way, chatting about one thing or another, seeking to capture the interest of other people, then waiting more or less patiently while someone else seeks enhancement so he can get back in the game again. Similar interactions occur over the card table or the back fence, in "bull sessions" or casual conversa-tions among friends in a thousand different settings. Each of these relationships provides the participants with important means of achieving enhancement of self.

The methods used by psychotherapists to aid their clients cover a vast range. Indeed, we know that almost *any* method will *sometimes* work with *some* people. Every now and then some new method of treatment bursts upon the public scene, attracting much attention and often heralded as the new panacea for all man's ills. These usually begin from some accidental discovery that a particular method worked effectively with several people, and thereafter the method is avidly tried by many others. Most of these unhappy persons are destined to be disappointed, but a few find the methods successful and their testimonials add to the prestige of the new approach. Success of the method may sometimes be quite phenomenal if enough people *begin to believe they will be helped*. Physicians are well aware that even some "physical" ills disappear when the patient believes strongly enough in the efficacy of the aspirin tablet his doctor prescribes for him.

It is not enough for the counselor to possess an armamentarium of methods that have worked in the past. Psychotherapy must be a precise, predictable process if human beings are to be helped in more than hit-or-miss fashion. Effective therapy must be predicated upon some underlying conception of the nature of human behavior, and its methods must be intimately related to those understandings. Modern psychotherapy is based upon the best understandings we are able to arrive at with respect to: (a) the nature of human beings and their behavior, (b) the nature and goals of the helping process, (c) tested methods of treatment, and (d) the nature and personality of the therapist himself. Each of these four variables of the therapeutic process has been given much study in recent years, and as we are able to find clearer and clearer understandings of each of these factors, modern psychotherapy has become a more and more precise and predictable process. Not all behavioral scientists see human behavior in exactly the same way. As a consequence a number of different "schools" of psychotherapy have grown up in recent years, each dependent upon its own interpretation of the four factors we have indicated above. Some of these have remained for long periods. Others have developed quickly and almost as quickly disappeared from the scene as they turned out to be based on fortuitous rather than predictable processes. Although the science of psychotherapy is new, we are nevertheless finding more and more effective ways of creating predictable and efficient helping relationships.

THE INTENSITY OF THE THERAPEUTIC RELATIONSHIP

Therapy differs from more casual relationships in concentrating upon only one of the members involved. The purpose of treatment is to help the client, and this requires that the counselor, teacher, or therapist subjugate his own immediate goals in the interest of his client, student, or counselee. This is not to say that the process provides no enhancement for the therapist. On the contrary, therapy has sometimes been facetiously defined as a situation in which "two people help each other." Therapists, of course, cannot suspend the universal action of the basic need to achieve maintenance and enhancement. Successful counseling is, itself, an enhancing experience for the counselor.

Fundamentally, psychological treatment consists in the provision of a good, helping, human relationship specially designed and concentrated for the peculiar requirements of a particular human being. Although there exist numerous schools of thought about how treatment ought to be done, and although each philosophy has developed its own concepts of what are appropriate and inappropriate methods of working with clients, all approaches seek to provide a good human relationship in one form or another. An interesting study by Fiedler found that experienced psychotherapists from different schools were more often in agreement about what constituted a "good" counseling relationship than were beginning-therapy students and experts from the same school of thought. This finding would seem to suggest that there is a "good" therapeutic relationship and that this relationship is arrived at by many therapists as a matter of experience irrespective of what school of thought they were trained in. Furthermore, in the same experiment, Fiedler found that "the man in the street," when asked to tell what he thought would be an ideal therapeutic relationship, described it in about the same terms as the "experts"! This would seem to imply that a good therapeutic relationship is not a magic quality, the exclusive prerogative of a specially trained few, but the crystallized, concentrated application of the best we know about a helping relationship for the assistance of a particular person in difficulty. This is usually not very different from what is good for any other individual but is provided for the patient with greater intensity and with particular reference to his peculiar need. It is not that people in psychological distress need a *different* kind of relationship, but rather that they need *more* of a *good* relationship than those who have less need for help.

THE DEPTH OF TREATMENT

Psychotherapy also differs from ordinary human relationships in the depth with which it is concerned. Earlier in this book we have seen that behavior is affected in the degree to which an individual discovers the personal meaning for him of any information, idea, concept, or experience. We have seen that the closer an event is perceived to the self, the more intense will be the individual's experience. The effective achievement of adequacy may require of the individual new perceptions at any point on this relationship scale. What is meant by "depth" in psychotherapy is simply the point on this continuum at which treatment is operating. The closer the exploration of the perceptual field to the self, the "deeper" the therapy. Depth of therapy is synonymous with personal reference or personal meaning.

We might think of all the data which a person needs in order to make an adjustment as lying upon a continuum stretching from information having a great deal of relationship to self at the center of the perceptual field, to information having little or no relationship to self at the outer edge (X to Y, Fig. 25). In order to live effectively in our society an individual will need to have information or data existing at all points along the continuum. Information at the extreme not-self end of the continuum has little or no effect upon behavior. This is the kind of information which bombards us every day and which passes in one ear and out the other.

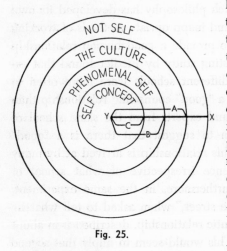

Fig. 25.

Data from the outside world and from the accumulated culture of our society, however, have a more important relationship to self. Here we need to discover the relationship to ourselves of the concepts and values accumulated by mankind in the course of his history. This traditionally is the primary task of education (section A, Fig. 25). It has the broad responsibility for helping the individual to develop an effective and satisfying relationship with the world around him.

Closer to the center of the perceptual field, people need to develop effective relationships with other people. These relationships are much closer to the core of self (section *B*, Fig. 25). Perceptions in this area have to do with the phenomenal self and the relationship of the individual to those people important to him. This is the area of the perceptual field of particular concern to group therapy.

Finally, at the very center of the perceptual field is the area of individual therapy (section *C*, Fig. 25). In this area the client is primarily concerned with discovering himself. The function of individual therapy is to assist the client to explore those very personal aspects of self involved in his self concept, values, ideals, etc.

Seen in this light, depth of therapy is a function of the personal character of the data under consideration. Education, group therapy, and individual therapy all deal with the perceptual field. Each attempts to aid the individual to explore the self and his relationships and varies from the others only in the area of its major concern. This is perhaps the most important distinction between psychotherapy and the functions of other agencies in assisting people to better adjustment. Therapy is only a more personal kind of exploration of the relationship of self to the external world. There are no clear-cut distinctions between individual therapy, group therapy, and education. These three kinds of adjustive experiences blend almost indistinguishably from one to another, differing only in emphasis. It must be clear from this analysis that therapy can never become the exclusive property of any profession. There can be no such thing as *the* psychotherapy. Psychotherapy is a "more or less" rather than an "all or none" activity in which many people in many professions engage in greater or lesser degree.

All therapies of whatever sort must affect human perceptions if they are to produce changes in behavior. The principles of perceptual psychology we have been exploring in this book will be found operating in whatever kind of psychotherapy we wish to examine. All methods of treatment will have a greater or lesser degree of consistency with our perceptual frame of reference. This will be true of much of psychoanalysis. It will be true also of the kinds of therapy advocated by such writers as Horney, Sullivan, Allen, May, Fromm, and many others. Perhaps most directly related to the views we have explored in this book, however, is the client-centered approach to treatment developed by Carl Rogers and his students. Indeed, so consistent is this view of therapy with the principles of perceptual psychology that, had it not developed prior to this frame of reference, it would certainly have had to be invented as an application of a perceptual view. The interested reader will find himself quickly at home in this field and a more detailed consideration of perceptual therapy can be found in many of the publications of client-centered counselors listed in the bibliography. In the remainder of this chapter we will confine ourselves to a few broad principles affecting the philosophy and practices of treatment growing out of a perceptual approach to behavior.

The Place of "Knowledge" in Treatment

We have seen in our discussion of the educational implications of a perceptual frame of reference that there may be a considerable disparity between what a person knows and what he does. Most so-called "maladjusted" behavior is not due to the fact that we do not know any better but that at the moment of action we *needed* to behave as we did. Not long ago I drove my car through a red light. Now, I am well aware that I should not go through red lights, but I did. Why did I? Because I was in a hurry to keep an appointment—I *needed* to behave as I did. Indeed, it wasn't until I had gone three blocks past the light that I was even aware of what I had done. My behavior was not a matter of not knowing, but of being unable to accept the perception at the moment of my action. The red light was perceived in the not-self portion of the phenomenal field because, had it been perceived as related to self, it would have been threatening to my satisfaction of need. Had I been able to perceive the red light as contributing to my need satisfaction, I would have stopped.

Knowledge is useful only if it is perceived as contributing to need satisfaction. It is even possible that some knowledge may place the threatened individual under greater threat than ever. Consequently, he will be driven to protect his existing organization and may, in the final analysis, be worse off than before. This serves to explain in some measure why it is that "telling people" is often violently resisted and may even result in increasing distress. Note how a client herself expresses this increased confusion from "telling" in the following excerpt:

CLIENT: You can think and think so long and you can try to talk yourself into things—you can tell yourself you are just timid, I talk myself out of it and philosophize and all that. I can forget for a while—for the time being—and then it comes back. Sometimes I feel so melancholy and then I tell myself I am just being self-centered, that there are many people worse off than I am. I might be blind for instance. I know it's silly to feel so badly about ordinary everyday things. It seems as though I should have control and not let things affect me so much. Maybe I'm not put together right—but I just can't. They told me I wasn't sociable enough with girls and ought to mingle with them more. And I try telling myself that is what I ought to do. But I can't seem to change myself that way—just by saying it to myself. It just makes more conflict inside and I don't have any satisfaction at all. (Pause) If by nature you're shy and retiring, you can work real hard and talk yourself into things sometimes and it may show on the outside but not on the inside. Then it hurts more than anything. Oh, I know psychology doesn't agree. It tells you a lot of things— they seem to think an individual can change and do anything he wants. I can't.

Somewhat later in counseling this client says:

CLIENT: They say when you know your faults and attack them—why you soon get over them. I've tried that for years but it's no good.
COUNSELOR: Mm hm.
CLIENT: It all sounds good in the books you read and the lectures you hear— but it doesn't work when you try to put it in practice. You just can't change a person to being boisterous and noisy when they are fundamentally shy. It can only be done on the outside. You can't force it on them, and I don't think you should. *It just makes a worse conflict than ever and that's all that remains—just the conflict.*

The meanings existing for the client must always be the major elements of concern in therapy, since it is change in these meanings that therapy is designed to foster. On the surface this seems like a very minor point, but it is amazing how often it has been overlooked in psychological and sociological treatment. It must always be recalled that client and therapist are operating in different frames of reference and what appears "good" to one may appear as exactly the opposite to the other. For example's sake, let us permit our imaginations to run freely for a moment and compare some common treatment techniques with what they *might* mean to the client:

TREATMENT TECHNIQUES	CLIENT MEANINGS
Telling a child to be good.	He thinks I'm bad!
Giving a needy client coal.	I can't support my family!
Warning a client to avoid daydreaming.	Good Lord! I'm going crazy!
Reassuring that "this is going to be all right."	He's afraid it isn't going to be all right.
Giving advice.	I can do that now—it's his responsibility—he told me to go ahead.
Foster-home placement.	They think my family is no good. Well, I'll show them guys!
Institutional placement.	I'm a real tough guy, I am. They gotta lock me up.

These seem like extreme examples, but unfortunately they often are not. The goal of therapy is to produce change in the client's meanings. Since behavior is a function of these meanings, therapy can only be successful if it produces a permanent change in meanings which will insure a consequent change in behavior.

To say that an individual in a severe psychological problem maintains his "maladjustment" because it gives him satisfaction is only partly true. It is not likely that he would enjoy and attempt to perpetuate this painful condition if he could perceive any better alternative. Rather, if he maintains his "maladjustment" it seems more likely that he does so because he *must* do so to maintain or enhance his phenomenal self in the situation as he sees it. Thus the client who says, "I know what I ought to do but I can't do it" is saying, in effect, that from a purely external or objective point of view, what he should do is clear, but from his own personal point of view his behavior is necessary to protect his organization. Knowledge can only contribute to need satisfaction if it is accepted into the individual's personal frame of reference. Therapy, to be successful, must produce some change in how people perceive. This is why treatment deals primarily with feelings, attitudes, convictions, and beliefs; what we sometimes call the "emotional" aspects of life. This is simply another way of saying that therapy is mainly concerned with those perceptions having a close and meaningful relationship to self. Successful therapy is rarely only a matter of helping people "know" better. Few of us misbehave because we do not know better. Like the farmer who told the county agent, "I ain't farmin' now half as well as I know how!" most of us already know far better than we behave. The problem of therapy is helping people explore their perceptions in such a way as to translate knowing into behaving. But how may this be done?

Two Kinds of Treatment

If the perceptual description of behavior we have outlined in this volume is accurate, it follows that all psychotherapy of whatever type must produce change in the client's perceptual field. Since change occurs through differentiation, to change behavior it will be necessary to bring about new differentiations either in the organization of the self concept or in the client's perception of the external world or both. This will be true whether we attempt (1) to assist a particular client to change his personal meanings by working with the client alone or (2) to induce a change in his field by changing his environment. Whether we work with the environment surrounding a client or with the client himself in a face-to-face situation our goal is the same. We hope to make possible new meanings in his perceptual field.

ENVIRONMENTAL TREATMENT

In Chapter 12 we described personal adequacy as a function of three things: (1) An essentially positive self concept, (2) a capacity for acceptance, and (3) a high degree of identification with others. Since therapy seeks to produce more adequate personalities, it follows that successful therapy must assist its clients to achieve a higher degree of these three characteristics than has been possible for them before. One of the ways in which this can be accomplished is by manipulating the environment in such a way that the individual is exposed to experiences from which he can learn to perceive himself in more positive ways, to be more accepting, or to identify more broadly with those about him.

Environmental therapy with children, for instance, often utilizes curriculum adjustment to make it possible for the child with feelings of failure and defeat to find success experiences. This gives him a new lease on his academic life, and he can then define himself and his abilities in more adequate terms. The same thing may be accomplished in foster-home placement. A child is removed from a home situation creating undesirable and harmful meanings to a foster home designed to produce different and more socially acceptable meanings in the youngster's perceptual field. Such methods are not confined to therapy. Families have been using environmental methods of dealing with children for ages. For instance, a certain family had tried for two years to get their 5-year-old to stop his persistent bed wetting but all to no avail. One evening while tucking in her son, the mother said "Son, when are you going to stop wetting the bed?"

The boy replied, "But Mom, I don't have to. I have a rubber sheet!" Once this meaning of the rubber sheet had been discovered, therapy was simple. Next day mother and son coöperated in making the bed and pointedly left off the sheet. And the child hasn't wet the bed since!

In environmental therapy the meaning changes we seek to bring about may be in the client's goals, his techniques, his self concept, his perceptions of others, or in all of these. In fact, it is probable that no change occurs in any one without some change in the others as well. Therapy on a goals-and-techniques level will often be all that is required to aid the threatened individual to more adequate behavior. Frequently it will be possible to assist the client to the differentiation of new goals and techniques which help him regain a feeling of adequacy and need satisfaction. So simple a measure as aiding an adolescent girl to discover more attractive methods of hair styling or helping an adolescent boy to a better understanding of the rudiments of etiquette in boy-girl relationships may go a long way toward helping them achieve greater feelings of adequacy and more effective behavior.

While many personality adjustments can be affected through change in the individual's goals and techniques, there is also danger that such a level of operation may be utilized when a more fundamental change is called for. Goals-and-techniques therapy is often palliative and, with the very threatened client, does not reduce the threat more than momentarily. With the self under threat in important ways, helping the individual only to the extent of discovering new goals and techniques may only result in making him dependent upon the therapist or, worse yet, cause him to feel he has not been helped at all. To help the man just out of prison to find a job may be only the beginning of therapy, yet, too often, it is as far as it ever gets. For deeply threatened personalities it is necessary that therapy aid clients to make fundamental changes in self organization. Sometimes this can be affected by environmental therapy, but unfortunately there are serious limits to this form of treatment.

LIMITATIONS OF ENVIRONMENTAL THERAPY

One of the most important of these limitations has to do with the varying worlds within which an individual moves. A growing child, for example, may be living in a number of cultural groups at once or in rapid succession, as illustrated in Fig. 26. His concept of himself, also, may have varying definitions with respect to each of the groups with which he comes in contact. In his earliest years, the child's self concept may be the result of his home experiences. The older he gets, however, the wider become the outside factors within which he moves as he passes from one cultural group to another. His self concept becomes defined with respect to his experience in these wider groups. At the same

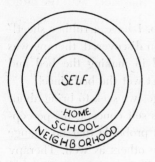

Fig. 26.

time, the possibility of producing changes in the external world to which
he is responding becomes increasingly more difficult. While it may be
possible for us to make some changes in small cultural groups, the amount
of change we can produce in larger ones becomes progressively less as
the size of the group increases. By the time an individual has reached
late adolescence, change in his external reality has become very nearly
impossible.

This principle is well illustrated in studies of foster-home placement.
Studies of this type of treatment are unanimous in their findings that the
earlier the child is placed, the more likely it is to be successful. Beyond the age of 9 or 10 such methods rapidly decrease in effectiveness.
Change in environment offers possibilities for helping children but seems
a distinctly limited and temporary measure for adolescents and adults.
It is a simple matter to remove candy from the neighborhood of a sick
child. The problems posed in removing alcohol from the environment
of an adult alcoholic, however, is a quite different matter!

Environmental therapy can operate effectively only when a subculture
to which the individual is responding is out of touch with a larger culture within which the individual is also behaving. For instance, it may
be useful and effective to remove a child from a family situation which
is in conflict with the demands of a larger social group. In this way the
child might be placed, let us say, in a foster home which was consistent
with the demands of the larger cultural group. But what about the situation wherein the child has a self concept considerably apart from both
larger and smaller groups in which he moves? This problem often
arises when delinquency of a child occurs in a middle-class family that
is not only well accepted in the community but intelligent and well
meaning in its attempts to do the right thing according to accepted
standards. In such a case the family is already consistent with the larger
cultural group definitions and the possibilities of environmental therapy
are extremely limited. The same situation often exists in the case of a
child with extremely severe feelings of jealousy and rejection, in a family
situation where every effort is made to help him feel wanted in the
family circle. Children often develop such feelings upon the arrival of a
baby brother or sister in the family group. The child is not rejected but
he thinks he is. Environmental treatment in a case of this kind is bound
to be extremely limited. It cannot remove the sibling, and to remove
the child from the home would only make matters worse. To send him

off to school or to camp, for instance, may appear to him as absolute proof of what he already believes!

The aim of all therapy of whatever type must be to aid the individual to a self concept adequate to deal with wider culture patterns in which he will move as an adult. What is more, the eventual goal of therapy must be to free the individual to operate on his own without the necessity for continuing manipulations of the world about him. A mature society cannot reorganize itself for each individual within its framework. Treatment must, in the long run, develop in the individual the ability to adjust to whatever happens; not protect him from the world in which he lives. Successful environmental treatment must contribute to a more positive view of self, to self acceptance and increased capacity for identification. Treatment which results in a degraded self, in failure of acceptance, or in feelings of rejection and isolation may temporarily solve some social problems but at a price, in the destruction of human potentialities, too great to afford. Much environmental treatment is little more than palliative, resulting in the temporary control of behavior so that it remains within socially tolerable limits, but may be accompanied by personal feelings of dependence and inadequacy that create still greater problems in the long run. Planning for environmental therapy must be done with a clear vision of the *meaning* of treatment measures in the perceptions of those they are applied to.

Individual Treatment Through Perception Change

As we have seen above, there are serious limitations upon the degree to which treatment can be accomplished by manipulation of the environment. Fortunately, we do not have to rely on this alone.. Perceptions can be affected and modified by change in environment. They can also be changed without reference to the environment at all. A great deal of the unhappiness and inadequacy suffered by people who seek treatment is the product of unfortunate perceptions of self and the world in which they live, and there is little or nothing to be contributed to the solution of their problems by environmental means. With a change in perceiving, however, they may be helped to achieve greater adequacy. They may even change their environments themselves!

It sometimes happens that people may be unwilling for one reason or another to change their environments. We are all familiar with the ostensibly simple solution "Well, if you don't like your job—quit!" But we are also aware that changing the situation is not so easy. It may even produce more problems than it settles. Many of our adjustments have to be made within ourselves in the perceptions we have of ourselves and the world we live in. This is well illustrated in the case of a woman the author once worked with. Mrs. Mabel Sargent was 38 years old and had been married about a year. For many years before her marriage she had nearly given up hope that she would ever find a suitable mate. Then Mr. Sargent appeared on the scene! He was handsome, a bachelor, only five years older than she and well able to support a wife. Best of all he fell deeply in love with Mabel, and they were married after a year's engagement. The only drawback to this picture was Mr. Sargent's 73-year-old mother. Mr. Sargent had lived with his mother all his life in the family homestead, and when the couple were married they moved in there. The elderly Mrs. Sargent resented her new daughter-in-law with a vicious and bitter fury that appeared when the two women were alone in the house. In the presence of others, it was expressed in subtle innuendo and cutting remarks having a quite different meaning for the uninformed hearer than for the wife at whom they were directed. The elder Mrs. Sargent seemed to all public eyes, and to her son as well, a paragon of grace and virtue, deeply fond of her new daughter-in-law. Poor Mabel, caught in this fix, could find no way out. She could not give up the man she had pined for so long, nor could she dispose of the old lady, although she carefully considered this alternative in the course of treatment! She could not even talk about her problem with her husband or friends, who thoroughly believed old Mrs. Sargent to be a gracious and kindly person. For a year Mabel sought vainly for a solution, becoming more and more distraught and physically ill over her insolvable dilemma. Finally, in therapy, she was helped to adjust to her problem by changing her perceptions of herself and the mother.

She came to see herself as a stronger, more adequate person than she had ever imagined and her mother-in-law as the pathetic, beaten, self-pitying old woman she truly was. With such changed perceptions she no longer felt so threatened and could even, on occasion, feel sorry for the elder Mrs. Sargent. Insteady of fighting her situation she learned to accept it, even though it was sometimes unpleasant. Instead of permitting her mother-in-law to drive her away, Mrs. Sargent decided she was a lot younger and would "just wait the old girl out!" These changes in perception made it possible to tolerate an admittedly bad situation so that despite the impossibility of changing the external scene, it was possible to live an effective and satisfying life.

Perceptions—The Data of Therapy

The emphasis of perceptual psychology upon an immediate rather than a historical understanding of the causation of behavior has important implications for treatment. When we believed behavior was exclusively a function of the forces exerted upon the individual, helping people through psychological treatment required that the therapist discover the nature of the forces which had produced his client's behavior. This often made it necessary for counselor and client to spend long hours probing into the client's past, "reliving" the experiences that had molded him in his present form. If it is true, however, that behavior is a function of perception, then it should be possible to assist people to better adjustment by helping them change their perceptions even if the counselor has no knowledge of the past. If perceptions can be changed, behavior must also change.

Once it was considered impossible to help a disturbed child without first producing changes in a child's parents. Psychotherapists, however, are now finding it possible to help children to new adjustment and happier lives even when there is little opportunity to make fundamental changes in family structure. Methods of play therapy, for example, dependent solely on assisting children to explore present perceptions of themselves and the world they live in, have produced startling results in helping disturbed youngsters.

The principle seems just as effective in therapy with adults. If people can be helped to change present perceptions it is often unnecessary to explore past experience. In my experience as a counselor over the past 20 years, I have often observed that the clients who spend most time exploring the past are almost exclusively from the upper-middle class. They have grown up in a generation deeply imbued with Freud's concept that behavior is the product of the things that have happened to us in the years of our growing up. As a consequence, they explore what they believe to be the causes of their behavior. Clients from lower socioeconomic groups who have had little opportunity to learn this theory of causation, talk very little about their pasts. Instead, they start right off to talk about their current perceptions expressed as feelings, attitudes, likes, and aversions. In the process of such exploration they often discover new ways of feeling or perceiving and their behavior changes accordingly, even though I often do not know the details of how they got into their current difficulty. People who spend most time exploring the past in counseling sooner or later come to a point where they say, "Well, this explains but it doesn't change," or "Now I know why I feel like I do but I still feel so!" If it is true that people behave according to present ways of seeing, then it follows that it should be possible to help them to better adjustment by changing present perceptions. Knowledge of the individual's past may be helpful in this. It is not always an essential. For many educators, psychologists, social workers, and psychiatrists this idea opens whole new avenues of approach to the problems of mental health.

PSYCHOLOGICAL TREATMENT AS PERCEPTION CHANGE

The man in the street sometimes sees psychotherapy as a terrifying relationship in which a client surrenders most of his dignity, and certainly all of his privacy, to an imposing Svengali who somehow rebuilds personality by trickery and guile. Even those less influenced by movie versions of therapy often think of it as a relationship in which an all-wise counselor advises or directs a client in trouble. This latter is the kind of relationship most of us have experienced in our visits to the physician. We are accustomed to taking our physical problems to the doctor, acquiescing more or less willingly in whatever diagnostic procedure he feels is necessary and attempting to carry out whatever treatment plan he devises for us. Physical conditions can often be observed by outsiders, but human perceptions are another matter. People's feelings, attitudes, and personal meanings lie inside the personality and are not open to direct observation. As a result the counselor-client relationship is quite different from that of doctor-patient. In the doctor-patient relationship it is the doctor who knows and the patient who does not, but in psychotherapy it is the client who perceives and the counselor who does not! The important data for psychological treatment are the perceptions of the client. To be successful, psychological treatment must produce some change in the client's perceptions of himself and the world in which he operates.

Whatever the frame of reference of the therapist, the production of change in behavior requires that therapy assist the client to make changes in his personal meanings. To do this effectively treatment methods must deal in one fashion or another with two basic problems:

(1) It must provide a situation which makes it possible for the client to explore his perceptions, and (2) it must assist the client in this process to the end that he may achieve a more adequate self organization as quickly and surely as possible.

THREAT COMPLICATES THERAPY

Persons seeking therapy are persons under threat. This feeling of threat is of extreme importance to the eventual adjustment of the individual and to therapy. The very existence of threat may prevent the maladjusted person from improving his position. For example, the housewife who cannot accept her roles as housekeeper, cook, nursemaid, laundress, and a hundred others, but conceives of herself as something quite different, finds herself constantly confronted by the hard realities of daily life. These are likely to appear to her expressly designed to frustrate and to force upon her the very facts from which she would prefer to escape. The pile of laundry reminds her that she is the laundress, mealtimes demand that she be cook, and baby's insistent wail may threaten her concept of herself to the point where any aspect of her daily life appears threatening and coercing beyond endurance.

Under threat and the necessity for self defense, the individual fails to differentiate clearly and accurately. His differentiations are likely to be false and misleading and provide no adequate basis for change. The maladjusted housewife we have mentioned above cannot see her tasks clearly. The woman next door who sells face powder at the local department store may appear to have a much better, more meaningful, and important task than her own. Feeling threatened by her daily tasks, it is difficult for her to accept them. Perceptions become distorted and differentiations become misleading or result in false conclusions. It becomes difficult or impossible to convince her that her job is important, meaningful, and dignified. The more threatened she feels, the more unlikely adequate differentiation becomes.

To be effective, therapy must aid its clients to deal with such threats. Many treatment failures are a direct outgrowth of the counselor's ineptitude in understanding and adjusting his behavior to his client's perceptions. It is common knowledge, for example, that "welfare cases" are often extremely unsympathetic and "downright ungrateful" to the social worker seeking to help them. With the best of intentions, the worker inquires into the home life of his client, discovers he needs coal, food, or assistance in finding a job. These "needs" he then seeks to satisfy often with no realization that this treatment may appear extremely threatening. For to the client they may appear only as invasions of his privacy, proof of his ineptitude in caring for his family, or a slur upon his manhood.

When ideas presented by the counselor are not consistent with the client's fundamental personality organization, they represent a threat and he can do nothing else but resist them. Mittelmann and Wolff have checked this experimentally. By measuring skin temperature of the client during psychoanalysis it could be observed that he showed no fear reactions until questions were posed which placed him in a threatened position. The same principle is put to work in the techniques of "lie detection." The stronger, more convincingly, threatening concepts are forced upon the client, the greater is the necessity for his resistance. Thus advice, persuasion, personal influence, suggestion, and other such counseling techniques may be readily effective when the advice or information given is consistent with the client's already existing phenomenal self. When they are not consistent, they are likely to be disturbing and may actually impede his progress by producing greater confusion or, worse still, force him into an even greater defense of his position.

It must be remembered that the organization which the client is attempting to maintain is a unique and *personal* organization which the counselor can probably never hope to know in its entirety. Even information which appears to the counselor to be complimentary to his client may actually be disturbing to his organization and resisted by him. To attack the client's organization in counseling is an extremely easy thing to do. Almost anyone is familiar in his own experience with counselor attacks expressed in such familiar phrases as:

"Now just a minute, young man . . ."
"Really, now, it's not as bad as all that."
"Look how many are worse off than you are."
"I've had more experience than you, son. Now take my advice."

or even:

"You're not so bad off—let me tell you about my experience!"

When people are threatened it is not always readily apparent to an outside observer. Many persons have learned through long experience to hide their feelings from others. Since early childhood most persons have been taught to be "gentlemen and ladies" and the threats they feel are not likely to be apparent upon casual observation. When threatened by a counselor, therefore, they are likely smilingly to agree with him and beat a hasty retreat, reserving their opinion of him and his methods for their friends and acquaintances. Or when threatened the client may find security in complete dependence on the counselor and take no responsibility himself.

To avoid attacking his client, the counselor must be possessed of a high degree of sensitivity to how things seem from his client's point of view. He must be able to perceive and forecast the effect of any action he takes from his client's point of view. This is not a task for an amateur. Even with long experience and great sensitivity on the part of the counselor, the best of therapists cannot always avoid such threats.

While it is of course possible to bring about changes in people's perceptions through force and coercion, we have seen in Chapter 9 that this is often an extremely hazardous and unpredictable approach. Most modern therapies attempt instead to create a situation which facilitates change in perception by removing the client from threat as much as practicable. This may be done in environmental therapy, for example, when a threatened child is placed in a secure foster home or when a mental patient is removed from the pressures which overwhelm him in daily life to the protection of a mental hospital. In individual treatment it may be accomplished by the relationship developed between client and counselor.

THE COUNSELING RELATIONSHIP

This relationship is not a trick but a human interaction between counselor and client (which makes possible the exploration of the client's perceptions and the discovery of new and more satisfying meanings of the self and the world.) By this relationship the counselor creates a situation in which his client can be temporarily freed from the hindering and restricting effect of threat. He attempts to provide his client with a kind of sheltered atmosphere in which he can be free to explore and examine even his most fearful and distressing perceptions without fear of censure or blame. This is a "special" kind of relationship designed to remove the client from the threats and frustrations of daily life. Here is how a young woman deeply fearful of men described her feeling to her counselor: "In here I can talk to you. But if I were to meet you in the hall, you would be just another man and I couldn't talk to you at all." And another client describes it so: "Well, I don't know what it is when I am in here, but here I feel that I can be perfectly honest with myself.

I don't have to put on an act." By making the relationship as non-threatening to his client as possible, the counselor thus makes it possible for the troubled client to drop his defenses and to explore his perceptions of self and the world with less necessity for avoidance, distortion, or self protection. By freeing the individual from threat, movement is made possible.

The relationship of therapy is created by much more than an absence of threat, however. It involves a very positive, active expression by the counselor of his own concern, understanding, and compassion which does more than free his client from threat. It actively supports and encourages him in the exploration of himself and his world. If treatment is very deep or intensive this relationship becomes a strong and personally meaningful experience for both counselor and client. To explore one's deepest, most personal self cannot be done on a superficial level or at arms' length. It requires that communication occur at the most fundamental and personal levels of "heart to heart" understanding. Depth psychotherapy is an intense, emotional, that is to say personally meaningful, experience. It is this "emotional" experience that makes possible the individual's exploration of his unique and private self.

How this therapeutic relationship is created between a counselor and his client will vary greatly depending upon the nature of the client and his problems and the understanding, skill, and personality of the therapist. Most therapists do not learn to create such atmospheres easily or quickly. Effective counseling relationships are learned for most people only through intense study and arduous self discipline.

The Exploration of Meaning

Having created a situation which permits the client to explore his perceptions freely, therapy must next assist the client to make this exploration and to arrive at new and more satisfying self definitions. Warm, permissive situations and secure relationships with a counselor make it possible to talk about one's deeper feelings but do not guarantee that such talk will occur. Having established a relationship which makes change possible, successful therapy still requires that some change take place in the individual's perceptions of himself and his world. This may be brought about by environmental methods in which the therapist attempts to expose his client to new experiences designed to give him new perceptions of himself and the world he lives in. The school psychologist, for example, does this when he places a child having difficulty with a particular teacher in another classroom where he will have an opportunity to work out a more satisfying relationship. Similar principles underlie the technique of foster-home placement, wherein a child is placed in a setting likely to produce more positive concepts of self.

In the face-to-face relationship of counseling, the therapist may attempt to help his client redefine self through the medium of language. To assure maximum help from the counseling period, it is necessary for the therapist to assist his client to explore those aspects of the phenomenal field most likely to be of assistance in helping him to reorganize his self concept. The counselor must aid his client to explore the crucial aspects of the field, namely the particular relationships of the client's experience to the self.

The talk which goes on in the counseling hour is not aimless talk. It is talk about the self and its relationships to the outside world which the counselor encourages in one fashion or another. He does this by discouraging talk in some directions and encouraging that which explores the self: its feelings, attitudes, beliefs, and convictions, the personal meanings existing for the client. In effect, he says by his behavior: "Here is the place to look." All counselors do this in one form or another and every method of counseling has devised its peculiar techniques for bringing about this personal exploration of meaning. In client-centered therapy, for example, it is accomplished in part by the counselor's sincere and consistent sympathetic understanding and in part by his basic technique called "recognition and acceptance of feeling." By this is meant that the counselor responds to his client by recognizing and accepting how he *feels* about the events he is describing. This is sometimes described as "mirroring" the client's feelings and, in a sense, that is what the therapist does. He attempts to reflect the essential feeling expressed by the client in clear and understandable terms. Sometimes he will recognize and accept the client's feelings by practically restating what he has said. For example:

CLIENT: I get so mad at her sometimes. She does things like that all the time.
COUNSELOR: Sometimes you feel very angry at her. I can see how you might feel that way.

Sometimes, too, the counselor may respond to the feeling in terms quite different from those used by the client, as in the following:

CLIENT: Yes, it is not at all clear to me. Should I keep it out of sight or keep it out in the open? I still don't know.
COUNSELOR: There are advantages in either direction.

In either event, however, the counselor attempts always to recognize and accept the feeling being expressed by his client. But why should he respond to his client's *feeling?* Why not to any other aspect of his client's statement?

In Chapter 11 we pointed out that what the individual is describing when he speaks of his emotions or feelings is, in reality, his personal reference. For instance, when I describe myself as "tired," I am describing my phenomenal field at this instant. In large part, this is a description of my awareness of my body state but includes, as well, all other aspects of my field at this moment, including the fact that I have just looked at the clock and discovered how very late it has become. My "feeling" is the meaning of events to me at this time. When the counselor concentrates attention on the "feelings" of his client, he is helping him to explore and differentiate out of the field the personal reference of events. This is why the therapeutic experience is likely to be a very emotional one. The more personal the exploration, the more emotional the experience will seem to be.

Many people in our society have been deeply hurt in the process of growing up, or have simply never learned to communicate with others on more than a fairly superficial level of meaning. They, almost literally, do not know how to look at themselves. In counseling, therefore, the therapist may have to "teach" his client where to look for the solution of his problems. He does this by the relationship he creates and the techniques he uses to direct the client's attention to the data of adjustment, that is, the individual's own ways of perceiving himself and the world about him. In emphasizing the client's feelings the counselor assists the client to an exploration of his field through an examination of the "meanings of events" for him. By recognizing and stating these meanings, clearly and sharply, he assists his client to further differentiations until, eventually, this process may arrive at those differentiations most troublesome or fear-producing for the client. Once that point has been reached new adjustments become possible.

This process of exploring meaning, which the adult carries on through the medium of language, is not available for children with vocabularies too limited to express their perceptions. Children can be helped, however, by therapy carried on in the language of play. Though children lack the vocabulary in terms of which to explore their perceptual field, they can achieve the same end through the manipulation of toys, paints, or the thousand and one materials at hand in a well-equipped play room. The play therapist provides the same facilitating atmosphere and assists the process of exploration of the child's own meanings expressed in his play activities. Thus, he might respond to the child sucking on a baby bottle: "Sometime, it is nice to be a baby. I know how you feel"; or to the child who has flushed the father doll down the toilet, "Sometimes you are very angry at the father doll." In this fashion he helps his young client explore his unique relationship to his world and in the process to arrive at more adequate ways of viewing himself and that world.

There is another way in which the relationship of psychotherapy helps the client to new and more adequate concepts of self. We have seen earlier that the adequate personality is characterized by three factors: a positive self, acceptance, and strong feelings of identification. By his behavior the therapist may be able to provide experiences for his client which help him begin to perceive himself as a more adequate person. The therapist treats his client *as though he were* lovable, likable, acceptable, and able. He accepts his client even when his client is unable to accept himself. This is an important experience for the inadequate personality. Self concepts are the products of our experience with the important people of our lives. Because his counselor treats him as though he were these positive things, little by little the client may come to believe in himself in these ways too. This does not, of course, happen quickly, for self concepts do not change so easily. Over a period of time, however, as he finds his counselor behaving consistently in these ways the client may begin to perceive himself in this light as well.

The warm, understanding relationship of the counseling experience and the deeply meaningful communication made possible by the personal character of the therapeutic relationship also provide the client with a strong feeling of identification. Perhaps for the first time in his life he finds it possible to identify successfully and meaningfully with another person, and this experience with the therapist increases the possibility of creating such relationships with other people as well. By his very behavior toward his client, the counselor is providing an important learning experience. In a very real sense he is teaching him to be adequate by treating him as though he were. For many threatened and inadequate personalities this is a new and wondrous experience. For deeply deprived personalities it may even prove extremely frightening as they feel desperately inadequate to deal with such strange and, in their experience, unusual behavior. Often they may be driven to test the genuineness of this relationship in ingenious and devious ways. To withstand this period of testing, the counselor must himself be capable of an extraordinary degree of patience, compassion, and firmness of position. This kind of experience in successful identification with the therapist can have tremendous value for the threatened and unhappy client. Through it he may be helped to identify more effectively with other people in his world.

With a clear differentiation of the relationship between self and the external world, facilitated by the creation of a situation that makes change possible and helped along by the therapist's assistance in the process of exploration of the field, the stage is set for a shift in the self concept. Under these circumstances such a redefinition of the phenomenal self and its relationship to external reality becomes not only possible but almost inevitable. But why should this be true?

The Outcome of Treatment—Self Reorganization

As we have seen, the threatened individual has a self concept inadequate to accept his perceptions of external events. Since his need is to maintain or enhance the organization of the phenomenal self, and since his perceptions of external affairs endanger that organization, he is driven to defend himself and is incapable of making any great change in the self concept. What is more, the selective effects of the self concept on perception makes the likelihood of any change in the self concept even more remote, for the client may not even be able to perceive the source of the threat to which he is exposed. Eventually, under these circumstances, the threat to the client's organization may become so great as to be almost intolerable yet he is unable to differentiate the nature of the terror to which he is exposed or what solutions are possible to him. The individual finds himself in a position where he cannot bear to remain as he is, yet cannot perceive any more adequate ways of behaving.

At this point in therapy we come to what appears at first glance a paradox—namely, that the same need to maintain and enhance the phenomenal self which brought the individual under threat in the first place operates to assist the client to a readjustment of his self concept and actually results in its change. Let us take an example to see how this comes about. Mr. Jones feels deeply threatened but cannot explain the source of his dread. So far as he is concerned he is just afraid of "something" but does not know what. Under these circumstances his need to maintain and enhance his organization causes him to defend his self concept, and he may be unable to perceive either the nature of the threat or the necessity for a reevaluation of his self concept in more adequate terms. In therapy he tells us of this threat which he feels but cannot "put his finger on." He describes it as vague and diffuse, and he is anxious and worried although he has nothing to worry about so far as he can see. As therapy progresses, he continues his exploration of his field and finally comes to differentiate clearly his own evaluation of himself and that of the events surrounding him. He tells us finally that he dislikes himself intensely. He feels he is a very unworthy person. What he is really afraid of is "What people will think of me?" Now with the situation clearly perceived, his need to maintain or enhance the phenomenal self brings him to a reorganization of his self concept in closer alignment with external reality. Anything else is impossible, for to remain as he is, is intolerable and keeps him under threat. The only thing which will remove the threat is to take the direction now clear to him as a result of his sharper differentiation of the situation. Before counseling, his need forced him to maintain his position because it was impossible for him to perceive that any other possibility existed. After he has achieved a clear differentiation of the situation in counseling it becomes intolerable to maintain his present self concept, and the maintenance and enhancement of the phenomenal self lies in making some change in its organization. Thus he may redefine himself as no better or worse than other men and really not such a bad person after all. With such a reorganization of self he may be able to like himself better and perceptions of external events will appear less threatening. In other words, if it becomes clear that enhancement of the phenomenal self is to be achieved by reorganization, the organism will move in that direction, providing the threat to his present position is dissipated.

It is just this sort of shift in the organization of the self concept which is characteristic of all successful therapies. While therapy is a device by which such changes are facilitated, the same types of changes are made repeatedly in the life of the average person. The very act of growing up involves a continuous process of reorganization or modification of the self concept as one moves from childhood, to youth, to manhood, to marriage, to middle age, and finally to old age. So long as the threat to the existing phenomenal self is not too great, reorganization continues smoothly as the person perceives the changes occurring in himself and his surroundings. Under extreme threat, however, the individual's self concept may become encysted. This often happens in children who feel threatened when parents push too hard for grown-up skills. When pressures become too great, individuals may feel so threatened and inadequate that they are forced to defend the existing self and so become incapable of change. The failing student in school may find the work demanded of him so overwhelming that he seeks to avoid it entirely, thus avoiding the very efforts that might solve his problem. Counseling is a method of breaking such a log jam and getting things moving again by making change in self definition possible once more. Psychological growth is a process of change in self definitions, and it is this kind of growth that treatment encourages and facilitates.

The Permanence of Change

Changes brought about in therapy may often be remarkably permanent. There is good reason why this should be true. Perhaps the greatest number of cases in which the self has become seriously threatened are due to the movement of the individual from one cultural group to another. This includes, of course, those many situations in which adult maladjustments are hang-overs from childhood self definitions. A great many of our maladjustments seem to arise from this early period of life when differentiations are far less clear than is true in adulthood, and when the child may even lack the necessary symbols in terms of which more adequate differentiations can be made.

A fundamental reorganization of self made as an adolescent or as an adult may, therefore, have a highly permanent effect for two reasons: (1) The individual has shucked off the inadequate self definitions imposed upon him as a child and is now better able to make clearer and more adequate ones than was possible to him in earlier days. (2) As a growing child, the individual moved into wider and wider cultural groups: from family to neighborhood group, to school, to gang, to social groups, etc. We have seen that this movement from one subculture to another is often the source of threatening perceptions, as the self concept formed in one group becomes inadequate to deal with the new group. When, however, the individual has reached adult status, he is no longer moving into such drastically different subcultures. His horizons have expanded and now include most of those groups in which he will move as an adult. Because he is no longer so likely to be moving from subculture to wider culture and because he has a greater differentiating ability, he is less exposed to new and upsetting relationships of self to the world about him. An adequate self definition effectively operating with people and events is less likely to be upset by ordinary exigencies of life. In fact, if emerging events are not too overwhelming, the experience of dealing successfully with them may be the very means by which even greater adequacy is achieved.

CHAPTER **20**

The Exploration of Meaning

H O W effectively we are able to operate with other people and how adequately we are able to contribute our full share to the society in which we live will depend in large part upon the understandings we have about the behavior of others. The more understanding we have, the more efficiently we can govern our own behavior in living and working with them. Whether we are aware of it or not, we all have perceptions about other people. Such understandings may exist all the way from some vague feeling like "people are generally nice," or "most people can't be trusted," to the highly differentiated and precise descriptions of the research psychologist. Whether vague or exact, however, all of us behave in terms of what we have come to believe is "so" about other people and their motivations.

To understand the behavior of another person it is necessary to understand how things seem to him, to have some grasp of the nature of his phenomenal field. In particular, we need to know how he perceives himself and the world in which he operates. Perceptions, however, are an internal matter not open to direct observation by an outsider, and this, at first glance, might seem to confront us with an impossible task.

THE INADEQUACY OF INTROSPECTION

Logically, it would seem that if we would like to know how a person sees himself or the world about him, the thing to do would be to ask him. This is the technique, widely used in the psychology of 40 to 50 years ago, known as "introspection." Psychologists of those days, however, were forced to give up this method of approach to human meaning as too inaccurate and unreliable, and it seems no more useful for our purposes today than it did then. This is perhaps best illustrated by the difficulties we incur when we try to understand the phenomenal self of another by asking him how he sees himself. His reply is not a description of his phenomenal self, but rather his "self report."

The self report is the individual's self description as he reports it to an outside observer. It represents what the individual *says* he is. Like any other act, the self report is a behavior revealing in more or less degree what is going on within the organism. It is an expressive behavior produced by the perceptual field including the phenomenal self. The self report and the self concept, however, are by no means synonymous. One is a behavior, the other a perceptual organization which can be more or less closely approximated by inference from behavior. Confusion of these two concepts can lead to similar confusion in our thinking. There are even a number of experiments in the psychological literature designed to study the self concept but which, in fact, are studies of the self report.

The self report, like any other behavior, is a product of the individual's *total* phenomenal field. This perceptual field, it is true, contains all other perceptions of which he is capable as well. Any behavior is always the product of the individual's perceptions of himself *and his perceptions of the situation in which he is involved.* The self report, like any other behavior, is thus a product of *both* the subject's perceptions of self and of not self. How accurate a description of the phenomenal self the self report is likely to be is dependent at least upon the following factors:

1. *The clarity of the subject's awareness.* We have already seen that the phenomenal self varies in degrees of clarity. Some concepts of self at any moment are in clear figure while others may be immersed in ground. Thus the businessman whose concept of himself as a father is largely in eclipse during the hours he spends in his office may become keenly aware of himself in this role as he enters the door of his home. The concepts of self held by an individual vary widely with respect to their clarity at any moment, and whether or not they may be reported to others will depend in part upon whether they can be called into clear figure at the moment they are asked for. There may also be wide variations in the clarity of self perceptions of a more permanent character. Some concepts of self, for example, may exist only at very low levels of awareness for most of our lives. Still others, like the adolescent's slowly emerging concept of himself as an adult, may be quite unclear for very long periods of time. Attempts to report such undifferentiated perceptions to others may well prove impossible.

2. *The lack of adequate symbols for expression.* The perceived self

may also be unreportable because the individual does not possess the necessary symbols in which self perceptions may be adequately expressed. Despite the extent of our language there are times when it is impossible for us truly to express the richness of our experience in the limited vocabularies we possess. Words are notoriously inadequate to convey our full meanings. Even when we are able to express ourselves with some degree of accuracy we always run the risk that the words we use may not mean the same things to others as they mean to us. The degree to which the self report approaches the phenomenal self is thus open to all the errors involved in any other human communication and cannot be accepted as a one-to-one relationship without control of these variables.

3. *The social expectancy.* In our society it is customary, indeed, practically necessary, for the individual to hide his true concepts of himself even if he is able to report them accurately. Though a given person may think of himself as "very charming" or as "very stupid," he certainly would be most unlikely to express such feelings even under the most unusual circumstances. Each of us is always surrounded by the society in which he lives. We can never quite escape the effects of this society no matter how hard we may try. We are always aware of the approval and disapproval of others and the things we say about ourselves must always be more or less affected by these perceptions. Our perceptual fields are seldom free from such societal expectancies.

4. *Coöperation of the subject.* Subjects who are asked to coöperate in an exploration of their perceived selves have complete control over any attempt to approach the problem by way of self reports. If they do not wish to reveal an aspect of self, they can dissemble as they please or refuse to coöperate at all. They do not even have to reveal the fact of their lack of coöperation, if indeed they are aware of such a decision at all. A subject may agree to coöperate in an exploration of his self concept with the best of intentions, but be quite unable to give the desired information accurately for reasons of which he, himself, may not be clearly aware.

5. *Freedom from threat and the degree of personal adequacy.* Still another factor affecting the credibility of the self report will be the degree of personal adequacy felt by the subject. In general, the more adequate the individual feels, the more likely his self report will approach an accurate description of the phenomenal self, other factors being equal. The more threatened and inadequate the personality, the less is the

likelihood that he will be able to give an accurate report of his concepts of self. The more threatened, inadequate, or maladjusted the individual, the more vulnerable his concepts of self and the greater will be the necessity for him to defend the self. Poor as they may be, the concepts we have of ourselves are all we possess and the smaller, more insignificant our precious horde, the more vigorously it must be defended.

6. *Change in field organization.* Most important of all as a factor contributing to error in the use of the self report is the change in field organization brought about by the request for such a report. The organization of the phenomenal field when the individual is behaving with self only partly in figure is not the same as that when the self is clearly and sharply in focus. The reader can test this for himself. Until this moment he may have been intent on capturing the meaning of these paragraphs, but if we now ask him to tell us "how" he is reading, at once his field changes. A field organized with respect to the attainment of some goal outside the self is not the same as a field organized with the self in sharp figure. The very act of turning attention to self requires a reorganization of the field and this, of course, changes the character of what can be reported.

The Place of Inference in Perception Study

Understanding other people's perceptions is not new to us. Everyone has been doing this more or less successfully since childhood. Whenever we have to deal with other people, but particularly when we are trying to communicate with them in one way or another, we are sensitive to how they may be perceiving what we are saying or doing and we adjust our own behavior accordingly. In explaining an idea to a friend, we observe his reactions as we speak and adjust our explanation in terms of the inferences we make about how it is seeming to him. In a similar fashion, the teacher observes the child's reactions to the lesson and shifts and changes his own behavior accordingly to assure understanding of the point he seeks to convey. All of us develop this kind of informal sensitivity to the perceptions of others. Indeed, without it we could hardly continue to live in our complex, coöperative society. We make such inferences so automatically that we are seldom keenly aware of how we are doing it.

Children make such inferences when they deduce from the behavior of the adult that "Mother is angry!" or "Aunt Sue wants to kiss me." It is also what the grownup does when he infers that "John is not happy with Alice" or "the boss feels sore about something this morning." In a sense, people are always telling us about their perceptions by the ways in which they behave. Our problem is one of developing sensitivity to others and skill in making inferences from the behavior we are able to observe. These inferences provide the basis, the frame of reference, on which our own behavior can be founded when it is necessary for us to deal with other people. They provide the raw data for effective human relationships.

As a point of departure for estimating the potential effectiveness of such an approach in the prediction of human behavior we may take the findings of Sorokin and Berger, that individuals can predict accurately about 80 percent of their activities for the next 24 hours. These predictions were naturally made by the individual on the basis of his own perceptual field, and it might be a natural assumption that an outside observer, basing his view of the field on inference, would not do as well. As a matter of fact, the observer using the perceptual approach can often do much better than the subject himself.

The observer cannot, of course, reconstruct the subject's present field with the richness, warmth, and detail that it actually has. His most precise approximation of that field is only a plan or schema of its general characteristics. But in drawing inferences about the future field and the future behavior of the subject, he has two advantages that the subject does not have. For one thing, the observer's field includes not only his approximation of the subject's field but a great deal of other knowledge as well. The subject's predictions of his future behavior are based upon his present field exclusively, but the observer, with a broader field, can predict, as the subject cannot, impingements of new experience and their effect upon the field. Johnson, secretly planning to punch Smith in the nose, has knowledge of Smith's future field and behavior which is not, at the moment, accessible to Smith. So does Jones, who has just written Smith a letter asking for money, and Miss Anderson, who has just put an F on young Smith's report card. Of course, none of these people can accurately predict Smith's response to their advances from this knowledge alone. But they do have information pertinent to his future field which is denied him and, if they know him well, they can predict what he will do when the predicted events occur.

The observer has one other advantage over the subject. The subject is a prisoner within his own present field and is sharply aware only of

the present figure. Material in the ground is at such a low level of awareness that it is available only in the form of vague feelings and "hunches,"
if at all. Even if the ground material has been in sharp figure in the past
it has very little influence at the moment. On the other hand the observer, if he has had an opportunity to study the individual's phenomenal field in the past, is aware of a great deal of this material, once figure
and now ground, which is out of the subject's reach at the moment, but
which under predictable conditions, under the stress of another situation, will emerge into figure again. In other words the behaver himself
can be aware only of his present field; the observer, who has his own
field, can be aware of much of the subject's ground material which
provides most of the raw material for the future field. Furthermore, since
the observer can view the subject's field unemotionally, without personal involvement, he can be aware of the subject's characteristic distortions and use this knowledge in predicting the kind and degree of distortion of new material. The subject, again, cannot do this for himself
because to him the distorted field is reality. In a situation where the
subject is well known to the observer, and his field has been thoroughly
explored by acceptable methods, and where the latter is also well
acquainted with the situation in which the subject is to find himself, the
prediction should fall little below complete accuracy.

Although most people develop enough sensitivity about the perceptions of others to make it possible for them to live fairly successfully,
such undisciplined kinds of observation hardly suffice for professional
workers. Teachers, social workers, psychologists, physicians, and others
who have social responsibilities for dealing with human problems, need
much more precise understandings of the perceptions of their students,
clients, and patients than is required for the more casual relationships
satisfactory for the purposes of the ordinary citizen. The inferences applied workers make about the perceptual fields of people call for much
more disciplined and controlled observations. The research worker will
need even more precise and accurate understandings than the applied
worker for his highly specialized and exacting purposes.

What distinguishes the research worker from the applied worker or
ordinary citizen is not that he seeks for something different in understanding, but only that he brings to the task a higher degree of care and
precision. The researcher, the teacher, and the man-in-the-street all need
to understand the perceptions of others. Most of us make inferences
about others' perceptions in the vague and undisciplined ways we have

learned in the process of our growing up, and this is ordinarily quite satisfactory for our daily purposes. The teacher, however, needs more precise understandings for his purposes and so must exert greater discipline and care in his observations. Such observations in turn will probably not be sufficiently precise for the research worker.

It should not be supposed that because each of these three approaches the problem of understanding perception with differing degrees of order and precision that one is "better" than another. On the contrary, each approach is useful and efficient for its own purposes. The methods appropriate to each of these levels is hardly suitable for the others. Thus the researcher finds the layman's ways too uncontrolled for research demands, while the layman finds the researcher's methods too detailed and cumbersome for the immediate action required in day-to-day and moment-to-moment living. The professional worker, on the other hand, uses methods lying somewhere between these extremes. His methods are at once more precise than the layman's and broader in scope than the researcher's.

In general, understanding the meanings of other people is accomplished by a process of observation, inference making, and testing of inferences. This is what the teacher does as he attempts to deal with the problem of Jimmy's difficulties in reading. He observes Jimmy read and infers, "It may be the child does not see well." Having made this observation, he checks his inference by having the child's eyes examined. If this proves inaccurate, he observes some more and makes other inferences. Perhaps Jimmy is not seeing the differences between l and t, or n and m. Or maybe the child sees the whole process of reading as a threatening failure experience. Through this kind of process of inferring and checking, the teacher is able to arrive at a workable understanding of how reading seems to Jimmy. This is the same kind of procedure used by mothers inferring why the baby is crying, or by psychologists attempting to diagnose the difficulties of a client. Through a continuous process of observing, inferring, testing, observing, inferring, testing, we may, over a period of time, come closer and closer to an accurate appraisal of the meanings existing for other people. Furthermore, we may do this informally, as we do in daily life, or we may carry on the process more exactly, exerting careful control and using highly refined techniques of observation and testing as the research scientist does in carrying out an experiment. At first glance this approach to the study of meaning may seem to some to be mystical and "unscientific." There is a widespread illusion that things can only be "true" or scientific if they can be physically measured. Actually, it is only when science is able to make inferences about things that it is able to progress beyond the immediate and the palpable to deal with the abstract and remote. A science limited only to that which is directly observable would never be able to deal with such matters as electricity, atomic physics, or the mysteries of human disease.

The making of inferences in itself is neither scientific nor unscientific. It is a technique of exploration. What makes a science is the care and discipline with which the data, whatever they may be, are collected, checked, and reported. The data used by the behavioral scientist studying the phenomenal self are exactly the same as those used by psychologists studying any other human characteristic, namely the observed behavior of the subject. For some purposes it is enough to deal only with behavior on this level as, for example, when we are trying to determine how many people taking the college entrance examination will probably graduate. When, however, we seek to predict what a *particular* individual will do, it is necessary for us to understand his motivations, desires, wants, goals, and perceptions of self and the world about him. The perceptual psychologist, interested in the study of meaning, accomplishes this by making inferences from the behavior he observes. Because he has different goals in view, he utilizes different methods of approach to his problem which make it possible to explore questions unapproachable in other frames of reference.

THE OBSERVER AS AN INSTRUMENT FOR RESEARCH

Human beings seem so much more variable than machines that a science which utilizes inferences for its data may at first glance appear hopelessly open to error. Indeed, it is true that the exploration of people's perceptions through a process of inference places a great deal more responsibility upon the observer than is true in the physical sciences. The making of inferences requires of the investigator that he be much more than a mechanist, concerned with the manipulation of external or physical factors alone. He must be able to see the world as others see it and be able to put himself in his client's place. This requires that he utilize his imagination and creative abilities to the utmost of his capacities while at the same time practicing upon himself the most rigid personal discipline with respect to his own prejudices and meanings. When inferences are made, the observer himself is acting as an instrument of research.

The direct observation of data, by itself, provides little help in the solution of problems in any science. There are, for example, no situations in which a single isolated datum is important. Nor do such data become much more useful simply by adding one to another. Data only become truly significant when subjected to the mediation or interpretation of human meaning. Creating a dynamic process from meaningless data is the indispensable function of the observer. Making inferences introduces a further variable to the process of observation, it is true. However, the use of human creativity in science does not produce an invalidation; only a further variable to be recognized and controlled. Properly used with full realization of its assets and liabilities, the human instrument deserves to be treated like any other fine instrument, with care and respect.

Exploring the Perceptual Field

How is it possible to explore so complex, unique, and apparently impregnable an organization as the perceptual field? Since the total field is made up of the individual's meanings of events past, present, and future, it may appear that the problem of understanding another's field is a completely hopeless task. Indeed it would be, if it were necessary for us to know and understand all the meanings of events for the individual in the course of his entire life history. Actually, the picture is by no means so bleak, for even without understanding the entire life history of an individual, many professional workers are making highly accurate predictions in their daily work.

While the exploration of the individual's total field in detail is almost impossible, the differentiations of certain aspects of the field are distinctly within the range of investigation. It will be recalled from our previous discussion that, while the behavior of the individual is always a result of the total organization of the perceptual field, certain differentiations become so important in the production of behavior as to serve as effective guides to what the individual will or will not do in any circumstance. These differentiations are the phenomenal self, the individual's perceptions of the world about him, and the goals, values, and techniques he has differentiated in the course of his experiences. These

loom so large in the production of behavior that it is possible to understand how people behave with great accuracy once an understanding has
been achieved of their character and operation in the individual's total
field of meaning. It is these four major types of differentiation within the
field with which perceptual diagnosis and research must be concerned:
(1) the individual's self concept, (2) the meanings of certain external
events for him, (3) the goals and values which he has differentiated to
satisfy need, and (4) the characteristic techniques by which he attempts
to reach his goals.

THE EXPLORATION OF THE SELF

Since the phenomenal self provides the very core of the individual's
perceptual field, any understanding of the nature of the individual's
field must, of necessity, be concerned with the peculiar organization of
concepts which go to make up his self concept. We have seen that the
self concept is composed of many definitions of self and that these definitions vary in at least two respects: (a) the degree of importance or
centrality of the concept—that is, aspects of self will vary in the degree
to which they seem to their possessor to be true, important, or basic
aspects of his own personality, and (b) the specificity or generality of
concepts—that is, one may wish to explore some broad sweeping aspect
of self like a feeling of adequacy, or a more specific concept of self
like the kind of driver he conceives of himself as being. The aspects
of self we seek to explore will vary in terms of these factors. What is
more, the techniques we use to explore these aspects will have to be
chosen in the light of these considerations. Methods which help us understand the central or general aspects of the self may prove inadequate
to aid us in understanding concepts of the self which are specific to
particular situations.

What aspects of self are explored, of course, will be determined by
the purposes of the observer. Different people will be interested in quite
different portions of the same person's self structure. The teacher, for
example, may be interested in the student's concept of self as able or
unable to do mathematics. The parent, on the other hand, may be more
concerned about a child's concepts of self as loved or accepted. The
foreman in the plant may be quite unconcerned about such matters but
be deeply interested in his employee's self concepts as a member of the
production team or as a member of the union. The clinical psychologist,
looking at the same person, may be particularly interested in those

aspects of the self in which the individual seems to feel most inadequate or deficient.

Since behavior is always a function of the total phenomenal field, the same behavior can even be utilized by different observers working from quite different frames of reference to infer different aspects of self. Thus it is possible that the teacher, psychologist, parent, foreman, or casual acquaintance might each observe the very same behavior and infer from it quite different concepts of self. Nor would one of these inferences necessarily be more "right" than another. They might all be quite accurate although each represents only a limited aspect of self.

EXPLORING THE INDIVIDUAL'S PRIVATE WORLD

Since the individual's behavior is always a function of how he sees himself and how he sees the situation in which he is involved, a real understanding of the perceptual field of another will require that we know, in addition to his phenomenal self, something of this situation. We will need to explore the private world of the subject. Through the same process of inference, prediction, and testing used to determine the phenomenal self and its various aspects, we may discover the meaning of his world for a particular subject. Such inferences can be made with respect to some particular portion: how he perceives, for instance, a political candidate, a motion-picture star, a particular brand of laundry detergent, or his fourth grade teacher. Or we may be interested in a much broader sample of the phenomenal field, as, for example, when we seek to assess a person's intelligence.

THE EXPLORATION OF GOALS AND VALUES

In a previous chapter we have seen that the goals and values differentiated in the phenomenal field have an ordering and selecting effect upon perception. Goals and values, then, are important factors to be explored in assessing people's meanings. With a knowledge of the goals and values important to a subject we are in a position to make much more accurate inferences regarding the ways in which he is likely to perceive a given event. People who value Communism do not see the same events as they are seen by those who value Capitalism. Knowing the existence of such goals and values in a personality helps us to make far more accurate inferences as to the meanings governing his behavior and consequently to predict what he will do in many situations.

Traditional tests of attitudes, personality, interests, likes, and preferences provide interesting clues to the goals and values existing in a particular person's phenomenal field. Public-opinion polls, interviews, and questionnaires of a less formal character have also been used to assess perceptions. Understanding of an individual's goals and values may be informal as we make such observations in our daily contacts or may be carefully measured as the research psychologist examines them. In either case, our awareness provides us with important clues to his perceptual field, which in turn will make it possible for us to predict what he will perceive and how he will behave in other situations.

THE EXPLORATION OF TECHNIQUES

Other important meanings in the perceptual field are the techniques which the individual has differentiated as means of satisfying his need. Many of these become highly characteristic of people and an understanding of them makes possible a high degree of accuracy in the prediction of behavior. Floyd Allport and his students, for example, have carried on fruitful researches in the prediction of behavior from inferences made about "what the individual is characteristically trying to do." Using such inferences, or "teleonomic trends," as Allport calls them, experimenters have been able to forecast with amazing accuracy the behavior of their subjects. The techniques people differentiate as appropriate to satisfy their needs can provide important clues to the nature of personality if we can find ways of discovering what they are.

Ways of Exploring the Perceptual Field

A vast number of materials are now available to the student hoping to explore the phenomenal field. These range from devices like the Rorschach Ink Blots, which have a very simple structure, to tests like the Minnesota Multiphasic Inventory, an extensive and complex battery of statements about self. They range, too, from casual observations to highly organized and directed observations utilized by researchers in the psychological laboratory. Indeed, the development of new techniques for exploring perception is one of the most active areas of psychological research, and new instruments are developed almost daily. Many older techniques of exploration designed by social scientists in years past for quite other purposes may also lend themselves to the needs of the worker desiring to explore human perception. Even children's games and the methods of salesmen and interviewers, on occasion, have contributed to our insights. The number of these methods is so vast and sometimes so technical as to be impossible of inclusion in this book. We shall therefore attempt to do no more than suggest some of these devices and the ways in which they may be used for exploring perception.

OBJECTIVE DATA IN PERCEPTUAL EXPLORATION

The exploration of meaning must begin at the same point as all other exploration of behavior, with some kind of external observation. Though we are concerned with the individual's meanings, these are always meanings of something. It will be necessary, therefore, to begin our exploration with external observations from which it will be possible for us to make inferences as to the nature of the individual's perceptual field. For the most part these inferences will be of the character, "Now why did he do that?" "Under what circumstances would a person have done that?" or "What meaning would one have to have about this or that event to make one act like that?" Such inferences cannot be made in a vacuum. It will be necessary to use objective, external observations of behavior as the basis for interpretations.

Since the collection of objective facts has for so long been conceived as the primary task of psychology, the techniques for obtaining them are extremely numerous and, for the most part, so well known that we shall not pause at this point to do more than attempt to classify them. In general, they fall into three broad types: the observer's observations, the observations of others, and various forms of controlled observations.

In the first of these classes, the psychologist makes direct observations of the individual and his environment. He attempts to describe these in as nearly exact terms as possible. For example, the clinician working with a particular child may visit the child's schoolroom to observe his behavior in that setting, or he may visit the child's home with an eye to observing the home conditions which surround him, or he may make more or less informal observations in his own office, clinic, or laboratory. In any event, he is seeking to establish the nature of the objective facts by means of his own personal observations.

In the case of observations made by others, the psychologist accepts the report of other witnesses whom he regards as reliable. Thus, he may ask for reports from teachers, employers, friends, and acquaintances of his subject. Frequently these reports may also be obtained from court records, school reports, and various forms of documentary material. To assure a measure of greater accuracy these may, furthermore, be subjected to certain tests of reliability and validity.

The third group includes a tremendous number of special devices constructed for the purpose of making controlled observations. These constitute the traditional and most acceptable observations in the external frame of reference. The techniques used vary widely from attempts to control observations in life situations by such means as taking time samples, successive observations, and the use of laboratory experimentation, to various forms of traditional psychological tests. All are based on the same principle of attempting to obtain accuracy and regularity through the restriction and control of observation to the point where agreement in observation (reliability) is possible. Many of these are oriented toward establishing the relationship of the individual to the "normal" group. The number of these instruments now in use is so large that it would be impossible for us to do justice to them here. Instead of attempting such a discussion we shall push on to examine the nature of more strictly perceptual data.

Exploring the Individual's Personal Field

At least four techniques of investigation into the individual's personal meanings are already in more or less widely accepted use or show promise of possible development for that purpose. These are: (1) information obtained from the individual himself, (2) inferences from observed behavior, (3) the use of projective techniques, and (4) the protocols of therapy.

INFORMATION FROM THE INDIVIDUAL HIMSELF

People are always telling us about themselves, their feelings, attitudes, and ways of seeing. All kinds of expressive behavior may give important clues to the nature of the perceptual field, providing we can learn to look and to hear. What people have to say about themselves, their feelings, beliefs, attitudes, problems, worries, concerns, or even simple descriptions of events going on about them are all behaviors derived from the perceptual field. Reading such behavior backward, then, should give us important insights into the field states which produced them. Some of the kinds of data we can use for this purpose are the things people say about themselves and others in conversation, in letters and various forms of personal documents like diaries, journals, or auto-biographies.

We have already seen in our discussion of the self report some of the pitfalls involved in accepting statements about self at face value or as having a one-to-one relationship to the phenomenal field. In spite of these difficulties, however, it is possible to use the subject's own descriptions of events, providing we remain keenly aware of the possibilities of error and make appropriate corrections. We can do this by concerning ourselves less with what is said and more with the probable meaning of such statements to the behaver. These meanings, for the most part, will be expressed in what the layman calls "feelings." It will be recalled from our previous discussion that feelings are the individual's attempts to describe his field state at any moment. Thus, by attending to the feelings which the individual is expressing, we may arrive at a more or less accurate description of the meanings which exist for him. This will be possible even when the words he uses describing himself or the events around him are intentionally distorted to give another impression. For instance, when a mother brings her 7-year-old son to the psychological clinic with the statement "My son is failing first grade. How can I ever face my friends?" it is not difficult to infer the meanings that exist in the mother's field or to decide whose self esteem is wounded by the child's failure. Frequently, such simple expressions may be more revealing of personal meanings than any number of more exact techniques of observation.

WAYS OF OBTAINING THE SUBJECT'S OWN REPORT. Techniques of obtaining the subject's own report vary greatly both in degree of structure and the degree to which they are revealing of the client's personal meanings. They vary in structure from unrestricted, casual conversations to highly restricted and exact responses like those on many tests or questionnaires. They will vary also in the degree to which they will provide data about personal meaning, depending upon the individual's need to protect himself.

INFORMAL CONVERSATION ABOUT SELF. Conversations may often be highly revealing of the person's meanings, particularly if he does not feel threatened by the circumstances in which he finds himself, or if he becomes so involved in a conversation that he loses sight of the potential threats which exist. It is a common observation that "bull sessions" and conversations with fellow passengers on trains and buses may often give the individual a sufficient feeling of temporary protection from threat that he is able to speak quite openly of even his deepest feelings. Sometimes, too, this occurs when a subject is extremely upset or angry, and when his field has become sufficiently narrowed so that he does not perceive the threat which exists in the larger field. Under the effects of alcohol a similar tendency may be noted. In this case, the absence of threat appears to be due to the blurring of the field rather than to an extreme narrowing, but results in the same failure to perceive threat. Certain drugs like sodium pentathol and sodium amytal also appear to depend for their effectiveness on this principle.

The practiced clinician soon learns to be on the alert for such expressions of meaning as they reveal themselves in the course of conversation. He learns to be particularly alert to such aspects of the person's behavior as varying tones and inflections of speaking, unusual modes of expression, and the degree of certainty or conviction with which the individual makes his statements. With experience, he learns that most people do not seriously call themselves "the black sheep of my family," for example, or express themselves vehemently about other people unless these things have important and often highly revealing meanings for them.

DIARIES AND LETTERS. These forms of personal documents have often been used in literature and in sociology but have only recently been of much concern to psychologists in the study of personality. Nevertheless, such materials in which the individual "talks to himself" are often extremely useful for purposes of getting at the meanings which motivate behavior. They may be much more expressive than what the client says in conversation, if in his letters, for instance, he is writing to others whom he feels he can trust.

In the following excerpts from an adolescent's diary note how meanings are expressed which would be most difficult to approach in a face-to-face conversation.

After six weeks of daily entries each saying "No job yet," "Still no job!" and the like, is the revealing entry:

I wish I could get a job!! What must Dad and Mother think? Here Sis has a job and I haven't!!

I felt disgusted with the whole world today.

The sooner I get out of this town the better I'll like it. It was all right for a while—but now! Gosh! It'll be great when I get to college and on my own hook.

Took Sally home from the library. She's not mad at me!! Gosh, it's great to love a girl like her!!

The three of us were not going to speak to any girls today! We all failed!

Joe got kicked out of the basketball game so I went with him. We resolved to always stick together.

THE USE OF AUTOBIOGRAPHY.   Like diaries and letters, autobiography has not been extensively used in psychological research because of the common objections to the introspective method. Perceptual psychology, too, must reject the introspective method. The use of inference, however, makes possible the effective employment of a number of sources of data about behavior not available to more traditional approaches. Since perceptual research is not primarily concerned with the accuracy or inaccuracy of external evaluation but in the meanings of events to the individual, the very inaccuracies of autobiography may often become important facts for understanding the individual. This is particularly true in clinical psychology where the concern is with the individual's differentiations of the phenomenal self and its relationship to objective events. The clinician does not say, "This is not true in terms of the objective facts but is the way my client sees them and *that is important.*" *It is even possible that it may be the very inaccuracy of report that gives the clinician his important clues to personality.*

The use of autobiography in psychologiacl research may vary widely from highly uncontrolled materials on the one hand to such highly controlled assignments on the other as to resemble a questionnaire. Whatever their nature, autobiographies may provide us most important clues into the fundamental meanings which make up the individual's phenomenal field. Such insights into personal meanings as are revealed in the following small excerpt from an autobiography are a valuable source of information and ought not to be overlooked as valuable devices for exploring meaning:

When I was ten years old my father died very suddenly. As far as we knew he was all right, till one night he had indigestion, went to the kitchen for some soda, and fell over. He lived for about twelve more hours under an oxygen tent, and then died. It was a heart attack. So one minute I had a father and next thing I didn't have one. It was so sudden and unexpected that I couldn't believe it. It left me with a very insecure feeling, as though there wasn't anything stable that I could depend on. Things just happened after that. Then my mother's attitude and being away all day running my father's store after he died emphasized this feeling even more. My mother was adjusting to the shock by constant activity. So my mother's constant running around and doing things gave me still less to hold on to.

THE USE OF TESTS AND QUESTIONNAIRES. A great many tests in current use have important values for perceptual research. This is particularly true of some of the better personality inventories, which may often be highly revealing of individual meanings. For purposes of exploring the phenomenal field, however, the normative scores obtained from these tests will tell us little about the personal meanings of events for the client. Most test scores are external descriptions or summary statements of the subject's behavior traits. For the most part, the individual items of the inventory are likely to prove of greater value as sources of data about people's meanings. Most of our intelligence tests, for example, are in reality no more than tests of the differentiations characteristic of the subject. The trend in modern clinical use of such standard intelligence tests as the Stanford-Binet is to emphasize the study of test items while laying less and less emphasis upon total scores. In fact, the real measure of a good psychometrician lies in the degree to which the worker can make interpretations from the differentiations he observes in the item analysis of the test.

Standardized tests provide us with important means of making observations about people in a common setting and comparing these with the performance of others. For purposes of perceptual research and diagnosis, however, we may be less interested in the subject's status with respect to others who have taken the test than we are in what his peculiar and individual responses to the test items tell us about the meaning existing in his perceptual organization. In exploring personal meaning, therefore, we can also use a large number of unstandardized tests or even special tests devised for a particular problem or a particular person. The test is used as a vehicle for observing uniqueness rather than likeness or difference.

Many commonly used questionnaires and interest inventories may also prove useful in exploring the individual's perceptual field. As in other tests, the individual items of the inventories will usually be found to be more useful for exploring meaning than the normative scores they produce. Statements by the subject that he would rather be a plumber than an actor, or a pharmacist than a teacher, may render us much more important insights than a percentile score indicating a "tendency toward" some large field of work.

Even closer to the needs of perceptual research are such tests as the

Mooney Problems Check List and others of its type. Such tests ask the subject to indicate in a large number of problems, attitudes, ideas, or the like, those which he feels are of greatest concern to him. In this way a fairly direct approach is made to exploring the personal meanings that exist for the individual. Many of our modern attitude tests have similar important cues to offer for the exploration of meanings.

INFERENCES FROM OBSERVED BEHAVIOR

A second important source of perceptual data lies in the inferences it may be possible for us to make from the behavior we observe. This is a technique all of us use in daily life. When our hostess begins to be uneasy and finds it difficult to stifle a yawn, we must know that it is time to go home. In the same way, we are constantly modifying our behavior as we make judgments of what others like or dislike, as we infer what the car driver is going to do when we cross the street, and as we build our sales appeal on what we think our customers want.

UNCONTROLLED BEHAVIOR SITUATIONS. Observations may be made of people behaving in various kinds of uncontrolled situations. With children, for example, we can observe behavior in nursery school, in free play on the playground, or in any number of free and relaxed settings. With adults observations can occur at dinner, on the streetcar, or in any of a thousand other activities not under direct control of the observer. From such observations, if we are alive to the meanings which produce behavior, a great deal of insight may be gained into the nature of the individual's field.

THE USE OF CONTROLLED OBSERVATIONS. For the experimental psychologist who is testing a theory much more controlled observations must be necessary. Psychologists have been making controlled observations of subjects in a great variety of situations for many years. A great deal of this already published research may be found to be highly profitable when observed from a perceptual viewpoint. For example, a great many of the experiments conducted on the level of aspiration are distinctly pertinent to the problems of perception. The same is true of the interesting experiments in child behavior carried on by Lewin and his students. Observations of children made under such controlled conditions are often revealing of important dynamic aspects of behavior. For instance, the work of Barker, Dembo, and Lewin, who experimented with children's reactions to the interposition of a barrier between the child and an assortment of beautiful playthings, was designed to observe the behavior of children when confronted with frustration. These same experiments provide interesting data from which it is possible to infer a good deal about the personal meanings existing for these children, although such inferences were not the primary purpose of the experiment when it was designed.

EXPRESSIVE MOVEMENT AND CONVERSATION.   If our fundamental hypothesis that all behavior is a function of the perceptual field is correct, then all activities of the individual should be revealing of meaning if we could but discover the means of interpreting them. This includes such expressive movements as writing, characteristic body gestures, or any other activity engaged in by the individual in the course of his daily life.

Even the subject's conversation about other people has vast possibilities for use as a device to approach the meanings of events for the individual. It is common observation that we respond to the behavior of others in terms of our own needs and meanings. Thus, even the most impartial Republican or Democratic newspaper cannot avoid a bias in its reporting. In the same way individuals are unlikely to be deeply concerned about behavior of others unless that concern is in some fashion meaningful to themselves. Actually, a person's conversation about other people is likely to be a very potent projection of his own attitudes and feelings if the observer is sufficiently keen to be aware of such meanings.

INTERPRETATIONS FROM PROJECTIVE DEVICES

To this point we have spoken of methods of exploring personal meaning in use from time immemorial. In more recent years, however, psychologists have opened a whole new means of approach to the exploration of the perceptual field. These are the projective devices. Since the individual's behavior is a function of his perceptual field, his behavior must be the result of the meanings which make up his field. If we supply a person, then, with a situation in which he is free to respond as he pleases, presumably he will invest the situation we provide with his own personal meanings. The stronger his need, the stronger should these meanings be expressed. This is the fundamental principle of projection and is the basic idea upon which a large number of modern methods for the exploration of personality have been constructed. Projective instruments are designed to confront the subject with some sort of ambiguous situation as an ink blot, a vague picture, an incomplete sentence, or an unfinished plot. In responding to such ambiguity the individual is necessarily thrown upon his own resources to interpret them, and the perceptions he reports in his responses give interesting clues to the nature of the perceptions making up his unique perceptual field.

Projective techniques have another aspect which further increases the likelihood that they will reveal the individual's meanings. This is the fact that most projective devices are designed to give the individual a feeling of protection which removes him from the threat involved in revealing meanings in ordinary life situations. By making the projective instrument a story, a play, or something of the kind, the subject is given a feeling of protection in that he can always pass off his responses as being "just a story" or a fantasy which "no one could possibly imagine had anything to do with himself." As a consequence, under this kind of protection persons responding to projective instruments often reveal to the skilled interpreter some of their most basic and personal meanings.

A vast literature has accumulated on the production, interpretation, and use of such instruments. Several hundred may be found in current use. Most of these are alike in providing some kind of standard setting to which subjects are asked to respond, but the designers of projective instruments have shown a high degree of ingenuity in the kinds of situations their subjects are asked to respond to. These range from the almost completely unstructured Stern "Cloud Pictures" to the highly structured and precisely controlled projections of some sentence-completion tests.

THE RORSCHACH INK BLOTS. Undoubtedly the best known and most widely used of the projective instruments is the Rorschach Ink Blots. This device consists of a series of ink blots to which the individual is asked to respond by telling the examiner what he "sees" in the blots. Whatever he says he "sees," of course, can only be the product of his own experience, and the meanings with which he invests the blots provide a revealing sample of the nature of his perceptual field. The typical Rorschach interview often provides a fascinating and helpful source of data from which it is possible to make important inferences about the perceptions of individuals. The Rorschach Ink Blots have been subjected to more study and research than any other projective instrument and over the years a number of systems have been devised for interpreting the responses of the subject to the blots.

PICTURE STORY TESTS. A more structured type of projective instrument is the Picture Story Test, of which the Thematic Apperception Test is perhaps one of the best known. These tests provide the subject with a series of pictures which are vague representations of social situations. Some, like the Thematic Apperception Test, are quite general in the kinds of meanings they seek to explore, while others are designed for use with particular groups of people or in certain limited kinds of situations. Symonds, for example, has produced a test for use with adolescents. Other tests have been constructed with pictures of Negroes to explore the dynamics of prejudice, or with pictures of children in school to examine the perceptions of children about school and teachers. Since all of us live in a society, and since our adjustment or lack of it is to the social situations in which we operate, the particular meanings social situations have for us constitute a major source of our problems. It is these kinds of meanings the picture story tests seek to explore.

COMPLETION TESTS. Another type of projective instrument in wide use is the Completion Tests. Instead of a pictorial representation these devices provide some kind of written statement purposely left incomplete, which the subject is then asked to finish. Sometimes these may be in the form of sentences like: "I used to think——" or "People often seem to me——" or "Teachers nearly always——." Sometimes the material presented to the subject may be a more lengthy description of a situation or predicament which the individual is then asked to resolve by writing out "what he would do."

An example of this type of instrument is the Situations Test designed to explore the perceptions of school administrators. The test consists of a short description of an interchange between an administrator and one of his teachers up to the point where some decision and action are called for. At this point the story ends and the administrator is asked to tell how he would have handled the problem. From this data it is possible to gain considerable understanding of how the administrator sees himself, his job, his school, his teachers, the children, and the curriculum.

ACTION TECHNIQUES. Still another kind of projective technique has the subject act out his perceptions in free play or in some more structured form of role playing or dramatic presentation. Psychodrama, for example, asks the subject to act some part either from his own or another person's life. The situations and roles he is asked to play may be quite freely chosen or they may be specifically designed by the examiner to explore some particular aspect of the individual's perceptual field. As a subject acts a role he automatically invests it with his own meanings and feelings and these provide important clues to his personal frame of reference.

PLAY DIAGNOSIS.   With children, play provides an approach not possible by other means, since young subjects usually do not possess the necessary concepts to express problems verbally, even if they felt free to do so. Through play, the language of childhood, the child is capable of manipulating his environment and making differentiations not otherwise possible to one with so limited a vocabulary. For example, while it may be very difficult, if not impossible, for the child to define his own position with respect to his parents and the world about him in terms of language, in play he can manipulate both the dolls that represent his parents and the rest of the world to his heart's content and may be able to arrive at new perceptions and relationships in the course of such manipulations. The skilled observer can infer meanings which the child himself is unable to put in words.

The operation of the individual's need in restricting the perceptual field may often be most clearly observed in child play. Play is not mere manipulation but appears to be strongly driven in specific directions closely allied with the individual's own problems. For example, when the mother of one little girl went to a mental hospital and was confined for months, the child was not told where her mother had gone or why. In fact, the entire matter became a subject about which no one would speak. The little girl became more and more anxious about the matter and with the passage of time and no word from her mother, more and more of her play time was spent in playing "hospital." She developed a veritable passion for this type of play and induced other children in the neighborhood to participate with her as well. With the return of her mother to the family circle this play was dropped at once. The stronger the need, the more the behavior will be directed toward the satisfaction of need, whether it be in play or in any other behavior. The operation of this principle makes play diagnosis and all other free projective techniques remarkably sensitive for the investigation of adjustment.

That perceptions revealed in projective instruments are a function of the individual's need seems true but it should not be supposed that the perceptions revealed by the subject and those which activate his behavior in other circumstances are one and the same. It must be recalled that projective devices are specially designed to remove the ordinary barriers to the subject's expression and behavior. The Thematic Apperception Test, for example, asks its subject for "as dramatic a story" as he can produce. Since it is often presented as a test of imagination, the client is likely to take the examiner at his word and let his fancy roam freely and exaggeratedly in his story plots. As a result, the stories he tells are often unrestrained, bizarre, and even violent in the feelings represented. Since the client is protected by the very projection the test attempts to elicit and is encouraged in his fantasies, this is a perfectly natural consequence and requires that the interpreter be extremely wary of equating the strength of the feelings expressed in the projective instrument with the strength of the need existing in the client's perceptual field. Our behavior in daily life is a function of the *total* perceptual field, including our awareness of the normal controls of our society. Projective instruments *sample* the perceptual field under special circumstances with normal controls removed. They do not describe it fully.

Despite the difficulties posed by the use of projective instruments, they are the most exciting and productive means of exploring the perceptual field open to us. We have only briefly touched upon this fascinating field here. That is all we can do in this volume. The reader may wish to explore this matter much further through reference to some of the standard texts on projective instruments.

PROTOCOLS OF THERAPY

With the development of increasingly refined techniques of psychotherapy and particularly with the development of techniques of recording therapeutic sessions, a whole new field of approach to perception has been laid open. In the protocols of therapy we are given an opportunity to observe not only the state of affairs in the individual's organization at any one time, but also the nature and direction of change which occurs in that organization. Like the physician's use of radioactive particles in the blood stream or the use of the fluoroscope, the protocols of therapy give us a priceless opportunity to observe the innermost recesses of personality. As Rogers has pointed out: "The fact that these verbal expressions of inner dynamics are preserved by electrical recording makes possible a detailed analysis of a sort not heretofore possible. Recording has given us a microscope by which we may examine at leisure, and in minute detail, almost every aspect of what was, in its occurrence, a fleeting moment impossible of accurate observation."

In the course of therapy the client reveals a great deal of information relative to his characteristic organization. He talks of himself, of his ways of seeing things, of the meanings of events for him and in so doing reveals to the observer many aspects of the perceptual field. What is more, he does this often with great freedom and clarity. As was true of the projective devices, he feels protected by the counseling atmosphere and under the cloak of this protection can feel free to express his thoughts, desires, dreams, hopes, and plans.

In therapy the client is often free to explore the meanings of events in his personal organization with a minimum of distortion. As a result, what the client has to express will often represent an effective picture of his field from moment to moment. The following statements from the Case of Edith Moore show the meaning of events for the client at any moment, and make possible the observation of change (differentiation) in these meanings as the interview proceeds.

> I want to do this. I don't know why I can't get started.
> I don't know what stops me. There must be a reason.
> If I could find the reason, maybe I could accomplish something.
> I am afraid that people will say something that will hurt me.
> It is hard to put myself in a position where I know I will be hurt.
> And again I might not be hurt and then I would get over the fear.
> I want to avoid people's remarks. I ought to do it anyway then maybe it wouldn't be so bad the next time.

The possibilities inherent in this technique have only begun to be explored. It seems likely that the use of recordings for the investigation of the dynamics of group discussion might similarly lead to important insights into the perception of persons in a wide variety of social settings.

The exploration of human meaning, we have seen, is fundamentally a problem of learning to read behavior backward. It is possible to discover the meanings existing for people through a process of inference from the behaviors we see them engaging in. Some of the methods of doing this have long been a part of the "common sense" of the "average man" and with care and discipline can still provide us with means for understanding. Others are comparatively new inventions of the psychologist and psychotherapist requiring much more know-how and sophistication. For the man in the street, for the practical worker in human relations, or for the scientist in the laboratory, however, the fundamental problem is the same. The key to understanding behavior, whether it be our own or other people's, lies in large measure in the skill we develop in the exploration and understanding of the nature of people's perceptions.

References

The number of authors whose work has important bearings upon the point of view represented by this volume is so large that, to avoid extensive footnoting and protect readibility, it has seemed wise to handle the documentation of this text by means of this list of references. When the contribution of a particular author has been specifically mentioned by name, the reader may find the appropriate reference to his work by turning directly to the Bibliography. For the most part, the names of authors and detailed descriptions of research do not appear in the text itself. However, by the use of this list of references the reader may be guided to the appropriate bibliographical item pertinent to the discussion throughout these pages.

This book is printed with 39 lines to the page. The work of each author listed in the bibliography is indexed at the point in the text to which his work seems most relevant. Numbers preceding the name of the author refer to page and line of this volume. The number following the author's name indicates the item in the bibliography particularly referred to. Items listed immediately under chapter headings and without page and line numbers are general references of interest throughout an entire chapter.

To locate the points in the volume where the work of a particular author has seemed most pertinent, refer to the Index.

CHAPTER 3.   What Do People Need?

CHAPTER 7. The Development of the Phenomenal Self

CHAPTER 8. The Effect of Self on Perceiving

Page Line

Goodman, 260; Torrance, 579
155   1   Cantril, 122; Centers, 129; Stagner, 555
155 11 Cohen, 142; Frenkel-Brunswik, 237; Friedenberg, 242
155 26 Adler, 5; Farberow, 216

Page Line

157 11 Raimy, 467, 468
157 24 Hartley, 278
158 13 Friedenberg, 242; Rogers, 482
158 22 Aidman, 7
158 36 Chapman, 130
159 39 Hartley, 278; Hastings, 280

CHAPTER 9. The Availability of Perception in the Field

166 10 Hogan, 291
166 39 Masserman, 391
168 35 Hastorf, 281
170 23 Bowlby, 99; Hogan, 291; Janis, 309; Walsh, 586
171 12 Hamilton, 275
171 14 Bettelheim, 69
171 20 Ausubel, 38; Beier, 58; Bruner, 108; Davis, 184; Diethelm, 190; Eichler, 204; Gaier, 250; Hastings, 280; Korchin, 336; Laffal, 342; Lantz, 344; Lanzetta, 345; Postman, 450, 451
171 38 Allport, 21; Barker, 49; Brown, 103; Cowen, 165, 167, 168, 169; Frenkel-Brunswik, 237; Janis, 309; Korchin, 336; McGinnies, 397; Roethlisberger, 478; Rokeach, 492; Smock, 538
172 14 Katz, 322; McKellar, 403; Postman, 448
172 32 Alexander, 11
172 37 Levanway, 355
173 2 Keister, 323
173 14 Cowen, 168, 169; Frenkel-Brunswik, 327; Keister, 323; Lazarus, 347; Rokeach, 492; Smock, 538
173 20 Adorno, 6; Brown, 103; Dorris, 195; Frenkel-Brunswik, 237
173 23 Bettelheim, 69; Buchenholtz,

112; Eriksen, 210; Murray, 421
174 17 Bowlby, 99; Krall, 337; McCarthy, 394
174 36 Rogers, 483
175 4 Crandall, 171; Keister, 323, 324
175 33 Combs, 161
175 37 Bettelheim, 69
177 18 Beier, 58; Freud, 241; Liddell, 370; Zander, 616
177 21 Tomkins, 576
177 34 Ausubel, 38; Lantz, 344
177 38 Beier, 59; Freud, 239; Gaier, 250
178 1 Pomeroy, 445
178 8 Rogers, 482; Thetford, 568
178 21 Diethelm, 190
178 33 Bruner, 109; Friedenberg, 242
178 35 Chodorkoff, 135
180 2 Toynbee, 580
180 16 Flanders, 225
180 19 Coch, 140
180 39 Lanzetta, 345
182 16 Mead, 406
183 29 Ausubel, 38
184 15 Bergman, 66
184 25 Murphy, 419
185 14 Lecky, 350
187 6 Eriksen, 210, 211; Tagiuri, 563
187 29 Belmont, 61
188 36 Adorno, 6

CHAPTER 10. Learning, Forgetting, and Problem Solving

Hilgard, 288; Snygg, 544
190 20 Adams, 3; Barnhart, 51; Brigden, 101; Snygg, 544

191 10 Adams, 3; Lashley, 346; Pavlov, 434

CHAPTER 11.   The Nature of Capacities, Emotion, and Feeling

CHAPTER 12. The Adequate Personality

CHAPTER 13.   The Inadequate Personality: The Dynamics of Failure

CHAPTER 17. The Goals and Purposes of Education

Page Line

Kelley, 325
368 5 Bills, 81
369 11 Rivers, 476
369 20 Kelley, 325
369 36 Williams, 605
370 1 Olson, 430
370 6 Lifton, 371
370 26 Torrance, 578
372 9 Katz, 321
372 26 Asch, 34
372 37 Jersild, 314
373 22 Hildreth, 286
375 10 Lecky, 350
377 25 Benjamins, 64

Page Line

377 33 Bovard, 95
378 18 Anderson, 30
378 24 Bills, 76
378 27 Bovard, 98; Coch, 140
378 33 Keister, 323
379 1 McCarthy, 394
379 30 Amatora, 22; Corey, 163
379 34 Howard, 299
380 12 Boger, 92
380 25 Bills, 76
381 10 Combs, 157
381 15 Tentative Social Studies Program, 566

CHAPTER 18. The Teaching Relationship

383 11 Combs, 152; Kelley, 325; Moustakas, 417
385 15 Combs, 153; Gaier, 250; Torrance, 578
386 13 Janis, 309
388 12 Asch, 34; Bills, 77; Fiedler, 221; Gordon, 263; Schwebel, 507
388 19 Bills, 81; Bovard, 97; Thompson, 572
389 6 McCarthy, 394
389 14 Bills, 77; Combs, 158; Johnson, 315
390 2 Diller, 191
390 8 Faw, 217; Fiedler, 221; Johnson, 315
390 15 Asch, 34; Gordon, 263; Lippitt, 377
390 28 Alexander, 11; Amatora, 22; Anderson, 30; Bixler, 86
390 32 McCarthy, 394
391 12 Walsh, 586
391 18 Potter, 454

392 7 Lippitt, 377
393 30 Bovard, 95
395 25 Asch, 34; Axline, 40; Bills, 77, 78; Bixler, 86; Faw, 217; Fiedler, 221, 222; Monroe, 412; Roseborough, 494; Sheldon, 519
396 31 Coch, 140
397 39 Zimet, 617
398 10 Gordon, 263; Johnson, 315
398 15 Blocksma, 88
399 19 Anderson, 30; Blocksma, 88; Gage, 249; Preston, 460
402 19 Lepage, 353
402 39 Preston, 460
403 18 Corey, 163; Gage, 249
403 24 Combs, 158
406 21 Alexander, 11; Amatora, 22; Flanders, 225
406 35 Corey, 163
407 38 Wispe, 606, 607

CHAPTER 19. The Personal Approach to Treatment

Combs, 145, 151; Rogers, 482
414 5 Pugh, 465
414 34 Rotter, 497
415 19 Fiedler, 221, 222
417 34 Alexander, 10; Allen, 12; Freud, 238, 239, 240; Horney, 294; Rogers, 482, 485;

Sullivan, 561
418 4 Brown, 102; Butler, 116; Combs, 143, 153; Haigh, 268; Porter, 447; Seeman, 510; Sheerer, 518; Snyder, 539, 540; Stock, 560
418 27 Horrocks, 297

CHAPTER 20.   The Exploration of Meaning

Bibliography

1. Abel, T. M. Free design of limited scope as a personality index. *Charact. & Pers.*, 1938, 7: 50-62.

2. Abernethy, Ethel. The effect of sorority pressures on the results of a self-inventory. *J. Soc. Psychol.*, 1954, 40: 177-183.

3. Adams, D. K. A restatement of the problem of learning. *Brit J. Psychol.*, 1931, 22: 150-178.

4. Adler, A. Notes regarding the dynamics of the self. *Brit. J. Med. Psychol.*, 1951, 24: 97-106.

5. Adler, A. *Understanding human nature.* New York: Greenberg, 1927.

6. Adorno, W. *The authoritarian personality.* New York: Harper, 1950.

7. Aidman, T. Changes in self perception as related to changes in perception of one's environment. *Amer. Psychologist*, 1948, 3: 286.

8. Aldrich, C. A., and Aldrich, Mary M. *Babies are human beings.* New York: Macmillan, 1938.

9. Alexander, F. *Psychosomatic medicine.* New York: Norton, 1950.

10. Alexander, F., French, T. M., and others. *Psychoanalytic therapy: Principles and application.* New York: Ronald Press, 1946.

11. Alexander, T. Certain characteristics of the self as related to affection. *Child Develop.*, 1951, 22: 285-290.

12. Allen, F. *Psychotherapy with children.* New York: Norton, 1942.

13. Allison, H. W., and Allison, Sarah G. Personality changes following transorbital lobotomy. *J. Abnorm. Soc. Psychol.*, 1954, 49: 219-223.

14. Allport, F. H. Teleonomic description in the study of personality. *Charact. & Pers.*, 1937, 5: 202-214.

15. Allport, F. *Theories of perception and the concept of structure.* New York: Wiley, 1955.

16. Allport, G. W. *Becoming.* New Haven: Yale Univ. Press, 1955.

17. Allport, G. W. *Personality.* New York: Holt, 1937.

18. Allport, G. W. The ego in contemporary psychology. *Psychol. Rev.*, 1943, 50: 451-478.

19. Allport, G. W. The psychologist's frame of reference. *Psychol. Bull.*, 1940, 37: 1-28.

20. Allport, G. W. The use of personal documents in psychological science. *Soc. Sci. Res. Coun. Bull.*, 1942.

21. Allport, G. W., and Postman, L. *The psychology of rumor.* New York: Henry Holt, 1947.

22. Amatora, S. A. Similarity in teacher and pupil personality. *J. Psychol.*, 1954, 37: 45-51.

23. Ambriere, Francis. *The long holiday.* Chicago: Ziff-Davis, 1948.

24. Ames, A. *An interpretative manual: The nature of our perceptions, prehensions and behavior.* Princeton: Princeton Univ. Press, 1955.

25. Ames, A. Visual Perception and the rotating trapezoidal window. *Psychol. Monogr.*, 1951, 65-67.

26. Ames, Louise B. The sense of self of nursery school children as manifested by their verbal behavior. *J. Genet. Psychol.*, 1952, *81:* 193-232.

27. Amster, F. Differential use of play in treatment of young children. *Amer. J. Orthopsychiat.*, 1943, *13:* 62-69.

28. Anderson, Camilla M. The self-image: A theory of dynamics of behavior. *Ment. Hyg.*, 1952, *36:* 227-244.

29. Anderson, H. H., and Anderson, Gladys L. *An introduction to projective techniques.* New York: Prentice-Hall, 1951.

30. Anderson, H. H., and Brewer, J. Studies of teachers' classroom personalities, I. Dominative and socially integrative behavior of kindergarten teachers. *Appl. Psychol. Monogr.*, 1945, No. 6, 157.

31. Angyal, A. *Foundations for a science of personality.* New York: Commonwealth Fund, 1941.

32. Ansbacher, H. L., and Ansbacher, Rowena (eds.). *The individual psychology of Alfred Adler.* New York: Basic Books, 1956.

33. Arnold, D. L., and Mooney, R. L. A student's problem check list for junior high school. *Educ. Res. Bull.*, 1943, *22:* 42-48.

34. Asch, M. J. Nondirective teaching in psychology: An experimental study. *Psychol. Monogr.*, 1951, *65* (4).

35. Asch, S. E. Effects of group pressure upon the modification and distortion of judgments. In G. E. Swanson, T. M. Newcomb, and E. L. Hartley (eds.), *Readings in social psychology.* (2nd ed.) New York: Holt, 1952.

36. Asch, S. E. *Social psychology.* New York: Prentice-Hall, 1952.

37. Asher, E. J. The inadequacy of current intelligence tests for testing Kentucky mountain children. *J. Genet. Psychol.*, 1935, *46:* 480-486.

38. Ausubel, D. P., Schiff, H. M., and Goldman, M. Qualitative characteristics in the learning process associated with anxiety. *J. Abnorm. Soc. Psychol.*, 1953, *48:* 537-547.

39. Axline, Virginia M. Mental deficiency—Symptom or disease? *J. Consult. Psychol.*, 1949, *13:* 313-327.

40. Axline, Virginia M. Nondirective therapy for poor readers. *J. Consult. Psychol.*, 1947, *11:* 61-69.

41. Axline, Virginia M. *Play therapy.* Boston: Houghton Mifflin, 1947.

42. Axline, Virginia M. Play therapy experiences as described by child participants. *J. Consult. Psychol.*, 1950, *14:* 53-63.

43. Bach, G. R. Young children's play fantasies. *Psychol. Monogr.*, 1945, 59, No. 2.

44. Bagby, J. A cross cultural study of perceptual predominance in binocular rivalry. 1956 (to be published).

45. Bakan, D. A reconsideration of the problem of introspection. *Psychol. Bull.*, 1954, *51:* 105-118.

46. Bakay, Eva., and Shiller, P. H. Manipulative correction of visually presented figures. *Amer. J. sychol.*, 1948, *61:* 487-501.

47. Balester, R. J. The self concept and juvenile delinquency. Unpublished doctor's dissertation, Vanderbilt Univ., 1956.

48. Banham, Katharine M. Senescence and the emotions: A genetic study. *J. Genet. Psychol.*, 1951, 78: 175-183.

49. Barker, R., Dembo, T., and Lewin, K. (Studies in topological and vector psychology: II.) Frustration and regression: An experiment with young children. *Univ. Iowa Stud. Child Welf.*, 1941, 18, No. 1.

50. Barker, R. G., Kounin, J. S., and Wright, H. F. (eds.). *Child behavior and development; a course of representative studies.* New York: McGraw-Hill, 1943.

51. Barnhart, E. N. Stages in the construction of children's drawings as revealed through a recording device. *Psychol. Bull.*, 1940, 37: 581.

52. Barry, J. R. The relation of verbal reactions to adjustment level. *J. Abnorm. Soc. Psychol.*, 1950, 45: 647-658.

53. Bartlett, F. C. *Remembering: a study in experimental and social psychology.* Cambridge, Mass.: University Press, 1932.

54. Bartley, S. H. *Principles of perception.* New York: Harpers, 1958.

55. Baruch, Dorothy W. Aggression during doll play in a preschool. *Amer. J. Orthopsychiat.*, 1941, 11: 252-260.

56. Baruch, Dorothy W. *New ways in discipline: You and your child today.* New York: Whittlesey House, 1949.

57. Bass, B. M., McGehee, C. R., Hawkins, W. C., Young, P. C., and Gebel, A. S. Personality variables related to leaderless group discussion behavior. *J. Abnorm. Soc. Psychol.*, 1953, 48: 120-128.

58. Beier, E. G. The effect of induced anxiety on the flexibility of intellectual functioning. *Psychol. Monogr.*, 1951, 65, No. 9.

59. Beier, E. G. The effects of Rohrschach interpretation on intellectual functioning of adjusted, questionably adjusted and maladjusted subjects. *J. Proj. Tech.*, 1953, 17: 66-69.

60. Bell, G. B., and Hall, H. E., Jr. The relationship between leadership and empathy. *J. Abnorm. Soc. Psychol.*, 1954, 49: 156-157.

61. Belmont, Lillian, and Birch, H. G. Re-individualizing the repression hypothesis. *J. Abnorm. Soc. Psychol.*, 1951, 46: 226-235.

62. Bender, L. Art and therapy in the mental disturbances of children. *J. Nerv. Ment. Dis.*, 1937, 86: 249-263.

63. Benedict, Ruth. *Patterns of culture.* New York: Houghton Mifflin, 1934.

64. Benjamins, J. Changes in performance in relation to influences upon self-conceptualization. *J. Abnorm. Soc. Psychol.*, 1950, 45: 473-480.

65. Berger, E. M. The relation between expressed acceptance of self and expressed acceptance of others. *J. Abnorm. Soc. Psychol.*, 1952, 47: 778-782.

66. Bergman, D. V. Counseling method and client responses. *J. Consult. Psychol.*, 1951, 15: 216-224.

67. Bernhardt, K., and Snygg, D. The effect of cues upon the choice of the shorter path. *J. Comp. Psychol.*, 1937, 24: 269-276.

68. Bertocci, P. A. The psychological self, the ego, and personality. *Psychol. Rev.*, 1945, 52: 91-99.

69. Bettelheim, B. Individual and mass behavior in extreme situations. *J. Abnorm. Soc. Psychol.*, 1943, *38*: 417-452.

70. Bevan, W. Perception: Evaluation of a concept. *Psychol. Rev.*, 1958, *55*: 34-55.

71. Bexton, W. H., Heron, W., and Scott, T. H. Effects of decreased variation in the sensory environment. *Canad. J. Psychol.*, 1954, *8*: 70-76.

72. Bice, H. Factors in self concept of child with cerebral palsy. *Ment. Hyg., N. Y.*, 1954, *38*: 120-131.

73. Bierl, J. Changes in interpersonal perceptions following social interaction. *J. Abnorm. Soc. Psychol.*, 1953, *48*: 61-66.

74. Bills, R. E. Attributes of successful educational leaders. In R. L. Hopper (ed.), Interdisciplinary research in educational administration. *Bull. Bureau Sch. Serv.* Lexington, Kentucky: Coll. Educ., Univ. Kentucky, 1953, 16-38.

75. Bills, R. E. A comparison of scores on the index of adjustment and values with behavior in level-of-aspiration tasks. *J. Consult. Psychol.*, 1953, *17*: 206-212.

76. Bills, R. E. The effect of a value on learning. *J. Pers.*, 1952, *21*: 217-222.

77. Bills, R. E. An investigation of student centered teaching. *J. Educ. Res.*, 1952, *46*: 313-319.

78. Bills, R. E. Personality changes during student centered teaching. *J. Educ. Res.*, 1956, *50*: 121-126.

79. Bills, R. E. Play therapy with well adjusted retarded readers. *J. Consult. Psychol.*, 1950, *14*: 246-249.

80. Bills, R. E. Self concepts and Rorschach signs of depression. *J. Consult. Psychol.*, 1954, *18*: 135-137.

81. Bills, R. E., and McGehee, C. R. The effect of attitude toward psychology in a learning experiment. *J. Pers.*, 1955, *23*: 499-500.

82. Bills, R. E., Vance, E. L., and McLean, O. S. An index of adjustment and values. *J. Consult. Psychol.*, 1951, *15*: 257-261.

83. Bird, C. *Social psychology.* New York: Appleton-Century, 1940.

84. Bird, C., and Monachesi, E. D. Prejudice and discontent. *J. Abnorm. Soc. Psychol.*, 1954, *49*: 29-35.

85. Bishop, Barbara M. Mother-child interaction and the social behavior of children. *Psychol. Monogr.*, 1951, *65*, No. 11 (Whole No. 328).

86. Bixler, R. H. Treatment of a reading problem through nondirective play therapy. *J. Consult. Psychol.*, 1945, *9*: 105-118.

87. Blake, R. R., and Ramsey, G. V. *Perception: An approach to personality.* New York: Ronald Press, 1951.

88. Blocksma, D. D. Leader flexibility in group guidance situations. *Educ. Psychol. Measmt.*, 1949, *9*: 531-535.

89. Blos, P. The adolescent personality. New York: Appleton-Century, 1941.

90. Boas, F. The relation between physical and mental development. *Science*, 1941, *93*: 339-342.

91. Bogardus, E. S. Changes in racial distances. *Int. J. Opin. Attitude Res.*, 1947, *1* (4): 55-62.

92. Boger, J. H. An experimental study of the effects of perceptual training on group I. Q. test scores of elementary pupils in rural ungraded schools. *J. Educ. Res.*, 1952, *46:* 43-52.

93. Boring, E. G. A history of introspection. *Psychol. Bull.*, 1953, *50:* 169-189.

94. Bossard, J. H. S. *The sociology of child development.* New York: Harper, 1948.

95. Bovard, E. W., Jr. Clinical insight as a function of group process. *J. Abnorm. Soc. Psychol.*, 1952, *47:* 534-539.

96. Bovard, E. W., Jr. Conformity to social norms in stable and temporary groups. *Science,* 1953, *117:* 361-363.

97. Bovard, E. W., Jr. The experimental production of interpersonal affect. *J. Abnorm. Soc. Psychol.*, 1951, *46:* 521-528.

98. Bovard, E. W., Jr. Group structure and perception. *J. Abnorm. Soc. Psychol.*, 1951, *46:* 398-405.

99. Bowlby, J. *Child care and the growth of love.* London: Penguin Books, 1953.

100. Breckenridge, Marian E., and Vincent, E. L. *Child development: Physical and psychological growth through the school years.* Philadelphia: Saunders, 1943.

101. Brigden, R. L. Tachistoscopic study of the differentiation of perception. *Psychol. Monogr.*, 1933, *44:* 163-166.

102. Bown, O. An investigation of the therapeutic relationship in client-centered psychotherapy. Unpublished doctoral dissertation, Univ. of Chicago, 1954.

103. Brown, R. W. A determinant of the relationship between rigidity and authoritarianism. *J. Abnorm. Soc. Psychol.*, 1953, *48:* 469-476.

104. Brown, R. W., and Lenneberg, E. H. A study in language and cognition. *J. Abnorm. Soc. Psychol.*, 1954, *49:* 454-462.

105. Brownfain, J. J. Stability of the self-concept as a dimension of personality. *J. Abnorm. Soc. Psychol.*, 1952, *47:* 597-606.

106. Bruner, J. S., and Goodman, C. C. Value and need as organizing factors in perception. *J. Abnorm. Soc. Psychol.*, 1947, *42:* 33-44.

107. Bruner, J. S., and Krech, D. *Personal and social factors in perception.* Durham, N. C.: Duke Univ. Press, 1950.

108. Bruner, J. S., and Postman, L. Emotional selectivity in perception and reaction. *J. Pers.*, 1947, *16:* 69-77.

109. Bruner, J. S., and Postman, L. On the perception of incongruity: A paradigm. *J. Pers.*, 1949, *18:* 206-223.

110. Bruner, J. S., and Postman, L. The symbolic value as an organizing factor in perception. *J. Soc. Psychol.*, 1948, *27:* 203-208.

111. Bryan, W. L., and Harter, N. Studies on the telegraphic language. *Psychol. Rev.*, 1899, *6:* 346-375.

112. Buchenholtz, B., and Frank, R. J. The concepts of the self in acute traumatic neurosis of war. *J. Nerv. Ment. Dis.*, 1948, *107:* 55-61.

113. Bugental, J. F. T., and Zelen, S. L. Investigations into the 'self-concept.' I. The W-A-Y technique. *J. Pers.*, 1950, *18:* 483-498.

114. Burkholder, P. R. Cooperation and conflict among primitive organisms. *Amer. Scientist,* 1952, *10:* 601-631.

115. Burtt, H. E. An experimental study of early childhood memory: Final report. *J. Genet. Psychol.,* 1941, *58:* 435-439.

116. Butler, J. M. The interaction of client and therapist. *J. Abnorm. Psychol.,* 1952, *47:* 366-378.

117. Calvin, A. D., and Holtzman, W. H. Adjustment and the discrepancy between self concept and inferred self. *J. Consult. Psychol.,* 1953, *17:* 39-44.

118. Cannon, W. B. *The way of an investigator: A scientist's experiences in medical research.* New York: Norton, 1945.

119. Cannon, W. B. *The wisdom of the body.* New York: Norton, 1932.

120. Cantril, H. An inquiry concerning the characteristics of man. *J. Abnorm. Soc. Psychol.,* 1950, *45:* 490-503.

121. Cantril, H. The nature of social perception. *Trans. N. Y. Acad. Sci.,* 1948, *10:* 143-153.

122. Cantril, H. Perception and interpersonal relations. *Amer. J. Psychiat.,* 1957, *114:* 119-126.

123. Cantril, H. The prediction of social events. *J. Abnorm. Soc. Psychol.,* 1938, *33:* 364-389.

124. Carlson, A. J., and Johnson, V. *The machinery of the body.* (4th ed.) Chicago: Univ. of Chicago Press, 1953.

125. Carmichael, L. (ed.) *Manual of child psychology.* New York: Wiley, 1946.

126. Carmichael, L., Hogen, H. P., and Walter, A. A. An experimental study of the effect of language on the reproduction of visually perceived form. *J. Exper. Psychol.,* 1932, *15:* 73-86.

127. Carter, L. F., and Schooler, K. Value, need, and other factors in perception. *Psychol. Rev.,* 1949, *56:* 200-207.

128. Centers, R. The American class structure: A psychological analysis. In G. E. Swanson, T. M. Newcomb, and E. L. Hartley (eds.), *Readings in social psychology.* (Rev. ed.) New York: Holt, 1952.

129. Centers, R. Nominal variation and class identification: The working and laboring classes. *J. Abnorm. Soc. Psychol.,* 1950, *45:* 195-215.

130. Chapman, D. W., and Volkmann, J. A social determinant of the level of aspiration. *J. Abnorm. Soc. Psychol.,* 1939, *34:* 225-238.

131. Chein, I. The logic of prediction: Some observations on Dr. Sarbin's exposition. *Psychol. Rev.,* 1945, *52:* 175-179.

132. Child, I. L., and Whiting, J. W. M. Determinants of level of aspiration: Evidence from everyday life. *J. Abnorm. Soc. Psychol.,* 1949, *44:* 303-314.

133. Child, I. L., and Whiting, J. W. M. Effects of goal attainment: Relaxation versus renewed striving. *J. Abnorm. Soc. Psychol.,* 1950, *45:* 667-681.

134. Chodorkoff, B. Adjustment and the discrepancy between the perceived and the ideal self. *J. Clin. Psychol.,* 1954, *10:* 266-268.

135. Chodorkoff, B. Self-perception, perceptual defense, and adjustment. *J. Abnorm. Soc. Psychol.,* 1954, *49:* 508-512.

136. Chowdhry, Kamla, and Newcomb, T. M. The relative abilities of leaders

and non-leaders to estimate opinions of their own groups. *J. Abnorm. Soc. Psychol.*, 1952, 47: 51-57.

137. Clark, K. B., and Clark, Mamie P. Racial identification and preference in Negro children. In G. E. Swanson, T. M. Newcomb, and E. L. Hartley (eds.), *Readings in social psychology.* (Rev. ed.) New York: Henry Holt, 1952, 551-560.

138. Clark, K. B., and Clark, M. P. Skin color as a factor in racial identification of Negro preschool children, *J. Soc. Psychol.* 1940, 11: 159-169.

139. Clark, R. S., Heron, W., Fetherstonhaugh, M. L., Forgays, D. G., and Hebb, D. O. Individual differences in dogs: Preliminary report on the effects of early experience. *Canad. J. Psychol.*, 1951, 5: 150-156.

140. Coch, L., and French, J. R. P., Jr. Overcoming resistance to change. *Hum. Relat.*, 1948, 1: 512-532.

141. Coffin, T. E. Some conditions of suggestion and suggestibility: A study of some attitudinal and situational factors influencing the process of suggestion. *Psychol. Monogr.*, 1941, 53, No. 4.

142. Cohen, L. D. Level-of-aspiration behavior and feelings of adequacy and self-acceptance. *J. Abnorm. Soc. Psychol.*, 1954, 49: 84-86.

143. Combs, A. W. Basic aspects of non-directive therapy. *Amer. J. Orthopsychiat.*, 1946, 16: 589-607.

144. Combs, A. W. A comparative study of motivations as revealed in thematic apperception stories and autobiography. *J. Clin. Psychol.*, 1947, 3: 65-75.

145. Combs, A. W. Counseling as a learning process. *J. of Counsel. Psychol.*, 1954, 1: 31-36.

146. Combs, A. W. Intelligence from a perceptual point of view. *J. Abnorm. Soc. Psychol.*, 1952, 47: 662-673.

147. Combs, A. W. A method of analysis for the Thematic Apperception Test and Autobiography. *J. Clin. Psychol.*, 1945, 2: 167-174.

148. Combs, A. W. The myth of competition. *Childh. Educ.*, 1957, 33: 364-369.

149. Combs, A. W. New horizons in field research: The self concept. *Ed. Leadership.*, 1958, 15: 315-319.

150. Combs, A. W. A phenomenological approach to adjustment theory. *J. Abnorm. Soc. Psychol.*, 1949, 44: 29-35.

151. Combs, A. W. Phenomenological concepts in non-directive therapy. *J. Consult. Psychol.*, 1948, 12: 197-208.

152. Combs, A. W. The psychology of the college student. *In What Should Higher Education Be Doing in 1954?* Hempstead, N. Y.: Hofstra College, 1954, 31-35.

153. Combs, A. W. Some dynamic aspects of non-directive therapy. *Ann. N. Y. Acad. Sci.*, 1948, 49: 878-888.

154. Combs, A. W. The use of personal experience in Thematic Apperception Test story plots. *J. Clin. Psychol.*, 1946, 2: 357-363.

155. Combs, A. W. The validity and reliability of interpretation from autobiography and Thematic Apperception Test. *J. Clin. Psychol.*, 1946, 2: 240-247.

156. Combs, A. W., and Cowen, W. L. Follow-up study of 32 cases treated

by nondirective psychotherapy. *J. Abnorm. Soc. Psychol.*, 1950, *45:* 232-258.

157. Combs, A. W., and Fisk, R. S. Problems and research needs in administration. *J. Soc. Issues*, 1954, *10:* 49-58.

158. Combs, A. W., Fisk, R. S., Fine, H. F., Zimet, C. N., Wiberley, J. A., and Nesbitt, D. A. The Syracuse studies. *J. Soc. Issues*, 1954, *10:* 5-24.

159. Combs, A. W., and Snygg, D. Implications of the phenomenological approach for the evaluation of psychotherapy. *Psych. Serv. Center J.*, 1950, *2:* 96-103.

160. Combs, A. W., and Soper, D. W. The self, its derivate terms and research. *J. Indiv. Psychol.*, 1957, *13:* 134-145.

161. Combs, A. W., and Taylor, C. The effect of perception of mild degrees of threat on performance. *J. Abnorm. Soc. Psychol.*, 1952, *47:* 420-424.

162. Conrad, Dorothy. An empirical study of the concept of psychotherapeutic success. *J. Consult. Psychol.*, 1952, *16:* 92-97.

163. Corey, S. M. *Action research to improve school practices.* New York: Bureau of Publications, Teachers College, Columbia Univ., 1953, 47-61.

164. Covner, B. J. Studies in phonographic recordings of verbal material: I. The use of phonographic recordings in counseling practice and research. *J. Consult. Psychol.*, 1942, *6:* 105-113.

165. Cowen, E. L. The influence of varying degrees of psychological stress on problem-solving rigidity. *J. Abnorm. Soc. Psychol.*, 1952, *47:* 512-519.

166. Cowen, E. L. The negative self concept as a personality measure. *J. Consult. Psychol.*, 1954, *18:* 138-142.

167. Cowen, E. L. Stress reduction and problem-solving rigidity. *J. Consult. Psychol.*, 1952, *16:* 425-428.

168. Cowen, E., and Beier, E. The influence of "threat expectancy" on perception. *J. Pers.*, 1950, *19:* 85-94.

169. Cowen, E. L., and Thompson, G. G. Problem solving rigidity and personality structure. *J. Abnorm. Soc. Psychol.*, 1951, *46:* 165-176.

170. Crafts, L. W., Schneirla, T. C., Robinson, E. E., and Gilbert, R. W. *Recent experiments in psychology.* New York: McGraw-Hill, 1938.

171. Crandall, V. J. Induced frustration and punishment-reward expectancy in thematic apperception stories. *J. Consult. Psychol.*, 1951, *15:* 400-404.

172. Creelman, Marjorie. Accuracy of the concept of self as a criterion in differential diagnosis. *Persona.*, 1949, *1* (2): 21-25.

173. Cronbach, L. J. *Essentials of psychological testing.* New York: Harper, 1949.

174. Cruickshank, W. M. Qualitative analysis of intelligence test responses. *J. Clin. Psychol.*, 1947, *3:* 381-386.

175. Crutchfield, R. S. Conformity and character. *Amer. Psychologist,* 1955, *10:* 191-198.

176. Cunningham, Ruth, and others. *Group behavior of boys and girls.* New York: Bureau of Publications, Teachers College, Columbia Univ., 1951.

177. Dashiell, J. *Fundamentals of general psychology.* Boston: Houghton Mifflin, 1937.

178. Davidoff, M. A study of empathy and correlations of prejudice toward a minority group. *Purdue Univ. Stud. Higher Educ.*, 1949, No. 67.

179. Davis, A. *Social class influences upon learning.* Cambridge, Mass.: Harvard Univ. Press, 1948.

180. Davis, A., and Dollard, J. *Children of bondage: The personality development of Negro youth in the urban South.* Washington, D. C.: American Council on Education, 1940.

181. Davis, A., Gardner, B. B., and Gardner, Mary. *Deep South.* Chicago: Univ. of Chicago Press, 1941.

182. Davis, A., and Havighurst, R. J. *Father of the man: How your child gets his personality.* Boston: Houghton Mifflin, 1947.

183. Davis, Clara. Self selection of diets: An experiment with infants. *The Trained Nurse and Hospital Review.*, 1931, *86:* 629-634.

184. Davis, D. R. Increase in strength of a secondary drive as a cause of disorganization. *Quart. J. Exp. Psychol.*, 1948, *1:* 22-28.

185. Davis, K. Final note on a case of extreme isolation. *Amer. J. Sociol.*, 1947, *52:* 432-437.

186. Dempsey, E. W. *Homeostasis.* In S. S. Stephens (ed.), *Handbook of experimental psychology.* New York: Wiley, 1951.

187. Despert, J. A method for the study of personality reactions in pre-school age children by means of analysis of their play. *J. Psychol.*, 1940, *9:* 17-29.

188. Dewey, E. *Behavior development of infants.* New York: Columbia Univ. Press, 1935.

189. Diehl, H. The ritual of science. *J. Psychol.*, 1941, *12:* 13-19.

190. Diethelm, O., and Jones, M. Influence of anxiety on attention, learning, retention and thinking. *Arch. Neurol. Psychiat.*, 1947, *58:* 325-336.

191. Diller, L. Conscious and unconscious self-attitudes after success and failure. *J. Pers.*, 1954, *23:* 1-12.

192. Dockeray, F. C., and Rice, G. Responses of newborn infants to pain stimulation. *Ohio State Univ. Stud.*, 1934, *12:* 82-93.

193. Dollard, J. *Criteria for the life history.* New Haven: Yale Univ. Press, 1935.

194. Dollard, J. *Frustration and Aggression.* New Haven: Yale Univ. Press, 1939.

195. Dorris, R. J., Levinson, D. J., and Hanfmann, Eugenia. Authoritarian personality studies by a new variation of the sentence completion technique. *J. Abnorm. Psychol.*, 1954, *49:* 99-108.

196. Driscoll, Gertrude. *How to study the behavior of children.* New York: Bureau of Publications, Teachers College, Columbia Univ., 1941, *8:* 1-84.

197. Dubois, Rachael-Davis. *Get together Americans.* New York: Harper, 1943.

198. Dunlap, K. *Habits: Their making and unmaking.* New York: Liveright, 1932.

199. Dymond, Rosalind. Personality and empathy. *J. Consult. Psychol.*, 1950, *14:* 343-350.

200. Dymond, Rosalind. A scale for the measure of empathic ability. *J. Consult. Psychol.*, 1949, *13:* 127-133.

201. Dymond, Rosalind. The relation of accuracy of perception of the spouse and marital happiness. *Amer. Psychol.*, 1953, *8:* 344.

202. Dymond, Rosalind, Hughes, Anne, and Raabe, Virginia. Measurable changes in empathy with age. *J. Consult. Psychol.*, 1952, *16:* 202-206.

203. Edwards, W. The theory of decision making. *Psychol. Bull.*, 1954, *51:* 380-417.

204. Eichler, R. Experimental stress and alleged Rorschach indices of anxiety. *J. Abnorm. Soc. Psychol.*, 1951, *46:* 344-355.

205. Elkin, F. Specialists interpret the case of Harold Holzer. *J. Abnorm. Soc. Psychol.*, 1947, *42:* 99-111.

206. Elkisch, P. Children's drawings in a projective technique. *Psychol. Monog.*, 1945, *58*, No. 1.

207. Engel, E. The role of content in binocular resolution. *Amer. J. Psychol.*, 1956, *69:* 87-91.

208. Engel, Mary. *The stability of the self concept in adolescence.* Unpublished doctoral dissertation, Peabody College, 1956.

209. Epstein, S. Unconscious self-evaluation in a normal and schizophrenic group. *J. Abnorm. Soc. Psychol.*, 1955, *50:* 65-70.

210. Eriksen, C. Defense against ego threat in memory and perception. *J. Abnorm. Soc. Psychol.*, 1952, *47:* 230-235.

211. Eriksen, C. Perceptual defense as a function of unacceptable needs. *J. Abnorm. Soc. Psychol.*, 1951, *46:* 557-564.

212. Eriksen, C. Psychological defenses and "ego strength" in the recall of completed and incompleted tasks. *J. Abnorm. Soc. Psychol.*, 1954, *49:* 45-50.

213. Eriksen, C., and Lazarus, R. Perceptual defense and projective tests. *J. Abnorm. Soc. Psychol.*, 1952, *47:* 302-308.

214. Evans, R. Personal values as factors in anti-Semitism. *J. Abnorm. Soc. Psychol.*, 1952, *47:* 749-756.

215. Evvard, J. Is the appetite of swine a reliable indication of physiological needs? *Proc. Iowa Acad. Sci.*, 1916, *22:* 375-411.

216. Farberow, N. L., and Sarbin, T. R. A clinical study of role and self in hypnotic age regression. *Amer. Psychologist*, 1950, *5:* 305.

217. Faw, V. A psychotherapeutic method of teaching psychology. *Amer. Psychologist*, 1949, *4:* 104-109.

218. Feingold, G. Q. Intelligence of the first generation of immigrant groups. *J. Educ. Psychol.*, 1924, *15:* 65-83.

219. Festinger, L., Pepitone, A., and Newcomb, T. Some consequences of de-individuation in a group. *J. Abnorm. Soc. Psychol.*, 1952, *47:* 382-389.

220. Fey, W. F. Acceptance by others and its relation to acceptance of self and others: A revaluation. *J. Abnorm. Soc. Psychol.*, 1955, *50:* 274-276.

221. Fiedler, F. E. A comparison of therapeutic relationships in psychoanalytic, nondirective and Adlerian therapy. *J. Consult. Psychol.*, 1950, *14:* 436-445.

222. Fiedler, F. E. The concept of an ideal therapeutic relationship. *J. Consult. Psychol.*, 1950, *14:* 239-245.

223. Fischer, R. P. Schilder's mind: Perception and thought and goals and desires of man. *Psychol. Bull.*, 1944, *41:* 30-40.

224. Fitts, W. H. *The role of the self-concept in social perception.* Unpublished doctoral dissertation, Vanderbilt Univ., 1954.

225. Flanders, N. A. Personal-social anxiety as a factor in experimental learning situations. *J. Educ. Res.,* 1951, *45:* 100-110.

226. Fleming, Louise, and Snyder, W. U. Social and personal changes following non-directive group play therapy. *Amer. J. Orthopsychiat.,* 1947, *17:* 101-116.

227. Fletcher, J. M. Homeostasis as an explanatory principle in psychology. *Psychol. Rev.,* 1942, *49:* 80-87.

228. Flowerman, S. H. The use of propaganda to reduce prejudice: A refutation. *Int. J. Opin. Attitude Res.,* 1949, *3:* 99-108.

229. Frank, L. K. The fundamental needs of the child. *Mental Hyg.,* 1938, *22:* 353-379.

230. Frank, L. K. *Projective methods.* Springfield, Ill.: C. C. Thomas, 1948.

231. Frank, L. K. Projective methods for the study of personality. *J. Psychol.,* 1939, *8:* 389-413.

232. Franklin, J. C., Schiele, B. C., Brozek, J., and Keys, A. Observations of human behavior in experimental semi-starvation and rehabilitation. *J. Clin. Psychol.,* 1948, *4:* 28-45.

233. Freeman, F. N., Holzinger, K. J., and Mitchell, B. C. The influence of environment on the intelligence, school achievement and conduct of foster children. *Yearb. Nat. Soc. Stud. Educ.,* 1928, *27:* Part I, 102-217.

234. Freeman, G. L. *The energetics of human behavior.* Ithaca, N. Y.: Cornell Univ. Press, 1948.

235. Frenkel-Brunswik, Else. Distortion of reality in perception and social outlook. *Amer. Psychologist,* 1949, *4:* 253.

236. Frenkel-Brunswik, Else. Mechanisms of self-deception. *J. Soc. Psychol.,* 1939, *10:* 409-420.

237. Frenkel-Brunswik, Else. A study of prejudice in children. *Hum. Relat.,* 1948, *1:* 295-306.

238. Freud, A. *Introduction to technic of child analysis.* Washington: Nervous and Mental Disease Pub. Co., 1928.

239. Freud, S. *A general introduction to psychoanalysis.* Garden City, N.Y.: Garden City Publishing Co., 1920.

240. Freud, S. *An outline of psychoanalysis.* New York: Norton, 1949.

241. Freud, S. *The problem of anxiety.* New York: Norton, 1936.

242. Friedenberg, E. Z., and Roth, J. A. *Self-perception in the university: A study of successful and unsuccessful graduate students.* Chicago: Univ. of Chicago Press, 1954.

243. Friedman, I. Phenomenal, ideal, and projected conceptions of self. *J. Abnorm. Soc. Psychol.,* 1955, *51:* 611-615.

244. Fromm, E. *The art of loving.* New York: Harper, 1956.

245. Fromm, E. *Psychoanalysis and religion.* New Haven: Yale Univ. Press, 1950.

246. Frymier, J. R. The relationship of certain behavioral characteristics to perception. Unpublished doctoral dissertation, Univ. of Florida, 1957.

247. Funkenstein, D. H. The physiology of fear and anger. *Sci. Amer.*, 1955, *192* (5): 74-80.

248. Gage, N. L. Accuracy of social perception and effectiveness in interpersonal relationships. *J. Personality*, 1953, *22*: 128-141.

249. Gage, N. L. Explorations in the understanding of others. *Educ. Psychol. Measmt.*, 1953, *13*: 14-26.

250. Gaier, E. L. Selected personality variables and the learning process. *Psychol. Monogr.*, 1952, *66*, No. 17 (whole No. 349).

251. Geig, A. C. Learning disability in intelligent children. *Med. Ann. Dist. Columbia*, 6, No. 9.

252. Gerard, R. W. *Unresting Cells.* New York: Harper, 1949.

253. Gesell, A., Ilg, F. L., Ames, L. B., and Bullis, G. E. *The child from five to ten.* New York: Harper, 1946.

254. Gesell, A., Thompson, H., and Amatruda, C. S. *The psychology of early growth.* New York: Macmillan, 1938.

255. Gibson, J. J., and Crooks, L. E. A. A theoretical field-analysis of automobile driving. *Amer. J. Psychol.*, 1938, *51*: 453-471.

256. Gilchrist, J. C., Ludeman, J. F., and Lysak, W. Values as determinants of word-recognition thresholds. *J. Abnorm. Soc. Psychol.*, 1954, *49*: 423-426.

257. Goldstein, K. *The organism.* New York: American Book Co., 1939.

258. Goodenough, Florence. *The measurement of intelligence by drawings.* Yonkers-on-Hudson, N. Y.: World Book, 1926.

259. Goodenough, Florence. Racial differences in the intelligence of school children. *J. Exp. Psychol.*, 1926, *9*: 388-397.

260. Goodman, H. Self-insight, empathy and perceptual distortion: A study of the relationships between measures of self-insight, empathy, and perceptual distortion as obtained from ratings made by individuals on themselves and others in their group. *Dissertation Abstr.*, 1953, *13*: 120.

261. Goodman, Mary E. *Race awareness in young children.* Cambridge, Mass.: Addison-Wesley Press, 1952.

262. Gordon, H. Mental and scholastic tests among retarded children. London: Bureau of Education, Educational Pamphlet No. 44, 1923.

263. Gordon, T. *Group-centered leadership: A way of releasing the creative power of groups.* Boston: Houghton Mifflin, 1955.

264. Gould, R. J. Some sociological determinants of goal striving. *J. Soc. Psychol.*, 1941, *13*: 461-473.

265. Greer, F. L., Galanter, E. H., and Nordie, P. G. Interpersonal knowledge and individual and group effectiveness. *J. Abnorm. Soc. Psychol.* 1954, *49*: 411-414.

266. Grossack, M. M. Some effects of cooperation and competition upon small group behavior. *J. Abnorm. Soc. Psychol.*, 1954, *49*: 341-348.

267. Grover, K. B. The use of English compositions to gain understandings of pupils. *Sch. Rev.*, 1946, *54*: 605-610.

268. Haigh, G. Defensive behavior in client-centered therapy. *J. Consult. Psychol.*, 1949, *13*: 181-189.

269. Haigh, G., and Fiske, D. W. Corroboration of personal values as selective factors in perception. *J. Abnorm. Soc. Psychol.*, 1952, *47*: 394-398.

270. Haimowitz, Natalie R., and Haimowitz, M. L. Personality changes in client-centered therapy. In W. Wolff and J. A. Precker (eds.), *Success in psychotherapy.* New York: Grune & Stratton, 1952, 63-93.

271. Haller, M. W. The reaction of infants to changes in raw intensity and pitch of pure tone. *J. Genet. Psychol.*, 1932, *40*: 162-180.

272. Hallowell, A. I. Cultural factors in the structuralization of perception. In J. H. Rohrer and M. Sherif (eds.), *Social psychology at the crossroads.* New York: Harper, 1951.

273. Halpern, H. M. Empathy, similarity and self-satisfaction. *J. Consult. Psychol.*, 1955, *19*: 449-452.

274. Halpin, A. W. James Clerk Maxwell on the dynamical and the statistical modes of thought about man. *J. Abnorm. Soc. Psychol.*, 1951, *46*: 257.

275. Hamilton, G. V. A study of perseverance reactions in primates and rodents. *Behav. Monogr.*, 1916, *3*: No. 13.

276. Hanlon, T. E., Hopstaetter, P. R., and Connor, J. P. Congruence of self and ideal self in relation to personality adjustment. *J. Consult. Psychol.*, 1954, *18*: 215-218.

277. Hartley, E. L. *Problems in prejudice.* New York: King's Crown Press, 1946.

278. Hartley, Margaret. Changes in the self-concept during psychotherapy. Unpublished doctoral dissertation, Univ. of Chicago, 1951.

279. Hartshorne, H., and May, M. A. *Studies in the nature of character.* I. Studies in Deceit. Book 1: General methods and results. Book 2: Statistical methods and results. New York: Macmillan, 1928.

280. Hastings, P. K. A relationship between visual perception and level of personal security. *J. Abnorm. Soc. Psychol.*, 1952, *47*: 552-560.

281. Hastorf, A. H., and Cantril, H. They saw a game: A case study. *J. Abnorm. Soc. Psychol.*, 1954, *49*: 129-134.

282. Havighurst, R. J., Robinson, Myra Z., and Dorr, Mildred. The development of the ideal self in childhood and adolescence. *J. Educ. Res.*, 1946, *40*: 241-257.

283. Hebb, D. O. *The organization of behavior: A neuropsychological theory.* New York: Wiley, 1949.

284. Henry, J., and Henry, Z. Doll play of Pilaga Indian children: An experimental and field analysis of the behavior of the Pilaga Indian children. *Res. Monogr. Amer. Orthopsychiat. Ass.*, 1944, 4.

285. Hildreth, G. *The child mind in evolution: A study of developmental sequences in drawing.* New York: King's Crown Press, 1941.

286. Hildreth, G. *Learning the three r's.* Philadelphia Educ. Pubs., 1936.

287. Hilgard, E. R. Human motives and the concept of self. *Amer. Psychologist*, 1949, *4*: 374-382.

288. Hilgard, E. R. *Theories of learning.* New York: Appleton-Century-Crofts, 1948.

289. Hinckley, E. D., and Rethlingshafer, Dorothy A. Value judgments of heights of men by college students. *J. Psychol.*, 1951, *31*: 257-262.

290. Hoffman, M. L. Some psychodynamic factors in compulsive conformity. *J. Abnorm. Soc. Psychol.*, 1953, *48:* 383-393.

291. Hogan, R. A. A theory of threat and defense. *J. Consult. Psychol.*, 1952, *16:* 417-424.

292. Hollander, E. P. Authoritarianism and leadership choice in a military setting. *J. Abnorm. Soc. Psychol.*, 1954, *49:* 365-370.

293. Hollingshead, A. B. *Elmtown's youth.* New York: J. Wiley, 1949.

294. Horney, Karen. *The neurotic personality of our time.* New York: W. W. Norton, 1937.

295. Horowitz, E. L. The development of attitude toward the negro. *Arch. Psychol.*, 1936, No. 194.

296. Horowitz, E. L. Some aspects of the development of patriotism in children. *Sociometry*, 1940, *3:* 329-341.

297. Horrocks, J. E. The relationship between knowledge of human development and ability to use such knowledge. *J. Appl. Psychol.*, 1946, *20:* 501-508.

298. Hovland, C. I., and Sherif, M. Judgmental phenomena and scales of attitude measurement: Item displacement in Thurstone scales. *J. Abnorm. Soc. Psychol.*, 1952, *47:* 822-832.

299. Howard, A. R., and Kelly, G. A. A theoretical approach to psychological movement. *J. Abnorm. Soc. Psychol.*, 1954, *49:* 399-404.

300. Hull, C. L. *Hypnosis and suggestibility.* New York: Appleton-Century, 1931.

301. Huntley, C. W. Judgments of self based upon records of expressive behavior. *J. Abnorm. Soc. Psychol.*, 1940, *35:* 398-427.

302. Husserl, E. *Ideas: General introduction to pure phenomenology.* London: Unwin, 1952.

303. Husserl, E. *Logische untersuchungen.* Halle, Germany: Niemeyer, 1921.

304. Immergluck, Ludwig. The role of set in perceptual judgment. *J. Psychol.*, 1952, *34:* 181-189.

305. Ittelson, W. H. *The Ames demonstrations in perception.* Princeton: Princeton Univ. Press, 1952.

306. Ittelson, W. H. The constancies in perceptual theory. *Psychol. Rev.*, 1951, *58:* 285-294.

307. Jahoda, G. Political attitudes and judgments of other people. *J. Abnorm. Soc. Psychol.*, 1954, *49:* 330-334.

308. James, W. *The principles of psychology.* New York: Henry Holt, 1890.

309. Janis, I. L., and Feshbach, S. Effects of fear-arousing communications. *J. Abnorm. Soc. Psychol.*, 1953, *48:* 78-92.

310. Jastak, J. A rigorous criterion of feeble-mindedness. *J. Abnorm. Soc. Psychol.*, 1949, *44:* 367-378.

311. Jenkins, Gladys G., Shacter, Helen, and Bauer, W. W. *These are your children: How they develop and how to guide them.* Chicago: Scott, Foresman, 1949.

312. Jensen, M. B. Mental deterioration following carbon monoxide poisoning. *J. Abnorm. Soc. Psychol.*, 1950, *45:* 146-153.

313. Jersild, A. T. *Child psychology.* New York: Prentice-Hall, 1954.

314. Jersild, A. T., and Tasch, Ruth. *Children's interests and what they suggest for education.* New York: Bureau of Publications, Teachers College, Columbia Univ., 1949.

315. Johnson, D. M., and Smith, H. C. Democratic leadership in the college classroom. *Psychol. Monogr.*, 1953, 67 (No. 361).

316. Johnson, T. F. Conceptions of parents held by adolescents. *J. Abnorm. Soc. Psychol.*, 1952, 47: 783-789.

317. Kanner, Leo. *Child psychiatry.* (3rd ed.) Springfield, Ill.: Thomas, 1957.

318. Kardiner, A. *The individual and his society.* New York: Columbia Univ. Press, 1939.

319. Kates, S. L. Subjects' evaluations of annoying situations after being described as well adjusted and poorly adjusted. *J. Consult. Psychol.*, 1952, 16: 429-434.

320. Katz, D., and Braley, K. Racial sterotypes of one hundred college students. *J. Abnorm. Soc. Psychol.*, 1933, 28: 280-290.

321. Katz, D., Maccoby, N., and Morse, Nancy C. *Productivity, supervision, and morale in an office situation.* Part I. Ann Arbor: Institute for Social Research, Univ. of Michigan, 1950.

322. Katz, I. Emotional expression in failure: A new hypothesis. *J. Abnorm. Soc. Psychol.*, 1950, 45: 329-349.

323. Keister, M. E. The behavior of young children in failure. *Univ. Iowa Stud. Child Welf.*, 1938, 14: 27-82.

324. Keister, M. E., and Updegraff, R. A study of children's reactions to failure and an experimental attempt to modify them. *Child Develop.*, 1937, 8: 241-248.

325. Kelley, E. C. *Education for what is real.* New York: Harper, 1947.

326. Kilpatrick, W. H., and Van Til, W. *Intercultural attitudes in the making; parents, youth leaders, and teachers at work.* New York: Harper, 1947.

327. Kimball, Barbara. The sentence-completion technique in a study of scholastic underachievement. *J. Consult. Psychol.*, 1952, 16: 353-358.

328. Kinsey, A. C., Pomeroy, W. B., and Martin, C. E. *Sexual behavior in the human male.* Philadelphia: Saunders, 1948.

329. Klein, G. S. The personal world through perception. In R. R. Blake, and G. V. Ramsey, *Perception.* New York: Ronald Press, 1951, 328-355.

330. Klein, G. S., Schlesinger, H. J., and Meister, D. E. The effect of personal values on perception: An experimental critique. *Psychol. Rev.*, 1951, 58: 96-112.

331. Kluckhohn, C., and Leighton, D. *The Navaho.* Cambridge: Harvard Univ. Press, 1946.

332. Koffka, K. Perception: An introduction to the gestalt-theorie. *Psychol. Bull.*, 1922, 19: 531-585.

333. Koffka, K. *Principles of Gestalt psychology.* New York: Harcourt, Brace, 1935.

334. Köhler, W. *Dynamics in psychology.* New York: Liveright, 1940.

335. Köhler, W. Psychological remarks on some questions of anthropology. *Amer. J. Psychol.*, 1937, *50:* 271-288.

336. Korchin, S. J., and Basowitz, H. Perceptual adequacy in a life stress. *J. Psychol.*, 1954, *38:* 495-502.

337. Krall, Vita. Personality characteristics of accident repeating children. *J. Abnorm. Soc. Psychol.*, 1953, *48:* 99-107.

338. Krasnogorski, N. I. The conditioned reflex and children's neuroses. *Amer. J. of Diseases of Child.*, 1925, *30:* 753-768.

339. Krech, D. The challenge and the promise. *J. Soc. Issues*, 1946, *2:* 34-46.

340. Kutner, B., Wilkens, Carol, and Yarrow, Penny. Verbal attitudes and overt behavior involving racial prejudice. *J. Abnorm. Soc. Psychol.*, 1952, *47:* 649-652.

341. Landsman, T. Four phenomenologies. *J. Ind. Psychol.*, 1958, *14:* 29-37.

342. Laffal, J. The learning and retention of words with association disturbances. *J. Abnorm. Soc. Psychol.*, 1952, *47:* 454-462.

343. Lange, C. G., and James, W. *The emotions.* Baltimore: Williams & Wilkins, 1922.

344. Lantz, Beatrice. Some dynamic aspects of success and failure. *Psychol. Monogr.*, 1945, *59:* No. 1.

345. Lanzetta, J. T., Haefner, D., Langham, P., and Axelrod, H. Some effects of situational threat on group behavior. *J. Abnorm. Soc. Psychol.*, 1954, *49:* 445-453.

346. Lashley, K. S. Nervous mechanisms in learning. In C. Murchison (ed.), *A handbook of general experimental psychology.* Worcester, Mass.: Clark Univ. Press, 1934, 456-496.

347. Lazarus, R. S., and Longo, N. The consistency of psychological defenses against threat. *J. Abnorm. Soc. Psychol.*, 1953, *48:* 495-499.

348. Lazarus, R. S., and McCleary, R. A. Autonomic discrimination with awareness: A study of subception. *Psychol. Rev.*, 1951, *58:* 113-122.

349. Lazarsfeld, P. F., Berelson, B., and Gaudet, H. *The people's choice.* New York: Duell, Sloan & Pearce, 1944.

350. Lecky, P. *Self-consistency: A theory of personality.* New York: Island Press, 1945.

351. Lee, Dorothy. Notes on the conception of the self among the Wintu Indians. *J. Abnorm. Soc. Psychol.*, 1950, *45:* 538-543.

352. Leeper, R. A study of a neglected portion of the field of learning—The development of sensory organization. *J. Genet. Psychol.*, 1935, *46:* 41-75.

353. LePage, W. R., and Lett, R. P. A study of teaching methods in engineering. *J. Eng. Educ.*, 1954, *44:* 317-324.

354. Leuba, C., and Lucas, C. The effects of attitudes on descriptions of pictures. *J. Exp. Psychol.*, 1945, *35:* 517-524.

355. Levanway, R. W. The effect of stress on expressed attitude toward self and others. *J. Abnorm. Soc. Psychol.*, 1955, *50:* 225-226.

356. Levine, J. M., and Murphy, G. The learning and forgetting of controversial material. *J. Abnorm. Soc. Psychol.*, 1943, *38:* 507-517.

357. Levine, R., Chein, I., and Murphy, G. The relation of the intensity of

the need to the amount of perceptual distortion: A preliminary report. *J. Psychol.*, 1942, *13:* 283-293.

358. Levy, D. M. *Maternal over-protection*. New York: Columbia Univ. Press, 1943.

359. Levy, D. M. Studies in sibling rivalry. *Res. Monogr. Amer. Orthopsychiat. Ass.*, 1937, No. 2.

360. Levy, L. H. Sexual symbolism: A validity study. *J. Consult. Psychol.*, 1954, *18:* 43-46.

361. Lewin, K. The conflict between Aristotelian and Galilean modes of thought in contemporary psychology. *J. Genet. Psychol.*, 1931, 5: 141-177.

362. Lewin, K. Defining the "field at a given time." *Psychol. Rev.*, 1943, *50:* 292-310.

363. Lewin, K. *A dynamic theory of personality*. New York: McGraw-Hill, 1935.

364. Lewin, K. *Field theory in social science*. (Ed. by D. Cartwright.) New York: Harper, 1951.

365. Lewin, K. Group decision and social change. In G. E. Swanson, T. M. Newcomb, and E. L. Hartley (eds.), *Readings in social psychology*. (2nd ed.) New York: Henry Holt, 1952, 459-473.

366. Lewin, K. *Principles of topological science*. New York: McGraw-Hill, 1936.

367. Lewin, K., Dembo, T., Festinger, L., and Sears, P. S. Level of aspiration. In J. McV. Hunt (ed.), *Personality and the behavior disorders*. New York: Ronald Press, 1944.

368. Lewin, K., Lippitt, R., and White, R. K. Patterns of aggressive behavior in experimentally created "social climates." *J. Soc. Psychol.*, 1939, *10:* 271-299.

369. Lewis, Claudia. Children of the Cumberland. New York: Columbia Univ. Press, 1946.

370. Liddell, H. S. Conditioned reflex method and experimental neurosis. In J. McV. Hunt (ed.), *Personality and the behavior disorders*. New York: Ronald Press, 1944.

371. Lifton, W. M. A study of the changes in self concept and content knowledge in students taking a course in counseling techniques. *Microfilm Abstr.*, 1951, *11* (1): 55-56.

372. Lindgren, H. C., and Robinson, Jacqueline. An evaluation of Dymond's Test of Insight and Empathy. *J. Consult. Psychol.*, 1953, *17:* 172-176.

373. Lindzey, G., and Rogalsky, S. Prejudice and identification of minority group membership. *J. Abnorm. Soc. Psychol.*, 1950, *45:* 37-53.

374. Linton, R. (ed.) *Acculturation in seven American Indian tribes*. New York: Appleton-Century, 1940.

375. Linton, R. *The cultural background of personality*. New York: Appleton-Century, 1945.

376. Linton, R., Fisher, Mary, and Ryan, W. *Culture and personality*. Washington, D. C.: American Council on Education, 1941.

377. Lippitt, R., and White, R. K. An experimental study of leadership and group life. In G. E. Swanson, T. M. Newcomb, and E. L. Hartley (eds.), *Readings in social psychology*. (Rev. ed.) New York: Henry Holt, 1952.

378. Maas, H. S. Personal and group factors in leaders' social perception. *J. Abnorm. Soc. Psychol.*, 1950, *45:* 54-63.

379. MacLeod, R. B. The phenomenological approach to social psychology. *Psychol. Rev.*, 1947, *54:* 193-210.

380. Maier, N. R. F. Reasoning and learning. *Psychol. Rev.*, 1931, *38:* 332-346.

381. Maier, N. R. F. Reasoning in children. *J. Comp. Psychol.*, 1936, *21:* 357-366.

382. Maier, N. R. F. Reasoning in humans, I. *J. Comp. Psychol.*, 1930, *10:* 115-143.

383. Maier, N. R. F. Reasoning in humans, II. The solution of a problem and its appearance in consciousness. *J. Comp. Psychol.*, 1931, *12:* 181-194.

384. Maier, N. R. F. *Studies of abnormal behavior in the rat.* New York: Harper, 1939.

385. Marks, E. S. Skin color judgments of Negro college students. *J. Abnorm. Psychol.*, 1943, *38:* 370-376.

386. Martin, W. E., Gross, N., and Darley, J. G. Studies of group behavior: leaders, followers, and isolates in small organized groups. *J. Abnorm. Soc. Psychol.*, 1952, *47:* 838-842.

387. Maslow, A. H. Dynamics of personality organization. *Psychol. Rev.*, 1943, *50:* 514-539.

388. Maslow, A. H. *Motivation and personality.* New York: Harper, 1954.

389. Maslow, A. H. Self-actualizing people: A study of psychological health. *Personality*, 1950, Symposium No. 1, 11-34.

390. Maslow, A. H., and Mittleman, B. *Principles of abnormal psychology.* New York: Harper, 1941.

391. Masserman, J. H., and Balken, E. R. The clinical application of phantasy studies. *J. Psychol.*, 1938, *6:* 81-88.

392. Mausner, B., and Siegel, A. The effect of variation in "value" on perceptual thresholds. *J. Abnorm. Soc. Psychol.*, 1950, *45:* 760-763.

393. Mayo, E. *The human problems of an industrial civilization.* Boston: Harvard Univ. Graduate School of Business Administration, 1946.

394. McCarthy, Dorothea. Personality and learning. *Amer. Coun. Educ. Stud.*, 1949, *13* (35): 93-96.

395. McClelland, D. C., and Atkinson, J. W. The projective expression of needs: I. The effect of different intensities of the hunger drive on perception. *J. Psychol.*, 1948, *25:* 205-222.

396. McConnell, J. Abstract behavior among the Tepehuan. *J. Abnorm. Soc. Psychol.*, 1954, *49:* 109-110.

397. McGinnies, E. Emotionality and perceptual defense. *Psychol. Rev.*, 1949, *56:* 244-251.

398. McGinnies, E. Personal values as determinants of word association. *J. Abnorm. Soc. Psychol.*, 1950, *45:* 28-36.

399. McGinnies, E., and Adornetto, J. Perceptual defense in normal and schizophrenic observers. *J. Abnorm. Soc. Psychol.*, 1952, *47:* 833-837.

400. McGinnies, E., and Bowles, W. Personal values as determinants of perceptual fixation. *J. Personality*, 1949, *18:* 224-235.

401. McGranahan, D. V. The psychology of language, *Psychol. Bull.*, 1936, *33:* 178-216.
402. McIntyre, C. J. Acceptance by others and its relation to acceptance of self and others. *J. Abnorm. Soc. Psychol.*, 1952, *47:* 624-625.
403. McKellar, P. Provocation to anger and the development of attitudes of hostility. *Brit. J. Psychol.*, 1950, *40:* 104-114.
404. McQuitty, L. L. A measure of personality integration in relation to the concept of self. *J. Personality*, 1950, *18:* 461-482.
405. Mead, G. H. *Mind, self and society from the standpoint of a social behaviorist.* Chicago: Univ. of Chicago Press, 1934.
406. Mead, M. (ed.) *Cultural patterns and technical change.* Paris: UNESCO, 1953.
407. Mead, M. *From the south seas.* New York: Morrow, 1939.
408. Mercer, Margaret, and Hecker, O. The use of Tolserol (myanesin) in psychological testing. *J. Clin. Psychol.*, 1951, *7:* 263-266.
409. Merker, F. *Die Masai.* Berlin, 1904.
410. Miller, J. G. Discrimination without awareness. *Amer. J. Psychol.*, 1939, *52:* 562-578.
411. Mittelmann, B., and Wolff, H. G. Emotion and skin temperature observations on patients during psychotherapeutic (psychoanalysis) interviews. *Psychosom. Med.*, 1943, *5:* 211-231.
412. Monroe, Ruth L. Diagnosis of learning disabilities through a projective technique. *J. Consult. Psychol.*, 1949, *13:* 390-395.
413. Moreno, J. L. Psychodrama and society. In A. A. Roback (ed.), *Present-day psychology.* New York: Philosophical Library, 1955, 679-686.
414. Morgan, C. D., and Murray, H. A. A method for investigating phantasies: The thematic apperception test. *Arch. Neurol. Psychiat.*, Chicago, 1935, *34:* 289-306.
415. Morse, Nancy C., and Allport, F. H. The causation of anti-Semitism: An investigation of seven hypotheses. *J. Psychol.*, 1952, *34:* 197-233.
416. Moustakas, C. E. *Children in play therapy.* New York: McGraw-Hill, 1953.
417. Moustakas, C. E. *The teacher and the child.* New York: McGraw-Hill, 1956.
418. Mowrer, O. H., and Kluckhohn, C. Dynamic theory of personality. In J. McV. Hunt (ed.), *Personality and the behavior disorders.* New York: Ronald Press, 1944, 69-135.
419. Murphy, G. *Personality: A biosocial approach to origin and structure.* New York: Harper, 1947.
420. Murphy, G., Murphy, Lois, and Newcomb, T. M. *Experimental social psychology.* (2nd ed.) New York: Harper, 1937.
421. Murray, H. A. The effect of fear upon estimates of the maliciousness of other personalities. *J. Soc. Psychol.*, 1933, *4:* 310-329.
422. Murray, H. A. *Explorations in personality.* New York: Oxford Univ. Press, 1938.
423. Mussen, P. H. Differences between the TAT responses of Negro and white boys. *J. Consult. Psychol.*, 1953, *17:* 373-376.

424. Mussen, P. H. Some personality and social factors related to changes in children's attitudes toward Negroes. *J. Abnorm. Soc. Psychol.*, 1950, *45*: 423-441.

425. Mussen, P. H., and Jones, Mary. Self-conception motivations, and interpersonal attitudes of late-and-early-maturing boys. *Child Develop.*, 1957, *28*: 243-256.

426. Neilon, Patricia. Shirley's babies after fifteen years: A personality study. *J. Genet. Psychol.*, 1948, *73*: 175-186.

427. Norman, R. D., and Ainsworth, Patricia. The relationships among projection, empathy, reality and adjustment, operationally defined. *J. Consult. Psychol.*, 1954, *18*: 53-58.

428. O'Connor, Patricia. Ethnocentrism, "intolerance of ambiguity," and abstract reasoning ability. *J. Abnorm. Soc. Psychol.*, 1952, *47*: 526-530.

429. Olson, W. C. *Child development.* Boston: D. C. Heath, 1949.

430. Olson, W. C. Self-selection as a principle of curriculum and method. *Educ. Digest*, 1945, *10*: 17-19.

431. Omwake, Katherine T. The relation between acceptance of self and acceptance of others shown by three personality inventories. *J. Consult. Psychol.*, 1954, *18*: 443-446.

432. Ort, R. S. A study of role-conflicts as related to happiness in marriage. *J. Abnorm. Soc. Psychol.*, 1950, *45*: 691-699.

433. Osgood, C. E. *Method and theory in experimental psychology.* New York: Oxford Univ. Press, 1953.

434. Pavlov, I. P. *Lectures on conditioned reflexes.* Vol. II. Conditioned reflexes and psychiatry. (Trans. & ed. by W. H. Gantt.) New York: International Publishers, 1941.

435. Pearl, D. Ethnocentrism and the self concept. *J. Soc. Psychol.*, 1954, *40*: 137-147.

436. Perrin, F. A. C. An experimental and introspective study of the human learning process in the maze. *Psychol. Monogr.*, 1914, *16*, No. 4.

437. Peterson, R. C., and Thurstone, L. L. *Motion pictures and the social attitudes of children.* New York: Macmillan, 1933.

438. Phillips, E. L. Attitudes toward self and others: A brief questionnaire report. *J. Consult. Psychol.*, 1951, *15*: 79-81.

439. Piaget, J. *The child's conception of the world.* New York: Harcourt Brace, 1929.

440. Piaget, J. *Judgment and reasoning in the child.* New York: Harcourt Brace, 1928.

441. Piaget, J. Principal factors determining intellectual evolution from childhood to adult life. In E. D. Adrian, and others, *Factors determining human behavior.* Cambridge, Mass.: Harvard Univ. Press, 1937, 32-48.

442. Pintler, M. H. Doll play as a function of the experimenter—child interaction and initial organization of materials. *Child Develop.*, 1945, *16*: 145-166.

443. Plant, J. S. *The envelope: A study of the impact of the world upon the child.* New York: Commonwealth Fund, 1950.

444. Plant, J. S. *Personality and the cultural pattern.* New York: Commonwealth Fund, 1937.

445. Pomeroy, D. S. Ameliorative effects of "counseling" upon maze peformance following experimentally induced stress. *Amer. Psychol.,* 1950, *5:* 327.

446. Porter, E. H., Jr. The development and evaluation of a measure of counseling interview procedures. *Educ. Psychol. Measmt.,* 1943, *3:* 106-126.

447. Porter, E. H., Jr. The development and evaluation of a measure of counseling interview procedures. *Educ. Psychol. Measmt.,* 1943, *3:* 215-238.

448. Postman, L., Bronson, Wanda C., and Gropper, G. L. Is there a mechanism of perceptual defense? *J. Abnorm. Soc. Psychol.,* 1953, *48:* 215-244.

449. Postman, L., and Bruner, J. S. Multiplicity of set as a determinant of perceptual behavior. *J. Exp. Psychol.,* 1949, *39:* 369-377.

450. Postman, L., and Bruner, J. S. Perception under stress. *Psychol. Rev.,* 1948, *55:* 314-323.

451. Postman, L., Bruner, J. S., and Walk, R. D. The perception of error. *Brit. J. Psychol.,* 1951, *42:* 1-10.

452. Postman, L., Bruner, J. S., and McGinnies, E. Personal values as selective factors in perception. *J. Abnorm. Soc. Psychol.,* 1948, *43:* 142-154.

453. Postman, L., and Schneider, B. H. Personal values, visual recognition, and recall. *Psychol. Rev.,* 1951, *58:* 271-284.

454. Potter, Muriel. The use of limits in reading therapy. *J. Consult. Psychol.,* 1950, *14:* 250-255.

455. Pottle, H. *An analysis of errors made in arithmetic addition.* Unpublished doctoral dissertation, Univ. of Toronto, 1937.

456. Poull, Louise. The effect of improvement in nutrition on the mental capacity of young children. *Child Develop.,* 1938, *9:* 123-126.

457. Pratt, K. C., Nelson, A. K., and Sun, K. H. The behavior of the newborn infant. *Ohio State Univ. Stud. Contr. Psychol.,* 1930, No. 10.

458. Precker, J. A. Similarity of valuings as a factor in selection of peers and near-authority figures. *J. Abnorm. Soc. Psychol.,* 1952, *47:* 406-414.

459. Prescott, D. A. *Emotion and the educative process.* Washington: Amer. Council on Educ., 1938.

460. Preston, M. S., and Heintz, R. K. Effects of participatory vs. supervisory leadership on group judgment. *J. Abnorm. Soc. Psychol.,* 1949, *44:* 345-355.

461. Prince, M. *Clinical and experimental studies in personality.* Cambridge, Mass.: Sci-Art Publishers, 1939.

462. Prince, W. F. The Doris case of multiple personality. *Proc. Amer. Soc. Psychol.,* res., 1915, *9:* 1916, *10.*

463. Proshansky, H. A projective method for the study of attitudes. *J. Abnorm. Soc. Psychol.,* 1943, *38:* 393-395.

464. Proshansky, H., and Murphy, G. The effects of reward and punishment on perception. *J. Psychol.,* 1942, *13:* 295-305.

465. Pugh, R. W. A specific relapse phenomenon during the course of electric convulsive therapy. *J. Consult. Psychol.,* 1953, *17:* 87-91.

466. Pullen, M. S., and Stagner, R. Rigidity and shock therapy of psychotics: An experimental study. *J. Consult. Psychol.,* 1953, *17:* 79-86.

467. Raimy, V. C. The self-concept as a factor in counseling and personality organization. Unpublished doctoral dissertation, Ohio State Univ., 1943.

468. Raimy, V. C. Self reference in counseling interviews. *J. Consult. Psychol.*, 1948, *12:* 153-163.

469. Rapaport, D., Gill, M., and Schafer, R. *Diagnostic psychological testing.* (2 vols.) Chicago: Year Book Publishers, 1945-46.

470. Raymaker, H. *Relationships between the self concept, self ideal concept and maladjustment.* Unpublished doctoral dissertation, Vanderbilt Univ., 1956.

471. Reeves, J. M., and Goldman, L. Social class perceptions and school maladjustment. *Personnel & Guidance J.*, 1957, *35:* 414-419.

472. Ribble, Margaret A. Infantile experience in relation to personality development. In J. McV. Hunt (ed.), *Personality and the behavior disorders.* New York: Ronald Press, 1944, 621-651.

473. Ribble, Margaret A. *The rights of infants: Early psychological needs and their satisfaction.* New York: Columbia Univ. Press, 1943.

474. Richter, C. P. Biology of drives. *Psychosom. Med.*, 1941, *3:* 105-110.

475. Riesen, A. H. Arrested vision. *Scientific Amer.*, 1950, *183:* 16-19.

476. Rivers, W. H. R. *The Todas.* New York: Macmillan, 1906.

477. Roethlisberger, F. J. *Management and morale.* Cambridge, Mass.: Harvard Univ. Press, 1941.

478. Roethlisberger, F. J., and Dickson, W. J. *Management and the worker.* Cambridge: Harvard Univ. Press, 1939.

479. Roethlisberger, F. J. *Management and morale.* Cambridge, Mass.: Harvard Univ. Press, 1941.

480. Rogers, C. R. The attitude and orientation of the counselor in client-centered therapy. *J. Consult. Psychol.*, 1949, *13:* 82-94.

481. Rogers, C. R. *Becoming a person.* (Pamphlet.) Hogg Fdn. for Mental Hygiene, Univ. of Texas, 1956.

482. Rogers, C. R. *Client-centered therapy.* Boston: Houghton Mifflin, 1951.

483. Rogers, C. R. *The clinical treatment of the problem child.* Boston, Houghton Mifflin, 1939.

484. Rogers, C. R. The concept of the fully functioning person. (Mimeographed statement.) Univ. of Chicago, 1957.

485. Rogers, C. R. *Counseling and psychotherapy.* Boston: Houghton Mifflin, 1942.

486. Rogers, C. R. Significant aspects of client-centered therapy. *Amer. Psychologist*, 1946, *1:* 415-422.

487. Rogers, C. R. Some observations on the organization of personality. *Amer. Psychologist*, 1947, *2:* 358-368.

488. Rogers, C. R., and Dymond, Rosalind F. *Psychotherapy and personality change.* Chicago: Univ. of Chicago Press, 1954.

489. Rogers, C. R., and Skinner, B. F. Some issues concerning the control of behavior. *Science*, 1956, *124:* 1057-1066.

490. Rohde, A. R. Explorations in personality by the sentence completion method. *J. Appl. Psychol.*, 1946, *30:* 169-181.

491. Rokeach, M. Attitude as a determinant of distortions in recall. *J. Abnorm. Soc. Psychol.*, 1952, *47:* 482-488.

492. Rokeach, M. The effect of perception time upon rigidity and concreteness of thinking. *J. Exp. Psychol.*, 1950, *40:* 206-216.

493. Rorschach, H. *Psychodiagnostik.* New York: Grune & Stratton, 1942.

494. Roseborough, Mary E. Experimental studies of small groups. *Psychol. Bull.* 1953, *50:* 275-303.

495. Rosenstock, I. M. Perceptual aspects of repression. *J. Abnorm. Soc. Psychol.*, 1951, *46:* 304-315.

496. Rosenzweig, S. An outline of frustration theory. In J. McV. Hunt (ed.), *Personality and the behavior disorders.* New York: Ronald Press, 1944, 379-388.

497. Rotter, J. B. The nature and treatment of stuttering: A clinical approach. *J. Abnorm. Soc. Psychol.*, 1944, *39:* 150-173.

498. Sanford, R. N. The effects of abstinence from food from imaginal processes: A preliminary experiment. *J. Psychol.*, 1936, *2:* 129-136.

499. Sanford, R. N. The effects of abstinence from food upon imaginal processes: A further experiment. *J. Psychol.*, 1937, *3:* 145-159.

500. Sarbin, T. R. The logic of prediction in psychology. *Psychol. Rev.*, 1944, *51:* 210-228.

501. Schafer, R., and Murphy, G. The role of autism in figure-ground relationship. *J. Exp. Psychol.*, 1943, *32:* 335-343.

502. Schein, E. The effect of group interaction on judgment of physical stimuli. Unpublished master's thesis, Stanford Univ., 1949.

503. Schmidt, B. Changes in personal, social, and intellectual behavior of children originally classified as feeble-minded. *Psychol. Monogr.*, 1946, *60,* No. 5.

504. Schneirla, T. C. The nature of ant learning. II. *J. Comp. Psychol.*, 1943, *35:* 149-176.

505. Schneirla, T. C. Studies in the nature of ant learning. I. *J. Comp. Psychol.*, 1941, *32:* 41-82.

506. Schrodinger, E. *What is life?* New York: Macmillan, 1945.

507. Schwebel, M., and Asch, M. J. Research possibilities in nondirective teaching. *J. Educ. Psychol.*, 1948, *39:* 359-369.

508. Scodel, A., and Mussen, P. Social perceptions of authoritarians and non-authoritarians. *J. Abnorm. Soc. Psychol.*, 1953, *48:* 181-184.

509. Sears, R. R. Experimental studies of projection: I. Attribution of traits. *J. Soc. Psychol.*, 1936, *7:* 151-163.

510. Seeman, J. A study of the process of non-directive therapy. *J. Consult. Psychol.*, 1949, *13:* 157-168.

511. Selye, H. *The physiology and pathology of exposure to stress.* Montreal: Acta, Inc., 1950.

512. Selye, H., and Fortier, C. Adaptive reactions to stress. *Res. Publ. Ass. Nerv. Ment. Dis.*, 1950, *29:* 3-18.

513. Selye, H., and Fortier, C. Adaptive reactions to stress. *Psychosom. Med.*, 1950, *12:* 149-157.

514. Seymour, A. H., and Whitaker, J. E. J. An experiment on nutrition. *Occup. Psychol.*, 1938, *12:* 215-223.

515. Shaffer, L. F. *The psychology of adjustment.* Boston: Houghton Mifflin, 1936.

516. Shaw. C. R. *The Jack-Roller.* Chicago: Univ. of Chicago Press, 1930.

517. Shaw, C. R., and Moore, M. E. *The natural history of a delinquent career.* Chicago: Univ. of Chicago Press, 1931.

518. Sheerer, Elizabeth T. An analysis of the relationship between acceptance of and respect for self and acceptance of and respect for others in ten counseling cases. *J. Consult. Psychol.*, 1949, *13:* 169-175.

519. Sheldon, W. D., and Landsman, T. An investigation of non-directive group therapy with students in academic difficulty. *J. Consult. Psychol.*, 1950, *14:* 210-215.

520. Sherif, M. An experimental approach to the study of attitudes. *Sociometry*, 1937, *1:* 90-98.

521. Sherif, M. A preliminary study of intergroup relations, in J. S. Rohrer and M. Sherif, *Social psychology at the crossroads.* New York: Harper, 1951, 388-424.

522. Sherif, M. *The psychology of social norms.* New York: Harper, 1936.

523. Sherif, M. A study of some social factors in perception. *Arch. Psychol.*, New York, 1935, No. 187.

524. Sherif, M., and Cantril, H. *The psychology of ego involvements.* New York: Wiley, 1947.

525. Sherif, M., and Sherif, Carolyn. *Groups in harmony and tension.* New York: Harper, 1953.

526. Sherif, M., and Sherif, Carolyn. *An outline of social psychology.* New York: Harper, 1956.

527. Sherif, M., White, B. J., and Harvey, O. J. Status in experimentally produced groups. *Amer. J. Sociol.*, 1955, *60:* 370-379.

528. Sherman, M., and Henry, T. R. *Hollow folk.* New York: Crowell, 1933.

529. Shirley, Mary. *The first two years.* Minneapolis: Univ. of Minnesota Press, 1933, Vol. 3.

530. Siipola, E. M. A group study of some effects of preparatory set. *Psychol. Monogr.*, 1935, *46*, No. 210.

531. Skeels, H. M., and Fillmore, E. A. The mental development of children from underprivileged homes. *J. Genet. Psychol.*, 1937, *50:* 427-439.

532. Slotkin, J. S. Social psychiatry of a Menomini community. *J. Abnorm. Psychol.*, 1953, *48:* 10-16.

533. Small, L. Personality determinants of vocational choice. *Psychol. Monogr.* 1953, *67* (1), (No. 351).

534. Smith, A. *An inquiry into the nature and causes of the wealth of nations.* London: Strahan and Cadell, 1796.

535. Smith, M. B. The phenomenological approach in personality theory: Some critical remarks. *J. Abnorm. Soc. Psychol.*, 1950, *45:* 516-522.

536. Smith, S. Language and non-verbal test performance of racial groups in

Honolulu before and after a fourteen-year interval. *J. Gen. Psychol.*, 1942, *26:* 51-93.

537. Smith, W. M. Past experience and the perception of visual size. *Amer. J. Psychol.*, 1952, *65:* 389-403.

538. Smock, C. D. The influence of psychological stress on the intolerance of ambiguity. *J. Abnorm. Soc. Psychol.*, 1955, *50:* 177-182.

539. Snyder, U. An investigation of the nature of non-directive psychotherapy. *J. Gen. Psychol.*, 1945, *33:* 192-224.

540. Snyder, W. U. *Casebook of non-directive counseling.* Boston: Houghton Mifflin, 1947.

541. Snygg, D. Configurational aspects of tachistoscopic observation. Unpublished doctoral dissertation, Univ. of Iowa, 1931.

542. Snygg, D. Maze learning as perception. *J. Genet. Psychol.*, 1936, *49:* 231-239.

543. Snygg, D. Mazes in which rats take the longer path to food. *J. Psychol.*, 1935–1936, *1:* 153-166.

544. Snygg, D. The need for a phenomenological system of psychology. *Psychol. Rev.*, 1941, *48:* 404-424.

545. Snygg, D. The psychological basis of human values. In D. Ward (ed.), *Goals of economic life.* New York: Hopkins Bros., 1953, 5-57.

546. Snygg, D. The relative difficulty of mechanically equivalent tasks: I. Human learning. *J. Genet. Psychol.*, 1935, *47:* 299-320.

547. Snygg, D. The relative difficulty of mechanically equivalent tasks: II. Animal learning. *J. Genet. Psychol.*, 1935, *47:* 321-336.

548. Snygg, D., and Combs, A. W. The phenomenological approach and the problems of "unconscious" behavior. *J. Abnorm. Soc. Psychol.*, 1950, *45:* 523-528.

549. Society for the Psychological Study of Social Issues. *Soc. Psychol. Stud. Soc. Issues Newsletter,* Nov., 1956.

550. Solomon, R. L., and Howes, D. G. Word frequency, personal values and visual duration thresholds. *Psychol. Rev.*, 1951, *58:* 256-270.

551. Soper, D. W., and Combs, A. W. Planning future research in education. *Educ. Leadership,* 1957, *14:* 315-318.

552. Sorokin, P. A., and Berger, C. F. *Time-budgets of human behavior.* Cambridge: Harvard Univ. Press, 1939.

553. Spitz, R. A. Hospitalism. In A. Freud, and others, *The psychoanalytic study of the child.* New York: International Univ. Press, 1945.

554. Spock, B. *The common sense book of baby and child care.* New York: Duell, Sloan & Pearce, 1946.

555. Stagner, R. Stereotypes of workers and executives among college men. *J. Abnorm. Soc. Psychol.*, 1950, *45:* 743-748.

556. Stern, W. M. Cloud pictures. *Charact. & Pers.*, 1937, *6:* 132-146.

557. Stephenson, W. A. A statistical approach to typology: the study of trait-universes. *J. Clin. Psychol.*, 1950, *6:* 26-37.

558. Stevenson, I. Language and non-verbal test performances of racial groups

in Honolulu before and after a fourteen-year interval. *J. Gen. Psychol.*, 1942, *26:* 51-93.

559. Stewart, Naomi. A.G.C.T. scores of Army personnel grouped by occupation. *Occupations,* 1947, *26:* 5-41.

560. Stock, D. An investigation into the interrelations between the self-concept and feelings directed toward other persons and groups. *J. Consult. Psychol.*, 1949, *13:* 176-180.

561. Sullivan, H. S. *Conceptions of modern psychiatry.* Washington, D. C.: William Alanson White Psychiatric Foundation, 1947.

562. Symonds, P. N. Criteria for the selection of pictures for the investigation of adolescent phantasies. *Psychol. Bull.,* 1938, *35:* 641.

563. Tagiuri, R., Blake, R. R., and Bruner, J. S. Some determinants of the perception of positive and negative feelings in others. *J. Abnorm. Soc. Psychol.*, 1953, *48·* 585-592.

564. Taylor, C., and Combs, A. W. Self-acceptance and adjustment. *J. Consult. Psychol.*, 1952, *16:* 89-91.

565. Taylor, D. M. Consistency of the self-concept. Unpublished doctoral dissertation, Vanderbilt Univ., 1953.

566. Tentative social studies program, Campus Elementary School, Oswego State Teachers College, Oswego, New York, 1945.

567. Terman, L. M. *Genetic studies of genius.* Stanford, Calif.: Stanford Univ. Press, 1925.

568. Thetford, W. N. An objective measure of frustration tolerance in evaluating psychotherapy. In W. Wolff and J. A. Precker (eds.), *Success in psychotherapy.* New York: Grune & Stratton, 1952.

569. Thibaut, J. W., and Coules, J. The role of communication in the reduction of interpersonal hostility. *J. Abnorm. Soc. Psychol.*, 1952, *47:* 770-777.

570. Thigpen, C. H., and Cleckley, H. A case of multiple personality. *J. Abnorm. Soc. Psychol.*, 1954, *49:* 135-151.

571. Thistlethwaite, D. Attitude and structure as factors in the distortion of reasoning. *J. Abnorm. Soc. Psychol.*, 1950, *45:* 442-458.

572. Thompson, G. G. The social and emotional development of preschool children under two types of educational program. *Psychol. Monogr.*, 1944, *56:* No. 5.

573. Thompson, Laura. Perception patterns in three Indian tribes. *Psychiatry,* 1951, *14:* 255-263.

574. Thrasher, F. M. *The gang.* Chicago: Univ. of Chicago Press, 1927.

575. Tolor, A. Teachers' judgments of the popularity of children from their human figure drawings. *J. Clin. Psychol.*, 1955, *11:* 158-162.

576. Tomkins, S. S. Experimental study of anxiety. *J. Psychol.*, 1943, *15:* 307-313.

577. Tomkins, S. S. *The Thematic Apperception Test: The theory and technique of interpretation.* New York: Grune & Stratton, 1947.

578. Torrance, P. The phenomenon of resistance in learning. *J. Abnorm. Soc. Psychol.*, 1950, *45:* 592-597.

579. Torrance, P. Rationalizations about test performance as a function of self-concepts. *J. Soc. Psychol.*, 1954, *39:* 211-217.

580. Toynbee, A. J. *A study of history.* London: Oxford Univ. Press, 1935–1939.

581. Tresselt, M. E. The influence of amount of practice upon the formation of a scale of judgement. *J. Exp. Psychol.*, 1947, *37:* 251-260.

582. Twersky, V. On the physical basis of the perception of obstacles by the blind. *Amer. J. Psychol.*, 1951, *64:* 409-416.

583. Ugurel-Semin, Refia. Moral behavior and moral judgment of children. *J. Abnorm. Soc. Psychol.*, 1952, *47:* 463-474.

584. U. S. Federal Security Agency. Children's Bureau. *Infant care.* Washington: U. S. Government Printing Office, 1945.

585. Vargas, M. J. Changes in self-awareness during client-centered therapy. In C. R. Rogers and R. Dymond (eds.), *Psychotherapy and personality change.* Chicago: Univ. of Chicago Press, 1954.

586. Walsh, Ann M. *Self concepts of bright boys with learning difficulties.* New York: Bureau of Publications, Teachers College, Columbia Univ., 1956.

587. Wapner, S., and Witkin, H. A. The role of visual factors in the maintenance of body-balance. *Amer. J. Psychol.*, 1950, *63:* 385-408.

588. Warner, W. L., and Lunt, P. S. *The social life of a modern community.* New Haven: Yale Univ. Press, 1941.

589. Watson, J. B. *Psychology.* Philadelphia: Lippincott, 1919.

590. Watson, J. B. *Psychology: From the standpoint of a behaviorist.* (3rd ed.) Philadelphia: Lippincott, 1929.

591. Wechsler, D. *The measurement of adult intelligence.* (3rd ed.) Baltimore: Williams and Wilkins, 1944.

592. Wechsler, D., and Hartogs, R. The clinical measurement of anxiety. *Psychiat. Quart.*, 1945, *19:* 618-635.

593. Wees, W. R., and Line, W. The influence of the form of a presentation upon reproduction: The principle of determination. *Brit. J. Psychol.*, 1937, *28:* 167-189.

594. Weingarten, Erica M. A study of selective perception in clinical judgment. *J. Pers.*, 1949, *17:* 369-406.

595. Wellman, B. L. The effect of pre-school attendance upon the I.Q. *J. Exp. Educ.*, 1933, *1:* 48-69.

596. Wellman, B. L. Growth in intelligence under differing school environments. *J. Exp. Educ.*, 1934, *3:* 59-83.

597. Wells, F. L., and Ruesch, J. (eds.). *Mental examiners' handbook.* New York: Psychological Corporation, 1942.

598. Werner, H., Wapner, S., and Chandler, K. A. Experiments on sensory-tonic field theory of perception: II. Effect of supported and unsupported tilt of the body on the visual perception of verticality. *J. Exp. Psychol.*, 1951, *42:* 346-350.

599. Wertheimer, M. Laws of perceptual form. In W. O. Ellis (ed.), *A source book of gestalt psychology.* New York: Harcourt, Brace, 1939.

600. Wever, E. G., and Zener, K. E. The method of absolute judgment in psychophysics. *Psychol. Rev.*, 1928, *35:* 466-493.
601. Wheeler, L. R. A comparative study of the intelligence of East Tennessee mountain children. *J. Educ. Psychol.*, 1942, *33:* 321-334.
602. Whorf, B. Science and linguistics, *Technology Rev.*, 1940, *42*(6): 229-231 and 247-248.
603. Whyte, W. F. *Street corner society.* Chicago: Univ. of Chicago Press, 1943.
604. Wieder, G. S. Group procedures modifying attitudes of prejudice in the college classroom. *J. Educ. Psychol.*, 1954, *45:* 332-344.
605. Williams, H. D. An experiment on self-directed education. *Sch. Soc.*, 1930, *31:* 715-718.
606. Wispe, L. G. Evaluating section teaching methods in the introductory course. *J. Educ. Res.*, 1951, *45:* 161-186.
607. Wispe, L. G. Teaching methods research. *Amer. Psychologist*, 1953, *8:* 147-149.
608. Wittreich, W. J. The honiphenomenon. *J. Abnorm. Soc. Psychol.*, 1952, *47:* 705-712.
609. Wolfenstein, Martha. The emergence of fun morality. *J. Soc. Issues*, 1951, *7*(4): 15-25.
610. Woodrow, H. The problem of general quantitative laws in psychology. *Psychol. Bull.*, 1942, *39:* 1-27.
611. Worchel, P., and Berry, J. H. The perception of obstacles by the deaf. *J. Exp. Psychol.*, 1952, *43:* 187-194.
612. Young, K. *Personality and problems of adjustment.* New York: Crofts, 1940.
613. Young, P. T. Studies of food preference, appetite and dietary habit. VI. Habit, palatability and diet as factors regulating the selection of food by the rat. *J. Comp. Psychol.*, 1946, *39:* 139-176.
614. Young, P. T. Studies of food preference, appetite and dietary habit. V. Technique for testing food preference and the significance of results obtained with different methods. *Comp. Psychol. Monogr.*, 1945, *19:* No. 1.
615. Young, P. T. The experimental analysis of appetite. *Psychol. Bull.*, 1941, *38:* 129-164.
616. Zander, A. T. A study of experimental frustration. *Psychol. Monogr.*, 1944, *56*, No. 3.
617. Zimet, C. N., and Fine, H. J. Personality changes with a group therapeutic experience in a human relations seminar. *J. Abnorm. Soc. Psychol.*, 1955, *51:* 68-73.
618. Zimet, C. N., and Fine, H. J. A quantitative method of scoring picture story tests. *J. Clin. Psychol.*, 1955, *11:* 24-28.
619. Zorbaugh, H. W. *Gold coast and slum.* Chicago: Univ. of Chicago Press, 1929.

Index

SPECIAL NOTE: *All authors whose work was consulted in developing this frame of reference have been listed in this index whether such authors are specifically named in the text or not. Where the author's work is not specifically indicated in the text, the reader may find the work referred to by consulting the proper page number in the References (pages 466-479).*

511